Creation and Ecology

"This is an excellent, well-conceived, very timely book in every way. Simkins brings together (1) a deep and thorough critical knowledge of biblical texts, including the historical contexts, perspective, and agenda of whole books as well as the function of particular passages; (2) a clear history of the development of the climate crisis and how it has been interrelated with the development of capitalism and theories of political economy that have rationalized both; (3) incisive criticism of the severely problematic neoliberal ideology that still prevails in public discourse; and (4) a remarkable critical grasp of how the political economy evident in biblical texts provides resources for imagining an alternative to the relentless growth inherent in capitalism that is driving the climate crisis. A must-read for clergy, students, laity, and all climate activists."

—**RICHARD A. HORSLEY**
Author of *Jesus and Empire* and *Covenant Economics*

"What does it look like to read the Hebrew Bible with both socio-economic sophistication and theological depth, while also reckoning with the human and planetary realities of the Anthropocene Epoch? This book may be the first serious attempt to answer that complex question. Simkins makes the bold and timely proposal that Israel's Scriptures in their social specificity offer an alternative vision to guide our own ineluctably *economic* existence."

—**ELLEN F. DAVIS**
Author of *Scripture, Culture, and Agriculture*

"This pioneering work, in the face of climate change, forces us to relate ecology, economics, and the Bible in a radical new way, that might be called eco-economic hermeneutics. Especially challenging is the claim that the ancient Israelite political economy might contribute to a positive new approach to our natural world, even though Simkins admits that the circumstances of climate change challenge biblical cosmology. I recommend this volume as a way to—as Simkins says—redeem creation."

—**NORMAN HABEL**
Author of *The Birth, the Curse and the Greening of Earth*

"Unlike many books on this topic, which relate biblical texts directly to the topic of ecology, this profound, learned, important, and disturbing book insists—convincingly—that cogent reflection on our ecological crisis requires critical analysis of forms of political economy, ancient and modern. Only by radically changing our capitalist system, Ronald Simkins argues, do we have any hope of avoiding the coming collapse. This demands our urgent attention."

—**DAVID G. HORRELL**
Author of *The Bible and the Environment*

"*Creation and Ecology*'s interdisciplinary work at significant intersections—the ancient and contemporary, economy and ecology—is vital for facing the civilizational threat of climate change. This book uniquely bridges the hermeneutical gap, while respecting the significant differences between antiquity and today, with rigor and integrity. It unflinchingly sees beyond the sacred veneer of an economy that values wealth above the lives of people and the planet and outlines meaningful pathways for addressing the current crisis."

—**CRYSTAL L. HALL**
Author of *Insights from Reading the Bible with the Poor*

"*Creation and Ecology* is as exceptional as it is timely. Synthesizing ecological hermeneutics with the most recent research on biblical economics, Simkins offers readers much-needed guidance in both understanding the economic nature of our environmental crisis and also in formulating effective biblical responses to the ecological and social consequences of climate change."

—**MATTHEW J. M. COOMBER**
Editor of *Bible and Justice*

"Ron Simkins has integrated his interests in political economy and creation. Simkins presents a compelling case that careful reflection on biblical texts can inspire better approaches to the current environmental crisis. Scholars will find the content both sophisticated and engaged with ongoing research. Lay readers will find the arguments as cogent and accessible. This work will reward all readers with enriched understandings on creation and ecology during a most crucial time."

—**ROGER NAM**
Professor of Hebrew Bible, Emory University

Creation and Ecology

The Political Economy of Ancient Israel
and the Environmental Crisis

RONALD A. SIMKINS

▲ CASCADE *Books* • Eugene, Oregon

CREATION AND ECOLOGY
The Political Economy of Ancient Israel and the Environmental Crisis

Copyright © 2020 Ronald A. Simkins. All rights reserved. Except for brief quotations in critical publications or reviews, no part of this book may be reproduced in any manner without prior written permission from the publisher. Write: Permissions, Wipf and Stock Publishers, 199 W. 8th Ave., Suite 3, Eugene, OR 97401.

Cascade Books
An Imprint of Wipf and Stock Publishers
199 W. 8th Ave., Suite 3
Eugene, OR 97401

www.wipfandstock.com

PAPERBACK ISBN: 978-1-5326-9872-9
HARDCOVER ISBN: 978-1-5326-9873-6
EBOOK ISBN: 978-1-5326-9874-3

Cataloguing-in-Publication data:

Names: Simkins, Ronald A., author.

Title: Creation and ecology : the political economy of ancient Israel and the environmental crisis / Ronald A. Simkins.

Description: Eugene, OR: Cascade Books, 2020. | Includes bibliographical references and index.

Identifiers: ISBN: 978-1-5326-9872-9 (paperback). | ISBN: 978-1-5326-9873-6 (hardcover). | ISBN: 978-1-5326-9874-3 (ebook).

Subjects: LCSH: Creation—Biblical teaching. | Human ecology—Biblical teaching. | Nature—Biblical teaching. | Bible. Old Testament—Criticism, interpretation, etc.

Classification: BS1199 N34 S55 2021 (print). | BS1199 (ebook).

12/22/20

Some of the material in chapter 4 was previously published in an earlier form in "The Embodied World: Creation Metaphors in the Ancient Near East," *Biblical Theology Bulletin* 44.1 (2014) 40–53. doi:10.1177/0146107913514203.

Some of material in chapter 5 was previously published in an earlier form. "The Bible and Anthropocentrism: Putting Humans in Their Place," *Dialectical Anthropology* 38 (2014) 397–413. Used by permission from Springer Nature.

An earlier form of chapter 8 was published as "Creation and Theodicy in the Context of Climate Change: A New Cosmology for the Anthropocene?" in *Religion and Reform*, edited by Ronald A. Simkins and Zachary B. Smith, 232–49. Journal of Religion & Society Supplement Series 18 (2019). http://www.creighton.edu/jrs/toc/ss18.html.

For Allison, Kelsey, and Michael

&

For Asher

For the younger generations who will inherit this world,

and my hope for a better one

Contents

Preface | ix

Introduction | 1

PART I: CREATION

1 Creation and Gender | 27

2 Creation and Political Economy | 55

3 Creation and Society | 91

4 Creation and the Body | 116

PART II: ECOLOGY

5 Ecology and Religion | 149

6 Ecology and Political Economy | 178

7 Ecology and the Anthropocene | 230

8 Ecology and Theodicy | 264

Conclusion | 281

Bibliography | 309
Ancient Documents Index | 353

Preface

THIS BOOK WAS WRITTEN during the COVID-19 pandemic. Although I mention the pandemic briefly in the final chapter, I otherwise resisted the temptation to link the pandemic with climate change, which is the subject of this book. Not that there is no legitimate connection between the two, especially in regard to economic concerns, but I feared that any linkage would undermine or distract from the veracity of my argument here. Nevertheless, the pandemic provided a surreal context for writing about climate change. As I wrote about the need to lessen production and consumption and transition to a low-energy society in order to reduce the burning of fossil fuels, the pandemic was forcing this upon society. Retail outlets and businesses closed, leading to a record 34 percent reduction in the GDP for the second quarter of 2020. Farmers were forced to kill some of their herds and flocks because they could not be processed for consumption. The price of oil dropped into negative territory and was stored in tankers offshore because transportation was drastically reduced and production of fossil fuels could not be slowed fast enough. Indeed, for a few months in the spring of 2020, the *increase* in carbon dioxide emissions into the atmosphere significantly slowed. Then came the summer of 2020; states rushed to reopen their economies, with the President's urging, despite rising infections of the virus. I needed no other lesson. At least in the United States, economic growth is more important than everything else, regardless of how many lives are endangered and die. Presently, as I write this, more than 170,000 U.S. Americans have died from the coronavirus, with a thousand deaths added to the total each day, yet schools are preparing to open, people debate whether they should wear masks, and the stock market repeatedly hits new highs. The United States is wholly unprepared for addressing climate change and for the economic sacrifices that addressing it effectively will entail. The rest of the world has had mixed results regarding the pandemic—some better, some worse—but most are probably no better off regarding climate change. Despite the wide diversity in politics and political affiliation around the globe—liberal or conservative, democratic or authoritarian—economic growth is largely still god, and it determines public policy and economic strategy around the globe. This is the problem for which I wrote this book.

This book is the culmination of thirty years of research, and it integrates several fields that I have written on separately: political economy, creation, gender, and the environment. Some might call it my magnum opus. I am not so comfortable with the term magnum—that is for others to decide—but it is certainly the opus of my career. Many of the ideas in the book have been introduced and partly explored in earlier publications, but they have been developed and synthesized here in a new way with a new thesis and argument. This book has been inspired and influenced by the work of many individuals, across several disciplines, some of whom I have had discussions with over the years, and many of whom I have never met but voraciously consumed their publications. Their influence is evident throughout this book in multiple citations, and I hope that I have done their work justice, especially in interdisciplinary matters, but the final synthesis is my own.

Although the research for this book extended over many years, the writing of it was made possible by and occurred within a year-long sabbatical from the Creighton College of Arts and Sciences in which I teach. I am thankful to Dean Bridget Keegan for granting and funding my sabbatical request and for her confidence that I would use the time well. I also extend thanks to Nicolae Roddy, Matthew J. M. Coomber, and Crystal Hall, who read and commented on the manuscript. The book is better because of them.

Finally, this book is dedicated to my daughters and son-in-law, and to my grandson. They were born into a world already aware of the dangers of climate change, and they and their generations will inherit a world that is shaped by the actions or inactions of my generation to curb the crisis. They are the reason why we should care about climate change, for the most catastrophic effects will happen to them and to our future descendants and generations. To paraphrase Jeremiah 31:29–30, children should not have to suffer the consequences of their parents' sins, but with climate change this seems inevitable. Our legacy should not be, that when faced with climate change, we did nothing. My generation largely has seemed unwilling to address the economic causes of the climate crisis—economic growth, capitalism, and free market are upheld as sacred truths, even by many religious adherents. This book, I hope, effectively challenges this thinking and provides an alternative framework for addressing climate change, along with a call for change. My hope is that the younger generations, who have known no world without climate change, will more readily embrace the difficult economic consequences that are necessary for a better world, will push for economic changes, and will hold us accountable.

August 2020

Introduction

Reading the Bible in the Environmental Crisis

THE FOCUS ON POLITICAL ECONOMY

THIS IS A BOOK about the current environmental crisis, which threatens severe consequences from climate change, degradation of the soil, and loss of biodiversity, and what the Bible might contribute in response. Although each of these environmental problems is significant in its own right, and each will have different effects on the human community, all are interrelated and share a similar cause. For this reason, before I address the environmental crisis, which will be the focus of Part II, I must first take a tour of the political economy of ancient Israel.[1] To some readers, this might seem to be an unnecessary detour, and it is not generally characteristic of the many excellent books on the Bible and the environment (see, e.g., Horrell 2010; Bauckham 2010; Tull 2013; compare the agrarian reading of the Bible in Davis 2009b). However, I have become convinced that the central cause of the environmental crisis is how we humans have mediated the relationship between society and nature, and this mediation is all about political economy.[2] That is, through our productive relations and powers, we creatures of the natural world have constructed society from the materials of the natural world, and through doing so have depleted natural resources, polluted natural environments, and altered natural processes. The current environmental crisis is a product of our current political economy, which entails not only our politics, ideology, and religion, but primarily our economic system. Because the crisis is economic at its core, it is helpful to place the Bible first within its own economic context in order to explore how it may contribute in responding to the crisis.

---

1. The expression "ancient Israel" is a scholarly construct used to designate the people who lived in the southern Levant and produced the Bible. It is used for convenience to encompass the historical kingdoms of Israel and Judah, as well as the people who preceded the formation of the states (the so-called tribal period) and the province of Yehud during the Persian empire.

2. Political economy refers both to a social-scientific discipline and to the holistically defined human society the discipline investigates (on the discipline broadly, see Roseberry 1988b; on the use of political economy with precapitalist societies, see Donham 1999; Léons and Rothstein 1979).

Let me take a step back and unpack this. Humans (*homo sapiens*) are creatures of the natural world. We evolved out of earlier hominids and share in the material substance, dependencies, and limitations of all other creatures in the natural world. We are also social beings, a trait that we share with some other creatures, and so we have formed social groups from our earliest emergence as a species. Somewhere along the path of our evolution, we developed a self-consciousness, apparently unique among earth's creatures, that enables us to perceive ourselves as distinct from the rest of the natural world. We are fully natural beings, yet we perceive (feel, believe, know) ourselves to be *more than* natural beings. For the ancient Israelites, this "more" was expressed in terms of the "knowledge of good and evil" (Yahwist creation myth) or the "image of God" (Priestly creation myth). In modern society, we tend to understand this "more" in terms of our cognitive faculties. Whether this "more" is understood as rationality, creativity, morality, or spirituality (or any combination of the four), we demonstrate our uniqueness by constructing a society that is distinct from the natural world in which we live. Although like all creatures we live from the foodstuffs grown and produced from the natural world, we also create our own products: from the buildings in which we live and work, to the industries that produce our stuff, to the infrastructure that supports our living. We can even grow our own vegetables and meat in a laboratory (Little 2019). As a human creation, we treat society as if it is independent from the natural world, an embodiment of our uniqueness; it is unlike the natural societies, for example, of ants, bees, or a pride of lions. Human society exploits the natural world for its resources, acting as if the natural world cannot impinge on society, yet society is wholly embedded in the world of nature. Everything we produce in society comes from the natural world; it is the only source of matter for our many material products, including the food that is produced in a laboratory. Even our intellectual products—our philosophy and religion, and our institutions for governing, learning, and the arts—have a material basis and are thus dependent on the natural world. Human society may be distinct, i.e., different, from the rest of the natural world, but it is not independent from it. Society is an extension of the natural world from which we humans have labored to transform materials (e.g., iron, rubber, petroleum, stone, among many others) into our own created products that make up society (such as asphalt roads and automobiles).

In short, our mediation of the relationship between society and nature involves an economic process. Material is extracted from the natural world and transformed into social products through human labor, which takes place within economic relations (the organization and structure of labor in production). Although the formation of economic relations is necessary for our livelihood, such relations are neither natural nor benign. Economic relations are social and structure society, and they impact the natural world; the mediation between nature and society produces effects that reverberate in each. Moreover, economic relations cannot be separated from the energy required to make them productive. Without energy, which must also be extracted from the natural world, an economy cannot produce. Not all economic relations, however, produce the same consequences; some relations are more destructive than others. Although the economic relations of the ancient world produced harmful environmental effects, such as deforestation and salination of the soil (see Hughes 1975; Redman 1999), the degradation of the natural world was limited by the structure of the relations and by the limited supply and flow of energy available. Their economic relations were not structured to produce economic growth. Indeed, ancient economies did not experience any sustained, per capita growth. Their primary source of energy was from the food they consumed. For hundreds of thousands of years, early humans lived from gathering wild plants and hunting animals. Beginning around twelve thousand years ago, humans began growing their own food and raising animals for their meat, secondary products, and muscle. But agriculture only supplied a modest surplus of energy beyond subsistence needs, limiting the growth of the economy. Wind and flowing water also contributed to the energy supply, and certainly benefited those who could exploit it, but it represented only a small portion of the overall economy.

The dominant economic relations of our society, in contrast, are capitalist relations of production, and they have had an especially destructive effect on the natural world. Capitalist relations are structured to facilitate economic growth, and the ever-growing capitalist economy is powered by, and dependent upon, the burning of cheap fossil fuels. Beginning in the eighteenth century with the burning of coal for the steam engine, and accelerating at the end of the nineteenth century with the many uses for petroleum and natural gas, capitalist relations have consumed the energy from decayed plants and animals, which had been sequestered within the earth. As with the ancient economies, the contemporary capitalist economy is fueled by solar energy, converted through photosynthesis into organic material. But unlike the ancients who were dependent on renewable natural cycles for their energy, capitalist relations have drawn down within two hundred years the energy stock that took the natural world millions of years to produce. Although fossil fuel reserves remain, existing sources are diminishing and new sources are increasingly costly to extract. The energy from fossil fuels have empowered capitalist relations to extract numerous resources from the natural world—today, over one hundred billion tonnes per year (Carrington 2020)—transform those resources into varied products that make up society, and degrade and pollute the natural world. Moreover, burning of fossil fuels has released long-sequestered carbon into the atmosphere—hundreds of gigatons of carbon dioxide, and increasing (Frumhoff 2014)—causing global warming and the climate to change. The current environmental crisis is a result of our own mediation between nature and society as human labor, governed by capitalist social relations of production and empowered by fossil fuels, has exploited the natural world without regard for the consequences, both for the natural world and for society. As climate change is making abundantly clear, human degradation of the natural world—in this case, the disruption of the carbon cycle by spewing too much carbon dioxide into the atmosphere—already has had serious consequences for society and portends much worse to come (Wallace-Wells 2019).

Because our mediation of the relationship between society and nature is determined by our political economy, the solution to the crisis must entail a change in the political economy. Primarily, we need to transform our economic relations and the energy they consume. The two are linked together. Politics, ideology, and religion may play a role because they determine, in part, the economic relations of the society, but they are not effective apart from their contribution to the political economy. Only when our economic relations are no longer structured around growth, and the energy we consume produces substantially less greenhouse gases will we be able to respond effectively to the current environmental crisis. All other actions, such as conserving water and electricity and reducing, reusing, and recycling materials, as virtuous and necessary as they might be, simply treat the *symptoms* of the crisis rather than its *causes*. Without addressing economic relations and the energy required for their production, the environmental crisis will persist. Our current political economy—the way we mediate the relationship between society and nature—is simply not sustainable within the natural systems of Earth.

The environmental crisis is first and foremost an economic problem. It is also a political problem, a humanist problem, and a religious problem, but it is our economy and its unquenchable thirst for energy that is propelling the crisis forward. This book thus begins in Part I by focusing on the political economy of ancient Israel. I do this for two reasons. First, I want to provide the appropriate context for understanding the biblical texts that were produced by the Israelite political economy. Because my concern is with the mediation between society and nature, I focus explicitly on creation in the Bible as a lens through which to explore ancient Israel's political economy. Although modern conceptions of creation emphasize cosmology and evolutionary biology with no attention to human society, ancient conceptions of creation emphasize human society and its connection to the material world. Ancient Israel's creation myths are no different, and they will provide insight into how the Israelites understood their mediation between society and nature.

Second, the political economy of ancient Israel provides an example of an alternative economic base by which to contrast our current capitalist economy. In particular, the Israelite political economy suggests possibilities for how contemporary societies may function without economic growth and by consuming less energy. In this regard, I must tread carefully; I am not suggesting that we can reconstitute the political economy of the ancient Israelites, nor would I want to. Norman Gottwald raised this caution many years ago: "No ethical prescription or mode from the Bible can be lifted out and employed today without considering its context and ours. Broadly speaking, there is no good reason to believe that we can ever return to earlier modes of production such as prevailed in biblical times" (1993, 345). He indicated further that any linkage between the ancient and the contemporary economies will be "perspectival and motivational rather than prescriptive and technical" (1993, 345). Although Gottwald was primarily concerned with economic inequality, oppression, and poverty, his caution is equally relevant to environmental concerns. Yet, in terms of the environment, two critical issues provide a contextual link between the capitalist political economy and the ancient Israelite political economy—namely, the role played by economic growth and the consumption of energy. In other words, despite the differences between the ancient and the contemporary economies, *the necessary remedy for the capitalist economy*—restructure economic property and social relations to eliminate the need for growth and reduce the use of energy, especially fossil fuels—*was a characteristic of the ancient economy*. Therefore, in Part II of this book, I will explore how the political economy of ancient Israel, as expressed through its religion and biblical texts, might support alternatives to our current environmentally destructive capitalist relations.

THE DEBATE OVER CLIMATE CHANGE

Although the environmental crisis involves many problems with our mediation between society and nature, climate change may be viewed as representative of the crisis. Not only is the root cause of climate change—the burning of fossil fuels to power an ever-growing economy—the cause of so many other environmental problems, but its consequences will also affect so many other natural and social systems: a recent literature review identified 467 ways by which human health, water, food, the economy, infrastructure, and security already have been adversely affected by the consequences of climate change, and these will only intensify as climate change increases (Mora et al. 2018). At this point in the introduction, some might expect an overview of climate change and a defense that it is real. I have decided not to provide one, except to note, as I have already and will do again, that climate change is the result of burning fossil fuels.[3] The science of climate change is well known in academic circles and has been widely accepted by the populace, and the consequences of climate change have been stated, perhaps *ad nauseum*, in various media and in the press. I assume all this in what follows. If the reader needs more information, or some assurance that climate change is real, I recommend the scientific assessments of the Intergovernmental Panel on Climate Change (IPCC), which are available online. For a more popular presentation, I recommend Naomi Klein's *This Changes Everything: Capitalism vs. The Climate*, which not only lays out the facts about climate change, but connects it to the demands of capitalism, a thesis I contribute to here. David Wallace-Wells' *The Uninhabitable Earth: Life after Warming* describes in chilling detail many of the

---

3. Climate change is actually the result of numerous greenhouse gases in the atmosphere, produced in multiple ways and from multiple sources; but carbon dioxide emissions from burning fossil fuels is the overwhelming cause and will be the primary focus of our discussion of climate change in this work.

inevitable consequences of unchecked climate change, though primarily their impact on humans and society, and Paul Hawken's *Drawdown: The Most Comprehensive Plan Ever Proposed to Reverse Global Warming* provides a compelling analysis of the many ways we can mitigate the consequences of climate change. This book is too long for me to repeat what is already well known or is accessible elsewhere, so if you need more information, please turn to these sources.

Climate change, unfortunately, has become a contentious and divisive issue in political and religious circles, with conservatives of various stripes often denying that climate change is a problem or rejecting solutions as unnecessary or economically untenable. This stands in contrast to a near universal acceptance of climate change within the scientific community (see Thompson 2010; Oreskes 2004; IPCC 2014). The reasons for this denial or complacency in the face of what many would label as a crisis are complex. A prominent reason is economics: if the scientific consensus on climate change is true, then our current capitalist economic system and consumption of fossil fuels must change (and this is the primary argument of this book). For many who are benefiting from the current economy, this price is too high, especially when the worst consequences of climate change will not be realized for many years; it is easier to reject or simply ignore climate change. A recent letter to the *Wall Street Journal* (Firsch 2020) insightfully notes that as long as climate activists demand the disassembly of capitalism to address the climate crisis, people on the right will continue to deny its existence. Those who are financially or ideologically invested in the current economic system (from neoliberal thinktanks to petroleum corporations) have cynically rejected the scientific research, including their own research, and have funded disinformation campaigns to dissuade the public of its veracity (Klein 2014, 38–46; Oreskes and Conway 2010; Frumhoff and Oreskes 2015). Many others are simply complacent because of the economic costs. Even though most U.S. Americans acknowledge the reality of climate change, most are unwilling to significantly alter the economy or prioritize climate change over other economic issues such as jobs and health care (Jamieson 2006). This is true for many liberals as well as conservatives.

Many conservatives, and especially conservative Christians, have rejected climate change because environmentalism in general and climate change in particular have become politicized; climate change is viewed as part of the package of liberal politics. Despite the fact that George H. W. Bush pledged to fight climate change when its potential effects were first becoming widely known in the 1980s, by the time his son, George W. Bush, became president, Republicans overwhelmingly rejected climate change, primarily for economic reasons (see Rich 2019). Barack Obama became president in 2008, campaigning, in part, to fight against climate change, then Donald J. Trump became president in 2016, claiming that climate change is a hoax. Democrats and Republicans have aligned themselves on the issue accordingly, with only minor exceptions. Conservative Christians, for their part, have largely aligned with Republicans and have shared their skepticism and denial of climate change (there are a few notable exceptions, such as the Evangelical Environmental Network and the Evangelical Climate Initiative; see Hayhoe 2019). Some conservative Christians have treated climate change, along with environmentalism, not only as a liberal political threat but also as a neo-pagan or atheistic threat to their faith (Zaleha and Szasz 2015; Cornwall Alliance 2009), and it is to the religious dimensions of the climate change debate that I want to give attention here.

At a religious level, climate change *should* appear to be uncontroversial for Christians. The Bible, for obvious reasons, does not specifically address climate change, nor does it suggest that humans cannot alter the climate. Instead, the Bible presents a world in which human behavior, whether it is righteous following God's laws or sinful contrary to God's commands, will have consequences in the world. Climate change could easily be understood to be the consequence of our collective human failure to exercise appropriately our divinely-appointed stewardship role in creation. Moreover, the science of climate change is uncontroversial within the scientific community, and it does not seem to challenge significant theological doctrines. In other words, unlike the debate between creation and evolution, or the many other religion versus science debates where significant theological issues are at stake, embracing the scientific consensus on climate change requires no accommodation in reading the Bible or with Christian doctrine. The recognition of anthropogenic climate change is compatible with the Christian faith. Or so it would seem. But reality is much more complicated. Although a minority of Evangelicals, for example, embrace climate change and have issued a call to address it (Evangelical Climate Initiative 2006), the majority do not and the National Association of Evangelicals has refused to take a stand on the issue (Cooperman 2006; they have issued a document regarding the effects of climate change on the poor, see Boorse 2011). Some conservative Christians reject or ignore climate change because of their eschatological orientation. Because they believe that Jesus will imminently return, probably within their own lifetime, the long-term dangers posed by climate change are deemed irrelevant, or the coming catastrophe is believed to fit within God's plan for the end-times (Barker and Bearce 2012; Nichols 2019). Other conservative Christians reject climate change, and many of the ancillary ideas associated with it, as incompatible with the biblical worldview (see Cornwall Alliance 2009). In none of these cases, however, is the issue simply what the Bible claims, though many biblical texts may be cited, or what the faith believes.

Because of the post-modern critique, we recognize that all readings of the Bible, or the readings of any other text for that matter, are dependent on the context of the readers—their historical-social location, ideology, and identity. It is not surprising, therefore, that many conservative Christians read their Bible in relation to climate change yet construct religious beliefs about climate change that are similar in effect to the beliefs of their conservative political and economic allies. Their readings of the Bible have been shaped by their political and economic beliefs. But dependency is not determinacy, and it is too facile to claim that such conservative Christians have simply imposed their political and economic views onto the Bible, as if such readings were inevitable. They are not. Other readings are possible. Nevertheless, such readings are chosen because they fit a particular political economy, which the potential consequences of climate change threaten to unravel, and they are divinely sanctified by the authority that the readers have given to them. Although the situation posed by climate change is unique, the religious debate over climate change shares many features with other debates between science and religion, and the Bible's role in these debates may offer us some insight into the current situation.

Two Modes of Reading the Bible

The battles between religion and the sciences, broadly understood, have often been fought by Christians on the battlefield of the Bible. Although the first salvo in any given battle began with science—a new discovery or the formulation of a new theory—the battle itself was frequently fought over competing interpretations of the Bible: for example, whether the Bible assumes a heliocentric or a geocentric view of the world; whether the temporal framework in the Bible is compatible with the geologically derived age of the earth; and, of course, foremost among other conflicts, whether the stories in Genesis can be reconciled with Darwinian evolution (Brown 2010, 6). The new science was either rejected, in total or in part, as incompatible with the truth revealed in Scripture, or if the science was embraced for the most part, then the interpretation of the biblical texts was accommodated to this new knowledge in such a way as to uphold the Bible's authority. The crux of the debate, however, was not simply the meaning of one or another biblical passage, but rather the nature and source of biblical authority and its relation to other authorities (scientific, ecclesial, political). What ostensibly has played out as a battle between religion and science is predominantly a conflict among church leaders, theologians, and other Bible readers over whether the Bible's authority is compatible with the results of the new science. Consequently, the battles between religion and science, including the religious debate over climate change, cannot be resolved for the religious combatants through recourse to newer and better science, or better science education, but rather must be addressed on the basis of the character of the Bible and the nature of the authority imputed to it. Only when the authority given to the Bible is understood to be compatible with the procedures and results of climate science, in our current situation, will the religious denial of climate change yield to more productive dialogue and understanding.

Through most of the history of Christianity, the Bible was read confessionally; it was a present, living word through which its readers heard the Word of God. Although made up of numerous texts, produced over hundreds of years, the collection of diverse biblical texts into a scriptural canon emphasized their unitary meaning. Moreover, the Bible was read through the unifying focal lens of the life and work of Jesus Christ as expressed through the creeds and church teaching, and difficult or problematic biblical passages were interpreted in reference to other biblical passages. Despite apparent contradictions or inconsistencies in the texts, the Bible was recognized to be perfectly harmonious, with no meaningful mistakes; it was divinely inspired, given by God first to Israel and then to the church.[4] The Bible's authority was embedded in the church, which provided the context for its interpretation. Through this scriptural mode of reading, the meaning of the Bible was expressed through the church and its authority was thus transparent. However, the rise of philology and textualization during the Renaissance and the fracturing of religious authority during the Reformation undermined this scriptural mode of reading the Bible and laid the groundwork for an alternative mode of reading (Legaspi 2010).

The academic mode of reading the Bible, which is characteristic of modern biblical studies, had its origin in the Enlightenment university of eighteenth-century Germany. According to Michael Legaspi (2010), this new, academic mode of reading the Bible developed as a political and moral response to the moribund Bible inherited from the Reformation. The division of the Western church during the Reformation had disembedded the Bible from the Roman Catholic Church so that its authority was located in the text, apart from the church's authority. With the reformers' emphasis on Scripture, the Bible's authority not only superseded the Roman Catholic Church's right to pronounce authoritatively on it, but also enabled the Bible to be used in opposition to those parts of the tradition that the reformers viewed as pernicious. Because the Bible was independently authoritative, its meaning should be singular and self-contained, according to the plain sense of the text. But such a unitary meaning often escaped its interpreters; instead, the authority and meaning of the Bible was contested by competing, emerging churches. The result was the Bible could no longer simply be read confessionally. Rather than promoting the unity of the church, the interpretations of the Bible catalyzed and reinforced the fractures. By the eighteenth century, such scriptural readings of the Bible "only seemed to perpetuate war, obscurantism, and senseless religious division . . ." (Legaspi 2010, 10).

While the Reformation separated the Bible's authority from the Roman Catholic Church, the legacy of the Renaissance served to undermine the authority of the Bible entirely. The Bible as sacred cripture was initially untouched by the discipline of philology because it was viewed as a uniquely authoritative text. It was incomparable to other texts because of its divine authorship, and so was immune to the vagaries of history. The differences between various versions of the Bible and their multiple manuscripts, however, raised the specter of error, and so philology was employed in the service of the church to determine the authentic manuscripts. Nevertheless, Erasmus' and the reformers' use of philology also served to demonstrate that the Bible

---

4. James Kugel (2007) argues that the scriptural mode of reading the Bible, for Jews and Christians, was based on four assumptions: 1) the Bible is fundamentally cryptic; 2) the Bible is filled with instruction for its readers; 3) the Bible contains no contradictions or mistakes; and 4) the Bible is divinely given.

had a history. As more ancient texts came to light and as the Bible itself was textualized, humanist scholars began to recognize the Bible's contingency—the Bible was not exceptional but rather the product of historical human authors. By the end of the seventeenth century, the Bible's exceptionalism and the authority it engendered was no longer readily apparent (see McCalla 2006, 28–39).

The new, academic mode of reading the Bible emerged in the eighteenth century as a way to shore up the failing authority of the Bible. For the German Enlightenment scholars—Gotthold Lessing, Johann Semler, and, most notably, Johann Michaelis, among others—the Bible belonged to a foreign, ancient world, and as such was a dead literary corpus like the Greek and Roman classics. Moreover, because the ancient biblical texts were discontinuous with contemporary Christianity, the Bible could no longer speak as a unifying scripture for the church. Nevertheless, these scholars sought to preserve the cultural relevance of the Bible for public life; the Bible possessed a cultural authority, like the classics, which could reinforce the ideal social and political values of the modern state. The Bible was interpreted like the classics. Rather than reading the Bible within a confessional context, these scholars placed the biblical texts in their ancient historical and cultural contexts; they sought to get behind the texts in order to understand the events that produced them. "Instead of looking *through* the Bible in order to understand *the truth about the world*, eighteenth-century scholars looked directly at the text, endeavoring to find new, ever more satisfactory frames of cultural and historical reference by which to understand *the meaning of the text*" (Legaspi 2010, 26).

The often-contentious relationship between the academic and scriptural modes of reading the Bible—two modes sharing the same text but with different understandings of authority—mirrors in many ways the core conflict in the religion and science debates (on the history of this conflict, see McCalla 2006). In the debate over Darwinian evolution, for example, the credibility of the science was only a secondary issue. The primary battle was over the nature and interpretation of the beginning chapters of Genesis.[5] For those adopting an academic mode of reading, the stories in Genesis can be divided into two distinct traditions, each representing a distinct historical period in Israelite history and religion. Moreover, the similarities these traditions share with Mesopotamian creation myths (despite some historical and cultural differences) indicate that the biblical stories share a similar mythic worldview. For such readers, the Genesis stories, as ancient tales or myths, were irrelevant to the modern quest to understand human origins and biological diversity, which Darwinian evolution sought to explain. For those embracing the scriptural mode of reading the Bible, however,

---

5. This was also the case for the Scopes trial of 1925, by far the most significant forum for the so-called religion and science debate in the U.S. According the McCalla, only Clarence Darrow seemed to think the focus of the debate was the incompatibility between religion and science. "Everyone else, on both sides, recognized the trial as an outlying skirmish in the battle for Christian America between Fundamentalists and their theologically liberal and moderate opponents . . . whose embrace of biblical criticism and theistic evolution betrayed the inerrant Bible and the true faith" (2006, 164).

the academic interpretation of Genesis undermines the Christian faith more so than evolutionary science because it challenges the very authority and truth of the Bible. For scriptural readers, the stories in Genesis, in accord with the Christian tradition, attest to God as the one who creates humans in his image and brings all other life into being. Such a meaning of the Bible is inspired and infallible, and so cannot simply be dismissed as ancient mythic thinking. Moreover, the biblical text makes no room for Darwinian evolution, which would deny the central role of God in the creation of life. Therefore, scriptural readers often reject the academic interpretation of Genesis, along with its ally Darwinian evolution, as examples of fallen-human error.

Although the debates over the meaning of the Bible in relation to the natural sciences were the most public and sensational, they were far from being the most frequent and significant. Beginning in the nineteenth century, biblical higher criticism, which characterizes the academic mode of reading the Bible, has repeatedly challenged the scriptural reader's understanding of the nature of the Bible and its interpretation. First, biblical critics used philology and literary and form criticisms to construct new understandings of the origin, composition, and dating of the biblical texts. Second, scholars used historical analysis and tradition criticisms in conjunction with archaeological results to rewrite an ancient history, which challenged the historical veracity of the Bible's foundational stories. Third, biblical critics placed the biblical traditions in the context of the history of religions and employed social-scientific criticisms to develop new understandings of the Israelite religion and worldview. This dismantled many of what had previously been understood as the Israelites' distinctive characteristics. In other words, most modern biblical critics, like their eighteenth-century forebearers, view the Bible as unexceptional and interpret it as a product of its ancient historical, cultural, and social contexts.

Within the Western world where this distinction developed, the academic mode of reading came to dominate biblical scholarship and liberal Protestant Christianity,[6] while the scriptural mode of reading persisted in various forms in conservative ecclesial contexts.[7] Many Bible readers, in fact, have attempted to embody both modes of reading. On the one hand, they critically read the Bible in its ancient context; on

---

6. Gordon Kaufman (1971) articulates the liberal Christian understanding of the Bible: it is a historical text of a people's experience and understanding of God. The Bible continues to be valuable, though not authoritative, as the principle historical reports about God, and therefore an indispensable source for the knowledge of God.

7. Reading the Bible in the Roman Catholic Church follows a different history than in Protestantism largely because the authority of the Bible was never disembedded from the church. Roman Catholics never embraced an independent authority of the Bible and so their scriptural mode of reading the Bible continued to be mediated by the teaching of the church. On the negative side, conflicts with science, such as in the Galileo affair, pitted the authority of the church against the new science. On the positive side, however, the church could more easily learn from the sciences and so its authority could clear the way for a fruitful dialogue between scriptural and academic readers of the Bible. The Pontifical Biblical Commission's document, *The Interpretation of the Bible in the Church* (1993), is a product of such dialogue.

the other hand, they seek to hear a text that continues to speak the Word of God. They have approached the two modes of reading much like Stephen J. Gould's "non-overlapping magisteria" (1997): science can tell us about the historical and material world, whereas the Bible can tell us about the spiritual world (see Denis Lamoureux's approach below). What ultimately distinguishes the two modes of reading, however, is the nature and scope of biblical authority, and the scriptural mode in particular has been increasingly shaped in response to the academic mode. Scriptural readers have learned from and embraced some of the methods of interpretation used by academic readers. They have incorporated many of the useful insights of academic criticisms in order to better understand the Bible in its ancient context. Yet, when issues of authority arise, the two modes part ways. For many scriptural readers, the presuppositions of the academic mode of reading, which rejects the intrinsic authority of the Bible, make this interpretive framework untenable. The anti-supernatural bias of academic readers, for example, is believed to distort their understanding of the Bible. The Bible, for scriptural readers, does not reflect ancient superstitious or mythic thinking, but the actual engagement of God in our world. Thus, scriptural readers are more likely to accept the biblical text at its face value—what the Bible overtly claims, rather than what academic criticisms might suggest. Moreover, scriptural readers are not content simply to understand the ancient contextual meaning of the Bible; they also seek to read the biblical text as the living Word of God, which continues to speak to contemporary believers.

According to the academic mode of reading, the Bible possesses no intrinsic authority, but only that which was historically ascribed to it by the church or others. The meaning of the Bible is historically and culturally contingent, and its interpretation is subject only to reason and the growing canons of humanistic and scientific knowledge. This mode of reading the Bible cannot conflict with new scientific discoveries or knowledge because such new knowledge would contribute to a new reading of the Bible. The scriptural mode of reading, in contrast, presumes the Bible is intrinsically and, in many ecclesial contexts, exclusively authoritative as the Word of God. Although the Bible is often recognized to have a history, the production of the Bible is nevertheless proclaimed to be divinely inspired. For many scriptural readers, the Bible's interpretation is subject to the Bible itself, for the Bible's meaning, properly understood, is singular and without error. New scientific knowledge may indeed conflict with the scriptural reading of the Bible when the science challenges or contradicts the assumed meaning of the biblical text. Under such circumstances, the relationship between the Bible's meaning and the scientific knowledge will be negotiated in such a way as to preserve the Bible's authority (see Harlow 2010; Kurka 2013). In some cases, the scientific knowledge will be rejected as the product of fallen-human error, but in other cases, either the meaning of the Bible or the significance of the scientific knowledge will be accommodated to the other (see Schneider 2012). In most cases, the authority of the Bible is bolstered by emphasizing dogmas such as divine verbal

INTRODUCTION

inspiration and inerrancy, which preclude any debate that might challenge that authority. This is what has happened with debate over climate change.

THE BIBLE AND ITS AMBIGUOUS AUTHORITY

For scriptural readers, the intrinsic authority of the Bible would seem to settle controversial issues that might challenge their faith. Unfortunately, what precisely is authoritative and its significance alludes us. A common claim is that the intended meaning of the sacred writers is authoritative. But who determines the intention of writers who are long dead? By what criteria do we adjudicate between possible intentions? Even if we could discern their intentions (which we cannot), is everything they intended authoritative? Because biblical authority is linked with divine inspiration, perhaps the writers' intention is not decisive. What role did God play in the composition of the text? Can we separate God's intentions from the writers' intentions? The notion of biblical authority does not answer these questions. Nor can other claims of biblical authority—where it is located and its significance—be resolved with unanimity. Authority, when exclusively ascribed to the text of the Bible, provides no help in adjudicating between competing interpretations of the Bible, nor can it contribute to how a particular biblical text *should* be interpreted. For this reason, in part, the Protestant tradition has fragmented into so many distinct church bodies, with each claiming authority for their distinctive understanding of the Bible and practice. When the Bible's authority was disembedded from the Roman Catholic Church at the Reformation, biblical authority lost its anchor; it is now like a ship floating at sea, subject to all the winds, waves, and currents that its readers bring to interpreting the biblical text. Biblical authority can determine no particular meaning, yet it can provide divine sanction for every interpretation gleaned from the biblical text. In other words, biblical authority is a human product, mediated by churches, and used by the faithful to legitimate particular understandings and practices based on their readings of the Bible.

I am not claiming, of course, that the Bible does not have authority. Such a claim would be patently and demonstrably false—many people have changed their thinking and behavior based on their reading of the Bible. Rather, my claim is that our understanding of the location and significance of biblical authority is contingent on our social-historical location, ideology, and identity, just as our interpretations are contingent. The problem for scriptural readers, who give priority to their understanding of the Bible over the knowledge gleaned from the sciences, is that their conception of biblical authority simply reinforces their interpretation of the Bible—indeed, it gives it divine sanction. It becomes a self-perpetuating circular enterprise with no external criteria by which to assess their understanding. Academic readers of the Bible do not face *this particular problem*. Although their interpretations of the Bible are just as contingent, they read the Bible in relation to numerous external issues and datasets, which have the effect of disrupting such contingencies with new information. Their interpretations are not endlessly circular, though they certainly may be biased; their use of external material in their interpretations, however, serves to isolate and thus reduce their biases. In order to illustrate this problem with scriptural readings of the Bible, let me turn to a critical issue that should be settled: the historicity of Adam. Although early readers of the Bible may have believed that Adam and Eve were the actual first human beings in the world, the modern sciences have dispelled any such naïveté. Moreover, our understanding of myths no longer leads us to expect Adam and Eve to have been real individuals. Nevertheless, for many scriptural readers, the historicity of Adam is a real concern.

The recent evangelical debates over the historical Adam are a direct result of the recent mapping of the human genome and subsequent genomic research (Ostling 2011). Prior to this research, scriptural readers of the Bible could accommodate varying degrees of evolutionary science without challenging biblical authority; their belief in God's special creation of humans was compatible with the evolutionary science.[8] They would argue, for example, that God intervened in the evolution of humans and created Adam and Eve as the first *modern* humans, from which all other modern humans are descended, or that modern humans were similarly created by God, but Adam and Eve were a more recent human couple, dating perhaps to the early Neolithic period, with whom God initiated a special relationship as representative of humankind (see Young 1995). In either case, the biblical authority was defended, and the truth of the Bible was upheld in relation to the overwhelming evidence of evolution. Moreover, the scientific research on mitochondrial DNA and Y-chromosome sequences seemed to support the biblical idea of a common human ancestor in the relatively recent past; human evolution, it was argued, had experienced a population bottleneck from which modern humans had emerged.

All this changed with recent genomic research. The genomic evidence suggests that the human population has not experienced an extreme population bottleneck for at least the last nine million years,[9] and that modern humans descend from an interbreeding population of at least several thousand (Venema 2010). In other words, the genomic evidence rules out the possibility that a historical Adam and Eve were the biological ancestors of all modern humans. This was, of course, not surprising news

---

8. The Catholic Church has essentially taught the same. In *Humani Generis*, Pius XII reluctantly accepted evolution, but insisted that "Catholic faith obliges us to hold that souls are immediately created by God" (1950, §36). Moreover, Pius (1950, §37) insisted that any form of polygenism—that all humans did not originate from a single human pair (Adam and Eve)—must be rejected and is incompatible with the church's teaching on original sin. John Paul II (1997), writing before the mapping of the human genome and the understanding of its implications for human evolution, reaffirmed Pius' teaching, especially with regard to the soul, but also acknowledged that the Church's understanding of Scripture must be informed by the results of the latest scientific research.

9. The most recent bottleneck was caused by the eruption of Toba, a large volcano in Sumatra, approximately 74,000 years ago. Afterwards, the human population may have shrunk to as few as 10,000 individuals (Smil 2019, 309), but too many individuals to have enabled a common human male or female ancestor.

to academic biblical critics, who had long ago abandoned any pretense of a historical primordial couple. When compared with other ancient Near Eastern creation stories such as Atrahasis, Adapa, and Enuma Elish, biblical critics recognized that the Genesis creation stories are of the same genre and serve similar purposes, and while Adam and Eve have mythic and literary roles in the narrative, they are not historical figures. Scriptural readers of the Bible, however, could not so easily come to this conclusion because so much more was at stake for them. As a story of historical, that is, real individuals, the garden narrative in Genesis 2–3 explains how sin historically came into the world through human rebellion, accompanied by spiritual death. Moreover, Jesus seems to refer to a real Adam and Eve (Matt 19:4), and Paul contrasts Adam's sin, which brought death for all humans, with Jesus' righteousness, which brings justification for all (Rom 5:12–20). For scriptural readers, the loss of a historical Adam challenges fundamental aspects of Christian theology, but more importantly, it challenges the authority of the Bible. It raises the question of whether the Bible is made up of a patchwork of true and false texts: if the story of human sin and death is fictional, can we trust the gospel, which offers the remedy? The loss of a historical Adam, for many, would appear to undermine the Bible's authority as a whole, and so call into question the truth of the Bible.

A recent book on the historical Adam has brought together four evangelical scholars, each with a different relationship to evolutionary science, to discuss the significance of Adam's existence or non-existence for Christian faith and practice and for the Christian worldview and theology (Barrett and Caneday 2013). What is not at issue in the discussion is the authority of the Bible, which is assumed and fortified throughout the discussion. Instead, each scholar demonstrates how his interpretation of the Bible, in negotiation with or rejection of evolutionary science, reinforces the authority of the Bible for Christian life and theology.

At one extreme, William D. Barrick (2013), a young-earth creationist (the earth is only six to ten thousand years old), predictably rejects evolutionary science in favor of a literalistic reading of the Genesis creation stories, including a literal historical Adam. His view of the scope of biblical authority demands that the claims of science should be rejected if they contradict what the Bible says, because only the Bible is inspired and inerrant. The authority of the Bible ensures its truth, and so his literal understanding of the garden narrative in Genesis is reinforced by his view of biblical authority.

At the other extreme, Denis O. Lamoureux (2013) embraces evolutionary creation and argues that Adam was not a historical person. Interestingly, he begins his discussion with a rather long rehearsal of his spiritual and intellectual pilgrimage in order to assure his audience that he is a faithful Christian. When he deals with the creation stories of Genesis, he places them in their Near Eastern context and makes the case that the biblical texts present the world in terms of an ancient science, which does not align with modern scientific facts. Nevertheless, and here is his scriptural move, God accommodated the biblical authors of Genesis by using the science of their day in order to communicate his teaching. Similarly, God also employed "an ancient understanding of human origins—the *de novo* creation of the first man Adam—as an incidental vessel to deliver inerrant spiritual truths" (2013, 61). In other words, although there was no historical Adam, biblical authority remains secure because it was God, as the divine author of Scripture, who told the fictional story about Adam; and God did so because only through such a story, using the ancient science of the day, could God's truth be intelligible to the ancient biblical authors and the ancient Israelite audience. Lamoureux's embrace of biblical authority does not result in a self-reinforcing interpretation of the Genesis narrative because he includes much scientific and Near Eastern knowledge in his reading of the Bible. But his understanding of biblical authority is quite circumscribed; it guarantees only the spiritual truth of the Bible, not its historical or scientific veracity (cf. Enns 2012).

The intermediary positions of John H. Walton (2013), who takes no stand on evolution, and C. John Collins (2013), who is an old-earth creationist, demand more negotiation between science and their interpretations of Genesis in order to uphold the Bible's authority, and as such their view of biblical authority only moderately reinforces their interpretations of Genesis. Walton's unique approach to the Genesis creation stories is his claim that they are not addressing material origins, but functionalities. The literary characters of Adam and Eve function as archetypes of humans in their relationship to God, and of men and women in God's created order. The Bible makes no scientific or historical claim about material human origins, and is thus compatible with a theistic evolution (though he does not embrace it). Nevertheless, Walton believes in a historical Adam and Eve, though they might not be the first humans, because they are linked into a genealogy and their historical actions best explain how sin and death come to all humans. Although the Bible does not make claims about the actual origin of humans, he believes it does make claims about the historical actions of Adam and Eve—that they were selected out from other humans by God for a unique archetypal (i.e., representative) relationship, yet they rebelled against God, condemning all humans to death through sin. For Walton, this interpretation affirms biblical authority and thus "adheres to inerrancy in that it is distinguishing between claims the Bible makes and, more importantly, to claims that it does not make" (2013, 117; cf. Walton 2012). Yet, it is only because of Walton's embrace of biblical authority that he can argue for the historicity of Adam and Eve—the Bible treats them as real, historical individuals, and thus it must be so.

C. John Collins argues that because the garden story in Genesis 2–3 is the first part of the biblical story of salvation-history, which tells the story of God's creation and redemption through the ancestors, the exodus, and beyond, it should be interpreted as referring to real, actual, historical events. Both Jesus and Paul assumed the garden story to be narrating real events, and so also affirmed this interpretation. Thus, Adam and Eve should be understood to have been real, historical individuals who were not only supernaturally created by God in the image of God, but also the ancestors of humankind (see further Collins 2011). For Collins, the authority of the Bible demands that its story be recognized as real, as having actually happened, without a literalistic interpretation. The Bible does not give a scientific, historical description of the beginning, but rather tells the story "after the manner of a popular poet" (2013, 173). In other words, Collins makes room for some forms of evolution and a geologically ancient earth, but nevertheless sees humans as the special creation of God. He recognizes the scientific problems with a single human couple as the progenitors of all humans, and so accepts the possibility that Adam and Eve were not the only humans at the beginning. If Adam and Eve were two among many humans, he suggests that Adam may have been the chieftain of the original human tribe, and thus representative of all humans. For Collins, biblical authority, and the inerrancy that derives from it, enables some accommodation of the interpretation of the Bible to modern science, but within the limits set by the real world that the Bible presents (cf. Collins 2010). Yet, there is no reason to expect the Bible to present the real world through the garden narrative other than his conception of biblical authority. Collins' and Walton's interpretations of Adam and Eve are equally circular regarding their historicity.

In the case of each of these evangelical scholars, one's relationship to the science was predetermined by one's commitment to a particular conception of biblical authority. Moreover, each of their understandings of biblical authority and its implications for interpreting Genesis is different, for the Bible's authority rests on the Bible alone; it is self-validating and not subject to or embedded in any ecclesial (or other) authority. There would appear to be no way to adjudicate between the different positions on biblical authority, nor between their interpretations, given their views of biblical authority. Thus, the debate in which the scholars engage leaves the reader uncertain about whether biblical authority requires the existence of Adam, or is compatible with the non-existence of Adam. This uncertainty regarding the significance of Adam is highlighted in the final section of the book, where two scholars with pastoral experience comment on the significance of Adam for Christian faith. For Gregory Boyd (2013), the historical Adam is insignificant to Christian faith, and so faith is secure whether or not there was a real Adam. For Philip Ryken (2013), in contrast, a historical Adam is central to Christian faith, and without the historical Adam, one cannot rightly understand the world or Christian faith. Within the scriptural mode of reading the Bible, it is unclear how these differences can be reconciled, and biblical authority offers no help.

The problem is not that each of these evangelical scholars has a different understanding of Genesis—all interpreters differ in their interpretations to some extent. Rather, it is that their interpretations are shaped by an understanding of biblical authority that has no definitive content. According to one understanding of biblical authority, much of what we have learned from the natural sciences can be embraced, but according to a different understanding of biblical authority, somethings taught by the natural sciences contradict what God has revealed in Scripture and so must be rejected. With no authority outside of the Bible by which to validate its meaning, biblical authority is subject to the biases of its readers. Many churches and religious institutions historically have attempted to compensate for the ambiguity of biblical authority by formalizing confessions or statements of faith. Confessions such as the Nicene Creed, Apostles' Creed, or Westminster Confession function to re-embed the Bible within a shared tradition of Christianity. Statements of faith are generally more particular to the specific institutions issuing them. However, neither confessions nor statements of faith are able to resolve the ambiguity of biblical authority but only to concretize a historically contingent notion of biblical authority. Both confessions and statements of faith are historically fixed, limited in what they address, and reflect the interpretive controversies during their formulation. For example, Wheaton College, perhaps the most prominent evangelical school, declares in its Statement of Faith: "WE BELIEVE that God directly created Adam and Eve, the historical parents of the entire human race; and that they were created in His own image, distinct from all other living creatures, and in a state of original righteousness." The Statement of Faith was originally written in 1924, a year before the Scopes trial, and reflects the religious debates over evolution at that time. It precluded particular readings of the Bible, such as Adam and Eve are mythological figures. Today, in light of what we know about the nature of literary texts and especially the science from genomic research, this statement appears wholly arbitrary and out of step with a realist view of the world. Nevertheless, the Statement of Faith upholds and reinforces a particular notion of biblical authority, which validates a Bible that is "verbally inspired by God and inerrant in the original writing," and so makes human evolution incompatible with the Bible.

THE BIBLE AND CLIMATE CHANGE

The Bible can make important contributions to discussion of the current environmental crisis that climate change represents. Its values and worldview challenge how humans mediate the relationship between society and the natural world. For Christians who read the Bible academically, the biblical values and worldview may add an additional voice, from their religious tradition, to their conversations over how to respond to climate change. For the majority of Christians, perhaps over a billion people worldwide, who read the Bible scripturally in some form, the authority of the Bible can compel Christians to act on behalf of the common world we share with all peoples and creatures of Earth. Roman Catholic Christians are better situated than many conservative Protestants to address the coming crisis posed by climate change. For Roman Catholicism, the Bible remains embedded in the church. As expressed during the Second Vatican Council,

> But the task of authentically interpreting the word of God, whether written or handed on, has been entrusted exclusively to the living teaching office of the Church, whose authority is exercised in the name of Jesus Christ. This teaching office is not above the word of God, but serves it, teaching only what has been handed on, listening to it devoutly, guarding it scrupulously and explaining it faithfully in accord with a divine commission and with the help of the Holy Spirit, it draws from this one deposit of faith everything which it presents for belief as divinely revealed. (*Dei Verbum*, Vatican II 1965, §10)

Unlike the confessions and statements of faith, the teaching office of the Catholic Church is dynamic. Although the church's teaching may conflict with what is taught by the sciences—such as with the Galileo affair—the church may also learn from the sciences, as it has done. The Roman Catholic Church now embraces scientific cosmology and evolution, and Pope Francis has recently issued *Laudato Si'* (2015), an encyclical teaching about human responsibility for addressing climate change. Orthodoxy, under the leadership of the Ecumenical Patriarch Bartholomew, has followed a similar path. Many Protestant denominations, including a few Evangelical groups, have issued their own statements on climate change (see the many documents collected by GreenFaith 2018). These statements, however, lack the formal authority that might persuade church members to act on behalf of the environment, which the Roman Catholic encyclicals do have. Nevertheless, they do guide church members in their scriptural reading of the Bible, hopefully instilling the legitimacy of environmental concern.

For some conservative Protestants, such church statements on behalf of climate change are evidence of the church's surrender to liberal politics rather than a legitimate voice in the climate debate. Their political and economic ideology has distorted their reading of the Bible, which has been justified and sanctified by their understanding of biblical authority. I am not in a position to re-define biblical authority for such scriptural readers. This is a matter of faith and may be stubbornly resistant to external arguments. Nevertheless, any biblical authority worthy of adherence at least should be *consistent with the real world*, which we know, in part, through the sciences and other academic disciplines—not through a blind acceptance but a dialogue that does not preclude what might be learned from the sciences on non-scientific grounds. And the science of climate change does not challenge any traditional Christian doctrines: not the authority of the Bible, the role of humans in the creation, nor the significance of God's redemption. In any case, the marshalling of more climate science will not alter their denial, nor can the debate be engaged simply over their interpretations of the Bible. The obstacles are political and economic. For this reason, it is critical that our approach to the Bible and climate change focuses on political economy.

The current environmental crisis is the result of the political economy that has dominated the world since the industrial revolution. It has been the means by which we altered the natural world and have extracted resources and materials from it to build our society. This political economy has transcended significant ideological divisions—neither the centralized states of the Russian Federation nor the People's Republic of China are exempt. It is a political economy rooted in the unlimited growth of capitalist relations and powered by fossil fuels—what Andreas Malm (2016) calls a "fossil economy." This political economy also funds climate denial, whether it is masked by religious piety or exposed as simple self-interest. But the current political economy is unsustainable, both in terms of how we extract from and degrade the natural world, and how our society has become dependent on such extraction. It will not last. It will either result in some form of collapse, necessitated by our degradation of the natural world—our mediation has consequences for both society and nature—or it will be abandoned in favor of something else. Our exploration of the ancient Israelite political economy will offer such an alternative. Not as a replacement for our current political economy—all political economies are historical and so none can be reconstituted—but as a dialogue partner in conversation on how to address the crisis of climate change and its many environmental and social consequences.

THE PLAN OF THE BOOK

In the chapters of Part I, I explore the ancient Israelite political economy by focusing on the Israelites' mediation between society and nature, which is expressed through their myths and metaphors of creation. The household was the primary productive unit of their political economy, and the productive relations between husband and wife were the primary means by which households engaged with the natural world. These household relations were also gendered relations, and thus in chapter 1 I explore the gendered nature of these productive relations as articulated through the Yahwist creation myth. The myth presents the normative gender roles of the Israelites as complementary, constructing a metaphor between agriculture and procreation, so that the man is a farmer and his wife bears children. But the relationship between the husband and wife is also hierarchical in that the woman is dependent upon her husband for her productivity. Moreover, the gendered household relationship is replicated in the political economy in other productive relations and in the Israelites' relationship to Yhwh.

In chapter 2, I explore the relationship between society and nature more fully. From the earliest times, humans have constructed society from their labor in the natural world, which was empowered primarily by solar energy derived from plants via photosynthesis. Through the use of tools and animal muscle, humans were able to supplement their own muscle in providing for their own subsistence, but because of the limited availability of energy, ancient human economies, including ancient Israel's, experienced virtually no per capita growth. Whatever economic growth resulted from their labors was consumed by the modest population growth of the society. As a result, new social relations of production emerged as a means by which some could

INTRODUCTION

benefit from the labor of others. The focus of this chapter is on the role of energy in the economy, its capture through productive inequalities and naturalization through gender relations, and thus how the political economy mediated the Israelites relationship with the natural world.

Whereas chapter 2 focuses on how the ancient Israelite political economy engaged with the natural world for energy and material to construct society, chapter 3 turns to the role of the political economy in the history of ancient Israelite society. Drawing on a prominent distinction between the earlier Yahwist and later Priestly creation myths, I propose that a fundamental conflict within the political economy of ancient Israel was over the composition and loyalty of the household—whether the husband and wife and their children were aligned with extended kinship relations, their *mishpahah*, or with the centralized Israelite or Persian administration. The conflict over the household enables us to recognize that the two creation myths represent historically and socially distinct political economies.

I round off Part I by returning in chapter 4 to issues of gender and explore how the natural world functioned as an extended body. The ancient Israelites' experience of their physical bodies was in relation to their experience of nature, which functioned as their extended body. As a result, their experience of the natural world through subsistence agriculture shaped their understanding of their gendered bodies. Their understanding of the physical body was further replicated onto the social body, shaping the ancient Israelite understanding of creation, their social values, ritual regulations, and their gendered perception of space. The ancient Israelites' physical bodies, through their gendered labor, thus mediated the relationship between their extended body in the natural world and the social body of society.

In Part II, I turn to the current environmental crisis and explore what the biblical tradition, a product of the ancient Israelites' political economy, might contribute in response to it. The focus of the previous chapters is on the relationship between society and nature: through labor, humans construct or build up society from what is extracted from the natural world. Early human societies were quite modest in their extraction and had little *permanent* impact on the natural world other than the killing off of the megafauna. The great societies of the ancient Near East and the Mediterranean, from which Western civilization was born, had more serious and lasting effects on the natural world. Deforestation and salination of the soil are still evident today, as well as a significant reduction in the faunal diversity attested in the ancient record, but their effect on the natural world remained localized. No societies in the past have impacted the natural world to the extent of our current society, which is the product of capitalist relations, requiring unlimited growth, powered by the burning of fossil fuels, and causing global consequences. Not only have we seriously degraded the natural world, our increasing consumption of fossil fuels threatens to undermine the very civilization that the burning of fossil fuels has made possible. We cannot continue with "business as usual"; our society and civilization are not sustainable with their present structure and metabolism. A change is required.

Religion is often approached as the basis for such change by giving a moral framework to the environmental crisis, though the biblical religion has also been accused of fostering destructive values toward nature. In chapter 5, I explore the religion of ancient Israel in relation to the role of humans in creation. Contrary to the arguments and assumptions of some, the ancient Israelites were not anthropocentric. Though they did see humans are distinct within the creation, the world was not created for humans, nor was the world given to humans to use as they pleased. Instead, the ancient Israelites were theocentric. They were dependent upon God and their labor in the natural world was mediated by their relationship to God. The ancient Israelites' theocentrism shaped their values toward the natural world.

In chapter 6, I assess the political economy of the current environmental crisis. All economic activity has an impact on the natural world, but economic activity organized by capitalist property relations and social relations of production is particularly problematic because of capitalism's need for continual economic growth. Growth is built into the structure of capitalism—it cannot survive without growth—and it is dependent on the energy supplied from fossil fuels, which produce climate change. The current environmental crisis is thus the inevitable consequence of capitalist relations. As a result, the solution to the environmental crisis must entail a transformation of economic activity so that it is not dependent on growth or fossil fuels, and as such it cannot be capitalism.

Humans have always impacted their environment, but climate change is unique in scope and scale. By burning fossil fuels to excess, we have altered the climate and pushed the planet into a new geological trajectory. Thus, some Earth system scientists have argued that the planet is transitioning from the stable Holocene Epoch, during which human civilization emerged and flourished, into a new epoch that has been called the Anthropocene. What waits for us in the Anthropocene is uncertain, but it is unlikely to be a good era for humans, as the ecomodernists claim. To mitigate the effects of climate change, a significantly vocal group of scientists have begun exploring ways to geoengineer the atmosphere—to cool the planet artificially, or to remove carbon dioxide from the atmosphere—and thus save the planet for human civilization. Chapter 7 addresses the consequences of the Anthropocene and the challenges its poses for understanding human nature.

The Bible was composed during the Holocene Epoch, which was characterized by a stable climate enabling humans and human civilization to grow and flourish. The biblical cosmology, as expressed through its creation stories and other texts, is a product of that era. Now that the planet has entered a new geological epoch—the Anthropocene, as many Earth system scientists claim—which is characterized by anthropogenic climate change, among other human impacts, the biblical cosmology raises questions of theodicy: Is the creation of God faulty? Is God ultimately responsible for

INTRODUCTION

the dire consequences and suffering that humans will experience as a result of climate change? Chapter 8 considers how the changing circumstances of climate change challenge the biblical cosmology, and whether the biblical cosmology remains relevant in the Anthropocene.

In the final chapter of the book, the conclusion, I consider how societies have collapsed in the past and whether climate change poses such a threat for our contemporary human civilization—I suggest that it does. After laying out a potential economic framework for addressing climate change, I explore the role of collapse in the biblical tradition and how it links the fate humankind with the rest of the natural world—that there is no human redemption apart from the redemption of creation. I end the book on a theological note by addressing the role of human sin in climate change and the need for lamentation and repentance.

Part I
CREATION

1

Creation and Gender

THE HOUSEHOLD AND ITS DIVISIONS

THE FUNDAMENTAL SOCIAL AND economic unit of the political economy of ancient Israel was the household—the *bet ab* ("house of the father") in the Hebrew Bible (Bendor 1996; Hardin 2011; Wilk and Rathje 1982). It consisted minimally of a married father and mother and their children. But the household was not an ancient version of our nuclear family, for it generally also included other family members such as the father's widowed mother, a younger brother and his wife, an unmarried sister, and a second wife or concubine.[1] If the father's son was married, he and his wife and their children would also have been included in the household. All of these people would have lived in the same dwelling—typically, a three or four room pillared house—or perhaps in multiple attached dwellings sharing walls and a courtyard (Stager 1985). The household included domestic animals, primarily sheep and goats, and maybe a cow or an ox; if the household was well-off, servants and a resident alien also may have belonged to it. Together, the members of the typical household contributed to its production—farming, herding, and cultivating fruit trees and vines—and its reproduction—bearing, raising, and educating children, processing and preparing foodstuffs (e.g., grinding flour and making bread), and weaving cloths and making pottery for household usage (see Meyers 1988, 128–38). Although there was a clearly recognized division of labor, the production of the household at times obscured the boundaries, with everyone contributing where labor was needed, especially during peak labor-demand periods such as the harvest.

---

1. Recently, Cynthia Chapman (2016) has argued convincingly that the household also included one or more mother houses (*bet em*). Mother houses, whose sons would inherit from their father, were nested within the father's house (*bet ab*); non-inheriting sons were part of mother houses that were loosely connected to their father's house, and would have separated in time.

Part I: Creation

The members of the household can be divided into hierarchies of age and gender.[2] Children, youths, and young adults, for example, owe honor to their parents and other elders, both male and female. This may take the form of deference, but also obedience and the granting of prestige because of the knowledge, skill, or wisdom that comes with age. Age would appear to represent an uncontested hierarchy because everyone moves up the hierarchy through the reproduction of the household: children become parents and the younger become older to be replaced by newly born children. Yet, the Bible admonishes the young to honor their parents (Exod 20:12) and warns those who would strike or curse their parents on penalty of death (Exod 21:15, 17), suggesting that the age hierarchy, even if contested, was non-negotiable. The age hierarchy, however, did not exempt children from labor; they contributed to the production and reproduction of the household as soon as they were physically able, each according to his or her own gender. And the elderly continued in their household labor until they were no longer able—there was no age at which one could retire.

Gender, rather than age, was the basis for the household division of labor.[3] Men and boys engaged primarily in the production of the household and women and girls in its reproduction (see Meyers 1988, 139–64). By working in the field with their father, tending the sheep and goats, and pruning the vines and fruit trees, Israelite boys learned how to become men. Similarly, Israelite girls learned how to become women by helping their mother with younger children and preparing meals. It was primarily through their labor in the household that boys and girls were socialized into their gender roles. Gender is not natural or biologically determined, and so one of the implicit functions of the household was the reproduction of gendered men and women. Indeed, the labor of the household was determinative of the construction of gender in ancient Israel.

Although social roles or activities are an indication of gender, gender is not simply a set of roles or identities but rather a pervasive ordering of relationships based on the perceived differences between men and women. Gender is a process that extends beyond the household to encompass social structures and institutions. It is a way of signifying relationships of power (Scott 1986, 1067). "Gender is present in the processes, practices, images and ideologies, and distributions of power in the various

---

2. Not all social relationships in ancient Israel were structured hierarchically, nor was there a single hierarchy that included all hierarchical relationships. Thus, Meyers (2006) prefers the model of heterarchy, in which many, diverse structures are laterally connected rather than vertically, as a more accurate characterization of ancient Israel. Heterarchy is indeed useful to include many social relations, particular among gendered groups (for example, local women's networks formed to share labor or skills) and the interrelationship of different groupings, which might not otherwise be incorporated into a model of hierarchy. But our focus is on the social relations structured by a power differential, which are generally (always?) hierarchical or expected to be so.

3. Wealthy households that attracted or acquired non-kin members, such as slaves, indentured servants, resident aliens, or Levites, would also have been structured by a hierarchy based on status that may have shaped the division of labor. In other words, slaves and servants may have been assigned tasks, based on their status rather than gender, which neither free males nor females would have done.

sectors of social life" (Acker 1992, 567). Gender is thus evident not only in household relations but also in extended kinship relations, patron–client relations, and in the relationship between the king and his subjects, though gender may be masked by the age hierarchy. Gender also depicts the relationship between Yhwh and his people. It is characteristic of social interactions such as hospitality and acts of generosity, service and servitude, and especially warfare. The political economy encompasses all of these social relations and interactions, and so is gendered by them. Thus, our investigation of the political economy must begin with gender, which marks the fundamental social relations of production in ancient Israel.

GENDER, SEX, AND AMBIGUITY

Understanding the construction of gender has a notable history over the past few decades (see Scott 1986; Moore 1988, 12–30). Previously, scholars defined gender as the culturally specific patterns that are imposed on the biological differences of sex. The biological distinction between male and female was assumed to be a natural, given trait of all persons, whereas gender was an identity that was culturally assigned, based on one's sex, and into which one was socialized. Thus, according to Simone de Beauvoir, "one is not born, but rather becomes, a woman" (1973, 301; see Butler 1986). The same could be said of a man.

Although this distinction between a biologically-given sex and a culturally constructed gender proved useful—for example, in reconciling the culturally diverse expressions of gender with an assumed universal gender asymmetry (see Ortner 1989–90)—the distinction could not be sustained, either empirically or theoretically. At the empirical level, the distinction between sex and gender assumes that, biologically, the world displays a clear sexual dimorphism, populated by distinct males and females. But biological sex turns out not to be as binary as the distinction assumes. Rather than occurring as a sexual dimorphism, male and female forms are simply the end points on a continuum of intersexual human forms, with the male pseudo-hermaphrodite, the true hermaphrodite, and the female pseudo-hermaphrodite being the most recognizable (see Fausto-Sterling). Moreover, at the level of sex chromosomes, which would presumably determine biological sex, over 70 combinations have been detected (Gudorf 1994, 4). Sex determination—whether someone is a male or female—turns out to be an effect of gender (see also Hood-Williams).

At the theoretical level, the distinction between biological sex and constructed gender suggests the possibility of a radical discontinuity that does not seem to play out in the real world. At most, biological sex only supplies "a suggestive and ambiguous backdrop to the cultural organization of gender" (Ortner and Whitehead 1981, 1), yet biological males are usually associated with masculine concepts of gender and biological females with feminine concepts of gender. This is unexpected, given that the cultural construction of gender would seem to sever any necessary link between a given sex and a particular gender. "When the constructed status of gender is theorized as radically independent of sex, gender itself becomes a free-floating artifice, with the consequence that *man* and *masculine* might just as easily signify a female body as a male one, and *woman* and *feminine* a male body as easily as a female one" (Butler 2006, 9). But such is not the case. Instead, given that sex turns out to be an effect of gender, the cultural construction of gender, in relation to sex, is dialectical: one becomes a gender within the constraints of the deeply-held, cultural norms of gender (Butler 1986).

Rather than understanding gender as a cultural construction of biological sex, gender is better understood to be the discursive origin of sex and to be performatively produced—"that is, constituting the identity it is purported to be" (Butler 2006, 34). Gender is not an essence or substance, but a series of acts that produce the effect of an identity, or a self-understanding, which gives the appearance of a natural state of being. Gender is always a doing: "Doing gender means creating differences between girls and boys and women and men, differences that are not natural, essential, or biological. Once the differences have been constructed, they are used to reinforce the 'essentialness' of gender" (West and Zimmerman 1987, 137). Gender is generative in compelling certain kinds of behavior, and concealing through its naturalization in the context of the body (Morris 1995, 573).[4]

The performative constitution (the "doing") of gender is best discerned at the margins where gender behavior seems ambiguous or even contradictory. In the majority of cases, men and women conform to the culturally determined, normative gender expectations, which reinforce the naturalization of gender and mask the organizing schemes, or structured worldview assumptions (see Kearney 1984, 41–64), of gender behavior. Seemingly ambiguous or contradictory gender behavior, however, does not conform to what is expected naturally—that is, one's gender behavior does not seem to fit one's gender identification—and thus enables insight beneath the process of naturalization. In the biblical tradition, such marginal cases are evident when men are represented like women, or when women are represented like or are representative of men.[5] For example, Israelite men, in several prophetic texts, are col-

---

4. Although gender differences are the basis for defining sexual differences, especially in ambiguous biological cases, it is through the physical sexual differences that the gender differences themselves are naturalized. Maurice Godelier recognized this dialectical relationship between sex and gender long before the "post-constructionist" treatment of gender, as typified by Butler and others: "Sex-related differences between bodies are continually summoned as testimony to social relations and phenomena that have nothing to do with sexuality. Not only as testimony to, but also testimony for—in other words, as legitimation" (1981, 17).

5. More broadly in the ancient Near East, this type of gender ambiguity may be evidence of third and perhaps even fourth gender individuals (see the discussion of McCaffrey 2002). In the biblical tradition, however, examples of this type of gender ambiguity are determined by context and do not form what may be interpreted as an essential understanding of gender (cf. Asher-Greve 2002). There is also little evidence of a third gender, other than perhaps the references to the eunuch (on the problem of the eunuch in the biblical tradition, see Lemos 2011).

lectively represented as the wife of Yhwh, and biblical women such as Deborah, Jael, and Judith behave like men, whereas women like Hannah and the prostitutes who petition Solomon are representative of men. In all of these cases, the gender behavior of the characters is either unexpected or unexpectedly valued in relation to the gender norms of biblical Israel. This gender ambiguity provides a window into the organizational schemes of Israelite gender and a means by which to understand how gender in biblical Israel was performatively constituted.

Neutral Gender?

Tikva Frymer-Kensky (1992, 2002) addressed these and other cases of gender ambiguity in two important volumes and reached a rather unconventional conclusion that needs to be considered in this context. Distinguishing the biblical portrayal of women from the lives of actual women in ancient Israel and Judah, she notes that there is nothing distinctly female about the way women are portrayed in the Bible, nor are the goals and strategies of women distinctly feminine—they are shared by men. She acknowledges that women in biblical Israel are socially subordinate to men, and that men have the right to control a woman's sexuality, but she insists that women are not essentially inferior. She concludes: "The Bible presents no characteristics of human behavior as 'female' or 'male,' no division of attributes between the poles of 'feminine' and 'masculine,' no hint of distinctions of such polarities as male aggressivity–female receptivity, male out-thrusting–female containment, male subjecthood–female objecthood, ... or any other polarities by which we are accustomed to think of gender distinctions" (1992, 141). According to Frymer-Kensky, Israel had a unique gender-neutral ideology, based on the ontological parity of all humans, and the examples of gender ambiguity are made possible because of the dissonance between this gender ideology and the Bible's patriarchal social structure.

Although insightful in recognizing the ontological parity between men and women in the Bible, Frymer-Kensky's conception of the Bible's anthropology as gender-neutral (or gender-blind) is problematic. Some characteristics of human behavior are presented as either male or female—namely, those involved with procreation. Men have "seed" and thus rule over the process of procreation, whereas women are dependent on such "seed" to fulfill their purpose of bearing children. Numerous biblical laws seem designed to protect or reinforce this very distinction between men and women.[6]

---

6. See especially the laws in Leviticus 18 that define women in terms of the nakedness of a man and regulate the man's sexual activity. The concern in these laws is not simply incest, but also the preservation or proper use of a man's seed. Thus, when a man has sexual relations with a kinsman's wife ("copulates for seed," v. 20), the preservation of his seed becomes confused with his kinsman's seed (see Milgrom 2000, 1567; Eilberg-Schwartz 1990, 183). Similarly, when a man has sexual relations with a menstruating woman ("uncovers her nakedness," v. 19), his seed is wasted. In Leviticus 15, the impurity that results from ejaculation and menstruation are taken up in great detail. Although the priestly treatment of these two impurities are parallel, here as elsewhere the male-produced impurity

Although Frymer-Kensky acknowledges that men and women have different social roles in the biblical tradition, this is apparently not significant for her interpretation. She claims, for example, "gender [in the biblical tradition] is a matter of biology and social roles, it is not a question of basic nature or identity" (1992, 141), and then, "the differences between male and female are only a question of genitalia rather than of character" (1992, 142). Frymer-Kensky seems to view gender as social and biological traits that adhere to, and even distort, the essential human character. But such human character is only evident through the action and discourse of gendered human beings, and differently gendered human beings may express the same character or human nature without diminishing the significance of their gender. Frymer-Kensky's understanding of gender seems to be governed by polar and essentialist assumptions. Her distinction between a socially constructed gender and an essentially-given identity is simply mistaken. One cannot explain the biblical cases of gender ambiguity, or even normative gender, by removing gender from the problem.

NORMATIVE GENDER IN GENESIS 2-3

The normative gender roles of the Israelites are nowhere explicitly articulated in the biblical tradition, but expressions of these roles are found in abundance and are commonly characterized as patriarchal. Although a so-called patriarchal gender asymmetry is evident in every ancient historical society and can be found in some form in many, if not all, modern societies (see Ortner 1974), the concept of patriarchy is too universalizing to be useful for analysis. It leaves undisclosed the workings of gender and the articulation of gender asymmetry in specific cultural contexts (Butler 2006, 5–6; Meyers 1988, 24–46). In order to understand the normative gender roles of biblical Israel, I must explore the assumptions and structures that underlie the expressions of gender in the biblical texts, and there is no better place to start this analysis than with the so-called Yahwist creation myth in Gen 2:4b—3:24, where a prominent purpose of the myth is to articulate and naturalize the gender roles of the first human couple.

The composition and date of the narrative traditions in Genesis are debated by scholars. Whereas scholars forty years ago could assert with confidence that the garden narrative in Gen 2:4b—3:24 belonged to the Yahwist (J) source of the Pentateuch and that it dated from the early period of the Judean monarchy, such a consensus no longer exists (for an overview, see the essays in Gertz et al. 2016). Without taking a position on the several current competing compositional models (see Albertz 2018; Baden 2012), it is reasonable to argue that significant portions of the non-Priestly material in Genesis—most notably the primeval history and the Jacob narrative, which

---

is less severe than the female-produced impurity. Nicole Ruane argues that the prohibition against intercourse with a menstruating woman is to avoid the mixing of male and female impurities and so keeps the male and female genders distinct (2013, 181–83).

have traditionally been associated with the Yahwist source (Carr 1996, 233–89)—have their origin during the monarchic period of Israel and Judah. The specific date of the narrative, whether from the early or later monarchic period, remains unclear and should not distract us from the narrative's import for understanding normative Israelite gender (see the cautions in Sommer 2011).

The Yahwist creation myth, like all myths, is a sacred and symbolic story that encodes, generally through metaphors, the fundamental assumptions and values of the culture, including gender (Clifford 1994, 1–10; Sproul 1979, 1–30; Doniger O'Flaherty 1988, 25–33). Through a series of word plays and a rite of passage, the Yahwist myth builds a metaphor between procreation and agriculture by comparing the husband's role in procreation to the farmer who tills the arable land and plants seed in the land, and the wife's role to the arable land that is sown and brings forth new life. In the biblical tradition, as in the ancient Near East generally (Asher-Greve 2002, 16), gender is associated with one's role in procreation.

Two Gendered Relationships

The first half of the Yahwist creation myth is structured around YHWH-Elohim's[7] creation of two gendered pairs: a man (*adam*) to work the arable land (*adamah*), and a wife (*ishah*) to help the husband (*ish*). Each pair is initially constructed through a Hebrew wordplay, using the masculine and feminine forms of the same word (note the feminine ending *–ah*), but the gendered relationship is further developed in the telling of the myth. The resulting complex gendered relationship constructed from these pairs serves to naturalize the gender hierarchy in ancient Israel as well as the social relations of production and reproduction in the Israelite household.

Although the myth begins by referring broadly to YHWH "making earth and heavens" (Gen 2:4b), the focus of the Yahwist myth is exclusively on YHWH's creation of living beings (*nepesh hayyah*), first the man, then the animals and birds, and finally the woman. The material world—a lifeless earth—is preexistent in the story, but it is not suitable for human (or presumably, animal) habitation. Biblical creation myths, like their Near Eastern counterparts, always begin the story of creation with preexisting matter. Rarely does God create something out of nothing (the creation of light in Gen 1:3 is an exception). Rather, God creates by ordering, separating, or, in the case of this myth, forming the existing material of the world. In typical Near Eastern fashion,[8]

---

7. Throughout Genesis 2–3, YHWH is referred to by the compound name YHWH-Elohim, probably best translated as "YHWH, a god" (see Westermann 1984, 198–99). The compound name only occurs here and once in Exodus 9:30. Throughout our discussion of the Yahwist creation myth, however, I will refer to the deity only as YHWH for the sake of simplicity. All translations of the Hebrew Bible are the author's unless otherwise noted. Chapter and verse designations follow the English versions.

8. Bernard Batto argues that the Yahwist has reshaped earlier mythic traditions, especially the myth of Atrahasis (1992, 41–72; for the text and translation of Atrahasis, see Lambert and Millard 1999; Dalley 1991, 1–38). There are indeed many parallels between the Yahwist creation myth (which

the Yahwist creation myth describes the condition of the world when Yhwh began to create—what was lacking in the preexisting world and why: the earth was a (mostly) dry, lifeless desert with no pasturage or field crops (Hiebert 1996, 37–38) because Yhwh had not yet sent rain and there was no man to cultivate the land (Gen 2:5).[9] Thus, in order to remedy what the earth lacks, Yhwh first creates a man (*adam*) by forming him out of the dirt or soil (*'apar*)[10] from the arable land (*adamah*), which had been moistened by water welling up (*ed*) from the earth (Gen 2:6–7; see Zevit 2013, 79–80). The purpose of the man's creation is implied by the statement of what was lacking: the man is created to cultivate the arable land; and this purpose is affirmed in Genesis 3:23 when Yhwh expels the man from the garden.

The creation of the man (*adam*) from the arable land (*adamah*) constructs a gendered relationship between the two. On the one hand, the relationship is agricultural. Prior to the man's creation, the arable land was unproductive. Now, as the man cultivates the land through tilling and sowing seed, the land will produce vegetation to support human society. On the other hand, the relationship is procreative; the man is born from the arable land like a child from its mother. Human creation from soil (or clay) is a common Near Eastern metaphor for procreation, with the forming of the soil analogous to the work of God in a woman's womb during gestation. In the Mesopotamian myth of Atrahasis, for example, Enki's treading of clay and Nintu-Mami's pinching off of fourteen pieces in order to create humans are juxtaposed and linked to a description of the process and rites of childbirth.

The myth of Atrahasis contains two accounts of human creation. Whereas the first account presents the creation of humans in an abstract and general way, the second account details the process by which humans are created out of clay:

> Far-sighted Enki and wise Mami
> Went into the room of fate.
> The womb-goddesses were assembled.
> He trod the clay in her presence;
> She kept reciting an incantation,

---

extends through Gen 8:22) and the myth of Atrahasis, in structure, themes, and specific images and content, some of which are helpful in our interpretation. The myth of Atrahasis, however, gives little attention to issues of gender.

9. Terje Stordalen (1992, 10–13) divides Genesis 2:5 into four parts so that the lack of pasturage is because Yhwh had not yet sent rain, and the lack of field crops is because there was no man to cultivate the arable land. The separation of Yhwh's and the man's responsibilities into two distinct spatial areas, however, does not fit with the rest of the myth where the withholding of Yhwh's rain (the curse on the arable land) affects the cultivatable land that the man will work.

10. Hebrew *'apar* is usually translated "dust" or "dirt," but I have chosen to translate it "soil." Although in many usages, there is little difference between dirt or soil, in agricultural studies, dirt is lifeless, without the microbes, fungi, and organic matter that constitute soil. This is not a distinction that the Israelites would have made, but it is an important distinction regarding the nature of the arable land, so I also employ it here: Yhwh creates the man out of the rich topsoil that constitutes the arable land.

> For Enki, staying in her presence, made her recite it.
>
> When she had finished her incantation,
>
> She pinched off fourteen pieces (of clay),
>
> (And set) seven pieces on the right,
>
> Seven on the left.
>
> Between them she put down a mud brick.
>
> She made use of (?) a reed, opened it (?) to cut the umbilical cord,
>
> Called up the wise and knowledgeable
>
> Womb-goddesses, seven and seven.
>
> Seven created males,
>
> Seven created females,
>
> For the womb-goddess is creator of fate. (I 249–60; S iii 1–11; Dalley 1991, 16–17]

This passage uses several complex metaphors. It begins by describing the process of making bricks. Like a brick-maker, Enki prepares the clay by stomping it with his feet, but in this context his actions serve as a metaphor for the shaping of the fetus in the womb. Mami (also known as Nintu, which are names for the great mother goddess Ninhursag), recites incantations so that the fetus will be born properly. This was a common task of Near Eastern midwifes (Beckman 1983). After her incantation, she pinches off fourteen pieces of clay, which is analogous to the movement of the fetus into the birth canal. Finally, Mami puts down a mud brick as a birthstool (Lambert and Miller 1999, 259), and then delivers seven males and seven females.

The metaphorical association between the fashioning of clay and the process of childbirth is made explicit in the following lines of the myth which give instructions for performing the rituals appropriate for a woman giving birth to a baby. When a woman gives birth, a mud brick should be put in the birthing house for seven days in honor of Mami, and the mother shall sever herself from the baby by cutting the umbilical cord (S iii 15–19). The next lines of the myth repeat Mami's role in the creation of humans, but with more specific detail: the womb-goddesses count the months; when the tenth month arrives, Nintu uses a staff and opens the womb (I 277–84). Nintu-Mami unambiguously acts as a divine midwife and delivers the birth of humans, who were fashioned from clay from their mother—ostensibly the earth.

Most scholars have compared Yhwh's creation of the man not to Enki and Mami's creation in Atrahasis, but rather to Khnum's fashioning of humans on his potter's wheel (Gordon 1982, 203–4; Hoffmeier 1984, 47; Westermann 1984, 203). Indeed, this comparison with the Egyptian creator god is appropriate. Yhwh's creation of the man from the soil does evoke the image of a potter who forms a vessel from clay on his wheel. But as the Great Hymn to Khnum makes clear, the ancient Egyptians also attributed to Khnum the necessary and critical task of forming human fetuses during gestation:

PART I: CREATION

> He fashioned gods and men,
> He has formed flocks and herds;
> He made birds as well as fishes,
> He created bulls, engendered cows.
> He knotted the flow of blood to the bones,
> Formed in his workshop as his handiwork,
> So the breath of life is within everything,
> Blood bound with semen in the bones,
> To knit the bones from start.
> He makes women give birth when the womb is ready,
> So as to open . . . as he wishes;
> He soothes suffering by his will,
> Relieves throats, lets everyone breathe,
> To give life to the young in the womb. (Esna 250; Lichtheim 1980, 112)

Like a potter shapes a vessel on his wheel, so Khnum forms the fetus in the womb. In fact, without Khnum's contribution conception cannot take place. Or, as the Admonitions of Ipuwer state: "Lo, women are barren, none conceive, Khnum does not fashion because of the state of the land" (2, 4; Lichtheim 1973, 151).

Khnum's role during the birth process has been illustrated on a number of wall carvings in the temple of Deir el Bahari that depict the birth of Hatshepsut, Egypt's prominent female king (for drawings of the wall carvings, see Naville 1896, XLVI–LV). In the first relevant scene, the chief god Amun, who assumes the form of the king, is tastefully depicted having intercourse with the queen Iahmes, Hatshepsut's mother (Gordon 1977). After the intercourse, the next scene portrays Khnum fashioning Hatshepsut on his potter's wheel. Then in the following scenes, Khnum and his spouse Heket, a birth-goddess, lead the pregnant queen to the birth chamber where she delivers Hatshepsut. According to these carvings, Khnum is the one who forms and shapes the fetus during gestation. His work and skill as a potter serve as a metaphor for his activity in the womb during pregnancy (Morenz 1973, 183–84; Gordon 1982, 206).

Returning to the Yahwist creation myth, YHWH's forming the man from the soil of the arable land should be interpreted as a metaphor for the man's birth from the land (the *adamah*). YHWH acts as a potter by forming the human fetus in the womb of the earth (see Ps 139:15 for the same metaphor), then YHWH acts as a midwife by delivering the man out of the ground, breathing into its nostrils the breath of life. The use of the procreative metaphor for the man's creation, however, is incomplete, for the metaphor suggests no entailments regarding conception. Unlike in the Atrahasis myth where the mother goddess Nintu-Mami insists that Enki must first give her clay before she can create humans (I 203), the Yahwist myth assigns no sexually-analogous role to Yhwh (Yhwh may be referred to as Israel's father elsewhere in the biblical tradition, but never in reference to procreation; see Deut 1:31; 8:5; Jer 3:19; 31:9). The land can give birth to a man, but the earth is not a mother goddess and Yhwh has no sexual partner. In the religion of the biblical tradition, sexuality is not a characteristic of the divine realm.[11]

The gendered relationship between the man (*adam*) and the arable land (*adamah*) is based on a mutual dependency. The female *adamah* is dependent upon the labor or work of the male *adam* to produce vegetation. Without the man working the arable land through tilling and sowing, the land would remain lifeless, lacking pasturage and field crops. The man supplies, in part, what the arable land lacks: tilling and sowing. It was for this work, the text suggests, that the man was created. The man, for his part, is bound to the arable land. He was created from the soil of the land, and when he dies, he will return to the land as soil (Gen 3:19). He is also dependent on the arable land to produce the crops for his subsistence. The mutual dependency between the man and the arable land is evident by the Hebrew verb *'abad*, which is used to define their relationship. When used with inanimate objects, *'abad* means "to work" and connotes a dominance over that which is worked: the man will thus dominate the land through his work to produce vegetation. However, when *'abad* is used with personal objects, it means "to serve" and denotes submission. In the myth, the arable land is also the mother from which the man was born, and thus the man will serve the land, through his tilling and sowing, so that it will produce vegetation. The use of *'abad* to characterize the gendered relationship between the man and the arable land produces a non-hierarchical relationship. The gendered relationship between the man and the arable land is complicated because the relationship between them is twofold. On the one hand, the man was created to work the land, and this relationship will mirror the man's relationship to his wife. On the other hand, the man was born from and serves the land. The land is like a mother to the man, and his submission to her reflects the age hierarchy.

Other dependencies highlighted by the myth must also be noted. The relationship between the man and the arable land is not dyadic. There are three partners in the relationship because the arable land is also dependent on Yhwh sending rain and the man is dependent on Yhwh for his creation from the land—that is, for forming him out of the soil. These dependencies, however, are different in kind and complicate the relationship between the man and the arable land. Whereas the land is dependent on Yhwh for its *continued* production, the man is dependent only for his *initial* creation. But the man's creation was, in fact, a production of the land, calling into question the arable land's need for the man's work. In other words, the arable land only has an

---

11. There is biblical and archaeological evidence to suggest that the goddess Asherah played a role in Israelite cultic practices (Olyan 1988; Dever 2005). The evidence is ambiguous, however, whether she was believed to be the wife of Yhwh, and there is no evidence that Yhwh and Asherah engaged in sexual intercourse in myth or ritual. Even when Yhwh is represented in bodily form, no reference is made to his midsection, to genitals (on making Yhwh sexless, see Eilberg-Schwartz 1994).

indirect or secondary dependence on the man, for the land can be productive from the work of Yhwh alone. Thus, the land can bring forth trees as Yhwh plants a garden in Eden (Gen 2:8–9). Because Yhwh's relationship to the land supersedes the man's relationship to the land, the man's dependency on the land for subsistence is mediated by Yhwh. The arable land will only be productive when Yhwh sends rain. Outside the Yahwist creation myth, Yhwh's mediation of Israel's dependence on the land is formalized through covenant. Yhwh owns the land (Lev 25:23), gives it to his people (Exod 6:8), and rains upon it so that it is fertile and fruitful (Deut 11:13–17); Israel's relationship to Yhwh in covenant determines Israel's relationship to the land.

Although no hierarchy is articulated between the man and the arable land, the relationship between Yhwh and the man is certainly hierarchical. As his compound name repeatedly reminds us, Yhwh is a god (*Elohim*) and the man is not. In the Yahwist creation myth, their hierarchical relationship is fully expressed when Yhwh puts the man in his garden, rather than leaving him to cultivate the arable land for which he was created.[12] The planting of the garden was the work of Yhwh alone—no need for the man to cultivate (*'abad*) the land for it to grow—and man is placed in the garden to tend (*'abad*) it and guard it (Gen 2:15).[13] Moreover, Yhwh mediates the man's access to the production of the garden: the man may eat from all the fruit trees in the garden, but he is prohibited from eating the fruit from the tree of the knowledge of good and evil on penalty of death (Gen 2:16–17). Why the man is moved from the arable land to Yhwh's garden is not stated in the myth, but at the end of the story the man is sent out of the garden to work the arable land.[14] In other words, the man was created to

---

12. In Genesis 2:20–24, the garden is described as the source of a river that splits into four branches. Although the name of some of the branches are well known—e.g., the Tigris and Euphrates—the myth is presenting primarily symbolism rather than simply geography. A four-branched stream that encircles the world is a common motif in the ancient Near East and would attest to Yhwh's divine sovereignty and the fertility that has its origin in it (see Batto 2013b, 109–12). Building on this and other royal themes, Nicolas Wyatt (2014) has argued that the garden is a royal garden located in Jerusalem and the setting for the royal cult. The *adam* in the garden, as its gardener, was thus originally a type of king (as in Ezekiel 28; see also Callender 2000, 62–65). Certainly, royal themes are evident in the garden, as noted, but in the Yahwist narrative the king in the garden would be Yhwh. It is Yhwh's garden: he plants it, walks about in it, and it remains his after the man is sent out of the garden. The *adam* is best interpreted as a typical Israelite farmer whose life is dependent on cultivating the arable land for his subsistence (see Hiebert 1996; Kennedy 1990; Yee 2003, 68–70). In the end, the *adam* does not belong in the garden once he eats the fruit of knowledge (Gen 3:22–23).

13. Although *'abad* is used for the man's working of the arable land and in the garden, two different kinds of work and labor are envisioned. Working the arable land requires tilling, followed by the sowing of seed and weeding. This is the hard work of farming. Working in the garden, however, would include the tending, fertilizing, and pruning of trees, for the garden is an orchard, not a vegetable garden. Such gardens in the ancient world belonged to kings, whose tending of their gardens would have been leisurely work. Servants would have been employed for the difficult work of landscaping the garden and the construction of waterworks to irrigate the garden. This hard labor would presumably have been carried out by Yhwh in his initial creation of the garden. The man is put in the garden only after its completion (on Near Eastern gardens, see Meyers 2012, 146–51; Zevit 2013, 114–18).

14. James Kennedy (1990, 5) suggests that the man was created to labor in God's garden. This would run counter to what is suggested in Genesis 2:5, that a man was needed to work the arable land,

cultivate the arable land and there is where he belongs. He was not created to tend the garden and so it was not intended to be his home (contrary to Stordalen 1992).[15]

After Yhwh placed the man in the garden, Yhwh realized that it was not good for the man to be alone. Thus, Yhwh decides to make a suitable (Hebrew *kenegdo*, "to correspond to") helper for him (Gen 2:18). Because the man was created from the arable land, Yhwh also tries to form the man's helper from the land, but is unsuccessful. Yhwh brings each of the creatures that he creates—born from the arable land like the man—to the man to name them, but no suitable helper was found (Gen 2:19–20). So, Yhwh tries a different approach. He puts the man to sleep, takes a bone (*tsela'*, traditionally translated "rib," though see Zevit 2013, 140–50) from his body, and from it builds a woman. When Yhwh brings the new creature to the man, he immediately recognizes that she is suitable, that is, corresponding to him: she is bone of his bone, and flesh of his flesh. Moreover, she is *ishah*, a wife, because she was taken from *ish*, her husband, paralleling and reversing the relationship of the *adam* who was born from the *adamah* (Gen 2:21–23). The terms *ish* and *ishah* are gendered social terms that can be used generally of a man and a woman, but in this context refer to a husband and a wife, and thus the myth provides an explanation for marriage (Gen 2:24).

The specific gender roles of the *ish* and *ishah* are not stated, though the character of their gendered relationship, which is contested by scholars, has begun to take shape. Phyllis Trible (1978, 94–105) has argued, for example, that both the *ish* and the *ishah* have their origin in the *adam* (who was previously sexually undifferentiated), and thus they represent complementary parts of the human creature, without subordination of one to the other. Her reading of the text is plausible up to a point—*ish* and *ishah* represent a complementary pair—but her claim that the *adam* was without gender, an "earth creature," and that the gendered relationship of *ish* and *ishah* lacks hierarchy is not sustainable (Lanser 1988). The man is only known as *ish* in the context of the marital relationship (Gen 2:23, 24; 3:6) in order to emphasize their gendered relationship. Elsewhere in the story, the man is referred to as *adam* (Gen 2:25; 3:17, 20, 21, 22, 24) and the woman is always *ishah*, and, as argued above, the *adam* is presented as male in relationship to the female *adamah*. Moreover, traces of hierarchy can be discerned in the relationship of *ish* and *ishah*, even prior to eating the fruit of knowledge in Genesis 3.

First, the woman was created to be the man's helper (*'ezer*). Being a helper does not indicate a subordinate *status*—even Yhwh can be described as a helper. Helping is a relational term, not an indication of status, but as such it has a subordinating *function*. In other words, regardless of status, a person who helps does not work on his or her own task but assists others in their tasks. Helping puts oneself in a secondary

---

and is fulfilled in Genesis 3:23, when Yhwh sends the man out of the garden to work the land. The man's time in the garden may contribute to, but is not the purpose of the man's creation.

15. Lawrence Stager (1999, 2000) has argued that the garden of Yhwh in the creation myth was replicated in the Jerusalem temple as the earthly dwelling of God.

or subordinate position in relation to the task to be accomplished (Clines 1990). How the woman helps the man is not stated in this context, though by the end of the myth it becomes clear that she assists the man through reproduction.

Second, the man identifies the woman as *ishah*. This has traditionally been interpreted as an act of naming, which in the ancient Near East was viewed as an act of dominance or sovereignty (von Rad 1972, 83; Westermann 1984, 228–29; Wenham 1987, 68). Trible, in contrast, distinguishes between the man's naming of the animals and his "calling" (*qara*) the woman *ishah*. The usual Hebrew form of naming is "to call the name of," which the man uses for the animals, but when the man calls the woman *ishah*, the Hebrew term "name" (*shem*) is absent. "Hence, in calling the woman, the man is not establishing his power over her but rejoicing in their mutuality" (Trible 1978, 100). However, as Lanser (1988, 73) indicates, the Yahwist narrative simply uses an abbreviated syntactic form for naming, perhaps because it is set in direct discourse, but the reader should assume the man is naming the woman nonetheless. Although Trible's interpretation does not hold, that does not mean that the man is thereby "establishing his power over" the woman (compare Gen 16:13, where Hagar names YHWH, but certainly does not establish power over him). The function of the man's naming in this context is to find a helper who corresponds to him—that is, it is an act of discernment (see Ramsey 1988). Whereas the man's ability or right to name indicates his dominant position vis-à-vis the animals and the woman, his *purpose* in naming is not to establish such power, a dominance which is already assumed, but to identify which creature will be a suitable helper. Calling the woman *ishah* and himself *ish* signaled both the woman's suitability to help and their gendered relationship.

Like the relationship between *adam* and *adamah*, the relationship between *ish* and *ishah* expresses a mutual dependency. Unlike the former relationship, however, the relationship between the husband and the wife is not without a suggestion of hierarchy. The woman was created from a piece of the man, analogous to the man being created from the soil of the arable land. The husband and wife thus share the same substance, just as the man, as soil, is composed of the same substance as the arable land. Because the wife comes from the man, the myth suggests that she is dependent on her husband. Whereas the man is dependent on the land for his subsistence, it is unclear in this context why the woman is dependent on her husband. Moreover, the basis of this dependency does not reflect the universal experience that all humans come from women through birth.[16] Indeed, this relationship is acknowledged in the myth when the man is born from the arable land, and when the man later names his wife Eve because she will be the mother of all living (Gen 3:20). Our contemporary, scientific understanding of procreation—that new life is dependent on sperm *and* ovum, that each partner contributes half of the needed genetic material—is relatively

---

16. As a qualification, the acknowledgment of transgender identity includes the recognition that a man may have a uterus and ovaries and thus give birth to a child, just as a woman may supply the needed sperm.

new and dependent on technologies that the ancient Israelites did not have.[17] As a result, the ancient Israelites understood the process of procreation differently, based on their experience of the world, and is symbolized in the myth by the woman being created from a piece of her husband. The character of the woman's dependency on her husband, however, remains unspecified at this point in the myth.

As for the man, he is dependent on the woman for her help, and here we can recognize a trace of hierarchy. Although not addressing issues of status, the woman was created to assist the man in his tasks. Her work will be subordinate or supplementary to his work, but at this point the myth leaves undefined the wife's specific help on which the man depends. A trace of hierarchy is also recognizable in the myth's reluctance to use *ish* to refer to the man. Immediately after the woman's creation, where *ish* and *ishah* are used to emphasize the human couple's gendered and marital relationship (Gen 2:23–24), they are referred to as *adam* and *ishah*, suggesting an asymmetrical relationship. While the woman's orientation is to her husband, her *ish*, the man's orientation is to the arable land, the *adamah*. Elsewhere only in Genesis 3:6 is the man again referred to as *ish*, but here the woman is the subject of the text and thus also reflects her orientation—she is giving the fruit to "her husband." The switch from *ish* to *adam* in relation to *ishah*, though not explained in the myth, reflects the ancient Israelite gender hierarchy.

A Rite of Passage

By the end of Genesis 2, the man and his wife, *adam* and *ishah*, exist in a liminal condition with their gender roles undefined. Their liminal condition is expressed by their nakedness: they are naked before each other without experiencing shame (Gen 2:25; Sasson 1985). Their nakedness is not surprising. The man (and by extension, the woman) were created out of soil, along with all the animals, so nakedness may be presumed. The lack of shame, however, is unexpected. Shame is a positive value referring to one's concern for reputation (which is honor; see Gilmore 1987; Malina 2001, 27–56; Bechtel 1991). It separates humans from animals and honorable people from fools, who lack shame and have no concern for their reputation. Because the exposure of one's naked body is shameful, leading one to hide or cover up, the human couple's lack of shame suggests that they do not yet understand nor experience the significance of their nakedness. That is, they are like children unaware of the sexual significance of their bodies—they have no sexual awareness (Bechtel 1995, 17). They are not animals,

17. For most peoples of the world, procreation in general and paternity in particular (maternity, for obvious reasons, has not generated the same kind of uncertainty), have been culturally defined (Barnes 1973; Monberg 1975; Delaney 1986). Most of the physical process of procreation remains beyond what is visible and requires rather sophisticated technology and an understanding of cellular biology to understand adequately. As a result, the ancient Near Eastern peoples and most of the Western tradition has understood production in terms of what was readily visible and seemingly analogous—namely, agriculture (Delaney 1986 and 1991; duBois 1988).

who are also unaware of their nakedness, but they are not yet fully human for they lack shame, or at the least, they have not yet matured or grown up. The man and his wife are liminal, and in the remainder of the myth they are transformed, undergoing a rite of passage, leaving behind their childlike natures and becoming fully adult humans (Niditch 1985, 31–34). In the process, they become aware of their gender roles and what it means to be a man or a woman in ancient Israel.

The catalyst for the human couple's transformation is eating the fruit from the tree of the knowledge of good and evil, which Yhwh had prohibited to the man, and the transformation itself is signaled by the man and his wife's awareness of their nakedness. Before they eat the fruit, they are naked with no shame; after they eat the fruit, they have a sense of shame ("their eyes are open") and so they cover themselves with fig leaves. The knowledge of good and evil is a merism referring to all knowledge or cultural knowledge (Wallace 1985, 115–32; Oden 1981; Westermann 1984, 242–45). The fruit represents the knowledge that distinguishes humans from animals, or even adults from children. It is what makes humans "like God" (Gen 3:5). Although the myth does not spell out how humans will be like God, the larger context of the myth suggests that it is through procreation and agriculture—the two activities that express Yhwh's relationship to the arable land. By bearing children and growing crops, humans create like God. It is for this reason that the myth presents sexual awareness as the effect of eating the fruit. Before eating the fruit, when the man and his wife were naked and lacked sexual awareness, they were not yet able, like children, to procreate. When they eat the fruit of knowledge, however, the man and his wife become sexually aware—an awareness of their bodies that characterizes them as adults—and they are ready to procreate.[18]

Human sexuality in procreation, and its analogue in agriculture, not only makes humans like God, it distinguishes them from the rest of Yhwh's creatures. Although both animals and humans engage in a process of reproduction, animal reproduction is a wholly natural event. Human reproduction is also natural; it involves a physical engagement with another body and the transference of semen. But human procreation is also social. It entails the bonding of the human pair, the formation of a household, and the creation of social structures through kinship. It also entails numerous emotions that promote and reinforce the social construction of family. Unlike the reproduction of animals, human sexuality mediates the relation between nature and society. It is through sexual labor, like agricultural labor, that humans create society from

---

18. A striking parallel to the transformation of the human couple is present in the Epic of Gilgamesh. Like *adam*, Enkidu is created out of clay but lives like a wild animal. He is a *lullu*, a primitive man. When Enkidu has a sexual encounter with a harlot, however, he is transformed into an *awilum*, a civilized man. Rather than living and running with the animals, Enkidu now clothes himself, eats bread and drinks beer, anoints his body with oil, and becomes like any other man. After their sex, the harlot speaks to Enkidu: "I am looking at you, Enkidu, you are godlike" (Dalley 1991, 137). For careful analysis of this episode, see Walls 2001, 18–34. As with the Yahwist myth, sexual intercourse, and the procreation that comes from it, separates humans from the animals and makes them "like God."

the material world of nature, and so distinguish themselves from other creatures—it makes humans like God.

The rite of passage is set within the narrative context of a dialogue between the woman and a serpent. Although the woman was created to help the man, to assist him in his work, here the woman takes the dominant role with her husband passively listening to the conversation. The serpent's purpose in the conversation appears simply to challenge the legitimacy of Yhwh's prohibition—the serpent's character or motivation is never developed. After initially questioning Yhwh's prohibition against eating the fruit in the garden (Gen 3:1), the serpent points out, truthfully, that eating the forbidden fruit will not cause death and it will make them like God, knowing good and evil (Gen 3:4–5). For the woman's part, she demonstrates intelligence and reason. She rejects the initial false choice suggested by the serpent, builds on Yhwh's prohibition by suggesting that it is best not to even touch the fruit (Gen 3:2–3), and finally concludes that it is reasonable to eat it: the fruit was good for food, looked appetizing, and made one wise (Gen 3:6). After she eats the fruit, the woman gives some to her husband (here he is defined in relation to her as *ish*, not *adam*), who is with her, and he eats it also. The silence of the man through the dialogue is deafening and has led some commentators in the past to assume that he was not even present (see Parker 2013). Presumably, the man agrees with his wife's reasoning, but it is odd that he does not contribute to the conversation, especially since Yhwh specifically prohibited *him* from eating the fruit. His passivity suggests that he is simply submissive to his wife, yielding to her reasoning and following her instructions, and that she thus speaks for and represents the human couple to others (cf. Chapman 2019; Kalmanofsky 2017, 36–39).

Once the human couple are transformed by eating the fruit, Yhwh explains to them the consequences of their new knowledge. Scholars differ in their interpretation of these consequences. Traditionally, they have been interpreted as Yhwh's punishment of the human couple for eating the forbidden fruit (see Westermann 1984, 252–67; von Rad 1972, 91–98; Yee 2003, 72–77). Other scholars, for different reasons, reject this interpretation and argue that the consequences are simply the natural, logical, or inevitable result of the human couple's acquisition of knowledge (see Meyer 1988, 86–88; Barr 1992, 1–20; Naidoff 1978). The narrative logic supports both interpretations to some extent,[19] though the degree of punishment is much less than traditionally assumed. In either case, the consequences of their knowledge prescribe the gender roles of the man and his wife.

Yhwh first addresses the woman: "I will multiply your toils and your pregnancies, and in travail you will bear children" (Gen 3:16; see Meyers 1988, 95–121). Because the woman now has knowledge and an awareness of her sexuality, childbirth is possible.

---

19. It is important to note that only the serpent (and by extension, the rest of the animals) and the arable land are "cursed"; the man and his wife are not cursed despite being the only ones who actually ate the forbidden fruit.

She will bear children, but such births will be painful. Her life will be filled with the labors that are characteristic of a mother and wife in ancient Israel. Yet the woman's role as mother will be dependent upon her husband, for her husband will rule over her.[20] The context of procreation defines the purpose of the man's dominance. The woman's gendered task of bearing children is dependent upon her husband's sperm, and thus he will have control over her sexuality and pregnancies. The woman's relationship to her husband is analogous to the man's relationship to the arable land. Just as the arable land is dependent upon the work of the man to till and sow it to produce vegetation, the woman is dependent upon her husband to impregnate her. It is through bearing her husband's children that the woman helps him.

Although Yhwh presents the woman's gender role in relation to her husband, the man's gender role is described in relation to the arable land (Gen 3:17–19). The man's newly acquired knowledge and awareness of sexuality is expressed, not in terms of procreation, but in terms of farming. The man now has the knowledge to work the arable land, which is the purpose for which he was created. No longer will the man live off the fruit of Yhwh's garden (the consequences for the man foreshadow his being expelled from the garden in Gen 3:23).[21] The man will be like Yhwh in his role of working the soil. Just as Yhwh planted a garden and caused trees to sprout up from the earth, the man will also bring forth vegetation from the lifeless land. Yet the man's labor will be made more difficult by Yhwh's curse of the arable land.

Yhwh's curse of the land indicates a punishment for the man. The land is cursed "on account of" the man because he listened to the voice of his wife and ate what Yhwh had forbidden (Gen 3:17). The man was created to work the arable land, but Yhwh's cursing of the land makes his task much more laborious: it will require toil and sweat, but will produce thorns and thistles. The man will eat from field crops all his life—presumably in contrast to eating from the fruit trees in the garden—until he returns to the arable land from which he was created. As noted above, Yhwh mediates the man's relationship to the arable land. Because of what the man has done, Yhwh will withhold his fertilizing rains so that the land does not readily yield its bounty. But only for a time. Unlike the curse on the animals, Yhwh removes this curse after the flood when Yhwh establishes the seasonal cycle of the Levant, which includes winter rains (Gen 5:29; 8:20–22). In other words, Yhwh uses the condition of the arable land

20. The role of the woman's *teshuqah*, often translated "desire," will be addressed below.

21. Up to this point in the myth, the tree of life has played virtually no role other than characterizing Yhwh's garden as a place where immortality is possible. Despite no prohibition, the narrative assumes that the humans had not yet eaten from the tree of life. But after the human couple are transformed through the fruit of knowledge, this might change. Perhaps their transformation also included an awareness of their own mortality, which is common for adults but rarely for children. The possibility of immortality, however, makes the garden incompatible with the newly transformed humans. Therefore, Yhwh expels the man from the garden: "lest the man reach out his hand and take also from the tree of life, eat it, and live forever" (Gen 3:22). In ways similar to other ancient Near Eastern myths, such as the Epic of Gilgamesh and the Myth of Adapa, the Yahwist creation myth emphasizes that immortality is beyond human grasp (see Barr 1992).

to punish the man, but only for a period of time; the status or role of the man himself is not changed. The woman receives no comparable punishment, but as the man's wife, she will experience the consequences of the man's increased and ineffectual labor.

Through the rite of passage initiated by eating the forbidden fruit of knowledge, the Yahwist creation myth presents the normative gender roles of Israelite men and women in terms of the complementary relationship of male farmers and female child bearers. By structuring the story through the parallel relationships of *adam* and *adamah* and *ish* and *ishah*, the Yahwist creates a metaphor between agriculture and procreation. Then, after eating the fruit of knowledge, Yhwh prescribes the man and woman's gender roles as the consequences of their newly acquired knowledge: just as a man tills and sows the arable land to produce his crops, so the husband will sow his semen in his wife to produce children; similarly, the wife, like the arable land, receives and nurtures the semen until it is delivered and born from her body, just as vegetation sprouts from seed sown in the land. Moreover, the myth naturalizes the gender roles in the context of the male and female body. Their gender roles are linked to cultural understandings of their bodies, which were created by Yhwh.

GENDER HIERARCHY AND SIN

Although a trace of hierarchy was already evident between the man and his wife before they ate the fruit of knowledge, after they are transformed through the rite of passage, the gendered hierarchy between the man and his wife is fully articulated. First, the myth indicates that the man and his wife mutually depend on one another. The woman is dependent on the man in order to bear children; he has the seed that she lacks. Similarly, the man is dependent on his wife—he cannot bear children alone, and she will be the mother of all living (Gen 3:20)—but the myth masks his dependency by subordinating his wife's "help" and by emphasizing the man's role in farming rather than procreation.[22] Second, the man is punished because he "listened to the voice of his wife" (Gen 3:17). Throughout the woman's conversation with the serpent, the man was submissive and therefore he followed her reasoning in eating the forbidden fruit. The man yielded to his wife, which led him to disregard Yhwh's prohibition. Third, Yhwh emphasizes to the woman that her husband will rule over her (Gen 3:16). Yhwh thus clarifies the gender hierarchy that was inchoate before eating the fruit, which the woman subverted through her conversation with the serpent (see Kalmanofsky 2017, 28–46).

22. Outside the Yahwist creation myth, the man's dependency on his wife for procreation is transferred to Yhwh, who mediates the production of children just as he mediates the production of the arable land. Although the man has the power to "sow seed" in the woman to produce children, only Yhwh opens and closes the womb (Gen 16:2; 25:21; 29:31; 30:2, 17, 22), just as Yhwh brings fertility to the land through rain. In other words, rather than emphasizing the man's dependency on both the woman and the land, the myth and the biblical tradition at large masks this dependency by emphasizing that the man's ability to work the arable land and impregnate his wife is dependent on Yhwh.

Part I: Creation

The gender hierarchy can be summarized by the final clause of Yhwh's address to the woman, which is traditionally translated: "your desire (*teshuqah*) will be for your husband, and he will rule (*mashal*) over you" (Gen 3:16). As noted above, the immediate context of this clause would seem to place the woman's desire and the husband's rule within the framework of procreation. That is, the woman will seek sexual intimacy with her husband to procreate despite the labor pangs associated with childbirth, yet the husband controls the procreative process because he possesses the necessary seed. In other words, the husband's rule over his wife in procreation is simply another way of expressing the wife's dependency on her husband. Of course, the history of the interpretation of this clause has not limited the context of the man's rule to procreation, and perhaps for good reason. On the one hand, it seems disproportionate to characterize the woman's dependency on the man's seed as his rule over her. On the other hand, such an interpretation begs the question of why the woman's relationship to her husband is framed as "desire" and his relationship to her is framed as "rule." In the family stories of Genesis, and beyond, wives simply do not desire their husbands, and it is not at all clear how husbands are ruling over their wives, not least of which in the context of procreation. Most of the women in Genesis are barren and dependent upon God to open their womb; their husbands are as powerless as the wives. It would seem, therefore, that an adequate interpretation of this clause in Genesis 3:16 must reach beyond its immediate context.

The garden narrative does not stand as an isolated tale in Genesis. Its narrative trajectory continues at least through Genesis 8, where Yhwh brings to an end the curse on the land and finally initiates the annual cycle of rain needed for agriculture (Gen 8:20–22). In the story immediately following the garden narrative—the story of Cain and Abel (Gen 4:1–16)—scholars have noted numerous structural, thematic, and semantic similarities, especially with Genesis 3 (Westermann 1984, 284–87, 292–93, 303; Clark 1971, 195–201; Hauser 1980). Most notable for our purpose is Yhwh's speech to Cain in verses 6–7, where Yhwh states in regard to sin, "its desire (*teshuqah*) is for you, but you must rule (*mashal*) over it." Although most commentators have noted the close similarities between this statement to Cain and what Yhwh says about the woman in Genesis 3:16—the statements differ only in terms of the persons addressed—few commentators have interpreted the statements in light of each other.[23] But given the many connections between the garden narrative and the story of Cain and Abel, it seems unlikely that the similarities between the statements in Gen 3:16 and 4:7 are coincidental. Rather, by connecting *teshuqah* and *mashal* in two different

---

23. Skinner (1930, 107) is suspicious of the verbal resemblances between Genesis 3:16 and 4:7 and suggests that the latter is simply a textual corruption that began when a copyist's eye wandered to the former, perhaps in an adjacent column. Westermann argues that God's speech in Genesis 4:6–7 is a later addition that was inserted to ascribe full responsibility to Cain for Abel's murder. The lynchpin for this conclusion is the similarities between Genesis 3:16 and 4:7: "This mechanical citation which gives the words a quite different meaning in the new context . . . is the surest sign that 4:6–7 must be a subsequent addition or modification" (1984, 300).

contexts, the Yahwist constructs a complex structural metaphor in which a wife's relationship to her husband is comparable to Cain's encounter with sin.

Yhwh's speech to Cain needs to be put in context. The story begins with the man and his wife, now known as Adam and Eve, procreating with the help of Yhwh and producing two sons: the elder Cain, who works the arable land, and his younger brother Abel, who tends the sheep.[24] After a period of time, each of the brothers offers a sacrifice to Yhwh from the produce of their labors: Cain offers the fruit of the land, and Abel offers the fat from the firstborn of his flock. Both vegetable and animal sacrifices are acceptable offerings, and indeed, both are expected from Yhwh, according to the Israelite laws. Nevertheless, Yhwh looks on Abel and his offering, but does not look on Cain and his offering, leading Cain to become angry and his face to fall (Gen 4:4–5).

The story gives no explanation for why Yhwh gives attention to Abel's offering and not Cain's offering. A common interpretation is that Cain did not offer his best to Yhwh, or did so begrudgingly (see Craig 112; Wenham 1987, 104). Some commentators, however, acknowledge that the silence in the text is significant (see von Rad 1972, 104; Westermann 1984, 296; cf. Spina 1992). At the very least, the Yahwist did not care to explain why Yhwh chose Abel over Cain. The important point for understanding the story is that Yhwh did so, and this makes Cain understandably angry. His sacrifice, which was presumably intended to honor or petition Yhwh, was ignored. Perhaps Cain was angry because Yhwh chose to recognize his younger brother over him. Perhaps Cain thought that the elder brother should be first in Yhwh's sight and should rank higher (see also Perry 2005).[25] Cain was thus infuriated when Yhwh chose otherwise. The remainder of the story explains how Cain reacts to Yhwh's choice.

In Gen 4:6–7, Yhwh speaks directly to Cain, first with three rhetorical questions that should assuage his anger: "Why are you angry? Why has your face fallen? If you do well, will your face not be lifted up?" Yhwh assures Cain that there is no reason for his anger. His sacrifice was not rejected; Yhwh has no fault against Cain. If he continues to do well, Yhwh will be pleased. The speech of Yhwh then ends with a warning to Cain: "Sin is lying at the door; its desire is for you, but you must rule over

---

24. The terse phrase *et yhwh*, which literally means, "with Yhwh," may be interpreted as "with the help of Yhwh," or "alongside with Yhwh." The former understanding emphasizes Yhwh's role in procreation, not only in opening the womb, but also in shaping the fetus within the womb. Yhwh's role in Eve's womb is comparable to Yhwh's role in forming the *adam* out of the soil of the *adamah* (cf. van Wolde 1991, 27). The latter understanding would imply that the woman has created a man just as Yhwh created a man. This understanding is less likely given the subordinate role that the woman plays in relation to the man in procreation.

25. Van Wolde (1991, 29) adds to this characterization of Cain's anger that Abel himself was a blunderer, making Yhwh's choice of him even more insulting. She bases her interpretation on Abel's name, which means "breath" or "vapor," and assumes that Abel did not amount to much in the opinion of others. The meaning of Abel's name, which uncharacteristically is not exploited by the Yahwist, is more likely an indication of his brief and transitory life.

it."[26] Yhwh's speech turns the tables on Cain by focusing on Cain's choice of behavior rather than on Yhwh's choice of sacrifice. Cain's sin is under his own control, should he exercise it. Sin is personified, perhaps as an animal, lying at the entrance to Cain's house as a way of indicating that Cain is not inherently sinful; his anger need not result in sin. Instead, if Cain simply rules over the sin—that is, controls his sinful inclinations—he will not sin. His relationship with Yhwh, and consequently with the arable land, will remain productive. Cain's condition is entirely dependent upon his own choice.

Returning to the parallel relationships between the man and his wife and Cain and sin, the key terms of these relationships are *teshuqah* and *mashal*. The latter term is unproblematic in the Hebrew text. It is a common verb used to express power or dominion over a subordinate or dependent. The meaning of *teshuqah*, however, is not certain. It is a rare term that only occurs in Gen 3:16; 4:7 and in Song of Songs 7:10. Its etymology is also uncertain. Many compare the term to Arabic *shaqa*, which means "to desire" or "to excite desire," but it should instead be connected to Arabic *saqa*, meaning, "to urge, drive, impel." Its use with *mashal* in the parallel verses of Genesis should also have a similar force of meaning. For example, *teshuqah* should not be positive in one verse but negative in the other. Ultimately, the meaning of *teshuqah* must come from its context, but the meaning should be consonant with its use in both verses.

Susan Foh argues for the meaning of *teshuqah* by giving primacy to its use in Gen 4:7. She reads this verse to imply that Cain is in an active struggle with sin—that sin seeks to possess or control him, and he struggles to master it. Thus, *teshuqah* refers to a "desire to control," and in the context of Gen 3:16, "The woman has the same sort of desire for her husband that sin has for Cain, a desire to possess or control him" (1979, 381; she is followed by several commentators, including Wenham 1987, 81–82; Hamilton 1990, 202; cf. Yee 2003, 71). Foh's interpretation begins with the assumption that sin's desire to control and Cain's rule in Gen 4:7 are antithetical, but this is not necessarily the case (indeed, it might be easier to resist sin if the relationship is antagonistic). Sin is described as lying at the door with the verb *rabats*, which is used predominantly of herd animals, but occasionally of wild animals, resting or lying down. It does not imply conflict or aggression. The key element of the text's orientational metaphor is that sin is located *at the door*, the border between the inside and outside of a house. Sin can remain outside the house where it belongs, or it can enter and take up residence inside the house. The choice is Cain's. The use of *teshuqah* in Song of Songs also belies Foh's interpretation; in that context, *teshuqah* is clearly positive: "I belong to my beloved, and his *teshuqah* is for me."

---

26. The text of Genesis is corrupt here, probably from haplography, and should be emended following the analysis of Hendel 1998, 45–46 (cf. Speiser 1982, 32–33, who tries to make sense of the text without emendation, but his analysis, while addressing some problems, raises new ones).

If the conflict between sin and Cain is reduced, then another possible understanding of *teshuqah* presents itself. *Teshuqah* may mean "impulse" or "urge" (Aurin 2008) and in relation to *mashal*, it may have the sense of "devotion" (Macintosh 2016) or "dependency" (Deurloo 1987). In other words, sin's impulse is simply to enter Cain's house. The Yahwist is not emphasizing the power of sin to control Cain but rather Cain's power to control sin: sin is dependent upon Cain and is subject to his rule. Cain simply fails to exercise his rule over sin, allowing sin to take up residence in his house and, in the end, to characterize Cain's actions. When this interpretation of *teshuqah* is applied to the woman in Gen 3:16, the emphasis would again fall on the husband's domination of his wife. Her *teshuqah* for her husband would ultimately be expressed in her submission or obedience to him (this was also recognized by Ibn Ezra 1988, 73, who interpreted *teshuqah* as "obedience"). Finally, in the Song of Songs, *teshuqah* would express the mutual dependency between the beloved and his lover; the man's *teshuqah*, "dependency," is toward his lover, who belongs to him.[27]

In the parallel relationships between the man and his wife, and between Cain and sin, the Yahwist is articulating an asymmetrical, hierarchical relationship to which both partners are (or should be) committed (Cain, of course, fails in his role). The husband and Cain act in relation to their partners as the dominant members in the relationship; the man's and Cain's "rule" is not tyrannical nor a unilateral exploitation (though, in the man's relationship to his wife it has the potential to become so). The woman and sin, however, are not simple passive recipients of their partners' domination; their urge or impulse is toward their partner. They seek union, intimacy, and partnership—the possibilities are multiple—but their actions are nevertheless expressed as deference and submission to their partners' will.

By constructing a complex metaphor comparing the man's relationship with his wife to Cain's relationship to sin, the Yahwist sheds light on the nature of the gender hierarchy. Although metaphors are often constructed to make a comparison in one direction, the effect of the metaphor is to create new meaning through entailments that work in both directions. In other words, each relationship expands our understanding of the other relationship. In fact, when viewed in light of each other, the two relationships may be characterized as positive and negative examples of the same fundamentally asymmetrical relationship. When the dominant member of the relationship "rules" appropriately, the subordinate member's "impulse" is directed or confined within appropriate boundaries. However, if the dominant member fails to exercise rule, then the subordinate's "impulse" may become distorted and sin may result. This relational dynamic is clear in regard to Cain who failed to restrain sin and thus killed his brother; it is less obvious with regard to the man and his wife, whose relationship

---

27. Joel Lohr (2011) argues, based on how the ancients translate *teshuqah*, that its meaning is related to the similar sounding *teshubah*, "return," though the specific nuance is perhaps lost. In this case, a parallel is constructed between what Yhwh says about the woman in Genesis 3:16 and the man in Genesis 3:19: Just as the man will "return" to the soil from which he was created, the woman will "return" to her husband from whom she was created.

is not developed in the myth beyond the description of their gender roles. The man's passivity during the woman's conversation with the serpent may be interpreted as his failure to "rule" his wife: the man yielded to her reasoning and ate the forbidden fruit, and Yhwh cursed the arable land because of him. If this is the case, it needs to be qualified. The husband's "rule" and the wife's "impulse" does not seem to preclude the wife taking the initiative or acting independently of her husband, nor does it suggest that the husband cannot yield to his wife, as attested in many biblical examples.[28] Only one gendered relationship in the biblical tradition is regularly subject to critique, and this is the relationship between Israelite men and foreign, or strange, women (the relationship between Boaz and Ruth is a notable exception). As most clearly illustrated in Solomon's marriage to many foreign women, the "impulse" of the wife and the failure of the husband to "rule" may result in the worship of foreign gods—Solomon's wives "turned away his heart after other gods" (1 Kgs 11:4). At stake in the relational dynamic between the husband and the wife, as well as the relationship between Cain and sin, is the man's relationship to Yhwh (Ruth, who has adopted the worship of Yhwh, does not pose the same threat to Boaz). The Yahwist's use of this complex metaphor to place sin within the framework of the gender hierarchy indicates that an inappropriate relationship between a man and his wife—when the wife coerces her husband away from Yhwh—may lead to sin.

WORLDVIEW, GENDER AMBIGUITY, AND SOCIAL STRUCTURE

Gender is a fundamental component of a people's worldview, which is made up of assumptions that are rarely articulated. Worldview assumptions generally operate beneath the surface of linguistic expressions and social behavior and thus must be inferred. We rarely articulate, for example, what it means to be "male" or "female" or something in between; we simply speak and act according to culturally shared assumptions that we have learned, reproduced, and sometimes reified. Fortunately, the mythic character of the Yahwist creation story and its focus on gender relations brings some of these assumptions to the surface of the narrative. These assumptions form the image of a bounded, hierarchical relationship in which the subordinate member depends on a dominant member who governs the subordinate. The dependency of the subordinate is based on a deficiency that the dominant member can supply. Although both members are dependent on and benefit from the relationship, the assumptions seem to express primarily the asymmetrical dependency of the subordinate. These assumptions are historically and culturally specific, but have unfortunately contributed to a history of patriarchy and misogyny. For the ancient Israelites, this hierarchical

---

28. For example, from the Yahwist tradition: Abram yields to Sarai's need for a child by taking Hagar as his wife (Gen 16), then sends Ishmael away as his wife demands (Gen 21); Rebekah instructs Jacob to deceive his father Isaac for the blessing; Rachel steals her father's household gods, intensifying the conflict between her father Laban and her husband Jacob (Gen 31).

image had its origin in the experience of agriculture and procreation, and it functioned within their worldview to organize and structure gender behavior.

Worldview assumptions regarding gender, however, are not limited to individual males and females. As part of the fundamental assumptions in the Israelite worldview, this gendered hierarchical image should be expected to organize and structure the people's perception of other similar hierarchical relationships (see Kearney 1984, 52–64; cf. Gilmore 1996), such as the relationship between kings and their people, patrons and their clients, empires and their vassal nations, and Yhwh and his people Israel. In other words, gender in ancient Israel is a constitutive element of multiple social relationships "within which or by means of which power is articulated" (Scott 1986, 1069), and it is legitimated, or naturalized, by the culturally perceived differences between men and women. All relations of production in ancient Israel, which are based on a power differential, are thus gendered—they are gender relations, structured and organized according to the gender hierarchy (Haug 2002, 2005). This gives rise to certain gender ambiguities, in which the social relations of power involve men and women in roles contrary to their gender expectation, which are their roles in the husband–wife relationship. Attention to these gender ambiguities further uncovers the ancient Israelite understanding of gender and the worldview assumptions on which it is based.

Scholars have long noticed, for example, that covenant language is gendered so that Yhwh is a husband in relation to the people of Israel, his wife (on the problems arising from this gender ambiguity, see Eilberg-Schwartz 1994). Explicit examples of this gendered relationship are attested in several prophetic texts (Hos 2; Jer 2–3; Ezek 16, 23), where Yhwh is described as a male husband to his female people (Israel or Judah; Samaria or Jerusalem), who are even presented with a female body (see Kamionkowski 2003). Generally, the marital metaphor is used to emphasize how the people have abandoned Yhwh for other gods, as a wife commits adultery in her pursuit of other lovers. Although the metaphor is persuasive in emphasizing the severity of the people's sins—what Israelite husband would not be enraged at his wife's adultery?—the metaphor would not work unless the largely male audience of the texts could identify with being the female wife of Yhwh. Without the Israelite men's recognition and acceptance that they are indeed like women in relation to Yhwh, the metaphor rings hollow or is at least irrelevant. Gender is not simply an indication of biological differences. Rather, because the Israelites' understanding of their biological differences and their gender behavior are both expressions of their gendered hierarchical worldview assumptions, Israelite men can identify with being the wife of Yhwh: Israelite men, through covenant, are bound to and dependent upon Yhwh, who rules over them. Because of the shared hierarchical image that defines the gendered relationship between husbands and wives and between Yhwh and his people, Israelite men will identify as husbands in one relationship and metaphorically as a wife in the other (see Carr 2000). Covenant relations are also gender relations.

In a similar way, the relationship between a king and his people is like the relationship between a husband and his wife. Thus, in the story of Solomon and the two prostitutes who fight over a child (1 Kgs 3:16–28), which functions in the larger narrative to illustrate the wisdom of Solomon in ruling his people, Solomon takes on the role of a husband, which is lacking for the prostitutes, to restore order to their lives. They are representative of an unruly people, primarily Israelite men, without a king.

A political relationship that is frequently represented in the biblical tradition, however, is between the people of Israel and a foreign king who oppresses them. This exploitive relationship is a distortion of Israel's gendered hierarchical image. Nevertheless, in such exploitive situations, women who prevail, usually with the help of Yhwh, are held up as models for the Israelite men in their own struggles. For example, the barren Hannah was provoked severely by her rival, fertile wife Peninnah for years because she was barren, but when Yhwh finally gives Hannah a child, her victory over Peninnah is presented as a victory for Israelite men who have suffered similarly under oppression:

> The barren has borne seven,
>> but she who has many children is forlorn . . .
> [Yhwh] raises up the poor from the soil;
>> he lifts up the needy from the ash heap,
> to make them sit with princes
>> and inherit a seat of honor. (1 Sam 2:5, 8)

Because gender is an expression of a social hierarchy, a relationship of power, rather than biology, Israelite men can identify with women who are powerless and with whom they share the same subordinate position within a hierarchical relationship.

It is less problematic in the biblical narrative when a woman acts like a man, for such behavior shares rather than challenges the hierarchically dominant gender behavior of men (contra Kalmanofsky 2017, 47–67). Thus, Deborah can serve as a judge for the Israelites and lead them into battle, and Judith, through the cunning and deceit of the powerless, can behead the general Holofernes, causing panic and flight among his troops, so that the Israelites are victorious in battle.

Similarly, though seemingly in a rather mundane way, Jael, in the absence of her husband, can offer hospitality and protection to a fleeing Sisera, an ally of her husband's clan. In this case, however, the relationship between Jael and Sisera goes awry when he begins making demands on her. In offering hospitality to Sisera, Jael takes the dominant, generally male, position in the relationship and she would expect Sisera to assume the subordinate, generally female, position, as was appropriate and customary for guests. But Sisera acts otherwise. Perhaps because he is a man in relation to a woman, or a general who does not want to be reminded of his own shameful defeat, he nevertheless asserts himself into the dominant role of the relationship. He refuses to relinquish his position of power. As the general of the oppressive King Jabin, Sisera was used to dominating over others and, as his mother attests, to raping women (Judg 5:30). By giving orders to Jael, Sisera ceased acting like a guest and retained the identity of a general and perhaps a rapist. Although the narrative in Judges 4 is silent on this matter, the parallel poetic account in Judges 5 implies with double entendre that Sisera was positioned over against Jael when she struck him dead (Judg 5:25–27).[29] At the very least, when Sisera insisted on his position as a man in relation to Jael, he posed a threat to her and she killed him for it. Jael's role as host was based on status—it was her tent, and her husband was absent—she had no power. Thus, she kills Sisera as a woman threatened by a man who is not her husband, and so she became a model for Israelite men. The male commander of the Israelite militia, Barak, defeated and slaughtered the Canaanite army with the help of YHWH, yet it is the female Jael who is praised in the song: "Most blessed of women be Jael, the wife of Heber the Kenite, of tent-dwelling women most blessed" (Judg 5:24). Like the Israelites who were oppressed by King Jabin, Jael was forced into the subordinate position by Sisera, but she refused to let him oppress her. With tent peg and mallet in hand, she struck a blow for a subjugated and oppressed Israel.

Gender in biblical Israel is an expression of power in a hierarchical relationship. It signifies the power differential that results from the different roles that men and women have in procreation, as culturally understood through the metaphor of agriculture. The most prominent and fundamental relationship was between husbands and wives, where the husband was the dominant, ruling member because he possessed the seed necessary for procreation, whereas the wife was dependent upon his seed to fulfill her primary social role. Gender is also contextual and varies according to the social relationship that it signifies. Thus, in other social relations, a man or a woman might take on different gendered roles depending on the circumstances—whether it be a patron or a client, a host or a guest, the king or his subjects, a foreign conqueror or an oppressed people—giving rise to various gender ambiguities.[30] Yet despite these ambiguities, the gender hierarchy is reproduced because it is based on a power differential, not on a biological difference. This is especially true with regard to the covenantal relationship between YHWH and the people, where YHWH is the dominant male and Israelite men assume the female, subordinate role. In this relationship, YHWH has all the power and Israel is wholly dependent on him, and thus YHWH, the

---

29. Kalmanofsky, reading Judges 4 independently of Judges 5, argues that, because Deborah and Jael take on male roles, the story "works to compromise the roles Deborah and Yael play and does not bestow glory upon them" (2017, 62). She recognizes that the song in Judges 5 preserves a different perspective on the narrative. Our interpretation, in contrast, gives priority to Judges 5, which is possibly the source material for the story in Judges 4 (see Halpern 1988, 76–103).

30. This is primarily true of men who engage in multiple public roles and thus may assume ambiguous gender roles. Women, in contrast, rarely engage in public roles and thus rarely assume such ambiguous roles. Deborah, as noted above, was an exception. Jael was able to assume an ambiguous gender role in a domestic context because her husband was absent and so she could represent her household.

consummate male, may take the men of Israel as his wife. Through their faithfulness, devotion, and submission to Yhwh, the Israelite men reproduce the gender hierarchy, even as they act contrary to their own maleness. This has two consequences. On the one hand, Yhwh's role as husband establishes male authority and models exemplary male behavior; on the other hand, Yhwh's male role challenges the role of human men, both in their relationship to the arable land and to their wives (see Eilberg-Schwartz 1994, 137–62). Men must still till and sow, but Yhwh brings fertility to the land and opens the wombs of women. Thus, the Yahwist creation myth and other biblical texts present an ideology in which Yhwh mediates the work or labor of men, based on the gendered covenantal relationship between Yhwh and the men. In other words, Israelite men must assume the female role in covenantal relation to Yhwh so that their male role through their labor is efficacious.

2

Creation and Political Economy

NATURE AND SOCIETY

POLITICAL ECONOMY ARTICULATES THE relationship between society and nature. It regulates how humans utilize the natural world in economic production within the context of a structured social system, as noted by Marx, "all production is appropriation of nature on the part of an individual within and through a specific form of society" (1973, 87). In other words, human labor in production mediates the relationship between society and nature. This relationship, however, has been quite contested with significant consequences. How one understands this relationship will shape not only one's understanding of the political economy but also one's response to current environmental crises such as climate change (see Schultz 2000). Therefore, before turning to ancient Israel's political economy, it is essential that I elucidate clearly the relationship between society and nature.

The binary of society and nature is similar to the human–nature, history–nature, and culture–nature binaries, all of which are the legacy of Cartesian dualism and deeply rooted in Greek philosophy. This dualism, based on the substantive distinction between mind and body, is often reflected in the definitions of the terms. Nature has been defined in terms of the collective physical world—plants, animals, streams, and fields—that is, all the products of the earth, as opposed to humans and human creations. Society, in contrast, has been defined in terms of collective humans and their creations. Society and nature, therefore, have been understood to be two distinct substances or arenas (a substance dualism). In other words, nature has been interpreted as simply the inert material world in which human culture and history and society takes place. The dichotomy between society and nature has had a significant effect on biblical interpretation, especially during the twentieth century, and it has been well documented and critiqued elsewhere (see Hiebert 1996, 3–29; Simkins 1991, 3–75;

1994). Our focus here instead will be on the political economic implications of this dichotomy and its resolution.

Although Cartesian dualism proved to be a philosophical dead-end, and most scholarly disciplines now reject such dualisms, the dichotomy between society and nature is alive and well in the most influential of academic disciplines: economics. Its most popular school of thought, neoclassical economics and its heirs, especially neo-liberalism, posit that the economy is a self-maintaining circular flow between households and firms. Land, capital, and labor (the productive input) flows from households to firms, where goods and services are produced and flow back to households. The added circulation of money, where households receive wages and profits from their inputs and firms receive income from consumption and investment, results in essentially a perpetual motion machine. Indeed, not only does the circular flow keep flowing, but it grows continually as profits from the production are reinvested into the firms. Finally, factor and product markets regulate the flow between households and firms. They regulate, for example, the resources used in production, the costs of the products, and the wages paid for labor. What is absent from this model is the role of nature in the process of production.

In the neoclassical economy, nature has no substantive relation to society. It is simply an input stock for production, which can be used however market forces direct. The natural stock is assumed to be free, though extraction of the resources may add to the costs of production. Moreover, nature has no limits within this configuration, for market forces will shift production to new resources, sometimes aided by new technologies, whenever one resource becomes too scarce to profit from its production or the product itself becomes less valuable to households due to rising costs or other market factors. Although the neoclassical economic model is essentially a closed system, the circular flow in fact leaks. Such leaks are referred to as externalities—costs and benefits that occur outside of the circle of production. A positive externality, for example, occurs when a farmer plants an apple orchard, which may benefit a nearby beekeeper. The apple farmer provides a source of nectar for the bees, whose benefit is external to the farmer's own production. Most externalities, however, are negative and take the form of pollution or environmental degradation. Such negative externalities may result in additional costs to a firm for production, or they may be borne by households without compensation. The government, which otherwise is not included in the circular flow of the economy, may step in to subsidize production for its positive externalities or tax and regulate production to reduce its negative externalities.

The relationship between society and nature is highlighted by the notion of externality. In the neoclassical economy, nature is simply the arena in which the production of human society takes place. We may extract resources from the stock it holds for our production, and we may pollute it as a result, but it is external to human society, offering only benefits and charging costs. Neoclassical economics even expects the gradual and absolute dematerialization of the economy, further removing society from nature.[1] Thus, it ignores natural limits, both in terms of the economy's use of natural resources and economic growth.[2] This is why neoclassical economists and the governments they advise have no adequate response to the crisis of climate change. From this perspective, climate change is simply a negative externality. It should be able to be solved, in the short term, through a combination of regulation (e.g., limiting the pollutants that coal-burning electric plants can put into the atmosphere, or converting them to use natural gas) and subsidies (e.g., tax benefits for households installing roof-top solar panels, or electric utilities using windmills). Cap and trade schemes or moderate carbon taxes are also possible options (see IMF 2019). In the long term, the expectation is that renewable technologies will make fossil fuels unnecessary (compare York 2012) or even harmless through the development of technologies such as carbon capture and sequestration (compare Wilberforce et al. 2019; Anderson and Peters 2016; Smith et al. 2016). In no case, however, can neoclassical economists entertain the possibility that the problem of climate change is with *production* itself. Whereas climate change is viewed as a problem in nature, production is the core of society and thus not directly related to climate change, which is only an externality.[3] Neoclassical economics is unable to offer adequate climate change solutions because its understanding of society and nature precludes the destructive engagement of society *in* nature that has resulted in climate change. A better economic understanding of society and nature is needed (for a full critique, see Hall and Klitgaard 2012, esp. 131–41).

Fortunately, other economic approaches integrate society and nature. Both ecological economics and biophysical economics, for example, recognize that the economy is embedded within the natural world. These economic approaches are related, but each has a distinct focus. Ecological economics[4] is transdisciplinary, bridging the

---

1. Although relative dematerialization is evident in a number of production processes due to better materials and design—for example, automobile engines have continuously produced more power with less materials in their construction—there has been no absolute dematerialization of the economy. In fact, many cases of relative dematerialization are offset by a rise in material use elsewhere—automobiles have gotten larger and heavier, requiring much more materials, despite a more efficient engine (see Smil 2019, 392–94; Ward et al. 2016; Wiedmann et al. 2015; Bunker 1996).

2. Neoclassical economics holds that the scarcity of natural resources is worked out in the market. If one resource becomes too expensive due to scarcity, then the market generates human-made substitutes to meet demand. This leads to the idea of infinite substitutability. The problem is that for many essential natural resources, there are no adequate substitutes (see Ayres 2005; Graedel et al. 2015).

3. Against the dichotomy of society and nature that neoclassical economics presumes, Andreas Malm recognizes what he calls the "paradox of historicized nature": the more that humans shape nature through their production, the more intensely nature affects human lives (2018, 72–77). Nature cannot be treated as a mere stock, and its disruption is not simply an externality. Human society and its production are integrated with nature in such a way that society's use of nature has ramifications for society itself.

4. Ecological economics should not be confused with environmental economics, which is a subdiscipline of neoclassical economics. Although environmental economics gives attention to the use of nature and environmental policy to reduce pollution, the natural world is defined in terms of "natural capital" (as a stock) and waste pollution remains an externality.

gap between ecology and economics. It views "the socioeconomic system as a part of the overall ecosphere, emphasizing carrying capacity and scale issues in relation to the growth of the human population and its activities, and the development of fair systems of property rights and wealth distribution" (Constanza 1996, 980). Biophysical economics, instead, seeks to "become more a *biophysical* science that reflects the actual conditions in real-world economies, one that focuses on resources and energy and not one that treats them simply as a commodity or as an externality" (Hall and Klitgaard 2012, 8). The analysis in the following sections and in later chapters of this book draw upon these economic approaches, but here I want to address their common starting point—that society is embedded in nature—and explore the implications of this relationship for addressing environmental crises such as climate change.

Even when one rejects the dichotomy between society and nature, their integration remains complex and disputed. Constructionism tends to collapse nature into society (Vogel 1996), whereas new materialism tends to collapse society into nature (LeCain 2015; Latour 2004, 2017). However, a critical realist and historical materialist approach (Malm 2018; Foster et al. 2010), which I adopt here, argues that society remains distinct *within* nature. Society is that which is produced from nature through our labor, whereas part of the natural world remains unmediated, distinct and not incorporated into society.[5] Against those who would collapse nature and society, nature is neither simply raw materials awaiting human use, nor simply a social product. It is rather a complex system that transcends any human use of it. The mediation between society and nature always leaves a surplus in nature (see Fremaux and Berry 2019).

Because society is embedded in nature, both are substantively material. Humans are physical, living creatures similar to all other creatures, and the stuff of society—buildings, roads, things—is material that has been appropriated and transformed from nature through production. Society has emerged from nature with its own unique properties. It shares some of the properties of nature, those that can be articulated and explored through the natural sciences, for example, but it has other properties for which there is no counterpart in nature, such as art and literature, gender and kinship, politics and religion.[6] "Society . . . has, in the very last instance, natural components. But they are arrayed in relations *out of which a society emerges*, as a system with novel properties *that are nowhere to be found in nature*—even laws of motion that no human bodies, not even local relations between two or three of them, have in and of themselves" (Malm 2018, 70). Society, then, as an emergent whole is more than the sum of its material parts. To use a natural metaphor, society is like a tree that emerges from the soil of a large field. The tree and the field are both material substances, yet the tree

---

5. In technical terms, I adopt a substance monism with a property dualism. Constructivists and Neo-materialists, in contrast, hold a substance and property monism in their collapse of society and nature. In critique of the latter, see Malm 2019.

6. This understanding of the relationship between society and nature is similar to how non-reductive physicalism treats the mind-body problem (see Murphy and Brown 2007).

is not identical with the field. It remains distinct as it grows within the field, for the tree has different properties than the field. For example, the tree requires sunlight for photosynthesis, whereas the soil of the field is less dependent on light. Nevertheless, the tree is not independent of the soil. Its roots reach deep into the earth from where it extracts water and nutrients necessary for its life, and each fall it drops its leaves, which enrich the soil as they decompose.

This understanding of relationship between society and nature meshes well with the ancient Israelites' conception.[7] Returning to the Yahwist creation myth, the relationship between society and nature is articulated through the man's creation from the arable land. The man (*adam*) is born from the land and shares the same substance. He is a dirt-creature, along with all the other animals, and he will return to the dirt when he dies. The man wholly belongs to the natural world. Yet the man is also distinct from the rest of nature through his knowledge, which makes him like God. As such, the man is also a creator. He and his wife will create children to form a household. He will cultivate and sow the land for crops from which he will sustain his family. He will use domesticated animals for their secondary products—wool and milk—and harness an ox or donkey to pull his plow and his cart and to thresh his grain. His wife will process the grain by grinding it into flour, then making bread, cakes, and perhaps beer for the nourishment of her family. She will take wool from the sheep and hair from the goats and cattle and weave textiles for clothes. The man will take mud from the earth, form it into bricks, and build his house on a stone foundation. Other mud, his wife will shape into bowls and pots, and after they are transformed by heat, they can be used to cook food and store wine and oil. In all of these ways and others, the human couple will construct a household—the fundamental component of society—from and within the natural world. Whereas nature is Yhwh's creation, which includes humans, society is a human creation.

Because humans belong to both nature as a part of God's creation, and society as creators themselves, a dialectical relationship exists between society and nature. In other words, when humans appropriate nature through their labor in the construction of society, they change themselves and the natural world. Drawing upon organic processes, Marx referred to the exchange between humans and nature as a social metabolism. Just as the soil of the arable land, for example, has a metabolism consisting of the nutrient cycle, so also there is a social metabolism between society and nature, which is mediated through human labor:

---

7. The Hebrew Bible has no word for the abstract concepts of society and nature. These concepts are represented only through their concrete parts, such as the house (*bet*) and the city (*'ir*) or the earth (*erets*) and the land (*adamah*). And, of course, humans are representative of society, even though they are also conceived as part of nature. A complex expression in Ps 24:1 largely corresponds to the concept of nature, but unlike the modern definition, it would seem to include humans: "the earth and its fullness, the world and all that lives in it." No comparable expression exists for society; such expressions as "the whole congregation of Israelites" (Num 1:2) refer primarily to people, and perhaps their animals, but not to the things and institutions that also make up society.

Part I: Creation

> Labour is, first of all, a process between man and nature, a process by which man, through his own actions, mediates, regulates and controls the metabolism between himself and nature. He confronts the materials of nature as a force of nature. He sets in motion the natural forces which belong to his own body, his arms, legs, head and hands, in order to appropriate the materials of nature in a form adapted to his own needs. Through this movement he acts upon external nature and changes it, and in this way he simultaneously changes his own nature. (Marx 2004, 353)

This metabolism is expressed directly in the Yahwist myth where the man is created to cultivate the arable land. His labor mediates his relationship to the land; it will bring life to the earth, as Yhwh intends, or it will disrupt the natural world, which in fact happens. The arable land is dependent upon the man for its production. And thus, contingent on his labor, the man will either sustain his household and create the base for society or threaten his own survival by spoiling nature. "Due to the interpenetration of society and nature, humans have the potential to alter the conditions of life in ways that surpass natural limits and undermine the reproduction of natural systems" (Foster et al. 2010, 403). When the man eats from the forbidden fruit, his actions have repercussions through both society and nature.

In contrast to neoclassical economics, an economics or political economy that embeds society in nature has a conceptual framework that can adequately address an environmental crisis such as climate change. It is able to account for and explain climate change as a problem with human production, at the interface of society and nature. Because climate change is a result of human production—the burning of fossil fuels that empower capitalist relations of production—any viable solution must also address human production. It is not an externality that requires only modest modifications to production or compensation to those affected. Rather, it challenges how contemporary production mediates the integral relationship between society and nature.

The concept of social metabolism is helpful here. Like the nutrient cycle of plants, it is the circulation of energy and matter between society and nature. The metabolism of agricultural land, for example, which produces nitrogen-rich grains and vegetables, requires the replenishment of its lost nitrogen, phosphorus, and potassium. This happened traditionally when the vegetative waste was returned to the land, the land laid fallow for a season or nitrogen-enriching cover crops were used, and animal manure was worked into the field. Similarly, the relationship between society and nature can be understood as a social metabolism: human society is dependent upon the natural world for it construction and continuance. When our mediation between society and nature degrades or depletes the natural world, our social metabolism is disrupted and threatens our social well-being. In industrial agriculture when the crop is shipped off to distant cities, where it is consumed and becomes waste there, a metabolic rift is created in the agricultural land's nutrient cycle—the nutrients it needs are not returned to the land. This rift can be closed by supplying the land with chemically produced fertilizers, but not without negative consequences for both nature and society. The synthetic fertilizers kill beneficial microbial life in the soil and much of the added nutrients leech into groundwater or get washed off into creeks and rivers, eventually forming algae blooms and dead zones in larger bodies of water. The synthetic fertilizers deplete the soil of other nutrients, creating an increasing dependence on them, and so their production uses increasing amounts of fossil fuels, contributing to climate change. In other words, when industrial agriculture attempts to solve the metabolic rift caused by its own production without addressing the production itself, it creates a further disruption or rift in the social metabolism—the exchange between society and nature (Foster et al. 2010; Clark and York 2008).

The social metabolic rift that has resulted in climate change touches on virtually every aspect of the contemporary political economy, for every social metabolism consists of a set of productive social relations and energy to empower them. The metabolism of subsistence agriculture, for example, runs on the productive relations of the household and on solar energy, as the plants convert sunlight to glucose though photosynthesis, feeding both humans and animals. The contemporary economy and its social metabolism, in contrast, consists of capitalist productive relations and is powered primarily (about 80%) on energy produced from fossil fuels, the burning of which is the cause of climate change. One cannot address climate change without tackling the problems associated with capitalist relations of production and the energy on which they are dependent.

God and Nature

Before turning to address the role of energy in the political economy, I must address another definition of nature, which plays a particularly important role in the ancient political economy. In addition to the collective physical world, nature can refer to the processes and forces that create and regulate the physical world. Thus, the growth of crops in agricultural may be explained by natural processes such as photosynthesis and the appropriate amounts of water and heat, much of which is beyond human control. Humans may cultivate the soil, apply fertilizer, and even irrigate the crops, but humans have no control over whether the seed sprouts, how the plant converts sunlight into growth, or possibly the source of water for the plants—whether it rains or there is a nearby body of water from which to irrigate—which is generally attributed to nature.

In the ancient Near East, including ancient Israel, the processes and forces of nature were attributed to the gods. Whereas modern people, who live largely in a secular society, especially in the west, recognize the difference between a natural or a personal causality, the ancient Near Eastern peoples thought only in terms of a personal causality.[8] If the cause of some event was not a human person, then it must have been a divine person. Humans may plow the land, but only gods can cause the sky to rain and the plants to grow. The gods were the forces in and behind natural phenomena; they were the causal agents of natural events. "Everything on earth, all objects and events, came forth from the god's actions and their will, and fitted into some kind of general plan that *they* had in mind" (Bottéro 1992, 105–6). The Bible, for example, is filled with language attributing to Yhwh rain, wind, and earthquakes, and with Yhwh represented with phenomena associated with the thunderstorm (see Ps 29 or 65, among many other texts). These are not metaphors attributing to God natural events, as modern people might interpret them, but rather, in the ancient Israelites' mind, they attest to Yhwh's literal engagement with the natural world. This is especially clear in the covenantal traditions, where Yhwh's role in nature is made conditional on Israel's behavior.

> If you obey my commandments which I [Moses] am commanding you today, to love Yhwh your God and to serve him will all your heart and life, then he will send rain on your land in its season, the early and springtime rains, and you will gather your grain, wine, and oil; and he will give grass in your field for your livestock, and you will eat and be satiated. Be careful, lest you are seduced and turn away to serve other gods and worship them. Yhwh will become enraged against you and he will stop up the heavens, so there will be no rain and the arable land will not produce its crop, and you will perish quickly off the good land that Yhwh is giving to you. (Deut 11:13–17)

From this text and others (see, especially, the blessings and curses in Lev 26 and Deut 28) it is clear that the Israelites understood that Yhwh caused the rain to fall or its opposite by stopping up the heavens. This use of personal causality for expressing natural processes is not the result of covenant theology but rather what made covenant theology possible. Because the Israelite worldview recognized personal causality rather than natural causality, the Israelites' relationship to the natural world could be framed in terms of their relationship to Yhwh their God (see Gaiser 2003). This is significant for articulating the political economy of ancient Israel; according to the Israelites' own ideology, Yhwh contributes to or hinders their production in a rather predictable way.[9] Human labor may mediate the interface between society and nature, but in ancient Israel, as we have already seen in the discussion of the Yahwist creation myth, the productivity of human labor itself is made possible by Yhwh.

---

8. The ancient Near Eastern peoples did not speculate about causality as did the later Greek philosophers, including Aristotle, who delineated four types of causality—material, formal, efficient, and final. None of these types of causality, however, fully accounts for the processes and forces of nature.

9. Without questioning God's role in the natural world, the Book of Job challenges its connection to human behavior.

ENERGY AND LIMITED GROWTH

If labor is what mediates the relationship between society and nature, energy creates the power of labor. All societies and their economies—past, present, and future—are dependent on energy. It is the only universal currency (Smil 2017), without which life is not possible, and when converted into usable forms, it has enabled the development of human civilization from subsistence-based villages to modern, affluent technological cities within a relatively brief period of human history. Although there is an abundant availability of energy, both in stock and flow, its conversion to useful work has traditionally constrained the development of civilization, which experienced zero to marginal economic growth per capita for millennia. Only with the introduction of inexpensive fossil fuels—coal, petroleum, and natural gas—has human civilization had sufficient energy for its reproduction and also surplus energy to fund human development in the arts and sciences, with new technologies, resulting in substantial per capita economic growth.[10]

There are limited sources of energy in our world. By far the most abundant source is sunlight, which produces 1.367 kilowatts for every square meter it strikes on the earth (known as the solar constant; Smil 2016a, 43). This is actually just a fraction of the sun's energy (most of it is lost in space), but it is still 10,000 times more energy than is currently needed by contemporary civilization (Sivaram 2018, 59). Other sources of energy include the wind, which is caused by the uneven heating of the earth by the sun; the movement of water in rivers and tides, which is made possible by solar radiation and caused by gravity; geothermal and geotectonic forces within the earth; and radioactive decay. The problem has never been the amount of energy available, but rather the human ability to harness the energy for useful purposes. Fortunately, the natural world has supplied the most effective technology for capturing and storing energy: photosynthesis.

> Humans use the products of photosynthesis for all or most all of our fuels simply because there is no alternative on the scale we need. This is because nature, the source of our fuels, has favored the storage of solar energy in the hydrocarbon bonds of plants and animals. The reasons are that these elements

---

10. Although it impossible to measure economic growth in the ancient world precisely, scholars have estimated that annual per capita growth was a mere fraction of 1%. This does not mean that there was no absolute growth in the ancient world. The economy grew slowly with the population, but whatever economic growth that did materialize was absorbed by the new population, resulting in a near-zero, net growth per capita. This rather stagnate situation changed with the introduction of fossil fuels, after which per capita growth ranged from just over 1% to as high as 8% (Japan between 1950 and 1973), along with a rapid population growth. Energy is not the sole variable for explaining modern economic growth—education, health, demographic shifts, trade, income inequality, and corruption also play a role—but energy is the necessary condition for growth (see Smil 2019, 406–36). As noted by Robert Ayers, "energy is the stuff of the universe . . . the economic system is essentially a system for extracting, processing and transforming energy as resources into energy embodied in products and services" (2017, 40).

are abundant and "cheap" to a plant, and most important, capable of forming *reduced*, or low oxygen, energy-containing chemical compounds. (Hall and Klitgaard 2012, 71)

All humans have thus met their metabolic needs with carbohydrates from their food, and modern society has developed from the energy supplied by the hydrocarbons in coal, petroleum, and natural gas. The energy from wind was harnessed in the ancient world through sails and later the windmill; the kinetic energy from the flow of water was harnessed through the water wheel. The other sources of energy were only harnessed in the modern era, but all non-solar sources supply only a small percentage of the energy used on the planet today, and especially in the ancient world.

Hunter-Gatherers

Homo Sapiens first arrived in the Levant approximately 100,000 years ago as migrating small bands of hunter-gatherers (Brooke 2014, 83–96). They were consumers more so than producers, taking and subsisting off of the solar energy that the natural world freely provided through photosynthesis. They gathered wild grains, cereals, legumes and pulses, tubers and rhizomes, nuts, and fruits, which grew in abundance around the fertile crescent. This vegetable diet was supplemented with meat from hunting a variety of ungulates and smaller mammals and reptiles, and from fishing. These animals converted the carbohydrates in the plants, many of which humans could not digest, into other nutrients that enriched the human body's metabolism. The hunter-gatherers had significant expenditures of energy in their hunting and gathering and also in their migrations, which were determined by the availability of the food supply, access to water and shelter, and probably the presence of other hunter-gatherers. Their survival was primarily an act of balancing energy: consuming more calories through their foodstuffs than they expended through their various activities. Hunter-gatherers formed a simple society with little, if any social structure; production was limited primarily to tools and the making of clothes; and there were no infrastructure costs. The energy required for survival was thus minimal: little more than the energy required by the sum of the individual metabolisms of the band plus the energy required in hunting and gathering and migrating when necessary.

The temporal distance is too great to be able to document the success and failure of the Paleolithic hunter-gatherer bands. Research on contemporary hunter-gatherers, however, suggests that, while their lifestyle is poor and they live a meager existence, certainly by modern civilizational standards, they also easily meet and surpass the energy requirements for their survival. It has been estimated, for example, that the !Kung Bushmen of the Kalahari in southern Africa, were able to collect in foodstuffs, through their hunting and gathering, ten times the calories that they expended, which easily met their metabolic and social needs (Hall and Klitgaard 2012, 42–44; Lee

1968). Overall, hunting and gathering from the natural world's bounty proved to be a successful survival strategy, for it sustained the human population—*Homo sapiens* and their ancestors—for hundreds of thousands of years. Although it supported only a meager life, human social needs were equally meager.

The hunter-gatherers were dependent on their own muscles as prime movers. They were unable to harness the power of animals, and they had no machines. They did, however, have tools, which made their delivery of energy much more efficient. Wood digging sticks, for example, helped them dig up edible roots and tubers; stone bifacial blades enabled them to cut up animal parts or plants; scrapers and awls aided them in cleaning animal hides and making simple coverings for themselves. It is possible that the bow and arrow had been invented by hunter-gatherers, but no direct evidence has been found. They did fashion clubs and stone pointed spears for hunting. They also discovered fire (evidence suggests a million years ago; see Berna et al. 2012), which preserved their energy by keeping them warm; it could be used to keep away predatory animals and it aided in hunting by easily clearing brush. Most importantly, fire was used to cook their food, which aided in digestion, releasing more nutrients from the food, and so increased the metabolic energy they received from the food. Fire also enabled them to dry animal meat for longer preservation.

Human societies require a surplus of energy in order to survive and a large surplus to grow, whether it be demographically, economically, or through social complexity. Humans, like all living plants and animals must conform to the "law of evolutionary energetics":

> If you are to survive you must produce or capture more energy than you use to obtain it, if you are to reproduce you must have a large surplus beyond metabolic needs, and if your species are to prosper over evolutionary time you must have a very large surplus for the average individual to compensate for the large losses that occur to the majority of the population. (Hall et al. 2009, 29)

The modest energy surplus from hunting and gathering enabled the social bands to reproduce themselves with modest demographic growth (Aimé and Austerlitz 2017), but no economic growth or increase in social complexity can be detected from the archaeological record. The adverse climate of the cold, dry, glacial Pleistocene perhaps even hindered growth (see Brooke 2014). Energy surplus, or net energy, occurs when a society captures and stores more energy than is required for it to reproduce itself, and three variables are helpful for understanding its potential and use in society: quantity (how much energy), quality (what kind of energy), and flow (rate of delivery of the energy; its potential power) (Hall and Klitgaard 2012, 41). For the hunter-gatherer bands, the quantity of energy depended on the available food supply, which was stored in its natural state (quality) and thus available only for a limited time for consumption, and the flow was dependent on the hunter-gatherer's own biological metabolism. Given the energy quality and flow of naturally occurring foodstuffs, the hunter-gatherer's energy surplus would remain small regardless of the quantity of foodstuffs available to them.

A formula that is often used to measure surplus energy is called, "energy return on investment" or EROI. It is a ratio of the energy gained from an energy-gathering activity divided by the energy required to get that energy (see Hall and Klitgaard 2012, 309–20). The ratio, of course, should be positive and more than one, otherwise one is losing energy, and because of entropy, the ratio needs to be significantly more than one. As noted above, for example, the !Kung Bushmen's food gathering activities had an EROI of 10:1, which might seem large on the face of it, but given its quality (food from gathering and hunting) and its flow (requiring daily consumption), a high 10:1 EROI is perhaps needed for the Bushmen's reproduction.[11] Moreover, some (many?) of the Bushmen (the elderly and small children) did not participate in the food-gathering activities and thus the EROI needs to be high to compensate for the inability of some to contribute. In comparison to modern Western society, a bare minimum EROI for social reproduction has been calculated at 3.3:1, but this is largely a survival level, leaving little energy for much of what we value about civilization (Hall and Klitgaard 2012, 319). A minimum EROI for the reproduction of Western society would be closer to 11:1 (Fizaine and Court 2016), comparable to the EROI of hunter-gatherer societies, but requiring a different quantity, quality, and flow from the energy.

Agriculture and Settled Society

When the climate suddenly changed with the warm, moist Holocene around 11,700 years ago, the human population in the Levant began settling down in small hamlets or villages and gradually took up agriculture mixed with animal husbandry. Instead of being simple consumers of what the natural world provided, humans became producers of their own food, which transformed human society. This social transformation, which was made possible by the domestication of plants and animals,[12] can be linked to the stabilization of the climate. During the preceding glacial Pleistocene, the climate was too cool and dry to support vigorous plant growth, and the carbon dioxide levels were too low for the C_3 plants that are the founder crops of agriculture, such as emmer, einkorn, barley, and some legumes (see Brooke 2014, 121–52). Nevertheless, despite the favorable conditions of the Holocene, it is unclear why humans embarked

---

11. Based on empirical data, Glaub and Hall (2017) calculated that the !Kung Bushmen's hunting of the kudu through persistence (pursuing the animal in the heat of day until it reaches a point of hypothermia, and then killing it at close range) produced an extremely high EROI ranging from 26:1 to 69:1, depending on the number of hunters involved. This form of hunting would compensate for the less efficient gathering of other forms of food.

12. Domestication is a two-way street. While humans domesticated plants and animals, humans were also domesticated so that humans became caretakers of certain plants and animals, affecting the human diet, lifestyle, and economy. Humans have been changed as much through domestication as the plants and animals.

down the road to agriculture in the first place (see Scott 2017). Scholars have argued that there must have been population pressures requiring more food, that the allure of settled life demanded new food sources, or simply that domestication was the gradual, unintended coevolution between humans, plants, and animals (see Simmons 2007). Perhaps there were multiple causes. In any case, the reason humans turned to agriculture need not distract us, for once agriculture was adopted (including its sibling animal husbandry), humans became dependent on it and never returned to hunting and gathering as the primary mode of subsistence.[13]

The transition to fully developed agriculture, including farmed crops, trees and vines, and domesticated animals, took a few thousand years and provided obvious benefits with a large food supply (see Zeder 2011; Asouti and Fuller 2103; Fuller et al. 2011). Farming provided a large, annual crop of grains, which could be stored until the next harvest, and were consumed in the form of bread, cakes, and beer. The olive tree supplied the primary source of fat in the diet and fuel for lamps; the grape vine was grown for the wine that could be produced from it, and other trees—date, fig, pomegranate, pistachio, and almond—supplemented the diet with their perennial fruits and nuts. Vegetable gardens, growing onions, leeks, garlic, lentils, chick-peas, and beans, rounded out the people's largely vegetarian diet. Animals were kept primarily for their secondary products. Small animals, such as sheep and goats, provide milk and wool or hair, whereas cattle and donkeys were used for traction and carrying loads. The animals also provided meat for special occasions such as religious feasts or as a backup food supply when the harvests failed or were inadequate (see Borowski 1998). The immediate benefit of the agricultural bounty was a growing population—still modest by contemporary standards, but noticeably more than for hunter-gatherers—and most of the surplus energy was translated into this growth. Hunting wilding game, as a cheap source of meat, continued to supplement the food supply, but as a decreasingly smaller percentage.[14]

The costs of agriculture, however, dramatically increased the energy demands on the people. The land first needed to be cleared and then cultivated. Initially, this was done with hand tools, but when the plow was invented, it could be pulled by an ox or donkey, and it enabled humans to cultivate larger fields. After the seeds were planted, the field needed to be repeatedly weeded and cultivated or the tendency of the land to return to its original state (a process known as ecological succession) would impair the crop, reducing its yield in the process. Although not the most intensive labor,

---

13. Subsistence is often used with a negative connotation and is associated with poverty. It is used here and elsewhere in this book to refer to a positive minimal existence in which one produces food and what is required for maintaining life rather than accumulating wealth to purchase food and the needs of life (see Mies and Bennholdt-Thomsen 1999, 19–22).

14. The population grew despite being less healthy. Diminished health is attested primarily from the archaeological record by individuals with smaller stature and less bone density, and is the result of several causes: deficient diet due to a lack of variety in the crops grown; poor harvests; and infectious diseases as a result of the growing population, among others (see Mummert 2011).

the care and protection of the crops during the several months of growth probably consumed the most energy of all tasks. More labor was needed at harvest time, during which the grain was picked with its stalks, then threshed and winnowed, before it could be stored. Tools were invented to aid in all of these tasks. Finally, little agricultural produce was eaten in its natural or harvested state (fruits and nuts would be the exception), and so had to be processed for consumption. Grain was ground into flour from which it could be baked or cooked into a variety of foods, with bread being the most common. Olives were crushed and pressed for their oil; grapes were pressed for their juice, which was stored in jars for fermentation. Animals needed to be fed or taken a distance from the crops for grazing; after the harvest, they would be grazed on the remains in the fields so that they would also leave their manure for fertilizer.

Beyond the energy cost for the production of food were the infrastructure costs, for agriculture requires a settled community. Thus, a house had to be built along with silos or lined pits and pottery vessels in which to store the agricultural produce. Tools were made, initially out of wood and stone, but eventually bronze and then iron was used. An oven would need to be constructed for baking, a hearth for cooking; heating fuel—wood, dung, straw—would need to be gathered and stored. A source of water would be essential: water was either hauled from a spring or river and stored in jars, collected from rain in a cistern cut out of the bedrock, or drawn from a well dug down to the water table. All of these basic tasks, and many others, required energy that had to be supplied from the agricultural produce because human muscle continued to be the prime mover of human societies. Animal muscle also played a significant role, especially in pulling the plow and hauling material in a cart or on the animal's back, but domestic animals also require human labor, and hence energy, to take care of them.

Although agriculture enabled humans to produce significantly more foodstuffs, it also required much more energy expenditures. And this does not account for climate variations or pest infestations or other catastrophes that frequently reduced the harvest and adversely impacted the people. Nor is this unique to the early periods of agriculture:

> Regardless of the historical period, environmental setting, or prevailing mode of cropping and intensification, no traditional agriculture could consistently produce enough food to eliminate extensive malnutrition. All of them were vulnerable to major famines, and even the societies practicing the most intensive cultivation were not immune to recurrent catastrophes, with droughts and floods being the most common natural triggers. (Smil 2017, 121)

Agriculture was an unreliable source of energy, easily affected by climate and pests; it could produce little more than what was required for basic human needs. But as long as human muscle was the prime mover, the development and complexity of human society would be linked to it. Humans would find further ways of substituting animal labor for human labor, such as harnessing an animal to pull a threshing sledge or turn a grinding stone, but such animals required either a share of the agricultural production or pasturage that took land out of production. Although the energy from wind and flowing water had been harnessed for transportation by the time of the Israelites, in later periods wind and flowing water energy would become more significant prime movers contributing to the growth of human society. Yet there was little to no economic growth per capita. Economic growth was largely offset by the slow population growth, which consumed much of the surplus energy that continued to come predominantly from agriculture. The remaining surplus energy supported the growing complexity of human societies, with some notable collapses, such as the fall of the Roman empire (see Tainter 1988). It would not be until humans discovered new sources of energy (fossil fuels) and were thus able to create new prime movers (the steam and internal combustion engines) that significant economic growth per capita would be possible. Economic growth in agricultural societies, such as ancient Israel, was hindered by the limits of agriculture itself (see Smil 2017, 120–26).[15]

Increasing Surplus Energy

The societal EROI of the early agricultural communities is difficult to measure (there are few modern analogs, see Martinez-Alier 2011), but it would appear to be less than that of hunter-gatherers, though sufficient for the societies to grow and increase in social complexity. Hunter-gatherers mostly lived within the energy balance between what their ecosystem provided and the energy they expended, and they did so for hundreds of thousands of years. Beginning with agricultural societies, however, humans sought more and more ways to capture surplus energy. More energy was needed because human production led to more wants and desires than what the natural world could provide without human production. Richard Heinberg (2003, 19–32) introduced a helpful classification scheme of five strategies humans have used for extracting an energy surplus from the natural world: takeover, tool use, specialization, scope enlargement, and drawdown.

Takeover is the most fundamental human strategy in engaging the natural world. It occurs when humans divert the life-supporting capacity of the natural world from supporting other fauna and flora to supporting humans. For the hunter-gatherers, takeover occurred when they migrated to a new region, after depleting the food stock of the previous one, or when they cleared brush with fire to make hunting more accessible. For agricultural societies, takeover occurs when land is cleared for cultivation, and a wide variety of vegetation is replaced by a few, selected crops. The domestication

---

15. Todd Buchholz (1988) argues that ancient Israel's laws were responsible for hindering economic growth by restricting economic transactions. Unfortunately, his analysis is rooted in neoclassical economics and he assumes a market, capitalist society; he misunderstands the character of the ancient economy. Moreover, his interpretation cannot account for the fact that no ancient society experienced per capita economic growth.

of plants and animals itself is a form of the takeover strategy. Once agriculture has been introduced into a region, however, the ability of takeover to increase energy surplus is limited. The energy gained by adding new fields would be offset by the additional labor required and the increased distance from the household or village.

Tool use refers to simple hand tools, more complex technologies such as the olive press, and even the machines and technologies that characterize the contemporary world. As noted above, tools make the use of muscle energy more efficient, enabling more work to be done with the same amount of energy. Tools also enable humans to convert external sources of energy into work. Through use of a sail, for example, humans convert the kinetic energy in wind into a force that can propel humans in a boat. A windmill will convert the same wind energy into mechanical power that can be used to pump water or generate electricity. But tools also enable humans to adapt to their environment. The southern Mesopotamian plain, for example, was too arid to support a large population though agriculture, but through an elaborate irrigation system, Mesopotamia was able to produce an abundance of grain and was home to the world's first human civilization (see Postgate 1994, 173–90; Liverani 1998). There is a tradeoff on energy with tool use, however, because the production of tools and machines requires energy. The Mesopotamian canal system required an enormous amount of energy through human labor, not just for digging the canals, but also for their regular maintenance. Nevertheless, the crops irrigated by the canals provided an even larger supply of energy, justifying the labor on the canals. Many tools in the ancient world were hand-made, requiring only human energy, but some required energy from an external source, generally heat from fire. Metal tools, such as the metal tipped plow, the knife, and weapons of war, thus required access to fuels that could produce sufficient heat to process the metal ores as well as the energy surplus to mine and smelt the ores (see, generally, Baker 2019).

The strategy of specialization entails the organization of society, including the division of labor and the development of occupations, some of which may be linked to the use and control of tools. Hunter-gatherers basically had an egalitarian division of labor between men and women. Although the men typically hunted and the women gathered plant foods and small animals, they contributed equally to the material livelihood of the band (Halperin 1980). In agricultural societies, a much more defined gendered division of labor emerged. Men dominated the agricultural tasks and other tasks away from the house, whereas women worked in and around the house, raising and educating children, processing foodstuffs and preparing meals, tending to the animals, and growing vegetables (Burton and White 1984; Ember 1983; Burton et al. 1977; Murdock and Provost 1973; Meyers 2007). Women may have participated in textile production (Costin 2013), but men dominated in other industries. At the core of specialization is the redistribution of energy so that some people benefit from the energy expenditure of others. This included first and foremost the use of slaves, who in the ancient Near East were captured in war or became slaves because of debt.

Their muscle energy and labor belonged to another, who may force them to work on tasks for which they might be reluctant to volunteer, such as quarrying, mining, or fighting in war. Another form of specialization was tied to control of specific tools or knowledge. Thus, a craftsman would benefit from the labors of others; although the mechanism would vary depending on the complexity of the society, the craftsman ultimately exchanged the product of his craft for food and other subsistence needs. Similarly, a priest exchanged his religious knowledge and skills for the production of others. Specialization is the means by which muscle energy is captured through the social hierarchy, as subordinates labor for the benefit of their superiors.

Scope enlargement takes place when one captures energies from regions and people beyond one's control, through trade or conquest. The trade of obsidian from sources in Turkey to the rest of the Near East is attested already during the Neolithic period. In later periods, metal ores were similarly traded. In the Levant, for example, copper ore is plentiful, but the strength of bronze could not be exploited without trading for tin, which is not found in the region. In the contemporary world, this form of scope enlargement is attested through globalization, as nations seek cheaper sources of labor and larger markets for their products. In the ancient world, however, the strategy of scope enlargement was exercised primarily through conquest—simply plundering a neighboring people for slaves and for their resources and goods. This became the basis for the great empires of the ancient world, and it continued into the modern world with colonization.

Finally, drawdown is an exclusively modern strategy for extracting an energy surplus by drawing down non-renewable energy sources such as fossil fuels and uranium. Drawdown has been a successful strategy for capturing energy and producing economic growth, along with the many benefits that come with it. But it also has serious negative consequences, such as pollution, climate change, and dependence on a limited and diminishing resource. Nevertheless, drawdown is the only strategy that has produced sustained per capita economic growth.

The other four strategies, which were utilized in the ancient world, also have negative consequences. Only takeover and tool use exploit new sources of energy. The takeover strategy is intrinsic to the relationship between humans and nature and so risks defining the natural world in terms of human use and production. Because tools often require energy in their production, the making of tools can degrade the natural world. The making of bronze and iron, for example, resulted in the deforestation of much of the eastern Mediterranean (Hughes 1975, 68–86). The use of tools and technologies can also have unintended consequences. The irrigation of the southern Mesopotamian plain through canals eventually resulted in the salinization of the fields, as salt deposits were left behind when water evaporated from the poorly drained fields (Hughes 1975, 34–35; see Scott 2017, 195–202). Tool use also contributed to the social hierarchy as control and possession of tools was used by some people to justify domination over others. Similarly, specialization and scope enlargement result from the emergence of new social relations of production by which some people exercise power over other people through differential access to resources, tools, skills, and knowledge. Rather than enabling humans to capture new forms of energy, as with the first two strategies, specialization and scope enlargement simply enabled some people to capture the energy surplus from the production of other people. Thus, specialization and scope enlargement contributed to hierarchy and exploitation within society. Although these strategies for extracting an energy surplus failed to produce any per capita economic growth, they transformed the relationship between humans and the natural world and shaped the development of human society.

PRODUCTIVE RELATIONS IN ANCIENT ISRAEL

The ancient Israelite economy was similar to all ancient Near Eastern economies in that it was powered by the conversion of solar energy into human and animal muscle. Moreover, the effort to harness more energy than could be captured individually structured its economy. Because the available sources of energy were limited, primarily the result of photosynthesis, increasing energy surplus meant capturing it from the labor of others. To do this, some people exercised power over others by providing access to land, controlling the use of tools or animals, lending seed and other resources, supplying additional labor when needed, and protecting against theft and other harms. The historically determined, productive relations that developed were based on an unequal power differential so that the dominant member was able to extract some of the surplus energy from the subordinate member, through his labor directly or from the product of his labor. These productive relations were *productive inequalities* in that one person became dependent on another for their productive interaction with the natural world (Donham 1999, 58–65); these relations produced the social hierarchy in ancient Israel and were naturalized through gender relations.

The productive relations were determined by the productive powers in ancient Israel.[16] Unlike their Mesopotamian and Egyptian neighbors, the ancient Israelites and other peoples along the Levant engaged in dry farming. They were dependent on the annual winter rains for their crops. They practiced a diverse agriculture, with multiple grain crops and legumes, fruit and nut trees, along with grape vines, and supplemented with sheep and goats. Their tools were similar to those used by other peoples, many of which were "upgraded" from bronze to iron over time (see Borowski 1987; Hopkins 1985). Terracing was a new technology that the Israelites seemed to have exploited in the hill country, opening up new land for cultivation, conserving water, and preserving topsoil from erosion. Terracing also required extensive cooperation for its construction and maintenance, and thus was probably not common

---

16. Productive powers are "not simply raw materials or tools; more inclusively, they are human skills, productive knowledge, and even technical aspects of cooperation in the labor process, all of these being intentionally used to produce" (Donham 1999, 59).

until late in the monarchic period (Hopkins 1987). Most of the industries—grain processing and storage, oil and wine production, pottery production, textile weaving, tanning, and metallurgy—remained as small cottage crafts (see King and Stager 2001, 93–107, 129–76). The rise of the territorial kingdom or state distinguishes the Israelites from their Bronze Age predecessors, but Israel was not alone in this—the Levant as a whole was divided into numerous territorial kingdoms, with Aramean kingdoms in the north, and Israelite, Moabite, Ammonite, and Edomite kingdoms in the south (see Finkelstein 1999; Master 2001). Along the coast, the Phoenicians and Philistines continued in the Bronze Age tradition with a confederation of city states. Although the documentation is incomplete, the territorial states were culturally-defined areas in which the people followed a shared patron deity. For the Israelites, this was Yhwh.

Unfortunately, so much is unknown about the ancient Israelite economy, largely due to the lack of documentation. Unlike ancient Mesopotamian societies, from which most of the surviving written materials are economic in nature, few economic records have survived from ancient Israel (the Samaria ostraca are a notable exception; see Nam 2012; Niemann 2008). The Hebrew Bible, which supplies the bulk of textual information about ancient Israel, gives little and uneven attention to economic issues; the archaeological remains, in contrast, provide significant material information, but not unambiguously so, and their contribution is thus often contested. Nevertheless, we do know that ancient Israel was unlike the Mesopotamian societies in many ways due to historical, geographical, and environmental factors. Ancient Israel was not dependent on an irrigation infrastructure; there were no large centralized storehouses;[17] temples played a small material role in the economy, though they loomed large ideologically; the society was predominantly rural with only a few large urban centers; the administration and bureaucracy remained relatively small throughout its brief history. It is not my purpose here to reconstruct fully the political economy of ancient Israel. This has been done masterfully by Roland Boer in his *The Sacred Economy of Ancient Israel* (2015). Our focus, rather, is on the role of energy in the economy, its capture through productive inequalities and naturalization through gender relations, and thus how the political economy mediated the Israelites relationship with the natural world.

---

17. This statement depends on the interpretation of the abundant tripartite pillared buildings. John Currid (1992) makes the most convincing argument that the buildings should be interpreted as storehouses. His argument is most effective for the three tripartite pillared buildings at Beersheba; it is not as persuasive for interpreting other sites. Larry Herr (1988) interprets the buildings as marketplaces, though his argument works best for Tell Hadar. John Holladay (1986) had earlier argued that the buildings were best understood as stables, but this works best for the two large multi-building complexes at Megiddo (see Franklin 2017). In other words, the tripartite pillared buildings had multiple functions, one of which may have been as a storehouse. At most, the buildings would be regional storehouses; no tripartite pillared buildings have been found at Samaria or Jerusalem.

Part I: Creation

The Ideology of Labor

The Israelites interacted with the natural world through their labor, which was structured by their productive relations, but these historically and socially specific inequalities cannot be adequately understood apart from Israelite religion. This may be viewed as an odd statement when taking a historical materialist approach since attention is usually given to productive relations first, then to superstructure (i.e., the ideology, which is expressed through religion, law, and politics). But the two cannot be separated other than analytically; the productive relations cannot exist without the superstructure. They have a dialectical relationship so that the productive relations determine the superstructure even as they are dependent on the superstructure for their existence. "As systems of regularized social interaction, inequalities are inextricably embedded in superstructural meanings and practices" (Donham 1999, 195). Moreover, the ideological superstructure makes it possible for the productive inequalities to reproduce: ideology does not simply legitimate power, but rather "provides the very terms in which power regularly becomes power" (Donham 1999, 196). Before addressing the social relations of production in ancient Israel, it is helpful to explore the role of labor and work in Israelite religion.

Work in the ancient world was not easy for the vast majority of people. It was physically taxing, requiring much drudgery with little pleasure. Although hard work provided for one's own subsistence, it rarely improved one's life, and thus people sought to minimize the labor needed for any task. This has been the common experience of agricultural peasants around the world who have found themselves in the same situation: regardless of how hard they work, the land provides little more than is necessary to survive (see Foster 1965; Oakman 2018). If subsistence labor was arduous, how much more so was laboring for someone else's benefit. It is not surprising, then, that human labor and work were given a divine sanction.

In the Mesopotamian myth of Atrahasis, for example, humans are created for the sole purpose of work. The myth begins in a primordial time before humans when the gods did all the work of the earth:

> When the gods instead of man
> Did the work, bore the loads,
> The gods' load was too great
> The work too hard, the trouble too much,
> The great Anunnaki made the Igigi
> Carry the workload sevenfold. (I 1–6; Dalley 1991, 8)

Prior to the creation of humans, the Anunnaki (older gods) made all the Igigi (younger gods) do the work that was necessary for Mesopotamian society—populated exclusively by divine beings—to survive. The Igigi, for example, dug out the beds for the Euphrates and Tigris rivers; they dug out the channels for the irrigation canals that made agriculture possible in the southern Mesopotamian plain. But the Igigi's labors were too hard, and so they rebelled against the Anunnaki. They roused Ellil, their counselor-warrior, from his sleep and complained to him:

> Every single one of us gods declared war!
> We have put [a stop] to the digging.
> The load is excessive, it is killing us!
> Our work is too hard, the trouble is too much!
> So every single one of us gods
> Has agreed to complain to Ellil. (I 146–52; Dalley 1991, 12)

Ellil is moved by the burden of the Igigi. He presents their case to Anu, the head of the Anunnaki, who recognizes the justice of their cause and offers a solution:

> What are we complaining of?
> Their work was indeed too hard, their trouble was too much . . .
> Belet-ili the womb-goddess is present,
> Let the womb-goddess create offspring,
> And let man bear the load of the gods! (I 176–77, 190–91; Dalley 1991, 13, 14–15)

The myth of Atrahasis expresses clearly that humans were created to relieve the gods of their burdensome labor—humans will do the work rather than the gods—but in doing so, the myth masks the productive inequalities that structure the Mesopotamian economy. In the myth, the gods are represented by two classes: the Igigi who do the heavy labor building the infrastructure for agriculture, and the Anunnaki who benefit from and administer their labor. The creation of humans relieves the Igigi of their arduous work, but the administrative work of the Anunnaki, who never complained of their burden, has no human counterpart in the myth. In the real world of ancient Mesopotamia, the Anunnaki are representative of the king and royal administration for whom the masses labored, but in the myth these gods continue to govern the world. Thus, humans not only replace the gods (the Igigi), they also work on behalf of the gods (the Anunnaki). The role of the king and the royal administration are subsumed into the Anunnaki.

The role of human work in the biblical tradition is similar to that in Atrahasis, but with some subtle yet significant differences. In the Yahwist creation myth, which was addressed in the first chapter, the man is created to labor in the arable land. Yet, unlike the humans in the Mesopotamian myth, the man is not created to relieve Yhwh of his work but rather to work *with* Yhwh. Each has a contribution to make: the man will cultivate the soil and Yhwh will fertilize it with rain. Indeed, the man soon learns, through his disobedience, followed by Yhwh cursing the land, that his labor without Yhwh's contribution will be arduous and incomplete; despite the creative power of human labor, the man remains dependent upon Yhwh's contribution of rain. In other

Part I: Creation

words, in the Yahwist creation story, the created world is dependent upon human work, but humans are not alone in their labors. Yhwh also has a role to play in order for human labor to be fully productive—Yhwh mediates, or makes possible, the productivity of human labor.

Work is a focal theme of the Priestly creation myth in Genesis 1:1–2:3, but it is the work of God, not humans, that is at issue. In six days, God labors to create an ordered, differentiated, and inhabited world from what was originally formless and empty. Then, on the seventh day, God demonstrates his sovereignty over creation by resting from his labors. This account of creation depicts the work of God. Humans, of course, are assigned work when they are created by God on the sixth day and commanded to procreate, subdue the earth, and exercise dominion over all the creatures (Gen 1:28). For the Priestly scribes, human work is significant because humans were created in the image of God and God blessed and sanctified the seventh day. The myth does not define what it means by "image of God," though the context would suggest that humans are like God, especially in their labor (von Rad 1972, 60; Bird 1981, 137–44; Tigay 1984; Barr 1972, 19–20). In other words, like the Yahwist, the Priestly scribes depict humans as creators through their labor but define their relationship to God's work differently by linking their work to the Sabbath.

The origin of the seven-day week cycle and the Sabbath day in ancient Israel is not known, but the connection between the Sabbath and creation predates the Priestly creation myth (Levenson 1988, 66–77). Already in the Ten Commandments (which are incorporated into the Priestly tradition; see Dozeman 2009, 488–92), the sabbath-cycle in which humans labor for six days and rest on the seventh is justified by God's pattern of work and rest at creation (Exod 20:8–11, though compare a different tradition in Deut 5:12–15, where Sabbath is linked to the rest God provided Israel from slavery in Egypt). For the Priestly scribes, the Sabbath also ritualizes the human labor-rest cycle. Through keeping the Sabbath, the ritual mimesis of God's rest sacramentalizes human labor on the preceding six days, even as it also actualizes God's sovereignty over creation; it gives human labor cosmological significance (see Levenson 1988, 127). Humans, who are the image of God, are creators like God, and through their labor and rest, they replicate God's creative activity. Human labor neither replaces (as with the myth of Atrahasis) nor collaborates with (as with the Yahwist creation myth) God's work, but rather actualizes it by reinscribing God as sovereign and replicating God's work as God's agents.

Later, in the book of Exodus, the Priestly scribes further define human work by connecting the Sabbath with God's covenant at Mount Sinai:

> You will keep my Sabbaths, for this is a sign between me and you throughout your generations to know that I am Yhwh who sanctifies you ... The Israelites shall keep the Sabbath, observing the Sabbath throughout their generations as an eternal covenant. It is a sign forever between me and the Israelites because

in six days God made the heavens and the earth, and on the seventh day God rested and was refreshed. (Exod 31:13, 16–17)

As a sign, or better, a symbol of the covenant, the Israelites' observance of the Sabbath becomes an indication of their faithfulness to God's covenant. By connecting the Sabbath and God's covenant, the Priestly scribes clarify the character of human labor: only when human labor is in accord with God's covenant, upholding God as the sovereign over creation, will it replicate God's creative activity. When Israelites keep the covenant, their labor will be creative like God's work at the beginning. Or, to state the reverse, when the Israelites violate God's covenant, their labor will be unproductive and even do damage to God's creation. In the Priestly worldview, the covenant between God and Israel is embedded in creation and thereby mediates Israel's relationship to the creation. God structured the creation so that there is an inherent connection between human actions and their consequences. "This act/consequence cosmogony envisions such pervasive order in the closed circuit of creation that whatever humans do, whether for good or for ill, will necessarily have repercussions in nature as easily as among people" (Knight 1985, 150; see Koch 1983). Because humans are God's agents in creation, human labor, for the Priestly scribes, either builds upon and sustains, or is contrary to and undermines, God's own creative activity, and such work is defined in relation to the requirements of the covenant.

It is a common Near Eastern ideology, as expressed in the myth of Atrahasis, that humans are creators like gods, but there were multiple ways of understanding the specific relationship between humans and gods and the character of the labor that resulted from it. In the Yahwist creation myth, human labor is needed for the earth to flourish, but humans collaborate with Yhwh whose contribution is also necessary. The productivity of human labor is mediated by Yhwh. Although the Yahwist tradition does not link human labor to Yhwh's covenant with Israel—the tradition may not address the covenant[18]—it connects the curse of the land, which frustrates the man's labor, to his disobedience of Yhwh's prohibition. The Yahwist's understanding of human labor is thus consistent with conceptions of the covenant, especially in the Deuteronomic tradition, which emphasize obedience to Yhwh's commands (*mitsvoth*). The Priestly creation myth, on the other hand, presents humans as the representatives of God, created in God's image. As such, their labor builds on and replicates God's own work in creation. Because the Priestly scribes place human labor within a covenantal relationship marked by Sabbath, the mimetic role of human labor actualizes God's sovereign role in creation only when the people keep the covenant;

---

18. The traditional formulation of the Documentary Hypothesis attributed parts of Exodus 19, 24, and 32–34 to the Yahwist (J) source (see Noth 1981; von Rad 1984), but recent scholarship has debated whether the so-called Yahwist tradition extends into Exodus, or whether it is even a coherent source (see the essays in Dozeman and Schmid 2006). Although there are good reasons to identify a Yahwist tradition in Genesis, there are fewer compelling reasons to identify it in Exodus. In any case, the Yahwist creation myth does not link to the covenant as does the Priestly creation myth.

Part I: Creation

otherwise, human labor undermines God's creation (see the different consequences—blessings and curses—in Lev 26, for example). More generally, for both the Yahwist and the Priestly scribes, human labor takes place within relationship to God, whether through collaboration or covenant.

The Organization of Labor

Returning to the social relations of production, the ancient Israelite economy consisted of a hierarchy of productive inequalities. The ideological framework that allows for and explains the productive inequalities in ancient Israel was the relationship between Yhwh and the people (cf. Boer 2007, 39–41). Drawing upon the Yahwist understanding of human labor, which was a historical product of the monarchic period of Judah, this ideology emphasized that all human production was dependent on Yhwh who owned the land, brought rain and fertility, opened human and animal wombs, and otherwise blessed human production. The people's labor or work would be effectual only if they maintained a right relationship with Yhwh, which was expressed through obedience to Yhwh's commands and through their participation in the cult—whether by means of household shrines, regional sanctuaries, or state temples—with offerings and sacrifices, tithes, and festivals. The ideological relationship between Yhwh and the people both justified the productive inequalities and made the inequalities possible. First, the undisputable hierarchy between Yhwh and the people defined the hierarchies between Israelites: the relations were based on power differentials in which one member was dependent on the other. Second, the power differential also gendered the productive relations, though rarely is this explicit in the language of the relations, except for the marital couple. The productive inequalities are often framed in terms of kinship language—father and son, for example—but this is used to mask the gendering of the production relations, which involved only men, and the threat that such relations might pose to the kinship structure of the society (see further discussion below and in the next chapter). The relationship between Yhwh and the people, though more commonly expressed in gendered language, was also framed in kinship language, especially when the emphasis was on the people's obedience to Yhwh (see McCarthy 1978; Medved 2016; Knobnya 2011). The age-kinship hierarchy was similar to the gender hierarchy, reflecting the same power differential between the members, and thus could be used interchangeably. In Jeremiah 3, for example, the prophet can refer to the relationship between Yhwh and Israel/Judah using both the gender and the age-kinship hierarchy, with each emphasizing faithlessness—ancient Israel as faithless sons and as a faithless wife. The ideological relationship between Yhwh and the people contributed to the reproduction of the productive inequalities in ancient Israel.

The household (*bet ab*), as introduced in the previous chapter, was the primary productive unit in ancient Israel (on the physical house, see Hardin 2010), and its production was structured by the hierarchical relationship between the husband and the wife. The household was largely self-sufficient and strived simply for a subsistence survival.[19] Economic growth was not expected, and the meager surplus that might be produced by the household was necessary to supply seed for the next planting season, feed the household during the lean time before the next harvest, and provide a hedge against a poor harvest the following year, which might be caused by an adverse climate, disease and pestilence, or war (Boer 2015, 53–81). Labor was supplied by all members of the household, and any division of labor dissolved during periods of intense labor need, such as planting and especially during the harvest (García Bachmann 2013). Nevertheless, the husband generally labored in the fields, away from the house, along with other men and boys of the household. The wife, and other women and girls, tended to work in and around the house. This division of labor was legitimized and naturalized by the gender ideology, in which the process of procreation, including the contribution of the husband and wife, was likened to agriculture. The husband was the possessor of seed. Whether in sowing a field or impregnating his wife, the husband controlled production; the wife, like a field, required her husband's labor in order to produce. According to the ideology, she was dependent on her husband to participate in the household production; and indeed, the gender ideology masked the many ways in which the wife, and other women, contributed to the production of the household (see Ebeling 2010). The gender ideology not only defined the inequitable role of each in the household production, it naturalized the inequality in the culturally defined, bodily differences between males and females. The productive relations were *gendered relations*. Moreover, the wife's dependence on her husband was structurally similar to the people's dependence on YHWH, which further determined the productive inequality between the husband and wife even as it gendered the relationship between YHWH and the people.

Households were not isolated structures but were integrated into larger socioeconomic institutions, the most immediate of which was the *mishpahah* ("clan" or "lineage").[20] The *mishpahah* was an extended kinship unit. In the genealogies, in particular, it represented a subdivision of the tribe, and was probably tied to a specific region of the tribe. There were four to eight *mishpahoth* per tribe, though Dan had only one *mishpahah* (Num 26:42). The *mishpahah* could also be subdivided by *mishpahoth*, as the *mishpahah* of Perez (of the tribe of Judah), is subdivided into the *mishpahoth*

---

19. Following Sahlins (1972), scholars have commonly subsumed the household production into a domestic mode of production, but households are not sufficient for a mode of production; they belong to a larger community, which constitutes an important relation of production (Roseberry 1986, 1988a; Donham 1981).

20. The Hebrew use of terms for social units is more fluid than their English translations suggest. For example, a *bet ab* may refer to the whole *mishpahah* rather than a subdivision of it. There seems to be some overlap in the terms (Lemche 1985, 260–72). Nevertheless, a clear hierarchy is also evident in many uses of these terms (see Josh 7:14–18): the *bet ab* is subsumed in the *mishpahah*, a number of which make up the *shevet* ("tribe").

of Hezron and Hamul (Num 26:19–22). Outside the genealogies, *mishpahah* is also used to refer to a smaller kinship unit, composed of multiple households (*bet aboth*), and overlapping in space with the village or town and its land (Gen 24:38; 2 Sam 20:6; see Faust 2000; Halpern 1991, 49–59).[21] The use of *mishpahah* in these contexts may overlap with *bet ab*. It is this latter, non-genealogical use of *mishpahah* that is the focus here.

The importance and composition of the *mishpahah* has been debated by scholars. Gottwald suggested that it was the most important social unit in early Israel, and that it functioned as a protective association of families, "which operated to preserve the minimal conditions for the integrity of each of its member families by extending mutual help as needed to supply male heirs, to keep or recover land, to rescue members from debt slavery, and to avenge murder" (1979, 267). For Gottwald, the *mishpahah* was primarily a social organization rather than a genetic one. Other scholars, such as Bendor (1996, 67–86), give priority to the *bet ab* and argue that the *mishpahah* was primarily a genetic group, growing out the *bet ab*. The evidence, meager though it might be, suggests a genetic connection among the members of a *mishpahah*, but the *mishpahah* also functioned to protect and take care of its members. The social importance of the *mishpahah* is unclear from the biblical tradition. The term occurs mostly in genealogical contexts, which are predominantly in the Priestly tradition; it occurs frequently in Joshua 13–21, which focuses on the division of the land among the Israelite tribes in the Deuteronomistic tradition (see Na'aman 2005, 331–61); *mishpahah* is used about fifty other times in texts from the monarchic period and the Priestly tradition. The *mishpahah* does not seem to have played a significant role in the post-exilic period. Politically, *mishpahah* is never used in conjunction with political terms—such as "elder" (*zaqan*), "head" (*rosh*), or "prince" (*nasi*)—indicating that the *mishpahah* had no political role in itself (Lemche 1985, 270–72). Nevertheless, the commonly referenced "elders of the town" (*ziqne 'ir*, Deut 21:19, and other texts) probably designated the heads of households, *bet aboth*, who, in smaller towns, where the *mishpahah* was coterminous with the town, would have assumed leadership over the *mishpahah* as well. In larger towns, the "elders of the town" may have belonged to separate *mishpahoth*, and thus would have formed a leadership body distinct from the *mishpahah* (see Willis 2001; Reviv 1989).

The economic role of the *mishpahah* was more significant. Although the evidence is scant and indirect, scholars have long argued that some of the land belonged primarily to the *mishpahah* (see Num 26 and Josh 13–17, where the land is apportioned to the *mishpahoth*),[22] and shares to the land were redistributed on a regular ba-

---

21. The spatial aspect of the *mishpahah* was signified not only by the physical structures of the village and the land belonging to it, but also by the tomb of the ancestor, by whose name the village was known. Rituals such as feeding the dead through burial offerings, sacrifice (1 Sam 20:6), and feasting (*marzeah*) would have functioned to reinforce the identity of the *mishpahah* and their connection to the land (see Brichto 1973; Bloch-Smith 1992, 111–12).

22. Some land seems to have been owned by the *bet ab*. Numbers 27:1–11, for example, is

sis (see Bendor 1996, 141–60; Levine 1996). The individual *bet ab*, then, had usufruct rights—the right to use the land for its production. Redistribution of the land would have been done by lots, perhaps annually, and apportioned according to the needs and ability of each *bet ab* (Boer 2015, 71–74).[23] All household heads would have participated in the redistribution of the land, in part to ensure an equitable share, but the distribution itself would have been controlled by the elder members of the *mishpahah*. The households of the *mishpahah* would have aided each other in their production by sharing, for example, an ox for plowing, tools, an oven, or an oil or wine press; contributing labor to building terraces, digging a well, quarrying out a cistern, or building the town wall; compensating for lost labor due to illness or injury. The women may have gathered to share knowledge and skills and train the next generation of girls in grinding and baking bread, weaving textiles, or other crafts of the household (Meyers 2007). The men may have gathered, not only to redistribute the land, but also to coordinate and diversify their crops, set aside fallow land for grazing of their animals, and make arrangements for the marriage of their children.

The *mishpahah* was patrilineal and patrilocal; it was an endogamous group, defining the limits of a preferred marriage partner (Num 36:5–9; Gen 24:38; see Steinberg 1993, 5–34). The structure of the *mishpahah* extended the structure of the household, the *bet ab*. The productive relations remained the same, structured along the gender hierarchy with males and females, and along the age hierarchy with elder and junior kin members (see Siskind). The *mishpahah* had a dynamic relationship with the household. As the family of endogamy, the *mishpahah* regulated the reproduction of the household, and through the redistribution of community land, the *mishpahah* provided the household with the means of production. As the household grew and divided, new households would be incorporated into the *mishpahah* until the *mishpahah*, having spread to another village or town, would itself be divided. When the households of the *mishpahah* were unable to reproduce, through infertility, disease, or war, the *mishpahah* would contract around the remaining households until only a single *bet ab* remained, when it might form a new *mishpahah* through its own reproduction (Bendor 1996, 77–82).

---

concerned that daughters receive a share of their father's "inheritance" (*nahalah*), when he does not have a son, instead of the land being returned to his *mishpahah* (see Blenkinsopp 1997, 54–55). The situation is unfortunately ambiguous. The father's inheritance may refer simply to his allotted share of the clan's *nahalah*, rather than to a permanent possession—it refers to the usufruct, not the land itself. In Numbers 36, on the other hand, the kinsmen fear that the daughter's share would be permanently lost from the *mishpahah* if they married outside of the *mishpahah*, suggesting a permanent division of the land rather than a periodic reallocation (Bendor 1996, 161–64). In any case, the *bet ab* may have acquired its own land through a royal grant (Levine 1996, 229–33; Ben-Barak 1981) or through other non-kin relations.

23. The meager evidence from the biblical tradition on the ancient Israelite land tenure system is often compared to the *musha'* tenure practices of the Ottoman period (see Guillaume 2012, 28–55; Nadan 2006, 261–98).

Part I: Creation

The Israelite *mishpahah* is most visible during the Iron I period (approximately 1200–1000 BCE) with the rapid increase of many small villages in the central hill county (see Stager 1985). These are small, unfortified sites, with a cluster of houses and no public buildings or monumental architecture; the material remains attest to a subsistence economy, with locally made, utilitarian pottery and simple agricultural installations. No luxury items were found and, along with the rather uniform architecture, there is no evidence of social stratification or social classes (see Lemos 2010, 159–79, and sources cited there). The society was not egalitarian—it was structured hierarchically along lines of age and gender—but there were few economic differences attested among the people. The *mishpahah* was a social institution that supported the ongoing subsistence struggles of its households (see Faust 2011). The productive inequalities of the *mishpahah* overlapped with those of the household and perhaps contributed to a power differential and an unequal distribution of the production among the households. But meager differences in wealth resulting from production were probably leveled by such mechanisms as the giving of bridewealth in marriage, which functioned to compensate the father of the bride for her lost labor and ensure that all property remained within the *mishpahah* (Lemos 2010). Other mechanisms might have included shared feasting at religious celebrations, where the people's relationship to Yhwh was also renewed, as well as acts of generosity, such as providing aid to a failing household from the production surplus of a more successful household, thus converting ephemeral surplus into longer lasting honor and prestige. These and other mechanisms functioned to balance the inequities, but their purpose was not equality but the successful subsistence of the *mishpahah*. In other words, whatever energy surplus was captured by the productive relations of the *mishpahah* was consumed by population growth rather than by creating material artifacts that signal social class and stratification.

Although the kinship relations of the *mishpahah* served to mitigate inequalities, social and economic inequalities resulted nevertheless. These inequalities were largely due to differential access to fertile land and material resources, size of the labor force, and ability, effort, and opportunity. By the middle of the Iron II period (approximately 1000–587 BCE), ancient Israel and Judah were fully stratified kingdoms, with evidence of both conspicuous wealth and poverty (see Holladay 1995; Dever 1995; cf. Faust 2012). It is not uncommon for kin to exploit their own for personal or patrimonial advantage (Black 1972), and thus some households exploited the production of others. These productive inequalities led to the formation of non-kin productive relations, both for the successful households seeking to expand their control over the labor of others, and the unsuccessful households seeking relief from and advantage over their own kin (Eisenstadt and Roniger 1984, 206). These relations were based on a generalized exchange with one member having an unequal access to and control of the productive powers. These new productive inequalities may be called patron–client relations (see Wolf 1966; Campbell 1964; Gellner and Waterbury 1977).

In the biblical tradition, or in the ancient Near Eastern languages in general, no technical terms are used for patron–client relations. This is an etic, heuristic category when applied to ancient Israel, and is not without debate. Niels Peter Lemche, who pioneered the use of patron–client relations for understanding socio-economic relations in ancient Israel, applied the concept broadly to a wide range of non-kin, unequal relations that were based on *hesed*, "loyalty" (1995a, 1995b, 1996; cf. Liverani 1979, 1983, 1990, who captures the concept of patronage without the language). For Lemche, patronage underlies the dominant political systems of the ancient Near East, including Israel (see Hobbs 1997; Schloen 2001; Pfoh 2009a). Others have defined patron–client relations more narrowly, based on the emic use of the terms in the late Roman Republic (Wallace-Hadrill 1989). For these scholars, the category of patron–client relations is only appropriate when the relations are also voluntary, informal, and not legally binding (Crook 2006; Westbrook 2009). This critique is reasonable when the ancient Israelite patron–client relations, for example, are compared with those of the late Roman Republic, but otherwise is an unnecessary restriction of the heuristic category. The critique is less relevant when seeking to understand a common element in diverse, yet similar relations. Moreover, the comprehensive comparative study of Eisenstadt and Roniger (1984) demonstrates that there is variation among patron–client relations, including their formality, their legality, and how the relationship is established. It is possible, and helpful (the purpose of heuristic categories), to treat contractual suzerain–vassal relations, coercive tributary relations between a king and his people, and personal relations between a superior and subordinate as specific types of patron–client relations so that patronage is interpreted as a system of political-economic relations (see also Pfoh 2009a, 113–60).

Patronage is a system of productive relations rooted in an unequal distribution of power and goods, and expressed socially through a generalized exchange of different types of resources. The structure of these relations is hierarchical. Patrons are those who have access to goods and the centers of power, whereas clients are in need of such access. In fact, patronage is most prominent in those societies that are characterized by "highly elaborated hierarchies of rank and position, often related to the differential access of various groups to the center" (Eisenstadt and Roniger 1984, 209–10). In spite of the social and economic hierarchy, the exchange between patrons and clients is based on reciprocity, and the relationship between them is idealized as friendship and expressed in terms of kinship. The patron is a "father" to his clients, who honor him as "sons" and faithful "servants." Patron–client relations are foremost personal bonds to which one's identity and honor is committed. The bonds are held together by mutual commitments of loyalty, though rarely ever formalized. The patron commits himself to protect and support his clients, and the client commits himself to serve his patron. By means of these interpersonal obligations, exercised through a generalized exchange, patron–client relations function to regulate and mitigate the effects of economic inequalities in a way that the kinship structure of the *mishpahah* was unable.

Part I: Creation

Because patronage is an etic category and thus not identified by the language of the Bible, explicit examples of patron–client relations in the biblical tradition are few. The use of kinship terminology for non-kin relations, however, is often a clear indication of patron–client relations. Saul, for example, is a strong man who attracted numerous clients into his service. He used gifts of fields and vineyards and appointments to military rank to secure their loyalty to him in his conflict with David (1 Sam 22:7–8). David, for his part, claimed to be a faithful client to Saul, acknowledging him as his "father" (1 Sam 24:11). After David spared Saul's life (a second time), Saul also acknowledged this relationship, repeatedly addressing David as his "son" (1 Sam 26:17–25), and thus recognizing David as a loyal client. During his conflict with Saul, David also encountered Nabal, to whom he was willing to submit as a client; he addressed him as "your son David," but Nabal refused David's request (1 Sam 25:2–13). David also had his own clients for whom he was a patron: all those in distress and in debt who gathered to him (1 Sam 22:2). Elisha addressed Elijah as his patron by calling him "father" (2 Kgs 2:12). The "sons of the prophets" (2 Kgs 2:3, and elsewhere) were probably clients of a senior, patron prophet. The servants of Naaman similarly addressed their patron as "father" (2 Kgs 5:13). Second Kings 16:5–9 describes the patron–client relationship between Ahaz and Tiglath-pileser III. In order to gain protection against the assault of Rezin and Pekah, Ahaz sought to become the client of the great Assyrian king. He initiated the relationship by seeking military help from Tiglath-pileser as his "servant and son." Ahaz then demonstrated his loyalty and friendship by sending gifts of silver and gold. Tiglath-pileser reciprocated by rescuing Ahaz from his enemies. This suzerain–vassal relationship, though it is unknown whether it was formalized with a treaty, is also an expression of patronage, and Judah under Ahaz became a client kingdom of the Assyrians. These are the primary references that explicitly attest to patron–client relations; the biblical tradition simply gives little attention to social and economic relations beyond kinship relations and royal affairs. Patron–client relations in ancient Israel thus need to be inferred from their common occurrence in the Levant (Pfoh 2009b, 2013), the social stratification of ancient Israel attested from archaeology (Dever 1995; Maeir and Shai 2016), and the ideological relationship between Yhwh and the people, which is an expression of a patron–client relationship (see Hobbs 1997; Olivier 1996; Tucker 2007; Noll 2012, 182–214).

Productive relations, like gender relations, express a power differential. The patron was often a strongman, acquiring his possessions by exploitation and force (from weaker and unsuccessful kinsmen, for example) or from royal grants in service to the king. The patron had control of land, work animals and tools, seed and orchards, and craft resources (such as metal ores or wool); he had access to water and the sources of power. But the patron often lacked labor to work his land or utilize his resources, so he would welcome, if not recruit, clients into his service, and he would secure their labor through debt. A patron may rent a parcel of his land to a client, from whom he would expect a portion of its production (generally a third) as rent. He would make loans to his clients—either with hacksilver money or with resources such as seed—and secure the loan with the client's labor. Given that traditional agriculture only produced meager surpluses, the client would rarely be able to pay back the loan *and* secure the resources for the next year's crops and his household's subsistence. So, the client would need to extend the loan, or take out a new loan. The patron did not expect the client to pay back the loan; indeed, he would prefer the client continually to be in his debt, for debt was simply the means by which the patron secured the client's labor and service (Boer 2015, 156–63; Guillaume 2010b). For clients who worked their own land but were in debt to their patron with loans, the debt became a means by which the patron could confiscate their land through foreclosure, turning the clients into tenant farmers on their own land. Clients also may have been in debt morally to the patron, who provided a service for the client, such as providing favorable access to the king or an official, or supplied a favor, such as lending the client an ox to plow his field. Although such debt was intangible, it was no less real and may have been reciprocated with labor or a valuable gift.

Although the relationship between patron and client could, and probably did, become exploitive (see Houston 2008, 44–48, 99–134), the patron had an interest in the success of the client. Because the patron benefited from the production of the client, the patron also needed to ensure the reproduction of the client's household. If he undermined his client's subsistence through over-exploitation, he also would suffer the consequences by either losing the client or subsidizing the client's subsistence at his own expense. As a result, the relationship between patron and client was framed as a personal relationship based on friendship and reciprocity: each member exchanged what the other needed, with the hope that both would benefit. In addition to a material exchange, the patron and client also exchanged intangibles. The client offered love, honor, and support to the patron in exchange for the patron's protection, loyalty, access and influence, help, and the promise of reciprocity.

> The client "buys," as it were, protection, first, against the exigencies of markets or nature; second, against the arbitrariness or weakness of the centre, or against the demands of other strong people or groups. The price the client pays is not just the rendering of a specific service but his acceptance of the patron's control over his (the client's) access to markets and to public goods, as well as over his ability fully to convert some of his own resources. (Eisenstadt and Roniger 1984, 214)

The exchange between patron and clients entailed a material imbalance in favor of the patron, but the personal nature of the relationship and the claim to reciprocity concealed the inequality of the relationship (see Sahlins 1972, 134).

The productive inequality of patron–client relations is structurally similar to the productive inequalities of the gendered household: the client's production is dependent on the material goods and resources that the patron provides. Moreover, like the gendered household relations of husband and wife, patron–client relations also are reflected in the ideological relationship between Yhwh and the people (see Noll 2012, 182–214). Yhwh is the divine patron who owns the land of Israel and controls its fertility. He gives the Israelites access to his land and shows loyalty (*hesed*) to them. As clients, the Israelites work his land, returning a portion to him in tithes and sacrifices, and love Yhwh by keeping his commands (Deut 6:5–9). If the Israelites are faithful clients, Yhwh will provide them with abundance and protection from their enemies. This is the ideology of the covenant, especially as expressed in its Deuteronomic form, which is modeled on a suzerain–vassal relationship. The homology between the gendered household relations of husband and wife and patron–client relations functions to gender and naturalize the latter. The ideological relationship between Yhwh and his people, who is both patron and husband to his client wife Israel, reinforces the gendering of patron–client relations, while making the reproduction of the productive inequalities of the relationship possible.

The use of kinship language to describe patron–client relations, however, requires further comment. Although men more conventionally identify their male relationships in terms of the age hierarchy rather than the gender hierarchy, kinship language was used to mask the threat that patron–client relations posed to the larger kinship system—to the *mishpahah*, in particular. Patron–client relations cut across kinship boundaries, for both the patron and the client. The power and affluence of the patron, for example, was based on the number and success of his non-kin clients. With regard to his own *mishpahah*, the patron either has appropriated its households into his own production, if he was the elder of the *mishpahah* (this appears to be the case with Saul), or has created a set of productive relations in competition with his *mishpahah* (this is the case with David). As for the client, his loyalty and obligations would be to his non-kin patron, not to his *mishpahah*. Indeed, the failure of a man's *mishpahah* to address the subsistence needs of his own household was a significant reason for which he might engage in a patron–client relation with a successful non-kin outsider. Patronage attracted households away from their *mishpahah*, and kinship language concealed this threat by extending kinship to include the patron–client relation.

Productive relations within the royal or elite sector of ancient Israel were specific types of patron–client relations: the estates and tributary relations (see Boer 2015, 110–45). Estates were common economic institutions in Mesopotamia during the third and second millennium BCE, and they belonged primarily to the palace and temple complexes (see Liverani 1984). By the first millennium, they had been replaced by family controlled, private firms, such as the Egibi (Neo-Babylonian) and Murashu (Persian) firms. There were no firms in ancient Israel—the society was probably too small and not as developed as Mesopotamia—and the nature and extent of agricultural estates (including latifundia) in ancient Israel is debated (see evidence cited in Faust 2011, 267–69; see Premnath 2003; cf. Houston 2008). In any case, the garden in the Yahwist creation myth is similar to a royal estate. The man's labor is appropriated by Yhwh, the king, to work his garden as its caretaker; he labors for Yhwh in exchange for food and protection, rather than work his own land—the fields for which he was created. In ancient Israel, the *lamelek* ("belonging to the king") inscriptions on the handles of storage jars are the best evidence for such estates (Rainey 1982; see Feig 2003, for a possible royal winery), but their interpretation has been debated (see Lipschits 2012). In any case, the productive relations of estates would consist of the patron (the king, a royal official, or a wealthy landowner) and his laboring clients.

Tributary relations were the primary means of financing the state apparatus. They are similar to patron–client relations but differ in the substantial power differential between the parties and in the purpose of the relationship. They were relations between the king and his people and were expressed in the form of taxes and corvée labor. The royal ideology (2 Sam 7; Pss 2, 72, 89) held the king to be the adopted son of Yhwh, and thus the relationship between the king and his people replicated the relationship between Yhwh and the people. Indeed, the royal ideology provided the cognitive framework that justified the king's extraction of the people's resources and labor (see 1 Sam 8:11–17; Yee 2017; Manning 2018, 188–89). Like patron–client relations, tributary relations were reciprocal: the king extracted resources and labor in exchange for a just social order and protection for the people (1 Sam 8:20). The king was limited in what he could extract—too much extraction would cut into the subsistence of the Israelite households, reducing what was available to live on and leading to rebellion. The rebellion and separation of the northern tribes after Solomon's death, in fact, is attributed to Solomon's excessive extraction, which was a burden on the people (1 Kgs 12:1–19). Unlike patron–client relations, however, the king was not vested in the success of the Israelite households. Tributary relations were largely parasitical on the people; the king provided order and peace for the people to labor, then extracted his share from their meager surpluses. The king's own bounty, acquired from his subjects, his estates, and from plunder, was used to build relations with other elite patrons, with whom he had a patron–client relation and to whom he would give land grants and administrative roles, and to support his retainers, all of whom would give loyalty and service to the king in exchange. When ancient Israel became subject to foreign empires, they also imposed tribute on the people (mediated either through the king or, later, the governor), further increasing the burden of their subsistence.

Slave relations were structurally similar to tributary and patron–client relations but different in kind—there was no reciprocity. Slaves were created largely through warfare, they may have been male or female, and their labor and their bodies belonged wholly to their masters. They had few recognized rights other than the right to live, they could be mistreated and abused (though see Exod 21:26–27), and women slaves would have been used sexually as well as for their physical labor (see García Bachmann 2013, 115–60; Callender 1998).[24] The appropriation of slave labor, however, was

---

24. Debt servitude was also a form of slavery, but it was temporary situation until the debt was paid or remitted, and within the context of patronage may have been beneficial to the debt-slave.

not without minimal obligations. The master would need to house, clothe, and feed the slaves (this is little different from one's obligation to take care of one's animals; see Marx 1973, 489), which would have made the owning of slaves a costly matter (cf. Glass 2000). As a result, we might expect to find slaves working for the elite or the more affluent households, but not in ordinary households struggling for subsistence. Nevertheless, slavery provided the most efficient way to transfer the surplus of labor from one individual to another.[25] It is difficult to know how pervasive slaves were in ancient Israel. In the biblical tradition, the vocabulary used refers to both slaves and servants, making it difficult to quantify them. The male servant/slave (*'ebed*), for example, may refer to a war slave, a debt slave, any subordinate in the society, and even the second most powerful person in the kingdom, the "servant of the king." One might expect that slaves were relatively few in ancient Israel, given the little attention to them in the biblical tradition, though slavery played a more prominent economic role in the ancient Near East than generally acknowledged. Slave relations, in any case, would have been subordinate to and supplemented the production of other relations, whether they were household, patron–client, or tributary relations (see Culbertson 2011; Baker 2001).

Other productive relations include trade relations, the nature and extent of which is debated (see Manning 2018, 233–61; Boer 2015, 163–90; Elat 1979). Trade networks had long existed in the ancient Near East, and archaeology attests to the trade of obsidian from as early as the Neolithic period (ca. 8500–4300 BCE), with trade in metal ores beginning in the Chalcolithic period (ca. 4300–3300 BCE). But whereas trade is everywhere attested, the ancient Near East did not have a market economy—that is, items traded were not commodified and profit maximization was not the imperative (contra Master 2014).[26] Instead, trade democratized access to geographically

---

25. Although the economic role of slavery in the ancient Near East is debated (see Scott 2017, 150–82), by the time of the Roman empire slavery had become the primary means of capturing energy for production. Slavery remained a dominant energy source until it was replaced by fossil fuels, beginning with coal in the eighteenth century (Nikiforuk 2012).

26. Trade of goods in the ancient world was different than contemporary global, capitalist trade. At the local level, trade was based on the use-value of the products, and one product was traded directly for another. In long distance trade, use-values were still the basis of exchange, even though a product may be more valuable in one region over another; most prices were conventional or set by the state according to their use-value. Some products were traded directly for other products (C–C), as in the second millennium Old Assyrian trade with Anatolia (see Kuhrt 1998), or the products were traded based on their value in money, such as silver (C–M–C). This latter form of exchange is how the Deuteronomic reformers wanted people who lived far from Jerusalem to consume their title: exchange a tenth of one's produce for silver, go to Jerusalem, buy food with the silver, and consume it there (Deut 14:24–26). Ancient long-distance trade functioned primarily for the benefit of royal houses and the elite and was regulated (through taxes and set prices) toward that goal. Commodification, which is characteristic of modern, globalized market-based trade, uses exchange-values of commodities to produce more money (M–C–M′). In other words, a capitalist invests money (M) in labor and the means of production in order to produce a desired product (C), which he sells on the market for a larger sum (M′) than he invested. More importantly, capitalist trade is based on market imperatives, such as competition, accumulation, profit-maximization, and increasing labor-productivity. Capitalist

limited resources and specialized crafts, and often served intangible purposes such as prestige and honor. Physical marketplaces are rarely attested archaeologically—there were probably few, if any, permanent structures—but they would be expected primarily around the gates of the large cities. It may be that the residents of such cities, engaged in administrative or other non-productive occupations, were provisioned, in part, through exchanges at the marketplace (Hunt 1991).

Overland trade always remained limited in quantity and focused on rare raw materials or luxury goods for the elite (see Singer-Avitz 1999). It was generally under royal control (Elat 1979), and only contributed to small sectors of the larger economy. Holladay (1995, 383–86; 2006) argued that control of the trade routes out of the Arabian desert contributed substantially to financing the monarchy in Jerusalem (Solomon's meeting with the Queen of Sheba would be understood in terms of trade negotiation; 1 Kgs 10:1–13). Other scholars, such as Hopkins (1996, 136–38), question the extent of Judah's control or the amount of wealth generated by this trade, at least during the early years of the kingdom. In any case, it is unclear what, if any, economic impact such trade had on the non-elite Israelite households. During the latter part of the kingdom of Judah, and later, maritime trade around the Mediterranean played a significant role for the Phoenician and Philistine city states, and some material evidence of the trade has been found in excavations throughout the land of Israel, mostly in the form of pottery (see Master 2003). The small scale of the foreign remains, however, suggests an equally small economic role for trade, at least for the average Israelite household. Perhaps, a local patron benefited from the exchange of luxury items. Ancient Israel's orientation was inland rather than toward the Mediterranean, and did not directly participate in the Mediterranean trade. Those who primarily benefited from trade—sea-going or overland—would have been the elite, without contributing to the subsistence of the Israelite household (see Coomber 2010, 77–134).

It remains uncertain how trade impacted the ancient Israelite economy. The king and the elites' desire for luxury items or resources through trade may have led to further extraction from the Israelite households. Some prophetic texts suggest as much (see Dearman 1988; Chaney 2017; Premnath 2003). Patrons who controlled large surpluses may have benefited, but not the average Israelite household. Trade was not conducted for the benefit of the average household. For ancient Israel, trade relations should be considered as emergent productive relations (Williams 1977, 121–27); they stood largely outside of the political economy of ancient Israel, never fully integrated into it as they were in the Phoenician and Philistine city states. Moreover, trade relations play no role in the ideology, confirming their marginal relationship to the political economy of ancient Israel.

Ancient Israel had an agrarian economy dominated by a hierarchy of productive relations and governed by an ideology espousing the relationship between Yhwh and

---

trade is thus structurally different from trade in the ancient world.

the people. The Israelites engaged the natural world through their productive relations and produced enough for their subsistence, but the productive inequalities also enabled some to capture the energy surplus from others and thereby create a hierarchical society with material evidence of social stratification. Indeed, the productive relations functioned to rationalize and preserve the inequalities. The production of the Israelites, according to their ideology, was contingent on their relationship to Yhwh—to be productive, Yhwh's mediation was necessary, especially for the dominant member of the productive relations. It was through Yhwh that their labor was efficacious. Although the husband, the patron, and the king embodied the male gender in relation to their subordinates (wife, client, and subject peoples), providing like Yhwh what the productive relation needed, in relation to Yhwh they assumed the female gender in their submission and obedience to him, just as clients and the people take on the female gender in relation to their patron and king. The gendered relationship between Yhwh and the people made the reproduction of the household, patron–client relations, and tributary relations possible. Moreover, the patron–client relations and tributary relations replicated and integrated the household relations into their own production. Yet, despite the hierarchy of productive inequalities, all were dependent on Yhwh, from the king to the husband of a household.

Through the work of the productive relations, the growth produced by the ancient Israelite economy was consumed by its growing population. Economic and population growth largely mirrored each other. Such a broad summary, however, conceals the fragility and the inequities of the ancient economy. During times of peace and stability, the productive relations of ancient Israel contributed to an uneven economic growth and thus to the stratification of society. And such economic growth may have been substantial for some members of society. Poor climate—resulting in drought or erratic rains, irregular temperatures, and unseasonable sirocco winds—was a frequent and unpredictable occurrence hindering growth (see Baly 1974, 69–76). Pestilence, disease, and war also disrupted production, so that periods of economic growth were offset by periods of contraction. Through the ups and downs of economic growth, however, there does not appear to have been any noticeable *per capita* economic growth across the population. Individually, some gained economically while others declined because those who experienced economic growth benefited from the production of others. In other words, the economic gain of some, primarily the elite, was at the expense of others. The individual economic condition of most Israelites would have decreased as their economic surplus was extracted by patrons and the royal class, including from the tribute imposed by the great empires of Assyria, Neo-Babylonia, and Persia. The agrarian economy of ancient Israelite society limited the possibility of economic growth, even as its productive inequalities shifted the economic surplus up the hierarchy of relations, from households to patrons to the king.

3

Creation and Society

CONFLICT OVER THE HOUSEHOLD

IN CAPITALIST SOCIETIES, WEALTH is usually the basis for power. Bill Gates and Elon Musk, for example, are able to wield power—social and political influence—because they are wealthy, and their wealth preceded and enabled the power they now exercise. In ancient precapitalist societies, such as ancient Israel, however, wealth generally proceeded from power. Those with power could exploit new avenues of wealth by transforming the relations of production. The social conflict in precapitalist societies may be expressed by a tension between an economic base and a newly evolving superstructure, resulting from the exercise of power, rather than a conflict between class relations as in capitalist societies. "Tension in precapitalist societies between the economic base and the superstructure is therefore not between social groups that are denied access to the means of resources or socially segregated into classes and exploited, but rather in the activity of individuals who attempt to increase their political power at the expense of kin members" (Tuden 1979, 26–27). The exercise of power in ancient Israel shaped the political economy and this is particularly evident in the treatment and composition of the Israelite household, the society's basic productive unit.

Saul and David were strongmen. They may have had popular support, but their kingdoms were founded on their exercise of power over others. Before Saul and David, during the so-called tribal period, household and kinship relations were the primary productive relations of the society and dominated its mode of production. The rise of Saul and David to prominence, however, attests to the formation of patron–client relations as well, but these relations do not appear to have dominated the society as a whole. In other words, household and kinship relations continued to dominate. From archaeological remains and the biblical description, the kingdoms of Saul and David do not appear to have fundamentally transformed the base of the economy.[1] Solomon inherited his kingdom, but apparently not without conflict (1 Kgs 1–2). He too was a strongman, but unlike Saul and David, he succeeded in transforming the mode of production in ancient Israel. This is attested in the archaeological remains, with monumental architecture first appearing during this period (Mazar 1990, 375–402).[2] Similarly, the biblical narrative of Solomon describes a socially stratified society. The construction of the royal temple in Jerusalem probably made the difference. Supported by the royal ideology, which originated with the temple, Solomon dominated the political economy with tributary relations, through which he extracted resources and labor from the people. Patron–client relations are attested with his officials, whom he charged with mediating his extraction from the people. The continuation of other patron–client relations, though not mentioned in regard to Solomon's kingdom, can be assumed from the description of Saul and David's reigns. Unlike his predecessors, however, Solomon was able to incorporate all other productive relations into the functioning of his own tributary relations. He was able to extract resources and labor from the people, and through the ideology of the temple, his extraction was sanctioned by Yhwh.

A brief glimpse of the political economy of Solomon's kingdom is presented in 1 Kings 4–5: the kingdom had a small administration, but reorganized the people into administrative districts, which Solomon taxed for his administration's support; he created a large horse and chariot force, for which he taxed the people for its upkeep, and he forced thousands of Israelites into corvée labor for his many building projects (compare 1 Sam 8:11–17). It is difficult to measure the scale of Solomon's economic extraction, but the biblical text suggests that it was excessive for the scale of the kingdom: the economic burden he placed on the people, especially the northern tribes, was the reason given for the dissolution of his kingdom following his death (1 Kgs 12). The administration of the kingdom itself is small by Mesopotamian standards, but it fits a patrimonial kingdom, using kinship ideology to encompass all of the people within the household of the king (Master 2001; Schloen 2001; Stager 2003). Solomon's

---

1. Despite the idealism of the biblical portrait of David, his kingdom, based on patron–client relations, is nevertheless presented as fragile as the relations themselves. Thus, David's affair with Bathsheba, the wife of a prominent client, threatens to unravel the web of relations that make up his power base, and so he seeks to hide his actions by killing Uriah (2 Sam 11–12). The rebellions of Absalom (2 Sam 15–19) and Sheba (2 Sam 20) illustrate the fragility of David's power base when the people align with other patrons. Finally, the failure of David's census (2 Sam 24), which is a common characteristic of tributary states, attests to David's dependence on the loyalty of his clients. Unlike tributary relations, David is not able to act for his own self-interest without also benefiting his clients.

2. This does not include Khirbet Qeiyafa, which, if the excavator is correct, is dated to the early tenth century BCE—that is, to the period of David (Garfinkel and Ganor 2008). It has two monumental four chamber gates and a centrally located palace or administrative building. If belonging to the kingdom of David, the social stratification attested at this site would be unique. The date of the site and the ethnicity of its inhabitants, however, has been challenged (see, e.g., Na'aman 2017).

kingdom was the House of David (2 Sam 7),³ named after the founder of the dynasty, just as the northern kingdom later came to be known as the House of Omri. The royal ideology of the temple justified and reinforced Solomon's ability to extract economic resources and labor from the people. He was Yhwh's adopted son; the agent of God for the people. His rule replicated Yhwh's rule, and the people thus owed their allegiance and resources to him (see Levenson 1985, 89–184). In other words, the people's relationship to Yhwh now included the king, who acted on Yhwh's behalf.

The role of the kinship system from Solomon's period and later has been the subject of debate. Because the interests of kings tend to be contrary to the interests of ordinary households, many scholars have argued that the tributary nature of the monarchy led to the demise of the kinship structure that characterized pre-monarchical Israel (see Blenkinsopp 1997, 86–88; Gottwald 1986, 84; Chaney 2017). The administrative districts enacted by Solomon, for example, ignored significant tribal boundaries, undermining kinship relations. Indeed, we have no reason to doubt the monarchy's exploitation of ordinary households. Unfortunately, we know little about the *mishpahah* and the kinship structure during the monarchic period, but the little evidence that remains suggests that some of the kinship structure remained intact.⁴ The eighth-century BCE Samaria ostraca, for example, attest to the continuing viability of *mishpahoth* of the tribe of Manasseh, matching what we know from the later Priestly genealogies (see Vanderhooft 2009). Whether the subdivisions of the *mishpahah* in the towns and villages continued to function is unknown. In any case, the biblical record does not give evidence of an ideology undermining kinship relations from this period of the monarchy (Bendor 1996, 219–21). Nevertheless, the monarchy's use of kinship ideology, conceiving the kingdom as the house of David, functioned to incorporate the Israelite households into its own production; it would have promoted the production of the ordinary households with no attention to larger, superstructural kinship units. By incorporating all households within the household of the king, extended kinship relations were rendered unnecessary. The tributary relations of Solomon's kingdom were sufficient to extract resources and labor from the Israelite households without an explicit ideological assault on extended kinship relations.

Although the royal theology does not address local kinship relations, other biblical texts present conflicting images of the household—of both its composition and its relation to other households. Some biblical texts that have their origin during the

3. In addition to the biblical tradition, the "house of David" is attested in the Tel Dan inscription (Biran and Naveh 1993; see Athas 2003) and possibly in the Mesha inscription (cautiously held by Lemaire 1994; against his reading, see Finkelstein, Na'aman, and Römer 2019).

4. Based on the average size of houses in cities in comparison to larger houses in villages, Faust (1999) has argued that the city houses were occupied by nuclear families, whereas the villages housed the traditional extended family. While this may be true in some cases, house size is often a factor of location rather than family size. Houses within walled cities simply have less space to work with than more open and expansive villages. Moreover, the size of the house does not correlate with the configuration of the household family—whether it is nuclear or extended. A single house in the city may be part of a cluster of houses forming a single extended household (see Brody 2011).

period of the monarchy (e.g., Deuteronomy) place the focus of the household on the paterfamilias and his relationship to his wife and their children, but give little attention to his obligation to the larger extended family, in his *bet ab* or his *mishpahah*. In contrast, other biblical texts that reflect life in early Israel (e.g., Judges) or the postexilic period (e.g., the Priestly tradition) embed the husband, wife, and children in an extended family, the *mishpahah*, and emphasize their familial obligations to it.

These two conflicting images of the household are also present in the two creation myths of Genesis. In the earlier Yahwist myth, Yhwh creates a helper for the man from his own "bone and flesh," generally an expression used for extended family relations (see Gen 29:14; Judg 9:2; 2 Sam 5:1; 19:12–13). In the setting of the garden, the woman is created for the man, so that he will not be alone. They are identified as husband (*ish*) and wife (*ishah*) and set forth as an exemplar or even as an archetype of marriage: "Therefore a man leaves his father and his mother and clings to his wife, and they become one flesh" (Gen 2:24). The extended family—bone and flesh—has become a married couple. Notably, reference to their roles in procreation is absent here. At this point in the myth, the human couple at best is only a nascent household. They are like children, sexually unaware and lacking the knowledge necessary for family life. Only after the human couple disregard Yhwh's prohibition and eat the fruit from the tree of the knowledge of good and evil do they become aware of their gendered family roles. At this point, they know how to create "like God." Once they are expelled from the comfort and security of the garden, the man and his wife proceed to build the first household by having sexual relations and giving birth to Cain and Abel.

The presentation of the first household in the Yahwist creation myth is ambiguous at best. The role of children oddly plays no role in Yhwh's creation of man, nor of his wife once in the garden. Yhwh appears to make no provision for children, and indeed, without the prohibited knowledge of good and evil the human couple would seem to be incapable of procreation. The lack of concern for children is mirrored by the etiology of marriage, which describes a man's detachment to his own parents: He leaves his parents to join with his wife in marriage (on the parallel with Atrahasis, see Batto 2013, 86–95). Although leaving one's parents to get married seems wholly natural in contemporary society, it is an odd formulation in the patrilineal and patrilocal society of ancient Israel. In marriage a son would bring his wife into his father's household, and they would physically reside in or near his parent's house after marriage (Meyers 1988, 37–40). Commentators early in the last century commonly argued that this passage reflects memory of an earlier matriarchal society, but more recent commentators have rightly rejected this interpretation as untenable. Nevertheless, this passage seems to be in conflict with the recognition that ancient Israel was a patrilocal society. What would it mean for a man to "leave" his parents and "cling" to his wife? Because a son physically remained in or near his parent's house after marriage, scholars have interpreted the Hebrew verbs figuratively in terms of the man's loyalty and affection. Gerhard von Rad argues: "The alliance of one sex to another [in marriage] is seen as a divine ordinance of creation" (1972, 85). Claus Westermann suggests that this verse "points to the basic power of love between man and woman" (1984, 233). Gordon Wenham recognizes that this verse signals a shift in the man's obligations: "On marriage a man's priorities change. Beforehand his first obligations are to his parents: afterwards they are to his wife" (1987, 71). Anthropologists have recognized that the strength of the conjugal bond is in inverse proportion to the strength of the bonds between extended kin (see Cohen 1969, 665). By emphasizing the affective ties between husband and wife, the myth undermines the husband's bond to his consanguineous kin. In the garden the human couple stands alone with no connection to parents or children. The story highlights the significance of marriage at the expense of family. Whereas marriage is clearly presented as a divine institution, instituted by Yhwh at creation, the household is presented as a *human* institution, created as a result of the human couple's acquisition of knowledge by disobeying Yhwh's prohibition.

The Yahwist creation myth belongs to the monarchic period in ancient Israel. During the post-exilic period, after the collapse of the kingdom of Judah, the Priestly scribes revised the earlier primeval narrative to communicate a new message to the Judean community. Specifically, the Priestly scribes prefaced the story of the garden with a new myth of creation, and thereby shaped how subsequent readers would read the original tale. In this new creation myth, God creates humans male and female in God's own image, and commands the humans to be fruitful and multiply (Gen 1:26–28). That which the Yahwist myth presents as the consequence of human knowledge, acquired in disobedience to Yhwh, the Priestly scribes attribute to God's acts and directives. In this presentation of creation, the human couple is created for family and the creation of a household; procreation is the first of God's commands. The Priestly scribes' revision of the creation myth thus redeemed the role of the family in God's purpose for creation.

The conflicting views of the Israelite household represented in the two creation myths express a tension in the political economy of ancient Israel regarding the loyalties and obligations of the paterfamilias within the Israelite household. In the mode of production of early Israel, the productive relations were fellow kin, and the few biblical texts reflecting this period present the family within the context of an extended kinship network—the man's brothers, father, uncles, and cousins.[5] Israel's transition from a tribal society to a monarchical kingdom was accompanied by a similar shift from a mode of production based on kinship relations to a mode in which the productive relations were with non-kin members—patron–client and tributary relations. Because patron–client relations tended to undermine kinship relations, the biblical

---

5. Although the composition of no biblical text can be securely dated to the pre-monarchical period, a number of texts are rooted in this period and reflect the socio-economic conditions of this period. Most notably, the so-called Book of the Covenant or Covenant Code (Exod 20:22—23:19) reflects a family-based, agrarian society with little evidence of centralization (see Marshall 1993). The books of Joshua and Judges are composed from numerous pre-Deuteronomic sources that also reflect the pre-monarchical period (see Gottwald 1979, 150–87).

texts produced by the centralized custodians of power, such as the Yahwist narrative and Deuteronomy, emphasize the primacy of the marital unit and the resulting nuclear family at the expense of the extended family. This transition in the political economy was gradual, reaching its peak in monarchic Judah only in the late eighth and seventh centuries (see Halpern 1991).[6] Finally, with the collapse of the monarchy and the kingdom of Judah, a new configuration of productive relations emerged along with an emphasis on extended family relations. Texts produced during this period, such as the Priestly tradition,[7] again placed the human couple within the context of an extended family. Conflict over the household, whether the loyalties and obligations of the paterfamilias should be to his extended kin or to non-kin members of society, was a prominent force in shaping the political economy of ancient Israel.

POLITICAL ECONOMY DURING THE MONARCHY

Conflict over the household was not the only force shaping the political economy. Ancient Israel's conflict with other polities played an equally significant role, if not more so. The rise of the monarchy, first with Saul and then with David, can be tied to the formation of patron–client relations, which produced notable strongmen and powerful client bases who supported their ascendancy. Yet, the monarchy was also a response to military threats from neighboring polities—the Philistines on the west (1 Sam 13–14) and the Ammonites on the east (1 Sam 11)—against whom the earlier tribal society was unequipped to confront. The Assyrian assaults against Israel and then Judah, beginning in the mid-ninth century BCE with Shalmaneser III and culminating with Sennacherib's devastation of Judah in 701 BCE, had a profound effect on the political economy. The Assyrian assaults, of course, brought an end to an independent political economy in the northern kingdom of Israel by the end of the eighth century BCE. Many of its people were killed or exiled to foreign lands, and refugees from other lands were deported to Israel. The land that had made up the kingdom was divided up and exploited as provinces of the Assyrian empire. Judah's conflict with Assyria, in contrast, was not fatal but almost as catastrophic. Judah survived the assault of Sennacherib, it seems, by abandoning the countryside and holing up in a

---

6. Scholars have debated over what constitutes a state and when Judah should be classified as a state (see the essays in Fritz and Davies 1996; Master 2001). Jamieson-Drake (1991), for example, argued that scribal activity, a common characteristic of states, was not a feature of the kingdom of Judah until the late eighth and seventh centuries. More recently discovered early inscriptions have cast some doubt on his conclusions (see Tappy and McCarter 2008). Although statehood is an etic category, and thus I prefer the more loosely defined "kingdom," most scholars agree that Judah was a state by the end of the eighth century BCE, Israel perhaps as early as the early-ninth century BCE.

7. The Priestly tradition, as used here, incorporates the texts of the Priestly source (P) and the Holiness Code (H). The Holiness Code originally was identified with Leviticus 17–26, but some scholars associate texts originally identified as P with the Holiness school (see Knohl 1995; Stackert 2015). Because the extent of P and H and their chronological relationship is debated, our purposes are served best by simply dealing with the tradition after P and H were combined.

refortified Jerusalem (Halpern 1991; see Finkelstein 1994; Na'aman 2014). Although Sennacherib destroyed forty-six cities and towns—according to his own boast (Oriental Institute Prism), which archaeological excavations have largely confirmed—and exiled over two hundred thousand Judahites, a large, bulging population survived in Jerusalem to repopulate and rebuild the kingdom.

Although the economic base was slowly rebuilt during the largely peaceful years of the seventh century BCE—thanks in part to Manasseh's long reign and submission to Assyria—the devastation of Sennacherib's campaign had two effects on the ideological superstructure. First, the royal ideology appears to have encountered resistance in some elite, especially temple circles. The Deuteronomic school, for example, sought to reform the royal ideology, which had justified Hezekiah's rebellion against Assyria. Whereas the royal ideology held that the king was the adopted son of Yhwh (Ps 2:7), Deuteronomy diminishes the king. He is simply one of the Israelites, whom God will choose to reign over the people (Deut 17:14–15). Kingship in Deuteronomy becomes a concession to the people, and is an unneeded role. Every traditional role of the king—leading the army in wars, patron of the cult, administering justice—Deuteronomy assigns to others or simply encodes in the laws of Deuteronomy, its *Torah*. The power of the king would be diffused across a broad ruling class; tributary relations would be subsumed within patron–client relations. The only task remaining for the king is to read the Torah (Deut 17:18–20; see Levinson 2001; Knoppers 1996, 2001b); as a result, the king would no longer be in a position to rebel against Assyria (see Dutcher-Walls 2002). The unique relationship between Yhwh and the king in the royal ideology is replaced in Deuteronomy by the covenant relationship between Yhwh and the people (Levinson 2001).

Diminishment of the king's role is a significant feature of Deuteronomy's reform, yet no evidence of its reception or impact on the political economy has survived. In the Deuteronomistic narrative of 2 Kings, the book of the Torah that was found in the Jerusalem temple, usually identified as some form of Deuteronomy, was embraced by Josiah and became the basis for his reform (2 Kgs 22:8–23:25). But nothing in the narrative addresses Deuteronomy's diminishment of kingship. Instead, Josiah acts as a traditional king, contrary to the king's role in Deuteronomy, in holding the national celebration of Passover in Jerusalem. Elsewhere, the Deuteronomistic historian, who otherwise seems to follow Deuteronomy, embraces values that are contrary to Deuteronomy's law of the king (e.g., Solomon's wealth and many horses; see Knoppers 1996). In other words, the Deuteronomistic historian simply ignores Deuteronomy's reform of kingship. It is also unlikely that Manasseh and Josiah themselves would have embraced an ideological reform that diminished their own power. There is no reason to think that the political economy would have been impacted by Deuteronomy's ideological reform; tributary relations would have continued to dominate, though at a much lesser scale due to the crippling of the economic base and the tribute imposed by the Assyrians.

Part I: Creation

The second effect of Sennacherib's campaign on the ideological superstructure was in relation to the ancient Israel's kinship bonds: the ideology sought to redefine the household by strengthening the nuclear family—the paterfamilias with his wife and children—at the expense of more extended family relations in the *bet ab* or *mishpahah*. Historically, this ideological shift in the composition of the household is evident in Hezekiah's centralization of the worship of Yhwh and in his abandonment of the countryside in his preparation for rebellion against Assyria. By eliminating traditional shrines—high place (*bamah*), pillars (*matseboth*), and Asherah-pole (2 Kgs 18:4)—Hezekiah undercut the religious support of the household and *mishpahah* and replaced it with a state religion centered in the Jerusalem temple. Sennacherib's devastation of the countryside and exile of a large portion of the people further crippled kinship relations (Halpern 1991). Although there was probably some reconstitution of kinship relations in the aftermath and rebuilding of Judah's society, textual traditions from the late monarchy preserve an ideology that continued to undermine extended kinship relations. From these textual traditions, we can identify multiple ways in which the ideological superstructure sustained the political economy, especially the formation and functioning of patron–client and tributary relations. From the perspective of the Deuteronomic reform, patron–client relations would have also benefited from the reduction in tributary relations, but this latter aspect of the reform never materialized.

As mentioned previously, the use of kinship ideology to describe the kingdom of Judah as the House of David, functioned to incorporate all Israelite households within the king's house. At the same time, inclusion in the king's house served to weaken extended kinship bonds, especially relations to one's *mishpahah*, making them superfluous. Genealogies of all Israel served the same function. The genealogy of Jacob in the Yahwist tradition (Gen 29:31—30:24), for example, functions to incorporate all the Israelites, irrespective of their clan and tribal loyalties, within a single kinship group. Segmented genealogies, which are usually fluid in their configuration, function to express social relations between persons and to rank the status of groups and individuals. Indeed, the earliest lists of Israelite tribes differ in number and order depending on the prominence of the individual tribes and regions.[8] At some point during the monarchy, presumably early in the monarchy, the genealogy of the traditional twelve Israelite tribes was frozen in form. Rather than functioning to rank one tribe over another, it functioned in the religious or ideological sphere as an expression of the

---

8. In the tribal list in the Song of Deborah (Judg 5), for example, only ten tribes are listed and Ephraim is listed first. Moreover, Judah and Simeon are not listed at all, though they could be included in Benjamin (which is listed second) as an inclusive reference to the southern regions of Israel. Gilead is named instead of Gad, and Machir is included instead of Manasseh. Because of the particular configuration of the tribes and the prominence given to Ephraim, Benjamin and Machir (listed third), scholars have argued that this tribal list reflects the political situation of pre-monarchical Israel. Other early tribal lists, in Deuteronomy 33 and Genesis 49, similarly reflect the political situation of early monarchic Israel (see the thorough analysis of Halpern 1983, 109-64).

ideal Israel (see Wilson 1977, 193–95). All Israelites were presented as equal members of the family of Jacob. By giving precedence to the unity of Israel, the genealogy and narratives of Jacob function to diminish tribal and clan loyalties.

A second way in which the ideology weakened extended kinship relations was through political and religious centralization. Hezekiah's preparation for rebellion against Assyria included a program of dismantling shrines outside of Jerusalem, but Josiah's program of centralization was much more thorough and was inspired by Deuteronomy's reform program (2 Kgs 23:4–20). At the political level, the state should appoint judges and officials to oversee legal cases rather than tribal and clan leaders (Deut 16:18). The *mishpahah* would no longer be the domain in which the issues of justice were decided; individuals would thus take their cases directly to state officials. Whether Josiah enacted this political reform is unknown, for the Deuteronomistic historian focuses exclusively on the religious aspects of the reform. At the religious level, the state prohibited sacrifice to Yahweh outside of Jerusalem. All tithes, sacrifices, donations, and votive offerings, according to Deuteronomy, should be brought to the temple in Jerusalem (Deut 12:5–7); they should not be offered at local family shrines. The traditional household festivals of unleavened bread (Passover), weeks, and booths should also be held in Jerusalem (Deut 16:1–17). The Deuteronomic reform placed the household's worship of Yahweh under the sponsorship or patronage of the state (see Levinson 1997, 53–97).

The effects of centralization on the household can be illustrated by examining the laws regarding a man who has sexual relations with an unbetrothed virgin. In the Covenant Code, which reflects the customary practices of early Israel, the law states:

> When a man seduces a virgin who is not betrothed and lies with her, he shall give the bridewealth for her and make her his wife. If her father refuses to give her to him, he shall pay an amount equal to the bridewealth for virgins. (Exod 22:16–18)

According to this law, the father should be compensated for the loss of his daughter's virginity—an economic commodity to the father (see Pressler 1994). The father is also in control of whether or not the daughter is given in marriage to her seducer. In the Deuteronomic reform, however, the scribes revised the law in accordance with the ideology of the monarchy:

> If a man meets a young virgin who is not betrothed, and seizes her and lies with her, and they are discovered, the man who lay with her shall give fifty shekels of silver to the young woman's father, and she shall become his wife. Because he violated her, he shall not be permitted to divorce her as long as he lives. (Deut 22:28–29)

According to this formulation, the role of the father is taken out of the equation. He will still be compensated for his economic loss, but his compensation is fixed by the state and he appears to have no say in whether the seducer marries his daughter. Emphasis is placed instead on the requirement that the man marry the woman he seduced, and that he never divorce her. In other words, issues that had been a matter of concern for the household—whether and to whom a daughter is married, and the amount of bridewealth she will attract—are now removed from the jurisdiction of the paterfamilias and imposed on the household by law. At the same time, the law creates a new nuclear family—the seducer, the daughter of the household, and the children they will produce—that is not indebted to the paterfamilias since he did not arrange the marriage.

Several other laws similarly reduce the power of the paterfamilias over his kin (see also Stulman 1990, 1992). In Deuteronomy 21:15-17, a man who is married to two wives, each with sons, must designate his eldest son—whether or not he is born from his favorite wife—to be his firstborn. The law was promulgated to protect the rights of the eldest son to the double portion share of the inheritance, but the law also undermines the power of the father to determine his own heir. Deuteronomy 21:18-21 states that if a father and mother have a rebellious son, they must take their case before the elders of the town who will decide his fate. Likewise, if a wife is accused of not being a virgin at marriage, the father and mother of the wife take their evidence to the city elders who determine the merits of the charge (Deut 22:13-21). In both cases, issues of justice are taken out of the context of the household and assigned to state appointed officials.

A third way in which the ideological superstructure weakened extended kinship loyalties was by prohibiting the practice of consulting the dead. The ancient Israelites believed the dead offer both benevolent and malevolent powers; they were deified and sources of knowledge. The deified ancestors of the family, if properly attended through feeding and cult, secured the future prosperity of the family. Moreover, the practice of the cult of the dead provided potent symbols of the solidarity of the *bet ab* and the *mishpahah* (see Lewis 1989). The household's connection to their dead ancestors was integral to the future cohesion and success of the *mishpahah*, and thus a threat to the social formation of monarchic Judah. Although the size of tombs may reflect the diminishment of kinship ties,[9] the archaeological evidence suggests that the state ideology had little effect on a family's care and treatment of the dead. The mortuary practices and beliefs were too embedded in the society to be significantly challenged.[10] Instead, the state focused on the role of intermediaries (see Bloch-

---

9. Halpern (1991, 71-73) argues that a shift in the construction of the widely attested bench tombs can be detected. Although multi-chambered tombs were still used in the seventh century BCE, Halpern notes an increase in the use of single-chambered bench tombs, especially in the countryside. In Jerusalem these smaller tombs were being constructed in the eighth century or earlier. For Halpern, the single-chambered bench tombs placed the focus of the funerary cult on the individual, married couple, or the nuclear family in contrast to the extended family or clan, which was the focus of the traditional multi-chambered tombs.

10. A notable exception is that Deuteronomy prohibits the use of the tithe in feeding the dead

Smith 1992, 109–32). Several laws in Deuteronomy and the Holiness Code[11] prohibit necromancy and threaten its practitioners with death (Deut 18:10–11; Lev 19:26, 31; 20:6, 27). On the one hand, such a prohibition, along with the process of centralization, secured for the temple cult in Jerusalem a monopoly on divine intermediation. The prohibitions in the Holiness Code continued to serve this function for the post-exilic temple cult as they were incorporated in the Priestly composition. On the other hand, the prohibition against consulting the dead minimized the role that the deceased could play in the politics of the household and *mishpahah*. The post-exilic traditions' emphasis on genealogy (see below) perhaps compensated for this loss, as the later ideology sought to connect the household to the *mishpahah* through genealogy rather than necromancy.

Fourth, the ideological superstructure functioned to strengthen the nuclear family at the expense of extended kinship relations by emphasizing the importance of the conjugal bond between a husband and his wife (see Steinberg 1991). The ideology of the Yahwist creation myth, for example, emphasizes the affective ties between husband and wife and thereby undermines the husband's bond to his consanguineous kin. The husband and the wife are "one flesh." The message is clear: a man's loyalty and obligation to his parents, his siblings, and his extended kin—his *bet ab* and *mishpahah*—should be secondary to his devotion and responsibility to his wife. The man's independence from his parents that is highlighted in the primeval myth is also expressed negatively in Deuteronomy:

> Parents should not be put to death for their children, nor shall children be put to death for their parents; only for their own sins may persons be put to death. (Deut 24:16)

Like the emphasis on the conjugal bond, the importance placed on individual responsibility and guilt functioned to weaken the ties of the extended family.[12]

(Deut 26:14). Instead, the tithe was to be consumed in Jerusalem before the temple priests and to be shared with the landless—the Levites, aliens, orphans, and widows. In other words, the tithe functioned to reinforce an individual family's corporate solidarity with the nation at the expense of their connection to the extended family or clan through the funerary cult.

11. Scholars disagree over the date of the Holiness Code (Lev 17–26) and its relationship to the rest of the Priestly tradition. Although the composition of the text probably dates to the exilic period at the earliest, some of the material seems to have its origin in the period of the monarchy.

12. Kaminsky (1995, 119–23) cautions that the individualism of Deuteronomy should not be interpreted as similar to the radical individualism that characterizes contemporary Western culture. The individualism of Deuteronomy remains embedded in the collective responsibility of the nation (see Deut 26:16–19). A similar individualism has been attributed to Jeremiah 31:29–30 and Ezekiel 18 (Halpern 1991, 79–91). In the context of the destruction of Jerusalem by the Babylonians and the subsequent exile, both texts seek to refute the commonly embraced parable: "The fathers have eaten sour grapes, and the children's teeth are set on edge." The exilic generation of Judeans were placing the blame for the national catastrophe on the sins of the previous generation. Both Jeremiah and Ezekiel use the language of individualism to challenge the people to recognize their own guilt in the catastrophe. They reject the notion of trans-generational retribution, not corporate responsibility per

Part I: Creation

The conjugal bond of the nuclear family was also strengthened at the expense of the extended family relations through laws regulating sexual relations and prohibiting adultery. Deuteronomy carefully defines the different circumstances that result in adultery (Deut 22:22–27). At its root, adultery takes place when a man has sexual relations with another man's wife. Both the man and the woman should be executed. Adultery also occurs when a man has sexual relations with a woman betrothed to another man. Under these circumstances, if the sexual relations take place in the town, then both the man and the woman should be stoned to death. If the woman cries out for help, however, the assumption of the law is that only the man should be killed. She is a victim of rape rather than an adulteress. By a similar logic, if the sexual relations take place out in the open country, only the man should be executed. The woman receives no punishment, for no one would have heard the woman if she had cried out. Another law in Deuteronomy prohibits the restoration of a marriage if a man's former wife has married and divorced another man (Deut 21:10–14). The logic of this law implies that such a remarriage would be comparable to adultery. In regulating sexual behavior, these laws remove the matter from the jurisdiction of the paterfamilias or *mishpahah*, where it traditionally belonged, and place it in the hands of the central authority.

The conjugal bond and the nuclear family are also strengthened through laws that regulated marriage and divorce. I have already noted above the law regarding a man who has sexual relations with an unbetrothed virgin (Deut 22:28–29). By requiring the man to marry the woman, the law creates a new conjugal bond outside the jurisdiction of the paterfamilias. Moreover, by prohibiting the man from divorcing her, the law protects the social and economic security of the woman who might not otherwise be able to marry. In a similar way, Deuteronomy 21:10–14 regulates how a man may treat a woman captured in war. He may marry her, but he must first allow her one month to mourn her father and mother (perhaps also to ensure that she is not pregnant with her dead husband's child). If he is not satisfied with her, he must let her go free; he cannot treat her as a slave or sell her for money. As with the previous law, this law protects the woman by preserving the integrity of the conjugal bond. A man's sexual relations with a woman belong in the context of marriage. By restricting divorce, the law stresses the importance of the conjugal relationship. Elsewhere, the importance of the conjugal bond is stated directly:

> When a man is newly married, he shall not go out with the army or be charged with any related duty. He shall be free at home one year and will be happy with the wife whom he married. (Deut 24:5; compare Deut 20:7)

This law distinguishes the conjugal relationship from the larger extended family on which the burden of war or some other obligation might fall. A man's loyalty and

---

se (Kaminsky 1995, 139–78). Indeed, Ezekiel replaces responsibility for the catastrophe on the present exilic generation as a whole (see Joyce 1989, 35–55).

obligation belong first and foremost to his wife, and the development of this relationship supersedes other commitments.

The relationship between the nuclear and the extended family is highlighted in the law of the levirate marriage (Deut 25:5–10). The context of this law is the extended family of the large *bet ab*, where "brothers reside together" and have not yet divided into separate households—in other words, they have not yet divided the family inheritance following the death of their father. Within this context, if one brother dies and leaves a childless widow, she should be given in marriage to the other brother. The child that is born from that union will then represent the deceased brother (literally: "stand on the name of his dead brother") so that "his name may not be blotted out of Israel." At issue in this law is the deceased brother's inheritance rights from the family estate. His "name" (*shem*) refers essentially to his household which includes land tenure rights—it functions like a legal title (see Pressler 1993, 66–69; Westbrook 1991, 74–77). Without a descendant, a man cannot pass on his land rights in his name, and his share of the land would be divided among his brothers. It is uncertain whether the law is dealing with the usufruct of the *mishpahah*'s land, or land owned by the *bet ab*, which may be subdivided following the death of the paterfamilias. In any case, the law makes this provision for a man who has not yet established his household and dies prematurely without an heir: his brother should father an heir so that a household may be established in the dead man's name.

A brother might not want to act as a levir under some circumstances (e.g., he is already married and has a son). At the very least, he may not want the family shares of the land divided up into one more parcel for his deceased brother. Indeed, it is in the interests of the extended family, both the *bet ab* and the *mishpahah*, to have as few claims to the land as possible to reduce the land's fragmentation. Thus, the law provides a mechanism in case the brother refuses to act as a levir. First, the widow, for whom the levirate marriage custom also provides social and economic security, though this is not an explicit concern of the law, takes the case before the elders of the city. Then the elders confront the brother to persuade him to do his duty. Finally, if the brother still refuses, the widow of the deceased publicly shames the brother and his household (Deut 25:7–10). The law of the levirate marriage functions to protect the deceased's brother's right to maintain his name with a household and land. Moreover, the deceased's right outweighs the interests of the extended family and his right is publicly defended.

The law of the levirate marriage supports the interests of the individual family member, and hence the nuclear family, over the interests of the extended family. This conflict also lies behind the stories of the daughters of Zelophehad (Num 27:1–11; 36:1–12; see Ben-Barak 2006). In the story in Numbers 27, the five daughters of Zelophehad, who died with no male heirs, bring their request to inherit their father's land before Moses and the leaders of the people:

Part I: Creation

> Our father died in the wilderness; he was not among the company of those who gathered together against Yhwh in the company of Korah, but died for his own sin; and he had no sons. Why should the name of our father be taken away from his *mishpahah* because he had no son? Give us a possession among our father's brothers. (Num 27:3–4)

As with the law of the levirate marriage, the daughters' concern is the continuation of their father's name—or more precisely in this context, the inheritance of his land (*nahalah*). Without a male heir, Zelophehad's land would be given to his brothers, the other *mishpahoth*, "clans," of Gilead, a descendant of Manasseh (Num 26:30–33). If his daughters inherit the land, however, his name will continue for the land will be registered in the name of his household, which belongs to the *mishpahah* of Hepher, the father of Zelophehad. In other words, Zelophehad's share of the land will be divided into five parcels and registered in the names of Mahlah, Noah, Hoglah, Milcah and Tirzah, daughters of Zelophehad. The literary context of this story is set during the so-called wilderness wanderings, before the Israelites settle the land. The land for which the daughters are making a claim, then, is for a geographic portion of the land that Yhwh will give to the Israelites. It is interesting that Moses and the leaders of the people do not decide the case themselves. Rather, Moses takes the case to Yhwh, who decides in favor of the daughters' petition. The ideological superstructure roots itself in divine sanction. A new law is thus instituted at the command of Yhwh that if a man dies and has no son, his inheritance (*nahalah*) shall be given to his daughter. Only if he has no descendants should his inheritance be given to members of his *mishpahah* (Num 27:8–11).

Although the story of the daughters of Zelophehad is preserved in the Priestly tradition, it dates much earlier to the period of the monarchy. The tradition of Zelophehad's daughters is also preserved, for example, in the Deuteronomistic History (Josh 17:3–6), and might have its origin in explaining why the tribe of Manasseh possessed land on the west side of the Jordan, which is given to the five daughters of Zelophehad, in addition to the lands of Gilead and Bashan on the east side, which belong to the other five *mishpahoth* of Gilead (see Snaith 1966). The story also conveys an ideology that supports the interests of the household over those of the *mishpahah*, and so may have functioned to weaken extended kinship relations in those cases when a household failed to produce a son. In any case, by the time of the compilation of the book of Numbers in the post-exilic period, the precedent set by the daughters of Zelophehad raised concerns for the scribes of the Priestly tradition, now living under a new mode of production. Therefore, a new story, in Numbers 36, was added as an addendum to the book in order to mitigate the effects of the case law established in Numbers 27. In this story, the heads of the Gileadite *mishpahoth* bring a new case to Moses and the leaders of the people. In regard to the daughters of Zelophehad inheriting the land of their father, they complain:

> If they are married into another Israelite tribe, then their inheritance will be taken away from the allotted portion of our inheritance and the inheritance of our ancestors will be added to the tribe in which they marry; the allotted portion of our inheritance will be diminished. (Num 36:3)

If the daughters of Zelophehad marry outside of the tribe of Manasseh, then their father's land would be passed down to their heirs who would belong to another tribe, resulting in the reduction of the land apportioned to the tribe of Manasseh. As in the previous case of the daughters, this case is decided directly by God, who revises the original legislation. The daughters of Zelophehad will continue to inherit the land that would be apportioned to their father, but now they must marry into a *mishpahah* of their father's tribe—that is, one of the Gileadite *mishpahoth* (Num 36:6–8). The postexilic revision of the legislation thus ensured that no land would be transferred from one tribe to another. At the same time, the legislation balanced the interests of the individual household and *bet ab*, which were inherited in the tradition, with the interests of the extended kinship relations, the *mishpahah*. Moreover, the law extended the family of endogamy from the *mishpahah* to the tribe (*matteh*).

The Yahwist creation myth and the book of Deuteronomy more broadly, originating during the monarchical period, preserve an ideology that sought to promote patron–client and tributary relations by undermining extended kinship relations. This ideology enabled the elite in ancient Israel to incorporate the production of the Israelite households within their own production. Rooted in the power exercised by kings and their patrons, they were able to siphon off surplus from the Israelite households and exploit the labor of the households to support their growing affluence. The Assyrian assaults on Judah at the end of the eighth century BCE were devastating to the political economy; these events further weakened extended kinship relations by Hezekiah abandoning the countryside and Sennacherib exiling two hundred thousand victims of his onslaught. Perhaps, extended kinship relations were reconstituted in part during the long peaceful reign of Manasseh, during which he rebuilt the traditional shrines his father had destroyed (2 Kgs 21:3), but the royal ideology of the temple would have persisted unabated. By the time the Yahwist creation myth and Deuteronomy were produced, the weakening of kinship relations had become a *fait accompli*, and these texts functioned to support a more hierarchical configuration of the political economy.

POLITICAL ECONOMY AFTER THE MONARCHY

The political economy of ancient Israel received a fatal blow with the destruction of Jerusalem and its temple, the loss of the monarchy, the exile of the people to Babylon, and their eventual restoration under Persian rule. Judah was transformed from a sometime independent monarchical kingdom into a small, insignificant province of the Persian empire,[13] and its political economy was shaped accordingly. The political economy of the monarchy was dead, and without a king and temple could not be resurrected.[14] Instead, a new political economy was born in Persian Yehud, but not *de novo*.[15] The corpse of the old political economy, if you will, was picked over and reconfigured, and then reconstituted with an ideology reformed by the experience of collapse and rebirth. The political economy of Persian Yehud can only be loosely reconstructed. Despite the enormous literary production during this period, little of it is descriptive of the period itself. Moreover, the workings of the Persian empire are largely known from non-Persian sources (primarily Greek), and they give little concern to what was happening in Yehud. Nevertheless, the biblical texts from this period attest to ample ideologies, some of which took hold and shaped the political economy.

The Persian empire was a bureaucratic empire (Eisenstadt 1993), extracting large surpluses from the periphery to the center through tribute in precious metals and resources. The taxes imposed on the people of Yehud included a tribute to the king (*mindah* or *middat*), a poll tax (*belo*), and a land tax (*halak*). These taxes would have been paid to the satrap of the "Beyond the River" province, which included Yehud. In addition, a tax was levied to provide for the governor and his associates (the "governor's food," Neh 5:14–19). Finally, the people were obligated to serve in corvée labor when needed (Eph'al 1988, 158–59). The tribute owed to the Persian authorities placed a heavy economic burden on the people and was wealth taken out of the economy, impoverishing many people. Because information on the Persian administration is fragmentary or ambiguous, there is much scholarly debate over the relationship of the

---

13. The attention of the Persians during the early history of the empire, at least based on our sources, was focused on the Greeks in Asia Minor and in Greece. During the fifth century, Egypt repeatedly rebelled against Persia, eventually freeing itself in the fourth century, only to be dominated by Persia again under Artaxerxes III Ochus in 343 BCE. Similar, and sometimes coordinated, rebellions occurred in the Phoenician cities (see Cook 1983, 208–28). The Persian administration, in this context, would have wanted a stable and loyal Yehud, and perhaps this is the reason behind the appointments of Nehemiah and Ezra. Otherwise, no other attention seems to have been given to the province. Persian Yehud was much smaller than the kingdom of Judah. Most of the population was centered around Jerusalem in the hill country, with the southern Shephelah and the Beersheba valley and areas south largely abandoned. Recent studies suggest that a dryer climate during the sixth and fifth centuries BCE perhaps accounts for the abandonment of these southern regions (see Langgut and Lipschits 2017).

14. The prophets Haggai and Zachariah attempted to resuscitate the monarchical political economy with their temple ideology (see Anderson 1987, 91–126) and the hope that Zerubbabel would restore the monarchy, though admittedly still subservient to the Persians. How Zerubbabel, appointed governor by the Persians, received their scheme is unknown. He disappeared from historical view, and their scheme was unrealized, even after the temple was rebuilt.

15. I do not suggest by this that no political economy was operative during the intervening years, from the fall of Jerusalem in 586 BCE to the restoration of the community in Yehud after 539 BCE. Life in the land continued for some (see the essays in Lipschits and Blenkinsopp 2003). When the Judeans returned from exile, however, they did not integrate within the existing political economy of those who remained in the land, but rather they took control of the levers of power, limited though they might be as a subject people, and created their own political economy.

province to the Persian administration. Some scholars argue that the Persians maintained strict control over their provinces (Fried 2004), others that the Persians authorized and enforced local customs (Frei 2001), and still others that the local people had significant autonomy outside the Persian administration (Knoppers 2001a). Some scholars argue that the temple participated in the Persian tax system (Schaper 1995, 1997), whereas others note that the temple and priests do not benefit from it (Bedford 2007, 2015). These and other debates over Persian Yehud cannot be resolved here, but I can note the following. The Persian empire dominated all economies within its domain. Whatever autonomy was exercised within Yehud, it was nevertheless within the structures of the Persian political economy.[16] In the few texts describing life in Persian Yehud, power was exercised primarily by Persian officials and appointees (primarily Nehemiah and Ezra, but they are also the main subjects of the texts). They implement Persian policy, yet they seemed to have a measure of autonomy—they used their own judgment and persuaded the people to act rather than compelled them by virtue of their state authority (e.g., Ezra 9–10; Neh 5:1–13). The priests were not agents of the Persian administration; they had no power to compel the people to act, and they and the temple seemed to be dependent on voluntary donations from the people (Bedford 2015). Finally, communal identity and boundaries were an essential concern for the leaders of the restored exilic community (the *golah*)—recent immigrants from Babylon to the province of Yehud—especially in contrast to the people who were already in the land (the *'am ha'arets*). In other words, the political economy of Yehud defined a distinct and exclusive community of immigrants, recently returned from exile, within the Persian empire.

The Priestly tradition dates to the Persian period and attests to the ideology of the restored Judean community under the Persian empire, though some of its material had its origin during the period of the monarchy (against those who argue for an early date for P, see Blenkinsopp 1996; Meyer 2010). The dating of this tradition is speculative because the tradition itself maintains the fiction of being received (e.g., the laws from Sinai) and composed prior to Israel's settlement in the land. No indication of Persian administration or Persian dominance is found; and the lack of explicit sociopolitical clues in the text is perhaps intentional. For example, the Priestly creation myth, in contrast to the Yahwist myth, suggests no social structure or hierarchy. The human couple are created and treated together, and they are blessed and commanded to have children,[17] subdue the earth, and have dominion over all living creatures—with plural verbs directed at both the man and the woman (Gen 1:27–28). There is no reference to gender or gender hierarchy (on the Priestly conception of gender, see Erbele-Küster 2011, 2017), though kinship is prominent. As noted above, the human

---

16. This is a fatal flaw in Joel Weinberg's (1992) conception of the "citizen-temple community" (see Cataldo 2003).

17. God's command for the humans to "be fruitful and multiply" attests to the need to repopulate Yehud, following years of war and exile (see Guillaume 2015).

couple are called to create a household. Elsewhere in the Priestly tradition, the congregation (*'edah*) of Israel is divided into tribes and *mishpahoth*, as in the pre-monarchical period (see Num 1, 26). Outside of the Priestly tradition, *mishpahah* is rarely used in the post-exilic or Persian period; it is a reflection of ancient Israel's earlier kinship system. The *mishpahah* may be further subdivided into numerous households, but the Priestly tradition prefers the plural expression, *bet aboth* rather than *bet ab*. The specific nuances of the *bet aboth* are unclear from the Priestly tradition (the expression is also preferred in Ezra–Nehemiah and Chronicles), but it seems to be a post-exilic expression for the primary kinship units of the community during the Persian period (Weinberg 1992, 49–61), used similarly to *mishpahah* during the monarchical period. In the census of Numbers 1, for example, *bet aboth* could be interpreted as a parallel synonym for *mishpahoth*. More specifically, in Numbers 26:2, Moses and Eleazar are commanded to take a (new) census of the whole congregation by ancestral houses (*bet aboth*), but the actual census only refers to the *mishpahoth* of each tribe, with no mention of the *bet aboth*. In other words, the Priestly tradition reflects a kinship-based society, one formed around ancestral houses (*bet aboth*), but connected to the monarchical kinship system by the use of *mishpahah*.

The Priestly tradition also gives no indication of productive inequalities such as patron–client relations. This is peculiar in that texts describing the Persian period, Ezra–Nehemiah in particular, attest to such relations. Nehemiah refers multiple times to the "nobles and officials." The "officials" (*seganim*) probably belonged to the Persian administration and may have served as patrons to some in the Judean community, but the "nobles" (*horim*) were simply social elites and would have formed patron–client relations with others. Moreover, Nehemiah's use of the terms makes it clear that the *horim* and *seganim* were also members of the Judean community (e.g., Neh 5:7). The Priestly tradition does mention "elders," but these would function within the kinship system, probably as heads of the *bet aboth*, not as patrons. There is no reason to doubt that the economic base in Persian Yehud continued as it had in Judah under Assyrian domination a few centuries earlier. Large surpluses would have been extracted from the people as tribute to the Persian empire—for the benefit of the entire administration from the king and his court to the local governor and his officials. Patron–client relations would have functioned within Yehud to extract further surpluses from the *bet aboth* in exchange for loans, resources, and access to persons in power. Indeed, Nehemiah 5:1–13 suggests that the patrons—the *horim* and *seganim*—were excessively exploiting their Judean clients by charging interest and foreclosing on the loans (see Guillaume 2010a; Miller 2010; Fried 2015). The silence of the Priestly tradition on patron–client relations is thus surprising. Perhaps patron–client relations simply did not fit within the fictional pre-settlement, non-monarchical setting of the tradition, but it is more probably due to the prominence that patron–client relations played in the Persian administration. From the Persian king to his nobles, to satraps and local officials, the Persian administration was structured by patron–client relations through gift-giving. Subordinates would give to their superiors from what they extracted from the people, whereas the superiors would give gifts to their clients in order to incur their debt and obligation to them (see Knoppers 2015, 55–57; Briant 2002, 302–54, 388–406; Fried 2018). The Priestly tradition offered an alternative ideological superstructure to the political economy, emphasizing kinship relations within a divine covenant as a mode of resistance against the dominant patron–client relations of the empire.

The Priestly tradition also has no role for a king, Persian or Israelite, though scholars have long noted the royal imagery in the Priestly creation myth. God's commands to the human couple to subdue (*kabash*) the earth and have dominion (*radah*) over living creatures are typically used of kings. This is certainly true of *radah*; it is used, for example of Solomon's dominion over his territory (1 Kgs 4:24). The verb *kabash*, however, is used in the Priestly tradition to refer to God's allotment of the land to Israel (Num 32:22, 29; Josh 18:1); its use in this context suggests that God has allotted the earth to humankind (Smith 2010, 101–2). The creation of humans in the image (*tselem*) and likeness (*demuth*) of God (Gen 1:26–27) is undeniably a royal image, but not for the human couple. Both *tselem* and *demuth* are terms used for statues of a king,[18] which are representations of the king's sovereignty. Hammurabi, for example, erected the stela inscribed with his law code before a statue (*tsalmu*, "image") of himself in the temple of Marduk in Babylon. The statue of Hammurabi serves as a representation of the king and ensures the authority of his law code. Thus, Hammurabi invites anyone who has been wronged to come before his statue, read aloud his law code, and so hear Hammurabi's pronouncement of justice for his case (xlviii 3–58, in the epilogue). Similarly, in the Priestly creation myth, humans are the representatives of God's sovereignty over creation; God is the only king in the Priestly tradition. In their task of subduing the land and having dominion over living creatures, humans may labor as God's regents, not because they are sovereign themselves, but because their authorization comes from God. The human in creation is a recipient of God's blessing. Just as God blessed the fish and the birds so that they would fill the waters and the sky, so God blesses humans to also fill the earth and work towards its betterment. Humans as the image of God is central to the Priestly ideology of work, as discussed in the previous chapter. Because humans are created in the image of God, their labor, when in accord with God's covenant, actualizes God's sovereignty over creation—God's creation is realized through the following of God's laws (Gorman 1990).

Through the ideology of the Priestly tradition, the Priestly scribes hoped to construct an alternative political economy within the Persian empire. It would consist of

---

18. A statue of Had-yith'i, found at Tell Fakhariyeh in Syria, included a bilingual Akkadian-Aramaic inscription. While the Akkadian inscription refers to the statue as the *tsalmu* ("image") of the king, the Aramaic inscription uses both *tslm* ("image") and *dmwt'* ("likeness"). The inscription was published by Abou-Assaf, Bordreuil, and Millard 1982; see also Garr 2000; Smith 2010, 99–100.

the exilic community (the *golah*) being restored on their traditional family land, as other peoples had their own land (see Wöhrle 2015), producing as households linked together in kinship relations (*bet aboth*). The community would be self-sufficient, separate from the many peoples of the Persian empire; it would be a holy congregation, in covenant with God, who would dwell within the tabernacle (the rebuilt temple) in its center. Faithfulness to God's covenant would ensure God's blessing on the people and their labors; the people could realize God's sovereignty in creation even under Persian domination.

Although the Priestly tradition is unconcerned with social hierarchy per se, there is nevertheless a gendered hierarchy of holiness (see Miller 2000, 131–58; Erbele-Küster 2011, 2017). The Priestly tradition seeks to ensure that God, who is holy, may dwell in the midst of the congregation, within the rebuilt temple in Jerusalem. To do this, the Priestly scribes construct a spatial hierarchy of holiness around the tabernacle as well as a hierarchy of holy people (see George 2009; Jenson 1992). Priests and Levites, followed by Israelite men and women, are in covenant with God and so are holy but in different degrees; their proximity to God's presence in the tabernacle will varying according to their holiness. Men are more holy than women and thus have more immediate access to Yhwh through the cult. Other peoples are not holy and are excluded from the congregation. To maintain the holiness of the congregation, the Priestly scribes distinguished between all that is clean and pure and that which is unclean and impure. Eating only clean foods (Lev 11), for example, maintained the holiness of the congregation (Douglas 1966, 41–57). The people should avoid that which is unclean, though some impurities cannot be avoided because they are involuntary and common experiences of life. In any case, impurities should be cleansed, which may occur through the passage of time, or also require washing or sacrifice (see Wright 1987). Violations of the covenant also defile the people, but these always require repentance and sacrifice.

At the center of the Priestly program for an alternative community is the rebuilt temple in Jerusalem. Solomon's temple was a royal chapel. It was funded by the king and it supported the king with its royal theology. The Priestly temple, in contrast, would be for all Israel. God would dwell in the temple and meet the Israelites there, making them holy (Exod 29:43). Yet how to fund the temple without a king was a problem. It does not appear, nor is it likely, that the Persian administration funded the temple; the Persians would have expected the local population to have supported their own temple (Bedford 2015). The Priestly ideology thus had to make provisions for the funding of the temple and its service, and it did so through the tithe and gift offerings to God. In Deuteronomy, during the monarchical period, the tithe was designed to be consumed by the people. For two years it would be brought to Jerusalem and consumed there, but in the third year it would be stored in one's town and given to those who were landless—the Levite, alien, widow, and orphan (Deut 14:22–29). In the Priestly tradition, the tithes are given to the Priests and the Levites in exchange for their temple service (Lev 27:30–33; Num 18:21–32). The tithe, which represented one tenth of all agricultural and pastoral produce, and various gifts to God—from festivals and first fruits offerings, to freewill offerings and vows, to the half-shekel donation (Exod 30:13)—functioned similarly to the patron–client relations that characterized the Persian administration. These gifts to God were an economic exchange and an expression of the people's covenantal relationship to God; they were given in exchange for God's blessing (i.e., the fertility of their land, animals, and wives), favor, and protection (Herman 1991). The tithes and gifts in the Priestly tradition centralized the political economy around the temple and concretely actualized the covenant between God and his people.[19]

In order to ensure the temple's support, the Priestly tradition prohibited the slaughtering of animals by laypersons for meat. In the Deuteronomic reform, slaughtering of animals by laypersons was instituted as an accommodation for the centralization of sacrifice in Jerusalem (Deut 12:20–24). Because the Deuteronomic reform allowed sacrifice only at the temple in Jerusalem, and because the slaughter of domesticated animals was a holy act requiring sacrifice (hunting wild animals does not seem to have posed a problem), the necessary burden of travel to Jerusalem in order to eat meat was too much. The reformers thus distinguished between sacred and profane slaughter. Killing animals for meat was declared profane, and could be performed by anyone wherever they lived, as long as the blood of the animal was drained and poured on to the ground. The priests during the Persian period, however, recognized that such a diffusion of slaughter would also have centrifugal effects on the temple cult. It would devalue both the act of sacrifice and the role of the priests. Thus, the Priestly tradition bans profane slaughter on penalty of being "cut off from the people." The tradition equates those who slaughter in the open field to those sacrificing to "goat-demons" and "prostituting themselves" (Lev 17:3–7). Only by sacrificing animals to God at the temple can they be eaten; and as an offering before God, the priest will also get a share (Lev 7:28–36).

Unlike the patron–client relations, the people's exchange with God through tithes and gift offerings was not incompatible with, nor functioned to undermine, kinship relations. Moreover, kinship relations would enable the Judean community to remain distinct and separate from the "people of the land," and thus Judean kinship relations served as a form of resistance to the dominant patron–client relations of the Persian empire, which functioned to integrate the diverse peoples of the empire together. The Priestly tradition's concern and promotion of kinship relations is evident primarily through its genealogies, where it not only describes the families of Israel (e.g., Num 1, 26), but also places Israel in relation to other peoples (e.g., Gen 10; see

---

19. The Priestly centralization of the cult not only continued the centralizing program of the Deuteronomic tradition, but may have been directed against the rival Yahwist cult in Samaria, on Mount Gerizim. Conflict with the Samarian leadership is attested in Ezra–Nehemiah, and perhaps adds a further dimension to the ideology of the Priestly tradition.

Crüsemann 1996). The Priestly tradition's concern for kinship relations is also evident in places where it differs from Deuteronomy, which tends to undermine extended kinship relations.

The Deuteronomic reform, for example, gives little attention to sexual relations except in the case of adultery. The Priestly tradition, in contrast, gives extensive attention to sexual relations in Leviticus 18:6–18 and 20:10–21. Although the distinction is not always clear, these texts address two different issues. On the one hand, they refer to sexual relations with women that are prohibited because they are adulterous (e.g., "You shall not uncover the nakedness of your brother's wife; it is your brother's nakedness," Lev 18:16). On the other hand, sexual relations with other women are prohibited because they are incestuous (e.g., "You shall not uncover the nakedness of your father's wife's daughter, begotten by your father, since she is your sister," Lev 18:11). The Deuteronomic reform gives no attention to incest; because its focus is on the integrity of the nuclear family, incest is not a primary concern. When extended family members live within the same household, however, sexual relations within the family are more complicated and incest and adultery are a problem.[20] A man may have sexual relations with his first cousin or with his niece, but not with his aunt, his wife's sister (while his wife is living), or his daughter-in-law. In the Priestly tradition, a man's sexual activity is restricted in order to preserve the integrity and relations of his extended family.

A second example concerns widows and orphans, but here the difference is based on silence. Deuteronomy gives significant attention to the plight of the widow (*almanah*)[21] and orphan, who are without ancestral land and the means of subsistence. Thus, Deuteronomy provides for them with regulations: those who do have land should not harvest their crops fully, allowing for the widows and orphans to glean from their fields and orchards (Deut 24:19–21); every third year, the tithe should be given to the widows and orphans, along with the Levite and alien (Deut 14:29); and the widows and orphans should celebrate the festivals of weeks and booths in Jerusalem with those who have land and food (Deut 16:11, 14). The problem posed by widows and orphans in Deuteronomy is a product of the political economy during the

---

20. Even within the nuclear family, sexual relations between a father and his daughter pose a problem. It is unlikely that the scribes of the Priestly tradition would have considered such a sexual relationship legitimate. Rather, because a father controlled his daughter's sexuality until marriage, perhaps the scribes of the Priestly tradition did not have the authority to forbid such a relationship. In any case, it does not explicitly prohibit it.

21. Naomi Steinberg (2004, 327) has observed the Bible uses three distinct expressions for the widow, each of which designates a distinct social status. The *ishah-almanah* ("widow-wife") is a widow "who has redemption rights in her husband's ancestral estate which she exercises through her son." King Jeroboam's mother (1 Kgs 11:26), for example, is a widow of this status. The *eshet-hammet* ("wife of the dead") is a widow "whose husband had died before fathering an heir to exercise the redemption rights to his ancestral holdings." The law of the Levirate (Deut 25:5–10), for example, applies to a widow of this status, and Ruth is described this way (Ruth 4:5). And finally, the *almanah* is the destitute widow, whose deceased husband had no ancestral land.

monarchy. The productive inequalities of patronage sought to exploit the household for its own production. Cutting across kinship loyalties, patron–client relations pitted households in competition with each other for access to resources, and thus tended to weaken and even sever extended kinship ties. Consequently, the creation of widows and orphans through the tragic death of the household paterfamilias would leave such widows and orphans without the support of extended kinship relations. Moreover, because the widow and orphan also had no access to ancestral land, the dead paterfamilias's household had possibly subsisted as a tenant or sharecropper on his patron's land, perhaps as the result of indebtedness or some other hardship, or had otherwise not subsisted on his own land. The death of the paterfamilias would thus also leave the widow and orphan without an economic base on which to subsist. Their plight is also a product of the gender ideology, which holds that the wife, and her minor children by extension, is dependent upon the labor of her husband. Thus, widows and orphans were assumed to be unable either to form their own household or to join in patron–client relations. Widows and orphans would be unable to subsist on their own labor, and would consequently be an economic drain on the resources of a benevolent patron.[22] The political economy with the productive inequalities of patronage created the conditions for the impoverishment of widows and orphans, which it also sought to remedy through the Deuteronomic laws concerning this vulnerable disenfranchised group.

In contrast to Deuteronomy, widows and orphans, as an economically disenfranchised pair, are not mentioned in the Priestly tradition. Even when the Holiness Code prohibits a farmer from fully harvesting his grain or grapes, the gleanings are to be left for the poor ('*ani*) and the alien (Lev 19:9–10; 23:22). Perhaps the widow and orphan are simply included in the "poor" (they are distinguished from the poor in Deuteronomy, see Lohfink 1991), or perhaps they were simply not perceived to be a social problem that needed to be addressed. There is no certain evidence of why this might be the case, but a reasonable solution is that in the Priestly political economy widows and orphans were expected to be supported by their extended kinship relations. The two, sole brief references to widows in the Priestly tradition may lend support to this conclusion. Leviticus 21:14 states that a priest, who must marry a virgin, thus cannot marry a widow or a divorced woman, presumably because they are not virgins. This law would imply that others did marry widows, which would have reintegrated them into a family. Similarly, Leviticus 22:13 indicates that a widowed daughter of a priest, without children, may return to her father's house and eat from her father's food, which are sacred gifts and thus off-limits to lay people. Because the daughter had not borne children for her dead husband, she does not fully belong to her husband's

---

22. The extent of the economic problem posed by widows and orphans is unknown, but following the devastating Assyrian wars at the end of the eighth century BCE, one could reasonably argue that there had been a dramatic increase in widows and orphans as their husbands and fathers were killed in the wars.

family and so may return to her father's house until she marries again. The text assumes that widows may return to their father's house;[23] what is at issue in the text is whether she would be able to eat his sacred food, as she had before she was married. In any case, kinship relations play a dominant role in the Priestly political economy, in contrast to the earlier monarchical political economy, and thus explicit provision for widows and orphans was unnecessary.

It does not appear that the Priestly tradition was fully successful in its efforts to create an alternative political economy, at least not initially. By the time of Ezra and Nehemiah (ca. mid-fifth century BCE), the Judeans within Yehud were not keeping the Sabbath or bringing their tithes to the temple, and they were intermarrying with non-Judean women from the "people of the land" (on the date and composition of Ezra–Nehemiah, see Blenkinsopp 1988). Like Josiah, whose Deuteronomic-like reform was inspired by a book of Torah found in the temple, Ezra reads from the book of the Torah of Moses (Neh 8:1–8), which leads the people to confess and renew the covenant with God, committing themselves to separate from the people of the land, adhere to the Sabbath regulations, give a one-third shekel for temple service, and bring their tithes to the Levites (Neh 10:28–39). It is reasonable to conclude that Ezra's book of Torah consisted of some form of the Priestly tradition, for the response of the people corresponds to the values of the tradition.[24] The chronological relationship of the careers of Ezra and Nehemiah and the covenant renewal narrative (Neh 7:5b—10:39) is complicated and uncertain; the covenant renewal narrative was inserted secondarily into the "Nehemiah memoir." It is thus difficult to correlate events of the covenant renewal with other reforms by Ezra and Nehemiah. It is perhaps enough to simply note that the Priestly political economy was at best only gradually and partially implemented. In any case, this political economy would face new challenges when Alexander and the Macedonians conquered the Persian empire in the latter half of the fourth century BCE.

In summary, the Yahwist and Priestly creation myths are the products of two distinct political economies. The Yahwist creation myth, as well as Deuteronomy, emphasizes the integrity of the nuclear family at the expense of extended kinship relations. The ideology of this myth supports patron–client relations, which empower the

---

23. One might wonder whether the levirate marriage custom would have applied in this case—that is, the widowed daughter of the priest should have married one of her husband's kinsmen. It is possible that the levirate marriage custom was no longer practiced, or that it did not apply to priestly families (suggested by Lev 21:14, indicating that priests cannot marry widows). Or perhaps the text imagines that the dead husband did not have a share in an undivided estate, which is the context for the levirate custom in Deuteronomy 25:5–10.

24. Despite this correspondence with the Priestly tradition, the text of Ezra–Nehemiah presents an ideology more accommodating to the Persian administration than the Priestly tradition: Ezra is appointed by the Persians, multiple references are made of Persian support for the Judean community and the temple, and Nehemiah is a loyal Persian-appointed governor. Other biblical texts of the Persian period, such as Isaiah 40–55, Haggai, and Zechariah 1–8, are also accommodating to the Persian administration (Silverman 2019).

monarchy, and seek to undermine kinship relations. The Priestly creation myth, and the rest of the Priestly tradition, in contrast, stresses extended kinship relations. These relations serve as a hedge against the Persian administration, which was structured along the lines of patron–client relations. Rather than a monarchy, the Priestly tradition structures the people's relationship to God, who dwells in the temple, through patronage; the people donate their tithes and gifts to God in exchange for fertility and protection. Unlike the patron–client relations of the Persian administration, the centralization of the people's relationship to God reinforces their kinship relations as the people of God.

4

Creation and the Body

THE BODY, NATURE, AND SOCIETY

LABOR MEDIATES OUR RELATIONSHIP between nature and society, but labor is not disembodied. It is through the labor of our *bodies* that humans mediate nature and society. Our bodies are nature; their material composition connects us to the rest of the natural world—they share a material substance. Moreover, our natural bodies are dependent on what the rest of nature produces in order to live. As Marx (1975, 275–76) notes,

> Physically man lives only on these products of nature, whether they appear in the form of food, heating, clothes, a dwelling, etc. The universality of man appears in practice precisely in the universality which makes all nature his *inorganic* body—both inasmuch as nature is (1) the direct means of life, and (2) the material, the object, and the instrument of his life activity. Nature is man's *inorganic* body—nature, that is, insofar as it is not itself human body. Man *lives* on nature—means that nature is his *body*, with which he must remain in continuous interchange if he is not to die. That man's physical and spiritual life is linked to nature means simply that nature is linked to itself, for man is a part of nature.

Human labor was first and foremost a means of maintaining human physical existence, and as such, Marx claims, nature was an extension of the physical body.[1] Humans were not separate from nature nor was nature simply the passive stage on

---

1. Marx referred to nature as man's "inorganic body." In our contemporary use of language, this would seem to be an oxymoron at the least, for nature must surely be "organic" in our common use of the term. But Marx uses "inorganic" as it was used in the nineteenth century and in contrast to the human "organic body." In other worlds, our physical bodies are nature composed of organs (heart, liver, lungs, etc.), whereas the rest of nature, external to our bodies (soil, plants, stones, etc.) is inorganic, without organs (see further, Foster and Burkett 2000).

which the human drama played out. Rather, humans, through their bodies, were part and parcel of nature; nature supplied the "inorganic" conditions of their being, and so through their labor humans engaged the natural world for their subsistence.

As nature, the human body has physical needs, and humans supply those needs from the nature that is external to their bodies. They construct tools from nature as extensions of their bodies to meet these needs.[2] A rock, for example, is a piece of nature. But when used as an extension of the hand, it can grind grain into flour to make bread; or it can be struck by another rock to produce sharp flakes that can pierce and kill an animal and then cut its meat from the bones. With other tools, all constructed from nature—such as the plow, axe, sickle, threshing sledge, and harnesses for animals—humans are able to transform nature to grow crops on which to subsist. These are the conditions of human existence, and in this way external nature is an extension of human bodies; the natural world is the extended, "inorganic" body.

The ancient Israelites' relationship to the natural world was vastly different from the experience of most contemporary U.S. Americans. Labor on the land was the material, physical reality of the Israelites; they worked the land and lived off its production. The land was experienced as an extension of their bodies: "only cultivation of the soil posits the land as the individual's extended body" (Marx 1973, 493). The Israelites conceived their relationship to the natural world in realist, relational terms, and their dependence on the land is expressed repeatedly throughout the biblical tradition (Brueggemann 2002; Habel 1995). In the United States, however, where the human relationship to land is generally mediated by capitalist relations of production, most Americans are alienated from nature just as they are alienated from their own labor. Indeed, the alienation of nature makes possible the alienation of labor (Foster and Burkett 2000, 416). We have been separated from nature, alienated from our external bodies, as we moved off the land (sometimes voluntarily, sometimes through coercion and compulsion) into cities for employment. Less than twenty percent of U.S. Americans live in rural areas, and only a fraction of those sustain themselves directly on their own working of the land. Even agriculture has been transformed by capitalism so that farmers produce for others, often corporations, rather than for themselves and their neighbors. We sustain ourselves on commodities purchased through our wages or income (if self-employed), rather than subsisting from the land itself. Our inherent dependence on the natural world has been mystified by capitalist relations, which pretend to supply all our needs from production, based on an unlimited resource stock, which is distributed through a free market. Our alienation from nature (produced by capitalist relations) has created a metabolic and environmental rift separating the natural conditions of human existence from the experience of our active existence

---

2. While tools are made from nature, the natural world creates no tools. "They are *organs of the human brain, created by the human hand*; the power of knowledge, objectified" (Marx 1973, 706). Tools are human constructions from nature through our labor, and thus tools also mediate our relationship between nature and society.

(Foster et al. 2010; Foster and Burkett 2000). In a later chapter I will argue that we need to return to the land, the goal of which would be to restore our relationship with nature and so recognize nature as our real body. This was not a problem for the ancient Israelites.

Through the labor of our bodies in nature, and from the tools we have constructed from nature, we construct society with others. Whereas nature is an extension of the physical body, society becomes an amalgamation of many bodies—it becomes a social body, which is conceived and structured in relation to the physical body. A fundamental insight from anthropology, recognized in a wide variety of cultures—ancient and modern peoples, traditional and capitalist societies—is that the human body serves as a symbol of society (Synnott 1993). The physical body is a microcosm of society and thus replicates the powers and dangers of society, its complexities and boundaries. Dietary restrictions or sexual taboos, for example, are not mere vestiges of an earlier, less enlightened era, although they may become this. They correspond to social concerns regarding the composition of the family, relations between different communities, and control of property. The physical body, what it can eat, and with whom and when it can have sexual relations, is thus perceived according to the structures of society. In the words of Mary Douglas (1966, 115): "The body is a model which can stand for any bounded system. Its boundaries can represent any boundaries which are threatened or precarious. The body is a complex structure. The functions of its different parts and their relation afford a source of symbols for other complex structures."

As a symbol of society, the physical body and the social body have a dialectical relationship, or, in the words of Clifford Geertz (1973, 93–94), the human body functions both as a model *of* society and also as a model *for* society. The social perception of the physical body serves to justify and reinforce—to naturalize, even—the relations of the social body. The biblical dietary laws (Lev 11), for example, replicate the dangers to Israelite society represented by deities other than Yhwh, and thereby reinforce Israelite monolatry (Houston 1993). Also, as I demonstrated in chapter 1, the ancient Israelites' social experience of their body in procreation naturalized their gender relations. The body social is perceived as a macrocosm of the body physical. Again, according to Douglas (1970, 65): "The social body constrains the way the physical body is perceived. The physical experience of the body, always modified by the social categories through which it is known, sustains a particular view of society. There is a continual exchange of meaning between the two kinds of bodily experience so that each reinforces the categories of the other."

The people's experiences of the natural world shaped their perception of their physical bodies, which thereby shaped their perception of society, their social body. Their experience of their physical bodies and their social experiences in turn further reinforced their perception of the natural world. For the ancient Israelites, and the peoples of the ancient Near East generally, this analysis can be extended further. Because the laboring body mediated the relationship between nature and society, it also served as a symbol of the created world at large, the totality of the natural and social world of the people's experience. That is, the human body was the material basis for their understanding of creation, which encompassed their natural and social worlds. Because the ancient Israelites lived off the land and recognized nature to be their extended body, they conceived of Yhwh's creation of the world also in relation to their physical bodies, the understanding of which was determined by their social body. For example, because the ancient Israelites understood the procreation of their bodies in relation to agriculture—a socially constructed knowledge based on their experiences of the body and farming the land—the Yahwist could depict the creation of the man and the animals in Genesis 2 as a birth out of the arable land. The ancient Israelites' understanding of creation was thus rooted in the social experience of their physical bodies.

CREATION METAPHORS AND BODILY EXPERIENCES

A distinction needs to be made between the ancient Israelites' understanding of creation and our contemporary understanding, by which we generally refer to cosmology and evolution (see Clifford 1994, 1–10). Not only did the ancient Israelites lack our alienation from nature—and thus our understanding of creation is not rooted in the human body—but they also had different purposes for contemplating creation and employing creation discourse. For us, creation is a scientific and natural process. Cosmology presents the origin of the universe in terms of the impersonal interaction of physical forces over eons of time. Planet earth is presented as only one of trillions of bodies that formed in the expanding universe, eventually becoming the third planet in our solar system, which is located on one of the spiral arms of the Milky Way galaxy. Paleontology, a branch of biology, presents the origin of humans through evolution, going back approximately four million years ago to the emergence of an early hominid, *Ardipithecus ramidus* (Lovejoy 2009). *Homo sapiens* did not emerge on to the scene until around two hundred thousand years ago, having evolved from *Ardipithecus ramidus* (or another early hominid species). Other animal species each have their own evolutionary history, as do plants and other organisms. In all cases, evolution proceeded through natural causes and forces, such as natural selection, genetic drift, mutations, and gene flow.

The ancient Israelite understanding of creation was not a primitive science—it was not an attempt to explain the material origins of the world—nor were the ancient Israelites making historical claims. The ancient Israelites expressed their understanding of creation through myths, which are symbolic narratives, and poetic language filled with metaphors. Creation for the ancient Israelites was not an impersonal interaction of physical forces—the Israelites did not express such causality. Instead, creation was a drama in which Yhwh was the primary actor; the creation always resulted from personal causes. Through the use of metaphors, creation myths and poetic verses make an analogy between the beginning (as imagined by the ancient Israelites) and what the people experienced in their present world. In other words, creation myths are about the present world of the people. Significant relations and issues of their present world were symbolically projected back onto an imagined beginning. In poetic verses, employed in psalms, wisdom, and prophetic texts, creation metaphors are explicitly used in reference to the present.

At their core, creation myths address concerns about the people's present world; they provide answers to fundamental questions such as: Why is society organized into different classes of people, and into different professions? What is the purpose of society, or what is an individual's purpose in society? What is the role of men? Of women? Why hold certain values and not others? Why live according to certain social customs? Creation myths give meaning, value, and purpose to the people's lives in the here and now. They make sense of the present, not the past. Creation myths focus on relating the people's present experiences—the ordinary world around them—to what is normative, certain, and established by the gods. Creation myths proclaim: "This is the way the world *really is!*" They are descriptive, but also signal a prescriptive mandate: "This is the way the world *should be!*"

The biblical tradition attests to a diverse collection of metaphors used to describe the creation of the world populated with humans.[3] In addition to reflecting human procreation, which we have already seen in the Yahwist creation myth, these metaphors compare the process of creation to planting, plowing, fashioning clay vessels, speaking commands, separating and dividing materials, and conflict with a life-threatening enemy (compare Westermann 1984, 26–41). Yet all of these metaphors have their unity in the political economy of ancient Israel and are rooted in the ancient Israelites' experience of their body and its relationship to nature and society—their extended and social bodies.

Studies by Lakoff and Johnson (1990; Lakoff 1987; Johnson 1987) have demonstrated that the conceptual structure of our thought and language is meaningful because it is embodied. Meaning arises from "our collective biological capacities and our physical and social experiences as beings functioning in our environment" (Lakoff 1987, 267), and metaphors structure the way we organize and understand our bodily experience. Accordingly, Lakoff and Johnson argue that metaphors provide new entailments and new inferences from that experience, but they do not adequately take into account the role played by culture. Rarely do metaphors structure understanding *de novo*; rarely do metaphors give rise to new, previously unrecognized entailments and inferences. Rather than being productive of new understandings, metaphors ordinarily are constrained by existing cultural understandings. In other words, the

---

3. Westermann (1984, 22–25) distinguished between accounts of world creation and human creation, but this distinction does not hold up to the evidence. In the ancient Near East as a whole, though occasionally treated separately, they do not represent distinct traditions (Clifford and Collins 1992, 8–9).

selection of metaphors is a feature of culture—commonly shared understandings of a people. Metaphors are chosen to communicate a cultural understanding that the sender of the communication already has in mind (Quinn 1991).

This last point needs further elaboration. A metaphor is simply a mapping of some source domain onto a target domain. Although the target domain is usually abstract or intangible and so is dependent upon a source domain in order to clarify, describe, or illuminate it, the target domain is not unknown. Typically, there is a preexistent, culturally shared understanding underlying the target domain. People already understand what they want to communicate about the target domain. One metaphor is then chosen over another because it more readily maps onto this cultural understanding. The Israelites' experience of cultivating the land through farming, for example, provided the cultural context for understanding their experience of their body during procreation. In comparing agriculture (source domain) to the conception and birth of a child (target domain), the Israelites were not creating a new understanding of procreation—that it works like agriculture—but expressing a commonly shared understanding of procreation. A metaphor is selected because it corresponds to the cultural understanding that is being communicated.

The creation metaphors used by the ancient Israelites gave structure to their natural and social experiences, relating their bodily experiences to the world at large. However, these metaphors were not productive of new understandings, suggesting a previously unrecognized relationship between the body, nature, and society. The metaphors did not construct this relationship, but rather expressed what was already culturally understood. The creation metaphors were determined by the hierarchy of productive relations through which the ancient Israelites mediated their relationship between nature and society. The people chose these particular metaphors over others because they more readily fit their culturally shared understanding produced by these relations. The ancient Israelites' understanding of creation, which was a product of the Israelite political economy, determined their choice of metaphors.

CREATION AND PRODUCTIVE RELATIONS

The biblical creation metaphors, which are found in the creation myths and in poetic verses, are a product, specifically, of ancient Israel's productive relations, which are hierarchically related. In particular, metaphors that entail aspects of procreation and agriculture have their origin in the gendered productive relations of the household. They express fundamental experiences of husbands and wives in their relations with each other and with the natural world. Metaphors that entail order and structure through separation, differentiation, and boundaries, probably also have their origin in gendered household productive relations, but they are usually expressed through tributary relations. In other words, tributary relations, which subsumed household relations within their own functioning, also incorporated household bodily experiences to express their relationship to nature and society. Metaphors of speech and those entailing conflict may have their origin in tributary relations, but more fundamental connections to household productive relations are nevertheless evident. In all cases, Yhwh is the creator, assuming the role of the husband and the king. Although the metaphors express an Israelite understanding of creation, they are not unique to ancient Israel. The ancient Israelites conceived of creation similarly to their ancient Near Eastern neighbors, though with notable differences based on their monolatrous worldview. Thus, I will focus first on Mesopotamian and Egyptian myths and metaphors of creation before turning to the Bible and how the ancient Israelites understood creation as an expression of the relationship between the body, nature, and society.

Creation in Mesopotamia and Egypt

The Sumerian myth of Enki and Ninmah begins by describing the structure of the world that resulted from its initial creation—the fashioning of heaven and earth and the procreation of the gods. A great disparity existed between the major and the minor gods. On the minor gods fell the arduous task of maintaining the earth, particularly the annual work of dredging the rivers and canals of their accumulated silt:

> The gods were dredging the rivers, were piling up their silt on projecting bends—
> And the gods lugging the clay began complaining about the corvée. (10–11; Jacobsen 1987, 154)

Fearful to approach Enki, the gods bring their complaint to Namma, Enki's mother and the mother who bore all the major gods. She intercedes on behalf of the minor gods, and requests that Enki relieve their burden. With his ingenuity and wisdom, Enki considers the problem that Namma presents him. Remembering his own conception and birth from Namma, he conceives the idea of creating humans in the same way. Humans will be charged with the tasks of the minor gods so that it will be their duty to maintain the earth by dredging the rivers and canals. Thus, Enki requests that Namma give birth to humans:

> O mother mine, since the sire who was once provided with heir by you is still there, have the god's birth-chair put together!
> When you have drenched even the core of the Apsu's fathering clay
> Imma-en and Imma-shar can make the fetus bigger, and when you have put limbs on it
> may Ninmah act as your birth-helper,
> and may Ninimma, Shuzidanna, Ninmada, Ninshara, Ninbara
> Ninmug, Dududuh and Ereshguna
> assist you at your giving birth.

> O mother mine, when you have determined its mode of being, may Ninmah put together the birth-chair,
>
> and when, without any male, you have built it up in it, may you give birth to mankind! (30–38; Jacobsen 1987, 156–57)

Namma then gives birth to a human, Enki clothes it, and all the minor gods rejoice.

In this myth Namma is able to give birth to humankind "without any male" only because the "fathering clay of Apsu" is still within her. Namma, who is the power in the riverbed that gives birth to fresh spring water (Enki), takes on the more general role of mother earth in this myth. The fathering clay of Apsu was the clay beneath the surface of the earth from which the subterranean water (Enki) was born. The clay is analogous to semen; it provides what is essential for life to begin. Just as Enki was born out of Namma from this clay, so Namma can give birth to humans from the clay that remains. Humans are fashioned from the fathering clay of the Apsu and are born out of the earth, out of Namma, with the help of Ninmah who serves as a midwife.

The Akkadian myth of Atrahasis, which was discussed in chapters 1 and 2, begins similarly to Enki and Ninmah, but in this myth the gods actually revolt because of their heavy burden. Recognizing the injustice of the minor gods' fate, the major gods agree to Enki's plan to create humans to relieve the minor gods from their labor. Together, Enki and Nintu (= Mami, Belet-ili), the birth goddess, create humans. Enki supplies the clay, just as semen must by supplied for human creation, and Nintu mixes it with the blood of a rebel god to form humans. As noted earlier, Nintu then acts as a midwife, delivering the newly formed humans from the earth. In other words, the myth of Atrahasis presents the creation of humans, like the Yahwist creation myth, as a birth process in which the humans are conceived by Enki, formed in the womb of the earth by Nintu, and then born from the earth with the help of Nintu.

A different tradition on the creation of humans claims that humans sprouted from the ground like plants. In the introductory lines to a Sumerian hymn to E-engur, Enki's temple at Eridu, the text states:

> When destinies had been determined for all engendered things,
>
> When in the year known as "Abundance born in heaven,..."
>
> The people had broken through the ground like grass. (Jacobsen 1970, 112)

The Creation of the Pickax builds upon this metaphor. In this myth, Enlil separates the heaven from the earth so that humans can sprout up:

> The lord did verily produce the normal order,
>
> The lord whose decisions cannot be altered,
>
> Enlil, did verily speed to remove heaven from earth
>
> So that the seed from which grew the nation could sprout up from the field;
>
> did verily speed to bring the earth out from under heaven as a separate entity

Part I: Creation

> And bound up for her the gash in the "bond of heaven and earth" [= Duranki]
> So that the "flesh producer" [= Uzumua] could grow the vanguard of mankind. (Jacobsen 1970, 113)

Duranki and Uzumua were sacred spots in ancient Nippur, the temple city of Enlil. Duranki was the spot at which heaven (conceived as male) and earth (conceived as female) were attached, presumably, in sexual union. When Enlil separated them, he bound up the resulting wound in the earth so that Uzumua (located within Duranki?) could grow humankind. This text seems to have developed from the insight that seeds need to be covered by dirt in order to sprout; otherwise they will simply bake in the sun.

Having prepared the earth for life, Enlil creates the pickax, the indispensable tool of early agriculturalists, and marvels over its quality. Humans, however, had not sprouted as expected. Apparently, the hard crust of the earth prevented them from breaking through. Thus, Enlil uses his newly created pickax to free them:

> [He] drove his pickax into the "flesh producer."
> In the hole which he thus made was the vanguard of mankind
> And while the people of his land were breaking through the ground toward Enlil
> He eyed his black-headed ones in steadfast fashion. (Jacobsen 1970, 114)

This myth combines metaphors of procreation with metaphors of agriculture. Humans come from the sexual union of heaven and earth, but sprout up as vegetation once the hard crust of the ground is broken up through cultivation.

The most widely known Mesopotamian creation myth, the Enuma Elish, begins by describing the creation as the result of procreation. From the intermingling of the primordial waters—Apsu (fresh water) and Tiamat (salt water)—five generations of gods were born: Lahmu and Lahamu, Anshar and Kishar, Anu, Ea (= Enki), and eventually Marduk. But the creation had no structure; it was characterized by the fluid waters of Apsu and Tiamat, their parents, and the movement of the great gods repeatedly disturbed the rest of their parents and the minor gods. Apsu plotted against the gods, incited by Mummu, his vizier, but Ea overpowered him with a magic spell, killed him, and set up his dwelling on the corpse of Apsu—now the life-producing subterranean waters. Continually stirred up by the great gods, Tiamat was incited by the minor gods to avenge her husband's death. She marshaled a monstrous army to destroy her children, but Marduk killed her in battle and scattered her army.

With the defeat of those powers opposed to structure, Marduk is able to complete the creation by bringing order to the world. The world in the Enuma Elish is literally a female body, as Marduk constructs the world from the body of the slain Tiamat (see Ossendrijver 2016). First, he structures the waters of Tiamat:

> Bel [Marduk] rested, surveyed the corpse,
> In order to divide the lump by a clever scheme.

> He split her into two like a dried fish:
> One half of her he set up and stretched out as the heavens.
> He stretched the skin and appointed a watch
> With the instruction not to let her waters escape. (IV 135–40; Lambert 2013, 95)

He then arranges stations in the heavens for the gods to serve as the stars, moon, and sun, and makes them responsible for signaling the days, months, and years (V 1–46). The rest of Marduk's creation focuses on the terrestrial realm. Although the tablet is damaged, the basic outline can be discerned. Marduk takes the spittle of Tiamat and forms it into clouds. He creates rain and places it under his own control. He heaps up mountains on her head and on her udder, stopping up her bodily portals. These serve as pillars to hold up the roof of the sky. He then bores through the mountains in order to release the Tigris and the Euphrates from her eyes. Finally, he stretches her tail across the sky to form the Milky Way (V 47–62).

There is also a gender dimension to the Enuma Elish. Marduk, the male storm-god, wages war on an unruly female Tiamat. With her husband Apsu, Tiamat gave birth to the gods, but once Apsu was killed, Tiamat spawned only monsters without any male fertilization. They make up Tiamat's army (along with the minor rebel gods) with whom she seeks to kill her children: "In agreeing to destroy her offspring, even with the support of other of her children, Tiamat contravenes the basic bond of motherhood and irrevocably transgresses the boundaries of the domestic woman" (Sonik 2009, 91). Tiamat has become an unnatural mother, and for this she is killed by Marduk. Gwendolyn Leick (1994) argues that Tiamat and Apsu represent the splitting of the earlier Sumerian ENGUR, the primordial waters evident in the life-teeming marshes of the southern Mesopotamian plain. In Sumerian mythology, ENGUR is personified as the female Nammu, who can create spontaneously, and in the myth of Enki and Ninmah, this explains why the "fathering clay of Apsu," which enables her to bear children, is within her. In any case, the mingling of Apsu and Tiamat at the beginning of the Enuma Elish introduces sexuality and gender where perhaps there had originally been none. When Ea kills Apsu and builds his house over his corpse, the male Apsu becomes the life-teeming waters of the southern marshes, where Ea's temple and city, Eridu, are located. Similarly, when Marduk constructs the world from Tiamat's body, he bores wells into her body to release water from the Apsu to fill channels (V 58–60). The world created by Marduk is gendered with a female body fertilized by male waters flowing through it. Although not developed in the myth, the gender of the protagonists suggests that Marduk's killing of Tiamat and subsequent structuring of her body with firm boundaries restores Tiamat's proper, domesticated fertility; with the aid of Apsu, she will sustain the Mesopotamian population through an abundance of agriculture.

As in the Enuma Elish, the Theogony of Dunnu begins with the procreation of the gods, described with agricultural metaphors:

Part I: Creation

> At the very beginning Plow married Earth
> And they decided to establish a family and dominion.
> "We shall break up the virgin soil of the land into clods."
> In the clods of their virgin soil, they created Sea.
> The Furrows, of their own accord, begot the Cattle God.
> Together they built Dunnu forever as his refuge.
> Plow made unrestricted dominion for himself in Dunnu. (1–7; Dalley 1991, 279)

In the following lines, the Cattle God marries his mother Earth and kills his father Plow and takes over his dominion. Then the Cattle God marries his older sister Sea who kills Earth. The Cattle God and Sea in turn give birth to a son, the Flocks God, who kills his father and marries his mother. So the generations proceed through incestuous marriage and patricide.

According to this myth, the creation of the world resulted from both procreation and the killing of one's parents. The importance of procreation is understandable, but what is the purpose of killing one's parents? An insight from the Enuma Elish proves helpful. In that myth both Apsu and Tiamat are slain, but neither ceases to exist. Rather, they become inert matter, and they are ordered within the structure of creation. No longer are they active forces in the world. In the same way, each of the succeeding generations in the Theogony of Dunnu becomes part of the material structure of the world through its death, ceasing to serve as an active agent in the world (Jacobsen 1984, 15–16).

An early example of Egypt's creation theology[4] is known as the Heliopolitan cosmogony because it originated in the cult of Atum at Heliopolis, the biblical On. It presents the classical Egyptian doctrine of the procreation of the world. According to this theology, the creation of the world began at Heliopolis as a hillock emerging out of the primeval ocean Nun. On this hillock the lone god Atum procreated by himself: "Atum is he who once came into being, who masturbated in On. He took his phallus in his grasp that he might create orgasm by means of it, and so were born the twins Shu and Tefnut" (Faulkner 1969, 198). Because this first couple was thought to have been born from Atum's mouth, later formulations of the theology state that Atum spit them out (Morenz 1973, 163). As a male, Atum had the "seeds of life" within him, and thus his ejaculation creates life even without a female counterpart. The rest of the gods of the Ennead, however, are then born through conventional procreative means.

Another creation theology focuses on the work of Ptah, the chief god of Memphis. Ptah is the self-created one, and in the Hymn to Ptah, he is praised as the one who also creates the world:

---

4. The Egyptians did not document their mythology in narrative form, in myths, as did the Mesopotamians, but incorporated it in rituals, spells, and hymns. Egyptian theology of creation is reconstructed from these liturgical forms. On the Egyptian understanding of creation, see Lesko 1991.

> Greetings, Ptah, father of the gods,
>> Tatenen, eldest of the originals, . . .
> who begot himself by himself, without any developing having developed;
>> who crafted the world in the design of his heart,
> when his developments developed.
>> Model who gave birth to all that is,
> begetter who created what exists. (Berlin Papyrus 3–9; Allen 1988, 39–40)

An important characteristic of Egyptian creation theology that can be observed from this text is the mixture of both craftsman and birth metaphors. Ptah both fashions the world and gives birth to it. In the following lines of the hymn Ptah is also compared to Khnum, the god who creates on his potter's wheel. But Khnum, as illustrated below, is also responsible for creating the semen and fashioning the fetus in the womb (Morenz 1973, 162, 183–84). These two types of creation are thoroughly integrated in the Egyptian theology, and stem from the same cultural understanding of creation.

A third Egyptian creation theology that combines elements from the previous two theologies is the Memphite Theology. According to this theology, Ptah is the creator of even Atum and the rest of the Heliopolitan Ennead, but the mode of creation has been abstracted from the concrete craftsman and birth metaphors to an intangible intellectual creative principle. The creation comes into being through Ptah's efficacious word.

> There took shape in the heart, there took shape on the tongue the form of Atum. For the very great one is Ptah, who gave life to all the gods and their *kas* through this heart and through this tongue, in which Horus [= command] had taken shape as Ptah, in which Thoth [= perception] had taken shape as Ptah. Thus heart and tongue rule over all limbs in accordance with the teaching that the heart is in every body and the tongue is in every mouth of all gods, all men, all cattle, all creeping things, whatever lives, thinking whatever he wishes and commanding whatever he wishes. His Ennead is before him as teeth and lips. They are the semen and the hands of Atum. For the Ennead of Atum came into being through his semen and his fingers. But the Ennead is the teeth and lips in this mouth which pronounced the name of every living thing, from which Shu and Tefnut came forth, and which gave birth to the Ennead. . . Thus all the gods were born and his Ennead was completed. For every word of the god came about through what the heart devised and the tongue commanded. (Lichtheim 1980, 54)

In this theology, Ptah is identified with the creative principle that is actualized through his thoughts and speech. The Ennead of Atum translates Ptah's word into material reality. The model for this abstract understanding of creation appears to be the actual workings of the human mind. Just as humans conceptualize and plan and

Part I: Creation

then act on those plans, so also Ptah's conceptualizations result in the creation of the world. Similarly, the Ennead is the agent in Ptah's creating just as the human senses serve as agents of the mind (Allen 1988, 45): "Sight, hearing, breathing—they report to the heart, and it makes every understanding come forth. As to the tongue, it repeats what the heart has devised" (Lichtheim 1980, 54). But this understanding of creation is rooted in procreation, for although the creation is actualized by the teeth and lips of Ptah, "they are the semen and the hands of Atum." The thought and speech of Ptah serve as a metonym for procreation; they refer to the desire of the heart that initiates sexual intercourse, though in the case of the lone Atum, it remains masturbation.

Egyptian theology has little to say about the creation of humans; its primary focus is world creation and the emergence of the gods. However, short references to human creation can be gleaned from a variety of Egyptian texts. In the texts discovered at el-Amarna, for example, the sun-disk Aten is praised for creating all life, including humans:

> August God who fashioned himself,
> Who made every land, created what is in it,
> All peoples, herds, and flocks,
> All trees that grow from soil;
> They live when you dawn for them,
> You are mother and father of all that you made. . . .
> You are One yet a million lives are in you,
> To make them live you give the breath of life to their noises;
> By the sight of your rays all flowers exist,
> What lives and sprouts from the soil grows when you shine. (Short Hymn to Aten; Lichtheim 1976, 91–92)

There is an oscillation in this hymn between Aten's natural life-giving power as the sun and Aten's paternal character. Because Akhenaten, the chief patron of the Aten cult, proclaimed Aten to be the sole god of Egypt, Aten is described as both a father and a mother. This aspect of Aten is further elaborated upon in the Great Hymn to Aten, where Aten is praised for characteristics similar to both Enki and Nintu, his Mesopotamian counterparts in the creation process:

> Who makes seed grow in women,
> Who creates people from sperm;
> Who feeds the son in his mother's womb,
> Who soothes him to still his tears.
> Nurse in the womb,
> Giver of breath,
> To nourish all that he made.

> When he comes from the womb to breathe,
> On the day of his birth,
> You open wide his mouth,
> You supply his needs. (Lichtheim 1976, 97–98)

Like Enki, Aten supplies the semen that enables conception in the womb. And like Nintu, Aten shapes the fetus in the womb and acts as a divine midwife to deliver and care for the child at birth.

The foremost creator of humans in Egypt is Khnum. He is most characteristically portrayed as a potter who fashions both gods and humans on his potter's wheel: "He has fashioned humankind on the wheel; he has engendered gods in order to people the land and the sphere of the Great Ocean" (Esna 394; Sauneron and Yoyotte 1959, 73). In a hymn from his temple in Esna, Khnum is praised for creating every living thing on his wheel:

> You are the master of the wheel,
> Who is pleased to model on the wheel,
> The beneficent god who organizes the land,
> Who puts the seeds in contact with the land . . .
> You are the all-powerful one,
> And you have made humans on the wheel.
> You have created the gods;
> You have modeled the small and large cattle;
> You have formed everything on your wheel each day
> In your name of Khnum the potter. (Esna 319; Sauneron and Yoyotte 1959, 73)

In addition to fashioning humans on the potter's wheel, Khnum also supplies them with the breath necessary for life. He is the "god who forms bodies, the god who equips nostrils" (Lichtheim 1980, 115). "The sweet breath of wind goes out from him for the nostrils of gods and humans" (Esna 378; Sauneron and Yoyotte 1959, 74). As a potter, Khnum also plays a role in the birth process. In fact, these two aspects of Khnum's character are inseparable. As discussed in chapter 1, Khnum's fashioning of humans on the potter's wheel was thought to be analogous to his work within the womb. Ancient Egyptians believed that Khnum had a necessary and critical task within the birth process.

Creation in Ancient Israel

Creation in the Bible is described with metaphors similar in kind to those used in Mesopotamian and Egyptian creation myths. Yhwh creates by fighting a sea dragon, battling chaotic waters, separating the heavens and the earth, dividing the primeval waters, speaking, fashioning people out of clay, giving birth to people, delivering humans out of the womb, planting people in the land, and causing the earth to produce animal and plant life. These metaphors were not limited to descriptions of creation; most of the creation metaphors in the Bible were employed in extraneous (i.e., non-creation) contexts. Contrary to some scholars (von Rad 1984, 131–43; McCarthy 1967), this use of creation metaphors did not diminish the significance of creation or strip the metaphors of their cosmological character. Rather, the biblical scribes used these metaphors in order to put the extraneous subject matter within the context of Yhwh's activity in creation. In particular, they employed creation metaphors to describe the human condition—as creatures, humans are dependent upon Yhwh the creator—and the redemption of Israel—Yhwh will redeem Israel through a new creation (Simkins 1994, 82–120). Nevertheless, all the biblical creation metaphors are rooted in an understanding of creation that the ancient Israelites shared in common with their ancient Near Eastern neighbors.

The least developed creation metaphors in the Bible are those connected with agriculture. Nowhere do the biblical writers explicitly describe the creation of humans as sprouting from the earth. But humans are commonly known as the "seed" (*zeraʿ*) of their ancestors, they are repeatedly compared to plants (e.g., Isa 5:1–6; 40:6–8; Jer 17:8; Pss 1:3; 90:5–6; 103:15–16), and the redemption of Israel is likened to the sprouting of plants. Amos (9:15), who compares Israel's exile to a plant that has been uprooted, proclaims Yhwh's coming redemption for Israel in terms of replanting:

> I will plant them on their land
> and they will not again be rooted out
> from their land that I have given them,
>   says Yhwh your God.

Similarly, Jeremiah compares Israel to a plant: "I will rejoice in doing good to them, and I will plant them in this land in faithfulness, with all my heart and all my soul" (32:41). In a different context, Jeremiah (31:27–28) likens Israel and Judah to a land that Yhwh is going to replant:

> The days are surely coming, says Yhwh, when I will sow the house of Israel and the house of Judah with human seed and animal seed. And just as I have watched over them to root out, break down, overthrow, destroy, and bring evil, so I will watch over them to build and to plant, says Yhwh.

The Babylonians, at Yhwh's direction, had devastated the land; the people and their livestock had been slaughtered. But the prophet proclaims that in coming days Yhwh will redeem the land by bringing new life to it like a newly planted field, sowing it with seed to produce humans and animals. Redemption is compared to creation through the use of agricultural metaphors (cf. Frymer-Kensky 1987).

The creation of humans is described with metaphors of a potter fashioning clay (e.g., Isa 29:15–16; Jer 18:3–6). Yhwh's fashioning of humans from clay, however, is also related to Yhwh's activity in the womb, as in the Yahwist creation myth. The earth, when it is personified, serves as a womb in which the fetus gestates. The task of a potter in shaping and fashioning clay is thus analogous to the growth and development of the fetus within the womb. In questioning God as to why he was suffering, for example, Job (10:8–11) claimed that Yhwh fashioned him in the womb like a potter fashions clay:

> Your hands formed and made me;
>> and then turned and destroyed me.
> Remember that you molded me like clay;
>> and will you turn me to dirt?
> Did you not pour me out like milk
>> and curdle me like cheese?
> You clothed me with skin and flesh,
>> and knit me together with bones and sinews.

The analogous relationship between the human womb and the earth is made explicit in Psalm 139:13, 15:

> For you created my inward parts;
>> you knit me together in my mother's womb. . . .
> My frame was not hidden from you,
>> when I was being made in secret,
>> woven in the depths of the earth.

Although the metaphors of these passages present the creation of a single individual, they reflect the people's understanding of the creation of humankind.

Biblical metaphors that present the creation of the world emphasize the establishment of order and structure. God created the world by stretching out the heavens, setting the earth on its foundations, and establishing the boundary of the sea (Ps 104:1–9). Structure and order, however, were not without opposition. Frequently, the sea or the waters were personified as a threat whom Yhwh must defeat (see Ps 93:3–4). In Psalm 104:7 God simply rebukes the waters, causing them to flee (see Levenson 1988, 53–65). In Psalm 74:12–17, sometimes referred to as a conflict myth, the sea is personified as a dragon whom Yhwh defeated before creation:

> Yet God is my King from of old,
>> working salvation in the earth.
> You divided the sea by your might;
>> you broke the heads of the dragons in the waters.

Part I: Creation

> You crushed the heads of Leviathan;
>> you gave him as food for the desert creatures.
> You cut openings for springs and streams;
>> you dried up ever-flowing rivers.
> Yours is the day, yours also the night;
>> you established the luminaries and the sun.
> You have fixed all the boundaries of the earth;
>> you formed the summer and fall harvests.

By defeating Leviathan, God was able to bring structure to the world. Creation metaphors of conflict have their origin in tributary relations, and Yhwh's relationship to the world is comparable to a king's relationship to his people. As king, God established the order and structure of the world by defeating all threats to it, just as a human king brings order to his kingdom by repelling all threats to his domain. Once the creation is secured and ordered, God brings prosperity and abundance to the world; similarly, the prosperity of the earthly kingdom is a result of the king's supremacy (see Ps 72). The order and structure God brings to the creation, however, is not static. In the biblical tradition the world is frequently threatened; fluidity and disorder surmount the boundaries of the world. Leviathan is bound or disabled, but not fully extinguished. As a result, God's supremacy as king is repeatedly being challenged. God must defend his creation and protect the integrity of the world by again combating his foes (Levenson 1988). In the context of Psalm 74, the psalmist sings of God's primordial defeat of Leviathan to remind God of the present assault on creation—the Babylonians are destroying Jerusalem and the temple—and to call him to defend the world, the home of his people (Ps 74:22–23):

> Rise up, O God, plead your cause;
>> remember how the worthless taunt you all day long.
> Do not forget the clamor of you assailants,
>> the roar of your adversaries goes up continually.

Although both Leviathan and Tiamat are represented as aquatic sea monsters, significant differences shape the mythology of each. Tiamat is a primordial substance (along with Apsu) out of which the creation is formed, and her body becomes the natural world as Marduk orders and structures it. Leviathan, in contrast, is an external threat to the creation; it is primordial and continues to exist within the world—within both nature and society—but is separate from or a distinct entity within the creation. Yhwh does not create the natural world from Leviathan's body as does Marduk from Tiamat's body. Thus, the relationship between Yhwh, Leviathan, and the creation is more complicated than that between Marduk and Tiamat. Structurally, the relations between Yhwh and the natural world is gendered like the relationship between Yhwh and the Israelites. The gendered relationship is evident in the Yahwist creation myth as

Yhwh forms the *adam* from the dirt of the *adamah*. The earth with its arable land is perceived as a female in bearing a human and bringing forth vegetation. The Israelite conception of Yhwh as a king who defeats his enemies belongs to the ideology of tributary relations, and just as these relations are gendered, the structurally parallel relationship between Yhwh and the natural world is also gendered and so may also be compared to gendered household productive relations. Yhwh's role in the conflict myth is thus also like a husband who guards the sexual integrity of his wife against all external dangers. He repels and defeats any suitor or threat to his wife—whether it be the natural world or the people of Israel—he secures her fecundity for his own benefit and the benefit of his household. In the conflict myth, Yhwh demonstrates his supremacy as king over creation and as a husband over his household.

The Priestly creation myth (Gen 1:1—2:3) contains the most complex use of creation metaphors in the Bible. This myth represents Priestly doctrine—"ancient, sacred knowledge, preserved and handed on by many generations of priests, repeatedly pondered, taught, reformed and expanded most carefully and compactly by new reflections and experiences of faith" (von Rad 1972, 63)—and the creation metaphors have thus undergone a process of harmonization and abstraction. In this myth, God creates a world inhabited by representative types of creatures—heavenly bodies, birds, water creatures, earth creatures, and humans—through divine speech, which is presented as eight fiats, structured according to six days (two fiats on the third and the sixth day). However, only with the creation of light on the first day does God create by command alone. In all other cases the myth states that God "made," "separated," or "created" (with no specific method) something, or that the earth itself brings forth life, following God's speech. The dominant creation metaphors in the priestly myth are those of order and structure. God first separates light from darkness (Gen 1:4). Then God separates the waters above from the waters below by making a dome in the midst of the waters (Gen 1:7). Finally, God separates the waters from the land (Gen 1:9). In all these cases the divine fiat is the externalization of God's thought. It serves as a metonym for God's activity in separating and making. The divine fiat also serves as a metonym for God's activity in agriculture and procreation. Thus on the third day God commands, "Let the earth put forth vegetation" (Gen 1:11), and the earth produces vegetation. Although not explicitly stated in the text, this fiat is a metonym for God's sowing the earth with seed. Similarly, God's commands on the fifth day, "Let the waters bring forth swarms of living creatures" (Gen 1:20), and on the sixth day, "Let the earth bring forth living creatures" (Gen 1:24), serve as metonyms for God impregnating the waters and the earth. Yet in fulfillment of these commands the myth simply states that God "created" the sea monsters and fish (Gen 1:21) and "made" all the earth creatures (Gen 1:25). These creation metaphors have been abstracted so that the waters and the earth no longer give birth to their creatures.

The ancient Israelite understanding of creation, as attested through a variety of metaphors, set within the larger ancient Near Eastern context, was rooted in the bodily experiences of household productive relations. A fundamental experience of these relations was the procreation of a child, which was comparable to their experience of farming. Through sexual intercourse, a husband and wife created a new human being much like a man cultivates the land to produce crops for the subsistence of his household. This metaphorical relationship between procreation and agriculture was embedded in the language of the people so that Hebrew *zera'* refers to both "semen" and "offspring," on the one hand, and "seed," which is sown into the land, on the other hand. The Israelites experienced their physical bodies in relation to the natural world, their extended body, and thus the reproduction of the physical, organic body was understood in relation to the production of their extended, inorganic body.

The Israelites' understanding of creation was simply a projection of their own bodily experiences onto the divine realm. In the Mesopotamian world, a divine father, fertilizing a divine mother, engendered the creation. This process took the form of a male sky fertilizing a female earth or as the mingling of fresh (male) and salt (female) waters. The ancient Egyptians reversed these metaphors due to their environment with the Nile emerging from the male earth as the source of life, and the male sun passing though the body of the female sky. In every case, however, the male role in creation was active and life giving, whereas the female role was passive. Despite the fluidity by which the ancient Near Eastern peoples described the divine procreation of the world, they always attributed human origins to a mother earth. The type of metaphors the people employed, however, depended on whether they emphasized the male or the female role in the creation of humans. Agricultural metaphors illustrate the male role. A male deity creates a populated world by sowing seed and plowing the ground so that humans may sprout from the earth. The female role in the creation of humans entails conception, gestation, and birth, for which the people used the metaphor of a potter's clay. The mother earth is a passive agent in creation; her body is acted upon by others—a father and a midwife. Just as a potter mixes clay, pinches off a piece, and shapes it into a vessel, deities work on the body of mother earth so that she gives birth to humans. Humans are pieces of clay, taken from the earth, their mother, and shaped into living beings. The ancient Israelites shared this understanding of creation, though within the constraints of their monolatrous worldview: humans were created out of soil, born from the earth, which was presumably impregnated by Yhwh.

The ancient Israelites also experienced their bodies in relation to the order, structure, and boundaries of the natural world. The natural world displayed order and regularity through the seasonal cycle and the courses of the sun, moon, and stars. The world was marked off with boundaries that differentiated one region from another—the sky from the earth, the land from the sea, the desert from the fertile soil, two lands divided by a river, the city from its hinterland, one people from another. This perception of the natural world reflected the Israelites' experience of their bodies as ordered, structured, and bounded, with symmetrical limbs, digits, eyes, and ears; orifices (nose, mouth, and genitals) along the central axis of the body; the menstrual cycle aligned with the cycles of the moon; and bounded by skin. This experience of the physical body in relation to the natural world gave rise to perceptions of the social body (see below) and metaphors of creation. Thus, the Priestly scribes presented God's creation of the world in Genesis 1 through a series of separations (light from darkness, waters above from the waters below, land from the waters) and the ordering of the world into distinct environments with its unique inhabitants (the heavens for the luminaries, the sky for the birds, the seas for the fish and sea monsters, and the land for animals and humans). The Priestly scribes also framed the creation around the speech of God—God commands the creation to come into being. Speech is, of course, a common bodily experience, and although it is characteristic of most human experiences, the Priestly use of speech has its origin in tributary relations in which a king may accomplish his intentions by commanding others. Similarly, the creation metaphors of conflict also have their origin in tributary relations, as a king protects his people by fighting all external threats. As discussed above, however, creation metaphors of conflict may be rooted in gendered household productive relations, as a husband protects the sexual integrity of his wife from suitors.

GENDER AND THE SOCIAL BODY

The Israelites' experience of their bodies in procreation and as an ordered, structured, and bounded entity shaped their understanding of the social body. Because the Israelites' experience of their bodies was also gendered—that is, they experienced male and female bodies differently—their experience of their bodies also naturalized the gender hierarchy. As introduced in chapter 3, the Priestly scribes recognized boundaries as potential markers of holiness. In Leviticus 11–15, they regulated the bounded physical body so that it would reflect God's holiness and thereby preserve the holiness of the community, the social body. Only those who were holy could approach God through the cult. Through ritual regulations, the priests distinguished between clean and unclean foods, regular and irregular discharges of bodily fluids, and skin ailments. In all cases, the crossing or breaking of boundaries was at issue, for such were viewed as a threat to holiness. Food enters the body through the mouth, and thus only clean foods—those animals that fit appropriately within their environment are clean (Douglas 1966, 41–67)—should be consumed. Skin ailments may also violate the boundary of the skin, thus the priests were concerned to distinguish mild ailments that simply formed on the surface of the skin from those that penetrated the skin. The food and skin regulations are gender neutral—male and female bodies are the same in this regard. Through the Israelites' experience of their gendered bodies, however, the priests recognized a difference between male and female bodily discharges, and this difference served to subordinate the role of women in the cult (see Erbele-Küster 2011, 2017). A man's discharge (primarily semen) was conceived of as a "flow *out of* his flesh" (Lev 15:2), whereas a woman's discharge (primarily her menstrual blood) was a "flow *in her* flesh" (Lev 15:19), making a qualitative and gendered distinction between their flows. Both the man's and the woman's flow are unclean, but in different degrees. A man's flow of semen is unclean during sexual intercourse, and because the fluid crosses the boundary from the man to the woman, both are unclean until evening. Similarly, if the man has a discharge of semen apart from sexual relations, he is unclean until evening (Lev 15:16–18). A woman's regular flow of menstrual blood (*in* her flesh) make her ritually unclean for seven days, which is similar to the man's *irregular* discharge (*out of* his flesh) (compare Lev 15:19–24 with Lev 15:2–15). When a woman has an *irregular* discharge, not during the time of her menstruation, she is unclean for the duration of her discharge plus an additional seven days (Lev 15:25–30). In other words, a woman's bodily discharge causes her to be ritually unclean for a longer period than the man's discharge, preventing her from participating in the cult. This difference between men and women is reflected also in the uncleanliness produced by childbirth. When a mother bears a male child, she is unclean for seven days (as with her menstruation), but when she bears a female child, she is unclean for fourteen days (Lev 12:1–5). She is essentially doubly unclean because of the female child.

Other priestly texts, such as the Holiness Code's regulation of sexual intercourse in Leviticus 18, privilege the man and subordinate the woman on grounds other than purity. Sexual intercourse, of course, also crossed boundaries—from the insertion of the penis to the sharing of fluids—and thus produces ritual impurity, but these regulations are concerned primarily with the man's seed. The text distinguishes appropriate procreative sexual relations (between husband and wife) from inappropriate sexual relations (adulterous, incestuous, homosexual,[5] and bestial relations). The regulations seem to be concerned not just with the productivity of the man's seed, but also with how the child that would result from the sexual intercourse might affect the social body. Thus, sexual relations with one's wife during menstruation are prohibited (Lev 18:19) because such relations would be unproductive. A similar reason explains the prohibition against male with male and bestial relations (Lev 18:22–23). Sexual relations with a kinsmen's wife are prohibited (Lev 18:20), however, because the resulting child would confuse inheritance. Generally, sexual relations with near kin are prohibited (Lev 18:6) because they would disrupt and undermine household and kinship relations. Because the male body contains the seed for procreation, the sexual regulations are oriented toward the man (with whom he can have sex) and concern the productivity of his seed. The woman's body in the regulations, in contrast, is consistently described as the "nakedness" of a man. Whereas the man is presented as actively engaged in sexual relations, the woman is defined exclusively in relation to a man, for her sexuality belongs to a man. The exception would be the prostitute, for "only the prostitute owned her own sexuality" (Frymer-Kensky 1998, 89).

---

5. The text of Leviticus prohibits a man from "lying with a male as with a woman," which addresses a specific sexual act. It does not address the modern conception of same-sex gender orientation, as the term "homosexual" might imply.

Many readers of the Bible have argued that women in the biblical world were viewed as property. This is not unexpected since the biblical language itself often suggests as much. Daughters, for example, can be sold into slavery, most often to resolve a debt obligation, suggesting that they are simply property. But this is a function of the daughters age and dependence on her father rather than her gender, for sons can also be sold into slavery and mothers, in the absence of a father, can carry out the transaction (see Neh 5:1–5; 2 Kgs 4:1–7; cf. Deut 15:12–17).

Biblical language that draws on the procreation-agriculture metaphor especially suggests that women are viewed as property. Referring to a woman as a man's "nakedness" suggests that she belongs to a man like property. If a woman's body is like a field in which her husband sows seed to produce children, is not her body property like a field? Take, for example, the law regarding a man who has had sexual intercourse with a virgin to whom he is not engaged:

> When a man seduces a virgin who is not betrothed and lies with her, he shall give the bridewealth for her and make her his wife. If her father refuses to give her to him, he shall pay an amount equal to the bridewealth for virgins. (Exod 22:16–17)

This law suggests neither adultery (the virgin is not betrothed) nor rape (he seduces, or persuades her, rather than forces her), but the man is still responsible to compensate her father. The reference to the "bridewealth" (mohar) explains why. Under usual conditions, marriage was an economic exchange. The father of the bride would receive bridewealth—an assortment of goods with an agreed economic value—in exchange for his daughter going to her husband's family, where she would labor and supply children. With his daughter's loss of virginity, however, her economic value is diminished because virginity was cherished, and thus the man who seduced her must compensate her father, whether he marries her or not. As an economic asset belonging to the father, his daughter is like property. Similarly, a man may sell his daughter as an *amah*, which may be a slave, but in the context of Exodus 21:7–11 she is treated as a concubine or a secondary wife (see Fleishman 2011, 7–92).

Other texts treat men and women similarly, with no hint of property relations. Thus, whoever curses or strikes their father or mother should be put to death (Exod 21:15, 17)—the mother is treated no differently than the father. If a slaveowner abuses their male and female slaves, depending on the abuse, the slaveowner shall be punished if they die, or they shall go free if their eye or tooth is damaged (Exod 21:20–21, 26–27). In other words, even though slaves are property, a female slave should be treated no differently than a male slave under these circumstances, even though under different circumstances the slaveowner had access to his female slave's sexuality. Furthermore, crimes against women receive the same punishment as the same crimes against men. Because of these discrepancies, some scholars have argued that women are only the property of men in relation to their sexuality (Wegner 1988), but this would be a peculiar understanding of property, which is not usually partitioned according to function. Beginning by understanding the nature of property relations, T. M. Lemos (2017) has argued persuasively that women, as wives or mothers, in the biblical tradition are never viewed as property. They are never referred to as property; they are never sold or exchanged as property; and they are not inherited as property. Instead, the treatment of a woman's sexuality as belonging to her husband (or her father) is an expression of her subordination within the Israelite household. Unlike property, subordination may be contextual. The woman is subordinate in regard to her sexuality, but may exert dominance in the management of the household, in relation to her children, or while laboring in select tasks. The biblical tradition, however, masks the multiple ways in which a woman might express dominance by emphasizing her subordinate role in procreation as the defining characteristic of gendered household productive relations.

The Israelites' experience of their bodies further shaped the social body through the values of honor and shame.[6] These male and female social values, which reinforced the Israelites' gender roles, were naturalized by being rooted in the contribution of each in procreation: male honor (his publicly recognized reputation) was rooted in a man's ability to engender through his seed and thus build a household (see Hoffner 1966, 327),[7] whereas female shame (a positive value expressing her concern for reputation, and the means by which her honor was expressed) reflected a woman's ancillary, receptive role in procreation (Delaney 1987). A man's honor was an expression of his autonomy and dominance within the gender hierarchy, whereas a woman's honor was an expression of her dependency—and thus, positive shame. Because a man's power to create life from his seed takes place outside of himself, within the womb of a woman, a man's honor was also dependent upon his ability to ensure that the child born was from his own seed. A woman's womb, like the soil of the earth, is indiscriminately

---

6. Honor and shame, and especially its relation to gender and sexuality, were originally recognized as social values characterizing the unity of the Mediterranean, and they been much explored in what has become known as the anthropology of the Mediterranean (see Campbell 1964; Peristiany 1966; Davis 1977; Pitt-Rivers 1977; Gilmore 1982, 1987; Peristiany and Pitt-Rivers 1992). Mediterraneanism in general, and honor and shame in particular, have received extensive critique both from within and outside anthropology. One primary critique is that insufficient attention has been given to cultural distinctiveness within the Mediterranean as well as shared cultural connections outside of the region (see Herzfeld 1980, 1984, 1987; Wikan 1984; Coombe 1990; cf. Horden and Purcell 2000, 483–523). Honor and shame have been used productively in biblical studies (see Malina 1993; Olyan 1996; Matthews and Benjamin 1996; cf. Crook 2009).

7. Male honor is also the result of power—more power equates to more honor, and thus the king has the most honor in society. As a powerful warlord, David was thus equal in honor to the wealthy Nabal, but Nabal rejected David's request for food as from someone dishonorable because David had fled from the court of Saul (1 Sam 25:2–13). A woman, in contrast, has power in her ability to disrupt or undermine her husband's honor. Abigail, Nabal's wife, exerts power over her husband, and thus shames him, when she disregards his decision and brings an abundant supply of food to David to compensate for her husband's foolish behavior (1 Sam 25:18–31). The wealthy, and presumably powerful, Nabal is conquered by his socially-shrewd wife rather than by David, the powerful warlord.

fecund; she will conceive and bear the child from any seed sown into her. Therefore, just as a farmer distinguishes his own field from the vast expanse of open land and guards it against outside intrusion, an honorable man would cover, guard, and protect his wife (and his daughters and sisters by extension) from the encroachment of others, thereby bringing order to her fecundity and safeguarding the legitimacy of his paternity (note how YHWH safeguards Abraham's paternity of Isaac when Abraham gives his wife Sarah to Abimelech for a wife; Gen 20:1–18). A woman, on the other hand, would display honor by recognizing her dependence on her husband. Because a woman shares in the honor of her husband, she yields to her husband's ordering of her sexuality; to do otherwise would be shameless (compare Sir 26:1–27). Yet, a woman may also cultivate her own reputation, through honorable deeds and actions, especially in her interactions with other women (see Prov 31:10–31; Wikan 1984).

As long as a man displayed honor by fathering children, ensuring the sexual purity of his wife and daughters, and protecting his reputation, his social behavior affirmed and contributed to his male gender identity. However, if a man was unable to maintain his honor against the encroachment of others, then he was dishonored and disgraced. His inadequate behavior and dishonored status would call into question his masculinity. Because male gender identity and male honor were rooted in the dominant male sexual role, the significant loss of honor entailed a gender reversal. By losing honor, a man also lost what it meant to be a man; male gender identity was fragile and was dependent on a man's dominance and autonomy. When an Israelite man submitted to another, superior man, as in patron–client relations, or in his submission to YHWH in covenant relationship, he would take on the female subordinate role. He would embody shame in relation to the honor of his patron, king, or God, and he would share their honor. The man's shame, though characteristic of the female gender, was a positive value and expressed his *willful* submission to others. It was a characteristic of his subordinate relationship, but he nevertheless remained a man in the full sense. A man who has been dishonored or *forcefully* made to submit to others, however, embodies the female gender in a different sense. His manhood has been challenged; the dishonored man has become like a woman whose body has been abused by others.[8] His dishonor is *imposed* on him, and he is no longer considered a *real* man. Comparable ethnographies suggest that shamed men are feminized. They are perceived by others as effeminate or emasculated; they have become like women. The gender identity of a woman is less fragile. In a male oriented society like ancient Israel, a woman who acts like a man, that is, performs tasks usually belonging to men, may be admired or praised, as the biblical examples of Deborah, Jael, and Judith attest.

---

8. Although both men and women may be subordinate to other men, their subordination differs in how their bodies are treated. A woman's subordination entails access to her body, whereas a man's subordination does not (see Lemos 2017, 78–80). When a man is disgraced or his submission is forced, however, his body becomes accessible like a woman's body—symbolically, if not physically.

Part I: Creation

She may take on a male gendered role, yet she remains fully a woman, because her body lacks what is constitutive of manhood.

The language of gender reversal is most frequent in reference to war, where the defeated are dishonored and thus viewed as women (see Chapman 2004). Real, honorable men are skilled in war with the bow or the sword (see 2 Sam 1:22). They are "mighty warriors" (*gibbor*). Psalm 127:3–5 juxtaposes a man's sexual potency (many sons) with his prowess as a warrior (a quiver full of arrows), in celebrating the man whom Yhwh has made honorable. When mighty warriors die tragically in battle, they are celebrated, honored by their people (2 Sam 1:19–27; Hoffner 1966, 329). Of course, a soldier may die dishonorably, in which case he becomes a woman. Although no texts refer to Israelites in this manner, from the Hittite world an oath taken by soldiers threatens them with gender reversal if the oath is violated:

> Whoever breaks these oaths and does evil to the king (and) the queen (and) the princes, let these oaths change him from a man into a woman! Let them change his troops into women and cover their heads with a length of cloth! Let them break the bows, arrows (and) clubs in their hands and [let them put] in their hands distaff and mirror! (Pritchard 1969, 354)

As women, the cursed Hittite warriors will exchange their masculine weapons for a distaff and mirror. Similarly, David cursed Joab for betraying him by killing Abner so that his house would not be without someone "holding the spindle" (2 Sam 3:29)—that is, the males of his house would be like women (Hoffner 1966, 332). When referring to the enemy, in contrast, the biblical scribes hope that they will become like women in battle and be ravaged like women in their defeat. Thus, Jeremiah 51:30 prophesies:

> The warriors of Babylon have ceased to engage in battle,
> > they dwell in their strongholds;
> Their strength has dried up,
> > they have become women!

The prophet Nahum (3:13) uses similar language against Nineveh and its warriors:

> Look at your troops: they are women in your midst.
> The gates of your land will be opened to your enemies,
> Fire will devour your bars.

Although there were no clear lines of demarcation between men's space and women's space—the gendered private–public dichotomy is not adequate—men were generally oriented toward the public sphere and women were oriented toward the domestic sphere. Most women's activities took place in and around the house, as well as in other spaces frequented by women, such as wells, public ovens, and shops. Her association with the house along with her public representation of her husband's honor, produced a homology between the female body and the house. Like the female body, the house is bounded space with an entrance that is vulnerable to the encroachment of outsiders. It is a social space that a man marks off as belonging uniquely to himself, similar to selecting a wife from many available women; the house is sacred to the man, set apart from common, ordinary space. As the arable land is a piece of nature on which the man will subsist, the house is the piece of society through which the man will create and sustain his family. The wife's body thus mediates the relation between nature and society and thereby determines her husband's honor as he builds his household.

This relationship between the body, nature, and society is articulated in the Deuteronomic ideology of war. Because the ideology proclaimed that Yhwh would fight for Israel against its enemies, the size of the Israelite army was unimportant. As a result, certain men were excused from battle: the man who had built a new house, but had not yet used it; the man who had planted a vineyard, but had not yet harvested its fruit; and the betrothed man who had not yet consummated his marriage (Deut 20:5–7). This legislation compares the relationship between a man and his wife with his relationship to his agricultural work and to his house, creating a homology between the three. In each of these three cases, the focus of the legislation is on the incomplete status of the man's labor: He has committed his honor through farming, building a house, and marrying a woman (including procreation), but has not yet realized his honor through the completion of these tasks—reaping his harvest, living in his house, and fathering children with his wife. The man's honor and thus his manhood remain in the balance. Because the man's need to realize his honor is paramount, he is freed from military service. If he were to die in battle, he would be deprived of this fundamental honor rooted in his household, despite whatever honor he may have gained in battle (cf. Washington 1998). Elsewhere, the Deuteronomic legislation builds on this ideology by stating that the newly married man was exempt from military or other public service for one year (Deut 24:5). The man was given a year's reprieve in order to demonstrate his honor by building a household, which would have included constructing a house, impregnating his wife, and living from the labor of his farming.

Because the house was perceived in relation to a woman's body, the boundary of the house was critical to the man's honor. Unwanted intruders into a man's house were analogous to those who would assault his wife; they threatened to dishonor the man of the house if not repelled. For this reason, a creditor who gave a loan to a man must wait outside of the man's house to receive his pledge. He could not enter the house to take the pledge for himself (Deut 24:10–11). Such an act would have deprived the debtor of honor, and would have been analogous to assaulting his wife.

This symbolic relationship between a man's house and his wife is further illustrated by the Deuteronomic legislation concerning a man who charged that his wife was not a virgin at marriage (Deut 22:13–21). According to the legislation, if no evidence of her virginity could be found—that is, the wife's parents were unwilling to support their daughter (Fryer-Kensky 1998, 93–95; cf. Matthews 1998, 108–12)—the husband's charge was deemed true. The woman should be stoned to death by the men of the town at the entrance of her father's house because she had committed a shameful act by prostituting herself in her father's house. For our purposes, what is significant to note in this legislation is twofold. First, the daughter's crime, that she had sexual intercourse prior to marriage, and so dishonored her father, was identified with her father's house, regardless of where the sexual relations actually took place. The sexual rights to the daughter belonged to the father to give as he saw fit; her sexuality, like a cultivatable field, was an economic resource of his household that was exchangeable through marriage. The sexual violation of his daughter, therefore, represented an unlawful invasion into the father's house. Second, the execution of the daughter, if she is found guilty, takes place at the location that symbolized her crime—the entrance to her father's house. The sexual violation of the man's daughter is represented as an assault through the entrance of his house. The participation of the men of the city in her execution further sanctioned and reinforced the sacred boundaries represented by the house and the women of the household.[9]

Scholars have long noted that cities in ancient Israel, especially Jerusalem and Samaria, are commonly presented in the Bible with feminine images (see, e.g., Schmitt 1991). The city is presented as a virgin daughter (Isa 37:22), a wife (Isa 62:5), a mother (Isa 66:8–13), a widow (Lam 1:1), and a whore (Ezek 16:15–22). As a personified woman, the city is a further extension of the replication of the female body on to the house. The city was the collective house of its citizens; it represented the body social. Like the family house, the city enclosed space exclusive to its populace; it was bound by a city wall with vulnerable entrances at its gates; and the integrity of the city was representative of the collective honor of its inhabitants.

The biblical texts provide scores of references to the Israelites' collective shame as a result of the people's defeat in battle by their enemies or their forced submission to their enemies. Although many of the references describe the Israelites' dishonor in terms of military defeat generally, without further elaborating on the defeat, a significant number of references connect their dishonor to the invasion and destruction of the people's city. Nehemiah's mission to Jerusalem, for example, begins when he receives news about the condition of those who had not been taken captive but had remained in the city: they were suffering great shame because the walls of the city were

---

9. The law focuses exclusively on the daughter whose virginity is in question and not the man who had sexual intercourse with her because his identify was perhaps unknown. But the law also highlights how men and women are treated differently. A man who has sex with a virgin will be required to pay the bridewealth and marry her, but is otherwise not harmed (Deut 22:28–29), whereas the daughter who loses her virginity is executed, if found out after marriage to another man. The difference between the two scenarios is that the daughter's actions—the initial sexual relationship and its concealment—have doubly dishonored her father for which there is no compensation since she is married to another man.

broken down and its gates had been burned (Neh 1:3). After Nehemiah was appointed governor of Yehud and inspected the city, he addressed the populace (Neh 2:17):

> You see the trouble we are in, that Jerusalem is in ruins and its gates have been burned with fire. Come, let us rebuild the wall of Jerusalem, so that we may no longer suffer disgrace.

Even though Yehud was a province of the Persian empire and not an independent kingdom, the ruin of Jerusalem without a wall and gates was shameful to the people. It was a symbol of their shame among all the nations of the empire.

The book of Joel laments the shame of the Judeans because Jerusalem is being invaded by a powerful locust army that cannot be stopped (Joel 2:9):

> Into the city they rush,
>> on the wall they run,
> on to the houses they ascend,
>> through the windows they enter like a thief.

But unlike in Nehemiah, Jerusalem in the context of Joel was not destroyed; its wall remained intact. The shame that the people experienced was not due to the destruction of the city but rather to the devastation of its hinterland (Joel 1:11–12):

> Stand ashamed, O tillers of the soil!
>> Wail, O vinedressers!
> Because of the wheat and barley,
>> for the harvest of the field has perished!
> The vine is dried up,
>> and the fig is withered;
> The pomegranate, even the date palm and apple tree,
>> all the trees of the field are dried up—
> for joy has been put to shame by the peoples.

The locust plague, which is the context of the book of Joel, has devastated the crops of the hinterland of Jerusalem, including their vines and fruit trees. Stripping the vegetation bare, the hinterland appears to have been ravaged by drought (or possibly preceded by drought; see Simkins 1991). As a result, the inhabitants of Jerusalem have been put to shame by the peoples (*bene adam*, in contrast to the *bene tsiyyon*) that surround them. Nevertheless, Joel offers hope that Yhwh will drive the locust army away and restore the land so that "my people will never be ashamed again" (Joel 2:26, 27). Just as the body of the farmer's wife mediated the relationship between his arable land and his house, the female body also mediates the relationship between a city and its hinterland.

Part I: Creation

Because of the extended homology between the city and a female body, an assault against the city was perceived like rape. It was an unwanted violation of the collective social body; it was a penetration into the dominion of others; it was a defilement of sacred boundaries. The inhabitants of the city would attempt to defend their collective honor by repelling the invasion, but the loss of the city in battle collectively shamed its populace in a way comparable to a man who was shamed by the rape of his wife. The people of a destroyed city were without honor; they were perceived as women, like the female city, that had been raped.

In the prophetic invectives against foreign cities, rape imagery for the destruction of the city is especially prominent, though the actual act of rape is only implied, never described. Nahum first challenged the honor of Nineveh by calling her a whore (Nah 3:4), but her defeat in battle will secure her shame. Her genitals will be exposed before others (Nah 3:5):

> I am against you, says Yhwh with his armies,
>   and I will lift your skirt over your face;
> And I will show the nations your nakedness,
>   and the kingdoms your shame.

Nineveh's populace will have no desire to defend their collective honor, because her troops would become like women; her gates would be wide open inviting the rape from her foes (Nah 3:13). Jeremiah heralded the coming destruction of Babylon with similar language, announcing an assault so violent that she would be unable again to bear children, and all who pass by her would be appalled at her wounds (Jer 50:11–16). During the assault, the warriors of the city would have no strength to repel it; they would become like women (Jer 51:30; cf. Jer 50:37). Second Isaiah (the anonymous prophet of Isaiah 40–55) also proclaimed the destruction of Babylon using similar shame and rape imagery. Babylon, identified as a "virgin daughter," will be forced to abandon her luxurious life (Isa 47:1–3):

> Come down and sit in the dirt, virgin daughter of Babylon!
>   Sit on the ground where there is no throne, daughter of Chaldea!
>   For you will no longer be called tender and dainty.
> Take a hand-mill and grind flour,
>   remove your veil, strip off your robe,
>   bare your leg, cross the rivers.
> Your nakedness will be exposed,
>   and your shame will be seen.
> I will take vengeance,
>   and I will encounter no one [to stop me].

Creation and the Body

Although the set up for the rape of Babylon is clear, the meaning of the final line is uncertain. It may mean that Yhwh will find no survivor from Babylon's destruction, or, as interpreted here, that Yhwh will not encounter any man to defend Babylon's honor.

The ancient Israelites' experience in subsistence agriculture shaped their understanding of their gendered bodies; their physical bodies were understood in relation to their extended, inorganic body—the natural world. The bounded male body produced seed and thus created outside of the body; the female body, which received seed like the arable land, created new life within her body. These physical differences of the gendered human body were replicated on to the social body—the amalgamation of physical bodies in relationship—shaping the ancient Israelite understanding of creation, their social values, ritual regulations with a cultic hierarchy, and their gendered perception of space. The physical human body, through its gendered labor, thus mediated the relationship between nature (the extended body) and society (the social body). This relationship between the physical, extended, and social body has its origin in household productive relations as written on the body of the husband and wife. He works the arable land, together they produce children, and he protects the sexual integrity of his wife. When replicated onto tributary relations, the role of the king becomes conspicuously absent; his body is ineffectual, unable to protect his people. Instead, the focus is on the body social, which suffers the rape of an enemy onslaught, bringing shame on the people of the city and a reconfiguration of productive relations.

Part II
ECOLOGY

5

Ecology and Religion

RELIGION AND THE ENVIRONMENTAL CRISIS

RELIGION HAS NEVER BEEN far from discussion of the current environmental crisis. Although it might be sufficient to discuss the crisis simply in terms of its economic, political, or social issues—for example, capitalist relations are driving ever-increasing fossil fuel consumption; political leaders in Washington D.C. lack the conviction or the courage to enact legislation that would significantly curb fossil fuel emissions; and the poor and the most marginalized members of our society, and globally, have contributed the least to the crisis but will suffer the most—religion adds, perhaps, a necessary, moral dimension to the crisis. It can frame environmental issues in terms of what some might call sin and evil, as well as justice and blessing. Indeed, many books on religion and the environment (including my own, see Simkins 1994) suggest that the religion of the Bible provides such a moral framework for addressing the environmental crisis. Religion, like all ideology, may influence how human labor mediates the relationship between society and the natural world. For the ancient Israelites, their religion—their beliefs, rituals, and practices regarding Yhwh—was embedded in their family, social, and political life and so, we can expect, had a prominent influence on how they engaged with the natural world. It is more complicated in contemporary, secular society, where religion is often privatized and relegated to individual matters. The value of the contribution of religion is questionable when the problem posed by the environmental crisis is structural and systemic. Nevertheless, the issue has more often been whether religion, especially Western Christianity, has contributed to the rise of the environmental crisis rather than possibly to its resolution.

The Bible and religion have played a contested role in contemporary discussion about the environment since the mid-1960s. In 1967, Lynn White Jr., in a brief yet seminal essay, "The Historic Roots of Our Ecologic Crisis," traced the origins of modern Western science and technology to the Medieval Christian worldview that was inspired by the biblical cosmology. In so doing, he transformed the environmental crisis into a religious problem, with Western Christianity and the Bible bearing a huge burden of guilt. According to White, the biblical religion, with its idea of linear history and perpetual progress, disenchanted the natural world. Nature was transformed from a subject to be revered into an object to be used. "By destroying pagan animism, Christianity made it possible to exploit nature in a mood of indifference to the feelings of natural objects" (1967, 1205). Drawing on a dominant Western Christian reading of Genesis 1, White claimed that humans were created in the image of God as the culmination of creation. Based on this reading, White observed that "no item in the physical creation had any purpose save to serve man's purposes" (1967, 1205). He argued that this anthropocentric reading of the biblical creation, in contrast to the alternative Greco-Roman mythology, placed humans at the center of creation, separated humans from nature, and "insisted that it is God's will that man exploit nature for his proper ends" (1967, 1205). For White, this reading of the biblical creation was part and parcel of a medieval Latin worldview that demythologized nature and gave rise to technological exploitations of the natural world and eventually to science. Nature had become a mere object that could be exploited with indifference. From this cosmology, Western Christianity emerged as "the most anthropocentric religion the world has seen" (1967, 1205). Because, as White argued, modern science and technology developed out of and shared the axioms of this Christian matrix, the environmental crisis cannot be addressed simply with more science and technology. Instead, the problem is with religion: "What people do about their ecology depends on what they think about themselves in relation to things around them. Human ecology is deeply conditioned by beliefs about our nature and destiny—that is, by religion" (1967, 1205).

White was not the first scholar to blame Western Christianity for creating the conditions for the environmental crisis (see Taylor 2016, 277–86), but White uniquely offered religion as also the solution. White's charge that Western Christianity and its worldview bears a burden of guilt for the environmental crisis has been embraced by many environmental activists, especially by those for whom religion served as a convenient culprit, but it has met with stiff criticism from other quarters. Biblical scholars have challenged White's reading of the Genesis creation stories (Trible 1971; Barr 1972; Anderson 1975; Hiers 1984; though cf. Harrison 1999), historians have questioned White's argument linking the rise of modern science with the Western Christian worldview (Sessions 1974; Whitney 1993), and other scholars have noted that Western Christian civilizations are not unique in their abuse and exploitation of the environment (Tuan 1970; Dubos 1972; Hughes 1975; cf. Glacken 1976). Nevertheless, White's thesis that religion is decisive in the human treatment of the environment largely has been accepted (Derr 1975), influencing existing academic fields, and has generated new fields of study (Minteer and Manning 2005; Jenkins 2009).

Building on the thesis of Lynn White, the interrelationship between religion and the environment seemed apparent and became the subject of much scholarly research, especially in the fields of religious studies and environmental studies, which share analogous investigative interests in patterns of thought and behavior. As noted by Jenkins and Chapple, these two academic fields "share research phenomena where human interaction with environmental systems is influenced by religious systems and where religious traditions or forms of experience themselves change in relation to changing environments" (2011, 442). Numerous studies have been conducted to understand how religious affiliation, participation, and beliefs may affect environmental concern and activism (see, e.g., Guth et al. 1995; Sherkat and Ellison 2007; Truelove and Joireman 2009; Djupe and Hunt 2009; Djupe and Gwiasda 2010; Taylor, Van Wieren, and Zaleha 2016; Berry 2013, 457–59; and the literature cited therein), and religion scholars, especially, have sought to reform and leverage religious traditions in addressing the environmental crisis (see the series edited by Tucker and Grim 1997–2004; Gottlieb 2010). The religious dimension of the environmental crisis has become the legacy of Lynn White.

In the field of religion and ecology, for example, the dominant voices of Mary Evelyn Tucker and John Grim (2017) build on Lynn White's idea that religious worldviews shape environmental behavior. Along with many colleagues, they examine the world's major religious traditions seeking to uncover traditional environmental knowledge, especially perspectives regarding human–nature relationships. They evaluate the teachings of the religious traditions with regard to their relevance for the environmental crisis, focusing on attitudes, practices, and orientations toward the world. Finally, they seek to reconstruct the religious traditions by suggesting ways that the traditions can adapt to the new circumstances posed by the environmental crisis. As with White's critique, Tucker and Grim are critical of the anthropocentric orientation of many of the world's religious traditions, especially the Western religions, and of their dualism that separates humans from nature. Nevertheless, they believe that traditional environmental knowledge—how premodern humans understood themselves to be embedded within the natural world—is symbolically encoded within the religious traditions and can be retrieved. They thus seek to identify the religious ecologies and cosmologies through which religion functioned in the past in relation to the natural world and can do so again today. For Tucker and Grim, the scholarly task of religion and ecology is to retrieve, evaluate, and adapt sustainable religious worldviews that can contribute to the ethical changes needed for the environmental crisis. Although they recognize issues of consumption, economic growth, and population, Tucker and Grim focus on religious worldviews because they understand that the environmental crisis represents a religious crisis, and so, like White, they seek a religious solution.

The academic field of Bible and ecology, though less prominent in the academy, similarly emphasizes the interface between religion and religious worldviews and the environment, building on the work of Lynn White. Biblical scholars were some of the first critics of White's thesis, not for connecting religion to the environmental crisis, but rather for his blame of the biblical cosmology in Genesis. More recently, however, a group of biblical scholars and theologians associated with the Earth Bible Project have been "willing to accept White's challenge and entertain the suspicion that the Bible, too, may have contributed to the current crisis" (Habel 2000, 30). For these scholars, the problem is not with the Bible per se, though they are not willing to acquit the Bible of all blame, but rather with the way that the Bible has been and continues to be read. Recognizing that the Bible has been read from a dualistic, anthropocentric perspective, they offer a new hermeneutic, rooted in ecojustice principles, that gives attention to Earth and the Earth community. Earth is treated as a subject; it has a voice in the biblical text. And the task of the reader "is to take up the cause of Earth and the non-human members of the Earth community by sensing their presence in the text—whether their presence is suppressed, oppressed or celebrated" (Habel 2000, 35). In the end, the Earth Bible scholars approach the biblical tradition in much the same way that Tucker and Grim treat diverse religious traditions: through retrieval, evaluation, and adapting the text to the new environmental context. They believe that biblical tradition can transform our understanding of the human–nature relationship if the text is read in the right way.

There are, of course, many diverse voices in the fields of religion and ecology and Bible and ecology. Nevertheless, many scholars within these fields continue to work within the idealist framework set out by White: that the environmental crisis is rooted in an anthropocentric, dualistic religious cosmology and thus needs a religious solution. Ironically, White never *argued* this thesis in his essay. His argument begins in seventh-century northern Europe with the introduction of a new plow. The earlier plows in the Near East and the Mediterranean simply scratched the surface, which was sufficient for their light, dry soils. But in northern Europe, with heavy, sticky soils, an entirely new kind of plow was needed, one "equipped with a vertical knife to cut the line of the furrow, a horizontal share to slice the sod, and a moldboard to turn it over" (1967, 1205). This new kind of plow, which required as many as eight oxen to pull, transformed agriculture. It could no longer be subsistence farming based on the needs of the family because no family could own eight oxen. Instead, farming became cooperative and was limited only by the new capacity to till the earth. "Man's relation to the soil was profoundly changed. Formerly man had been part of nature; now he was the exploiter of nature" (1967, 1205). White notes that this conception is reflected in illustrated calendars. In older calendars, the months of the year were represented by passive personifications, but in the newer Frankish calendars, men are exploiting the natural world by plowing, harvesting, chopping trees, and butchering pigs.

White's argument is coherent up to this point. Then he makes an idealist turn, connecting the "novelties" of the plow and calendar with "larger intellectual patterns" (1967, 1205), namely, the anthropocentric and dualist Western Christian worldview. His argument simply *assumes* that the Western Christian worldview, with its new understanding of the relationship between humans and nature, laid the foundation for the development of modern science and technology and the exploitation of the natural world. Putting aside White's many historical claims, his argument assumes a causal relationship between a religious worldview and historical change with no evidence or justification. Moreover, he treats the religious worldview in isolation from economic, social, political, and other factors (see Whitney 1993). White's argument could have just as reasonably taken a historical-materialist turn, explaining how Medieval technological developments shaped and reinforced a particular theological strand within Christianity (see Santmire 1985). In other words, the Christian anthropocentrism that White identifies may have been a product of the Medieval economy rather than its foundation.

Recently, religion scholars have begun to question White's religious cosmology thesis—that what we think about the human–nature relationship really does matter, that religion is a sufficient agent of social change (see Taylor 2004; 2016, 296–97; Jenkins 2009; 2013).[1] Although the correlation between religious beliefs and environmental concern has been well documented, with mixed results, the material impact of religion on the environment, both positively and negatively, remains an open question (Taylor, Van Wieren, and Zaleha 2016). Many material factors contribute to human interaction with the environment, including economic, social, and technological factors, so that benevolent environmental behavior and actions are not simply a matter of thinking and believing appropriately. Religious values may be frustrated by other concerns, and material issues may prevent the realization of such values. There is often a disjunction between belief and practice. White's focus on religion as both the cause and solution to the environmental crisis has encouraged religious and biblical studies scholars to focus primarily on religious worldviews, with insufficient attention to how economic, social, and political systems help create and reinforce such worldviews and provide the means for implementing the values generated by those worldviews (Whitney 1993, 169). Religion remains, nevertheless, an important component in environmental discussions. It offers a language of moral seriousness within a value-oriented context that is helpful in shaping institutional and individual behavior, and it provides models for humane and compassionate engagement that are useful for environmental activism (Gottlieb 2007).

For Christianity, in particular, the Bible may play a significant role in its relationship to the environment. As a sacred and authoritative scripture, the Bible is a foundational source of Christian theology and provides ethical guidance within the context of the biblical worldview. The Bible's contribution to environmental discussions today, however, is complex and mixed at best (see Horrell 2010). On the one

---

1. Wendell Berry interestingly reverses the argument made by White. Rather than the Bible being the ideological and religious justification for environmental abuse, he argues that neglect and abuse of the environment leads to a misuse of the Bible: "The misuse of the Bible thus logically accompanies the abuse of Nature: if you are going to destroy creatures without respect, you will want to reduce them to 'materiality'; you will want to deny that there is a spirit or truth in them, just as you will want to believe that only holy or ensouled creatures are human or only Christian humans" (1993, 156).

hand, the biblical writers' experience of the natural world was so very different from much of the contemporary experience. Whereas the vast majority of Israelites lived in small agrarian villages eking out their existence in a subsistence economy, the modern, especially western, population is largely urban, technologically oriented, globally connected, and dependent on a surplus economy. As a result, the biblical values toward the natural world do not easily translate into contemporary environmental ethics.[2] On the other hand, the Bible's agrarian worldview offers a critique of and provides an alternative to the contemporary anthropocentric, materialistic, industrial worldview that has so often been destructive of the environment. Religion and the Bible may contribute to discussion of the current environmental crisis, but only when religion and the Bible are placed within their larger political-economic context.

THE BIBLE AND ANTHROPOCENTRISM

White's characterization of Western Christianity as the "most anthropocentric religion" is a ready-made weapon to discount what Christianity and the Bible might bring to environmental discussions. Indeed, it is difficult to image how a primary concern about and for *humans* can adequately express concern for the *non-human world*; anthropocentrism has resulted in human abuse of nature, not human concern for nature. Or so the argument goes, but this is largely assumed rather than demonstrated. The recognition that humans are different, to some degree, from every other creature even though we are fully embedded in nature—only humans can engage in a conversation about values, for example—may suggest a form of anthropocentrism, but does not preclude that humans should act responsibly in relation to the rest of the natural world. Indeed, this form of anthropocentrism seems to be inherent in the Christian tradition.

In two messages celebrating the World Day of Peace (2008, 2010) and in the encyclical *Caritas in Veritate* (2009), Pope Benedict XVI brought environmental issues to the forefront of the Roman Catholic Church's teaching, and he did so in a way that may be called thoroughly anthropocentric. Drawing on the same biblical tradition that White highlights, Genesis 1 and 2, and the affirmation of humans in Psalm 8, Benedict emphasized that humans are created in the "image of God," that the natural world is given to humankind by God, and that nature is subject to human use: "Nature is at our disposal not as 'a heap of scattered refuse,' but as a gift of the Creator who has given it an inbuilt order, enabling man to draw from it the principles needed in order 'to till it

---

2. In 2009, the *Journal for the Study of Religion, Nature and Culture* hosted a forum discussing and critiquing an essay by James A. Nash, where he argues against using the Bible as a moral authority in environmental debates. For Nash, the Bible is simply too historically and culturally bound to its ancient context and concerns to function as an adequate moral authority today, though he does argue that the Bible should be included in the dialogue. Nash's essay is followed by both appreciative and critical responses from Robb; Northcott; Childs; Davis; Faramelli; Deane-Drummond; Zaleha; and McDaniel.

and keep it' (Gen 2:15)" (2009, §48). Benedict tempers this anthropocentrism by underscoring human responsibilities toward the environment and that the environment belongs to all humans and to future generations, which would seemingly mitigate White's critique of the anthropocentrism of Western Christianity. But White's critique is aimed, not at this or that particular value that may characterize anthropocentrism, but at anthropocentrism's fundamental separation of humans from nature. Indeed, it is this separation that Benedict seems to be intent on upholding: "If the Church's magisterium expresses grave misgivings about notions of the environment inspired by ecocentrism and biocentrism, it is because such notions eliminate the difference of identity and worth between the human person and other living things ... such notions end up abolishing the distinctiveness and superior role of human beings" (2010, §13). Nature "is prior to us, and it has been given to us by God as the setting for our life" (2009, §48), and thus would seem to be separate from humans.

Francis's recent encyclical, *Laudato Si'* (2015), would also seem to support a form of anthropocentrism in his explicit rejection of biocentrism, for he is also concerned not to diminish the uniqueness of humans, and especially the unique responsibility humans share for environmental care. He, and Benedict before him, want to uphold that human beings have "unique capacities of knowledge, will, freedom and responsibility ..." (2015, §118). Francis links all humans, including those "excluded" (e.g., the poor and future generations), with all non-human creatures and the earth itself in solidarity, and thus, unlike Benedict, "moves toward a declaration of intrinsic value of all life. He stresses the importance of ecosystems, but he also proclaims that each organism is a 'creature of God' and therefore 'good and admirable in itself'" (Sideris 2018, 28, citing Francis 2015, §140). Although Francis recognizes the distinctiveness of humans, he does not assume a separation of humans from nature but sees all as part of God's creation: "Nature cannot be regarded as something separate from ourselves or as a mere setting in which we live. We are part of nature, included in it and thus in constant interaction with it" (2015, §139). Francis explicitly distances himself from anthropocentrism, which he modifies with adjectives such as "tyrannical," "excessive," "distorted," "misguided," and "modern," suggesting, perhaps, that it is not anthropocentrism per se that is problematic but what it has become in the current world.

Whereas Benedict's anthropocentrism, supposedly rooted in the biblical tradition, would appear to confirm White's critique of Western Christianity, Francis's understanding of the human–nature relationship, which shares the same tradition, cannot be called anthropocentric in White's sense, though his emphasis on the distinctiveness of humans remains anthropocentric for some (see Deane-Drummond 2016, 260). Many other Christian thinkers, who also are steeped in the biblical tradition, reject anthropocentrism outright and do so in accord with the biblical tradition (see, e.g., Rolston 1996; Berry 1993).[3] Indeed, St. Francis' own biocentrism (Mizzoni

---

3. Neither Holmes Rolston nor Wendell Berry denies that the Bible expresses anthropocentric concerns, but such concerns do not translate into the thoroughly anthropocentric worldview that

2008), which White held up as a remedy to Western Christianity's anthropocentrism, emerged from his own understanding of the biblical tradition, which does not separate humans from nature (Ruether 2011). Whether or not a particular expression of Christianity is anthropocentric is more dependent on the culture and values of its adherents than on the Bible itself (cf. Kopnina 2012). In fact, both Benedict's reading of the biblical creation and the dominant Western Christian understanding of that tradition, of which White is critical, exemplify a post-Cartesian reading of the Bible with the assumption that humankind is separate and distinct from the natural world (see Hoffman and Sandelands 2005, 149–55). Such anthropocentric readings of the Bible are imposed upon the text, reflecting cultural assumptions, rather than the result of understanding the text in its own social-historical context. Strands of Western Christianity may indeed be as anthropocentric as White claims, but only because contemporary Western culture, the offspring of the Enlightenment, is so anthropocentric.

The meaning and breadth of anthropocentrism has been contested (Hargrove 1992; Midgley 1994; Spitler 1982; Grey 1998; Norton 1984; Kopnina et al. 2018); there are stronger and weaker versions. Clive Hamilton (2017) argues that we need to distinguish between anthropocentrism as a scientific fact—that humans are the dominant creature and distinctive from all others—and anthropocentrism as a normative claim—that humans should dominate the world. From the context of the Anthropocene, in which humans have become a geological agent (see chapter 7), Hamilton argues that we need to be anthropocentric in the former sense if we are going to take responsibility for our degradation of the natural world and act to reverse it. In other words, like Francis, Hamilton emphasizes the distinctive qualities of humans without the self-centered baggage that often accompanies notions of anthropocentrism.

In environmental discussions, anthropocentrism is generally defined to mean that "human beings, and human beings only, are of intrinsic value (that is, valuable in and of themselves) and that non-human nature is valuable only insofar as it is valuable for human purposes (that is, valuable instrumentally—extrinsically—for its ability to serve human ends)" (Keller 2010, 4). According to this understanding, the biblical worldview is simply not anthropocentric. Although the Bible gives a great deal of attention to humans—it is indeed a text for and about humans—and so expresses human or anthropocentric concerns, humans are everywhere in the Bible embedded in the larger context of the creation and especially in their relationship to God. If humans have intrinsic value in the biblical tradition, then so does the rest of the natural world because humans and the rest of the natural world are valuable as part of God's creation—an ecocentric worldview, if you will. But the creation itself has value

---

environmental activists often denounce. Instead, they recognize that such anthropocentric concerns are set within a larger worldview, in which humans are but one of God's many creatures and concerns. As Rolston nicely summarizes this stance: "So biblical writers put humans in their place; there is a people-to-people ethic of concern for any viable human ecology, and this takes place in a sphere swarming with creatures that are also of concern. Depending on the focus, this ethic is anthropocentric, or biocentric, or theocentric, but it is environmental at every scale" (1996, 26).

only in as much as it is the creation *of God*, who remains in relationship with it. God imputes the creation—humans, animals, the land—with value, and God the creator is the measure of all that is good and right in the world. The biblical worldview is first and foremost *theocentric*.[4]

THE CASE AGAINST ANTHROPOCENTRISM IN THE BIBLICAL TRADITION

The hallmark texts for expressing anthropocentrism in the biblical tradition, cited by both Benedict and Lynn White, and by others, are Genesis 1 and Psalm 8. In Genesis 1, for example, God creates the human couple on the sixth and final day of creation, creating them in the image of God, and blessing them with the command, "Be fruitful and multiply, and fill the earth and subdue it; and have dominion over the fish of the sea and over the birds of the air and over every living thing that moves upon the earth" (Gen 1:28). On the surface, this text might seem to place humans at the pinnacle of creation with all of nature given to them for their use. But on closer examination and in the context of the biblical tradition as a whole, being in the image of God has its limits. The human couple may come together in sexual intercourse, for example, but only God opens the womb so that a woman may bear a child. The man may subdue the earth through tilling and sowing, but only God brings the rain that softens the soil and causes the seed to germinate. Humans are blessed with dominion over living creatures, but they are not free to eat them—at least not yet in the Genesis narrative. When God does finally permit humans to eat living creatures, God places restrictions on how they should be killed (i.e., the creatures should be drained of blood; Gen 9:3–4) and which animals can be eaten (i.e., no unclean creature should be eaten; Lev 11). Human dominion only extends to the animal world; it does not encompass the climate, water resources, or natural processes (see Kay 1989, 222). Moreover, as the rest of the biblical tradition makes clear, the exercise of human dominion over the animal world is unrealized; wild animals remain outside the scope of human rule. As mentioned in our discussion of the Yahwist creation myth, God's covenant relationship with humans mediates the efficacy of their labor in the natural world. Human dominion in the image of God remains subject to God.

---

4. Although Bron Taylor criticizes Christianity as being inherently anthropocentric, the religion expressed in the biblical tradition, when taking its premodern, pre-scientific context into account, would correspond to his definition of "dark green religion." According to the biblical religion, all creation is sacred (though not divine; see Berry 1993, who emphasizes its holiness), and all creatures have intrinsic value, which is imputed by God. Using Taylor's own criteria, the biblical value system is "(1) based on a felt kinship with the rest of life . . . ; (2) accompanied by feelings of humility and a corresponding critique of human moral superiority . . . ; and (3) reinforced by metaphysics of interconnection and the idea of interdependence . . ." (2010, 13). These characteristics of "dark green religion" are evident, for example, in Psalm 104 and will be addressed in the argument below.

Part II: Ecology

Despite these limitations to being in the image of God, the Priestly scribes who composed Genesis 1 nevertheless affirmed the distinctive status of humankind. Humans alone in God's creation are singled out as being in the image of God, and humans alone are given dominion. Psalm 8:3–8 similarly highlights this distinctive status of humans:

> When I look at your heavens, the work of your fingers,
>> the moon and the stars that you have established;
> what are human beings that you remember them,
>> mortals that pay attention to them?
> Yet you have made them a little lower than God,
>> and crowned them with glory and honor.
> You have given them dominion over the works of your hands;
>> you have put all things under their feet,
> all sheep and oxen,
>> and also the beasts of the field,
> the birds of the air, and the fish of the sea,
>> whatever passes along the paths of the seas.

It is difficult to imagine a more anthropocentric claim! But the glory and honor of humans extolled in this psalm is at odds with so much of the representation of humans in the biblical tradition and with human experience generally. When have humans on this planet ever lived up to or realized such a lofty status? In the Genesis stories following the creation of humans, for example, human violence so corrupts the world that God destroys it with a flood and begins anew. In order to curb humankind's violent tendencies, God's blessing to Noah and his sons includes both concessions and limitations. Humans should again procreate and fill the earth (Gen 9:1), but absent is any reference to subduing the earth and having dominion over all living creatures. Instead, a fear and dread of humans will characterize the animal world. Their fear and dread are justified, for humans are given permission to kill and eat other living creatures. Their flesh may be eaten but not their blood, for their blood belongs to God (Gen 9:2–5). As a concession to the human propensity towards violence, God gives humans animal flesh for food, but as a reminder that God is the creator of all life—both humans and animals—God prohibits consumption of their blood and shedding of human blood.

The very context of Psalm 8 also challenges its claim of a lofty human status. Psalms 7–10 as a whole plead for God's justice and deliverance in the midst of human violence and oppression:

> O let the evil of the wicked come to an end . . .
> See how [the unrepentant] conceives trouble,

> becomes pregnant with mischief,
>> and gives birth to deception.
> He digs a well, and it puts him to shame,
>> and falls into the pit he has made.
> His trouble returns upon on his own head,
>> and on his own head his violence descends. (Ps 7:9, 14–16)

> Rise up, O Yhwh! Do not let humans prevail;
>> let the nations be judged before you.
> Appoint terror for them, O Yhwh;
>> let the nations know that they are only human. (Ps 9:19–20)

> In arrogance the wicked pursue the poor;
>> let them be caught in the schemes they have devised.
> For the wicked boast of the desires of their heart,
>> those greedy for gain curse and spurn Yhwh.
> In arrogance, the wicked say, "God will not seek it out";
>> all their thoughts are, "There is no God." (Ps 10:2–4)

So much for human glory and honor! The context of Psalm 8 exposes the false hope of anthropocentrism with the reality of human experience. Human dominion over creation has become a self-serving dominion of some humans over others. In its larger context, Psalm 8 is not a triumphal hymn, celebrating human ascendancy to near-God status. Rather, it is a hymn expressing the psalmist's amazement that, given the ignoble human condition, God has blessed humankind with such a distinctive status. The reality of the human condition, however, makes clear that the divinely-given status of humans is not yet realized. James Luther Mays is undoubtedly correct when he argues that the psalm expresses what might be called "an eschatological tension": Humans presently exist "between creation and realization, living an unfulfilled destiny in a flawed and perverted way" (2006, 34). Dominion is a hope, not a reality.

Finally, it is important to note that God's command to humankind to be fruitful and multiply, to subdue the earth, and to have dominion over all living creatures is placed in the context of blessing—"Then God blessed them . . ." (Gen 1:28)—and therefore remains dependent on God's own activity (see Kay 1989, 220). As blessing, subduing and having dominion are not inherent characteristics of humankind, nor a divine right given to humans. They are rather the expression of God's creative activity through the work of humans (just as procreation may be viewed, rightly so, as humans creating like God). Being in the image of God marks the distinctive status of humankind, but subduing and having dominion are only possible as God chooses to make it so. By blessing the humans, God *actualizes* human labor, which may be expressed in subduing the earth and having dominion over animals. Elsewhere in the biblical tradition, such blessing is linked to Israel's obedience to God's covenant (see Westermann 1978, 48). When Israel is faithful to the covenant, then God will ensure the prosperity of Israel through increasing the fruit of its womb, the fruit of its livestock, and the fruit of its arable land (Deut 28:11). However, when Israel is unfaithful to the covenant, its subduing and dominion will be ineffectual: its land will not yield food and its wombs and livestock will miscarry; the Israelites will die in the land due to disease, pestilence, and other afflictions, and the birds and animals will consume their corpses (Deut 28:15–68). God's blessing is made conditional upon Israel's actions, but even so, it is not Israel that produces the blessing. Blessing is wholly the activity of God; it is a means by which Yhwh mediates human labor. As the Deuteronomist reminds the Israelites:

> Do not say to yourself, "My power and the might of my own hands have created for me this wealth." But remember Yhwh your God, for he is the one who gives you to power to create wealth, so that he may confirm his covenant, which he swore to your ancestors, as he is doing today. (Deut 8:17–18)

Although Genesis 1 and Psalm 8 highlight the distinctive status of humankind in the creation, they do not do so from an anthropocentric worldview. The limits and failures of human dominion should dethrone any such notion. Instead, in the biblical tradition all creation, humankind included, is dependent upon God the creator. There is no conception of "nature" in the biblical world—either as the physical world distinct from humans, or as a causal and regulating physical force—only creation, which is "the earth and what fills it, the world and what lives in it" (Ps 24:1), and this was created by God, belongs to God, and is sustained by God. The biblical tradition expresses a theocentric worldview. Humans are part and parcel of creation, and have a distinctive status and role within creation. But humans are neither the measure of creation nor the purpose of creation.

THE PLACE OF HUMANS IN A THEOCENTRIC CONTEXT

Although the biblical tradition as a whole stems from the theocentric worldview of the biblical scribes, three biblical texts in particular offer alternative understandings of the status and role of humans within the creation: the Yahwist creation myth in Genesis 2–3, Psalm 104, and Job 38–42. Each of these texts challenges the prominent status ascribed to humans in Genesis 1 and Psalm 8 and highlights the relationship of humankind to the rest of the creation.

The Yahwist Creation Myth in Genesis 2–3

The Yahwist Creation myth in Genesis 2–3 predates the Priestly creation myth in Genesis 1, and is perhaps also the occasion for the Priestly scribes own formulation of humans being created in the image of God. For whereas the Priestly scribes boldly proclaim that humans are created to be distinctly different from all other living creatures, the Yahwist tradition admits to a much more ambiguous situation. Humans in the Yahwist myth are also like Yhwh and distinct from other creatures, but only because of their rebellion against Yhwh.[5]

In Genesis 2, the human creature is created out of the arable land to work the very land from which he was created. In all that happens subsequently in the myth, this fundamental bond between humankind and the land is never altered: Humans belong to the earth and return to it in their death. Human purpose in this world is also defined by this bond. Humans are created to bring life to the land through agriculture. Genesis 2:5 suggests that the earth is dependent upon humans for their labor, but it is also careful to note that agriculture is a collaborative effort: Humans will till and work the soil, and Yhwh will supply the rain. The Priestly command to "subdue the earth" says no more than this, though its formulation suppresses humankind's dependence on Yhwh's contribution to the work in favor of emphasizing God's blessing.

In the Yahwist myth, all animal life is created out of the arable land to help the man in his labor. And although no creature is a fitting partner for the man (literally, "corresponds to" the man), all creatures share the same substance and origin as that of the man. Humans and animals form a community of earth creatures (Hiebert 1996, 63), though the Yahwist never explores the benefits or ramifications of this community. Instead, attention is given to the disruption of this community through the human couple's eating of the fruit of knowledge. By eating the fruit, which had been forbidden by Yhwh, the humans become "like God knowing good and evil" (Gen 3:5). This new status differentiates humans from the rest of the earth creatures. Their relationship will no longer be characterized by "help" (cf. Hiebert 1996, 60), but rather by "enmity." Speaking to the serpent, Yhwh initiates this new relationship as a curse:

> I will put enmity between you and the woman,
>> and between your offspring and hers;
>
> he will strike your head,
>> and you will strike his heel. (Gen 3:15)

The serpent, which played a pivotal role in the human couple's rebellion, is representative of all domestic (*behemah*) and wild animals (*hayyat hassadeh*), and so just as the serpent is cursed, all animals are cursed. Humans and animals no longer belong

---

5. In chapter 1, I interpreted the Yahwist creation myth by focusing on the gendered roles of the man and his wife. Here, in contrast, I interpret the man and his wife together as humans and as a human couple, and focus instead on their shared relationship to Yhwh and the rest of creation.

to the same community; humans will exploit and subject animals to their own will, and slaughter those animals that pose a threat to the human community. The Priestly tradition also affirms this distinction between humans and animals with its emphasis on human dominion before the flood and the divine concession to eat animals after the flood. What is absent in the Priestly tradition is any hint that animals may do harm to humans.

Human rebellion to be like God has disrupted the state of creation (which is the basic meaning of "curse"). Not only does their new knowledge alter their relationship to animals, it also sows differentiation and dependency within the human community. Although their knowledge makes human community possible (through procreation), men and women will engage in distinct social roles, filled with toil, with one gender dominating the other. Moreover, the collaboration between Yhwh and humans is suspended: the arable land is cursed as Yhwh withholds the rain from the land. Human labor will yield only thorns and thistles, not the abundant agriculture for which humans were created (Gen 3:16–19).

The Yahwist creation myth wrestles with the ambiguities inherent in the status of humans in the world. Humans are mortal, fleshy creatures like all animals, yet humans are also like God with knowledge and creativity. Humans can produce new life like God and build magnificent creations, yet forces beyond their control may frustrate their labor. Humans may come together for community, yet they dominate, oppress, and even kill one another. The place of humans in this world is at once exalted and humble, and at the core of this ambiguity, for the Yahwist, is the act of human rebellion against Yhwh. The first humans simply decided to pursue their own desires rather than yield to Yhwh's prohibition. Eating the forbidden fruit did not corrupt humankind, nor did the human couple achieve a higher status with no effect from their disobedience. For the Yahwist, the status of humans in this world cannot be separated from the means by which they achieved their status. It is the nature of humans to be like God, yet also to rebel against Yhwh. Or as Yhwh in the Yahwist tradition points out after the flood, "the inclination of the human heart is evil from youth" (Gen 8:21).

The curses on the animals and on the arable land are the corollary of humankind's ambiguous status. The curse on the arable land appears to be Yhwh's first attempt at curbing the "evil inclination," but it is not successful. Human rebellion continues. Thus Yhwh revokes the curse on the arable land following the flood, as Yhwh promises to uphold the seasonal cycle that is characteristic of the eastern Mediterranean (Gen 8:20–22). Yhwh will address the "evil inclination" by other means.

The curse on the animals, however, is not alleviated, nor does the Yahwist tradition address it further, for the curse on the animals reflected the common Near Eastern understanding of the violent relationship between humans and especially wild animals. The Near Eastern conception of creation is limited, dynamic, and corresponds to the activity of the gods. In the Yahwist's myth, for example, the domain of creation is discernible in Yhwh's forming living creatures from the soil, the building of the woman, the human-divine collaboration in agriculture, and in Yhwh's planting and the man's tending of the garden. The dry, barren desert that existed prior to Yhwh's activity and that continues to characterize much of the landscape around Israel and in the Near East remains outside the bounds of creation (and thus Israel must be sustained by God when in the desert; see Feldt 2012). Although Yhwh created the animals and thus they are an expression of Yhwh's creative activity, the curse on the animals separates them from the creation. Domestic animals become part of the human community and so are incorporated into creation, but wild animals remain with the desert outside of creation and a threat to the human community. As such, the covenant and prophetic traditions treat wild animals as agents of God's judgment, and the violence and enmity that is characteristic of wild animals is comparable to that of enemy armies and hostile invaders (see Deut 28:26; Jer 15:3; Ezek 5:17; Isa 18:6; 34:11, 13–15; Hos 2:12). The roaming of wild animals in inhabited towns and sown fields signals the ruination of creation.

The threat of wild animals and the undoing of creation were real to the Israelites. Thus, God's blessing in the covenant formulation promises security from the wild animals in addition to seasonal rain and agricultural bounty:

> I will grant peace in the land, and you will lie down, and no one will terrify you; I will remove evil beasts from the land, and no sword will pass through your land. (Lev 26:6; see Ezek 34:25)

Within the current creation, peace between humans and animals is secured through covenant. The prophet Isaiah, in contrast, appears to envision a transformation of the creation when the hostility between humans and animals will be reconciled, when the curse on the animals will be annulled. In conjunction with a coming king who will reign in justice and righteousness, Isaiah proclaims, the creation will be transformed so that even the human and animal worlds will live in peace:

> A wolf will reside with a lamb,
>> a leopard will lie down with a kid,
> a calf and a lion and a fatling together,
>> and a little child will lead them.
> A cow and a bear will graze,
>> together, their young will lie down;
> and a lion will eat straw like an ox.
> A suckling child will play over the hole of a cobra,
>> and a weaned child will stretch his hand over a viper's den.
> They will neither hurt nor destroy
>> on my holy mountain;
> for the earth will be full of the knowledge of Yhwh
>> as the waters cover the sea. (Isa 11:6–9)

There will be peace between the domestic animals, representative of the human community, and wild animals; and in a wave to the Yahwist tradition, the offspring of the woman and the serpent will play together with no harm. But this will happen only when God makes it so—it is an eschatological vision of a new creation. Humans are unable to either restore or transform the creation; this is the work of God alone.

The Yahwist tradition attests to human dependence on Yhwh. Humans are not masters of their own history. They are dependent on Yhwh for the productivity of their labor, but they have rebelled against Yhwh, resulting in consequences beyond their control. The Yahwist creation myth does not have an anthropocentric view of the world, nor do the other cited texts. Humans might be distinct within creation, and through their actions may disrupt the creation, but they are nevertheless subject to Yhwh and dependent upon Yhwh for the restoration of creation. The worldview of the Yahwist creation myth is theocentric.

Psalm 104

In contrast to the Yahwist creation myth, and most of the biblical tradition (not to mention Near Eastern traditions generally), Psalm 104 and the speech of God in Job 38–42 do not present wild animals as hostile forces, inimical to creation. Indeed, these two texts, which share many similarities on this matter, give little attention to the role of humans in the world and instead focus on God's attention to and relationship with the wild creatures of this world.

Psalm 104 is not a creation account, detailing God's creation of the world, but rather a panoramic hymn praising God for continually sustaining the creation. Nevertheless, the hymn has explicit similarities with the Priestly creation myth in Genesis 1. Both traditions present the creation in a similar order, beginning first with light, then water and sky, land and vegetation, sun and moon. The reference to animals, humans, and sea creatures in the psalm deviates from the order that is found in Genesis 1, but like Genesis 1, focus is given to each in the psalm. The psalm and Genesis 1 also share much common vocabulary, which stands out in contrast to the vocabulary of other creation texts. Finally, only Genesis 1, with its general reference to the sea monsters (Hebrew *tanninim*), and Psalm 104, with its specific reference to Leviathan, present the beast(s) as one of God's creatures. Elsewhere, Leviathan, or the *tanninim*, represents a primordial sea dragon that God must defeat in battle to secure the order of creation (see, for example, Ps 74:13–14). In his speech to Job, God's defeat of the ferocious Leviathan is the object of his great boast before Job, but in Psalm 104, Leviathan is simply a creature that God formed to sport in the sea (Ps 104:26). The similarities between Psalm 104 and Genesis 1 have resulted in debate among scholars over which text is dependent on the other, with many scholars aligning themselves on either side of the issue (compare Levinson 1988, 54–65 and Berlin 2005 for two different interpretations of the relationship between these texts). The similarities between the two texts are real, but they do not demand literary dependence. Psalm 104 and Genesis 1 may simply be "relatively independent expressions of the same part of Israelite theology" (Craigie 1974, 18). In any case, it would be imprudent to base the interpretation of Psalm 104 on a conjectured literary relationship with Genesis 1.

Although the similarities between Psalm 104 and Genesis 1 are noteworthy, the differences between the texts are more significant for understanding the psalm. What looms large in Genesis 1 with its articulation of the status and role of humans is virtually absent in Psalm 104. The panoramic praise of the psalm is sung from a human perspective, and the animals described in each part of the psalm are referenced in relation to humans, but humans are not singled out as special or distinctive in the creation (except in terms of their wickedness; see below). Humankind is not presented in the image of God, nor do humans have dominion over all other living creatures. Instead, all creatures, including humans, are dependent upon God for their food and subsistence.

Significantly, all the creatures referenced in the psalm, with the possible exception of the "cattle" (*behemah*) in verse 14, are wild animals.[6] All of these creatures, including the "cattle" and especially Leviathan, live and carry out their tasks independently of humankind and human dominion. No creature serves humankind, not even the "cattle" (see Harrelson 1975, 20). Moreover, all of the animals are engaged in activities that resemble human tasks: drinking, eating, resting, sitting, having homes, going to work, returning home, and playing. The psalmist thinks of the animals and even Leviathan "as fellow creatures with whom he or she shared a common life" (Whitekettle 2011, 183).

In contrast to the wild animals discussed above, none of the creatures in Psalm 104, and most notably Leviathan, is outside of the bounds of creation. God's creative sustaining of the world encompasses all creatures. This is a similarity that Psalm 104 shares with Genesis 1, where God creates all creatures including the sea monsters. The harmonious creation of Genesis 1, however, is disrupted by the curse on the animals in Genesis 3. Indeed, the Priestly scribes endorse the Yahwist's depiction of this curse by accentuating the fear and dread that is on all animals following the flood (Gen 9:2). This is not the case in Psalm 104. There is no space or creature outside the sustaining creative activity of God.

The role of God in Psalm 104 corresponds to what we would call today the forces of nature. Whereas the scientific worldview would explain change in the world in term of natural causality—whether they are physical, chemical, or biological causes—the psalmist understood the world in terms of personal causality. All change in the world beyond individual agency—whether human or animal—belongs to God, and thus all

---

6. The Hebrew term *behemah* may refer to wild or domestic land animals, or to all land animals generally, but when it occurs in contrast to *hayyah* (v. 11), it usually refers to domestic land animals. The contrast that is made in v. 14, however, is not between wild and domestic animals, but between animals that eat grass (*tsir*) and humans that eat plants (*'eseb*). In this case, *behemah* may refer to all herbivore land animals, whether they are wild or domestic.

life is dependent on God. Whether it be the movement of the sun to light and heat the day and to signal the workday and seasonal chores, or the control of water that gushes forth from springs, fills riverbeds and the seas, or rains upon the land, it is God's activity alone that makes life possible. The distinction between humans and animals that is highlighted elsewhere in the biblical tradition is insignificant in the context of God's activity, for humans are as dependent upon God as all other creatures.[7] The mutual dependence of all creatures on God is stated no more clearly than in the psalm's depiction of the natural cycle of life and death. All creatures—humans and animals—are dependent upon God for life; and when they die, they return to the dirt from which they were created:

> These all look to you
>> to give them their food in due season;
> when you give to them, they gather it up;
>> when you open your hand, they are well satiated.
> When you hide your face, they are terrified;
>> when you take away their breath, they die
>> and return to the dirt.
> When you extend your breath, they are created;
>> and you renew the face of the arable land. (Ps 104:27–30)

Only in the last verse of the psalm are humans singled out as distinctive from other creatures: "Let sinners be consumed from the earth, and let the wicked be no more" (Ps 104:35). In contrast to the wild animals, whose presence elsewhere represents the undoing of creation, and in contrast to Leviathan, which elsewhere is the primordial threat to God's creation, this psalm lays the ruin of creation at human feet. Only humans, out of all creatures, pose a threat to God's creation because only humans stand in opposition to God. Thus, in awe of the beauty and wonder of God's creation, the psalmist prays that no humans would corrupt it. The world and all that is in it belongs to God (Ps 24:1), and so humans, in community with all other creatures, are fully dependent on God for their livelihood.[8]

---

7. William Brown argues that Psalm 104 offers a correction to the anthropic principle: Humans may have their place, but the creation was not designed around them. "If there is a 'principle' at work in creation according to the psalm, it is inclusively 'biotic' rather than anthropic" (2010, 153).

8. James Limburg claims that the "orientation of this psalm is not anthropocentric but rather geocentric, earth-centered" (1994, 344). Indeed, the psalm emphasizes that God's activity encompasses the earth rather than simply focuses on humans. It is a misnomer, however, to characterize the psalm as geocentric, for it is *God's* activity that is the focus of the psalm and it is dependence on *God* that all creation shares. The psalmist's worldview is theocentric, and certainly not anthropocentric.

The Speech of Yhwh in Job 38–42

Whereas Psalm 104 marginalizes the role of humans in the natural world, the speeches of Yhwh in the book of Job declare humans to be irrelevant. In response to Job's accusations that Yhwh has not properly governed the world, Yhwh addresses Job with a litany of rhetorical questions on the creation (Job 38:4–39:30) and then with a description of two beasts—Behemoth and Leviathan (Job 40:15–41:34)—whose very existence mocks Job's own sense of self-importance. Job, who thought that Yhwh should give attention to his innocent suffering, that Yhwh should give an account of his negligence in administering the creation, is silenced in the encounter between the splendors of creation and his own human limits (see Crenshaw 1992). The divine speeches in Job are radically non-anthropocentric: the world is simply not about humans.

In the first speech (Job 38:4–39:30), Yhwh mocks Job by questioning his role in or understanding of the vast creation, addressing issues of cosmology, meteorology, and zoology. The first speech shares many similarities with Psalm 104, emphasizing not only Yhwh's role in establishing and sustaining the creation, but also Yhwh's attention to the wild animals. Unlike Psalm 104, however, the description of Yhwh's creation in the first speech serves to emphasize the limits of human knowledge and dominion in the world. The creation is vastly greater than Job's experience, his understanding, and his control, and the many wild animals described by Yhwh are not only of no use to Job, but they have a relationship to Yhwh independent of humankind.

Although humans play virtually no role in God's creation depicted in the book of Job, three references to humans in the first divine speech may serve as hermeneutical clues for interpreting the speech. The first passage (Job 38:13–15) notes how the morning and dawn expose the wicked, shaking them out of the earth. Clearly not a favorable reference to humans, but it addresses Job's concerns for justice expressed earlier in the book. Yhwh and Yhwh's creation are not indifferent to evil. The second and third passages more directly address our focus here. Yhwh interrogates Job regarding his ability to sustain the creation with rain:

> Who has cut a channel for the flood,
>> and a way for the thunderbolt,
> to bring rain on a land where no one lives,
>> on the desert, which is empty of human life,
> to satisfy the ruin and desolate land,
>> and to make the ground grow grass? (Job 38:25–27)

In this text Yhwh sustains the creation, not for the sake of humans, but for its own sake in a land that does not include humans at all. The waste and desolate land is valuable to Yhwh and needs sustaining, not because it is of use to humans, but because it is part of Yhwh's creation (Tucker 1997, 14; Dick 2006, 266).

Part II: Ecology

The third hermeneutical clue is found in the description of the final creature mentioned in the first speech. Often translated "eagle," the *nesher* is a bird of prey that might be better understood to be the vulture in this context. After describing its home high in the rocky crag, the divine speech concludes:

> From there it searches for food;
>> its eyes see it from far away.
>
> Its chicks lick up blood;
>> and where the slain are, there it is. (Job 39:29–30)

Dead humans on a battlefield are no more than carrion for the birds of prey; so much for the glory of humans!

In the second divine speech (Job 40:15–41:34), Yhwh introduces Job to Behemoth and Leviathan, two mythological beasts that challenge Job's status and his dominion in creation. Behemoth, which is perhaps imagined like a hippopotamus, is described as a beast that Yhwh made just as he made Job (Job 40:15). What is comparable between the creations of Job and Behemoth is not stated, but the affinity between them suggests that Job is no more important to Yhwh than is Behemoth. Indeed, Behemoth's creation was "the first of the deeds of God" (Job 40:19). A similar statement is used of Wisdom in Proverbs 8:22, and it may imply not only first in a sequence, but also first in importance. Behemoth, created like Job, is nevertheless greater than Job. Leviathan too is beyond Job's equal. The ferocious Leviathan, who makes even the gods afraid (Job 41:25), can only be controlled by Yhwh. Human dominion is a charade before the likes of Leviathan:

> On earth it has no equal,
>> one made without fear.
>
> It sees everything that is lofty;
>> it is king over all that are proud. (Job 41:33–34)

The speeches of Yhwh in the book of Job do not address the role of humans in relation to domestic animals, or the task of humans in agriculture and other creative endeavors. In other words, the divine speeches do not intend to affirm the place of humans in the world, but rather to challenge those who, like Job, think the world revolves around them (see Dick 2006, 263–70). In other words, the speeches of Yhwh in Job are a critique of the anthropocentric view of the world (see Schifferdecker 2008, 63–102; Brown 2010, 115–40).

THEOCENTRISM AND THE RELATIONSHIP BETWEEN SOCIETY AND NATURE

Although the Bible has been read anthropocentrically—a Western cultural imposition on the Bible—anthropocentrism is not the biblical worldview. Humans in the biblical tradition may be distinct from other living creatures, and are assigned by God distinctive tasks within the creation. But being distinctive does not entitle them to use creation for their own purposes, nor are they the only beings with intrinsic value. They may subdue the earth and have dominion over some creatures as the Priestly creation myth hopes, but they remain subject to God. Indeed, that which makes humans distinctive in the biblical tradition cannot be separated from human rebellion against God—a point emphasized in the Yahwist creation myth but also underlying many other texts (especially in the covenant and prophetic traditions)—which the Bible characterizes as being inclined towards evil. Their actions have consequences in the world for which they are liable. Humans may make their own way in the world, but the world is not theirs to make, and they are ultimately answerable to God, the creator.

The biblical worldview is theocentric. Although this worldview shaped how the Israelites' labor mediated the relationship between society and nature, it did not determine their particular understanding of the role of humans within the natural world. All of the ancient Near Eastern societies had a theocentric worldview, but each understood the role of humans in the world differently. In the cultures of the southern Mesopotamian plain, for example, where agriculture was dependent on irrigation through canals from the Tigris and Euphrates rivers, humans were thought to have been created to do the work of the gods. In chapter 2, I discussed the myth of Atrahasis, in which humans were created to relieve the younger generation of gods, the Igigi, of their burdensome labor. The Igigi had been forced to dig out the river-beds of the Tigris and Euphrates, to dig out canals and clear channels for irrigation, and to make mud bricks for building. But humans, instead, were given these and other tasks to build up society.

The myth of Atrahasis served to legitimize a Mesopotamian king's mobilization of his people not only for the public good, such as building city walls and irrigating fields, but also to build temple and palace complexes and to work on his estates. The people were created for these tasks, just as the king was given and exercised the authority of Enlil, the chief god of the earth. This understanding of the role of humans endowed human labor with sacred significance. Human labor itself, apart from the gods, was creative and expanded the creation. It could transform a barren plain with irrigation into rich fields of grain, able to support cities and their large populations; it could transform mud into bricks from which to build cities with their temples, palaces, and ziggurats. Yet, the role of humans in the world remained subordinate to the will of the gods. Humans labored not for their own benefit nor even ultimately for the king, but rather for the gods for whom they were created to serve (Bottéro 2001, 98–103).

In the Nile valley of Egypt, the role of humans in the world was subordinate to the cosmic forces, which the Egyptians' understood based on their experience of the annual inundation of the Nile river, on which agriculture was dependent, and of the powerful, cyclical effects of the sun. For the ancient Egyptians, the world consisted of a relationship of beings (Ennead) who developed from Atum, the "lord of totality." Like a mound that emerges from the Nile's inundation when it recedes, Atum emerged from the infinitely expansive primeval waters (Nun), and then through self-development brought forth the other gods: Shu and Tefnut are the dry air and moisture that separate the earth Geb and the sky Nut. The cosmos was conceived as an inhabitable world surrounded by endless waters of darkness. Atum is also the sun god Re who sails across the sky during the day, and passes through the body of Nut at night to be reborn each morning. From Geb and Nut were born four deities whose roles are more social than natural: Osiris, the perfect being, was killed by Seth and became king of the underworld; Seth is the god of disorder; Isis is associated with healing; and Nephthys assists both Seth (as a consort) and Isis. A tenth god, Horus, is the son of Osiris and Isis, the living king of Egypt, and also a manifestation of the sun (Allen 1988, 8–12).

The Egyptians perceived of the world as a harmonious relationship of multiple divine beings. Because the creation was the unfolding and development of Atum, the Egyptians themselves, unlike the Mesopotamians and Israelites, did not think they were engaged in *bringing about* creation. Nevertheless, the Egyptians, especially the king and the priests who functioned as his substitutes, played a significant role in *maintaining* the creation through their role in the cult and preservation of justice (*maat*): "*maat* is order, the just measure of things that underlies the world; it is the perfect state of things toward which one should strive and which is in harmony with the creator god's intentions" (Hornung 1982, 213). Maat is like a material substance on which both gods and humans live. Through the offerings of the temple cult, the king and his priests return *maat* to the gods. Through his deeds and words, the king also bestows *maat* on his people, who are expected to live their lives in harmony with *maat*—to keep *maat* by doing and speaking *maat*—and thereby increase *maat* in the world.

Although the world was perceived as a harmonious unity, it was not without its dangers. The murder of Osiris by Seth disrupted the unity of the world, but more significantly the ordered world of existence was continuously threatened by nonexistence as represented by Apophis, an indestructible serpent who lives in the eternal waters of Nun and seeks to consume Re each night. There, in the primeval waters, Re is regenerated to be reborn at dawn, but at the risk of losing existence (Hornung 1982, 158–59). Only if the sun god's nocturnal cosmic journey was supported by the cult and justice would the forces of disintegration be pushed back so that Re could complete his journey. For this reason, Re installed a king on earth as his son and successor, "who was not a mortal human being but a mortal god sharing in the same substance as the sun-god" (Quirke 1992, 36). Through the king's participation in daily temple cults of the gods and by ensuring that justice (*maat*) was present in the land, the king maintained the good, harmonious created order of the world. Only through the king's role in preserving the cosmos were ordinary individuals able to participate in maintaining the creation through their own acts of justice (Quirke 1992, 70–103). The Egyptian conception of the world was fragile and thus required vigilance in preserving it through the cult and justice.

The biblical tradition presents the role of humans in the world differently from both the Mesopotamian and Egyptian perspectives but shares with them a similar theocentric perspective. In the biblical world of ancient Israel, humans have both a collaborative role in creation with Yhwh (as in Yahwist creation myth) and a representative role in the creation as the image of God (from the Priestly creation myth). Each of these roles mediates the relationship between society and nature differently (see the full discussion in chapter 2), but in both roles humans are fully embedded in the natural world as part of God's creation. Moreover, in both roles, humans are dependent upon and subject to God who created them. The world belongs not to humans but to God, who created and sustains it. The distinctive status and tasks assigned to humans may place humans above other creatures within a functional hierarchy, but even the role of humans pales in comparison to God's work in creation. In the biblical theocentric worldview, all creatures are valued and valuable; their worth derives from God. All alike are dependent upon God for creation and subsistence, and all alike are valuable to God as part of his creation. The world, inclusive of humans and animals, trees and plants, belongs to God because it is God's creation (Ps 24:1), and it is in relation to God that each part of creation has it value and worth. The biblical theocentric worldview thus offers a challenge to the anthropocentrism that has infected Western Christianity since the Enlightenment by dethroning humans from their artificial (human-made) precipice overlooking the natural world. Humans in the biblical tradition are part and parcel of the creation, along with the rest of the natural world, and their role within the creation cannot separate them from the creation.

THEOCENTRISM AND VALUES TOWARD NATURE

Just as the theocentric worldview does not determine the role of humans in the world, it does not determine one's values toward the natural world. The ancient Israelites may have recognized that they were embedded within the natural world, but a full range of values toward nature were possible and their preferences for one value over another depended on their social-historical context. A common human problem that all societies must address is the relationship between humans and nature. Kluckhohn and Strodtbeck (1973) postulated that there are only a limited range of possible solutions to this problem and that all alternative solutions are present in every society. For the human relationship to nature problem, they offered the solutions ranging from mastery-over-nature to harmony-with-nature and subjugation-to-nature. Preferences for one or another of these solutions, which may be characterized as value orientations, shape how humans actually engage with the natural world. The anthropocentric worldview that is embraced by many U.S. Americans, for example, is often expressed through a mastery-over-nature value orientation, enabling humans to use (and abuse) the resources of the natural world for their own purposes, though the other solutions may be preferred under certain circumstances. In contrast, the theocentric worldview held by the ancient Israelites favors the harmony-with-nature value orientation, but each of the solutions is found in the biblical tradition (see Simkins 1994).

The mastery-over-nature solution to the human relationship to nature problem is found only in a qualified form in the biblical tradition. Generally, this solution emphasizes the hierarchical relationship between humans and the rest of nature. Nature, in this orientation, consists of impersonal objects and forces, which humans may exploit for their own purposes, and perhaps with impunity. In the ancient Near East, this value orientation is found only in royal contexts and is characteristic of tributary relations of production. The Assyrian king, for example, demonstrated his mastery over nature by killing lions in a ritualized hunt (Watanabe 2002, 69–88). By killing the lion, a symbol of wild nature and thereby a threat to human society, the king demonstrated his power over nature and his ability, as a representative of the chief deity Ashur, to extend creation throughout the world. The king's hunt was commanded by the gods, and his actions were thus an extension of the gods' creative activity. In contrast, the epic tale of Gilgamesh and Enkidu killing the terrifying Huwawa, the guardian of the pine forest, and the Bull of Heaven expresses a mastery-over-nature value orientation that has run amok. Huwawa and the Bull of Heaven were the servants of Enlil and Anu, and thus by killing them, Gilgamesh and Enkidu defied the will of the gods. Enkidu is sentenced to die, while Gilgamesh is left to lament his friend's death and seek a way to overcome his own mortality. The epic tempers Gilgamesh and Enkidu's mastery-over-nature orientation by rejecting their arrogance. The mastery-over-nature orientation finds its limits in divine will. Rather than glorying in their mastery over Huwawa and the Bull of Heaven, the epic instead simply emphasizes the ways in which humans, or more particularly kings, achieve a measure of immortality through their creative works (Jacobsen 1976, 195–219).

In the biblical tradition, the mastery-over-nature value orientation is ascribed to humans in the Priestly creation myth with God's blessing for them to subdue the earth and have dominion over the animals. The role of humans in this myth is modelled on kings—the Hebrew verbs *kabash* ("subdue") and *radah* ("rule, have dominion") are regularly used of kings, and the "image of God" reflects the statues that kings erect of themselves in their territory. But, as I have discussed previously, such mastery is qualified in the Priestly tradition and should be understood as a hope rather than the reality of humans. Indeed, the hope of mastery-over-nature may have been the Priestly response to a prevailing subjugation-to-nature orientation that had settled on the Judean community, who had endured the traumatic consequences of the Babylonian destruction of Jerusalem and exile in a foreign land. The Priestly myth should be read to be offering hope to a disheartened and despairing community, rather than enabling humans to exploit the natural world for their own designs. Humans were created as part of the natural world to be representatives of God; they are not autonomous beings separate from nature, nor able to use the natural world in any way that pleases them.

The mastery-over-nature value orientation is also reflected in the Jerusalem royal theology. The king enthroned in Jerusalem was understood to be the son of Yhwh: "I [the king] will announce the decree of Yhwh: he said to me, 'you are my son; today I have begotten you'" (Ps 2:7). As the son of God, the king stands in relation to the creation in much the same way that Yhwh does. Yhwh had defeated the primordial powers, represented as the sea or an aquatic monster (Rahab or Leviathan), from which he created the world (Ps 74:12–17; 89:9–14). Similarly, Yahweh will give the king power to hold the unruly, but vanquished, sea at bay: "I [Yhwh] will set his hand on the sea, his right hand on the rivers" (Ps 89:25). The royal theology expects the king to be able to exert mastery over nature as Yhwh does. But though the psalms reflecting the royal theology repeatedly address Yhwh's power in and over creation, the king's mastery over nature is presented only as a *potential*:

> May he [the king] be like rain coming down on mown grass,
> > like showers watering the earth . . .
> May an abundance of grain be in the land,
> > on the tops of mountains may it wave,
> > its fruit like Lebanon.
> May [the people] blossom in the cities,
> > like the plants of the earth. (Ps 72:6, 16)

Empowered by Yhwh as his son, the king may indeed demonstrate a mastery over nature. More often than not, however, the psalms attest to the king's need for Yhwh's help, belying any facile dogma of the royal theology. Whatever power the king exercised over creation, he did so only in dependence on Yhwh. Like the value orientation of humans generally in the Priestly creation myth, the king's mastery-over-nature orientation, which was a product of his divine adoption, is qualified. It expressed hope that the king may participate in God's creative activity, as a son might do so in his father's work, but the historical reality of the Israelite kings rarely lived up to their lofty ideology.

The most commonly attested value orientation in the biblical tradition regarding the relationship between humans and nature is harmony-with-nature. This orientation is characteristic of household and patron–client relations of production, and is rooted in the similar, reified relations that the people have with Yhwh—that is, in covenant, Yhwh is a patron to the Israelites, his clients; and in marriage, Yhwh is a husband to his people, his wife. The harmony-with-nature orientation recognizes the integral link that humans share with the rest of the natural world: humans are part of nature. As result, human actions have consequences in nature, which also affect humans in turn. In the Yahwist creation myth, for example, the human couple's consumption of the fruit of knowledge had effects in the rest of nature—the animals and the arable land were cursed—and for the human couple themselves—there was enmity between humans and animals, the land withheld its produce, and the man ruled over his wife. Similarly, in the covenant tradition, the Israelites faithfulness to Yhwh's commands will have ramifications for the productivity of their land, crops, and herds, and for the well-being of their households (see, e.g., Deut 11:13–17; 28:1–68; Lev 26:3–45).

In the wisdom tradition, the link between humans and nature enables humans to learn about society from the natural world itself. For example, the natural world attests to the social dangers of being lazy:

> I passed by the field of a lazy man,
>> by the vineyard of a man with no sense;
> and look, it was overgrown with thistles,
>> the ground was covered with weeds,
>> and its stone wall was broken down.
> Then I saw and considered it;
>> I looked and received instruction.
> A little sleep, a little slumber,
>> a little folding of the hands to rest,
> and poverty will come to you like a robber,
>> and destitution like an armed man. (Prov 24:30–34)

Because humans are embedded in nature, a neglected plot of arable land in the natural world may communicate social knowledge.

The prophetic tradition both proclaims the coming of natural calamities in response to the people's sins, and uses the condition of the natural world to justify its social commentary. Hosea, for example, connects the people's sins with the condition of the natural world:

> Hear the word of Yhwh, O Israelites;
>> for Yhwh has a case against the inhabitants of the land.
> There is no faithfulness or loyalty,
>> and no knowledge of God in the land.
> Swearing, deceiving, and murder,
>> stealing and committing adultery break out;

> bloodshed follows bloodshed.
> Therefore, the land dries up,
> and all who live in it languish;
> the animals of the field,
> and the birds of the air,
> even the fish of the sea are perishing. (Hos 4:1–3)

For Hosea, the social condition of the people and the condition of the natural world go hand in hand. Throughout the biblical tradition, the ancient Israelites express the harmony-with-nature value orientation, attesting to their recognition that humans cannot be separated from the natural world and that their actions have consequences in nature.

The third solution to the human relationship nature problem is subjugation-to-nature. With this value orientation, humans feel powerless and oppressed in relation to the rest of the natural world. The will of God appears to be hostile toward them, or at least capricious, and humans have no power to change their plight. The subjugation-to-nature attitude is characteristic of catastrophes—natural, social, and political—in which the people's life and livelihood has been radically altered due to no perceived fault of their own. In ancient Israel, it resulted from a disruption of the traditional relations of production—household, patron–client, and even tributary relations—where other value orientations dominated. The subjugation-to-nature orientation is a solution of last resort, when the other value orientations are no longer possible or fail to make sense of the world.

The classic biblical example of the subjugation-to-nature value orientation can be found in the book of Job: Yhwh acts capriciously and Job's actions seem unconnected to his experience of the world. The opening prose framework of the book tells the story of a wealthy, pious man who tragically loses his wealth, his many children, and his health, apparently to satisfy a wager between Yhwh and the Accuser. Building on this story, the poetic body of the book focuses on Job's theological and ethical debate with his friends over the causes of his tragic condition. According to his friends, Job's condition is ultimately a result of his own (or his children's) sins. In other words, his friends express the harmony-with-nature orientation that is at home with the covenant theology discussed above. Job, on the other hand, rejects his friends' explanation and instead blames Yhwh, whom Job does not believe is just—that is, treating Job as he deserves. Job is expressing the subjugation-to-nature orientation and feels oppressed by Yhwh.

Job's subjugation-to-nature orientation offers no comfort when Yhwh finally responds to Job's accusations. In two speeches to Job, Yhwh not only emphasizes Job's irrelevance but also deconstructs the distinctive character of humans within the creation generally (see Crenshaw 1992). As discussed above, in the first speech (Job 38:4–39:30), Yhwh mocks Job by questioning his role in or understanding of the vast creation; Yhwh humbles Job by emphasizing the limits of his knowledge and his lack of dominion in the world. In the second divine speech (Job 40:15–41:34), Yhwh challenges Job's role within the creation by placing him in relationship to Behemoth and Leviathan. Both are beyond Job's equal. Behemoth is "the first of the great acts of God" (Job 40:19), and Leviathan is a ferocious beast that only Yhwh can control (Job 41:33–34). Whatever the historical circumstances of the book of Job—and many scholars think it is the destruction of Jerusalem by the Babylonians—the Israelites' conception of the role of humans in the world, their relationship to nature, as expressed in the book of Job, has been wholly undermined by their experiences. No longer are humans able to shape the world or collaborate with Yhwh in creation; they see themselves subjugated to the whims of a god whose will they cannot thwart and whose actions they cannot understand.

Each of the value orientations evident within the biblical tradition attests to a distinctive understanding of the relationship between humans and nature, and each emerged out of particular social-historical circumstances. All the orientations, however, share the same basic theocentric worldview. The theocentric worldview seems to have favored the harmony-with-nature orientation, and it qualified the mastery-over-nature orientation. Unlike the expression of mastery-over-nature within an anthropocentric worldview, which provides no regulation on how one might use or abuse the natural world, the theocentric worldview in ancient Israel provided limits to one's mastery over nature because one was dependent upon and subject to God. Regardless of their particular orientation to nature, the Israelites recognized their ultimate dependence on God and their orientation to nature was a reflection of their relationship to God.

Returning to the larger issue of the relationship between society and nature, does the theocentric worldview make a difference in the mediation between society and nature? It would seem so for the ancient Israelites. Their inherently religious ideology—that Yhwh is engaged in sustaining the world; that their relationship to Yhwh in covenant was determinative of the efficacy of their labor (J); or that as God's representatives, they actualized God's sovereign, creative activity through their labor (P)—would have shaped their relationship with nature and how they consumed the materials of the natural world in their construction of society. Their religious ideology was expressed predominantly with the harmony-with-nature value orientation. That is, they recognized that humans were embedded in the natural world as part of the creation and that their actions had consequences in nature. Unfortunately, we do not know the material consequences of their labor in mediating between society and nature, whether it was beneficial for or destructive of their environment. Their ideology would suggest they had a beneficial relationship with their environment, but we must be cautious here. Values, such as the harmony-with-nature orientation, are not always translated into effective action—there may be competing values that dominate, or the actions generated by the values may be ineffective. Moreover, human actions may have unintended consequences. The building of terraces, for example, is an effective technology to expand arable land, capture rainwater runoff, and prevent soil erosion. But if the terraces collapse, whether due to poor construction, a lack of maintenance, or even destabilization from an earthquake, the soil erosion may be worse than if the terraces had never been built. In any case, the ancient Israelites' impact on the environment would have been relatively meager and restorable—their population, technology, and subsistence economy limited the damage that could be done. In other words, their political economy, in which their religious ideology played a role, would have limited the damage or degradation done to their environment.

While we cannot detail the effects of the ancient Israelites' political economy on the natural world—it is too distant from us to know precisely—their impact on the natural world certainly paled in comparison to our current impact. The difference is largely a factor of scale (of population and society), technology (extreme differences in productivity and impact), energy consumption (fossil fuel stocks instead of renewable flows), and social relations of production (capitalist relations instead of agrarian relations)—that is, a difference in political economy, which includes religion as part of the superstructure. At issue for us here, however, is whether the biblical theocentric worldview can make a difference in *our* mediation between society and nature. Pope Francis thinks so, and his recent encyclical, calling "every person living on this planet" (2015, §3) to protect our "common home" from global environmental deterioration, is thoroughly theocentric. Theocentrism reminds us that the world is not ours to do with as we please—it belongs to God—and that humans, with all our creativity, ingenuity, and power, remain nevertheless subject to God—we are not masters of our own destiny (contrary to the dominant anthropocentric worldview; see Catton and Dunlap 1980, 17–18). Theocentrism has many of the same advantages as ecocentrism or biocentrism in that is places humans within a larger framework external to themselves. Yet it also allows for the distinctiveness of humans, which ecocentrism and biocentrism do not. Theocentrism risks becoming simply an idealist philosophy (see O'Keefe 2016), but when rooted in the material world of creation, as in the biblical tradition, theocentrism provides a necessary corrective to the anthropocentrism that has dominated the Western world. Nevertheless, theocentrism cannot be isolated from the rest of the political economy, especially from the consumption of energy and the social relations of production, through which we mediate the relationship between society and nature. The Bible's religious ideology will be effective only if it manages to transform our current capitalist relations, which are dependent on the consumption of fossil fuels, into productive relations that acknowledge the embeddedness of humans and society in the natural world.

6

Ecology and Political Economy

ECONOMIC CORE OF THE ENVIRONMENTAL CRISIS

MOST BIBLICAL AND RELIGIOUS studies scholars have addressed the current environmental crisis from within Lynn White's (1967) religious worldview framework, typically emphasizing religious values through which people might cherish and take care of the environment. Rosemary Radford Ruether is a notable exception. In the late 1970s, she published a short essay, summarizing her early environmental thought, in which she critiqued the Western religious responses to the environmental crisis. She recognized two distinct types of response: a romantic neo-animism, which sought to return to our primitive religious roots when humans were in harmony with nature, and a stewardship conservationism, which sought to conserve natural resources and be good stewards of the environment. Both approaches were inadequate for Ruether because "there was little recognition that [the environmental] crisis took place within a particular economic system" (1978, 1130). Ruether noted, for example, that the environmental movement was largely the product of the nations of the industrialized North, and religious environmental concern gave little or no attention to the other major religious social movements of the day, such as the liberation movements in the global South and especially in Latin America. In fact, the goals of environmentalism and the liberation movements were often at odds: the ecological balance of humanity with nature seemed to preclude development and the more equal distribution of economic goods for the global South. She discerned that both types of religious responses regarded the environmental crisis primarily "as a crisis between 'man' and 'nature,' rather than as a crisis resulting from the way in which a particular exploitative relationship between classes, races and nations used natural resources" (1978, 1130). For Ruether, the destruction of the natural environment and the social and economic exploitation of people in society are part and parcel of the same reality.

Ruether was ahead of her time in recognizing the political-economic base of the environmental crisis—not just that economic behavior in particular has degraded the natural world, but also that not everyone experiences the environmental crisis in the same way. The environmental crisis entails exploitation between humans and nature, and also among humans. The same logic of domination governs both—a domination that is inherent in capitalism. "It is no accident," she notes, "that nature is most devastated where poor people live" (1978, 1132). Both the natural world and the poor have been exploited for the benefit of capitalists. Thus, she argues that environmental concern must also entail questions of economic justice; that is, it must include ecojustice, which emphasizes "the reordering of access to and use of natural resources within a just economy" (1978, 1131).

Whereas Ruether pushed biblical and religious studies scholars concerned with the environment to address also economic concerns, a number of economically-oriented scholars—primarily ecosystem ecologists and environmental economists—in the early 1980s began challenging traditional neoclassical economics and its treatment of the environment. Neoclassical economics treats the natural world as if it were a subsystem of the macro-economy, a simple stock for material resources and a sink for waste (included as externalities in economic calculations). This relationship between the economy and the natural world, which is contrary to the results of basic science, is inadequate and unable to address the current environmental crisis. These scholars insisted, instead, that the economy must be viewed as a subsystem of the ecosystem, the larger natural world on which it is dependent. Ecological economics, as the new discipline came to be known, is based on the realization that the traditional economic "vision of unlimited growth is in fundamental conflict with the ecological perspective, which sees scale and carrying capacity limits as central to the analysis of any biophysical process" (Harris 1995, 18; see further Perrings 1995; Gowdy 2000). By inverting the neoclassical relationship between the economy and the ecosystem, it subverts notions of dematerialization, that the human economy can be decoupled from the natural environment, and undermines the neoclassical assumption that the current economic system is sustainable.[1]

It is now inadequate to frame the environmental crisis simply in terms of religious worldview and values, though few biblical and religious studies scholars concerned with the environment give sufficient attention to economic concerns, and it is irresponsible to address economic issues without acknowledging the consequences for the environment. The condition of the natural world is directly related to the expanse, throughput, and intensity of economic activity, for all economic activity, which is necessary for human living, alters the environment. An analytical tool that

---

1. Although a minority voice in economics generally, ecological economics, along with related approaches such as biophysical economics, continues to challenge neoclassical and now neoliberal economics. For an assessment and self-reflection on the discipline, see Anderson and M'Gonigle 2012; Spash 2019; Melgar-Melgar and Hall 2019; Daly 2019.

illustrates the relationship between the ecosystem and the economy is the IPAT formula (I = PAT) developed through a scientific exchange in the early 1970s (Ehrlich and Holdren 1971, 1972; Commoner 1972). The formula states that human impact on the environment (I) is equal to the population (P) times affluence (A), which includes both consumption and production, times the impact of technology (T). Although this formula is a mathematical identity and thus its evaluative function is limited (see Alcott 2009), its heuristic value is nevertheless significant. The formula makes clear that there are multiple economic forces driving the environmental crisis, that these forces do not act independently, and that their relationship is exponential rather than linear (for variations on the formula, see York, Rosa, and Dietz 2003).

The rapidly growing human population, for example, has been singled out as *the* environmental problem (Ehrlich 1970), but according to the IPAT formula it should not be isolated from the effects of affluence and technology (see Jackson 2009, 6–7). Population as a whole can be misleading because it is subject to species-type thinking—that is, all humans are lumped together in a single population assessment, when the affluence and technology use of individual humans varies considerably. Three hundred million U.S. Americans, for instance, have a far greater environmental impact than two billion inhabitants of the global South living in poverty. And even within the United States, a wide disparity between the wealthy and the poor creates an uneven responsibility for environmental impact. Nevertheless, population growth also cannot be ignored or dismissed (contra Francis 2015, §50), for a growing population requires an increasing material consumption just to maintain a livable subsistence. Global population growth needs to be slowed—many think it will peak naturally around 10 billion people (see Smil 2019, 303–31)—and even reduced, not through draconian measures but rather through education and women's rights, including reproductive rights, which tend to reduce population growth naturally (Zehner 2012, 187–222; see Cafaro and Crist 2012).

Although population cannot be neglected, affluence and technology are the drivers of environmental impact that are more easily addressed. Affluence, as an indicator of consumption, determines the mass of material resources that are extracted from the natural world (the throughput) for production, whereas the technology determines the intensity of the extraction and the rate of production. It is the exponential relationship of these economic forces, however, that is the most impactful on the environment. Using widely accepted figures, the environmental impact on the planet increased from 1900 to 1950 by almost eleven-fold (1100%), even though the individual increase of each component was rather modest (ranging from 40% to 290%). From 1950 to 2011, however, the increase in the human impact on the environment was one-hundred-thirty-four-fold (13,400%). Population, affluence, and technology each experienced significant increases over the six decades (ranging from 280% for population to 1040% for affluence), but their multiplication results in an exponential increase in environmental impact. This "great acceleration" in environmental impact since 1950, which can be identified in many environmental and economic scales, contributes to the rationale for recognizing a new epoch, the Anthropocene (Steffen, Persson, et al. 2011; see chapter 7).

Underlying all the components of the IPAT formula is the use of energy, which is essential to the functioning of the economy and thus also contributes to environmental impact. Life is dependent on energy, without which the population will not grow, technology will not operate, and production leading to affluence will cease. In the ancient world, the economy was dependent on solar energy, captured through photosynthesis and embodied in plants for food and biomass, such as wood, charcoal, straw, and dung. Some people were able to attain a modest level of affluence through harnessing the labor of others and eventually the use of wind and water flows. Most people, however, managed to harness only enough energy to provide for their own subsistence, using simple technologies and harnessing the labor of animals. As a result, the population grew very slowly, always less than 0.1 percent growth per year (Smil 2019, 318), and the economy grew on average only in pace with the population, producing no sustained per capita economic growth. But there was proportionally little environmental impact as well, and certainly not on a global scale.

In contrast, the modern, capitalist economy is fueled primarily (about 80%; REN21 2019) by fossil fuels. Embodying millions of years of solar energy, fossil fuels, as a mobile and possessable stock, released capitalist relations of production from the natural constraints that wind and water flows posed (Malm 2016), and produced self-sustaining economic growth. This growth, which produced historically unprecedented levels of affluence and technology, is inseparable from the energy that fueled it (Brown et al. 2011; Hall and Klitgaard 2012; Sorrell 2010, 1789–92; Stern 2011). The economy—the totality of production and consumption—has a metabolism that is fueled by energy, much like the metabolism of the human body is fueled by food. Without sufficient new inputs of energy, the economy cannot maintain its growth; a shortage of energy directly limits economic activity. Given this relationship between energy and the economy, it is not possible "to increase socially desirable goods and services substantially without concomitantly increasing the consumption of energy and other natural resources and without increasing environmental impacts that now include climate change, pollution, altered biogeochemical cycles, and reduced biodiversity" (Brown et al. 2011, 22). This is a problem for those concerned with economic justice, such as Ruether, since levels of affluence are so unequal across the planet. According to the UNDP's Human Development Report, as many as 2.7 billion people live in poverty—that is, they live on less than $2.50 per day—which was close to half the global population when the study for the report was completed (UNDP 2014, 19). Raising these people out of poverty will require the consumption of energy. Brown et al. (2011) estimated that it would take a five-fold increase in the rate of energy consumption (in 2006 figures), primarily from fossil fuels—which will produce a five-fold increase in environmental impact—to raise the global population to the standard of living (or level of affluence) in the U.S. The global population, of course, has increased since that study, and so also the energy requirement to meet the needs of the poor has increased proportionally.[2]

The role of technology in the IPAT formula has been contested. Some have argued that better technology can offset increases in population and affluence (e.g., Waggoner and Ausubel 2002)—an argument also made by the ecomodernists (see chapter 7). But technology is not neutral; it is a product of capitalist relations, whose logic demands ever increasing production. As a product, technology embodies materials and energy, and through its production it has a direct impact on the natural world. Short of aiding in the discovery of a new, relatively pollution-free source of energy, such as a breakthrough in nuclear fusion, technology might lower environmental impact by contributing to efficiency, squeezing more energy and productivity out of less natural resources. This would seem to reduce both energy and material demand, and it often does for each unit of production. But such efficiency also results, paradoxically, in more energy and material *consumption*. Jevon's paradox, as it has come to be known, is the recognition that increased efficiency generates increased demand of a natural resource, including fuel for energy, rather than decreased demand (Alcott 2005; Foster et al. 2010, 169–81; see Saunders 1992). More efficient gasoline engines, for example, have not resulted in less material-dense cars consuming less gasoline but rather more cars, often requiring more materials, driving more miles, and with more powerful engines. In other words, according to Jevon's paradox, gains in efficiency are offset by a rise in affluence, leading to an even greater human impact on the environment. This is simply the logic of capitalism; more efficient energy production and technological innovation result in greater economic growth because they increase the efficiency of production, reducing its cost per unit, and thus enabling more production, not less, in the quest for accumulation and maximizing profits. Technology in capitalist production increases the overall demand for energy and material resources, and so also increases the environmental impact of the economy (see York, Rosa, and Dietz 2005). Because of the logic of capitalism, Ellen Meiksins Wood (2017, 198) emphasizes that the use of technology does not reduce environmental impact:

> Capitalism can certainly produce and even profit from energy-efficient technologies, but its own inherent logic systematically prohibits their sustainable utilization. Just as the requirements of profit and capital accumulation inevitably drive production beyond consumption and beyond the limits of use,

---

2. Another way of approaching this issue is through the metric of ecological footprint, which measures how much of the ecosystem, translated into acres of the earth, a person uses. In the United States, for example, the third wealthiest nation in terms of biocapacity, each person is allotted 9.3 global acres but uses, on average, 17.2 global acres. In other words, the affluency of the average American is running almost a 100% global debt (see Kelly et al. 2015, for all the national and state figures). With a global population of 7 billion, there is approximately 2.3 global acres per person. This would mean that it would take approximately four earths to supply the global population with the standard of living allotted to the average U.S. American.

they also compel destruction long before the possibilities of use are exhausted. Whatever capitalism may do to enable the efficient use of resources, its own imperatives will always drive it further.

The exponential relationship between population, affluence, and technology make the current environmental crisis exceedingly difficult to address effectively. Moreover, as each of these components grows, as they inevitably will with a growing economy, the environmental crisis becomes all the more dire. Regardless of whatever religious worldview or values we might bring to the crisis, we have little chance of success in altering the current trajectory of the crisis without addressing its economic core. Climate change, for example, which is perhaps the most pressing environmental concern, but also connected to multiple other concerns, is the result of burning fossil fuels that power the economy. Yet, despite the globally recognized concern over climate change, expressed in the Kyoto Protocol (1997) and the Paris Climate Agreement (2015), consumption of fossil fuels continues to grow each year (Ritchie and Roser 2020) as the economy itself grows. Economic growth has produced social goods such as greater levels of affluence and development for more people, but such growth is also based on exploitation—through the expropriation of labor and material resources (Kallis 2018). Although the energy from fossil fuels has provided the conditions for economic growth, growth itself is the result of capitalist relations.

The sole rational goal of capitalist relations of production is accumulation of wealth through maximizing profit, and this is accomplished through increasing labor productivity and expanding production by reinvesting the surplus in technology and efficiency (see Malm 2016, 279–92). In other words, growth is built into the structure of capitalism, and without growth, capitalism cannot function and will produce crises of its own. Capitalist social relations will continue to produce as long as the production process is supplied with sufficient energy and material resources. Initially, capitalist production in eighteenth and early nineteenth-century England was dependent on the water wheel, but once capitalism embraced fossil fuels for its energy, economic growth became self-sustaining. Today, some industries continue to be dependent directly on fossil fuels, such as the steel and cement industries, transportation, and agriculture. Other production, however, is powered by electricity and thus is only indirectly dependent on fossil fuels, which power the giant turbines to produce electricity. Electricity is also produced by nuclear plants, windmills, hydroelectric dams, concentrated solar power plants, and solar photovoltaic panels, all of which contribute only a small portion of global energy produced. Renewable energy technologies are not sufficient to power the economic growth required by capitalist relations. Because the human impact on the environment is directly related to economic activity, and because continuing economic growth is dependent on the energy from fossil fuels that produce climate change, the current environmental crisis, as a product of capitalist relations, requires an economic solution freed from the fetters of unending growth.

Part II: Ecology

SOCIAL CONDITIONS OF ECONOMIC GROWTH

Neither sustained economic growth nor the capitalist relations that produce it are the natural or inevitable result of human evolution. They emerged late in human history at a specific place and during a specific time. Ellen Meiksins Wood (2017) argues that capitalist property and social relations emerged during the sixteenth and seventeenth centuries in England, beginning in the countryside, and then matured and spread to other nations during the eighteenth and nineteenth centuries. Andreas Malm (2016) addresses the link between capitalism and fossil fuel by demonstrating why the early capitalists favored the more expensive steam engine, powered by burning coal, over the less expensive and widely available waterwheel—the mobility and possessable stock of coal reinforced capitalist social and property relations in a way that the free water flow was incapable of doing. Rather than rehearse their arguments, some of which have already been mentioned, I will focus on the historically unique character of capitalist relations by comparing them to the economic relations of the ancient Israelites, which are typical of pre-capitalist relations.

Property relations of the ancient Israelites were based on *usufruct rights* rather than ownership (Guillaume 2012, 9–27). As the creator, all of the natural world belongs to Yhwh. Humans may utilize the natural world for their own subsistence, but they remain dependent on Yhwh for their production—all that we would attribute to nature, from sending the fertilizing rain to the development of new life in the womb. At the level of ideology, then, Yhwh owned all the land (Lev 25:23; Deut 19:14; see Ps 24:1), which was distributed by lot to the Israelite families (*mishpahoth*) as an inheritance (*nahalah*) (Josh 13–19; Num 26:52–56). Although not explicitly spelled out in the Bible, Yhwh's ownership of the land was perhaps the ideological basis for the annual tithe that the Israelites owed to God. At a practical level, the land was perhaps in trust to the king (see Miller 2015), so that land whose usufruct rights belonged to a state criminal may have reverted to the king's possession, but not even the king could contravene Yhwh's allotment of the land to the people (1 Kgs 21). Rather, the king would have guaranteed the people's usufruct rights.

Usufruct rights to the land may have been distributed among households or *bet aboth*, perhaps annually like the *musha* system during the Ottoman period (Guillaume 2012, 28–55).[3] The *nahalah* was land obtained through conquest, grant, or inheritance. At Yhwh's command, all Israelite *mishpahoth* received a *nahalah*, including towns and villages, from the land that was conquered from the Canaanites; then the tribes of the Israelites gave to the Levites towns and pasturage, each from their *nahalah* (Josh 21). Because no legal documents have survived from ancient Israel, it is

---

3. Land used for annual crops may have been distributed annually, based on the size of the household. Other land used for orchards and vineyards, however, is unlikely to have been distributed because they require a multiyear investment to reap any produce. This land may have been allotted to a single household and passed down from generation to generation. Land used exclusively for pasturage was probably shared in common.

unclear whether the *nahalah* could be sold—the story of Naboth's vineyard (1 Kgs 21) suggests that it cannot (see Russell 2014)—but nothing in the biblical texts prohibits it (see Dearman 1988, 67–70). Land could be confiscated by the king: Ahab confiscated Naboth's *nahalah* when he was falsely convicted and executed, and David seems to have confiscated Saul's ancestral land after his death (though it is not called *nahalah*). Kings could also grant land to their retainers (1 Sam 22:7–8; 2 Sam 9:7), which was perhaps also considered *nahalah* (Levine 1996, 229–31) and probably could be sold (Dearman 1988, 62–77).

Under Babylonian and Persian domination, the *nahalah* land tenure system gave way to the *ahuzzah* system. Like the *nahalah*, the *ahuzzah* was land that was acquired from Yhwh originally at the settlement of the land (Lev 14:34; Gen 17:8). Abraham, in contrast, purchased an *ahuzzah*-burial cave from Ephron the Hittite (Gen 23). Although this transaction was intended to be inheritable, hence Abraham sought permission from the Hittites (*Bnei Heth*), presumably the leaders of the community, and offered the full price (see Westbrook 1991, 24–35), among the Israelites only the usufruct rights of the land were sold. Because the land belonged to Yhwh, its usufruct rights could be sold for up to fifty years or confiscated because of debt, but the land itself could not be alienated from its original "possessor," who could reclaim it at the Jubilee (Lev 25:8–25) (Levine 1996, 237–43). Houses within a walled city could be permanently sold after a year, during which time they could be redeemed by their previous owners. But houses in unwalled villages or in the open country were treated like land and so could only be used for a period of time until the Jubilee (Lev 25:29–34). Ownership of land was not necessary in ancient Israel; family usufruct rights were sufficient to ensure that households were able to subsist on the land, and they reinforced Yhwh's ownership of and lordship over the creation.

Property relations in capitalism are based on *exclusive ownership* of the means of production. The beginnings of capitalist property relations can be detected in the sixteenth-century English enclosure movement when common and traditional use-rights to land were extinguished. Large landowners claimed exclusive ownership of land in order to put it to profitable use—*to improve it*, in their ideology—through sheep farming. In the seventeenth century, John Locke articulated the growing political and economic foundation for private property that is essential to capitalist property relations: individual private property is a natural right, given by God independent of the state, and is secured when a person "mixes his labour with it, thus joining it to something that is his own [his body]" (2017, §27). Locke would initially seem to connect property with one's own labor, that is, one's property is defined by what one actually produces (such as growing grain or picking an apple). Such indivisible produce can only be consumed by one person. But Locke extends ownership to the means of production: "A man owns whatever land he tills, plants, improves, cultivates, and can use the products of" (2017, §32). Furthermore, it is not labor per se that interests Locke, but labor put to the use of *improvement*, which in the seventeenth century referred to making land productive and profitable (see Wood 1984). One could improve land by using one's own labor or by appropriating the labor of others: "Thus when my horse bites off some grass, my servant cuts turf, or I dig up ore . . . the grass or turf or ore becomes my property" (2017, §28). Unimproved land, such as the land occupied by the Native Americans, or the common land with traditional use-rights in England, is a waste—it is of no use in the state of nature—and could thus be appropriated by others who would improve it. Land that is made productive, on the other hand, adds value to the land and contributes to the betterment of humankind. Locke recognized the limits of nature: one can only own what one can use; otherwise, it would be a waste (see Haddad 2003). But money changes the calculation. If the land produces more than a person can use, then the product can be converted into durable money, which does not spoil, and so the owner of the land may enlarge his possessions indefinitely. For Locke, the producers, who have a right to property, are those who appropriate the labor of others to create exchange value and thus profit (Wood 2017, 95–115).

Locke's understanding of property relations became the basis of land appropriation in the English countryside and the development of an agrarian capitalism. Aristocrats leased their appropriated lands to capitalist tenants, who farmed the land by hiring wage laborers, who once had common use-rights to the land. In the eighteenth century, these property relations structured the emerging industrial capitalism, first in the English cities, then in their colonies, and eventually became the dominant understanding of private property in the industrialized world. Capitalists own the means of production—that is, through their use of money, they have appropriated not only the natural resources, fossil fuels, and materials needed for production, but also the machines and technologies utilized in the production process. They also have appropriated the labor—muscles, skills, and knowledge—of others, who no longer could subsist on their own, in exchange for wages. The exchange value that results from production thus belongs to, is the exclusive property of, the capitalists. Despite being reified through the capitalist ideology, widely accepted, and codified into law by the modern nation-state, capitalist property relations, which make claims of exclusive ownership, are not natural nor inevitable. They remain only a social construction rooted in Locke's understanding of property and thus could be dissolved similarly by social agreement (the Fifth Amendment notwithstanding).

Capitalist property relations incorporate the natural world differently than do the Israelite property relations. Because the latter are based on usufruct rights, the ancient Israelites' relationship to the natural world was mediated by their relationship to Yhwh. Yhwh was the creator of the world; it belonged to Yhwh alone. But Yhwh was also in covenantal relationship with Israel, and so Yhwh would ensure their material abundance and prosperity if the Israelites remained faithful to Yhwh's covenant: Yhwh would ensure their possession and use of the land, its fertility, the abundance of their flock, and the well-being of their households (see Deut 11:13–17; 28:1–68; Lev 26:3–45). Locke, who takes an anthropocentric approach to the biblical tradition, also acknowledged the earth to be God's creation, which was given to humans in common (citing Ps 115:16). In other words, the earth and its resources *belong to* humans rather than to God. Moreover, according to Locke, God did not intend for the earth to remain in common: "since he gave it them for their benefit and for the greatest conveniences of life they could get from it, he can't have meant it always to remain common and uncultivated" (2017, §34). Locke interprets God's command for humans to subdue the earth as a call to improve it and thus take ownership of it through one's labor (2017, §32). Thus, according to Locke, it is God's will for humans to appropriate parts of the natural world—to take exclusive ownership of it—and to use it to benefit life.

For capitalist property relations, building on Locke's conception of property, the earth and all its resources are a free gift to humans—to those who can appropriate them and produce exchange value from them. Two corollaries follow from this. First, nature belongs only to those who can appropriate it and has value only through its appropriation. Even though nature is given to all humans in common, until it is worked or improved, it is waste; nature has no value in and of itself. Only the one who appropriates material from nature can claim exclusive ownership over it and thus use it however one sees fit. Value is created when it is improved—when labor is added to it. Only when a tree, for example, is cut down and used for fuel, or made into a piece of furniture, or used to build a house is value created from the wood. Second, unworked material from nature is a *free* gift and thus may be appropriated without cost for the material. The act of appropriation may entail costs and so add to the value to the material, but the material itself is free (because it has no value in the state of nature). As a result, capitalists can appropriate as much of the natural world as they need for production, and all of it and the exchange value they create from it will belong to them alone. For Locke, this was not a problem because the earth was believed to be so abundant that one person's appropriation of nature did not deprive another of equally appropriating nature. In today's world, however, the limits of the natural world are increasingly recognized (Haddad 2003). Nevertheless, capitalist property relations, which are reinforced by the state, enable capitalists to continue to extract natural resources without limit and to the deprivation of others.

From the perspective of the biblical tradition, which emphasizes that the natural world has value because it is the creation of God and that all Israelite households have usufruct rights in God's earth, capitalist property relations are exploitive of both the natural world, claiming exclusive ownership of what belongs to God, and of the rest of the population, who have an equal right in the use of nature. While it might be legitimate to claim exclusive ownership over the product of one's own labor when it cannot otherwise be shared, such as food or a piece of clothing, there is no *natural* right to ownership when the production is due to the labor of others, or when those who have an equal claim on the limited resource are not compensated. Marx (1992, 911) compares the absurdity of capitalist claims of exclusive ownership of nature to similar claims of ownership of humans in slavery:

> From the standpoint of a higher socio-economic formation, the private property of particular individuals in the earth will appear just as absurd as the private property of one man in other men. Even an entire society, a nation, or all simultaneously existing societies taken together, are not the owners of the earth. They are simply its possessors, its beneficiaries, and have to bequeath it in an improved state to succeeding generations, as *boni patres familias* [good heads of the household].

Ancient Israelite and capitalist social relations of production also differ in the way that surplus is created and extracted. As a subsistence economy, most ancient Israelites had access to the means of production—land, tools, animals—and surplus accrued during good years as a result of one's own labor. Household relations were the primary productive relations, and everyone in the household participated in the production, according to gender and age roles. Whatever surplus was produced by the household belonged to and sustained the household. Some Israelites also entered into patron–client relations, and all Israelites participated in the tributary relations of the royal house. Although households may have benefitted from these relations, especially from patronage, some of the household surplus was also extracted through the relationship. That is, the patron may have extracted some of the client's labor or a share of the client's production as rent in exchange for access to land, a loan of grain, or a political favor; and all households were subject to taxation by the state. The extraction of surplus, however, was based on *extra-economic factors*: political power linked with friendship and honor for the patron, and military and judicial power for the king. Divine sanction also played a role in extraction, especially in relation to the king.

In capitalist social relations, surplus is also created through labor, generally by improving materials from nature, but is extracted by *economic means* through wages. Workers, who no longer own or have access to the means of production, labor in exchange for wages, but the wages are less than the exchange value produced by their labor. This extra value—a surplus value that accrues for the capitalist—is built into the wage labor. The wage-laborers essentially work part of the day for free, continually adding value to the production without compensation. And because the workers are unable to provide for their own livelihood apart from such wage-labor, they have little choice but to give up their surplus value, accepting the deficient wage in order to purchase the necessities of life. Capitalist social relations are thus inherently exploitive: "Only in capitalism is the dominant mode of appropriation based on the complete dispossession of direct producers, who (unlike chattel slaves) are legally free and whose surplus labor is appropriated by purely 'economic' means" (Wood 2017, 96).

Capitalist social relations are also exploitive in terms of gender relations. Although the structures of capitalism do not create specific gender relations, unlike household relations in ancient Israel, they reinforce and exploit existing hierarchical or patriarchal understandings of gender. For example, capitalism gives no attention to the reproduction of its own laborers. It assumes that the unpaid labor of the wife, who is needed to nurture children, will supplement the husband's wage to maintain the household. The wife is doubly dependent: like the husband, she is dependent on the capitalist who owns the means of production, but she is also dependent on her husband who is paid in wages. If the wife does enter the workforce, she is often relegated to gender-specific jobs or is paid less for the same job as a man. "Family obligations that keep women out of the paid labor force for periods of time and the restricted opportunities and incomes available to many women when they do enter the paid labor force work in tandem to promote women's economic dependence" (Acker 1988, 475). The woman's economic dependence within the household is thus mediated by marital and kinship relations; it is determined by extra-economic relations that control the distribution of the husband's wage. The structures of capitalism promote household relations of distribution, which "embody and perpetuate male domination and the subordination of women" (Acker 1988, 497). Capitalism's exploitation of gender relations increases the surplus by appropriating the free labor used for the worker's reproduction or through reduced wages for a female workforce.

In order to maximize the surplus, the capitalist invests in technology that reduces the amount of labor required for production, thus increasing efficiency. Technology and innovation both simplified and specialized the skills necessary for production, thus reducing the wages of the laborers or increasing their productivity. The capitalist's continual reinvestment of the surplus for the purpose of increasing accumulation and profit-maximization provides the conditions for economic growth. Money is invested in machines and materials, labor is hired for the specific tasks of production, then the commodity is sold on the market for more money than was expended on its production. Reinvestment in the production process enables more workers to produce more commodities with more material, for the purpose of creating more profit. A growing surplus is realized when investment is put into better machines, requiring less labor, with fewer skills, and when labor is more tightly controlled. Once the production process was powered by energy-dense, fossil fuels—a mobile, possessable stock, which reinforced capitalist relations, and seemingly endless in supply—economic growth became self-sustaining (Malm 2016). As production increases through reinvestment more fossil fuel is consumed and more material resources are transformed into commodities. Self-sustaining growth, which is made possible by an equally growing extraction of materials *and* fossil fuel for energy, is a feature or property of capitalist relations. But continual growth in production is only possible if it is matched by continual growth in consumption, and this is made possible by the market in capitalism.

In ancient Israel, as well as the rest of the pre-capitalist world, markets functioned simply to provide goods that could be produced exclusively or more cheaply in one part of the world to other parts where they could not be produced at all or as cheaply. In the ancient world, much of the trade involved luxury or prestige items for the royal houses and the elite, but some trade was commercial in nature, where profit was made by buying cheap in one region and selling dear in another. The logic of these markets was simply the exchange of commensurable products; they made no demand on production. Profit, when it was the purpose of trade, which was rarely the case in the ancient world, resulted from regional differences, such as access to desired resources or valued skills. Markets did not alter the social relations of production; the ancients did not have a market society.

The market in capitalism functions differently than it did in the ancient and pre-capitalist world. The capitalist market is the "principal determinant and regulator of social reproduction" (Wood 2017, 97). Both the capitalist and the workers are dependent on the market. Workers are dependent on the market to sell their labor as a commodity, and the market will determine their wages. Capitalists are dependent on the market to buy the means of production and hire labor, as well as to sell their products in order to profit from their surplus value. The market, which is now global in scale, also functions to incorporate all production within the capitalist economy. Small family or independently owned businesses, for example, must also compete in the market just as large capitalist firms, but without the advantages of scale.

> Material life and social reproduction in capitalism are universally mediated by the market, so that all individuals must in one way or another enter into market relations in order to gain access to the means of life. This unique system of market-dependence means that the dictates of the capitalist market—its imperatives of competition, accumulation, profit-maximization, and increasing labour-productivity—regulate not only economic transactions but social relations in general. (Wood 2017, 7)

The market links production with consumption and thus creates the conditions so that both capitalists and workers need and benefit from economic growth. Capitalists need economic growth to realize profits on their investments, based on the dynamics of their social relations of production. Without economic growth, production must be reduced, entailing the laying off of workers, lest overproduction consumes the profit. Workers also need economic growth to ensure employment and perhaps a growing wage (though the workers' share of the economic growth is much smaller than the capitalists; see Piketty 2014). Economic growth provides the workers with an abundant, diverse supply of cheap products from which to purchase the necessities of life, and the means to buy occasionally even a few luxury goods.

Economic growth is a structural property of capitalist property and social relations, and without growth, capitalist relations cannot function (see Higgs 2014).[4]

---

4. Capitalism produces growth in spite of the fact that the contradictions of capitalism—such as the tendency towards overproduction—result in periodic and inevitable crises, typically known as recessions. These crises often require extra-economic relief, such as subsidies, which governments too willingly hand over. Not even capitalism—the only economic system to produce sustained per capita economic growth—can sustain growth indefinitely. It typically grows for a period, retracts in crisis,

Economic growth is also dependent on an abundance of energy, which is supplied predominantly by fossil fuels, to power the metabolism of capitalist relations. Without a sufficient reservoir and flow of energy, capitalist production will sputter and stall as it quickly uses up the available energy—production will contract, profits will fall, and accumulation will stop. Because of the intrinsic and essential relationship between capitalism and economic growth, no capitalist solution to the environmental crisis is possible. This is particularly true when put in the context of the market, for the market does not value the natural world. Like the labor of workers, it is a mere commodity to be purchased for as little as possible. Subject to the market, the natural world ceases to be the commons of all and becomes the property of a few.[5] The imperatives of the market—competition, accumulation, maximizing profit, and increasing labor-productivity—result in the exploitation of workers and the degradation of the natural world. At best, the growth of the inherent environmental impact produced by capitalism can be restrained or slowed, which is typically the aim, if not the result, of most environmental protection policies. The same can be said for carbon dioxide emissions, which result from the fossil fuels that power capitalist production. But in neither case, can the growth of environmental impact or carbon dioxide emissions be stopped. Capitalism will inevitably produce growth and thus increase environmental impact along with carbon dioxide emissions, or capitalism will give way to a different socio-economic configuration.

MATERIAL BASIS OF ECONOMIC ACTIVITY

The argument that I have been making is that *all economic activity* (affluence and technology in the IPAT formula) has an impact on the environment, and capitalism in particular, with its endless need for growth and its dependence on fossil fuels for energy, is the cause of the current environmental crisis. Consequently, its solution must entail economic activity without the need for growth or fossil fuels, and as such it cannot be capitalism. The fundament reason that economic activity has an impact on the environment is because all economic activity—production and consumption, and the energy that powers it—has a material basis. This was recognized by Marx (2004, 172):

---

and then repeats the cycle over again, with even more growth. Despite the havoc capitalism's ups and downs may produce, especially for the workers, the unending desire for accumulation and profit is what drives it forward.

5. Garrett Hardin (1968), in defense of private property, argued that land that is held in common will be abused by the self-interest of all those who have access to it. His "tragedy of the commons" has been applied to all resource use. However, his analysis is incomplete because he does not consider the specific political economy into which the land usage is subsumed; he assumes a universal set of social relations, which are capitalist. His "tragedy of the commons" is essentially a tragedy of the market (Bollier 2014, 21–36) or a tragedy of the commodity (Longo et al. 2015, 27–38).

Part II: Ecology

> Use-values like coats, linen, etc., in short, the physical bodies of commodities, are combinations of two elements, the material provided by nature, and labour. If we subtract the total amount of useful labour of different kinds which is contained in the coat, the linen, etc., *a material substratum is always left*. This substratum is furnished by nature without human intervention. When man engages in production, he can only proceed as nature does herself, i.e. he can only change the form of the materials. Furthermore, even in this work of modification he is constantly helped by natural forces. Labour is therefore not the only source of material wealth, i.e. of the use-values it produces. As William Petty says, labour is the father of material wealth, the earth is its mother. (emphasis added)

The material basis of the economy limits its economic growth; it is constrained by resource availability and absolutely limited by the biophysical, finite limits of the planet.[6] Capitalism, with its need for growth, is simply propelling the economy headlong into the environmental crises (Magdoff 2013), along with the pollution and environmental degradation that comes with it, crashing through planetary boundaries as if it were an automobile *accelerating* toward the side of a mountain in the distance.[7] Nevertheless, many environmentally conscious individuals, groups, and organizations continue to maintain that we can both address our environmental problems and grow the economy—embracing a "green capitalism." Their solution? Decouple the economy from its environmental impacts.

Decoupling has become a buzz-word in environmental circles and it commonly refers to breaking the link between good economic benefits and harmful environmental consequences. Because there is no easy way to measure the entire economy and its environmental impact, decoupling typically is applied to particular sectors. Thus, those concerned with climate change, for example, argue that we need to decouple

---

6. Resource depletion (or exhaustion) is generally not about the complete expenditure of a resource but rather its economically viable extraction. In other words, a resource will become far too expensive to extract before it no longer exists. Conventional petroleum, for example, can be extracted from $10 to $40 per barrel, but shale oil costs from $60 to $90 per barrel to extract; oil from the Alberta Tar Sands costs about $85 per barrel. On the day that I wrote this, crude oil was selling between $20 and $28 per barrel on the market, making the extraction of some oil not economically viable. Oil will be "depleted," not when the wells are dry but when it is no longer financially viable to continue extracting it. Nevertheless, there is also an absolute limit to how much oil is available, even if it is never reached.

7. Neoclassical economics, which gives little regard to the actual biophysical world, is unconcerned about material resource depletion because the market will resolve the problem. Either a cheaper, more abundant resource will shift demand away from the more expensive, depleted resource; it will become economical to recycle the depleted resource; human created capital will substitute for the depleted resource; or technology and innovation will reduce the demand on the depleted resource through efficiency (see Neumayer 2000). In other words, neoclassical economics assumes that although some resources may be depleted, many other viable resources will continue to be available for unlimited use. However, no adequate substitute exists—naturally occurring or human created—for many currently used resources (Graedel et al. 2015), and efficiency often leads to more use of the resource, following Jevon's paradox (Alcott 2005; Foster et al. 2010, 169–81).

energy or production from carbon dioxide emissions. The economy as a whole is often measured by gross domestic product (GDP), even though this metric does not include economic activity that is not commodified, such as housework, volunteer labor, or subsistence of any kind (Higgs 2014, 158–60). Relative decoupling occurs when economic growth increases more than the environmental impact; absolute decoupling occurs when economic growth increases while environmental impact actually decreases.

There is plenty of evidence of relative decoupling, especially when particular sectors of the economy and the environment are analyzed. As economies develop and mature, they become more efficient and the material intensity of the economy tends to decrease.[8] Several European nations, for example, have seen a relative decoupling of carbon dioxide emissions from GDP (Mikayilov et al. 2018; the U.S. experienced a modest relative decoupling in 2019). This is, perhaps, useful information, but it conceals as much as it reveals—namely, it does not *explain* the relative decoupling, and many causes are possible. One cause of relative decoupling is offshoring production. Many Europeans nations, as well as the United States, have moved much of their manufacturing to the global South, where labor is cheap, and so the associated carbon dioxide emissions are moved offshore as well. Another cause of relative decoupling is substitution. Converting coal burning plants to natural gas reduces the carbon dioxide emission by about half. The use of renewable energy, such as windmills and solar photovoltaic panels, would also reduce carbon dioxide emissions, though it would increase material usage instead. In any case, relative decoupling with regard to carbon dioxide emissions can be distorting. First, the globalized economy makes it difficult to sort out the emissions that should be credited to each nation. China produces far more annual carbon dioxide emissions than any other nation, but China also exports many of the commodities that embody those emissions to other nations. Second, the impact of carbon dioxide emissions on climate change is cumulative—carbon dioxide can remain in the atmosphere for thousands of years. While it might be helpful to know that the annual emissions of carbon dioxide have dropped in one or another nation, the global carbon dioxide emissions—the only figure that really matters—have continued to increase. In 2019, global emissions of carbon dioxide amounted to 36.8 billion tonnes, a 0.6 percent increase from 2018 and more than 4 percent increase

---

8. In most developed societies, the so-called knowledge economy plays an increasing role in the entire economy. Many professions in such societies are based on intellectual capital—education, research, law, medicine, finance, computer programming—and thus require much fewer material resources or fossil fuels for their production, leading to a relative decoupling of the local economy from environmental impact. But such decoupling can be deceptive. Since these professions are valued more than manufacturing, their higher salaries inflate the GDP relative to more intensive material and carbon-dioxide-emitting production. Moreover, these professions might lead to a reduction in materials and carbon dioxide emissions locally, but their higher standard of living, which correlates with more consumption, generally requires an increase in materials and carbon dioxide emissions globally.

from 2015 when the Paris Climate Agreement was signed (Global Carbon Project 2019).

When analyzed globally relative decoupling of carbon dioxide emission has not yet occurred. Similarly, total material resource use does not give any evidence of decoupling the economy from its material base (Hickel and Kallis 2019; UNEP 2016; Schandl et al. 2017; cf. Behrens et al. 2007). In fact, global material resource use has accelerated since 2000. Global GDP has grown from $15.4 trillion in 1970 to $51.7 trillion in 2010, with an annual increase of 3.1 percent (double the rate of population growth), but only 2.6 percent annual increase since 2000. Global material resource use, in contrast, has grown from 23.7 billion tonnes in 1970 to 70.1 billion tonnes in 2010, which translates into an average rate of 2.7 percent increase until 2000, then a 3.7 percent increase through 2010. When population is taken into account, material resource use rose from 6.4 tonnes per capita in 1970 to 7.9 tonnes per capita in 2000, a rather modest 0.8 percent increase per year over thirty years. Then, the per capita resource use surged to 10.1 tonnes by 2010, a 2.8 percent increase per year.[9] Much of the global increase in material resource use during the 2000s can be attributed to Asia and the Pacific due to their increasing transition from agrarian to industrial production. Whereas an increasing larger proportion of the production is taking place in Asia and the Pacific, consumption remains highest in Europe and North America (Wiedmann et al. 2015). Africa has the lowest annual material footprint with approximately 3 tonnes per person, Europe uses over 20 tonnes per person and North America uses over 30 tonnes per person.[10] In other words, the "richest countries consume on average 10 times as many materials as the poorest countries, and twice the world average, which demonstrates very unequal distribution of materials to support the standard of living" (UNEP 2016, 17).

Although some relative decoupling can be found within particular sectors, such as carbon dioxide emissions by nation, when production and consumption are taken into account and analyzed on a global scale, even relative decoupling tends to disappear. There definitely is no evidence for absolute decoupling, especially when the focus is global. With the shift of production to the global South, whatever gains in efficiency (and thus relative decoupling) that had accrued during the three decades from 1970 to 2000 were lost. In 2000, 1.2 kilograms of material were required on average to produce $1 of GDP, but by 2010, nearly 1.4 kilograms of material were needed to produce the same $1 (UNEP 2016, 40). Moreover, as more production becomes dependent on trade, it is important to note that global trade requires proportionally more material resources, "mobilizing much greater amounts of materials than direct

---

9. Recent figures suggest that these trends have continued to the present, with 92 billion tonnes of material extracted by 2017, translating to 12 tonnes per capita (see the data at MaterialFlows.net).

10. Due to the global financial crisis, beginning in 2008, the European and North American material footprints were reduced to 20 and 25 tonnes per capita respectfully. More recent data was not available.

traded flows indicate" (Schandl et al. 2017, 832). By 2010, 10 billion tonnes of globally traded goods required 30 billion tonnes of extracted material resources, and the amount of traded goods has continued to increase. Not all economic activity entails the same material intensity, and so shifting from one form of production to another may also entail a reduction in material resource use—a relative decoupling—or an increase in material use, as with trade. But all economic activity has a material basis, and thus contributes to environmental impact. Decoupling as a means to preserve the natural environment is largely a product of capitalist ideology that masks the cause of the environmental crisis and reinforces the continual need for economic growth (see Jackson 2009, 67–86).

The hope of decoupling the economy from environmental impact nevertheless persists in environmental circles. It is associated with concepts such as "sustainable development" and "green growth," and it undergirds international programs, such as the United Nations Sustainable Development Goals (SDG n.d.), and national initiatives, such as the Green New Deal.[11] The Sustainable Development Goals consist of seventeen goals, from eliminating poverty and hunger, reducing inequality and providing quality education, to protecting the environment along with economic growth. They were accepted in 2015 by the member nations of the U.N. as part of the "2030 Agenda for Sustainable Development," which provides a fifteen-year plan to accomplish the goals. Although some progress has been made, neither the speed nor the scale of the work is sufficient to reach the goals by 2030; the key to success in accomplishing the goals is "decoupling escalating resource use and environmental degradation from economic growth" (UNEP 2014, xii). Although decoupling is mentioned in the goals (goal 8 addresses economic growth; see §8.4 of the 2030 Agenda), the United Nations Environment Programme (UNEP) laid the foundation for the Sustainable Development Goals on two reports addressing decoupling (2011, 2014). These reports make the compelling case that decoupling environmental degradation and economic growth is essential for sustainable development. In this view, they are probably correct: because it requires economic growth, *sustainable* development is not possible *without decoupling*. But the possibility of decoupling remains largely theoretical and untethered from biophysical constraints.

To its credit, UNEP recognizes that sustainable development is not compatible with a *material* growth of the economy. Thus, UNEP links decoupling with the dematerialization of the economy, distinguishing between traditional physical economic growth (resource consumption) that is unsustainable and non-material economic

---

11. The Green New Deal, which has been proposed in several European nations and in the United States, is a framework for addressing climate change within a capitalist economy. Although not necessarily using the language of decoupling, the Green New Deal proposes to harness the growth of capitalism to produce good, high-wage jobs, rebuild and upgrade infrastructure, and increase clean manufacturing, while also decarbonizing the economy and addressing other environmental concerns. Despite many laudable goals, the Green New Deal, like most ideas employing "green capitalism" or "green growth," is based on irreconcilable contradictions (see Hickel and Kallis 2019).

growth that results from the flow of money and value. Sustainable development will occur when the developing nations transition from physical to non-material economic growth (2011, 33–35). However, such dematerialization of the economy is no more possible than absolute decoupling of economic growth from environmental degradation. Some sectors of any economy are less materially intense than others, such as the so-called knowledge economy in comparison with industrial manufacturing, and these sectors increase with development (Smil 2017, 348–49). But material resources are not simply a factor of production, they are also intrinsic to consumption. Any growth that results from monetary flow will eventually be realized with increased consumption, requiring increased material resources. Moreover, it is unclear how monetary flow is expected to grow without material growth. The economy is not a perpetual motion machine; its metabolism is dependent on the continual consumption of material and energy. Even naturally flowing solar, wind, and water energy require materials for their conversion to usable energy, and growth will not take place without energy.

In its second report, UNEP acknowledges that decoupling is not happening: "breaking the link between human well-being and resource consumption is necessary and possible but in reality is hardly happening" (2014, xii). According to the 2019 report on the Sustainable Development Goals, the global material footprint—how much material resources are being used globally per capita—has grown rapidly, outpacing population and economic growth. The needed dematerialization of the economy, or decoupling of economic growth from environmental impact, has not occurred *because it cannot*. The economy takes place within the biophysical, material world; it is the sum of our engagement with the material world and with one another. Economic growth is equally material at its base and likewise has material, i.e., environmental, consequences. The problem with decoupling is not simply that it does not work, but that it masks the real problem and allows for the continuation of business-as-usual: "even if decoupling is infeasible, it will take some time for this to be demonstrated to the satisfaction of its proponents as well as those merely using it as a smokescreen to continue business as usual for as long as they still can. Thus, the decoupling fantasy may allow us to maintain an increasingly destructive path with both the promise of success and demonstration of its impossibility deferred into the future" (Fletcher and Rammelt 2017, 463). Sustainable development is an oxymoron (see Hannis 2017; Higgs 2014, 105–62).

LIMITS OF RENEWABLE ENERGY

Although the economy cannot be decoupled from its material basis, including the environmental degradation that comes with it, the economy can be decoupled (relatively) from carbon dioxide emissions because energy can be produced from sources other than fossil fuels. The energy from wind and water flows were tapped in antiquity, but today we can extract kinetic energy from burning biofuels and electricity from nuclear fission, hydroelectric dams, biomass and geothermal sources, wind turbines, and solar radiation—all sources of renewable energy. Because climate change is primarily caused by excessive carbon dioxide emissions in the atmosphere as a result of burning fossil fuels, many have argued that society needs to shift from fossil fuels as the primary source of energy to a variety of carbon-dioxide-free, renewable sources.[12] Moreover, many environmentally concerned people claim, or assume, that economic growth can continue in a decarbonized, renewable energy powered world.[13] It cannot. Let me be clear: *society needs to transition to renewable sources of energy as soon as possible* (on the available technologies and sources, see Hawken 2017). But renewable energy technologies—at least the ones existing today—cannot meet all of society's current energy needs, let alone increasing needs due to economic growth. A society that is powered mostly by renewable energy technologies will be a society with less economic activity than today and, as a result, cannot be dependent on economic growth. It will thus not be a society governed by capitalist relations, for renewable energy will not be able to supply the economic growth capitalism requires.

Within the last two decades, energy studies have increasingly given attention to achieving 100 percent renewable energy (Hansen et al. 2019). Most of these studies have a regional or national focus—which allows carbon dioxide emissions to be outsourced to other regions—and few have addressed the more difficult transportation and industrial sectors of the economy. Most studies present only theoretical models of energy systems. At present, renewable energy cannot power ocean freighters or aircraft, produce sufficient heat for the production of cement or steal, and the hydrocarbons of fossil fuels are needed for many synthetic processes, such as producing plastics and fertilizer. Recently, Mark Jacobson, Mark Delucchi, and their team have published a series of articles attempting to demonstrate that 100 percent of the world's energy can be supplied by water, wind, and solar power, producing all new energy by 2030 and replacing existing energy by 2050 (with a 30% reduction in energy demand from efficiency—a historically unprecedented reduction in energy intensity), with energy costs that are similar to today's costs (Jacobson and Delucchi 2011; Delucchi and Jacobson 2011; Jacobson, Delucchi, Bazouin et al. 2015; Jacobson, Delucchi, Cameron, et al. 2015). Jacobson and Delucchi's studies were widely reported in the media and embraced by many environmentalists, but their vision of a global renewable energy

---

12. Nuclear power, even though it produces carbon-free electricity, is generally not considered in the mix of renewable energy technologies. The nuclear fuels—uranium, plutonium, and thorium—are not renewable, and pose other environmental problems. Moreover, the lifecycle of a nuclear power plant (fuel mining, transport, and enrichment, plant construction, and plant decommissioning) is dependent on fossil fuels and thus produces significant carbon dioxide emissions.

13. The Green New Deal (H. Res. 109, 116 Congress), for example, requires the federal government "to achieve net-zero greenhouse gas emissions," presumably through renewable energy technologies, and also "to create millions of good, high-wage jobs and ensure prosperity and economic security for all people of the United States." Renewable energy is assumed to be compatible with economic growth, if not the context for "green" new jobs.

system is not achievable. Vaclav Smil has characterized their work as "unbounded science and engineering fiction" (2016a, 243). To meet global energy needs, they propose installing 3.8 million 5-megawatt wind turbines (40 times the 2013 capacity), 49 thousand 300-megawatt solar plants (2700 times the 2018 capacity), 40 thousand 300-megawatt solar photovoltaic power plants and 1.7 billion 3-kilowatt rooftop systems (170 times the 2013 capacity, with no existing solar plants this large), 5350 100-megawatt geothermal power plants (a hundred-fold increase from today), 720 thousand 0.75-megawatt wave devices and 490 thousand 1-megawatt tidal turbines (only a handful existed in 2014), 270 new 1300-megawatt hydroelectric power plants, and energy for industry and transportation will be supplied with electrolytic hydrogen (Jacobson and Delucchi 2011; see Smil 2016a, 244). Some of these figures are wildly unrealistic; a non-existent hydrogen-based infrastructure would need to be created; and the existing electrical infrastructure would need to be expanded enormously and upgraded to a smart grid. Others have accused Jacobson and Delucchi of modelling errors; making incorrect, implausible, and unsupported assumptions; deploying technologies unproven at scale; and ignoring infrastructure costs (Clack et al. 2017). According to Smil, "the chances of a 100% water-wind-solar world to be ready by 2030 are nil" (2016a, 245; see Heard et al. 2017; Loftus et al. 2015; Floyd et al. 2020).

Any 100 percent renewable energy system will need to rely on wind and solar power for most of its energy. Hydroelectric and geothermal power are much more limited in their potential to expand (Heinberg and Fridley 2016, 66–68), and biofuels and biomass are limited by competing demands on productive land (for agriculture and forests); wave and tidal generators are not yet commercially viable, and there is no installed base. The problem with wind and solar power is that they are variable energy sources—that is, they convert energy only intermittently, when the wind is blowing and the sun is shining.[14] Solar energy can be captured with photovoltaic (PV) panels only during the day, and depending on the latitude, only during a limited number of hours during the middle of the day, and more during the summer than the winter. This regularity is interrupted by clouds, which significantly reduce the efficiency of the panels. Wind turbines can generate energy around the clock, but are dependent on a steady blowing wind. Typically, winds must reach 8 miles per hour for the turbines to generate (though the windmill blades will begin turning at 5 miles per hour). Fluctuating or excessive wind speeds reduce the generating capacity of the windmill. The intermittency of wind and solar energy creates a significant obstacle, if we are going to be dependent on these sources for a reliable, consistent flow of electricity.

There are three possible solutions for variable energy flows. First, and most consequential, is to adapt to an intermittent supply of energy. Although energy fluctuations can be minimized by spreading the energy sources across a wide area to take advantage of regional weather differences, it would require a more sophisticated

---

14. Hydroelectric is also a variable energy source (though not intermittent) in that drought can reduce the flow of rivers or lower reservoirs and thus lower the energy capacity of the power plant.

electrical grid than we presently have in the U.S. and the installation of an excessive number of wind turbines and solar power plants to compensate for regions where they are not producing, all of which would raise the cost of the energy considerably (Heard et al. 2017, 1129–30). And in the end, fluctuations in energy availability cannot be eliminated.[15] Adaptation to fluctuating energy flows would necessarily disrupt business-as-usual, because it would come with brownouts (reduced energy availability) and blackouts (no energy availability) at irregular and inconvenient times and for unpredictable durations. Many of our current energy uses are dependent on a regular, consistent availability of electricity, such as refrigeration, computers and electronics, manufacturing equipment, and especially health care equipment. A variable and unpredictable flow of energy will require not only economic changes but social as well. Lifestyle choices, social engagements and structures, and civic roles would need to accommodate a shifting and variable supply of energy and the disruptions it would cause.

Second, we can compensate for variable energy by deploying an energy storage system, but this would be limited in scale and duration. A backup set of batteries, for example, could compensate for the loss of energy to critical healthcare equipment, but not for all energy loss or an extended period of time, and batteries are resource intensive and become prohibitively expensive at scale.[16] An alternative is pumped storage hydropower, where surplus energy is used to pump water from a lower reservoir to an upper reservoir. When electricity is needed, water from the upper reservoir is released to flow down to the lower reservoir through power-generating turbines. The advantages of pumped storage hydropower are that it can store large amounts of energy and can release the energy very quickly; the disadvantages are that it is limited by geography—ideally, there should be an elevation difference of 1500 feet between the reservoirs—and water availability. Building reservoirs also has significant environmental consequences, including greenhouse gas emissions.[17] Concentrated solar power plants are also able to store energy by using hot molten salt, which powers steam turbines. During the day, the molten salt is heated by sunlight, which is directed and concentrated on the salt by a large array of mirrors, with temperatures

---

15. Variability is a fundamental difference between fossil fuels, which are a *stock* that can be stored and supplied at a continuous rate, and renewables, which are based on *flows* that are limited by the source (the sun, wind, or water) and subject to disruption. Variability is an inherent property of renewable energy, and so cannot be eliminated.

16. Lithium-ion batteries require cobalt, nickel, and especially lithium, and all have quite limited known reserves (Dominish 2019). With a modest growth in battery production each year, lithium reserves will be exhausted within fifty years (Heinberg and Fridley 2016, 73; see Vikström et al. 2013). In other words, we cannot simply electrify all the automobiles, more than a billion worldwide, as well as our electronics, and still have lithium to spare for storing intermittent electricity.

17. Although pumped storage hydropower is the most commonly used grid-level storage option, in the U.S. it produces only 2 percent of the electric grid's capacity (Heinberg and Fridley 2016, 54). Many more reservoir systems would need to be created for pumped storage hydropower to serve as an adequate backup for a 100 percent renewable energy system.

reaching above 435 degrees Fahrenheit; then at night, the residual heat of the molten salt is able to continue generating electricity for five to ten hours (see Hawken 2017, 31–33). Concentrated solar power plants also have their limits—relatively few power plants exist, they are capital intensive and less efficient that solar PV, and they cannot generate electricity around the clock. They are best located in subtropical deserts to maximize solar radiation, which is often far from large populations and have a shortage of water. The electricity generated from such power plants, however, is more easily integrated into the conventional grid (Hawken 2017, 13–15).

Third, the current, most widely used method of compensating for the variability of solar and wind power is to maintain an alternative, redundant way to generate electricity. Today, this is accomplished with fossil fuel power plants, which are supplemented by renewable energy, but the primary power source can shift: fossil fuel power plants could supplement renewable energy technologies when they are unable to produce. This is an expensive option because it requires two energy systems that are able to generate sufficient capacity. The fossil fuel power plants would also continue to produce carbon dioxide emissions. They would need to be continually running at low idle because they cannot be turned on quickly—that is, within seconds; they take minutes to hours to generate sufficient steam to turn the turbines, during which time there would be a disruption in the energy system. For those committed to a 100 percent renewable energy system, this would be the least preferable option, but fossil fuel power plants can be replaced with a renewable option: biomass power plants. Such power plants create a reliable and consistent flow of electricity just like fossil fuel power plants, but instead of burning coal or natural gas, they burn woodchips, woody crops, or discarded waste, all of which is renewable, if inefficient (see Heinberg and Fridley 2016, 65–66). Biomass power plants emit carbon dioxide, but they do not increase the atmospheric concentration since the carbon is already in circulation.[18] The problem with biomass power plants is the feedstock, and this is an issue of scale. Woody material that was grown on degraded land dedicated for this purpose and simple plant waste make an ideal feedstock, but such resources are limited. As more energy is required from biomass power plants, forests and crops grown on good agricultural land have been included in the feedstock, and this is an inefficient way to produce electricity. Biomass power plants can result in adverse land-use changes and deforestation, and can impact food security. At best, biomass power plants can supplement wind and solar power; they cannot fully replace wind and solar power when they are not producing unless the overall demand for electricity is within sustainable feedstock limits for biomass (Hawken 2017, 15–17). In any case, none of the three options for addressing the variability of wind and solar power are without

---

18. The problem with burning fossil fuels is that it releases enormous amounts of carbon dioxide into the atmosphere, which had been sequestered for millions of years. Burning biomass, in contrast, simply returns the carbon dioxide that the plants had pulled out of the air through photosynthesis. If not burned, the carbon will return to the atmosphere as methane when the plants decay.

significant economic, social, or environmental costs, and each of the options becomes more problematic with scale. On the other hand, all three options are feasible—in order to maintain a predominantly renewable energy system—if the need for energy is *significantly reduced*.

Renewable energy technologies, it is often claimed, produce "clean energy" or "green energy," especially in contrast to fossil fuels. And it is true that wind turbines and solar PV panels, for example, do not emit carbon dioxide while they are *producing* electricity, but they are far from "clean" or "green." All energy technologies have an environmental impact in their production and often on the landscape in which they are deployed (Moriarty and Honnery 2016, 2012). They depend on the mining and processing of metals and rare earth elements, often with the use of massive amounts of water, and their construction, installation, and recycling require fossil fuel powered industries. Through this process, carbon dioxide is emitted, waste is produced with toxic materials, the land is degraded, and water systems are polluted (on mineral extraction for renewable energy technology, see Dominish 2016). No renewable energy technology is self-producing, nor can it decommission itself—that is, it cannot be produced or dismantled and recycled from the electricity it generates.[19] All renewable energy technologies require machinery and industries that are unable to be powered by renewable energy: the manufacturing of concrete and steel for wind turbines, glass and solar cells for solar PV panels, and aluminum and silicon microchips for computers all require concentrated high temperatures that electricity or biofuels cannot deliver (Heinberg and Fridley 2016, 97). Moreover, while renewable energy technologies generate more carbon-free electricity than the fossil fuel energy required to produce them, the use of renewable energy technologies has not reduced fossil fuel consumption nor carbon dioxide emissions; they have simple contributed more energy—even a growing share—to feed a growing demand (York 2012). Renewable energy is subsidized by and dependent upon fossil fuels (Smil 2016b). Thus, a rapid increase in the mass production and installation of wind turbines and solar PV panels, or any other renewable energy technology, will require a similar increase in fossil fuel consumption and resource extraction, and will result in even more environmental degradation. Renewable energy technologies are needed to minimize the effects of climate change, but they cannot completely replace fossil fuels, which are needed for industry, and they entail their own environmental consequences (Fitz 2019; Hickel 2019b; see Moriarty and Honnery 2011).

---

19. Wind turbines have a useful life of twenty years; solar panels are usable for twenty-five to thirty years. Decommissioning of wind turbines is not cheap. The dismantling and removal of 134 wind turbines in a Minnesota windfarm, for example, cost $71 million, $523,000 per wind turbine, and this cost was not out of line with the decommissioning of other wind turbines (Orr 2019). Although much of the materials in a wind turbine can be recycled, the large blades cannot, so they are often buried in landfills. Most solar PV panels also end up in landfills, releasing their toxic materials into the earth (Xu et al. 2018).

Part II: Ecology

The limits of renewable energy are also evident in its density and in the net energy (EROI) that such renewable energy technologies produce. Energy (or power) density refers to the amount of energy within a given mass, volume, or area. For example, the best lithium-ion batteries store and deliver energy with a density of 0.5 megajoules per kilogram (House 2009). Batteries have a very low energy density, even at the theoretical maximum of 5 megajoules per kilogram (Heinberg and Fridley 2016, 56). The same kilogram of gasoline, in contrast, contains 46 megajoules of energy—a nearly 100-fold increase. Gasoline is thus a good fuel for transportation: it embodies a lot of energy without a lot of weight; natural gas, at 55 megajoules per kilogram would be even better. Batteries, on the other hand, are very heavy for the energy they deliver (the battery pack for a Tesla Model S is about 600 kilograms). Thus, batteries make a poor energy supply for cars and trucks, will never power airplanes, but are suitable for bicycles and scooters because much less energy is required (see Cooper 2020). Because the energy embodied in automobiles is about 75 megawatts (Heinberg and Fridley 2016, 83)—translating roughly into the energy of 2000 gallons of gasoline, or 60,000 miles of driving based on 30 miles per gallon—it is environmentally preferable simply to reduce the production and driving of automobiles in favor of alternative modes of transportation such as walking, biking, and public transportation with buses and light rail powered by the electric grid (Zehner 2013; Hawkins et al. 2012).

All renewable energy options face similar constraints based on power density, but instead of measuring their density by mass, a more appropriate measurement is the amount of power they produce in watts for each square meter of area devoted to its production. Natural gas has the greatest density, as high as 2000 watts per square meter, followed by coal with a density as high as 1000 watts per square meter (Smil 2016a, 211).[20] When used to generate electricity, which would be a better comparison with renewables, natural gas and coal have a median power density of 482 and 135 watts per square meter respectively (Zalk and Behrens 2018). Renewable energy is much less dense than fossil fuels, or nuclear, by two orders of magnitude. Solar energy systems vary widely in their power density, but they have a median of about 6.6 watts per square meter, whereas wind turbines have a median density of 1.84 watts per square meters.[21] Biomass power systems have the worst power density with a median

---

20. Power density calculations differ, sometimes considerably, across different studies largely as the result of variations in capacity factors. The capacity factor is the average power generated divided by the rated peak power, and thus can vary according to environmental conditions and the efficiency of the technology. Wind turbines, for example, have capacity factors ranging from 22 to 43 percent, whereas the capacity factors of solar PV systems range from 12 to 20 percent (Heinberg and Fridley 2018, 52). The review and analysis by Zalk and Behrens (2018) present the median and average power densities from multiple studies, and thus provide a reasonably reliable foundation for the discussion here.

21. In addition to converting wind into electricity, wind turbines also remove energy from wind flows (Miller et al. 2011). Thus, wind turbines must be spaced three to five turbine diameters apart in the cross-wind direction and six to ten turbine diameters in the downwind direction (Smil 2016a, 64). Moreover, when windfarms are larger than 100 square kilometers, the maximum power density that

at 0.08 watts per square meter, though the maximum calculation was 0.6 watts per square meter (Zalk and Behrens 2018). Biofuels are a little better with 0.3 watts per square meter (Smil 2016a, 88–91). Because renewable energy is so much less dense than fossil fuels, replacing fossil fuels with renewable energy would require the use of considerably more land space. In Great Britain, for example, when the per capita energy consumption is divided by its population density, the resulting 1.25 watts per square meter is the average consumption of energy per unit of area (McKay 2013). This is about the same power density that a mix of wind, solar, and bioenergy would provide, indicating that it would take the entire land mass of Great Britain to provide enough renewable energy for its population. The United States is better off since its population is less dense, but Smil calculates that it would take between 25 and 50 percent of the U.S. landmass to provide enough renewable energy to replace the fossil fuel-nuclear-hydroelectric energy used in 2012 (Smil 2016a, 246–47). Some countries, such as Japan, do not have enough landmass to supply a similar amount of renewable energy. Of course, some technologies, such as wind turbines, can be moved offshore, and some of the land needed for energy production can be used for other purposes: land used for wind turbines can be farmed, and solar PV panels can be installed on the roofs of houses and other buildings, though biomass and biofuels compete with forests and agricultural land. Nevertheless, the low density of renewable energy means that it cannot simply replace fossil fuel energy; space constraints will result in less available energy.

All energy systems require energy to produce energy. Net energy or energy return on investment (EROI), which was introduced in chapter 2, is the amount of energy the system produces minus the energy required to build, operate, and maintain the system. It takes very little energy, for example, to pick an apple off a tree in my neighbor's yard—the apple will provide lots of energy with little expenditure so that the net energy is high. However, if I want my own apple tree, I must spend lots of energy first by planting a tree, and then by cultivating and pruning it, perhaps for several years. I might have more satisfaction in picking and eating an apple from my own tree, but the net energy will be less initially (a loss per apple, but a gain for the whole harvest). Similarly, fossil fuels produce a high net energy or EROI. In the early years of the oil industry, oil was easy to find and extract, so its EROI was well over 100:1—that is, for every barrel of oil invested in extraction, more than 100 barrels were produced; or simply, oil supplied over 100 times more energy than needed for its production. As oil became more difficult to find and extract, thus requiring more energy, its EROI also dropped. Today, the EROI of conventional oil is between 12:1 and 35:1, depending on its source. Oil extracted from shale rock formations and the Tar sands has a much lower EROI of 5:1 or less. It is unlikely that oil reserves will be exhausted before it simply costs too much (in money and energy) to extract more of it (see Guilford et al.

---

can be achieved is 1 watt per square meter (Adams and Keith 2013).

2011). Other fossil fuels have similarly high EROIs: coal is around 30:1, and natural gas ranges from 10:1 to 80:1 (Hall and Klitgaard 2012, 313).

Renewable energy technologies can produce both high and low net energy. Hydroelectric power produces the highest EROI, with over 100:1, but it also has one of the lowest power densities. Similarly, wind turbines have an EROI of about 20:1, though individual turbines vary considerably due windspeed, power capacity of the turbine, and diameter of the rotor (Kubiszewski et al. 2010). With this EROI, wind power is competitive with fossil fuels, though its power density is similar to hydroelectric. Solar energy has the most contested EROI largely because it is unclear what energy costs should be included. EROI's range from a little over 2:1 to has high at 14:1. A review of 45 studies puts the average EROI for solar PV panels at 10:1 (Hall et al. 2014). The problem with wind and solar energy is that most all of the costs are incurred before the turbines and panels begin producing any energy, so they will always have a negative EROI initially. Wind and solar EROIs do not include the dismantling and decommissioning of the technologies, which can have substantial costs, especially given the relatively short life of the turbines and panels. Wind and solar EROIs can be expected to decline as energy output increases because more favorable locations for the turbines and panels will give way to less favorable ones (Moriarty and Honnery 2012, 2016). Storage of the variable electricity generated by wind turbines and solar panels would also reduce the EROI. Finally, biofuels have a very low EROI: ethanol and biodiesel have similar EROIs in the range of 0.8:1 to 1.6:1 (Hall and Klitgaard 2012, 313). Biofuel is only economically viable because it is heavily subsidized by fossil fuels and the government. Given its low EROI and the carbon dioxide emissions during production (from fossil fuels and the feedstock), biofuel is simply not a long-term viable energy solution. When it is produced from land that could be better used in regenerative agricultural production, it is little better than gasoline in terms of net carbon dioxide emissions. Its main purpose in the U.S., and why it is subsidized by the government, is to stabilize corn prices due to overproduction following the mandates of industrial agriculture (Wise 2019, 138–39).

The calculation of net energy or EROI is not without problems or controversy, and scholars disagree on where to draw the boundaries for what to include in the calculation. The front-loading of expenses and the variability of wind and solar energy is particularly problematic, especially in comparison to fossil fuels. Nevertheless, the concept of EROI provides a number of insights regarding the viability and limits of renewable energy. First, the generally lower EROI of renewable energy will require a larger percent of the economy to be devoted to energy production. Even if renewables are able to produce as much energy as our current fossil fuel energy system, the energy will be less useful: "as society transitions away from high-EROI fossil fuels its overall economic efficiency may decline, as a somewhat higher proportion of produced energy will have to be reinvested into further energy production" (Heinberg and Fridley 2016, 119). Second, the minimum EROI for the reproduction of Western society—which includes arts, education, medicine, and the sciences, and the infrastructure to support it—has been calculated to be 11:1 (Fizaine and Court 2016), which is perhaps the average EROI of a mix of renewables, depending on the contribution of biomass and biofuel. Or, perhaps renewables are unable to produce this much net energy. In any case, there is no surplus energy for economic growth.

Given the variability of renewable energy, the inadequacy of storage, its low density and relatively low EROI, renewable technologies cannot sufficiently produce current levels of energy, let along the energy we would need if economic growth continues. Moreover, regardless of how much energy renewable technologies can produce, we will not be able to fully eliminate fossil fuels. We will remain dependent on them for some critical transportation and industrial tasks, as well as for the reproduction of the renewable energy system. The only realistic solution for reducing the emissions of carbon dioxide into the atmosphere from the burning of fossil fuels is to transition to a mostly renewable energy system and *a low energy society*. Our consumption of energy, on which all economic activity is dependent, must be reduced, and we can afford to consume less. U.S. Americans consume a disproportionate amount of energy in the world: we consume twice the per capita energy of Europeans and Japanese, three times the per capita energy of Chinese, four to five times the per capita energy of Brazilians, and ten times the per capita energy of Indians (Ritchie and Roser 2018). The U.S. and other industrialized nations can and should consume less energy so that undeveloped and developing nations can consume more to raise their standard of living. Much of the energy used in the global South is increasingly devoted to supporting the industrialized North through international trade; the world would need a third more energy than is currently used for the global South to achieve a high level of development (Arto et al. 2016). In other words, the North has colonized the South for its energy to produce goods that might satisfy our insatiable appetite for consumption, rather than enable the South to use the energy for their own development. Renewable energy cannot sustain a high energy society, and it cannot power a continually growing economy—it cannot even power our current economy. If we want to address climate change and the current environmental crisis, we must radically reduce our consumption, to reduce production, to free up enough energy (primarily from fossil fuels) to build a renewable energy system sufficient to sustain a low energy society.

METABOLIC RIFT IN THE RELATIONSHIP BETWEEN SOCIETY AND NATURE

Nowhere is the material basis of the economy more evident than in agriculture, which is arguably the largest industry in the world and one of the most destructive of the natural world.[22] All people are dependent on the soil (or the sea) and what it pro-

---

22. Very quickly in this study I recognized that there is a disconnect between university research in agriculture, much of which is funded by industrial agricultural corporations and serves its interests,

duces, and cultivation is the most fundamental way in which humans engage with the natural world.[23] While there has been some decoupling of energy and carbon dioxide emissions, thanks to efficiency and renewable energy technologies, there is no possibility of decoupling human life from the soil and its products.[24] Nevertheless, industrial agriculture, based on market imperatives, has generated a series of rifts in the metabolic relationship between society and nature, contributing to the current environmental crisis. In the ancient world, much of the environmental degradation was associated with agriculture, but the people largely sought to live within the cycles of nature and so preserve the fertility of the land—it was the basis of their subsistence. Today, most agriculture in the industrial North and a growing proportion in the global South functions under a capitalist regime. Its emphasis is not preservation of the land nor feeding people with nutritious food, but rather increasing the intensive production of a commodity to be sold on the global market for a profit.

Capitalism was born in the English countryside in the sixteenth and seventeenth centuries with the reorganization of farming along new property and social relations (Wood 2017). When capitalist agriculture spread to the American colonies, it was aided by slave labor, which made it profitable for a couple of centuries. But in the nineteenth and twentieth centuries it became industrialized with machinery, chemical inputs, and specially-bred crops, and its production grew exponentially. With its compulsion to grow, capitalist agriculture slowly transformed the world, enabling the population to grow in pace. Today, the world produces much more food than it consumes, ranging from 75% to 100% more than what is needed, including a large portion of grain fed to animals. Yet over a billion people are malnourished or undernourished because they are unable to adequately access the market (Smil 2017, 313; IAASTD 2016, 4–6). Over 50 percent of the world lives in cities—over 80 percent in the United States—and the percentage grows each year because fossil fuels and machinery have reduced the need for agricultural labor (Smil 2019, 336–38), while at the same time contributing as much as 23 percent of the world's carbon dioxide emissions, according

---

and the other research done by a minority of academics outside the industrial agricultural establishment and the farmers themselves. I have especially been influenced by those engaged in regenerative agriculture and the research done at the Land Institute in Salina, Kansas. When not cited directly, I am dependent in this section on the following sources: Bell 2004; Montgomery 2017; Wise 2019; Mies and Bennholdt-Thomsen 1999; Clunies-Ross and Hildyard 1992; Perfecto, Vandermeer, and Wright 2019; Jackson 1980; Ohlson 2014; Schwartz 2103; and Brown 2018.

23. Some people, of course, have chosen to live off the sea and its produce, but only 0.3% of food comes from the sea (Pimentel 2006). For an analysis of fishing and aquaculture, see Longo et al. 2015. The focus here will be on the other 99.7% of food, which comes from the soil.

24. Hydroponics and aquaponics can enable the growth of vegetables, mostly greens, without soil, but this is not a material decoupling. Some of the necessary material nutrients of the soil are simply supplied by the circulation of nutrient rich water on the roots. Hydroponics and aquaponics represent only a small fraction of a percent of agricultural production, yet they have found their own niche in urban contexts supplying greens especially to restaurants. The produce contains little carbohydrates, proteins, or fat, and thus cannot ultimately sustain even a small population (Smil 2018).

to some calculations (IPCC 2020, 8).[25] While more land continues to be appropriated for agriculture each year—about half of all habitable land, three-quarters of which is dedicated to livestock (Ritchie and Roser 2019)—a third of all land is moderately to severely degraded due to erosion, salination, acidification, and chemical pollution, among other causes, with consequences for the quality of the food grown and the integrity of the ecosystem (FAO and ITPS 2015).

Farming has always been an assault of sorts on nature, and the natural world responds in kind. By clearing a field for planting, whether through plowing or burning, the farmer destroys the previous biological diversity that nature had supplied. Nature strikes back, if you will, by sending in a host of weeds (nature abhors a vacuum). Through a process known as "ecological succession," the natural world springs back, restoring the damage left by human activity. The natural world, from a human perspective, favors disorder and diversity, whereas agriculture is the process of imposing order and uniformity on the natural world. Thus, when the farmer plants a single crop in a field, nature introduces pathogens and pests that can wreak havoc on the crop, and they get worse each year that the same crop is planted. Moreover, the farmer soon learns that, despite the abundance of life growing in the natural world, the fertility of the soil is limited. After a few years of robbing the soil of its nutrients, crops, which require more nutrients than the less desirable weeds, will diminish, and the farmer will be forced to move on to a new field.

Over the years, farmers have learned to work with the natural world rather than against it. They refrain from tilling the soil whenever possible; they plant multiple crops together, usually with legumes, and rotate the crops regularly; they cover their fields with plant residues for mulch or with cover crops; they leave the land fallow for a season or more; they graze herd animals on the fields; they spread manure or compost on the fields. Some of these techniques were practiced in the ancient world, others are more recent innovations, but all lessen agriculture's assault on the natural world. Ancient and traditional agriculture was typically the business of the household. It was a holistic enterprise, in which the farm supplied the family's subsistence and all the resources (inputs) necessary for continual farming. Cities were dependent on the surrounding farms—their hinterland—for their necessary foodstuffs, but the farms were not usually dependent on the cities—at least not for their food or their ability to farm. Farms were largely self-sufficient.

---

25. Attributing 23 percent of carbon dioxide emissions to agriculture is problematic, if not deceptive. Much of the emissions are attributed to cows, which emit methane rather than carbon dioxide. Some of the emissions are attributed to soils, which emit nitrous oxide. The IPCC and others convert all the greenhouse gases into a carbon dioxide equivalent, but methane and carbon dioxide cannot be compared so simply. Methane is much more potent than carbon dioxide, but it remains in the atmosphere only about 10 years, whereas carbon dioxide remains in the atmosphere for hundreds, if not thousands, of years. The methane that is released by cows and other ruminants is also part of the methane cycle in which rotting vegetable matter is involved. In other words, the actual effect of agriculture on climate change is much less (the EPA claims it is 9% of greenhouse gases in the U.S.) than the 23 percent would lead one to believe (see Pitesky et al. 2009; Mitloehner 2018; Simon Fairlie 2018).

All of this changed with capitalist, industrial agriculture. Capitalism has always engaged in a war on subsistence. It needs to subsume all other economic activity within its own functioning to satisfy its unquenchable need for growth and in order to maximize profits. To this end, subsistence is a threat to capitalism because it is self-sufficient. Subsistence is independent of the capitalist market, both for the means and the distribution of production, and it challenges the naturalization of capitalist relations by offering an alternative to capitalism's exploitation of people and nature. The war on subsistence is most evident in its subsumption of subsistence farming in the global South. Using political and economic pressure, especially through loans from the International Monetary Fund, transnational corporations are imposing industrial agricultural practices on previously subsistence farmers under the banner of development. The farmers end up producing food for the market, but industrial practices have undermined their own subsistence and their ability to feed their neighbors. Instead of being self-sufficient, the people become dependent on a global market for their seeds, agricultural inputs, and their food, none of which they can generally afford (see Wise 2019).

When capitalism first emerged, subsistence farmers were evicted from land on which they had common or use-rights for years. Their subsistence farming impeded the profit of land-owning aristocrats, who consolidated common land within their own holdings, and then leased it out to capitalist farmers, who exploited the land for the greatest profit. Without access to land, the subsistence farmers were forced to work much of the same land that they had previously farmed, but now for wages as tenants. Many of the farmers, however, had no recourse but to migrate to the cities, where they formed the industrial workforce who had to sell their labor for wages in order to survive (Wood 2017). By undermining subsistence, capitalism undermines competition to its own production, increases its control over the means of production, including labor, and expands the market for its own products—all in order to maximize its own profits. This is as true of industrial agriculture as it is of Walmart's undermining of small family owned-and-operated retail stores in rural America—the dynamics and consequences are similar. In its war on subsistence or self-sufficiency with the family farm, the metabolic rifts generated by industrial agriculture have undermined rural communities, degraded the soil, and contributed to the current environmental crisis.[26]

A metabolism is simply the exchange of matter and energy; all life has a metabolic relationship with the natural world. Plants, for example, metabolize solar energy, carbon dioxide, and water to produce carbohydrates, from which the plants build biomass, and oxygen, which is released back into the air. But plants also need nutrients

---

26. In the United States, nothing illustrates this better than the Dust Bowl of the 1930s. Using techniques unsuited to the soil or the weather, farmers were encouraged by government policy to intensively plant a single variety of wheat, which undermined the soil's fertility, ultimately leading to the loss of millions of hectares of topsoil and the abandonment of many farms and rural communities (see Holleman 2018).

to grow. They receive these through a metabolic exchange with the microorganisms in the soil (which number in the billions for every spoonful). The plants exude a liquid portion of their carbohydrates through their roots, which the microorganisms consume, leaving nutrients to be taken up by the roots in exchange and excreting carbon in the soil as waste. The exchange between plants and microorganisms is managed by mycorrhizal fungi. These fungi extend the reach of the plant into the soil for nutrients through threadlike filaments called hyphae, bind soil particles into aggregates by secreting glomalin, and channel carbon into the soil, aiding microbial communities and creating soil organic matter (Johnson et al. 2017; see Montgomery 2017, 41–50; Schwartz 2013, 33–37).[27] When plant metabolism is fully functioning, plants flourish and carbon is sequestered in the soil.

Traditional agriculture has disrupted this plant metabolism in two ways. First, when the soil is disturbed through plowing or tilling, the carbon in the soil is oxidized and released into the air as carbon dioxide. Carbon is essential to the structure and life-sustaining properties of the soil. Its loss hinders the soil's ability to retain water and nutrients, foster microbial life, and sequester carbon.[28] Second, when plants are harvested and removed from the fields, rather than allowed to die naturally and decompose in the soil, the organic material and nutrients of the plants are taken away from the soil, reducing the soil's organic matter and its fertility. This happens whether the crops are consumed on the farm, in the city, or around the globe, if the plants' biomass is not returned to the soil. Combined, these disruptions create a metabolic rift in the nutrient cycle between plants and soil, diminishing the soil's ability to grow and sustain abundant crops. Farmers engaged in traditional and regenerative agriculture have found natural ways to mend this rift through no-till planting and mulching, composting and manuring, use of cover crops, and mob grazing of herd animals, sometimes referred to as managed grazing (for an example, see Brown 2018). In other words, they care for the *health of the soil* so that it will continue to support new life.[29] Industrial agriculture, in contrast, addresses this metabolic rift by focusing

---

27. The hyphae of the mycorrhizal fungi create a vast network that enables exchange of nutrients between the plants and the soil. When the soil is undisturbed, the mycorrhizal fungi's hyphae can extend deep into the soil, reaching otherwise untapped nutrients and sequestering carbon. Plowing or otherwise disturbing the soil breaks the fragile hyphae and disrupts the exchange network, limiting the depth of the plants' exchange with the soil.

28. The earth's soils represent the largest terrestrial reservoir of carbon, though much of it has been released through agriculture and other disturbances. Although estimates vary, scholars suggest as much as 133 billion tonnes of carbon, from a depth of two meters, has been released, adding approximately 63 ppm of carbon dioxide to the atmosphere (Bradford et al. 2019). Carbon can be restored to the soil naturally, but how much can be sequestered is debated; some suggest that carbon sequestration can offset as much as one third of the annual increase in atmospheric carbon dioxide (Machmuller et al. 2015).

29. There are many new approaches to farming that seek to work with nature rather than against it, much like traditional farming methods, but with better understandings of the soil's ecology. Many names are used to designate these approaches, including regenerative agriculture, conservation agriculture, sustainable agriculture, agroecology, and the Brown revolution. Although differences between

on the production of the plants. Its concern is *crop yield* and the profits it produces. Industrial agriculture thus introduces synthetic fertilizer and other chemicals to compensate for the deficiencies of the soil.

Plants get all but two of the minerals and nutrients they need from the soil, which are accessed through their roots with the help of the microbial community. Through photosynthesis, they get carbon, the source of energy for plant growth, from carbon dioxide in the air. Plants also need nitrogen, which is a major component in chlorophyll, needed for photosynthesis, and amino acids, the building blocks of proteins. Nitrogen occurs abundantly in the air as dinitrogen (N_2), but plants cannot use it in this inert state. Instead, it must be "fixed," which requires a specialized group of bacteria in the soil that live in symbiotic relationship to legumes. These bacteria break the bonds between the two nitrogen atoms of dinitrogen, producing reactive nitrogen (N), which plants can utilize. Nitrogen can also be returned to the soil through compost and manure. Early in the twentieth century, Fritz Haber and Carl Bosch discovered how to transform the nitrogen gas in the atmosphere into ammonia (NH_3), which became the basis of all synthetic nitrogen fertilizers. When applied to crops, the fertilizer (which often includes phosphorus and potassium) compensates for the nutrient depletion of the soil. By focusing exclusively on crop yields and using synthetic fertilizer, industrial agriculture has been able to overcome the natural limits of the soil that the metabolic rift in the nutrient cycle represents, and it has done so with great success in production, but not without significant environmental consequences.

Most of the reactive nitrogen in fertilizer that is applied to crops runs off into streams and leaches into groundwater, leading to algal blooms with dead zones and fish kills in the oceans and polluting aquifers and drinking water.[30] But reactive nitrogen is not limited to the fertilizer applied in the fields.[31] Additional reactive nitrogen is produced and added to the ecosystem from the burning of fossil fuels. It joins with other chemicals, producing severe air pollution (ground-level ozone) and nitrous oxide, a potent greenhouse gas. Ironically, for many wild plants, the nitrogen fertilizer is too nutrient-rich, resulting in their giving way to more vigorous plants and thus a loss of biodiversity. Biodiversity loss is also found in the soil, where the nutrient-rich fertilizer subverts the plants metabolic exchange with the microorganism in the soil. With an abundance of nitrogen and other minerals readily available through the

---

these approaches can be found, they all emphasize the long-term health of the soil as essential to agriculture. I will refer to all of these approaches under the rubric of regenerative agriculture, in contrast to industrial agriculture, which is not sustainable.

30. As I write this, my hometown newspaper, the *Omaha World-Herald*, reports that many small Nebraska towns are paying millions of dollars to build water pipelines to other towns or drill new wells because nitrate contamination—from synthetic nitrogen fertilizer—has polluted their drinking water, making it unsafe to drink according to federal standards (Walsh 2020).

31. Synthetic nitrogen has permeated the human body as well, so that "almost half of the nitrogen found in a typical human's muscle and organ tissue originated in the Haber–Bosch process" (Heinberg and Fridley 2016, 109).

fertilizer, the plants no longer need to work for their food, and so do not exude carbohydrates; the microorganisms die or become dormant as a result. There are also questions regarding human health consequences as a result of the excessive synthetic nitrogen in the ecosystem (Townsend and Howarth 2010). The earth's nitrogen cycle has been completely disrupted by human activity, which produces twice as much reactive nitrogen each year than all natural sources combined. The planetary boundary represented by the nitrogen cycle has long been crossed and is perhaps approaching a critical threshold (Steffen, Richardson, et al. 2015; see chapter 7), yet most agriculture in the world remains dependent on synthetically produced nitrogen fertilizer to meet the nutrient requirements of the crops.

The metabolic exchange between plants and the soil is a natural process, a nutrient cycle, but there is also a social metabolism that regulates the interchange between society and nature. Regenerative farmers, who are concerned about the long-term viability of their farming, seek to mend the metabolic rift of the nutrient cycle by working with nature, stimulating natural processes, and caring for the health of the soil. "Each mode of production creates a particular social metabolic order that determines the interchange between society and nature. Such interactions influence the ongoing reproduction of society and ecosystems" (Foster et al. 2010, 75). The social metabolism of pre-capitalist modes of production, including ancient Israel's, necessarily gave attention to natural processes; they were only able to sustain themselves if they worked with the natural world, which in the case of ancient Israel, was understood to be the work of God. Those who practice regenerative agriculture today benefit from the wisdom of the past, aided by a better understanding of plant and soil ecology.

Industrial agriculture, on the other hand, is unable to mend the metabolic rift in the plant's nutrient cycle because its focus is on maximizing profits, which translates into increasing crop yields. At best, by introducing synthetic fertilizer, industrial agriculture whitewashes over the metabolic rift. By subsuming the natural conditions of farming within the social metabolism of capitalism, industrial agriculture subjects nature to the demands of capital—that is, maximizing profits. It addresses only the immediate, symptomatic nutrient needs of the plants, and so fails to address the chronic condition of the soil. In its attempt to mend the metabolic rift of the nutrient cycle, industrial agriculture has simply exchanged one problem for another, generating additional, more serious rifts, such as overloading the earth's nitrogen cycle. As a capitalist enterprise, industrial agriculture has the tendency "to violate the natural conditions that ensure nature's vitality, undermining the base on which ecological and human sustainability depends" (Foster et al. 2010, 76).

Farming and animal husbandry are the most fundamental and historically significant ways in which humans have engaged with the natural world. But industrial agriculture, adhering to the demands of capital, has transformed agriculture from a collaborative venture with the earth into simply an exploitive commodity production. Guided by the need to maximize profit, industrial agriculture has generated a metabolic rift in the interchange between society and nature through a series of separations. First, industrial agriculture, like all capitalist enterprises, has separated people from the land. In part, this is related to capitalism's war on subsistence; capitalism can only thrive if people are dependent on wages for their subsistence rather than being self-sufficient. But capitalism also seeks to reduce labor costs through efficiency and technology. Thus, by mechanizing the farm, capitalism has reduced the number of people necessary for labor. In 1900, about 41 percent of the U.S. population worked on farms; in 2018 only 1.3 percent of the U.S. workforce was in farming (USDA 2005; 2020a). Consolidation has also reduced the number of farms, which peaked in 1935 with 6.8 million but fell to little over 2 million in the 1970s (USDA 2020b). The number of farms has continued to fall, but by an uncertain amount,[32] though the amount of land farmed has remained stable. The vast majority of farms are small, but the largest 3 percent of the farms account for 46 percent of all production (USDA 2020b). In 1930, 30 percent of farmers received some non-farm income, but by 2002, 93 percent of farm households had income from off the farm (USDA 2005). It is also worth noting that 39 percent of all farmland is leased or rented, and of that land, 80 percent is owned by non-farming landlords (USDA 2019b).

Although most farmland in the United States is individual or family owned (corporate ownership is a small percentage), far fewer people, as a percentage of the population, farm the land today than a hundred years ago, and many of them do not own the land they farm. There is nothing intrinsically wrong with fewer people choosing to farm, though it tends to distance society as a whole from the natural world. What is wrong is how the reduction in farmers and number of farms took place. Historically, farming was the means of subsistence for the majority of the population, and the harvest surplus would feed the nearby towns and cities. Foodstuffs were sold for their use-value, and a farmer's livelihood was tied to the quantity and quality of the harvests. With industrial agriculture, farming produced exchange value rather than use-value. The farmers' livelihood became dependent on the capitalist market and the uncontrollable variables of supply and demand, but the market never seemed to favor the farmers. In lean years, the farmers made little because of low production and the suppression of prices by gigantic agrobusinesses. In years of abundance, prices dropped and farmers still made little. Former U.S. Secretary of Agriculture, Earl Butz, famously said, "Get big, or get out," and farmers did. They invested in high-tech machines and more agrochemical inputs, and upgraded infrastructure, with the hope of increasing their profits. But most farmers have largely left the farm because of debt. Despite reducing labor costs with machinery, the vast majority of farmers have

---

32. According to the Census of Agriculture, a plot of land that grows fruit, vegetables, or animals is counted as a farm if "$1,000 or more of such products were raised and sold, *or normally would have been sold*, during the Census year" (USDA 2019, emphasis added). The $1,000 minimum was set in 1974 and has not been raised since. Thus, many small plots of land have been counted as farms, even if not actively used for farming. The definition of a farm has not been updated largely for political reasons.

not benefitted economically; most are dependent on some form of off-farm income. In 2018, 90 percent of farmers grossed less than $350,000 and half made less than $10,000 from their farms (USDA 2020b); and debt among farmers is a recurring issue, with the total debt of the farm sector rising to $426.6 billion in 2019, the sixth year of increase in a row. Most farmers have little, if any, margin for profit (farm bankruptcies surged 20% in 2019, hitting an eight-year high, see Huffstutter 2020). Who, then, has benefitted from the reduction of farmers and farms? A small percentage of large farms have benefitted from a number of advantages of scale, but the primary beneficiaries have been the handful of agrobusinesses separating the farmers from the consumers of their products.

The separation of producers and consumers was inevitable from urbanization. As people left the farms and rural communities for the cities, more and more of the agricultural produce would need to be transported to the cities to supply their growing need for food. Here is where the profit lies. Large multinational agrobusinesses control food production from farm to table. Once there were many companies, occupying different levels in the production process, but through vertical ("from seedling to supermarket") and horizontal integration, most food production is now controlled by only a few corporations—such as Cargill, Nestlé, Archer Daniels Midland, Tyson Foods, PepsiCo, and Kraft-Heinz. These corporations dominate the market, and thus control what farmers grow and the prices farmer are paid for their crops. Farmers only receive about 10 percent of the final cost of the food sold to consumers (Perfecto et al. 2019, 77). The goal of these corporations is, of course, profit, and they increase their profit through efficiency. Biological diversity, for crops or animals, simply slows the production process and reduces profit. Thus, because of corporate control of food processing and retailing, 75 percent of the world's food comes from just twelve plant species and five animal species. In fact, 60 percent of all food energy comes from five grain species: rice, wheat, maize, millet, and sorghum (IAASTD 2016, 45). In the United States, food travels on average about 1300 miles before reaching its final destination (Clunies-Ross and Hildyard 1992, 72). Food has been reduced to a simple commodity, among many others, for sale through the market.

Farmers are economically squeezed by agrobusinesses. On the one side, they control the farm's output (farmers cannot grow what they cannot sell). On the other side, a few large agrobusinesses—Syngenta, Bayer (recently merged with Monsanto), DowDuPont, and Cargill—control the inputs (seeds, fertilizers, and pesticides) needed for farming. Traditionally, most inputs were created on the farm. Farmers saved a portion of their seed for the following year, and the need for fertilizers and pesticides could be reduced (or eliminated) with good soil management. But industrial agriculture has separated the inputs from the farm itself. Farmers must now buy their seeds. Few companies sell (or develop) open-pollinated seeds, and the hybrid seeds sold by agrobusinesses do not reproduce themselves (or breed true).[33] Thus, farmers must

---

33. Hybrid seeds can be stabilized to reproduce, but this takes multiple generations of breeding

buy new seeds each year. Today, five corporations control 60 percent of all seed sales (IAASTD 2016, 44). Many of the hybrid seeds are genetically designed to work with particular fertilizers or pesticides, increasing the need for these inputs as well.

Fertilizer and pesticide use have grown exponentially since the 1950s (Horrigan et al. 2002, 446), but with diminishing returns. Around 1970, for example, a ton of synthetic fertilizer would yield an additional 15 to 20 tons in corn harvest, but by 1990 it was only adding an additional 5 to 10 tons (Clunes-Ross and Hildyard 1992, 61). Whereas fertilizer is used to supplement nature, pesticides (an inclusive term for insecticides, herbicides, and fungicides) are a direct assault on it. And they are losing; nature works to subvert their effectiveness. Glyphosate, the active ingredient in Monsanto's Roundup, encountered its first resistant weed in 1996. Now there are dozens. Insecticides and fungicides have encountered even more resistance, requiring more and more chemicals to counteract the pests' resistance—there are now about 1600 chemicals used in the battle against pests, and they have killed many beneficial insects and fungi as well. Fertilizers and pesticides are like a drug; the more one uses, the more one needs (Perfecto et al. 2019, 77–82; Horrigan et al. 2002, 446). Industrial agricultural inputs have increased the cost of farming, reducing the farmers' economic viability.

Finally, industrial agriculture has separated animal and crop production for the purposes of intensification and efficiency. This is unfortunate. Animals have traditionally grazed on crop residue, and they can also graze on cover crops, leaving plenty of manure in exchange. The animals' grazing on plants also stimulates the plants' exchange with the microbial community in the soil, increasing the soil's carbon sequestration. Moreover, the animals' hooves trample vegetation into the soil, further increasing its organic matter. But with their separation, the cropland becomes depleted without the animals manure, which becomes a waste that needs to be disposed—in 1997, the USDA estimated that animals produced 1.4 billion tons of waste, approximately 5 tons for every U.S. citizen at the time (Horrigan et al. 2002, 448–49). Although some animals are allowed to graze for food in pastures, most animals are commercially raised in concentrated animal feeding operations (CAFOs), consuming as much as 60 percent of the grain crop (Smil 2017, 313). When animals feed on pasture, they convert plants that are not edible to humans into protein that humans can eat, and so increase the food supply. But when they are fed grain, they convert edible human food into protein, and they do it very inefficiently: it takes 2 kilograms of grain to produce 1 kilogram of chicken, 4 kilograms for one kilogram of pork, and 7 kilograms for one kilogram of beef (Horrigan et al. 2002, 445).

The concentration of animals in feedlots and CAFOs is due in part to capitalism's need to maximize profits, but also to a growing desire for more meat in the diet,

---

and selecting plants for desired traits. Once the seeds become open-pollenated, farmers can save and use their own seeds, but this cuts the revenue stream for seed companies, which is counter to their purpose.

especially in the developing world—meat consumption in China, for example, has increased six-fold in the past 40 years. Nevertheless, meat consumption is highest in the U.S. with an average consumption per person of 118 kilograms per year; the European Union follows with 83 kilograms per year, whereas the world average is only 43 kilograms per year, and in undeveloped countries consumption is 14 kilograms per year or less (IAASTD 2016, 10). Such concentration of animals, however, is a threat to animal, human, and environmental health. Animals become vulnerable to disease and require antibiotics, which remain in their meat; they are crowded together like cargo, with a poor quality of life; and their manure, stored in large lagoons, is a constant source of pollution and pathogens, including Escherichia coli, salmonella, Cryptosporidium, and Pfiesteria piscicida (Marks 2001). Animals raised and fed on pastures have a superior quality of life, their manure and trampling aids the growing of crops, and their meat is more nutritious from eating the natural biodiversity of the pasture. Moreover, animals aid in the sequestering of carbon in the soil, and when trees are added to the pasture—a practice known as silvopasture—even more carbon is sequestered, among other benefits (Hawken 2017, 49–51).

By separating the people from the land, the producers from the consumers, agricultural inputs from the farm, and animals from the crops, industrial agriculture has created a rift in the metabolic relationship between society and nature. The result of this metabolic rift has been soil degradation and a contribution to climate change, among other problems. Soil degradation threatens the global food supply. Each year, 24 billion tons of topsoil are lost due to erosion at an estimated cost of $400 billion.[34] The soil organic matter, on average, has been diminished 50 to 65 percent from pre-cultivation levels (IAASTD 2016, 32–33). Although compensated in part by synthetic fertilizer, because it inhibits microbial exchange with the roots, more and more needs to be applied each year, leading to what may be called the "fertilizer treadmill" (Perfecto et al. 2019, 81). Pesticides also contribute to the degradation of the soil, killing microbial life and beneficial insects, as well as fostering the evolution of resistant pests. Industrial agriculture is made possible by an abundance of cheap fossil fuel, which is used to power large machinery, as a feedstock for agrochemicals, and to transport the agricultural products around the globe. In the United States, it takes ten calories of energy from fossil fuels to product one calorie of edible food (Clunies-Ross and Hildyard 1992, 38).[35] It is not surprising, then, that agriculture contributes to climate

34. Estimates vary widely in different reports. For example, some reports estimate as much as 75 billion tons of topsoil is lost each year due to erosion (Pimentel and Burgess 2013). I have chosen to follow more conservative estimates.

35. Generally, this would be a recipe for disaster. All species must produce or capture a large surplus of energy, beyond the energy used to obtain it, to meet their basic metabolic and reproductive needs. This is not the case with farming. This energy imbalance is only possible because farming draws down a reservoir stock of energy (fossil fuels) that took millions of years to create. Fossil fuels essentially subsidize the food industry, and they are able to do so because they produce so much more energy than is needed to extract and process them (with an EROI of about 20:1 on average for conventional petroleum).

change. More significantly, the degradation of the world's soils make agriculture more vulnerable to the consequences of climate change: the soils are unable to absorb heavy downpours or retain water for droughts, and the crops are less resilient to excessive heat because the soil remains hotter (Montgomery 2017; Brown 2018).

Industrial agriculture has subsumed farming and animal husbandry within the social metabolic order of capitalism, which "is inherently anti-ecological, since it systematically subordinates nature in its pursuit of endless accumulation and production on ever-larger scales" (Foster et al. 2010, 74). Disrupting traditional relationships between nature and society, industrial agriculture treats nature and natural processes as simply the means of commodity production, which can be improved and intensified with industrial technologies. Nature is no longer intrinsically valued; human life and society are not understood to be dependent upon nature. This is nowhere more evident than in some factory animal farms (CAFOs), where the animals are treated as simple commodities, meat on hooves, with no quality of life (see, e.g., Solotaroff 2013). Capitalism has ruined agriculture and distorted the metabolic interchange between society and nature, alienating people from the natural world on which they are dependent. And it is unnecessary, except to increase the profits of agrobusinesses. Small farms engaging more labor are more productive than large, mechanized farms (Sheng, Ding, and Huang 2019). Regenerative agricultural approaches, which care for the health of the soil, can produce healthier, more diverse crops with reduced need for industrial inputs. And returning animals to the farm can increase their health, the nutrition of their meat, and their quality of life, while also benefiting the cropland with manure and increasing organic matter in the soil.[36]

Unfortunately, farmers adopting regenerative agricultural approaches are fighting an uphill battle. Regardless of how they farm, most remain subject to the market and its demands. Some farmers have found outlets by dealing with consumers directly, through farmer's markets, CSAs (community supported agriculture), or direct relationships with restaurants and grocery stores, but these outlets can only distribute a small percentage of agricultural production. Many farmers have little financial margin due to debt. Although regenerative agriculture is less expensive because it requires less inputs, government farm subsidies, thanks to lobbying from agrobusinesses, favor industrial agricultural approaches: large farms with intensive monocultural production. Farmers can be penalized by utilizing cover crops, crop rotations, or diversifying their crops (see Bell 2004, 237–39; Clunies-Ross and Hildyard 1992, 83–84; Wise 2019; Montgomery 2017, 271–73). Nevertheless, regenerative agriculture is necessary to counter and subvert the exploitation of industrial agriculture and begin to heal the

---

36. Returning animals to the farm may result in a reduction of meat output, which would benefit the Western diets that consume too much meat. But using mob or managed grazing, which increases the density of herd animals per acre and rotates them frequently to prevent overgrazing, can be as productive as industrial animal management and benefit the soil and crops as well (see Brown 2018, 61–77; Schwartz 2013).

metabolic rift between society and nature.[37] According to Bell, "growing food is only one dimension of . . . the purpose of agriculture: *cultivation*—the care and tending of creation, human and nonhuman, social and ecological" (2004, 248).

POLITICAL ECONOMY IN A LIMITED WORLD

A continually growing economy is simply impossible; eventually, it will transgress the ecological limits of the planet and collapse. The economy is a subsystem of the biosphere and so is limited by it. Kenneth Boulding, an economist and social scientist of the mid-twentieth century, famously stated, "Anyone who believes exponential growth can go on forever in a finite world is either a madman or an economist." Neoliberal economists, like their neo-classical forebearers, have led us astray. Economic growth cannot continue forever; it is the historical anomaly. The current conception and experience of an unlimited growth economy, which is a property of capitalist social relations and only made possible through the exploitation of fossil fuels, is just a couple of hundred years old. The vast majority of the history of human civilization, including the history of the ancient Israelites that is reflected in the Bible, has been lived out within the context of an economy with little to no growth. Subsistence rather than surplus was largely the goal of production, and consumption was more closely tied to human need. There were, of course, notable historical exceptions, and history is filled with the rise and fall of individuals and regimes seeking to acquire more, generally by expropriating it from others, but from the dawn of agriculture (roughly 11,700 years ago) until the 1800s, there was not any appreciable per capita economic growth.

In order to address the environmental crisis and the dangers that climate change poses for human civilization, society must reject the demands of capitalism and leave growth behind (see Hueting 2010; Griethuysen 2010; Pirgmaier 2017). Climate change is the inevitable consequence of the fossil economy, which is "an economy of self-sustaining growth predicated on the growing consumption of fossil fuel, and therefore generating a sustained growth in emissions of carbon dioxide" (Malm 2016, 11). Capitalism and fossil fuels are now a package deal: there can be no sustained economic growth without fossil fuels, and capitalism, with its particular property and social relations, cannot survive without growth. Renewable energy cannot substitute for fossil fuels and sufficiently feed capitalism's appetite for growth. As a result, a significant reduction of fossil fuels, which is *required* in order to reduce the most severe

---

37. Most people will not farm directly, of course, though we should support public initiatives and policies that enable people to return to farming. Non-farmers can contribute to healing the metabolic rift between society and nature caused by industrial agriculture by gardening and growing their own food. Gardening also benefits from some of the practices of regenerative agriculture, including diversity and rotation of plants, composting, mulching, and keeping the soil covered. Whether this takes place in one's own yard, in cooperation with others in a public garden, or through the restoration of blighted urban areas, gardening connects one to nature and its cycles, provide nutritious food, and offers many health benefits (Soga et al. 2017; see Pollan 1991).

consequences of climate change, will *inevitably* lead to a reduction in economic activity and thus an end to economic growth.

Economic growth and fossil fuels are linked in capitalism. But because they are linked, we have not made any notable progress toward national or global goals of addressing climate change by reducing fossil fuel consumption. This is the Gordian knot that twenty-first-century human civilization faces, and whether and how it can be unraveled remains uncertain. Even though we might acknowledge the dangers that climate change poses, most are unwilling to prioritize economic solutions to the problem. This is especially true for U.S. Americans (see Jamieson 2006). Since we have benefitted disproportionally from the fossil economy, we must alter our lifestyle much more radically than others. For many in the global South, who have yet to experience the benefits of the fossil economy, their standard of living instead needs to be raised.

Any solution to climate change will require government intervention. The market cannot help us; it serves the capitalist system. In the end, there are only two basic options, one addressing the supply of fossil fuels and the other addressing their demand. We can deliberately curtail the supply of fossil fuels to minimally needed levels, though this might require nationalizing the fossil fuel industries. The loss of fossil fuels would have an immediate impact on the economy, reducing economic activity proportionally. The other option is to reduce demand for fossil fuels, either by making fossil fuels prohibitively expensive (through carbon taxes, for example), or deliberately reducing economic activity (as we experienced during the Covid-19 pandemic). Neither of these options are attractive, nor will they be without pain and suffering. Ideally, we should build and install renewable energy technologies to create a gradual transition—unfortunately, a new renewable energy system cannot be employed as rapidly as needed; such an extensive energy transition may take decades (Smil 2017, 440–41)—but the longer we wait, the more carbon dioxide is emitted into the atmosphere and the more severe the consequences will be. If we wait too long, the consequences of climate change will consume whatever economic growth we have managed to accumulate, and more (Wallace-Wells 2019). Nature will always have the final say.

However we act, economic growth will eventually disappear—whether we act to prevent the worst of climate change, or as a consequence of climate change—and we will need a new ideology that recognizes at last the limited world in which we have always lived. The capitalist ideology recognizes no limits; it holds out accumulation and maximal profit as the goal of economic life. It naturalizes the expropriation of nature and human labor: the inequitable use of natural resources by some to the exclusion of others, and the purchasing of someone's labor for less than its value—for as little as the market will allow. Capitalist ideology not only justifies capitalist exploitation, but also combats every attempt to reduce its demands, such as through unionizing labor and regulation, tariffs, or other forms of government intrusion, which would reduce its growth and potential for accumulation and profit. We must combat capitalist ideology with an alternative ideology that upholds economic and environmental justice and promotes sustainability within the constraints of a limited world. And this is where religion comes in, providing a sacred and moral foundation to the ideology. As Wendell Berry (2008, 39) notes:

> We are, after all, trying now to deal with the failure of scientists, technicians, and politicians to "think up" a version of human continuance that is economically probable and ecologically responsible, or perhaps even imaginable. If we go back into our tradition, we are going to find a concern with religion, which at a minimum shatters the selfish context of the individual life, and thus forces a consideration of what humans beings are and ought to be.

No religion, least of all the religion of an agrarian Iron Age, Near Eastern people, can provide an economic model for the contemporary world with all its complexity. Nevertheless, religion can contribute to an economic ideology that can challenge the basic assumptions of the capitalist ideology. The current capitalist economy needs growth to function, and thus a sustainable, limited economy without growth cannot be achieved without rethinking the demands, axioms, and values of the current economic system and restructuring economic relations. In particular, property relations and social relations of production need to be restructured to fit equitably and justly within a limited world. This is the economic world of the ancient Israelites, and the biblical scribes expected the Israelites to live their lives prosperously within such a limited world. Yet such a limited political economy was also not without its problems: selfishness, corruption, and exploitation are not unique to capitalism. Thus, the biblical scribes articulated within the Torah, the legal traditions of the Bible, a vision of how the people could live justly and equitably in their social and economic relations. The Bible offers an alternative way of being economic humans (*homo economicus*) and living well in a limited world.

Capitalist property relations, for example, are structured so that the products of the natural world are treated as a free-gift of nature. Land in the Americas was expropriated (that is, without exchange) from its native inhabitants and given to those who would improve it. Natural resources—fossil fuels, minerals, timber—can be mined and extracted with no cost for the resource itself. The natural world is viewed as a gift from God for humans to use and improve as they see fit. If the world were unlimited, as traditional economic theory treats it, so that one person's expropriation of nature does not affect another person's potential expropriation, then this might make a degree of sense, at least with regard to equity. Locke's ideas were conceived in this context. But the world is limited and the use of limited resources by some precludes the use of those resources by others and deprives them of the value that the limited quantity and scarcity of such resources would produce. Locke's interpretation aside, the Bible suggests an alternative ideology in which the world and all its resources belong to God, who created the world and so has claim to all that is in it (Ps 24:1).

This becomes explicit in Yhwh's relationship to Israel. Yhwh promises an inheritance of land to all the Israelite families, apportioned by lot according to their size (Num 26:52–56), but Yhwh also makes clear that the land belongs to him (Lev 25:23). The Israelites may use the land—they may possess its usufruct—but they do not own it. They may even sell the land, but only its usufruct is at stake, and then only for the years that remain until the next fifty-year-jubilee when everyone should return to their original possession (Lev 25:8–17). In the limited growth economy of the biblical world, everyone had a right to the use of land because no one owned the land and its resources except God, and those who did not possess land, such as Levites, resident aliens, widows and orphans, were to be supported by those who did (see below). This biblical tradition challenges the current economic understanding of property by suggesting that the earth and all its natural resources belong to the people of the earth, not simply to those who take it.

Historically, exclusive ownership of land and natural resources was initially the result of conquest and theft, and when capitalism emerged, further expropriation was justified by an ideology that enabled some to possess what is freely given to all. Although conquest is not absent from the biblical tradition—indeed, the Israelites take possession of the land from the Canaanites (a problematic legacy!)—the biblical tradition offers an alternative to capitalist private property with usufruct. The natural world, as the creation of God, is the commons of all (see Bollier 2014); it is a wealth that can be shared by all people. All inhabitants of the world have a right to usufruct in God's creation—to use some of the natural bounty of the world. Some land and resources, of course, will be taken out of the commons to be used exclusively, such as a plot of land on which to build a home and resources that are extracted for producing use-values. But when land and resources are appropriated to the exclusion of others, their use-value belongs to and should be compensated to others. In other words, contrary to capitalist property relations, someone should not be able to expropriate nature, which is common to all, with no costs.

The structure of social relations is more complicated because they are determined by the purpose of production. In capitalism, the purpose of production is accumulation and profit maximization. As a result, labor is treated simply as one of the forces of production, the costs of which should be minimized to increase profit. Capitalist social relations are exploitive of labor, and this is made possible through the use of money and the market. The market treats labor as a commodity, whose exchange value is determined by supply and demand, and thus the capitalists maintain their advantage by ensuring a constant reserve labor force (i.e., the unemployed). By paying laborers a wage with abstract money (i.e., it is a symbol of value), the actual value of the labor is further mystified, enabling capitalists to exploit the surplus labor for their own accumulation. The capitalists exploitation of labor has only been mitigated by unionization and government regulation, which demanded better wages (including a minimum wage), limited the workweek, secured benefits, and mandated safe working conditions. Yet, none of this has dampened the drive for accumulation and profit.

Most social relations in ancient Israel were household relations, which served the purpose of reproduction and subsistence. In fact, this is the most common purpose of all pre-capitalist social relations of production, and must be a fundamental feature of production in a limited world. Because the world is limited, production should not be for endless accumulation, but one's needs should be met. Subsistence is not simply "getting by" or a "meager existence." It is rather a self-sufficiency—living a full and happy life, independent and able to choose what, when, and how one produces (see Mies and Bennholdt-Thomsen 1999). The goal of reproduction also shapes the relationship between society and nature; it provides a historical trajectory to the relationship. Capitalist production is only concerned about immediate accumulation and profit. It has no long-term trajectory other than continually increasing accumulation and profit. It collapses history into the present "now," and nature need not be preserved for tomorrow. For household relations, in contrast, reproduction entails generational continuity and succession. The natural world is treated so that the next generation can also benefit from it. This is the driving force behind sustainability: meeting the needs of the present generation without compromising the ability of future generations to meet their own needs.

Household relations in ancient Israel were not always sufficient for subsistence. Households aligned with other households within their *mishpahah*, or with non-kin households forming patron–client relations, and all households were subsumed within the tributary relations of the king. Although the purpose of subsistence and reproduction continued, these relations had the potential—as all social relations do—for exploitation and injustice. An economic ideology for a limited world must include provisions for those who are unable to provide for their own subsistence, and here the biblical tradition can make a significant contribution.

Caring for the Poor and Needy

Concern for the poor and needy, those who have been unable to subsist sufficiently on their own, is represented imprecisely in the biblical tradition's earliest collection of laws, the so-called Book of the Covenant (Exod 20:22—23:19). Although there are explicit laws that make reference to the poor, it is not evident that such laws would be necessary. On the one hand, it is peculiar that the laws make reference to the poor at all; this is not true of other Near Eastern law codes. Although the prologues and epilogues of law codes, such as Hammurabi's code, describe how the king defends and cares for the poor, the laws themselves do not mention the poor (Lohfink 1991). This discrepancy between the laws and their framework is not found in the biblical laws, yet even so the biblical laws make only modest mention of the poor.

On the other hand, where the laws mention the poor, it is not always evident how the laws provide for the poor. In the Book of the Covenant, God's concern for the poor is unambiguous:

> You shall not mistreat a resident alien or oppress him, for you were aliens in the land of Egypt. You shall not abuse any widow or orphan. If you do abuse them, when they cry out to me, I will surely heed their cry; my wrath will burn, and I will kill you with the sword, and your wives will become widows and your children orphans. (Exod 22:21–24)

But the laws do not command the people to do anything on behalf of the poor—here singled out as the widow, the orphan, and the alien. The people should simply not take advantage of the poor's plight by doing anything that would be oppressive. Further examples are given in the following laws: If one lends to the poor, one should not charge interest, which would further impoverish the poor person, and if one takes a cloak in pledge of such a loan, it should be returned by evening because it may be the person's only cloak (Exod 22:25–27). God will punish those who oppress the poor—no other sanction is given—but in these laws God does not command care for the poor.

The failure of the Book of the Covenant to include provisions for the care of the poor is perhaps not surprising given that its Near Eastern analogues fail to mention the poor at all. Yet, it does beg the question of who does care for the poor. In the prologues and epilogues of the Near Eastern law codes, it is the king who establishes what the Bible labels as "justice and righteousness," which includes care for the poor and needy. The laws do not require the people to care for the poor because it is the king's role to ensure that their needs are met. A summary of David's reign as king states that he "administered justice and righteousness (*mishpat utsedakah*) for all his people" (2 Sam 8:15). Moshe Weinfeld has argued that *mishpat utsedakah*, when used in the prophets and Psalms, refers "primarily to the improvement of the conditions of the poor, which is undoubtedly accomplished through regulation issued by the king and his officials . . ." (1995, 35). The king's role in upholding "justice and righteousness" and his role in caring for the poor is made explicit in Ps 72:1–4:

> Give the king your justice, O God,
>   and your righteousness to a king's son.
> May he judge your people with righteousness,
>   and your poor with justice.
> May the mountains yield prosperity for the people,
>   and the hills, in righteousness.
> May he defend the cause of the poor of the people,
>   give deliverance to the children of the needy,
>   and crush the oppressor.

The king is the agent of God's justice and righteousness, and so should care for the poor and needy on behalf of God. As Weinfeld has made clear, judging "with righteousness" and "with justice" is not about the proper execution of judicial proceedings, but rather "social justice and equity, which is bound up with kindness and mercy" (1995, 36). How the king accomplishes this is unclear. Since the laws do not mention the king, and the royal psalms do not specify any particular tasks, it is likely that the poor and needy found help with their *mishpahah*, their extended kin relations. The laws function to warn the heads of the *mishpahoth* not to exploit their own kin, especially vulnerable widows and orphans, and the kings, like all heads of state, take credit for the people taking care of one another.

The only law in the Book of the Covenant that details a particular economic help that should be given to the poor is the law concerning a debt slave: "When you buy a male Hebrew slave, he shall serve six years, but in the seventh he shall go out a free person, without debt" (Exod 21:2). Debt servitude, as it is better called, was a common means of collateral used to secure and repay loans for an economically struggling household. For example, when a household had insufficient resources to sustain itself through the next agricultural cycle—due to low crop yield cause by drought or pestilence, or to a multitude of other unexpected causes—the head of the household might secure a loan from his patron in order to obtain sufficient resources for the household's subsistence and for the following year's plantings. Ideally, the next agricultural cycle would produce sufficient bounty to repay the loan, support the household, and include enough seed for the following season, but this was often not the case. The head of the household, or his children, might have to labor for the patron as a way to repay the loan. A household could be trapped in an endless cycle of debt, with the agricultural season producing enough for the household's survival or for repayment of the loan, but not for both. The law of the debt slave, however, put a limit on how long the debt cycle could continue: in the seventh year, the ledger is cleared and the head of the household or his son is freed from servitude (see Chirichigno 1993, 186–255).[38] In this way, the law of the debt slave functions to end the cycle of debt in much the same way as contemporary laws on personal bankruptcy, but here the obligation is placed on the patron to release his client from his debt.

Although most of the laws that address the poor in the Book of the Covenant do not give explicit reference to economic relief, the social context of the laws makes such reference unnecessary in most cases. The authority behind and responsibility for taking care of the poor and needy in ancient Israel was the king as the agent of God. The Book of the Covenant is probably the product of the early monarchic period and it assumes the role of the king as the administrator of justice and righteousness. The

---

38. The situation of a daughter subjected to debt servitude is more complicated because of her sexuality. She becomes a secondary wife in the household into which she is sold, and so is not freed in the seventh year. However, she cannot be sold like a slave, and if she is not properly treated as a wife, then she may go free (Exod 21:7–11).

king ensured that the poor and needy were taken care of by their *mishpahoth*. The exception is the law of the debt slave, which does spell out specific relief. Because the poor person in this context is subject to a third party, the patron to whom he has been subjected (or subjected himself) for debt service, the law limits the extent of such servitude. The patrons to whom impoverished Israelites became indebted thus shared in the responsibility to provide economic relief through the divine mandate to release their indentured servants after six years of servitude. The economic relief is made explicit when the role of the king can no longer be assumed.

Reform and Counter-Reform

When we turn to the later Deuteronomic and Priestly legislation, the laws that provide for the poor and needy specify particular measures of economic relief. Perhaps, this was due in part to the harsh criticism of the monarchy and its officials by the seventh-century prophets, who point out their failures to administer justice and righteousness on behalf of the poor and others. According to these prophets, the royal establishment had not been fulfilling its responsibility to care for the poor and needy. However, changes regarding the articulation of economic actions are probably due more to the changes forced upon the monarchy. Under Assyrian hegemony in the seventh century, the power and role of the monarchy had been circumscribed by this foreign domination (see Levinson 2001; Dutcher-Walls 2002). Then, shortly into the sixth century BCE, the monarchy ceased to exist with the sack of Jerusalem and exile of the people by the Babylonians. The Deuteronomic and Priestly scribes lived in a very different world vis-à-vis the monarchy than the scribes of the Book of the Covenant, and this is evident in their articulation of economic aid. The authority behind and responsibility for economic aid could no longer be the king. The authority instead became the legislation itself, which was attributed to God who communicated through Moses to the people, and the responsibility for the economic aid was placed in the hands of the people.

The relationship between the Deuteronomic and Priestly traditions is highly contested and cannot be resolved here. Nevertheless, some framework is needed to put their different laws in context. Although both works draw upon earlier legal and customary traditions, the formulations of the Deuteronomic and Priestly works date to the seventh and sixth century BCE respectively. Thus, the Deuteronomic work includes the role of a king, circumscribed though it is, whereas no king is present, or assumed, in the Priestly work. Both traditions are constructive, utopian, and reform oriented, but the Priestly work also seems to be responding in part to the Deuteronomic work, and thus I consider it to be a counter-reform.

The Deuteronomic legislation includes multiple laws providing food for the poor and systematic debt relief. Norbert Lohfink has argued that the Deuteronomic laws distinguish two economically disenfranchised groups: a group that does not possess landed property—the widow, orphan, alien, and Levite—and a second group referred to as the poor and needy (*ebyon* and *'ani*) who are subject to the repeatable and cyclical processes of indebtedness and debt servitude. This latter group may experience poverty for numerous social, economic, or environmental reasons, and so the Deuteronomic reform seeks to limit poverty to seven years and to protect the person who has been impoverished (Deut 15:1–18; 24:10–15). In a radical expansion and revision of the earlier law concerning the debt slave, the Deuteronomic law commands: "Every seventh year you will grant a remission (*shemittah*) of debts" (Deut 15:1). In the explanation of the law that follows, it is clear that the remission should occur every seventh year, regardless of when the loan was acquired, and that only debts to fellow community members ("his neighbor and his brother") are subject to remission. Indebtedness to non-Israelites, which presumably involve commercial loans, are not released. As with the earlier law concerning debt servitude, the Deuteronomic law also commands the release of debt slaves after six years, but includes daughters as well as sons (Deut 15:12–18). Moreover, the patron is commanded to send out the debt slave with a share of the bounty from his or her labor, providing a modest foundation on which to build economic security (see Chirichigno 1993, 256–301).

Similar remissions of debt were not uncommon in the ancient Near Eastern world, with the Edict of Ammisaduqa being the most well-known, which, like the remission in Deuteronomy, makes the distinction between personal and commercial debts and also includes the release of debt slaves. Such remissions were enacted by kings, generally when they came to power, as a proclamation of the character of their rule. The Deuteronomic remission, however, is proclaimed by Yhwh—it is the "remission of Yhwh" (Deut 15:2)—rather than the king, and it is scheduled every seven years in contrast to the ad hoc proclamations of the Near Eastern kings. Through Yhwh's proclamation of remission, the Deuteronomic scribes have transferred to the people the responsibility of debt relief that had previously belonged to the king.

In contrast to the poor and needy, the widow, orphan, alien, and Levite experience poverty as a condition of their socio-economic status: they are those who have no land on which to subsist. The Deuteronomic laws, therefore, require those who do have land to provide for them. Every third year, the tithe should be given to this impoverished group (Deut 14:28–29). During the pilgrimage festivals of Weeks and Booths, the widow, orphan, alien, and Levite will share in the people's food in Jerusalem (Deut 16:9–15). Finally, the widow, orphan, and alien should be given the gleanings of the grain, olive, and grape harvests (Deut 24:19–21). Without access to land, the widow, orphan, alien, and Levite are permanently unable to provide for their own subsistence and so are dependent on others. Although these provisions are the result of individual acts, they should not be confused with private acts of charity. In the Deuteronomic formulation, each provision is an expression of Israel's covenant with Yhwh; each is commanded as a fitting response to God's blessing and prior deliverance of Israel from bondage in Egypt. The Deuteronomic laws thus provide a minimum provision for the widow, orphan, alien, and Levite's survival; they are provided subsistence through the labor and production of others.

The Priestly scribes do not distinguish between two groups of poor people, as do the Deuteronomic scribes. Otherwise, the Priestly legislation similarly prohibits farmers from fully harvesting their grain or grapes so that the gleanings left behind may provide subsistence for the poor and the alien (Lev 19:9–10; 23:22). Elsewhere, the Priestly scribes make provision for the Levites, who will subsist off of the tithes (Lev 27:30–33; Num 18:21–24), but the plight of the widow and orphan is not mentioned. Their conspicuous absence in relation to the Deuteronomic legislation is probably the result of a change in political economy that transpired with Persian domination.

Comparable to the Deuteronomic remission, the Priestly jubilee (*yobel*) is concerned with the redemption of the Israelites' land and persons (Lev 25:8–55): every fifty years the (male) Israelites should return to their property (*ahuzzah*) and their family (*mishpahah*). Because the land belongs to YHWH, only a certain number of harvests, rather than the land itself, can be sold up to the year of jubilee when the land should return to the one who originally possessed it. The jubilee legislation also makes provision for the redemption of persons who may experience increasing levels of impoverishment. If an Israelite sells his property because of impoverishment, then a near-kinsmen (*go'el*) should redeem his land. If the Israelite is unable to provide for himself, he may become dependent on a patron with whom he will live as a resident alien (*ger*). And if the Israelite needs to sell himself into servitude, he should not be treated as a slave but as a hired laborer with the right of redemption: he may redeem himself through his wages, or his kin may redeem him. In any case, an Israelite's dependence or servitude should last only until the year of jubilee when we would be freed and restored on his land (see Fager 1993; Chirichigno 1993, 302–43).

As with the Deuteronomic remission, the responsibility for the economic relief is placed on the patron, on whom an impoverished Israelite might become dependent for provisions or to whom he might become indebted into servitude. In both cases, the patron should treat the impoverished man as his kin (Hebrew "brother"), providing for him without profit and treating him with the respect of a laborer who earns his keep. But the Priestly scribes also placed the responsibility on the man's *mishpahah*, his extended family beyond the household, who are charged with redeeming the man and his land. It is this emphasis on the family that perhaps accounts for the legislation's silence with regard to the widow and orphan. For the Priestly scribes, the recipients of economic relief are the Israelites who have usufruct rights to land, and the economic relief is constructed to ensure their redemption on their land. The widows and orphans, presumably, were expected to be cared for by their *mishpahoth*.

Ideology and Practice

All three legal traditions, each in its own distinctive way, provide for the subsistence of the poor and include measures for debt relief. Both types of provisions are essential to any economic ideology suitable for a limited world. Economic growth has covered a multitude of sins: it masks over inequalities and any number of injustices with the modest gains that manage to "trickle down" to the low wage-earning workers. Economic growth not only ensures further accumulation and profit for the capitalists, but is also a weapon used against any economic reform that might cut into those profits. In a limited world, the failures of the economic system to meet the needs of all must be addressed directly.

The concern for the poor and needy in the Book of the Covenant is quite modest and perhaps the most realized in ancient Israel. Beyond the family, the *mishpahah*, who would take care of their poor and needy, it largely assumes the role of the king in providing for their subsistence—for administering justice and righteousness—but it explicitly gives responsibility for limiting debt servitude to the patrons to whom such service was owed. The Deuteronomic and Priestly legislations build on these two aspects of economic aid with multiple laws providing subsistence for the poor and diverse methods of debt relief, but responsibility for the economic aid is put in the hands of the people—whether the subsistence farmer whose fields and orchards could be gleaned, the patron who provides food and loans, or the extended family who redeems lost land and indebted kin. Moreover, both the Deuteronomic and Priestly legislations broaden the extent of the economic aid, though in different and competing ways.

The biblical legislation is ideological, and perhaps even utopian in the Deuteronomic and Priestly legislation; it does not correspond directly with actual customs or legal practice in ancient Israel (Houston 2006, 169–203). Yet, the values expressed in the legislation do correspond in part to actual Israelite practice, though the evidence is meager. Most care for the poor and needy probably belonged to the *mishpahah*, and the Israelite kings, following in the well-established Near Eastern tradition, recognized the welfare of society to be their responsibility. The biblical prophets suggest as much when they criticize the kings and the elite (see, e.g., Amos 4:1–5; 6:4–7; 8:4–8; Mic 2:1–5). The Deuteronomic and Priestly provisions that the poor could glean in fields and orchards probably reflects actual rural customs, as depicted in the story of Ruth. Little burden would have been created for the farmers, and such a custom did not need a royal administration to implement.

Other provisions in the legislation, especially those concerning debt relief, do not appear to reflect the actual practices as formulated. Debt is a focal concern of the biblical economic legislation, and was as much of a problem in ancient Israel as it is today. In the ancient Israelite economy, debt was often the result of the exorbitant interest rate charged on loans. Generally set at a fixed rate between 20 and 33 percent per year (depending on whether it was a loan of silver or grain), and sometimes even much higher, loans were not often expected to be paid back. Instead, the creditor made loans to gain access to the collateral, which was usually either a portion of the usufruct of the debtor's land or the debtor's own labor. In fact, the lack of economic growth potentially kept the debtor in service to the creditor indefinitely (Boer 2015, 156–63). The biblical scribes, however, sought to reform this system: the Deuteronomic scribes introduced a seven-year cycle of debt remission and manumission (Deut 15:1–17), whereas the Priestly scribes introduced a more complicated system of redemption by kin, hired labor, and remission of debts within a fifty-year cycle (Lev 25:25–55). Both scribal groups agreed that interest, which exploited the needs of the debtor by forcing him into the service of others, should not be charged on loans to fellow Israelites (Lev 25:36–37; Deut 23:19–20; see Exod 22:25). In the contemporary economy, debt is built into the system itself with the fractional reserve banking system. Rather than national governments creating money interest-free, most money in circulation is created by commercial banks as credit entries in their customers' accounts in the form of interest-bearing loans. In other words, the circulation of money is dependent on debt, which must continually grow in aggregate to compensate for the money taken out of circulation through taxes and as bank capital to reduce the risk of insolvency (Sorrell 2010, 1797–801). The structure of the monetary system requires economic growth. Although current interest rates are not as exorbitant as those in the ancient world (with perhaps the exception of some credit cards and payday loan businesses), interest-bearing debt is not necessary for a monetary system. The government can create and distribute money without interest. By creating money without interest, the government would not be creating a system that perpetuates the cycle of debt that has been the ruin of so many, and would enable a sustainable economy in a limited world in which growth is not required.

The Bible gives only two examples of actual systematic debt relief. The prophetic book of Jeremiah, set during the last days of the kingdom of Judah, describes how King Zedekiah issued a proclamation of liberty (*deror*) to set free all Hebrew slaves, male and female, but afterwards the officials and the people of Jerusalem reneged on their covenant and returned the slaves to their former status (Jer 34:8–22). Although Zedekiah's remission has some similarities with the Deuteronomic formulation of debt remission, it differs in notable ways: it is promulgated ad hoc rather than after a seven-year interval, it is issued by the king's authority, and its purpose is to free all enslaved (indentured?) Judeans permanently from servitude rather than simply end a cycle of debt. Although Jeremiah alludes to the Deuteronomic legislation, his critique also suggests that Zedekiah's proclamation was unprecedented, and thus was unlikely to be based on the Deuteronomic legislation.

Later, during the Persian period, Nehemiah faces a situation in which Judeans were falling into debt, losing the usufruct of their land, and encumbering their sons and daughters with debt servitude—problems that the Deuteronomic and Priestly legislations aimed to prevent (Neh 5:1–13). Nehemiah blames the problem, in part, on the taking of interest on antichretic loans, and he demands that the nobles and officials restore the interest taken and the usufruct rights secured by the loans, essentially remitting the people's debt (see Fried 2015). Although the nobles and officials agree to his demands, they do so because of his authority as the Persian governor; Nehemiah does not appeal to the Deuteronomic or Priestly legal traditions. The text gives no evidence that Nehemiah's reform was based on common custom or earlier legal traditions, though the lack of any resistance or objection from the nobles and officials might suggest that it drew upon shared values and was at least not unprecedented.

The biblical tradition offers an alternative way of living well as economic human beings. From the perspective of a world of unlimited economic growth, these biblical ideas perhaps give the appearance of being unrealistic or simply utopian ideals. They are not. Rather, they are reforms that sought to ensure just economic relations in the ancient world, and they can contribute to a contemporary economic ideology for living well in a limited world. In his essay, "Faustian Economics: Hell Hath No Limits," Wendell Berry has argued that limits are essential to what it means to be human—this is a biblical idea, which was realized throughout the ancient Israelite political economy. Humans have always lived in a limited world, though this is often forgotten. The environmental crisis has reminded us of our limits. It is not a question of when we will reach our limits, we have already begun to do so, but rather how we encounter our limits. This, according to Berry (2008, 42), is the character of our being human:

> Whichever way we turn, from now on, we are going to find a limit beyond which there will be no more. To hit these limits at top speed is not a rational choice. To start slowing down, with the idea of avoiding catastrophe, *is* a rational choice, and a viable one if we can recover the necessary political sanity. Of course it makes sense to consider alternative energy sources, provided *they* make sense. But also we will have to re-examine the economic structures of our lives, and conform them to the tolerances and limits of our earthly places. Where there is no more, our one choice is to make the most and the best of what we have.

7

Ecology and the Anthropocene

THE DAWN OF THE ANTHROPOCENE

ALTHOUGH LIFE ON PLANET Earth seems to have begun near the end of the two-billion year-long Proterozoic Eon, plant and animal life did not appear in abundance until the Phanerozoic Eon, the eon in which we live, beginning 541 million years ago with the Paleozoic Era and Cambrian Period. Much of the history of the earth during this time is characterized by alternating periods of greenhouse and icehouse climates, through which biotic life evolved, flourished, and then contracted:

> The warm temperatures, vast shallow seas, and dispersed, low-lying continents of the Greenhouse eras would have hosted a great diversity of tropical communities of species, perhaps highly specialized and localized. The rifting of continents would have multiplied the evolutionary opportunities through founder effects of geographical isolation, . . . Greenhouses indeed saw a massive "escalation" in evolutionary diversity. Icehouse conditions would have been more conducive to less-specialized, more migratory species. (Brooke 2014, 48)

Life evolved in fits and starts, resulting in five mass extinctions (see Gould 1989). Although there is no single cause for the extinctions, the role played by climate is noteworthy, for "there is a very general relationship between mass extinctions and the ebb and flow of the Icehouse-Greenhouse cycle" (Brooke 2014, 49). Three of the five extinctions occurred in relation to the turn of the climate; the other two do not connect to the changing climate so easily.

We live during the Quaternary Period. It began about 2.6 million years ago as the third period of the Cenozoic Era, the 66 million years since the impact of a massive comet or asteroid that killed all the dinosaurs and initiated the planet's fifth mass extinction. The Quaternary Period includes two epochs. The much longer Pleistocene

Epoch is the period during which the earliest humans evolved. It is also characterized by cold glacial periods, which alternated with brief, warmer interglacial periods, first every 40,000 years and then every 100,000 years. Although humans were able to leave the relative warmth of Africa and migrate over much of the planet, they never progressed beyond small bands of hunter-gatherers. Perhaps their social development was hindered by the colder, unstable climate. Then, about 11,700 years ago, the earth quickly warmed (perhaps within a few decades) and the climate stabilized. Although this was simply the beginning of the most recent interglacial period, it also marked a significant break with the Pleistocene and so was designated as the Holocene Epoch (Zalasiewicz and Williams 2012). Its precise boundary with the Pleistocene, referred to colloquially as a "golden spike," was recently identified from an ice core drilled in central Greenland (Walker et al. 2009).

Humans played no active role in Earth's long geological history. Rather, the conditions of the earth largely hindered human development until the stable conditions of the Holocene. Having only existed for a brief period during the history of Earth, and despite altering their local environment through fire and agriculture, domesticating some animals and hunting others to extinction, deforesting some regions and salinizing soils, humans have had only a negligible impact on the earth. Until recently. Now the earth seems to be entering a new geological epoch due primarily to human activity. Primarily through our burning of fossil fuels, we have changed the climate by overloading the earth's carbon cycle. Through our impact on this and other Earth systems, we have pushed the planet into a new geological trajectory, the outcome of which is uncertain. The current environmental crisis is not simply a matter of inconvenience, an added burden to carrying on "business as usual," but a fundamental alteration of Earth as humans have known it. It requires an equally fundamental restructuring of political and economic relations in response. The dawn of a new geological epoch as a result of human activity challenges not only our relationship to the natural world but also the nature of being human.

The Holocene is the epoch of human civilization. Although much shorter than the Pleistocene, humans during the Holocene have flourished according to every metric. How much we can attribute to the new stable, warm climate, however, is uncertain. We do know that people soon began settling down in small villages, domesticated grains and legumes to produce their own food, and increased the rate of population growth (Smil 2019, 309–11). Some have argued that agriculture, which may be credited with the population growth, was impossible during the earlier glacial periods. The low levels of carbon dioxide in the atmosphere during those periods (180 ppm[1] during glacial maximums) would have severely impacted C3 plants, which make up the bulk of domesticated crops. With the onset of the warmer Holocene, the increasing carbon dioxide levels (up to 280 ppm) due to the melting glaciers enabled domestication of these crops (Brooke 2014, 125). But agriculture required more than

1. The metric ppm refers to the "parts per million" by volume of carbon dioxide in the atmosphere.

simply a warm, carbon-rich atmosphere; ecological (the variety and distribution of plants available), intellectual (a sufficient understanding of plant life), and social (co-operation and necessity) factors were also required. At most, we can claim that the warm, stable climate of the Holocene provided the conditions for human flourishing.

Although the climate of the Holocene is stable in comparison to earlier periods, its relatively minor changes have had significant effects on human civilization. For example, the Holocene is divided into three ages or stages based on noticeable changes in the climate (and identified in the stratigraphy of a Greenland ice core and in a stalagmite from a cave in India). About 8,200 years ago, the world experienced a sudden, though brief cooling, separating the Greenlandian Age from the Northgrippian Age. The current Meghalayan Age began around 4,200 years ago and was initiated by a two-hundred-year drought (Walker et al. 2018). In terms of human history, the 8,200-year-ago event correlates with the collapse of the Pre-Pottery Neolithic cultures in the Near East, the world's first settled peoples. The Pottery Neolithic cultures that emerged afterwards were much impoverished in relation to the previous cultures, despite having learned the technology of pottery production. Traces of the 4,200-year-ago drought can be found on all continents. The Old Kingdom of Egypt and Early Bronze cultures in the Levant came to an end, though the Third Dynasty of Ur on the southern Mesopotamian plain persisted for another two hundred years before collapsing. Similarly, the agricultural cultures in China and India also collapsed around this time. Did the change in climate cause the collapse of these civilizations? Probably not directly. Historians can identify social, political, and economic causes of collapse that are independent of climate change. Nevertheless, the mega-drought caused by the change in climate certainly magnified the effects of other causes, perhaps making the collapses inevitable. Other climactic changes during the Holocene, such as the Medieval warming (eleventh to fourteenth centuries), followed by the so-called "little ice age" (to the mid-nineteenth century), have been less pronounced and more difficult to link with significant historical changes. Perhaps, as human civilization has developed, it has become less impacted by changes in the climate. Or, maybe not.

The effects that anthropogenic climate change will have on human civilization are not fully known, though no respectable voices claim that they will be positive. Modest and catastrophic scenarios abound, and much depends, of course, on how much greenhouse gases, primarily carbon dioxide, we continue to put into the atmosphere. In May 2019, the Mauna Loa Observatory in Hawaii recorded the level of carbon dioxide in the atmosphere to be 415 ppm, which is much higher than the 240–280 ppm variability of carbon dioxide during most of the Holocene. The last time that carbon dioxide in the atmosphere reached the current level was during the Pliocene Epoch, the 2.7 million-year period that preceded the Quaternary Period. Although the living conditions of the Pliocene were radically different from those of today—it was 2°–3° C warmer than today, with little glacial and polar ice and snow cover; sea level was 25 meters higher so that most of Florida was underwater (Robinson et al. 2008)—the effects of the current level of carbon dioxide have been relatively modest in comparison: a 1° C rise in average temperature, resulting in severe weather, coastal flooding, and an increase in wildfires, among other less noticeable consequences such as loss of biodiversity. The oceans have absorbed some of the heat produced by rising levels of carbon dioxide, causing a lag in the climate response, perhaps from twenty-five to fifty years (Hansen et al. 2005). In other words, the Earth system, which includes the oceans and the climate, moves at a much slower rate than is generally discernable to living human beings; the full effects of what we do today will not be felt until many years later. It is not surprising, then, that the significance of the earth entering into a new epoch, the Anthropocene, as a result of anthropogenic climate change and the consequences of other human activity, might initially allude us.

In February of 2000, at the International Geosphere-Biosphere Program (IGBP) in Cuernavaca, Mexico, Paul J. Crutzen suggested—in frustration, it seems, from the report of the event—that the Holocene should no longer be referred to as the current epoch, because human activity has moved Earth into a new geological period, the Anthropocene. Crutzen did not invent the term; it had been used twenty years earlier by Eugene F. Stoermer, but had never caught on. Together, they published a proposal for a new epoch in the IGBP's newsletter later that year, then two years later Crutzen published a similar proposal to a wider audience in the popular and prestigious journal *Nature* (Crutzen and Stoermer 2000; Crutzen 2002; see Steffen, Persson, et al. 2011). Their argument claims that human activity, especially the burning of fossil fuels since the beginning of the Industrial Revolution in 1800, has pushed the planet out of the Holocene and into a new geological era. Although they highlight the rise of anthropogenic greenhouse gases, the evidence of which is visible in ice cores, they emphasize also the multiple ways in which humans have impacted the Earth systems: population explosion of humans and cattle, urbanization, human appropriation of land, loss of fisheries, pollution of various kinds, chemical production, and species extinction. They conclude their proposal by briefly addressing the significance of the new, human-produced epoch:

> Without major catastrophes like an enormous volcanic eruption, an unexpected epidemic, a large-scale nuclear war, an asteroid impact, a new ice age, or continued plundering of Earth's resources by partially still primitive technology . . . [humankind] will remain *a major geological force* for many millennia, maybe millions of years, to come. (Crutzen and Stoermer 2000, 18, emphasis added)

The concept of the Anthropocene is a product of Earth system science. This new science, with roots only in the 1970s and 80s, treats the earth as a single, integrated planetary system, comprising the atmosphere, biosphere, hydrosphere (including the cryosphere), and lithosphere (or geosphere). More specifically, "in the context of global change, the *Earth System* has come to mean the suite of interacting physical, chemical, and biological global-scale cycles (often called biogeochemical cycles) and energy fluxes which provide the conditions necessary for life on the planet" (Steffen et al. 2004, 7). The Anthropocene is not simply climate change. Although carbon dioxide in the atmosphere is a primary way by which to track the progression of the transition to the new epoch, the Anthropocene entails changes across the entire Earth system, with impacts in one sphere having effects throughout the other components of the Earth system. As a result, the Anthropocene is associated with a wide range of phenomena, including:

> an order-of-magnitude in erosion and sediment transport associated with urbanization and agriculture; marked and abrupt anthropogenic perturbations of the cycles of elements such as carbon, nitrogen, phosphorus and various metals together with new chemical compounds; environmental changes generated by these perturbations, including global warming, sea-level rise, ocean acidification and spreading oceanic "dead zones"; rapid changes in the biosphere both on land and in the sea, as a result of habitat loss, predation, explosion of domestic animal populations and species invasions; and the proliferation and global dispersion of many new "minerals" and "rocks" including concrete, fly ash and plastics, and the myriad "technofossils" produced from these and other materials. (SQS 2019)

Since Crutzen's proposal for the Anthropocene, a group of Earth system scientists have worked to further define, clarify, and even promote the Anthropocene as a new epoch (see Zalasiewicz et al. 2019). In order to more precisely identify the beginnings of the Anthropocene, they have tracked twelve features of the Earth system and twelve socio-economic trends from the year 1750, before the beginning of the Industrial Revolution, to 2010. For the socio-economic trends, they use indicators that identify major features of contemporary society, such as population, economic growth, resource use, urbanization, transportation, and communications. Similarly, they chose indicators that would track changes in the Earth system's structure and functioning, such as atmosphere composition, stratosphere ozone, the climate system, the water and nitrogen cycles, marine ecosystems, land systems, tropical forests, and terrestrial biosphere degradation (Steffen, Broadgate, et al. 2015). Significantly, with two qualified exceptions, all of the trends for both the Earth system and society follow the same exponential curve: there is a gradual growth or rise in the indicator from 1750 until an inflection point (or "knee") around 1950, then a dramatic upward turn until 2010, which is referred to as the "great acceleration."[2] One exception to the common trend is that the indicator for domesticated land showed a more dramatic rise before 1950 and a slower rate of growth after 1950. The other exception is that the indicator for marine fish capture rises dramatically beginning in 1950, then plateaus in the 1990s

---

2. Not all of the trends could be tracked from 1750. Either data was not available, such as from ocean acidification, or the feature did not exist, such as telecommunications. The available data, however, have largely aligned with the curves of the other features.

and falls slightly afterwards. Rather than attesting to a decrease in human impact on the Earth system, both of these exceptions provide evidence for the biophysical limits of the Earth system features. Most productive land on the planet has been appropriated for human use with little land remaining, and the oceans have been overfished, diminishing the potential for current catches. For all other indicators, however, no biophysical limits have yet to stop the growth, though in recent years it seems to have slowed in a few cases, forming perhaps the beginning of an S-curve. Humans have increasingly impacted the Earth system as the socio-economic trends have increased, and the years following the Second World War appear to be the inflection point of the great acceleration into the Anthropocene.[3]

What awaits human civilization in the Anthropocene is uncertain. Human activity has forced the Earth system from its previous trajectory into a "planetary *terra incognita*" (Steffen, Crutzen, and McNeill 2007, 614). At the very least, the Anthropocene "represents the beginning of a very rapid human-driven trajectory of the Earth System away from the glacial-interglacial limit cycle [which has characterized the Late Quaternary Period] toward new, hotter climatic conditions and a profoundly different biosphere" (Steffen et al. 2018, 8253). Or, as Clive Hamilton (2017) has noted, the Anthropocene represents a rupture in the earth's history. In the short term (decades?), the Anthropocene, driven by human activity, will be marked by instability due to the carbon dioxide already in the atmosphere and the emissions already committed from the built infrastructure—a process known as carbon lock-in (Unruh 2000). Carbon dioxide is a fuel for the Earth system—it magnifies the energy produced by the sun through the greenhouse effect—and the excessive amount in the atmosphere makes the Earth system unstable and unable to settle into a new, moderately warm trajectory. If we do not reduce our production of carbon dioxide and other greenhouse gases, the Earth system, through feedback loops integral to its own workings, will eventually settle into a trajectory that may be hostile, if not incompatible, with human life—similar to the greenhouse or hothouse climates that characterized Earth's earlier history (Steffen et al. 2018). In any case, we cannot return to the Holocene. Neither history nor the Earth system works in reverse, and the planet is now on a different trajectory. Our best hope—and perhaps the only viable solution—is to stop emitting carbon dioxide

---

3. Some scholars, especially some associated with ecomodernism, have argued that 1950, or even 1800 with the beginning of the Industrial Revolution, are arbitrary dates in the long history of human impacts on the environment. They argue that the Anthropocene only represents the culmination of a millennial long transition of human relations to the environment (see Bauer and Ellis 2018; Ellis 2015, 2011; Ellis et al. 2013). Admittedly, humans have always impacted their environments, but the Anthropocene is different in kind and degree from all earlier human impacts: it represents a synchronous *global* impact that is *geological* in scale. This has not occurred in human history until the so-called great acceleration, beginning in the post-World War II era (Zalasiewicz et al. 2018). The early dating of the Anthropocene is a form of denial—that the Anthropocene represents a *rupture* in the natural geological course of Earth as a result of the economic growth produced by capitalist relations and the burning of fossil fuels and other human activity.

into the atmosphere through the burning of fossil fuel, which will eventually reduce the energy in the Earth system, enabling it to stabilize with life-supportive conditions.

Human civilization emerged with the stable conditions of the Holocene, and it is uncertain how civilization will fare under very different conditions. Because the conditions that will dominate in the Anthropocene depend in part on what humans do now, some scientists have framed the transition from the Holocene into the Anthropocene by the concept of planetary boundaries. Although initially framed as a way of maintaining the state of the Holocene (Rockström et al. 2009), more recent formulations focus on "Holocene-like" conditions (Rockström 2015) as the planet moves out of the Holocene into a new epoch. The planetary boundaries are designed to provide a "safe operating space" for humankind based on the favorable conditions of the Holocene. They address two issues: "What are the processes and subsystems that keep Earth in a Holocene-like state, and what levels of human pressure on each of these could reach a threshold, thereby disrupting the continuity of the Earth system?" (Rockström 2015). Rather than regulating human behavior, the planetary boundaries are offered to decision-makers as an aid in choosing desirable courses for societal development (Steffen, Richardson, et al. 2015). They have been embraced by the United Nations High-Level Panel on Global Sustainability and the UN Environmental Program's Global Environmental Outlook. The planetary boundaries identify nine Earth system processes that are critical for Holocene-like conditions. They include climate change, biosphere integrity (genetic and functional diversity), biogeochemical flows (especially, nitrogen and phosphorus cycles), stratospheric ozone depletion, ocean acidification, freshwater use, land-system change, atmospheric aerosol loading, and the anthropogenic introduction of novel entities (such as CFCs and other synthetics chemicals). For each process, a threshold is identified which, if crossed, may lead to intolerable environmental changes. The boundary, which is meant to represent a safe operating space, is placed a reasonable distance below the threshold, and the threshold itself is expanded to create a warning zone of uncertainty. Beyond this zone, the Earth system processes enter a dangerous level in which human society might face a high risk of serious environmental impacts.

As of this writing, four planetary boundaries have been crossed: climate change and land-system change are in the threshold zone of uncertainty, and biosphere integrity (the genetic diversity component) and biogeochemical flows are in the dangerous level. This is not surprising, for the Anthropocene itself is defined in terms of changes in the Earth system that deviate significantly from the Holocene. In other words, if we had not crossed planetary boundaries, we would not be speaking of a new geological era—we would still be within the biophysical parameters of the Holocene. The planetary boundaries only attest to the current state of the Earth system in relation to the civilization-supporting conditions of the Holocene; they do not represent absolute boundaries or thresholds for human life in general. Some scholars, such as the ecomodernists, have even called into question the very nature of planetary boundaries and thresholds (Nordhaus et al. 2012), but more on them below. Although the planetary boundaries cannot keep us in the Holocene and transgressed boundaries are to be assumed, the planetary boundaries do help us to monitor our transition into the Anthropocene. They suggest ways by which we can stabilize the planet in a new moderate trajectory, or warn us as we approach potential tipping points that would force the planet into a very different trajectory, hostile to human life and civilization (see also Lenton et al. 2008).

Presently, the Anthropocene is only used informally. In order for it to become a formal designation in the Geological Time Scale, a number of hurdles must be overcome. First, the proposal needs a supermajority of support from the Subcommission on Quaternary Stratigraphy (SQS). To that end, the SQS appointed a working group on the Anthropocene in 2009, whose task is to evaluate and marshal the evidence for the Anthropocene as a *geological* time unit. The evidence should consist of biostratigraphical, sedimentological, and geochemical material changes similar in scale to material changes separating other epoch boundaries, such as between the Pleistocene and Holocene. The working group would also need to define a Global Stratigraphic Section and Point (the "golden spike"), which would mark the Holocene-Anthropocene boundary.[4] In May 2019, the Anthropocene Working Group voted overwhelmingly that the Anthropocene should be treated as a formal geological time unit and that the base of the Anthropocene (when it begins) should be set in the mid-twentieth century. The recently accumulating strata from the "great acceleration," along with the radionuclides from the fallout of thermonuclear bomb tests should provide the material for locating and defining the golden spike. After the SQS approves the proposal, it must be approved by its parent body, the International Commission on Stratigraphy, and then finally by the International Union of Geological Sciences, a process that will take many years. The Anthropocene will be formally defined on stratigraphic grounds (Waters et al. 2016; Zalasiewicz et al. 2011, 2017), but until then it calls attention informally to how broadly and deeply humans have altered the planet and the magnitude of the current environmental crisis.

THE SIGNIFICANCE OF THE ANTHROPOCENE

Because the concept of the Anthropocene rests on the premise that humans have significantly altered the Earth system, elevating humans to the role of a "major geological force," the Anthropocene has gained wide attention from the social sciences and humanities, where humans and human activity are a primary focus. And the concept

---

4. Some scholars have suggested, perhaps in jest, that one potential biostratigraphic marker of the Anthropocene is the broiler chicken. The chicken, which is anatomically distinct from its natural predecessors, has been genetically engineered to grow fast and large. It is found all over the planet, and as many as 22 billion exist at any one time. They will undoubtedly leave a mark in the fossil record and thus could signal the onset of the Anthropocene (Bennett et al. 2018).

of the Anthropocene has had no shortage of critics. Indeed, although some natural scientists have challenged the dating and utility of the Anthropocene concept (Ruddiman 2003; Visconti 2014), social scientists and humanists have unleashed the most scathing critiques. Some of the criticisms of the Anthropocene have resulted from the crossing of disciplinary boundaries, as is seen primarily in the debate over its name and what it implies. When Paul Crutzen blurted out the term "Anthropocene" at a scholarly meeting, he had not given it any prior thought, according to his own account, and it is a flawed term, as will become evident below. Nevertheless, for many Earth system scientists, the use of *anthropos* ("human"; all geological epochs are labeled "-cene") in defining the new epoch represented well its fundamental characteristic: "humans as the dominant force driving marked and globally near-synchronous changes to some key Earth processes" (Zalasiewicz et al. 2017, 208). From the perspective of their science, the Anthropocene name means no more than this, and Earth system scientists and geologists should be able to name and define a geological epoch as they think appropriate within their discipline (Angus 2016, 224–32; Hamilton 2017, 27–35; contrary to Ellis et al. 2016). The human and social *significance* of the Anthropocene, however, is not the purview of the natural sciences, but at least it should be in accord with the primary scientific—that is, geological—meaning of the Anthropocene. In other words, social science and humanities scholars must negotiate the significance of the Anthropocene in relation to how the term is used in Earth system sciences. To this end, three related cautions regarding the significance of the Anthropocene are in order.

First, the Anthropocene uses species language as appropriate for the Earth system sciences, but its social and human significance is not a feature or property of the species. Simply put, humans in general, as a species, have not altered the geological trajectory of the planet, nor is there any specific, inherent characteristic of the human species that explains the new geological epoch. Even the Earth system scientists note that the changes which introduced the Anthropocene, such as climate change, cannot be attributed to all humans—Crutzen (2002), for example, claimed that they have been caused by only 25 percent of the population. Climate change is the result of the excessive burning of fossil fuels, but this is not an inherent human trait; it is not a property of the species. Humans have subsisted for millennia without consuming fossil fuels, and many of those who have burned fossil fuels, such as the medieval Song Dynasty in China, consumed the fuel (coal) at a moderate rate without altering the carbon cycle. Only when fossil fuel was linked with capitalism did its consumption escalate and produce the conditions for climate change and the Anthropocene. Indeed, those most responsible for altering the planet and setting it on a new course represent a much smaller percentage of the population than Crutzen imagined. They are the class of capitalists, who have used the power of their money, wedded to the energy provided by the burning of fossil fuels—initially coal, but eventually oil and natural gas—to create what is appropriately called the fossil economy, which now dominates the planet (Malm 2016; see Angus 2016). It is the fossil economy and those driving it, not humans in general, that has produced climate change, which marks the transition of Earth from the Holocene to the Anthropocene. But I should be more specific.

Capitalism in the form of the fossil economy,[5] beginning around 1800 with the invention of the steam engine, enabled something never before seen on planet Earth: self-sustaining growth, which soon translated into an economy that experienced sustained per capita growth. The fossil economy is built on capitalist relations of production, which include the capitalists who own the means of production—the material resources and especially machines powered by fossil fuel—and workers who sell their labor in order to provide for their own livelihood. But what makes capitalist relations unique is that production is based on exchange value, which is unlimited, rather than use-value, and a portion of the surplus is reinvested into the production process; both exchange value and reinvestment contribute structurally to growth in production. In other words, capitalism is a process of accumulation. Growth is also a feature of consumption, without which the production process results in over-production, cutting into profits. Thus, the ideology of capitalism creates and justifies a *need* for continual consumption, in order to maintain a growing production and continual growth in profits. In creating self-sustaining economic growth, capitalist relations have depleted material resources, polluted environments, and have released billions of tonnes of carbon dioxide into the atmosphere by burning fossil fuels without limits, and all in the pursuit of endless accumulation.

Although Dipesh Chakrabarty recognizes the instrumental role that capitalism has played in climate change, he nevertheless claims that the Anthropocene is also about our role as a species: "the current crisis has brought into view certain other conditions for the existence of life in the human form that have no intrinsic connection to the logics of capitalist, nationalist, or socialist identities. They are connected rather to the history of life on this planet" (2009, 217). He acknowledges that nothing inherent to the human species has pushed us into the Anthropocene, and he is aware of the dangers of essentialism, yet he maintains that climate change, through scientific analysis, "shows . . . the effects of our actions as a species" (2009, 221). But here is the interdisciplinary problem, for while the natural sciences may treat humans as a species, such species-thinking distorts the social sciences and humanities. Species-thinking *is* essentialist, reductionist, or homogenizing of humans; it ignores differences and the particular histories of individual humans; it distorts the social sciences and humanities, which recognize the differences among humans and discern meaning

---

5. Capitalism did not originate with the fossil economy, but had existed for around two centuries prior to James Watt's invention of the steam engine. Capitalism initially emerged from market-driven, solar-powered agriculture (Wood 2017), and capitalist industry—beginning with textile production—was powered by flowing water. But the spatial-temporal features of these sources of energy and their common access inhibited the development of the capitalist economy. Fossil fuels, initially coal, with its mobility and private ownership, finally enabled the internal dynamics of capitalism to flourish (see Malm 2016).

from them (see Sideris 2016). It is unclear what Chakrabarty gains by emphasizing the species. He recognizes that we do not experience ourselves as part of a species, and thus thinking of ourselves as a species is at the limit of historical understanding. Nevertheless, for Chakrabarty, being a species is perhaps experienced in our shared sense of catastrophe that the Anthropocene might convey. But even here, species-thinking distorts. Until the moment of extinction, which erases all differences, humans will experience the Anthropocene differently based on social-historical location. We are not all in the same boat—the wealthy, the powerful, and the privileged will experience the consequences of climate change differently than the poor, the unimportant, and the masses. Human history has taught us as much. While we might agree with Chakrabarty that "the whole crisis cannot be *reduced* to a story of capitalism" (2009, 221, emphasis added), neither should human history be reduced through abstraction to the history of a species. Species-thinking only serves to mystify the social-historical causes of climate change, which has pushed us into the Anthropocene, and it serves only the interests of those responsible (Malm and Hornborg 2014).

Second, the effects of human activity on Earth might be like a "major geological force," but humans are not in control of the Anthropocene, nor should they be the only focus of concern in addressing its consequences. Much of the Anthropocene discourse tends to be anthropocentric as if the planet and its future is all about us (Crist 2013).[6] Humans are called to be planetary stewards in order to keep "the Earth's environment in a state conducive for further human development" (Steffen, Persson, et al. 2011, 741). Similarly, the purpose of the planetary boundaries is to provide a framework for the continual flourishing of *human society*. Humans are not only the cause of the earth's shift to the Anthropocene, but also viewed as the solution. In part, this is a consequence of species-thinking. If the human species, as a geological force, has caused climate change and set Earth on the trajectory to the Anthropocene, then some think that we can certainly guide our transition into the Anthropocene so that human society will continue as usual. But humans are *not* a geological force, even though the accumulated effects of our activity might have altered the course of the planet *like* a geological force. Humans are not unified like a force; we do not act with singular purpose, nor can we predict the consequences of our collective actions. We are not sitting in the driver's seat, able to steer the planet on any course than suits us

---

6. According to Clive Hamilton, we are *not anthropocentric enough*: "we refuse to face up to the profound importance of humans, ontologically and now practically, to the Earth and its future" (2017, 43). He proposes a weak form of anthropocentrism that takes responsibility for the powers we have exercised in degrading the earth. Although Hamilton's emphasis on human responsibility and action is critically important, framing it in terms of anthropocentrism confuses the conversation because of its inherent dangers—humans are accountable only to themselves. The biblical tradition also emphasizes human distinctiveness—what I think Hamilton means by anthropocentrism—but without neglecting that humans are also fully material creatures, like all other creatures, made out of the dirt by God. In this theocentric worldview, humans are accountable to God, who limits their behavior through law and covenant, which is rooted in the structure of creation itself.

best. Moreover, there is no driver's seat; the Earth system evolves and changes in ways that we do not fully understand, and certainly cannot control.

The anthropocentric discourse of the Anthropocene is also simply a product of our largely anthropocentric society. The discourse reflects the very worldview that enabled climate change and environmental degradation in the first place (see Crist 2019). It is a worldview that places human concerns, needs, and wants above all else, and thus it is not surprising that the Anthropocene discourse presents humans and the future of human society as the focal subject of concern. The loss of biodiversity, for example, is usually listed as one of the many indicators of the new epoch. But its significance for many seems to be the effect it might have on human civilization; it is not a focal concern in its own right. We may be in the midst of the sixth mass extinction, this time caused by humans (Kolbert 2014), which is an appropriate marker of a new geological period, but it is the future of human society alone which features in much of the discourse. The problem with this anthropocentric discourse is that it

> shrinks the discursive space for challenging the domination of the biosphere, offering instead a techno-scientific pitch for its rationalization and a pragmatic plea for resigning ourselves to its actuality. The very concept of the Anthropocene crystallizes human dominion, corralling the already-pliable-in-that-direction human mind into viewing our master identity as manifestly destined, quasi-natural, and sort of awesome. The Anthropocene accepts the humanization of Earth as reality, even though this is still contestable, partially reversible, and worthy of resistance and of inspiring a different vision. Yet the Anthropocene discourse perpetuates the concealment that the human takeover is (by now) an unexamined *choice*, one which human beings have it within both our power and our nature to rescind if only we focused our creative, critical gaze upon it. (Crist 2013, 141)

The Anthropocene is not about humans or human society. It is a geological epoch that has no intrinsic meaning but forebodes consequences for life, in all its diversity and abundance, on Earth. It represents a change in the Earth system—caused by some humans—that will reverberate throughout its many subsystems, possibly promoting new forms of life but also impeding, altering, and extinguishing the diversity of life as it exists.

Third, the Anthropocene challenges the modernist conceptual dichotomy between humans and nature. In 1980, Carolyn Merchant argued that the scientific revolution of the sixteenth and seventeenth century resulted in the "death of nature." Building on the Enlightenment distinction between subject and object, and under the power of the new mechanistic science, nature had been stripped down to its inert matter, interrogated and tortured like a witch on a rack to reveal its secrets. Merchant's own particular take is that nature was treated like a woman so that both could be dominated (see also Merchant 2006). A few years later, in 1989, Bill McKibben declared the "end of nature." Humans had so penetrated the natural world that no part remained unaffected by humans. Nature, as something distinct from human society, had come to an end; no untouched nature remained. Then came the Anthropocene, with humans now proclaimed as a "major geological force." Its anthropocentric discourse does not seem to offer a critique of the dichotomy between humans and nature, as the work of humans is credited with altering the natural course of the planet. Nevertheless, according to some of the Earth system scientists, this "phenomenon of global change represents a profound shift in the relationship between humans and the rest of nature" (Steffen, Crutzen, and McNeill 2007, 614). Unfortunately, they do not explain the character of this relationship, though their language might suggest that humans are at least part of nature. In their essay, however, they simply extend the modernist narrative into the future: humans, as a species, have always altered the natural world, first with the invention of fire, then by killing the megafauna, and domesticating plants and animals. Humans may have altered Earth's ecosystems, but before the Industrial Revolution humans "did not have the numbers, social and economic organization, or technologies needed to equal or dominate the great forces of Nature in magnitude or rate" (Steffen, Crutzen, and McNeill 2007, 615). Only with the consumption of fossil fuels did humans become a global geophysical force, the "profound shift," pushing the earth into a new geological trajectory.[7] It does not seem for these Earth system scientists that the relationship between humans and nature has fundamentally changed. Nature is still the object being altered by human subjects, though their impact on nature has become more intense. In fact, the scientists suggest that in the future we may need to consider "drastic options," using our geophysical power to adjust the trajectory of the planet through geoengineering solutions. For these scientists, the Anthropocene merely signals the shift from human dominion over small bits of nature to planetary dominion.

Other scholars recognize that the dichotomy between humans and nature is no longer applicable. Historians, for example, have generally understood the subject of history to be human affairs. Natural history, in contrast, rarely includes humans within its scope. For Dipesh Chakrabarty, however, this distinction is no longer relevant. Because humans have become geological agents in human history, "the distinction between human and natural histories . . . has begun to collapse" (2009, 207). It is for this reason that Chakrabarty attempts to integrate the contingent history of capitalism with the history of humans as a species. Timothy LeCain embraces the work of Chakrabarty and pushes it further by claiming that the "distinction between human and natural ontologies is at an end" (2016, 7). But whereas Chakrabarty at least maintains the *analytical* distinction between humans and nature—he distinguishes

---

7. Contrary to their claim, it was not the consumption of fossil fuels per se that made humans a geophysical force. The Chinese during the Song Dynasty also burned considerable coal, but they lacked the capitalist relations and the self-sustaining growth they produced. Only when capitalist relations were linked to the burning of fossil fuels did the fossil economy emerge and result in climate change. The Anthropocene, which has resulted from climate change, represents more properly a sociogenic rather than anthropogenic geological change (see Malm 2016).

between the histories of capitalism and the human species—LeCain eliminates the distinction entirely: "In collapsing human and natural ontologies, it becomes possible to understand coal and oil as creative ontological forces, to suggest that humans do not use fossil fuels so much as they become entangled with and created by them" (2016, 19). The new materialist perspective of LeCain does not recognize a distinction between humans and the rest of nature—all are material and energy. Humans are a product of the material world in which they live because all materials have agency. "Coal shaped the humans who used it far more than humans shaped coal" (2015, 21). But by attributing agency to all material things—anything that effects a change is an agent—LeCain also diminishes the agency of humans: "humans and their cultures are best understood not as the creators of their destiny and environment, but as products of a material world that is constantly creating and recreating them" (2015, 23). Agency becomes a meaningless trope and humans shed their responsibility for climate change and the Anthropocene (see Malm 2018).

Humans indeed belong wholly to the material world; no quibbling with the new materialists on this issue. Moreover, the concept of the Anthropocene resolves the dichotomy between humans and nature, but it does not eliminate the analytical need for a distinction between them (see Malm 2019). Humans have a history, which remains distinct from the history of the natural world, because humans have agency unlike the rest of the material world. Human history and natural history have not collapsed into a single, universal history, even though they intersect at the Anthropocene.[8] The history of climate change, for example, is the history of how humans formed particular social relations in production, how the capitalists in those relations favored the burning of coal to power their production due to its natural properties, and how the burning of coal enabled self-sustaining growth, but emitted increasing quantities of carbon dioxide. It is not the history of coal acting on humans. Coal was chosen because it was a privately owned, mobile stock that enabled capitalist control over labor; coal did not shape or determine capitalist relations, which preceded the use of coal, nor did it predispose capitalists into preferring it. Coal is simply material that humans have used to construct society. Humans are embedded in the natural, material world. We work with bits of nature to construct society, which remains part of the material world but with its own properties. Because everything is material, our construction of society from the natural world has effects in both society and nature.[9] Economic growth is one of those effects, climate change is another effect. The latter is the material, natural response to the excessive burning of fossil fuels, which is intrinsically

---

8. Human history and natural history remain distinct even in the Anthropocene because their subjects remain distinct—humans vs. non-human nature. They may intersect in as much as humans are wholly natural and have altered the rest of nature, but they will not unite. Even Chakrabarty (2009, 220–22) acknowledged that such a universal, undifferentiated history would be at the limits of historical understanding.

9. Andreas Malm called this the paradox of historicized nature: "The more profoundly humans have shaped nature over history, the more intensely nature comes to affect their lives" (2018, 76).

tied to the former. It is the result of human agency, and it can be stopped, though not without also social effects.

ECOMODERNISM AND THE GOOD ANTHROPOCENE

When Paul Crutzen proposed the Anthropocene, he viewed it as an unfortunate consequence of the expanding impact of human activity on the environment over the past three centuries. The many Earth system scientists he has worked with since have shared a similar opinion, recognizing that the Anthropocene poses significant challenges for human civilization. "A daunting task lies ahead for scientists and engineers to guide society towards environmentally sustainable management during the era of the Anthropocene" (Crutzen 2002, 23). Most other scholars have shared a similarly cautious, if not ominous, notion of what lies ahead. It is striking, then, that a group of scientists, activists, policy makers, and financiers—self-proclaimed ecomodernists—actually welcome the Anthropocene. With an unbridled optimism that technology and innovation can solve our environmental problems, they believe we can experience a good Anthropocene, if not a great one.

Michael Shellenberger and Ted Nordhaus, founders of the Breakthrough Institute, which is committed to modernizing environmentalism for the twenty-first century, gained public notoriety in 2004 when they distributed an essay at the Environmental Grantmakers Association proclaiming "The Death of Environmentalism." Based on interviews of 25 prominent environmental organization leaders, they argued that such organizations are politically unable to meet the challenges posed by climate change. In 2011, after embracing the ecomodernist philosophy, they published another essay defending modernism and its solutions for the environment. Aided by Bruno Latour, who served as a senior fellow at the Breakthrough Institute, their argument builds on his idea of hybrids: "technologies have not only been created by us, but have also helped create us.... Technology, in short, made us human." Technology, which is wholly natural and made from the raw materials of the earth, has always been used by humans to address our problems. Not using technology now when we face the challenge of climate change and other environmental problems will only make the problems worse. But the use of technology has both positive and negative, unintended consequences. The solution for the unintended consequences, they argue, is simply more and better technology. The technology may create new problems, but such problems are better than the old problems, just as "obesity is a better problem than hunger, and living in a hotter world is a better problem than living in one without electricity." The challenges of the Anthropocene, they cavalierly propose, can be solved with the nascent and promising technologies available today:

> Stabilizing greenhouse gas emissions will require a new generation of nuclear power plants to cheaply replace coal plants as well as, perhaps, to pull carbon

dioxide out of the atmosphere and power desalination plants to irrigate and grow forests in today's deserts. Pulling frontier agriculture back from forests will require massively increasing agricultural yields through genetic engineering. Replacing environmentally degrading cattle ranching may require growing meat in laboratories, which will gradually be viewed as less repulsive than today's cruel and deadly methods of meat production. And the solution to the species extinction problem will involve creating new habitats and new organisms, perhaps from the DNA of previously extinct ones.

In 2015, Shellenberger and Nordhaus joined sixteen others to produce *An Ecomodernist Manifesto*, where they layout their collective vision for the Anthropocene. They begin the manifesto by noting two traditional environmental ideals that can no longer be reconciled: they affirm that humans must shrink their impact on the environment, but reject that human societies can harmonize with nature. "A good Anthropocene demands that humans use their growing social, economic, and technological powers to make life better for people, stabilize the climate, and protect the natural world. . . . Intensifying many human activities—particularly farming, energy extraction, forestry, and settlement—so that they use less land and interfere less with the natural world is the key to decoupling human development from environmental impacts" (Asafu-Adjaye et al. 2015, 6–7). They note the paradox that although human activity has seriously degraded natural environments, humans, who would seemingly be dependent on the biosphere, continue to flourish. For them, the explanation is obvious: technology has reduced human dependence on the natural world (cf. Raudsepp-Hearne et al. 2010). Humans must therefore decouple human development from environmental impacts.

Decoupling human development from nature is not so simple—the laws of thermodynamics would indicate that absolute decoupling is an impossible task (see Ward et al. 2016; Bithas and Kalimeris 2017; Bunker 1996)—but the ecomodernists suggest three ways. First, people from rural communities should continue to move into the cities, which more efficiently use resources and reduce environmental impacts. Second, further agricultural intensification will require less land, which can be reforested, and fewer people to work the land. Third, transition to a world powered by zero-carbon energy sources that are power dense and highly scalable. High-efficiency solar cells offer the potential with further innovation, but the only present-day solution that can supply the many terawatts of power needed for a flourishing economy is nuclear fission.

> Urbanization, agricultural intensification, nuclear power, aquaculture, and desalination are all processes with a demonstrated potential to reduce human demands on the environment, allowing more room for non-human species. Suburbanization, low-yield farming, and many forms of renewable energy production, in contrast, generally require more land and resources and leave less room for nature. (Asafu-Adjaye et al. 2015, 18)

The ecomodernists present a rather fuzzy understanding of modernism. They claim that it should not be conflated with capitalism, but do not define it themselves other than to identify with the "long-term evolution of social, economic, political, and technological arrangements" that have benefitted human societies (Asafu-Adjaye et al. 2015, 18). But this "evolution" is coterminous with the history of capitalism, and while modernism cannot be conflated with capitalism, it is certainly made possible by the self-sustaining growth of capitalism. Both the ideology of modernism and the technology on which it relies are products of capitalist relations. The goal of all of it is further economic growth: "More-productive economies are wealthier economies, capable of meeting human needs while committing more of their economic surplus to non-economic amenities, including better human health, greater human freedom and opportunity, arts, culture, and the conservation of nature" (Asafu-Adjaye et al. 2015, 29). While this is true in part, greater productivity has also resulted in greater production of carbon dioxide emissions and greater degradation of the environment, not to mention growing economic inequality and all the social ills that come with it (see Piketty 2014; Wilkinson and Pickett 2009).

Perhaps the most fundamental objection to ecomodernism is its myopic view of history. Modernism is presented only in terms of its positive benefits, and the ecomodernists double down on it as the hope for the future:

> Modernization has liberated ever more people from lives of poverty and hard agricultural labor, women from chattel status, children and ethnic minorities from oppression, and societies from capricious and arbitrary governance. Greater resource productivity associated with modern socio-technological systems has allowed human societies to meet human needs with fewer resource inputs and less impact on the environment. (Asafu-Adjaye et al. 2015, 28–29)

But the ecomodernists fail to recognize all the harm produced by modernism. The very forces of modernism that brought good for some, also caused poverty and exploitation, colonialization and forced removal of people from their land, the loss of subsistence, and the exacerbation of social inequalities. Moreover, modernism has spawned numerous wars, including two devasting world wars, and terrorism. In myopically embracing modernism, the ecomodernists offer nothing other than more of the same. The global environmental crisis is a result of modernism; more modernism will not solve the crisis. Modernism is part of the problem and we need less of it, especially its unquenching thirst for economic growth, to navigate our way into the Anthropocene.

Many other claims by the ecomodernists are either misinformed or wildly unrealistic. Take decoupling, for example. If we could decouple human well-being from environmental impacts, then our global environmental crisis would be solved. But we cannot do this. There have been numerous cases of *relative* decoupling due to technology and efficiency, or shifting production from one region to another. But no *absolute* decoupling is possible, for a material base is inherent to all production. The ecomodernists suggest that relative decoupling takes place in cities. This is partially true when narrow sectors of the city are examined, but cities as a whole are more resource intensive than rural towns and village, and they produce much more waste per person, including greenhouse gases (Kennedy et al. 2015; Caradonna et al. 2015). The ecomodernists' comments on agriculture are equally problematic. Large intensive agriculture has become more labor efficient, hence much of the rural population has had to retreat to the cities for employment, but it has also seriously degraded the land with top-soil loss and chemical inputs that kill microbial life and pollute waterways from runoff. Moreover, large intensive agriculture is not as productive as smaller farms. Since the 1960s, beginning with the groundbreaking work of Amartya Sen, numerous studies have demonstrated that there is an inverse relationship between farm size and its productivity, due in part to an increase in farmworkers on smaller, more traditional farms (see, e.g., Sheng, Ding, and Huang 2019).[10] Finally, the ecomodernists' interest in nuclear power is understandable. It produces substantial energy without carbon emissions, though the building of nuclear power plants is carbon intensive. Moreover, shuttering nuclear plants is not beneficial if their electricity will simply be replaced by plants burning fossil fuel. But nuclear plants produce a very small percentage of the electricity being consumed today—much less than the electricity produced by renewable sources, which can replace nuclear power plants. In addition to the long-lasting radioactive waste produced by nuclear fission and the nuclear weapons threat posed by the processing of uranium, the scaling up of nuclear power plants to supply global energy needs faces innumerable economic, political, and social hurdles, not to mention a limited supply of accessible uranium, the mining of which is riddled with dangers to health and life (Caradonna et al. 2015).

GEOENGINEERING THE PLANET

Although not directly mentioned in the manifesto, the ecomodernist optimism regarding the power of technology to solve human problems provides the intellectual foundation for geoengineering (sometimes referred to as climate engineering), which is the intentional large-scale, human intervention in the earth's natural systems in order to counter or reverse the effects of climate change (see Morton 2015; Nicholson 2013; Keith 2000).[11] And some of the ecomodernists, most prominently David

---

10. The ecomodernists' manifesto presents farm labor as something to be "liberated from" rather than as a valuable, noble profession. Less labor engaged in farm work, however, is not social good; it is only a capitalist good so that there is an excess of labor for capitalist production.

11. The terms "intentional" and "large-scale" are critical to the definition of geoengineering. Climate change, which is unintentional, should not be understood as geoengineering, even though it is human-made. Similarly, the artificial fixing of nitrogen through the Haber-Bosch method should not viewed as geoengineering (contra Morton 2015) because it is not intentionally large-scale—it is not

Keith (2013), are engaged in geoengineering research and invested in geoengineering solutions. But the hope of geoengineering is not limited to the ecomodernists. Paul Crutzen (2006), in response to the "grossly disappointing international political response" to reduce greenhouse emissions, argued that research should explore artificially cooling the earth by injecting sulfur dioxide into the stratosphere, mimicking the cooling effects of a volcanic eruption.[12] Geoengineering is cautiously presented as an option in much of the Earth system science discourse on the Anthropocene. Indeed, geoengineering seems to be inherent in the anthropocentric ideology of the Anthropocene: the human geophysical force that altered the natural geological course of the planet through climate change can also adjust the effects of climate change to produce a good Anthropocene. Once a fringe idea of a few overly zealous technophiles, geoengineering has become an integral part of the conversation over climate change by policy makers in Washington, D.C. and elsewhere. In 2015, the National Academy of Sciences released two reports on geoengineering, recommending caution and further research. Building on these recommendations, the U.S. Senate in 2016 charged the Department of Energy to study how the earth might reflect more sunlight back into space to fight global warming (Cho 2016). Geoengineering research has been funded by government bodies, such as the National Science Foundation, and prominent philanthropists, such as Bill Gates. Even the Intergovernmental Panel on Climate Change offers geoengineering solutions as a way to mitigate climate change (IPCC 2018). Geoengineering is not going away, and as the carbon dioxide levels in the atmosphere continue to rise each year, its implementation becomes more likely.

Geoengineering may take two distinct forms that are different in purpose, scalability, costs, and risks: solar radiation management (SRM), which attempts to cool the earth primarily by increasing the albedo (reflectivity) of the atmosphere and the earth's surface, and carbon dioxide removal (CDR), which seeks to remove the carbon dioxide already in the atmosphere. Climate change is a property of the greenhouse effect. When sunlight enters the atmosphere, about a third of it is reflected back into space—from bright clouds and surfaces—and the rest is absorbed as heat into the landscape and oceans, producing ocean currents and winds, evaporation and storms, and photosynthesis. The heat caused by the sunlight then emits thermal, infrared radiation, some of which is trapped by greenhouse gases—primarily carbon dioxide, but also methane, nitrous oxide, water vapor, ozone, and chlorofluorocarbons—in the upper troposphere, further heating the atmosphere and the earth. The more greenhouse gases in the troposphere, the more heat is trapped and the more the climate is destabilized. The SRM solutions are designed to reflect more of the sun's radiation

---

intentionally altering Earth's nitrogen cycle, for example—though its *accumulative* effects have had a global impact.

12. Crutzen claims that his argument was meant to scare people into acting more effectively on mitigation of emissions, but his essay is often read as an endorsement of geoengineering (Morton 2015, 155).

back into space before its heat can be trapped in the atmosphere. A variety of options have been proposed under the SRM rubric. Marine cloud brightening would entail injecting sea-salt aerosols into low-lying clouds to increase their albedo; alternatively, cirrus cloud thinning, also through the injection of aerosols, would allow more thermal, infrared radiation to escape into space. Some have even proposed putting mirrors in space, either high in the stratosphere or in space between the earth and the sun, to reflect sunlight before it enters the troposphere. But the most frequently discussed technique, and the most plausibly implemented, is injecting a sulfate aerosol into the stratosphere, which would increase its albedo, reflecting some of the solar radiation and counteracting the greenhouse effect caused by carbon dioxide and other greenhouse gases (Irving et al. 2016).

At a theoretical level, the injection of a sulfate aerosol into the stratosphere would cool the planet, just as the relatively recent volcanic eruptions of El Chichón (1982) in Mexico and Mount Pinatubo (1991) in the Philippines, which spewed millions of tonnes of sulfur dioxide into the atmosphere, produced measurable global cooling. Such an effect, however, is brief; scientists estimate that the sulfate aerosol might remain in the stratosphere for one to two years at the most before falling back to Earth. To counteract the temperature rise from the carbon dioxide remaining in the atmosphere, the aerosol would need to be released in the stratosphere repeatedly, and, increasingly if carbon dioxide emissions continue to grow. Although the plan is simple and relatively cheap, the specifics are rather complicated and uncertain. How would the aerosol be delivered high in the stratosphere, above the ceiling of virtually all aircraft? Two options are being pursued: a redesigned U2-type aircraft that could carry a large payload, or a large weather balloon carrying a hose attached to a pump on the earth. Both options present obstacles, but most scholars seem confident that they can be overcome. If the aerosol is able to be delivered to the stratosphere, then another set of problems must be addressed. How much aerosol should be sprayed? What size of aerosol particles are needed for the desired effect? What spatial distribution of the aerosol will produce the desired effect? The best answers for these problems remain unknown because it is difficult to test possible solutions. There is no practice planet, so any experiment or test of an SRM solution is also an implementation of it. Most significantly, the consequences of this form of geoengineering also remain uncertain (MacMartin et al. 2016).[13]

Some consequences of sulfate aerosol injection are certain. It will not reduce the level of carbon dioxide in the atmosphere; it will only reduce the heat that might

---

13. Many consequences of SRM are likely unpredictable, and thus cannot be anticipated. For example, a recent study suggests that a decline in herbivore insect populations may be due to the increased carbon dioxide of climate change. Although the added carbon dioxide in the atmosphere may stimulate plant growth, it makes the plants less nutritious, with reduced concentrations of nitrogen, phosphorus, potassium, and sodium, thus reducing the insect population and the birds who feed on them (Welti et al. 2020). The Earth system is integrated in ways that we do not fully understand, so that changes in one subsystem have unexpected reverberations in another.

otherwise be caused by the greenhouse gases. Thus, ocean acidification, which is a consequence of too much carbon dioxide, will continue and perhaps increase. Other possible consequences can be extrapolated from the volcanic eruptions of El Chichón and Pinatubo. Computer modelling of sulfate aerosol solutions, for example, suggests that agriculture may benefit from the higher levels of carbon dioxide and reduced heat (Kravitz et al. 2013), but sulfate aerosol would also reduce and scatter the sunlight (perhaps resulting in the whitening of the sky). A more recent study of agriculture damage from the El Chichón and Pinatubo eruptions indicate that the reduced and scattered sunlight caused by a sulfate aerosol would result in reduced agricultural yields, cancelling any benefit from a cooler climate (Proctor et al. 2018). The reduction of sunlight from a sulfate aerosol may also cause many problems with the hydrological cycle. Less sunlight means less evaporation and thus less rain; following the eruption of Mount Pinatubo, there was a substantial decrease in precipitation over land and a record decrease in runoff and river discharge into the ocean (Trenberth and Dai 2007). When the Tambora volcano erupted in 1815, the annual Indian monsoon failed to materialize, southern China experienced famine, and New England had frost in July (Morton 2015, 86). Other notable consequences of injecting sulfate aerosol into the stratosphere is the probability that the sulfate will combine with the chlorofluorocarbons already in the atmosphere to damage the ozone further, and when mixed with water vapor, the sulfates will return to earth as acid rain. In other words, mitigating the heat effects of climate change by injecting sulfate aerosol into the stratosphere risks altering the Earth system in unpredictable and detrimental ways without addressing the fundamental cause of climate change: the emission of carbon dioxide from the burning of fossil fuels.

In addition to the environmental risks posed by geoengineering, especially of the SRM type, it poses several significant social risks. SRM is not a climate change solution; even its advocates argue that it must go hand in hand with the mitigation of carbon dioxide from the burning of fossil fuels. But such mitigation is not easy because of the way that fossil fuels are integrated into the global economy, and renewable energy only offers a partial solution at best. Thus, geoengineering may be viewed as an alternative (Plan B) to reducing carbon dioxide emissions (Plan A). Known as the "moral hazard" argument, it claims that as long as there is a Plan B (the possibility of geoengineering) people may be empowered to ignore the threat of climate change because Plan A (the mitigation of emissions) would be too difficult. The reality of the moral hazard risk is uncertain. Nevertheless, advocates of climate engineering insist that mitigation must take place (see Morton 2015, 158–62), but our mitigation of carbon emissions has been an abject failure—they continue to rise globally. Climate change deniers also tend to oppose the reduction of fossil fuels on economic grounds (see Klein 2014), contributing to a preference for geoengineering.

Another social risk posed by geoengineering concerns the governance of SRM—or, as it has been called, the "hand on the thermostat." Despite the technical challenges of sulfate aerosol injection in the stratosphere, it is a relatively inexpensive operation that many nations could perform as well as a number of wealthy individuals.[14] But who would control if, when, and how it is implemented, and by what means? Ideally, some globally accepted, governing body would need to be created to regulate the injection of sulfate aerosol—to control the thermostat. But whose interests would they represent? It is easy to imagine how one nation, which might be experiencing a drought or losing their forests because of acid rain, might object to the continuing use of sulfate aerosol, and might act unilaterally to stop it. Another nation might insist on an alternative implementation to produce a more favorable result for them. This social risk is even more problematic because it would be nearly impossible to link any specific weather event as the result of a particular implementation of SRM, which might destabilize geopolitical relations. Because there are many variables in the implementation of an aerosol injection into the stratosphere, and because its effects would have uneven consequences around the planet, this method of geoengineering is ripe for international conflict and poses numerous security hazards. After carefully assessing the conflict and security issues posed by SRM, one analyst concluded that "climate engineering generates more, not less, security politics, potentially giving birth not just to new consultative bodies, but also to undemocratic practices or—for the skeptics—contributing to creating an authoritarian global state" (Corry 2017, 308). Others have noted a paradox in that the technologies that make SRM capable of addressing the rising temperatures of climate change quickly and inexpensively are also likely to create, for these reasons, the greatest amount of social and physical conflict (Zürn and Schäfer 2013).

Finally, the so-called "termination shock" poses both social and environmental risks. Under its commonly proposed form of implementation, sulfate aerosol injection should only be used as a last resort, in case of emergency. According to Crutzen, "its possibility should not be used to justify inadequate climate policies, but merely to create a possibility to combat *potentially drastic climate heating*" (2006, 216, emphasis added). Under these circumstances, however, injection of sulfate aerosol would need to continue indefinitely, if not continually increase, for such a scenario implies that we would have failed to curtail the burning of fossil fuels. Although the injection of sulfate aerosol may cool the climate to an acceptable temperature, carbon dioxide would continue to accumulate in the atmosphere (and increase ocean acidity) past the dangerous levels that warranted the implementation of geoengineering in the first place. If the sulfate aerosol injections were to stop, then the temperature of the climate would rise quickly within a few years, surpassing any previous peak, and

---

14. Relatedly, some scholars have highlighted the injustice involved in SRM: "solar geoengineering research is being advocated for by a small group of primarily white men at elite institutions in the Global North, funded largely by billionaires or their philanthropic arms, who are increasingly adopting militarized approaches and logics. Solar geoengineering research advances an extreme, expert-elite technocratic intervention into the global climate system that would serve to further concentrate contemporary forms of political and economic power" (Stephens and Surprise 2020, 1).

wreaking havoc on the environment and planetary life in the process. In other words, the circumstances that would commit us to using sulfate aerosol injection, require us to continue employing the technology forever, locking future generations into SRM. And here we bump into the governance risks, mentioned above, for the plausibility of uninterrupted sulfate aerosol injections for multiple generations seems unlikely.

In response to this no-win situation, some scholars have proposed a more limited use of geoengineering to provide more time for emissions mitigation. Instead of using sulfate aerosol injection as a last resort, it could be implemented moderately *now*, along with a plan for mitigation of carbon emissions. Its purpose would be to lengthen the time before the carbon dioxide levels become dangerous and thus provide more time for mitigation, and to provide an opportunity to field test SRM to better understanding its benefits and risks. The aerosol injections would be limited below the risk of "termination shock"—that is, they would be designed only for modest, not optimal, temperature reduction—and they would be reduced in pace with the carbon emissions (Wigley 2006; Keith and MacMartin 2015). This approach at least is devised to minimize any adverse effects of the geoengineering and could be stopped at any time if the consequences became too great, but it is unclear if its benefits would be worth the risks.

Not all forms of geoengineering bear the same risks. In most cases, carbon dioxide removal (CDR) poses fewer risks, but the costs of some technologies are very expensive, and scalability is an issue for all technologies. Because CDR technologies remove carbon dioxide from the air, they are also referred to as negative emissions technologies and the most common of which is known as carbon capture and storage (CCS). It uses chemistry to separate the carbon dioxide from the fossil fuel, either before it is combusted, afterwards from its exhaust, or during an oxyfuel combustion (see Wilberforce et al. 2019). The technology has been used for years with coal-fired power plants, and it can capture from 85 to 95 percent of the carbon dioxide processed at the plant. But it is energy and water intensive, requiring an addition 10 to 40 percent more energy than the plant would produce otherwise, and much more water for cooling and emission scrubbing (Eldardiry and Habib 2018). Storage of the liquid carbon dioxide that is captured is also a problem. It can be pumped underground into porous rock formations, and especially into depleted oil fields. This is also costly because it needs to be transported from the power plant, either by truck or pipeline, and it can leak into the air during transportation and into the water table during storage. Capturing carbon dioxide from the atmosphere (direct air capture) is more complicated because its density is so much less than from the exhaust of a power plant. David Keith created the company Carbon Engineering to explore the potential of CCS from the air. In 2015, he started a pilot plant in British Columbia, and by 2018 he was able to offer some conclusions from his work. He believes that his plant can capture carbon dioxide from the air for a levelized cost between $94 and $232 per ton, in contrast to $600 per ton from previous estimates. This assumes that he can convert the captured carbon dioxide into synthetic fuels to be sold for about $1 per liter (Keith et al. 2018).[15] There are serious doubts, however, whether the technology can be scaled up to make a significant reduction in the carbon dioxide level of the atmosphere, which is *increasing* by over 40 billion tonnes of carbon dioxide per year.[16] Nevertheless, oil and gas companies are beginning to invest in commercializing CCS, including in Keith's Carbon Engineering.

Other forms of CDR attempt to exploit natural processes. Bioenergy with CCS builds on the notion of renewable biofuel by growing crops that extract carbon dioxide from the atmosphere as they grow, then burning those crops for energy, while capturing the carbon dioxide emissions and storing the emissions underground (see Anderson and Peters 2016). Biochar similarly uses renewable crops, which are super-heated in a low-oxygen environment, a process known as pyrolysis, to produce charcoal that stores the carbon dioxide in solid form. The charcoal is then buried in the ground or used as a soil enhancement. Other forms of CDR are afforestation or reforestation and soil carbon sequestration; they simply attempt to scale up the natural photosynthetic processes of carbon dioxide removal. It is problematic calling these latter two forms "technologies" because they represent natural processes that can be fostered through sustainable land management. Regenerative agriculture, practiced in conjunction with dense herding using holistic planned grazing, can sequester substantial carbon in the soil, and the carbon will increase in depth and remain there if the soil is not disturbed (i.e., plowed) and is protected with cover crops. While there is much potential in sequestering carbon in the soil naturally using sustainable agricultural techniques, the carbon can be released from the soil when farmers are unable to commit fully to the sustainable practices (Bossio et al. 2020; Poulton et al. 2018; see Bradford et al. 2019). All of these technologies, however, have biophysical, economic, and practical limits and thus, with the exception of soil carbon sequestration, cannot be expected to contribute significant mitigation of carbon emissions (see Smith et al. 2015; Smith 2016).

The one CDR technique that does pose serious risks is ocean seeding. The theory is that adding iron to the ocean stimulates the growth of phytoplankton, which consume carbon dioxide from the atmosphere. When phytoplankton die and sink to the ocean floor, then the consumed carbon dioxide will be sequestered, perhaps for centuries. Unfortunately, this process is only effective if the phytoplankton sink to the

---

15. Although the burning of synthetic fuels would release the carbon dioxide back into the atmosphere, it would not be new, previously sequestered carbon dioxide. Synthetic fuels would be a way to recycle the existing carbon dioxide in the atmosphere, which of course is already at levels too high.

16. Vaclav Smil (2011, 219) highlights the problem of scale that CCS faces: "This means that in order to sequester just a fifth of current CO_2 emissions we would have to create an entirely new worldwide absorption-gathering-compression-transportation-storage industry whose annual throughput would have to be about 70 percent larger than the annual volume now handled by the global crude oil industry whose immense infrastructure of wells, pipelines, compressor stations and storages took generations to build." And if we continue burning fossil fuels, the amount of carbon dioxide in the atmosphere and the task of CCS increases as well.

ocean floor, which is often not the case. Phytoplankton is crucial to the ocean food chain, and thus is often consumed by bacteria and zooplankton. In one experiment, the phytoplankton were consumed by a school of shrimp! Some estimates suggest that as little as 5 percent might reach the ocean floor without being consumed. If ocean currents bring the dead phytoplankton back to the surface, then the sequestered carbon dioxide will be released back into the atmosphere. More significantly, dumping iron into the ocean risks numerous side effects. Phytoplankton blooms release large amounts of gases—nitrous oxide, methane, and methyl halides that erode the ozone layer—which might counter any gain from carbon dioxide sequestration. The bacteria that results from the decay of dead phytoplankton consumes the oxygen in the water leaving behind dead zones. The effects of ocean seeding on ocean life and ecology is not fully known. In 2008, the U.N. Convention on Biological Diversity issued a moratorium on large scale commercial ocean seeding until the risks and benefits are better known (Tollefson 2008). But this did not stop the world's first climate-vigilante, Russ George, chief executive of Planktos Inc., who dumped 100 tonnes of iron sulfate into the ocean off the west coast of Canada in July 2012 (Lukacs 2012), highlighting the social risk of governance discussed above.

Putting aside the dangerous risks of solar radiation management, all geoengineering techniques fail to address the causes of climate change: the burning of fossil fuels, linked to capitalist relations, in order to produce self-sustaining economic growth. By dealing only with the symptoms, these geoengineering schemes simply postpone the essential need to address the cause of climate change. Moreover, geoengineering and its technology are a product of capitalist relations as much as climate change itself. They create profit from climate change, as in the case of carbon capture and storage technology, or promote business as usual, as is the case with solar radiation management. Even under the best of circumstances, geoengineering may allow us to continue business as usual a little longer, but the problem and consequences of climate change will fall on our children, grandchildren, and future generations. This is wrong—and dare I say *sinful*—since climate change is especially *our* problem. Although capitalist relations and the burning of fossil fuels were linked in the nineteenth century, it was not until the mid-twentieth century that carbon emissions escalated to dangerous levels. At the same time, other metrics of the Earth system were beginning to accelerate, signaling the planet's transition to the Anthropocene. Those living today did not create the conditions for climate change and the Anthropocene, but we are the first generations to experience it and recognize it, and thus *we* must do something about it.

HUMAN LIMITS AND THE NATURE OF BEING HUMAN

The Anthropocene challenges our understanding of human nature, especially with its anthropocentric discourse. It posits that humans are a geophysical force, able to alter the natural geological trajectory of the planet. Ecomodernism and advocates of geoengineering build on this assessment. With confidence in human technology and human innovation, they believe that humans, as planetary stewards, can continue to shape the planet, to mitigate the effects of climate change, and produce a good Anthropocene, with no natural limits to what humans could accomplish. As one ecomodernist claims:

> Ever since early humans discovered fire and the benefits of collaborative systems such as collective hunting and social learning, human systems, not the classic biophysical limits that still constrain other species, have set the wider envelope for human population growth and prosperity. It was not planetary boundaries, but human system boundaries that constrained human development in the Holocene, the geological epoch that we have just left. We should expect no less in the Anthropocene. . . . Yet the evidence shows clearly that the human enterprise has continued to expand beyond natural limits for millennia. Indeed, the history of human civilization might be characterized as a history of transgressing natural limits and thriving. (Ellis 2012).

For Erle Ellis, all human limits are self-imposed, but technological innovation has overcome them. The Bible also places confidence in humans, especially in the Priestly tradition. There, humans are created in the image of God; they are giving dominion over the earth as God's representatives. Through their labor, humans are able to actualize God's creation in the world. Psalm 8, reflecting the Priestly tradition, even claims that humans are only a little lower than God. But unlike the ecomodernists and the advocates of geoengineering, the Priestly tradition also recognizes the limits of being human. Human limits in the biblical tradition are the means through which the biblical scribes addressed the two interrelated properties of being human: capability, which ecomodernist and geoengineers readily embrace, and fallibility, which they often fail to consider (see Clingerman 2014).

In the Priestly tradition, humans are fully capable of transforming the earth through their labor, but are not God and thus have limits, which are inscribed in law. All humans are limited by a few regulations. They may eat meat from any bird, land animal, or fish, but not with its life, that is, its blood, nor should they shed human blood. Yet, if someone murders another, then other humans are empowered to execute justice (Gen 9:2–6). Life, symbolized by blood, belongs to God, and thus humans acknowledge their own limits—that they are not God—when they drain the blood of an animal before eating its meat, and when they respect other human life. For the Israelites, their limits are more fully defined because God has created a unique relationship with them. Because they are to be distinct from all other peoples, being holy to God and holy like God (Lev 19:2), their limits are circumscribed in relation to God's holiness. In other words, they are limited in what they can eat, with whom they can have sexual relations, what they can do on the Sabbath, the kind of fabrics they can wear, and the grain they sow, among other purity regulations, in order to protect the holiness of the community. As long as the Israelites live and act within God's proscriptions and maintain God's commandments, then their work will result in the earth and human life flourishing (Lev 26:3–13), and God may dwell in their midst. Sacrifices and offerings are instituted in order for the people to maintain their holiness if the boundaries of God's holiness are encroached (Lev 1–7). If the Israelites transgress their limits as inscribed in the law, then they and the earth will suffer consequences—sickness and disease; drought and plague, war and exile (Lev 26:14–39). For the Priestly tradition, humans are indeed powerful and capable, but limits are intrinsic to being human. They separate human and divine realms. With regard to the Israelites, limits are intrinsic to their covenantal relationship with God. They separate the Israelites from other people and make it possible for God to dwell among them.

Whereas intrinsic human limits in the Priestly tradition regulate human capabilities, in the Yahwist tradition human limits underscore human fallibility as humans repeatedly seek to transgress their limits. When the human couple transgress Yhwh's prohibition against eating the fruit of knowledge in the garden, Yhwh curses the arable land, reducing its productivity by withholding rain (Gen 3:17–19). Human agriculture had been dependent on Yhwh to supply the needed rain, but following the human rebellion against him, Yhwh leaves the human couple on their own to eke out a subsistence from the land without his rain. In other words, Yhwh's attempt to limit the human couple by forbidding the fruit of knowledge failed, so Yhwh, perhaps in frustration, limits the earth's ability to provide for the humans by refusing to send rain. Because the garden was also the home of the tree of life, which offered immortality, Yhwh expelled the human couple from the garden, lest they ignore that limit too. When Cain murders his brother, Yhwh curses Cain from the land so that it would not yield to him any produce, forcing him to be a wanderer on the earth (Gen 4:11–12). But instead, Cain settles down and builds the first city (Gen 4:17) and human civilization begins. A descendant of Cain, Lamech, then kills another man like his forebearer, but unlike Cain who tried to hide his sin, Lamech boasts of his murder and claims divine retribution on any who would seek vengeance (Gen 4:23–24). In a brief, enigmatic text, Yhwh limits the life of humans to one hundred and twenty years because they were engaging in sexual relations with divine beings (Gen 6:1–4). Finally, the abundance of human wickedness compels Yhwh to destroy all life with a flood, except the family of Noah and a selection of each of the animals (Gen 6:5—8:22). Through the Yahwist's early history, humans transgress their limits and Yhwh must act in response. Yhwh's attempt to limit or restrict human behavior fails so that Yhwh is sorry that he created humans at all. Unable to change or limit human behavior effectively, Yhwh destroys human and animal life with the hope of beginning again with Noah and his family, whom he favored.

In the Yahwist tradition, humans are particularly fallible; they repeatedly frustrate Yhwh's attempts to correct them—to keep them within boundaries appropriate to humans. The fruit of knowledge, for example, enabled humans to become like God. It blurred the distinction between humans and God, while distinguishing humans from all other creatures Yhwh created. This overlap of the human and divine realms proved to be acceptable to Yhwh, and is analogous to the Priestly tradition's use of "image of God" to describe the creation of humans. Unlike the tree of knowledge, however, Yhwh did not want the humans eating from the tree of life under any circumstance, so he expelled them from the garden to prevent them from becoming immortal, which would have dissolved the distinction between humans and God entirely. When Cain kills his brother and Lamech kills another, they similarly blur the distinction between humans and God. Humans become like God through their creating of new life through procreation, as a consequence of their newly acquired knowledge, but life itself belongs to God and to take life violates God's prerogatives. The Yahwist tradition in this regard is similar to the Priestly tradition's concern with blood, which belongs to God. Although procreation is endorsed by God in the Yahwist tradition, and commanded by God in the Priestly account, God's role in opening the womb nevertheless remains necessary. Humans can only give life with the help of God. Finally, when human daughters engage in sexual relations with divine beings (literally, the "sons of gods"), producing "mighty warriors of old, men of renown," the distinction between the human and divine realms is nearly dissolved. By limiting human life to 120 years, Yhwh thus reinforces the boundary of mortality between humans and God.[17]

Human fallibility, in the Yahwist tradition, is the reason Yhwh destroyed all life with the flood. Yhwh recognized humans to be inclined towards evil: "Yhwh saw that human evil was abundant on the earth, and every inclination of their inner thoughts was only evil continually. So Yhwh was sorry that he made humans on the earth, and it grieved him in his heart" (Gen 6:5–6). The Priestly tradition, in contrast, places the cause of the flood on human capability gone awry: "The earth was ruined in God's sight, and the earth was full of violence. God saw the earth and it was ruined because all flesh had corrupted its ways on the earth" (Gen 6:11–12). Rather than using their capabilities to build up creation, the Priestly scribes verdict was that humans had damaged the creation by transgressing their own limits—perhaps interpreting the earlier Yahwist stories of Cain, Lamech, and the divine-human sexual relations. The flood in the Priestly tradition reverses creation; the waters above and the waters below break through their boundaries, turning the earth back into a watery mass as it was before creation. When the waters of the flood gradually recede, Noah and his family leave the ark on New Year's day, the day of a new creation (Barré 1988). Noah and his family are blessed, like the original human couple, and then God articulates the limits of humankind regarding the shedding of blood. For the Yahwist tradition, the flood does not have a satisfactory resolution. Yhwh, perhaps in a fit of rage over

---

17. Although not explicitly mentioned in the myth, the text suggests that natural human death had not yet been instituted. In other words, humans were mortal in that they could be killed, but otherwise they would continue living forever. The institution of natural human death secures the distinction between humans and God.

human fallibility, doused the earth with forty days and nights of rain—the very thing he had withheld from the land because of their initial rebellion. But after the flood receded, Yhwh recognized that the humans who survived were no better than those he destroyed: "the inclination of the human heart was evil from youth" (Gen 8:21). If Yhwh had hoped to begin creation again with a better set of humans, then the flood was a complete failure. Thus Yhwh, resigned to the inherent fallibility of humans, restored the climate to its proper seasonal changes, and promised never to flood the earth again *because humans are fallible.*

Human capabilities have a dialectical relationship with human fallibilities. Human capabilities make possible fallibilities, which in turn shape and *limit* the capabilities. Human capabilities are the result of knowledge and reason, innovation and technology, moral discernment, spirituality, and judgment—all that makes humans different from other creatures—whereas human fallibility is the result of finitude—that which humans share with all other creatures. The Priestly tradition emphasizes primarily human capability because of its focus on world construction: humans should actualize God's creation through their work, and ancient Israel in particular should construct a community holy to God in the midst of Persian imperial domination. The Yahwist tradition, on the other hand, has less lofty goals; it is intent on reminding the ancient Israelites of their human limits, which is the source of conflict between them and God. Humans may be like God, but they are not God, and this distinction has consequences in the real political-economic world of the ancient Israelites. In the final story before the Yahwist shifts focus to ancient Israel's ancestors—the story of the Tower of Babel—the Yahwist provides a critique of the political economy of empire itself by emphasizing yet again human fallibility.

The Tower of Babel

The story of the Tower of Babel (Gen 11:1–9), as it has traditionally been called, depicts a conflict between the human population of the earth and Yhwh, but the brief myth does not articulate the nature of the conflict. It simply depicts a unified human population settling in one place and building a city and a tower. The ambiguity of the conflict has led to two distinct interpretations. In the Christian tradition, emphasis has been placed generally on human pride as the human population builds a tower whose top is in the heavens, whereas the Jewish tradition has emphasized the human desire not to be scattered over the earth, disregarding God's earlier command to fill the earth (Gen 1:28) (Harland 1998; Anderson 1978). Some scholars have sought to minimize the conflict entirely by emphasizing the etiological function of the story—that it presents the origin of world cultures, for example (Hiebert 2007; cf. Lacocque 2009). The story can be read in multiple ways because each of these interpretations is in part embodied in the story, and different readers bring different concerns to their interpretation of the text. Our purpose here is to read the story in relation to the Anthropocene and the challenges its poses regarding the nature of being human.

Although the unity of the story has been questioned (see Baden 2009), most scholars read the text as a coherent, single narrative. The story is well crafted and structured symmetrically or chiastically (following Wenham 1987). In the first part, the people migrate and settle, then plan and build a city and tower to make a name for themselves; in the second part, Yhwh responds and then reverses their actions: Yhwh confuses their language, scatters them, and they stop building the city. The structure of the story is highlighted in the following translation:

> Now the whole earth had one language and the same words.
>> When they journeyed eastward, they found a plain in the land of Shinar, and they settled there.
>>> They said to each other, "Come, let us make bricks and fire them thoroughly." They had bricks instead of stone, and bitumen instead of clay mortar. Then they said, "Come, let us make for ourselves a city and a tower with its top in the heavens in order to make a name for ourselves, lest we are scattered over the whole earth."
>>> Then Yhwh went down to inspect the city and the tower, which humankind had built.
>>> And Yhwh said, "Look, all of them are one people and have one language; this is the beginning of what they might do, and now nothing that they scheme to do will be impossible for them. Come, let us go down and confuse their language there so that they will not understand each other's speech."
>> So Yhwh scattered them from there over the whole earth, and they stopped building the city.
> Therefore, its name is called Babel, because there Yhwh confused the language of the whole earth, and from there Yhwh scattered them over the whole earth.

The story of the Tower of Babel has no precise Near Eastern analogues. Samuel Noah Kramer (1968) suggested a fragmentary Sumerian text, in which Enki confuses human languages, perhaps because of rivalry with Enlil, but it offers little interpretive aid other than suggesting a rivalry between the human population and Yhwh. The single language of the people is significant, but the Tower of Babel story focuses on the concern of the human population to make a name for themselves lest they be scattered. So the people construct a city and its tower in the plain of Shinar. This is the great city of Babylon ("Babel" in Hebrew), a name synonymous with empire and imperial power in the ancient Near East. From the time of Hammurabi, who first established Babylon as the core city of a great empire, Babylon remained the prominent imperial city, even when the core of the empire was elsewhere, such as in Assyria or Persia. Not until the prominence of Rome was another city more indicative of empire than Babylon, and then even here Babylon could serve as a cipher for Rome (e.g., in Revelation).

The tower itself most likely refers to the large ziggurat—a seven-story pyramid made from mudbricks, with a small temple at the top—called Etemenanki, built in the center of Babylon. An artificial mountain constructed on the Mesopotamian plain, it functioned as a cosmic mountain (Clifford 1972), an *axis mundi*, connecting Babylon with the heavens above and the netherworld below. Indeed, Etemenanki means "house of the foundation of heaven and earth." With its lofty temple in the heavens, Etemenanki complemented Marduk's primary temple, Esagil, which was built at the southern base of the ziggurat. The Enuma Elish claims that the city and its ziggurat were built by the Anunnaki, at Marduk's request, after he created humans:

> "Build Babylon, the task you have sought.
>> Let bricks for it be molded, and raise the shrine!"
> The Anunnaki wielded the pick.
>> For one year they made the needed bricks.
> When the second year arrived,
>> They raised the peak of Esagil, a replica of the Apsu.
> They built the lofty temple tower [ziggurat] of the Apsu
>> And for Anu, Enlil, Ea and him [Marduk] they established it as a dwelling.
> (VI.57–64; Lambert 2013, 113)

The origin of the actual ziggurat is unknown. It was partly destroyed by Sennacherib, while he was suppressing a Babylonian rebellion in 689 BCE; it was restored in part by his successors, and then fully rebuilt by Nebuchadnezzar II. City building and the construction of a ziggurat are the characteristics of kings (or gods) in royal inscriptions; making a name for oneself is also a royal attribute (Uehlinger 1990). But in the Tower of Babel story, it is the human population as a unified whole that has these royal aspirations rather than a king.

Although the narrative focuses on the speech and actions of the whole human population (the "whole earth"), we should be as suspicious of the claim of a unified humanity as we are of the species-thinking associated with the Anthropocene. The ancient Near East was not a democratic society; people did not make decisions in mass, and certainly a *people* did not think and act in concert without hierarchy and a leader, generally a king. Yet, in the story of the Tower of Babel they do. Thus, many early interpreters associated the events of this story with the reference to Nimrod in Genesis 10:8–10 (also a Yahwist text), whose kingdom is described as beginning in Babel (see van der Toorn and van der Horst 1990). In fact, one might imagine that the biblical scribes, by emphasizing the unified human population, were masking the tributary relations that would otherwise be expected: the "whole earth" was building the city and the tower because their king and his administration had compelled them to do so. But to what end? The biblical scribes elsewhere openly criticize kings, and empires have had no shortage of critics. Rather than concealing the power and authority wielded by a royal administration, the Yahwist's emphasis of a unified humanity suggests that they represent a unified, totalizing empire, with no opposition, enemies, or critics. All the people have one language and use the "same words"—or, as we might say colloquially, everyone is on the same page.

Empires in the ancient world were the single greatest political-economic achievement, and in the biblical tradition they are employed as a model of Yhwh's relationship to Israel. The covenant between Yhwh and Israel in the Deuteronomic tradition, for example, is modeled on the treaties that emperors would impose on their vassal states (see McCarthy 1978; Baltzer 1971; Levenson 1985). Empires united disparate peoples within a single political and economic system. Like capitalism, which seeks to incorporate all economic behavior within its own functioning, the centripetal force of empires attempted to incorporate more and more of the periphery under their control. But empires were not without opposition. Peripheral peoples often violently resisted the encroachment of empire, and rebellion within the empire was a perpetual problem. Moreover, political and ideological opposition to empire abounded. The biblical tradition, especially in the Prophets, is filled with critiques of the Assyrian and Babylonian empires and emperors.[18] The end of an empire was always finally the result of conflict, sometimes as the result of the ambition of another empire, sometimes as a consequence of the centrifugal forces of the peoples. In other words, opposition and conflict also regulated the size and duration of empires. But in the story of the Tower of Babel, the human empire is wholly united with no opposition or conflict, and thus Yhwh recognizes that "nothing that they scheme to do will be impossible for them" (Gen 11:6).

The issue for Yhwh in the story does not appear to be the people's construction of a city and a tower, nor is empire itself a problem. All peoples had built cities, some of which included ziggurat towers, and the world had seen several empires, two of which Yhwh would employ to punish his own people Israel. But all earthly cities and empires have limits. Not so with the united humanity in this story. If the entire human population can speak with one voice and marshal the power inherent in it, then the distinction between the human and divine realms may once again be blurred (see Blenkinsopp 2011, 168). Although Yhwh's realm is described far beyond human reach—Yhwh must "go down" to inspect the city and tower—the story presents the people and Yhwh as belonging to rival communities. The people exclaim, "Come, let us make bricks . . . Come, let us build a city and a tower . . ." (Gen 11:3–4). Yhwh assesses the situation, "Look, all of them are one people and have one language," and then responds, "Come, let us go down . . ." (Gen 11:6–7). Yhwh is not alone but dwells with a host of other divine beings, who together make up the divine council or

---

18. Norman Gottwald even claims that Israel "was born as an anti-imperial resistance movement" (2016, 3).

assembly. The reference to the divine assembly here is reminiscent of the first occasion in the Yahwist tradition when Yhwh consulted with them following the human couple's eating of the fruit of knowledge: "Look, the man has become like one of us, knowing good and evil . . ." (Gen 3:22). The two contexts are analogous. In the first, the human couple have transgressed one divinely-imposed limit—gaining knowledge by eating the forbidden fruit—making the humans *like* God, but then Yhwh, after consultation, imposes another limit on humans by preventing them from eating the fruit of the tree of life and becoming immortal. In the second, the human population again threatens to transgress human limits through their unity and single language, so Yhwh, again after consultation, goes down to the human community to confuse their language and scatter the people. In both cases, Yhwh is concerned to protect the distinction between the human and divine realms and thus Yhwh *limits* humans. By confusing the people's languages and scattering them over the earth, Yhwh introduces opposition and conflict into the people's political-economic ambitions. The building of the city and the tower comes to an end. Rather than being the "gate of the gods," (*bab ilum*, the popular Babylonian etymology of the city's name), Babel has become a "confusion" (making a pun with the Hebrew verb *balal*).

The story of the Tower of Babel resolves the potential overreach of human capability, as expressed through their unity and singular language, by introducing the conditions for human fallibility to emerge—the confusion of languages, which will give rise to opposition and conflict and thus regulate empire. In the Yahwist tradition, and in the Bible generally, human limits are intrinsic to being material creatures, the creation of God. Humans are like God, but are not gods, and so there is an absolute distinction between being human and being God. Mortality defines human existence. But there are also divine prerogatives, by means of which humans encroach on the divine realm. Murder is the most obvious, and giving and taking of life is recognized as belonging to God. Other divine prerogatives are not challenged by humans in the biblical tradition because the ancient Israelites could not imagine the capability to do so. Weather, for example, is always controlled by God. Yhwh causes the rain to fall on the land, and Yhwh may also withhold the rain. Although humans have often tried to persuade God into raining on the earth, humans have never been able to do so on their own (Donner 2007). Geoengineering suggests that humans are capable of altering the Earth's systems, presumably for the better. Whether or not this is within human capability is not yet known, but perhaps it is beyond the limits of where humans should go (Clingerman 2012). Human fallibility must also be taken into account, for it will undoubtedly play a role in any geoengineering project. Our continued inability to control the weather, let alone adequately predict it days and weeks into the future, should be a caution against any attempt to control Earth systems. As H. H. Lamb, a British meteorologist, noted, "an essential precaution [is] to wait until a scientific system for forecasting the behavior of the natural climate . . . has been devised and operated successfully for, perhaps, a hundred years" (quoted in Nicholson 2013, 327).

Because the story of the Tower of Babel also includes the building of a city and a tower, it also challenges the limits of human technology. The story does not critique the use of technology per se. Making mudbricks and using bitumen to build a city and tower was not problematic, but rather the means toward a problematic end: to remain a unified, totalizing empire. Similarly, the technology embraced by the ecomodernists and the geoengineers is not problematic on its own, but as the product of capitalist relations, it enables the continuation of the very political-economic relations that produced climate change in the first place. Although technology is a means by which humans may extend their appropriation of the natural world—it increases human capabilities—it also enhances the potential and increases the consequences of human fallibility. The limits of technology are determined by human limits, which result from the dialectical relationship between human capabilities and human fallibility. Joseph Blenkinsopp (2011, 170) summarizes well the contribution that the story of the Tower of Babel makes to our assessment of the limits of technology:

> The present reality of ecological degradation, global warming, the proliferation of nuclear and biological weapons, cloning, the spread of AIDS and the prospect of other pandemic diseases, could induce us to read the story of the unfinished tower and the abandoned city as a parable about the ambiguities and dangers of limitless technological progress. Our technologies are so much more advanced than those of the travelers from the east—for them it was a mere matter of using bricks instead of stone and putting up a seven-storey building—but it is to be doubted whether our wisdom, or our consciousness of the limitations of our moral capacity, is any greater. To quote a saying of Michel de Montaigne, "Presumption is our natural and original malady . . . It is by the vanity of this very imagination that man sets himself up as the equal of God."

8

Ecology and Theodicy

CHALLENGE OF CLIMATE CHANGE IN THE ANTHROPOCENE

THE BOOK OF JOB presents a classic example of theodicy. Job, who claims to have lived a righteous life, experiences various catastrophes for which he can identify no legitimate cause. His friends, drawing upon traditional theology, attempt to convince him that his suffering is justifiable, but Job will not be persuaded nor consoled by them and ultimately holds God responsible. When God finally responds to Job's accusations, God does so with a cosmology, which places Job's suffering and complaint within a larger, theocentric context. No satisfactory answer is given for Job's complaint, but the import of his suffering is diminished as he recognizes his own insignificance in God's creation.

In the past, during the long Holocene epoch, environmental degradation and pollution of the natural world was always partial and regional. Salination of the soil, deforestation, chemical spills, and air pollution all had limited effects. Although the consequences for humans were not insignificant, such environmental degradation and pollution never threatened all humans nor human civilization on a planetary scale. Climate change is different from all preceding environmental crises, and it challenges not only the role of humans in this world, but also the nature of God and the role of God in the creation.

The human situation in the context of climate change raises questions of theodicy that are similar to Job's, and traditional religious or theological understandings about the role of God or humans in the world, rooted in the biblical cosmologies, are, like the understandings of Job's friends, not necessarily helpful. The classic formulation of theodicy is whether an all-good, all-powerful God is compatible with a world in which there is evil. As a theodicy, the book of Job raises questions about whether God is just in his dealings with a suffering Job. Job assumes that he should not be suffering, that God has neglected his plight, or that God simply chooses not to relieve him of suffering. Job's friends respond to his complaints with traditional, biblical answers that reflect the common covenant theology—that Job has sinned, that his children have sinned, or that humans are treated better than their sins deserve. In all cases, Job's friends maintain that God is just and the problem is with Job. Job is not so sure. He yearns for a hearing before God in order to make the case for his unjust suffering, and he is confident of his triumph.

Most of the book of Job seems to put God on trial, with Job prosecuting his case against God and his friends as self-appointed witnesses on behalf of God. Yet, when God shows ups, he does not take the stand in his defense. Rather, he reverses roles with Job, becoming Job's accuser and putting him on defense, and God does this by rehearsing his role in creation and its unfathomable splendor. Job is made to see his insignificance and perhaps also the inconsequence of his suffering in comparison to God' marvelous creation. But Job is only one man. Even if we multiply his case by a thousand or a million or even a billion, Job's suffering is still limited or partial in relation to the entire human population and especially in relation to the whole creation. This is the worldview of the Holocene. The scope of the Anthropocene, in contrast, is inclusive; it encompasses the whole planet. Climate change, the particular crisis that marks the Anthropocene, is not just a regional disruption; it will not have a limited effect. All humans will experience its consequences, and human civilization on Earth is at stake. The biblical conception of God and God's role in creation might seem too small for the Anthropocene. Can the biblical cosmologies, like God's response to Job, continue to speak in the context of climate change, or do we need a new cosmology to face this new challenge?[1] Are the biblical cosmologies in response to climate change no better than the covenant theology of Job's friends in the face of his suffering? How might God respond to our accusation that climate change and the consequences it will bear are simply not fair or just, and that the fault lies with God and his creation?

Since Lynn White's critique of Christianity and its role in the current environmental crisis, the primary focus of environmental concern has shifted from issues of pollution and toxic chemicals, among other concerns, to the consequences of climate change. White himself ominously refers to climate change as one of the many ways in which humans have adversely impacted the environment, though he does not develop the comment. In contrast to the smog produced in medieval London by burning soft coal, he briefly warns that "our present combustion of fossil fuels threatens to change the chemistry of the globe's atmosphere as a whole, with consequences which

---

1. Because of the limited, pre-scientific understandings of so many religious cosmologies, including the biblical cosmologies, some scholars have proposed a new cosmology rooted in the scientific story of the universe. They assume that a commonly shared evolutionary cosmology, grounded in contemporary physics and biology, will instill in humans a more profound sense of connection with the real world and thus produce motivation for better care of the environment (see Swimme and Berry 1992). Whether such a scientific cosmology could instill values and motivate humans is doubtful; as a modern creation, it would lack the substantial power of myth. Nevertheless, it is also not without its own problems (see Sideris 2017).

we are only beginning to guess" (1967, 1204). This is somewhat surprising for an essay published in 1967. Although the potential of human-produced global warming was recognized by the end of the 1800s, it was not until the late 1970s and 1980s that a consensus emerged among climate scientists regarding the dangers posed by climate change and that many confirmed that global warming itself was well underway (Hughes 2009, 254–63; Rich 2019). Now, in 2020 as I write this, the reality of climate change is certain and its effects have already begun to be felt (see IPCC 2014).

Climate change poses a qualitatively different challenge to the biblical cosmology and Western Christianity than does the argument articulated by White. Whereas various forms of pollution and environmental degradation result from human exploitation and abuse of the natural world, accompanied perhaps by a corrupted and exploitive understanding of the human–nature relationship, climate change has resulted from an excessive release of a *naturally occurring gas*, primarily carbon dioxide from the burning of fossil fuels, which is *essential* to both faunal and floral life on this planet. Moreover, the excessive release of carbon dioxide in the atmosphere has largely been the byproduct of energy production, which, when joined with capitalist relations beginning around 1800, resulted in the first period of sustained per capita economic growth in human history (see Roser 2020). With this previously unprecedented economic growth has come increased standards of living, economic and social mobility, the lowering of child mortality, better health and longevity, and a rapidly increasing human population. In other words, in many ways, climate change is a consequence of the *success* of the human species on this planet.

The human success story, of course, has not been without its failures. Capitalist social relations, which are the engine of economic growth, are exploitive of laborers and the natural world, both of which are consumed for the capitalists' accumulation and profit. But all periods of human history have experienced exploitive social relations—tributary relations in the ancient world, slave relations in the classical world, feudal relations in the medieval period—all of which exploited the many for the benefit of a few. In terms of the environment, capitalist industries have produced an immense amount of inorganic and toxic pollutants, fouling the earth's land, waterways, and air, and causing the extinction of innumerable species. But not all pollution can be attributed to capitalism. Humans more broadly have regularly fouled the air, landscape, and waterways. Yet, as bad as human exploitation and environmental destruction might be, many hold out hope that it can be stopped; capitalist social relations can be made more just (or less exploitive) through regulation, and with time much of the pollution and adverse environmental effects can be reversed (the extinction of species being a notable exception). This is not the case with climate change. Once carbon dioxide is released, it can remain in the atmosphere for millennia. A large portion of the carbon dioxide may dissolve in the oceans within a hundred years, increasing its acidification, but other processes that might absorb carbon dioxide, such as photosynthesis, are much slower. Currently, too much carbon dioxide is being released for the earth's natural sinks to absorb, resulting in increasing levels of carbon dioxide in the atmosphere that will continue to warm the planet long into the future (Archer 2005).

Moreover, a capitalist global economy is dependent on an increasing level of energy (Brown et al. 2011), regardless of how just the social relations might be, so that a significant reduction of carbon dioxide in the atmosphere by reducing carbon-based energy production would entail severe, even catastrophic, economic consequences (see Hueting 2010)—not to mention difficult and unlikely political choices. Although clean renewable energy sources are gaining a larger percentage of the production of electricity globally, the total decarbonization of global energy production is not foreseeable given our current technology (Clack et al. 2017). A further complication is that a large portion of the global population, especially in the global South but also in parts of the industrial North, are poor, malnourished, suffer from sickness and disease, and otherwise lack many of the necessities of life. Raising their standard of living will require much more production of energy, further increasing the level of carbon dioxide in the atmosphere. In other words, unlike many other forms of pollution and degradation of the natural world, the cause of climate change—the release of carbon dioxide into the atmosphere by burning fossil fuels—cannot easily and will not entirely be reduced within sustainable limits; even if such limits could be obtained, the effects of the carbon dioxide already released could be felt for thousands of years.

The very success of the human species poses a problem for the long-term survival of human civilization: there are simply too many humans dependent on too much energy for the emission of carbon dioxide to remain within sustainable limits. This problem—the reality of the human environmental situation—posits a world that is incompatible with the biblical cosmology in Genesis 1. White (1967, 1205) criticized the anthropocentrism of the biblical cosmology—that as the image of God, humans transcend the natural world and the entire creation has no purpose but to serve human purposes. As we have already observed, numerous biblical scholars have noted White's misreading of the biblical text: humans remain part of the natural world and were created to be stewards of the creation. Instead of giving humans license to exploit the natural world, the biblical cosmology in Genesis 1 indicates that humans are responsible for the condition of creation, and, indeed, the pollution of the natural world is an indictment of our role as stewards of creation. Yet the excessive release of carbon dioxide in the atmosphere through the production of energy is not simply a *human* failure. On the one hand, it is the *unintended* product of a high standard of living generated by capitalist relations and an overly abundant human population, none of which is contrary to the Genesis 1 cosmology. On the other hand, the release of carbon dioxide is excessive and therefore problematic because of the limits of Earth's natural sinks to absorb it. Earth, the creation of God, does not seem to be able to support what some might call the flourishing of human culture and civilization that the production of energy has made possible.

Part II: Ecology

Climate change is incompatible with the biblical cosmology in Genesis 1 because this cosmology presents the reader with a *good, stable world*. At every stage in the creation, God proclaims his work to be good, and at the end, God evaluates the final product as "very good." There are also no opposing forces to God's sovereignty. Yet, this good, stable world cannot currently sustain the flourishing human community—perhaps, it is not as good as it needs to be. Within the world of Genesis 1, humans, like Job, must question God and God's ability to create a good world. The Genesis 1 cosmology in the context of climate change raises the specter of theodicy: Is the creation of God faulty? Is God ultimately responsible for the dire consequences and suffering that humans will experience as a result of climate change? Raising questions of theodicy is not itself problematic—the book of Job does exactly this. Where the Genesis 1 cosmology falls short, unlike the theodicy in the book of Job, is that it constructs a world that is unable to address the theodicy it poses. The Genesis 1 cosmology made sense of the world during the Holocene epoch, with its stable climate, but proves to be inadequate as the Anthropocene epoch dawns, where the effects of human flourishing are embedded in the very creation itself. If other biblical cosmologies would continue to be relevant, they must be able to take into account the challenge posed by climate change.

BIBLICAL COSMOLOGIES IN RESPONSE TO CLIMATE CHANGE

Psalm 104

Although Genesis 1 gets pride of place, the Bible includes numerous other cosmologies, incorporated into diverse genres. Psalm 104 presents a cosmology most similar to Genesis 1, but it is framed within a panoramic hymn praising God for continually sustaining the creation. Like Genesis 1, God constructs a habitable world: God stretches out the heavens like a tent (Ps 104:2); God sets the earth on its foundations, covers it with water, and then gathers the water within fixed boundaries (Ps 104:5–9); God makes the sun and the moon (Ps 104:19). Much of God's activity can be likened to the forces of nature: God transverses the sky wrapped in the light of the sun (Ps 104:1–4); God waters the ground with rain and makes springs gush forth to fill streams (Ps 104:10); God causes the grass and plants to grow (Ps 104:14). Unlike Genesis 1, however, humans play little role in this cosmology. They are not created in the image of God, nor are they blessed with specific commands from God. Rather, like other creatures, humans are fed and sustained by God (Ps 104:14–15) so that they can live out their lives doing that for which they were created—namely, to work during the day until evening (Ps 104:23). Although the particular work of humans is not specified, the content of the psalm suggests it would include tilling the ground and sowing seed, as well as planting, grafting, and pruning of grape vines and olive trees.

Nevertheless, the psalm emphasizes God's role in creation at the expense of the role of humans, as is fitting for a hymn of praise to God.

By emphasizing God's role in sustaining the creation, Psalm 104 places the burden for maintaining a stable world on God. Climate change would thus appear to be an indictment against God; contrary to what Psalm 104 claims, God has been negligent in sustaining the world from the deleterious effects of too much carbon dioxide in the atmosphere. Further evidence that Psalm 104 presents a world that is incompatible with climate change is found in the psalmist's reference to Leviathan (Ps 104:26). Elsewhere in the biblical tradition, Leviathan is a primordial sea-dragon that Yhwh must defeat to secure the stability of the created world. Leviathan may represent primordial or historical foes, but it embodies an alternative divine power structure (Ballentine 2015), which undermines God's creation and is a threat to human life. In Psalm 104, however, Leviathan is a creature, made by God, with which God plays. In this cosmology, not even Leviathan can pose a threat to the creation that God continually sustains. If Leviathan is harmless, how much less of a threat are humans? Yet, the psalm ends with the wish that "sinners be consumed from the earth" (Ps 104:35). Is this because humans when they sin against God pose a threat to creation? Probably not. The psalm presents God as too powerful and masterful to be threatened by humans; humans die and return to the dirt like all other creatures when God removes their breath (Ps 104:29). Rather, in the paean of God's wonderful creation, human sin is simply all that mars its beauty and splendor; it is analogous to human pollution that degrades the natural world. Such pollution can be stopped, and the environment can be restored; thus, the psalmist wishes for there to be no sinners. This is appropriate for the kind of damage to the environment that humans were capable of during the Holocene, but the long-lasting effects of too much carbon dioxide in the atmosphere that characterizes the Anthropocene is not so easily dismissed: the damage caused by climate change will continue long after humans cease to exist. In the end, Psalm 104, like Genesis 1, does not allow for a world with climate change because it does not envision a world beyond God's control nor a world which God does not adequately sustain. As such, Psalm 104 does not provide a cosmology that is relevant for the Anthropocene.

Yahwist Creation Myth

Whereas Psalm 104 suppresses the role of humans in the creation, the Yahwist creation myth in Genesis 2–3 focuses primarily on the role of humans. Humans are created to work the soil so that the earth will bring forth vegetation to sustain life. Moreover, humans are collaborators, or co-creators, with Yhwh in creation. The myth begins with a dry barren earth with no vegetation because it lacks humans to till the arable land and God has not yet rained upon the earth. So, Yhwh, through the birth process, first creates a human creature out of the dirt of the arable land, thus forever linking humans (*adam*) to the land (*adamah*) from which they were born (Gen 2:7). Then in an unanticipated move, Yhwh plants a garden and gives the man the task of tending it (Gen 2:8–9, 15). At this point, the reader expects God to begin raining upon the earth so that the man can till and sow it, which is why he was created. And indeed, at the end of the narrative, when the man is banned from the garden, he is sent out to work the fields (Gen 3:23). But now, the man is in Yhwh's garden, presumably because the man is not yet ready to fulfill his vocation. The garden proves to be liminal space: neither uncreated like the barren earth that surrounds it, nor a place created for humans. Instead, drawing upon the birth metaphor used in the man's own creation, it is a place where the human creature will grow up from childhood into adulthood, ready to live and create in the world on his own.

It is not long before the man is surrounded by other dirt creatures. In order to find a helper for the man—one who corresponds to him—God creates all the animals and birds out of the dirt, just has he created the man, but none of the creatures match up with the man (Gen 2:18–20). So, Yhwh tries a different approach; Yhwh takes part of the man—flesh and bone from his side—and builds another creature from it. This new creature indeed corresponds with the man, and she will be a wife (*ishah*) to him and he will be a husband (*ish*) to her (Gen 2:21–23). Together, they form the beginning of a family. Yet, the human couple are still like children: they are both naked and not ashamed (Gen 2:25). They have no awareness of their sexual differences, the sexual significance of their genitals, and thus have no reason to cover or hide them. Like Enkidu before he encounters the harlot (Epic of Gilgamesh I), the man and woman are more like animals than humans—at home with all the other creatures formed out of the arable land.

At the center of the garden is the tree of the knowledge of good and evil. Yhwh prohibits the consumption of the tree's fruit on penalty of death, yet the fruit is also what transforms the human couple from children into adults and distinguishes them from all other creatures. In a dialogue with the woman, a serpent challenges Yhwh's prohibition against eating the fruit: eating the fruit will not cause death and it will make one wise like God. For her part, the woman demonstrates intelligence in her understanding of Yhwh's prohibition, but then reasons that the fruit is worth eating: it is good for food, a delight to the eyes, and it makes one wise. So, she eats it, gives some to her husband who agrees with her reasoning, and they are transformed. They now understand the sexual significance of their bodies and seek to cover and hide their genitals (Gen 3:1–7).

What has happened to the human couple? Eating the forbidden fruit has given the human couple knowledge. The "knowledge of good and evil" is a merism, in which two contrasting parts—good and evil—represent the whole. The "knowledge of good and evil" is simply an all-inclusive expression for knowledge. With knowledge, the human couple have become like God. At the same time, they have become unlike other creatures, which do not have knowledge. The human couple are also like God in their sexual awareness; they understand the procreative potential of their bodies and will be able to create new life. Because the ancient Israelites, like all other ancient Near Eastern peoples, understood procreation in terms of agriculture, the man now also knows how to till and sow the arable land, just as he will inseminate his wife, to fulfill the vocation for which he was created.

Although the man and woman rebel against Yhwh's prohibition, eating the fruit of knowledge is also good for the human couple. Becoming adults with knowledge is necessary if humans are to be collaborators with Yhwh in creation. However, adulthood is not without its share of pain and suffering. In articulating the consequences of their newly gained knowledge, Yhwh not only affirms the benefits of knowledge but also the real-life hardships that come along with it (Gen 3:14–19). Human relations with the animals—the other creatures formed out of the soil—will not be what they once were. Human knowledge has changed the relationship and there will now be hostility between humans and animals. Humans will use animals for their own ends—for food, wool and hair, leather and parchment, and labor—but animals will also fear humans and attack them. The myth labels this transformation in their relationship as a "curse," which is not the way Yhwh had intended the creation to be. As for the woman, she will realize her knowledge by bearing many children, but this will be accompanied with much toil—life for an Israelite woman was not easy, with many tasks required for subsistence in addition to childcare. The childbirths themselves will be painful, and her need for her husband's seed will make her dependent upon him. The man will also experience much toil but in the fields that he will work all the days of his life. Surprisingly, Yhwh also decides to withhold the much-needed rain, which makes the man's work less productive and supportive of life. The rain was part of Yhwh's responsibility in collaborating with humans in creation, but now Yhwh is going to let the human couple manage on their own for a while. The myth also labels this as a "curse," but Yhwh decides against withholding the rain after a few generations (Gen 5:29; 8:21), though not without devastating consequences (the flood!). Finally, Yhwh affirms their new adult status by clothing the human couple with animal skins, and then sends them from the garden to live and work in the world for which they were created (Gen 3:21–24).

Unlike Genesis 1 and Psalm 104, the Yahwist creation myth limits Yhwh's role in the creation. Yhwh does not create alone but gives a substantial role to humans; Yhwh is not solely responsible for the state of the creation. Whereas Genesis 1 and Psalm 104 focus on God's role in creation, the Yahwist cosmology gives only brief attention to Yhwh's role: Yhwh creates the humans (and the animals and birds as a byproduct), plants a garden, and then does nothing else. The focus of the Yahwist cosmology is on humans—their status and development—and at the center of that focus is the human couple eating the fruit of knowledge, the meaning and significance of which is ambiguous. On the one hand, eating the fruit of knowledge enables the human couple to mature as adults—for the woman to bear children and for the man to work the land. This is clearly good for the humans and makes possible the development of human civilization. On the other hand, eating the fruit is a violation of Yhwh's prohibition, and the human couple's acquisition of knowledge also includes some negative consequences, such as pain and suffering. This ambiguity, which is inherent in the cosmology, enables the Yahwist cosmology to continue to be relevant in the context of climate change. The current situation that humans face with the excessive release of carbon dioxide during the production of energy is analogous to the human couple eating the fruit of knowledge in the myth. In both cases, that which is necessary for human development and success—the fruit of knowledge and energy—turns out to have *unintended consequences* that call into question the very success of the human project.

One notable dissimilarity between the human situation in relation to the production of energy and the human situation in the Yahwist myth is that the fruit of knowledge was forbidden to the human couple, whereas nothing analogous to a prohibition marks the production of energy from carbon-rich fossil fuels. But this difference between the two situations is more superficial than it initially seems. It is not the production of energy that is problematic per se, but rather its linkage with capitalist relations of production, which are inherently *exploitive* (Malm 2016). Moreover, a close reading of the Yahwist creation myth suggests that Yhwh expected the human couple to eat the fruit of knowledge despite the prohibition. Several textual clues point in this direction. First, the garden includes another notable tree, namely, the tree of life. Yhwh does not prohibit the humans from eating its fruit, but at the end of the story it is unambiguously clear that Yhwh does not want the humans to eat from the tree of life under any circumstances. It is for this reason, and this reason alone according to the text, that Yhwh expels the humans from the garden and places cherubim with a flaming sword at its entrance to prevent access to the tree of life. Yhwh accepts that the humans eat the fruit of knowledge but cannot accept and will not allow the humans to eat the fruit of life. Yet, whereas Yhwh prohibits eating the fruit of knowledge, no prohibition is stated regarding the tree of life. Second, Yhwh does not appear to be upset that the humans eat the fruit of knowledge. In what follows after their eating of the fruit, Yhwh simply explains to the human couple the natural and expected consequences of their new knowledge. There is no punishment for eating the fruit except, perhaps, Yhwh's temporary withholding of rain. But even here, the reason Yhwh withholds the rain is unclear: Is Yhwh making life more difficult for the humans because they ate the fruit and now have knowledge? Or, is Yhwh simply letting the humans experience the world on their own, without Yhwh's own contribution of rain, because they rebelled against him? If the former, then presumably Yhwh thought that it was wrong for the humans to eat the fruit; if the latter, then Yhwh is more concerned about the rebellious nature of humans and perhaps seeks to curb it—this latter theme is developed further in the Yahwist narrative that follows the garden scene. Third, the text is silent on why Yhwh prohibits the fruit of knowledge, yet the consequences of such knowledge are intrinsic goods: the creation of life through procreation and agriculture. Moreover, Yhwh's threat of death upon eating the fruit is hollow, as the serpent realizes; the humans do not die.[2] In the end, Yhwh's prohibition against eating the fruit does little more than signal the ambiguity of eating it, the consequences of which are both good and bad.

When read within the context of climate change, the ambiguity of eating the fruit of knowledge invites the reader to ponder the similar ambiguity of the production of energy. A continual abundant supply of energy has enabled human civilization to flourish in ways which were unimaginable even a century ago, but such energy has also made possible the production of weapons of mass destruction. No century has seen more human development and technological advancement than the twentieth century—and we might expect similar progress for the twenty-first century—yet no century has seen more death and destruction caused by human hands than the twentieth century. Energy can empower humans to achieve unimaginable dreams or bring about horrific terror.

Eating the fruit of knowledge produces a further ambiguity in the Yahwist cosmology regarding the status of humans. The child-like human couple are transformed from simple creatures of the soil into adult humans who are like God. They are no longer like the animals, yet they are not gods either. Being like God has its limits, and these limits are explored in the Yahwist narrative beyond the garden scene (Gen 4–11). Beginning with the expulsion of the human couple from the garden, Yhwh's purpose in the narrative at every turn is to limit humans who repeatedly seek to transgress divine boundaries—through murder, intercourse with divine beings, and making a name for a united humankind. Given the rebellious nature of humans—whose every inclination of the human heart is evil continually (Gen 6:5; 8:21)—they are not content simply to be like God but seek divine status themselves. Hence, Yhwh reminds the human couple after eating the fruit of knowledge that, despite their new status and potential, they are still dirt-creatures and will return to dirt in the end (Gen 3:19). The current challenge of climate change has similarly exposed the limits of the creation for human growth and development. A stable, inhabitable world can only tolerate so much carbon dioxide in the atmosphere, after which the flourishing and success of the human species itself can only diminish.

---

2. The assumption of the narrative is that the humans were always mortal, created from the dirt. Moreover, the presence of the tree of life in the garden and Yhwh's explicit desire that the humans not eat from it further attests to the mortality of the humans. The tree of life plays no role in the story until after the humans eat from the tree of knowledge because until their acquisition of knowledge, the human couple were perhaps unaware of their own mortality. Only with their "eyes open" does Yhwh fear that the human couple might eat of the fruit of the tree of life and live forever.

Part II: Ecology

The Conflict Myth

The single most referenced cosmology in the biblical tradition is the conflict myth. Simply put, the conflict myth is a topos that encompasses a battle between a divine warrior—most often a storm god—and his alternative—the personified sea, an aquatic monster, or even historical foes. The myth is about the divine warrior's kingship, and it is made universal through the creation of a cosmos. Several long narrative versions of the conflict myth have survived from the ancient Near East—the Enuma Elish with Marduk's battle and victory over Tiamat being the most well know today—but the Bible lacks any narrative expression of the myth. Instead, the biblical scribes utilized specific motifs of the conflict myth in many, varied contexts and genres, but largely to make the same ideological point: Yhwh is supreme over all other foes, divine and human (see Ballentine 2015).

One of the fullest expressions of the conflict myth is found in Psalm 74:12–17, the relevant portion of which reads as follows:

> God is my King from of old,
>> working salvation in the midst of the earth.
>
> You divided Sea with your might;
>> you broke the heads of the sea monsters in the waters.
>
> You crushed the heads of Leviathan;
>> you gave him as food for the desert creatures.
>
> You cut open spring and stream;
>> you dry up ever-flowing rivers.
>
> The day belongs to you, and also the night;
>> you established the luminaries and the sun.
>
> You fixed all the boundaries of the earth;
>> you made summer and winter.

According to this psalmist, God's creation entailed primarily a primordial battle against an aquatic foe, referred to here as Sea, sea monsters (*tanninim*), and Leviathan, but elsewhere also as Rahab, rivers, and waters. Based on parallels with more fully articulated Near Eastern versions of the conflict myth, we can presume that the aquatic foe in the Bible stands in opposition to God's kingship and is a threat to the stability of the world, though little attention is given to this in the biblical analogues. Instead, the focus of the biblical cosmology is on God's certain defeat of the foe and the stability of the world God creates from it.

This cosmology, which in Psalm 74 seems to be set in primordial time, gives the impression that God's aquatic foe was vanquished at the beginning of the world and so the world is created free from the threat it imposes. Indeed, this is how Genesis 1 developed out of the conflict myth, where the primordial aquatic foe is reduced simply to the inert "deep" (*tehom*, related to the Mesopotamian Tiamat) and the sea monsters are created on the fifth day with the other sea creatures. In the worldview of Genesis 1, no forces stand in opposition to God; this is not the case with the biblical use of the conflict myth. Although God's ability to defeat the aquatic foe is never in doubt, the foe is not exterminated in such a way as to purge it from the creation. Rather, God's victory more often entails the binding of the aquatic foe, restricting its effects within fixed limits. The sea and the waters are thus confined within boundaries that enable human, animal, and plant life to flourish; Leviathan remains bound by God like a fish on a hook (see Levenson 1988, 14–25). This cosmology thus imagines an inherently *unstable world* in which the aquatic foe is latent within the creation and may yet again break out in opposition against God. The *world remains stable* only because God vigilantly maintains the binding of his foe until God finally kills the beast at the end of time: "On that day, YHWH with his fierce, great, and mighty sword will punish Leviathan the fleeing serpent, Leviathan the twisting serpent, and he will kill the monster in the sea" (Isa 27:1).

Although God's aquatic foe remains bound from the creation of the world, its continual presence within the creation enables it to embody historical foes who may challenge God's sovereignty over the world. Within the biblical tradition, the conflict myth is used in association with two primary foes of Israel: Egypt, from whom God delivers the Israelites at the sea, and Babylon, who raises the question of God's supremacy by defeating Judah and destroying Jerusalem. Regarding the former, the conflict myth transforms God's historical deliverance of the Israelites from Egypt into a cosmology in which YHWH's supremacy is unrivalled. Early poetic and narrative traditions (Exod 15:1–12 and the Yahwist or pre-P portions of Exod 14) present the Exodus event as a conflict between Yahweh and the Pharaoh of Egypt, and the sea is simply the geographical location where the conflict takes place. But later mythologized traditions transformed the physical sea into YHWH's aquatic foe. Egypt is identified with the sea or simply fades into the background. Thus, for example, a psalmist (Ps 77:16–20) describes the event at the sea with the language of the conflict myth:

> When the waters saw you, O God,
>> when the waters saw you, they writhed;
>> even the depths trembled.
> Clouds poured out water;
>> the skies thundered;
>> your arrows flew about.
> The sound of your thunder was in the whirlwind;
>> your lightening lit up the world;
>> the earth trembled and shook.

> Your way was through the sea,
>> your path, through the mighty waters;
>> but your footprints were not seen.
> You led your people like a flock
>> by the hand of Moses and Aaron.

Yhwh is presented as the storm-god who defeats the aquatic foe and thereby delivers his people from Egypt. The vestiges of the conflict myth are still detectable in the later Priestly (P) portion of the narrative in Exodus 14, where God splits the sea for the Israelites to cross on dry ground (see Cross 1973, 112–44).

Later in Israel's history, in the context of Babylon's onslaught and destruction of Jerusalem, Egypt is again identified with God's aquatic foe. In two oracles, Ezekiel identifies the Pharaoh of Egypt as the sea monster (*tannin*), which God will hook in its jaws and throw onto the open field as food for the wild animals (Ezek 29:3–5; 32:2–5). Whereas the use of the conflict myth in these texts emphasizes God's supremacy over Egypt, the historical reality of Jerusalem's destruction by the Babylonians would seem to challenge God's supremacy. Does Nebuchadnezzar's victory demonstrate that Babylon's god, Marduk, is superior to Yhwh? According to the prophets and the biblical scribes, the answer is a resounding "No," but whether God would again act on behalf of his people is less certain. Thus, the author of Psalm 74 uses the conflict myth to remind God, who had defeated Leviathan and created the world, of his universal supremacy and to call upon God to remember his covenant and deliver his people from the devastation caused by the Babylonians (compare Psalm 89, which makes the same argument on behalf of Jerusalem's king). Other texts use the conflict myth to announce the inevitable and certain defeat of Babylon (see Jer 51:34–37; probably also Hab 3). With the defeat of the Babylonians by the Persians, an anonymous prophet of the Exile (Isa 51:9–11) could proclaim that Yhwh was once again defeating the aquatic foe and restoring stability to the creation:

> Awake, awake, put on strength,
>> O arm of Yhwh!
> Awake, as in days of old,
>> generations of long ago!
> Was it not you who cut Rahab in pieces
>> who pierced the sea monster?
> Was it not you who dried up the sea,
>> waters of the great deep;
> who made the depths of the sea
>> a way for the redeemed to pass over?
> So the ransomed of Yhwh will return and enter Zion with rejoicing,
>> and everlasting joy will be on their heads;

> They will obtain joy and gladness,
> > sorrow and sighing will flee.

Yhwh's deliverance of the Judean exiles from Babylon is viewed as a replication of Yhwh's previous deliverance of the Israelites from Egypt and Yhwh's primordial defeat of the aquatic foe, all of which are expressed with motifs from the conflict myth.

Because the conflict myth presupposes an inherently unstable world, it may continue to be relevant in a world that is being transformed through climate change. Although Yhwh is supreme in the conflict myth, Yhwh is not without opponents, whether they be mythical or historical. Unlike Genesis 1 and Psalm 104, which also emphasize God's supremacy, the conflict myth is able to address a world in which humans can destabilize the climate by producing too much carbon dioxide, even to the point of surpassing a planetary boundary, by recognizing that the creation itself is vulnerable to forces not in service to God's purposes. In the conflict myth, these forces are represented by the aquatic foe, which may be either primordial, suggesting that the creation is inherently unstable, or an historic foe, indicating a particular group of people, such as Babylon or Egypt, is in opposition to God. The latter understanding of the aquatic foe, however, constructs an imprecise analogy for the human situation in climate change; it would suggest that God's battle for the creation is a battle against humans—that humans have transgressed the limits that God established at creation, suggesting perhaps similarities with the Yahwist creation myth.

The historicization of the conflict myth in relation to climate change breaks down in two significant ways. First, unlike the humans in the garden, who rebel against God's prohibition, modern humans have not rebelled against God in their production of energy, which has produced greenhouse gases in dangerous amounts. Instead, the excessive emission of carbon dioxide is an unintended byproduct of energy production, and the quantities of the produced gas were initially benign, transgressing no planetary boundaries nor threatening the stability of the climate. Only with the increasing demands of the previous century for energy to power increasing production for an ever-growing and affluent population, which mark the success of the human species, have the consequences of too much carbon dioxide begun to have an effect. Second, God's role is significantly different in the conflict myth when compared to God's role in the Yahwist creation myth. In the latter, where human rebellion is ambiguous, God yields to the disrupting role that humans play in the creation, and acts to curb their rebellious behavior rather than destroy them (though God does eventually destroy them with the flood). The conflict myth, on the other hand, emphasizes God's mastery over creation: God cannot tolerate rebellion and will defeat all foes, restoring the order of creation. Thus, if the human role in climate change is likened to God's aquatic foe, then the conflict myth holds out the expectation that God will address the human threat to the creation: humans will suffer the consequences of their transgressions, and God's restoration of the creation may entail an alteration and reconfiguration of the human community. The conflict myth according to this interpretation, when read in the context of climate change, offers hope for the creation as a whole, but not for humans, whose success has become a threat to the creation itself.

If God's aquatic foe in the conflict myth is understood in terms of a primordial enemy, then reading the conflict myth in the context of climate change shifts the problem from the success of the human species to the inherent limits of the creation. Humans are not absolved of responsibility for climate change—at the very least, humans have collectively transgressed a planetary boundary with their production of energy; in mythic terms, they have unleashed the aquatic foe or sea monster from it bindings. However, the burden is placed on the inherent limits of the planet as experienced, for example, in the deficiency of the planet's natural sinks to absorb sufficient carbon dioxide for the continuing flourishing of the human community. According to this view, the stability of creation for humans cannot be taken for granted; it teeters on whether its numerous natural systems remain within the limits of the planet's ability to sustain human life. God's mastery over creation is challenged not by human flourishing per se but rather by the creation's limitation in supporting such flourishing.

BIBLICAL COSMOLOGY FOR AN UNSTABLE, LIMITED WORLD

Cosmologies are some of the myths by which we live our lives. They shape our thinking and values, they give structure and purpose to our lives, and they invite us to explore our place within the world. But a changing world requires a reassessment of whether the cosmologies continue to resonate in our new context. The biblical cosmologies were written during the stability of the Holocene era, and for over 2,500 years they have defined who Jews and Christians are in the world created by God. Lynn White argued that the biblical cosmology in Genesis 1, in particular, needed to be rejected or reformed because it was a root cause of human abuse of the natural world, but he largely misread the biblical text. Nevertheless, climate change poses a challenge for the biblical cosmologies that not even White anticipated. Climate change is the result of economic growth—the linking of capitalist social relations with the production of energy from fossil fuels—which has provided the conditions for developing and sustaining human society. It is the consequence of human success on this planet, and as such, climate change poses an unprecedented challenge for the biblical cosmologies.

Humankind's release of carbon dioxide through the burning of fossil fuels to produce energy has destabilized the climate; the flourishing of human life, that resulted from economic growth, has transgressed a planetary boundary, posing a risk for the long-term sustainability of the human community. The Yahwist creation myth and the conflict myth continue to resonate within the context of climate change. The Yahwist tradition places the burden on humans, who have a tendency to push beyond the limits of the creation. The human success story becomes the product of human arrogance or hubris, an unwillingness to live within the energy limits imposed by the creation. This is not so true in relation to our initial use of fossil fuels; unlike the fruit of knowledge, the limits of energy consumption were not so well known. For those who had been limited by energy from photosynthesis, wind, and water, the increasing amounts of energy that could be harnessed from fossil fuels perhaps seemed like a gift from God, and the adverse consequences from excessive carbon dioxide emissions were not initially understood. But the effects of burning fossil fuels have become well known, and the consequences of climate change can be recognized in the changing world around us: melting of the polar ice caps and glaciers, excessive heat and drought, polar plunges of cold air, raging fires, and unprecedented flooding. We now know that we have exceeded the planetary boundary for carbon dioxide and altered the climate. The burden is now on us to pull back from the boundary, to burn less fossil fuel and live on less energy that is mostly renewable, and so remain within creation's limits.

The use of the conflict myth in the biblical tradition, in particular, provides an appropriate cosmology for understanding the contemporary human situation facing the challenge of climate change because the conflict myth can make sense of an inherently unstable limited world. Moreover, the conflict myth can address the theodicy posed by the convergence of a flourishing human community, a limited world unable to sustain it, and God's inaction on behalf of the creation. When God's foe was historical, the conflict myth offered hope to God's people by reminding God of his past victories over his foes. They called on God to "awake, as in days of old" (Isa 51:9); they questioned how long God will hide his face (Ps 89:46); they pleaded for God to "rise up" and "remember" (Ps 74:18, 22). Such texts expressed confidence that God will eventually destroy the historic foe who is disrupting God's creation. The response to this theodicy is different when the foe is primordial, for such a foe is embedded in the very structure of creation itself. In some texts, the conflict myth offers an eschatological hope: that God will eventually kill the sea monster (Isa 27:1) so that the creation itself will be transformed anew. The conflict myth may articulate not only the creation of the world but also the consummation of the world (compare the *Urzeit-Endzeit* pattern argued by Gunkel 2006). A different response to this theodicy is offered by Yhwh's speech to Job, which employs motifs from the conflict myth to affirm that Yhwh alone remains supreme over creation even though the creation is inherently unstable. In questioning Job about the creation, Yhwh ends his speech by confronting Job with the terror of Leviathan (Job 41:18–21):

> Its sneezes flash forth light,
>   Its eyes are like the glow of dawn.
> Flaming torches go from its mouth,
>   Sparks of fire escape.
> Smoke comes out from his nostrils,
>   Sparks, blown and blazing.

> Its throat kindles coals,
>
>> Flames pour out its mouth...
>
> Gods are afraid at its terror,
>
>> They cower from its rampage.[3]

Although Yhwh makes very clear in his speech to Job that Yhwh (and Yhwh alone) can control Leviathan, the ferocious sea monster nevertheless remains within the creation. In the context of the book of Job, Leviathan's continual presence in the creation explains how innocent suffering is possible: it is neither incompatible with God's mastery over creation, nor necessarily the result of human sin. Similarly, when read in the context of climate change, the conflict myth, as utilized in the book of Job, acknowledges God's mastery over creation without putting the burden of the climate's instability exclusively on humans—it is built into the creation. Humans are not off the hook; we must transition away from a dependence on fossil fuels not simply because we have transgressed a limit but also because carbon dioxide emissions have destabilized the planet. During the Holocene Epoch, a delicate balance within the Earth systems enabled the flourishing of human life and civilization. Like Leviathan who had been bound at the beginning of time for creation to succeed, the sequestering of so much carbon within the crust of the earth brought stability to the Holocene for humans to flourish. Now, the sea monster has been unleashed; the burning of fossil fuels has released the long-stored carbon and pushed the planet into a new trajectory. The climate's inherent instability is neither a flaw in God's creation, nor an indication of God's failure to maintain the order of creation. The cosmology of the book of Job, when read in the context of climate change, enables us to hold God's mastery over creation in tension with the reality of an unstable climate.

As a response to climate change, Genesis 1 and Psalm 104 raise questions about God's creation and God's continuing role in sustaining creation. They remain compelling cosmologies regarding God's relationship to humans and the nature world, just as the covenant theology of Job's friends continues to speak about God's relationship to his people. But Genesis 1 and Psalm 104 are unable to address adequately the challenges posed by climate change just as covenant theology could not address Job's innocent suffering. Because these cosmologies place the burden of creation on God, they suggest in the face of climate change that God created an inadequate world or is unable to sustain it. The assumptions of these cosmologies are incompatible with a world experiencing climate change. Other cosmologies in the Bible either place the burden of creation on humans (the Yahwist creation myth) or assume that the world is inherently unstable (the conflict myth). These cosmologies will continue to prove relevant as we address and live with the consequences of a crisis of our own making, which is the character of the Anthropocene Epoch.

---

3. This translation is based in part on Pope 1965, 335–45.

Conclusion
This Is the Way the World Ends

This is the way the world ends
This is the way the world ends
This is the way the world ends
Not with a bang but a whimper.

—T. S. Elliot, "The Hollow Men," 1925

THE NATURE OF COLLAPSE

Ancient Israel was born out of collapse, which shaped not only the people's earliest political economy but also their identity. The kingdoms of the Late Bronze Age (1550–1200 BCE) had been integrated into a larger political economic system. The elite classes intermarried, traded luxury and prestige goods, and corresponded regularly. The small petty states of the southern Levant were specifically integrated into the Egyptian New Kingdom, but not without influence, or interference, from the Hurrians of Mitanni and the Hittites in Syria and Anatolia. Toward the end of the thirteenth century BCE, all of the kingdoms around the eastern Mediterranean and inland in Mesopotamia began collapsing. Only Egypt survived in recognizable form, though in a significantly diminished condition. The causes of the collapse are multiple and thus debated. Climatological and economic causes are at the forefront, but neither seem sufficient in themselves. The wave of destructions associated with the collapse, many of which, though not all, are attributed to the so-called Sea Peoples, may have been as much a consequence as a cause of the collapse. Whatever the specific causes, the collapse of the Late Bronze kingdoms was the end of the world of the Bronze Age (Cline 2014) but also the beginning of a new world, as cities were rebuilt and numerous small, unfortified hamlets began to emerge in the central hill country of Palestine.

Collapse can be catastrophic. It can be sudden and result in countless loss of lives—human and animal—as popular literature, television shows, and movies might depict, resulting from an asteroid impacting the planet, a thermonuclear war among nations, or an out-of-control deadly virus during a pandemic. More often than not, however, historical collapses have played out in slow motion, as if the end were inevitable but could not be rushed. The western Roman Empire and the Mayan civilization took centuries to collapse. When the end does come, it may seem unexpected to those not paying attention, but with hindsight it appears less so. Telltale signs were undoubtedly evident. Collapse should not be confused with political economic changes due to conquest or internal turmoil, or even with the gradual disintegration of society. The recent demise of the Soviet Union, for example, is better understood as a regime change and a reconfiguration of its political economy rather than as a collapse.[1] Collapse is the loss of social complexity and takes place in a power vacuum, apart from other social competitors; it is not the replacement of one form of social complexity with a different one. Collapse is usually presented as something to fear, as the end of the current order, the present way of life. And this is true, and collapse has all the connotations of death. But collapse also brings the possibility of something new, a better way of living, a chance to start over again—like new life in the spring following the death of winter. It is part of the natural cycle of life and death on this planet.

All premodern human societies eventually collapsed,[2] and we should not expect our current society to be an exception. "However much we like to think of ourselves as something special in world history, in fact industrial societies are subject to the same principles that caused earlier societies to collapse" (Tainter 1988, 216). As I have discussed, society is an extension of the natural world. It is the product of human labor, our own creation, but it remains embedded in nature. Society also has its own metabolism—like all natural systems—which is dependent on energy for its reproduction. The earliest human societies were quite simple and depended on little more than the regular flow of energy from the sun, which enabled the earth to produce and sustain an abundance of floral and faunal life. As societies became more complex, marked by inequality (differentiation, ranking, and unequal access to resources) and heterogeneity (multiple, distinctive social components), their energy requirements increased. More people became dependent on the production of others, and public projects and social goods required even more energy. Humans harnessed the labor of animals and other humans, and then eventually the energy from water and wind flows in order to meet the energy requirements of an increasingly complex society, but as long as the flow of energy was limited, a society's potential complexity was also

---

1. Although the Soviet Union did not collapse, some of its complexity was lost as many of the national republics broke away from Russia, the core of the Soviet Union.

2. This is perhaps an exaggeration. Some societies, such as the ancient Greeks, the Byzantines, and the Ottomans, were conquered or absorbed by others, none of which should be considered collapse. But no society can continue forever, and those that have not succumbed to another society have eventually collapsed.

limited. New sources of energy could be acquired through conquest and plunder, but this also required further complexity and energy costs, and the net gain in energy diminished over time. In the end, the available sources of energy could no longer support the complexity of society and it collapsed. What makes our current society different from all previous societies is that we rely on a previously little-tapped source of energy—fossil fuels—which combined with unique productive relations—capitalist relations—has fostered self-sustaining economic growth, resulting in an exponentially wealthier, more differentiated, and thus more complex society. But such an historically-extreme social complexity has come with an equally extraordinary energy cost, which not even fossil fuels can fund forever. All the while, we continue to contribute to climate change, the inescapable consequence of our social metabolism, with the potential to precipitate the collapse of our own society.

Joseph A. Tainter (1988) produced the definitive study on the collapse of complex societies. After analyzing the collapse of numerous premodern states—the western Roman Empire, the Mayan civilization, and the Chacoan society, among others—attributed to multiple causes—such as resource depletion, natural catastrophes, conflicts, and economic causes—he concluded that states collapse because they are no longer able to fulfill their purpose for being, which, in short, is to solve the perceived problems of the people. Whether to secure the well-being of the populace or to resolve conflict over differential access to resources, complexity is a sociopolitical solution to these fundamental problems of society, and such complexity comes with a cost:

> More complex societies are more costly to maintain than simpler ones, requiring greater support levels per capita. As societies increase in complexity, more networks are created among individuals, more hierarchical controls are created to regulate these networks, more information is processed, there is more centralization of information flow, there is increasing need to support specialists not directly involved in resource production, and the like. All of this complexity is dependent upon energy flow at a scale vastly greater than that characterizing small groups of self-sufficient foragers or agriculturalists. (Tainter 1988, 91–92)

Initially, the benefits of complexity far outweigh the necessary energy investments. But as complexity continues to grow, the benefits in proportion to the energy investment eventually begin to decrease. At some point, without the input of new energy sources, from the conquest of new lands or innovation, the cost of maintaining the complexity of society surpasses its benefits and the society becomes vulnerable to collapse.

Changes in the benefit/investment ratio help to explain why societies might begin to collapse: the benefits of sociopolitical complexity might simply not be worth the costs necessary to sustain it. Collapse may be an economic choice. But this explanation begs the question of why the benefits of complexity would be outpaced by the costs of complexity. Tainter tackles this question—and here is his unique contribution to understanding collapse—by recognizing that social evolution, like all natural systems, is subject to the laws of nature. In particular, Tainter argues that the law of diminishing returns, an economic form of the second law of thermodynamics (Smith and Smith 1996), impacts the benefit/investment ratio so that "investment in sociopolitical complexity as a problem-solving response often reaches a point of declining marginal returns" in additional benefits (Tainter 1988, 93).

Let me break this down a bit. The marginal return is what results from increasing the inputs in production, and specifically, it is the net gain from that increased input. The law of diminishing returns refers to the phenomenon that a constant increase in the inputs of production, such as more labor or better technology, results in a declining margin return. Although the total output will increase, the return for each additional unit of input will diminish. Agriculture is often used as an example. If you farm a field and use a modest amount of inputs—roughly $300 per acre for seeds, fertilizer, pesticide, irrigation, and fuel—you may produce 135 bushels of corn per acre. If you double your inputs to $600 per acre with better seeds, more fertilizer, better timed irrigation, and better equipment, your yield will also increase, but probably not double. You may produce a yield of 170 bushels of corn per acre. If, in the next year, you increase your inputs again, essentially tripling your inputs to $900 per acre, you may produce 190 bushels of corn per acre. Your yield has increased each year with a constant investment, but your marginal returns (35 bushels after the second year, and 20 bushels after the third year) have decreased. Tainter argues that diminishing marginal returns can be identified throughout the many, diverse components of complex societies: in resource extraction, information processing (including education and research and development), hierarchical specialization and bureaucracies, and economic activity (1988, 94–118).

The social metabolism of a complex society requires energy to sustain its complexity, and growth in complexity comes with an associated increased cost in energy. Because society is a system, its growth in complexity affects all of its component parts and all are linked in being subject to the law of diminishing returns. Thus, the energy needs of any one component of society will have reverberations throughout the rest of society. A failure in agriculture, for example, will incur energy costs in the hierarchy and bureaucracy, in other resource extraction and production, and perhaps in the military. A society becomes vulnerable to collapse when various forms of social, political, or economic stress combine with a declining marginal return from investments in complexity. Continued investment may be unable to sustain the society's complexity. Alternatively, the people, or a significant proportion of the people, may also choose not to continue investing in the society because social complexity is no longer an attractive problem-solving strategy—they may simply abandon the society, either physically through migration, or allowing it to decompose into a simpler form (Tainter 1988, 120–21). This is perhaps the best way to understand the collapse of the

CONCLUSION

Late Bronze kingdoms. An extended drought and economic failures stressed the societies beyond what could reasonably be sustained, precipitating the collapse, but many of the peoples may have hastened the collapse by abandoning their societies. Some of the Sea Peoples and the new settlements in the central hill country of Palestine may have been their descendants.

Does contemporary society face the threat of collapse? Tainter did not think so, at least not immediately. Collapse can only take place within a political vacuum, which does not exist in the contemporary world. All contemporary states are complex and linked in a global system so that no one state could collapse. It would either be absorbed by another state or, as in the recent case of Greece, propped up financially by its peers. Tainter believed that the competitive peer politics of the current world, with each state measured against its rivals, would require states to continue investing in complexity regardless of the cost or the greatly diminished marginal returns. He does acknowledge, however, that the *whole system* might collapse: "Collapse, if and when it comes again, will this time be global. No longer can any individual nation collapse. World civilization will disintegrate as a whole. Competitors who evolve as peers collapse in like manner" (1988, 214). Nevertheless, he believed that the competitive dynamics of peer politics would forestall any threat to collapse, and this reprieve should be used to develop new energy sources to maintain our economic well-being.

The complexity of contemporary society is made possible from the energy of fossil fuels. Although fossil fuels are limited and so their depletion would eventually undermine society's complexity, it is their contribution to climate change that poses the primary and more immediate threat of collapse. When Tainter did his study in the 1980s, the dangers of climate change were not widely discussed, and he makes only passing reference to them. Over thirty years later, the dangers of climate change are a present reality and what the future holds if climate change remains unchecked is better known (see Wallace-Wells 2019). There is a growing body of science-based literature both warning, and pronouncing the inevitability, of the collapse of human civilization (see, e.g., Ehrlich and Ehrlich 2013; Bendell 2018; Spratt and Dunlop 2018; Rupert and Alexander 2019). The costs associated with climate change will rapidly and progressively increase the costs of maintaining the complexity of society. Recent analysis suggests that climate change will cost hundreds of billions of current dollars per year for the United States alone by the end of the century (Martinich and Crimmins 2019). And this does not include additional societal costs to compensate for economic and other systemic losses, which will be substantial (DeFries et al. 2019), nor the loss of countless lives. Climate change has the potential to destabilize contemporary society in a way that Tainter did not foresee in the 1980s. Climate change will make the costs of maintaining the current complexity of the world's societies far beyond its benefits. And there are no alternative energy sources to fossil fuels, as Tainter had hoped. Renewable energy technologies can reduce the consumption of fossil fuels, but they cannot entirely replace them. And the net energy produced by renewable technologies (their EROI) is much less than fossil fuels, requiring more investment for the same benefit. Nuclear fission is not a favorable option. It is not renewable, would take decades to scale up, and comes with significant associated costs that make it untenable for many. Nuclear fusion, which has the potential to supply most, if not all, our energy needs, cannot be harnessed in a practical way. It is little better than the dilithium crystals that power warp drive in the world of *Star Trek*.

Climate change is a threat to world civilization, and it exacerbates the threat of other environmental concerns such as soil degradation and loss of biodiversity. Not only will climate change increase the costs of maintaining the complexity of society—all societies of the world—but curbing its impact requires that society transitions to a low energy economy, one that is sustainable without much use of fossil fuels. Such a society cannot be organized by capitalist property and social relations, which are dependent on a growing supply of energy for their social metabolism. Such a society will also need to be less complex than our current society because there will be less energy available to sustain it. Is such a transition possible? Tainter, during the years of the Cold War, was dismissive of intentional underdevelopment or degrowth, comparing any unilateral economic deceleration to unilateral disarmament (1988, 214). And he is probably correct with regard to individual nation states, especially with the close linkage of economic and military power. But climate change is a global threat and will require a global solution. No state, not even the United States, which is historically the largest producer of carbon dioxide emissions, can solve the crisis of climate change unilaterally. At the very least, all industrialized nations—those for whom fossil fuels power their economic growth—must act in concert and collaboration.

DOUGHNUT ECONOMICS

The current environmental crisis, which is marked by climate change, is a consequence of our economic system and its fixation on continual economic growth. The nearly singular goal of economics and the solution to all economic problems has been growth, especially as marked by the gross domestic product (GDP), for at least seventy years. But during those seventy years, we have degraded 75 percent of the world's soils, undermining the well-being of two fifths of the world's population (IPBES 2018); we have initiated the sixth mass extinction of species; and we have emitted so much carbon dioxide into the atmosphere from burning fossil fuels that we have altered the geological trajectory of the planet, pushing it into a new epoch. And these are just the consequences for the environment. The quest for unending growth has also produced one of the most inequitable societies in human history, where the bottom fifty percent of the world's population owns less than one percent of the wealth and the top one percent own forty-five percent of the world's wealth (Credit Suisse 2019), posing a threat to the world's democratic institutions. According to Thomas Piketty (2014, 1), increasing inequality is the inevitable consequence of capitalist relations:

> When the rate of return on capital exceeds the rate of growth of output and income, as it did in the nineteenth century and seems quite likely to do again in the twenty-first, capitalism automatically generates arbitrary and unsustainable inequalities that radically undermine the meritocratic values on which democratic societies are based.

In other words, economic growth is unequal and economic inequality belies the myth that capitalist growth is like a rising sea that raises all boats. A few benefit disproportionately, while most benefit little or not at all, so that increasing inequality results in a reduction of social mobility (see Chetty et al. 2017). Growth cannot continue to be the goal of economics.

Rather than focus on growth, Kate Raworth (2017) has recently argued that economics should focus on creating a safe and just space for humans to thrive. She takes a global approach and embeds the economy within the natural world, arguing that economics should foster human flourishing that is balanced between two boundaries, represented by the rings of a doughnut, in order to avoid human deprivation and planetary degradation. The inner ring of the doughnut forms the social foundation of economic activity that is necessary to meet the basic needs of human life. These include sufficient food, clean water and sanitation, access to energy and clean cooking facilities, access to education and healthcare, decent housing, a minimum income and decent work, and access to networks for information and social support, all of which should be achieved with gender equality, social equity, political voice, and peace and justice. Raworth has largely drawn upon the United Nation's Sustainable Development Goals, but has omitted any concern for economic growth. The outer ring of the doughnut forms the ecological ceiling, consisting of the nine planetary boundaries discussed earlier, within the limits of which economic activity must remain. An economy that remains between these two boundaries will allow all humans to thrive equitably and justly while also maintaining the Holocene-like conditions of the planet that made human civilization possible. Or so Raworth hopes.

Raworth has laid out a road map for an alternative economic goal—human prosperity within a flourishing web of life—to the "cuckoo goal" of GDP growth (2017, 51). In the process, she dispels many neoclassical and neoliberal assumptions, but she does not present an economic analysis to demonstrate that such an economy is possible. She acknowledges that four of the planetary boundaries have already been transgressed—climate change, land-system change, biosphere integrity, and biogeochemical flows—but does not explain how the economy can be pulled back within these boundaries. Instead, she highlights five factors that will determine whether such an economy is achievable: the stability of the human population, the distribution of the world's wealth, the lifestyle aspirations of the people, the technology used, and the governance structures needed to regulate the economy equitably (2017, 49–51). She does not assess what is necessary regarding each of these factors, nor does she make any specific proposals, but rather focuses on how to think economically within her framework. Raworth's roadmap is attractive, especially because of its recognition of social and environmental limits, but assessment of its feasibility has been left to others.

O'Neill et al. (2018) adopted Raworth's doughnut economics framework to analyze whether it is possible to meet the needs of the social foundation while remaining within the ecological ceiling. They analyzed over 150 nations in terms of eleven indicators of social outcomes (which largely overlapped with Raworth's social foundation) and seven biophysical boundaries[3] converted to per capita equivalents (as a way to measure the resource consumption of nations). They gave special attention to the provisioning systems, such as infrastructure, technology, manufacturing, government, communities, and markets, which mediate the relationship between resource use and the social outcome. Given that several of the planetary boundaries have already been breached, their conclusion is not surprising: "no country meets basic needs for its citizens at a globally sustainable level of resource use" (2018, 88). But their findings also attest to the severe social and economic inequalities across the global. They found that only sixteen nations remain within the biophysical boundaries, while forty-eight nations have transgressed at least six of them (the United States has transgressed all of the biophysical boundaries). Only three nations achieved all of the social outcomes, seven more nations achieved ten of them (the United States only achieved nine of the social outcomes), while thirty-five nations failed to achieve any of the social outcomes. Generally, the better a nation does in meeting the social outcomes, the worse it does in staying within the biophysical boundaries. The researchers think that the basic physical needs of the world's population, such as nutrition, sanitation, access to energy, and elimination of poverty, can be addressed within the biophysical boundaries, but qualitative needs, such as life satisfaction, healthy life expectancy, secondary education, democratic quality, social support, and equality, cannot be met without the provisioning systems becoming *two to six times* more efficient. Jason Hickel conducted a similar study and concluded: "Achieving a good life for all within planetary boundaries will require overshoot nations [such as the United States] to reduce their biophysical footprints by at least 40–50% on average from current levels (assuming poor nations can achieve social thresholds within planetary boundaries)" (2019a, 31). The doughnut may represent a "safe and just space" for humans to thrive—a better and more sustainable goal than growth—but such a goal cannot be achieved with our current economic system. Fossil capitalism cannot be contained within the doughnut's social and biophysical boundaries.

Presently, the world is on course for a global collapse of human of civilization. How soon this might occur will depend on how rapidly the effects of climate change accelerate. Earth scientists have identified numerous tipping elements in the Earth

---

3. Five of the biophysical boundaries correspond to the planetary boundaries: climate change, nitrogen and phosphorus loading, freshwater use, and land system change (measured in term of embodied human appropriation of net primary production). To these five they added two other measures of consumption that have biophysical limits: an ecological footprint (limited by the area of Earth's landmass) and a material footprint (limited by the mass of Earth's resources).

system that regulate the state of the climate, such as the massive ice sheets of the Arctic, Greenland, and Antarctica, the Atlantic thermohaline circulation (the so-called Gulf stream), the Amazon rainforest, the Indian summer monsoon, and permafrost (Lenton et al. 2008). Each of these elements has a tipping point, a threshold beyond which the element is qualitatively altered and accelerates climate change. These tipping elements are linked together like dominos, so that the tipping of one element cascades into the tipping of multiple elements. Recently, the Earth scientists recognized nine elements that are approaching their tipping points and thus signal a planetary emergency (Lenton et al. 2019). Although they acknowledge that not all scientists agree with their analysis of tipping points, they insist that the danger merits immediate action. Certainty does not seem to be possible in this case. Nevertheless, it is noteworthy that some scientists believe that the collapse of civilization may occur much sooner than many of us would imagine possible.

In order to slow climate change and stave off collapse, our economic system, which is responsible for climate change, must be radically transformed, and Raworth's doughnut economics provides an appropriate framework. It remains uncertain whether we can live fully within Raworth's "safe and just space"; it is unlikely that we will be able to pull back from the planetary boundaries that we have already transgressed, at least not for many years. Nevertheless, economic growth can no longer be the goal of economic policy, and capitalist relations can no longer be the means by which the relationship between society and nature is mediated. Rather, economics must recognize the biophysical limits of the planet and foster the well-being of all people, ensuring an adequate social foundation to meet basic human needs. As a result, we cannot expect the market to solve our problems, nor can market imperatives set the terms for social reproduction. The market is a function of the capitalist system, and can only exacerbate the problems caused by capitalism. The market cannot be the economic regulator: "wherever market imperatives regulate the economy and govern social reproduction, there will be no escape from exploitation" (Wood 2017, 195). Instead, the market *must be regulated* based on desirable social outcomes and to prevent excesses that would further encroach upon biophysical limits. Society can no longer be a market society. The economy can no longer be organized around growth for the benefit of a few, and so capitalist relations must be transformed into other productive relations.

Addressing climate change effectively will at the same time also undermine capitalist relations of production, for both are tied to the consumption of fossil fuels. Capitalist relations are dependent upon an abundance of energy, until now supplied by fossil fuels, in order to power their unquenchable appetite for growth; capitalist relations are not sustainable in a low energy society. In order to curb climate change, we need to drastically reduce the consumption of fossil fuels, transitioning to renewable sources of energy wherever possible. This cannot happen unless we also consume less goods and travel less miles so that production and the use of natural resources is also significantly reduced. Consumerism is the ideological reflex of capitalist production. It creates the need and justification for endless production, without which capitalism cannot exist. Consumerism plays on legitimate human desires such as pleasure and self-satisfaction, as well as on the baser impulses of greed and envy. It must be countered with an alternative ideology that places these desires and impulses within a context of material limits, economic sufficiency, shared responsibility, and environmental stewardship. Many religions, including Judaism and Christianity, are infused with these values and can supply the content for an alternative ideology.

A low energy society is also a less complex and locally oriented society. Ultimately, we need to live more simply. Reduced consumption is better for the natural world and for us. According to Patriarch Bartholomew (1997):

> Excessive consumption may be understood to issue from a worldview of estrangement from self, from land, from life, and from God. Consuming the fruits of the earth unrestrained, we become consumed ourselves, by avarice and greed. Excessive consumption leaves us emptied, out-of-touch with our deepest self.

Subsistence and household businesses should also be encouraged, and more people should return to the land. This has been the most successful economic strategy in human history, as well as the most exploited, and household relations that are *equitable and just* should be fostered as an alternative that is appropriate for a low-energy society (see Mies and Bennholdt-Thomsen 1999). Moreover, they also compensate for the reduced labor needed for production that will result from less consumption. Subsistence is also the best remedy to capitalist relations.

Social and economic inequality in the current world, much of it the result of the inherent exploitation of capitalist relations and their global siblings, colonialism and globalization, must be reduced. People in the industrial North need to reduce their standard of living—their ecological and material footprints (York et al. 2005; Wiedmann et al. 2015)—so that people in the global South can meet their basic needs within the biophysical boundaries of the planet. But there is also a great deal of inequality within industrial societies that must be challenged: "today's widening struggles cannot be fought simply on the boundaries of the system, that is, in the realm of *expropriation*, but require a return as well to the implicit issue of appropriation without equivalent within capitalist production itself, the realm of *exploitation*" (Foster and Clark 2020, 63). In other words, economic inequality has been built on capitalists' appropriation of labor and natural resources without any, or sufficient, exchange. Workers must be compensated adequately for their labor with a just and equitable share in the business that their labor has built. A universal basic income would also compensate all those who contribute to social reproduction. Capitalist property relations have enabled capitalists to claim natural resources, which belong to the earth for all its inhabitants to use, as their own, exclusive property. They have robbed nature, to which all people of Earth should have a share. Thus, expropriation of resources must become appropriation with equitable compensation. Similarly, much private property must give way to usufruct of the commons. Earth belongs to all its inhabitants—given to us in trust by God, its creator—so all should benefit from it and have an immediate stake in its care and preservation.

Capitalism is intrinsically linked to climate change and collapse. Not only is it the cause of climate change, but through climate change it threatens the collapse of human civilization. The connection of capitalism and collapse has been noted by Fredric Jameson, who quotes an anonymous aphorism, "Someone once said that it is easier to imagine the end of the world than to imagine the end of capitalism," but then notes, "We can now revise that and witness the attempt to imagine capitalism by way of imagining the end of the world" (2003, 76). Perhaps only with the end of the world—that is, through collapse—will capitalism come to an end, but its end will surely come because the biophysical limits of the planet are fixed. The natural world in which capitalism is embedded will have the last say. Can we curb the effects of climate change and stave off collapse? Honestly, I do not know. Capitalism's grip on the economy and the political establishment that benefits from it is firm and will fight and subvert any attempt to weaken it. I have suggested ways toward that goal, all of which require political leadership and cooperation globally, but anything that weakens the grip of capitalism is a step in the right direction.[4]

HUMAN SIN AND THE REDEMPTION OF CREATION

Collapse can be understood as a natural event, subject to natural laws. Just as natural ecosystems require a constant flow of energy, such as from the sun, so also human society, embedded in nature, requires an influx of energy to support not only human activity but also the complexity of society. Collapse will come about when society can no longer maintain the cost of its own complexity; it can be reduced to a mathematical equation, though the content of the specific variables—such as what cost/benefit ratio is society able, and willing, to tolerate—remain uncertain. Human society, as part of the natural world, is subject to the same ecological limits as other living systems. While humans may be more adaptable than many other species, aided in part by technologies, and thus can prolong society, not even humans can transcend the limits of the natural world. The potential of collapse may be measured in economic terms, but it is equally a strain on ecological systems. It is precipitated by human activity, and as such, collapse also has a moral character. Human produced climate change is undermining the stability of our society and we are culpable.

---

4. Given other concerns, I have given little attention to political theory, especially regarding sovereignty. But as the effects of climate change continue to increase, the nature and form of sovereignty becomes an especially critical issue for how we might navigate the crisis. For a description and analysis of the options, see Wainwright and Mann 2020.

One may take a laissez-faire approach to societal collapse, especially when it might not take place until the distant future, not unlike how one might approach natural catastrophes—it is out of our control. Indeed, this seems to be the dominant political attitude towards climate change, despite party affiliation and lip-service to the contrary. No significant policies have been enacted to reverse climate change, and few have been considered. The so-called Green New Deal would be a step in the right direction, but not even it can disavow economic growth and so it undermines its own merits. The politicians seem content to let nature take its course and adapt accordingly. But unlike a hurricane or an earthquake, climate change is not the result of natural systems; it is *not* nature taking its course. It is rather the reverberation in nature from human activity in society. Our construction of society through capitalist relations, powered by fossil fuels, has disrupted the Earth systems, and climate change, among other environmental degradations, is the result. Through our actions that cause climate change, we have overridden the natural course of the planet, pushed it into a new geological epoch, and hastened the collapse of society. A laissez-faire attitude is a form of denial that climate change is transforming the planet, posing a threat to the stability of society, and that humans are to blame.

Some humans are innocent. They have not contributed to climate change, nor participated in nor benefitted from the structures that caused climate change. Generally, those who have contributed the least to climate change because of their modest, underdeveloped economies will be most harmed by it because of their location in the most vulnerable areas of the planet and their inability to compensate for its effects. Like Job, they do not deserve the suffering that has and will fall upon them. They are largely the poor of the world, predominantly in the global South but also found in the industrial nations of the North. Their encounter with capitalism is primarily as victims of its exploitation. Although primary blame for climate change can be attributed to the class of capitalists, who have organized society for their production and benefit, blame must also be shared by all those who have benefitted from capitalism and its fossil economy, even while perhaps also being exploited. These are the majority of U.S. Americans and those in the industrialized nations that make up the middle class, who have benefitted from a growing economy and who consume a disproportionately large share of the earth's resources, including fossil fuels. There is plenty of fault to go around; climate change is the product of systemic abuse of the natural world and does not require intention. We—those reading this book are undoubtedly also in this group—share in a collective guilt by participating in and benefitting from the capitalist system, even though individually we might work to reverse climate change. In the biblical tradition, collective as well as individual wrong is called sin, and this applies equally to crimes against nature.

> For humans to cause species to become extinct and to destroy the biological diversity of God's creation, for humans to degrade the integrity of Earth by causing changes in its climate, by stripping the Earth of its natural forests, or

destroying its wetlands, for humans to injure other humans with disease, for humans to contaminate the Earth's waters, its land, its air, and its life, with poisonous substances, these are sins. (Bartholomew 1997)

Sin represents a violation, a wrongdoing against God, others, or the moral order that God created in the universe. Climate change is the result of such sin. For the capitalists, it is the sin of idolatry, serving the accumulation of money instead of God. The maximization of profit is their ultimate concern (Tillich 1957). For the majority of us who participate in the structures of capitalism, it is our collective failure in preventing the exploitation of others, both locally and globally, while also benefitting from it that marks our sin. The laptop I write this on, for example, is built with exploitative wages (in China) and from mineral extraction using child labor and violence (in the Democratic Republic of Congo), in order to keep the laptop cheap enough so that I can afford to replace it every few years. Closer to home, the inexpensive food I purchase at the grocery store is made possible by the agribusinesses that maximize their profits in part by depriving farmers of a just price for their products—justifying their price by recourse to the market, which measures only exchange value rather than the use value of the product. Finally, all who participate in the capitalists system share in the collective, systemic sin that has altered the natural geological course of the planet. The Anthropocene is not an indication of humankind coming of age, but an indictment of our inability to live within the natural, created boundaries of the earth, and our responsibility for all the harm, including the sixth mass extinction of species, that will result from it.

In the covenant tradition of the Bible, human sin is often linked with environmental consequences. Failure to follow God's laws, for example, may result in drought and pestilence, whereas fertility and abundance may follow from keeping the laws. This same linkage is also found in the prophetic tradition, but here the prophets use the condition of the natural world as evidence of the people's sins against God. Thus, Hosea (4:1–3) could declare:

> Hear the word of YHWH, O Israelites;
> > for YHWH has an indictment against the inhabitants of the land:
>
> There is no faithfulness or loyalty,
> > and no knowledge of God in the land.
>
> Swearing, deceiving, and murder,
> > stealing and committing adultery break out;
> > bloodshed follows bloodshed.
>
> Therefore the land dries up,
> > and all who live in it languish;
> > the animals of the field,
> > and the birds of the air,

> even the fish of the sea are perishing.

Hosea interpreted a drought as a sign that the people of Israel had sinned against God. Even more so, the reference to the animals, birds, and fish is a stock phrase used to refer to the creation (see Zeph 1:2–3). The drought, for Hosea, not only indicts the Israelites, but also heralds the collapse of creation (DeRoche 1981). This connection between human behavior and the state of creation is even more apparent in the prophecies of Jeremiah. Like Hosea, Jeremiah claims that a drought that is scorching Judah is the result of the sins of the people and as such is testifying against them (14:1–9). In fact, the sins of the people against God are so great that Jeremiah, in language reminiscent of the Priestly creation story, envisions the collapse of the creation (4:23–26):

> I looked on the earth, and lo, it was formless and empty;
> and to the heavens, and they had no light.
> I looked on the mountains, and lo, they were quaking,
> and all the hills shook back and forth.
> I looked, and lo, there was no one at all,
> and all the birds of the air had fled.
> I looked, and lo, the fruitful land was a desert,
> and all its cities were laid in ruins
> before Yhwh, before his fierce anger.

Linking human sin with natural catastrophes is problematic for the modern mind. Tornadoes, earthquakes, and floods, for example, can be explained by natural causes. When Pat Robertson, in 2005, suggested that hurricane Katrina was the result of God's anger over abortion, he was widely ridiculed, and certainly his facile theological judgment on this issue had no merit. The biblical prophet's mindset cannot easily be reconciled with what we know about the natural world (Kay 1988, 327). But in some ways, the biblical prophets had an advantage that we, who share the modern scientific mind, have lost, for the prophets understood no dichotomy between humans and nature. Although the prophets' moral understanding was rooted in an ancient covenant tradition and worldview that is not directly relevant to the current context, they nevertheless recognized that humans were fully part of the natural world—God's creation—and thus human actions will have reverberations throughout the natural world. Many in the modern world have been denying this at least since Descartes. Climate change is the material corrective to the dichotomy between humans and nature. It is a natural event with human causes. Because society is embedded in nature, what happens in society has reverberations into nature (and vice-versa). Climate change is the natural effect of human actions that can be called "sin," and unlike Robertson's simplistic assessment of a destructive hurricane, with climate change we can detail the causal links: the burning of fossil fuels to power a continually growing economy propelled by exploitive capitalist relations.

Conclusion

The story of humans in the Bible, from Adam and Eve, through Abraham, Moses, and David, to the prophets used to be called, and often still is, "salvation history." It was viewed as the history of God's relationship with humans, and especially Israel, and the prophets proclaimed God's coming salvation, which was understood primarily in historical, human terms. The problem with this understanding is that it is incomplete. First, God's relationship is with more than just humans, for humans are simply part of the creation. God's prophesied redemption includes the whole creation. Humans are in need of redemption because of their evil inclination and rebellion against God, but the rest of creation also needs to be redeemed. Not because it is evil or contrary to the purposes of God, but because it has been corrupted by human sin (see Rolston 1994). Second, the "salvation history" approach tends to gloss over the consequences of the people's sin, which can accumulate and cascade into the collapse of creation before the world is redeemed in a new creation. Human sin has real consequences, and the prophets did not neglect this, often detailing their wrongdoing, but human sin is also an assault on God and the order of creation—it is an attack on Yhwh's sovereignty over creation. And so, some of the prophets draw upon Yhwh's battle in the conflict myth to portray Yhwh's punishment and redemption of his people. As Yhwh goes out to battle those who challenge his kingship, the creation writhes and eventually collapses, but after his victory over opposing forces—human sinners or nations in the prophets' context—the world flourishes anew as Yhwh creates again (see Cross 1973, 162–63; Simkins 1994, 147–50). Creation followed by collapse and new creation was a common mythic pattern by which the prophets interpreted the effects of human sin and offered up the hope of God's redemption of creation. Few prophetic texts incorporate the whole mythic pattern, emphasizing instead either the collapse or the redemption of creation. The prophecy in Isaiah 34–35, in contrast, includes the whole pattern: Yhwh's battle is against the nations whose blood will be shed and whose land will become a waste, overrun by wild animals—a sign of the collapse of creation (Tucker 1997, 9–12)—then through a new creation, Yhwh will redeem his people from exile. Hosea 1–2 also uses the full mythic pattern, but rather than drawing upon Yhwh's cosmogonic battle like most other prophets, Hosea employs a household metaphor that resonates with the Yahwist creation myth.

It is uncertain whether Hosea knew the Yahwist creation myth. He does not cite it nor employ similar phraseology. He does seem to share with the myth, however, a similar understanding of the relationship between Yhwh, the land, and humans. Just as the Yahwist presents Yhwh and the land giving birth to the first human (*adam*), Hosea addresses Yhwh's relationship to the land (*erets* rather than *adamah*), who has given birth to more children—the people of Israel. And just as the first human and his wife rebel against Yhwh, with repercussions for the humans and the land, their mother, Hosea describes how Yhwh's wife, the land, pursued other lovers, with consequences for her and her children. In both cases, humans are linked to the land in their relationship to Yhwh, and agriculture requires the collaboration of humans (who work the land) and Yhwh (who sends rain).

Hosea's prophecy begins with Yhwh instructing Hosea to marry a promiscuous woman and have children of promiscuity "because the land is exceedingly promiscuous in turning away from Yhwh" (1:2). Like many other prophets, Hosea employs a sign-action to communicate his message; in this case, he uses his own household (whether real or fictive): "The prophet is to represent by his marriage and family life Yhwh's relationship to Israel as a relationship subverted by Israel's promiscuous behavior" (Bird 1997, 225). Hosea's initial statement is problematic; it is not clear how the land (*erets*) can be promiscuous, nor the way in which the children are promiscuous. If pushed too far, Hosea's metaphor might seem to break down. The land, which is the wife of Yhwh through most of the prophecy (Braaten 2001), would appear to be a metonym for the people of the land—namely, Israel. This is made explicit in Hosea 3, and the wife emerges as the Israelite people in a few passages in Hosea 2. It is Israel who has been promiscuous in its relationship with Yhwh. Identifying the land with the people of Israel as Yhwh's wife enables the prophet to emphasize the consequences of the people's sins on creation. The children are also the people of Israel, born from the land, their mother, and for this reason, they are also described as promiscuous—not born from promiscuity, as we might expect from the root metaphor, though the promiscuity of their mother makes their legitimacy questionable. The children's names are also signs of Yhwh's judgment on his people: Jezreel, for Yhwh will judge Israel for the bloodshed that brought the current dynasty to power; Lo-ruhamah, for Yhwh will no longer have pity on his people; and Lo-ammi, for Yhwh will no longer claim Israel as his people. In other words, the land and the children are treated together as the *household* of Yhwh, which has been promiscuous (Bird 1997, 226; Keefe 1995, 96–97).[5]

Hosea's metaphor of promiscuity in the household is powerful and shocking. In a society in which male honor was linked to the sexual control of women, Yhwh's marriage to a promiscuous woman exploits Israelite men's own anxieties over female sexuality and its control. "Sexual humiliation is symbolic of the most severe loss of honor: in fact, it is the means by which both women and the men of their families are shamed" (Streete 1997, 84). Promiscuity is also socially disruptive. The adultery that

---

5. Marvin Chaney differentiates the land from the children by introducing a class distinction. The land represents the male urban warrior elite of Israel, whereas the children are the Israelite lower classes, who suffer the guilt of their mother (the elite) as illegitimate bastards while being innocent of her crimes (2017, 175–204). This distinction, however, does not resolve all the problems with the metaphor. On the one hand, the children seem to be implicated in the mother's crime in Hos 2:8, where "they" use her silver and gold for Baal. On the other hand, the wife in Hos 2:14–20 cannot be restricted to just the elite but refers to all Israel. While many of Hosea's accusations undoubtedly focus on the crimes of the elite—elsewhere in the book he singles out king, priest, prophet, and princes—the land and children, as different representations of Israel, are best viewed as different aspects of Yhwh's household.

results from promiscuity is the "great sin" in the ancient Near East;[6] it disrupts the most fundamental bonds of society: the bond between a husband and his wife, and by metaphorical extension, the bond between a patron and his client, the king and his subjects, and in this case, God and his people. No Israelite could hear it and not understand Yhwh's right to exact judgment. So Yhwh threatens his wife with divorce proceedings, initially enlisting his children as allies, but then abruptly including them in her judgment (Hos 2:2–5):

> Plead with your mother, plead—
>> for she is not my wife,
>> and I am not her husband—
> that she removes her promiscuity from her face,
>> and her adultery from between her breasts,
> lest I strip her naked
>> and expose her as on the day she was born,
> and make her like a desert,
>> and turn her into a dry land,
>> and kill her with thirst.
> Upon her children also I will have no pity,
>> because they are children of promiscuity.
> For their mother has committed fornication;
>> she who conceived them has acted shamefully.
> For she said, "I will go after my lovers,
>> who give me my bread and my water,
>> my wool and my flax, my oil and my drink."

Because of her promiscuity, Yhwh will treat his wife like any other Israelite husband would: by violently reasserting his control over her sexuality. The marital relationship between Yhwh and Israel is bound by the social dynamics of patriarchal marriage in ancient Israel. The prophet uses violent sexual language to both shock his male elite audience on whom the blame falls and to vindicate Yhwh's role in the relationship (see Weems 1995). Yhwh had previously tried to prevent the land's promiscuity by hedging up her way with thorns and building a wall around her, but to no avail.[7] So Yhwh will strip her naked, exposing her before her lovers; Yhwh will

---

6. Chaney (2017, 185), following Bird (1997) and others, notes that Hosea emphasizes promiscuity (*zanah*) over adultery (*na'ap*). While in some contexts, this distinction is critical—promiscuity generally occurs outside of marriage contexts—in the marriage context of Hosea, it is a distinction without a difference: a wife's promiscuity *is* adulterous. Chaney's point that a wife's promiscuity calls into question a husband's paternity is well taken, but adultery does the same.

7. Reading the verbs in Hos 2:6–7 as past tense rather than as future with the NRSV and other versions (see Braaten 2001, 191).

deprive her of fertility by withholding his rain from her. She had assumed it was her lovers who endowed her with fertility, but she was mistaken.

> She did not know
> > that it was I who gave her
> > the grain, the wine, and the oil,
> and lavished upon her silver
> > and gold that they used for Baal. (Hos 2:8)

Thus, Yhwh will take back all his produce, bring an end to all her ritual celebrations, and lay waste the land, which will be overrun by wild animals (Hos 2:9–13). Yhwh will end his creative activity and allow the land to return to its dry, barren state as it was in the beginning (see Gen 2:5–6). Israel's sins, its promiscuity for lovers other than Yhwh, will result in the collapse of creation.

Hosea gives little indication in this prophecy regarding the specific sins of the people that constituted their promiscuity. There is a brief reference to Baal (Hos 2:8) or "the days of the Baals" (Hos 2:13), and a few more references to Baal or the Baals are scattered throughout the book, but evidence of extensive Baal worship in eighth-century Israel is lacking. Baal worship plays no role in other eighth-century prophets (Keefe 1995, 78), and Baal is not widely attested in personal names, which we might expect if Baal was worshipped during this period (Tigay 1986).[8] Baal is a rain-god to whom the people may have devoted themselves, but there is also no evidence of a fertility cult, belonging to Baal or any other god, that rivaled Yhwh at this time. Indeed, Hosea declares that Yhwh will bring an end to his own ritual celebrations: the land's exultations, festivals, new moon celebrations, sabbath, and assemblies (Hos 2:11). Traditional Yahwistic religious rituals, when mixed with promiscuity, are as problematic for Hosea as any so-called fertility rituals to Baal (against a fertility cult, see Keefe 1995, 76–89). Elsewhere in Hosea, the rituals are likened to idolatry (see Hos 4:12–19; 8:4–5; 10:5; 11:1–2; 13:2), which is perhaps a charge leveled against Yhwh's children in Hos 2:8, who take the silver and gold from Yhwh and use it for Baal. At the very least, it seems, Hosea is advocating for a narrower conception of Yhwh worship, stripped of its traditional and popular practices that Hosea deemed foreign (Yee 2003, 92–97).

Yet, the sins of Israel should not be understood as exclusively religious. Religion in the ancient world was embedded in the political and social structures of the society and reinforced those structures. The religious body was an expression of the social body, and both could be expressed by the sexual body. In other words, Israel's

---

8. In the biblical tradition, Baal is attested primarily in relation to the House of Omri or Ahab in ninth-century Israel, but that Baal is an import along with Jezebel, the Tyrian princess who marries Ahab. The stories of Elijah and Elisha (1 Kgs 17–2 Kgs 10) present a battle between Yhwh and Baal for the allegiance of the people of Israel, but that battle seems to come to an end with the extermination of the House of Ahab in Jehu's coup.

promiscuity may entail sociopolitical sins as well as religious sins. Indeed, "in a society that defines itself through 'proper' (here specifically a patriarchal) order of sexual relations, textual images of the sexual transgression of women ... figure the disintegration of societal bonds" (Keefe 1995, 89). What these sociopolitical sins might be is somewhat a matter of speculation. Hosea suggests that foreign alliances—with Assyria and Egypt in particular—along with the trade relations made possible through them, were involved (see Hos 8:9–10; 12:1). The many references in which Hosea singles out Israel's leaders, such as the king, priest, prophet, and princes, suggest that the elite and royal establishment had been oppressing the lower classes—accusations also made by other eighth-century prophets (i.e., Amos, Micah, and Isaiah; see Chaney 2017, 121–46; Premnath 2003; cf. Houston 2008)—but Hosea does not define the specific sins further. Regardless of the specific sins of the people, Hosea uses the image of Yhwh's promiscuous household to condemn Israelite society and to herald the inevitable collapse of creation.

Collapse, for Hosea, would be the end of the current sociopolitical kingdom of Israel, but not the end of Yhwh's relationship with his people. The collapse will initiate unexpectedly a new beginning. Although Yhwh, the wronged husband, had abused his adulterous wife, he now turns once again to woo her, bringing her into the desert and speaking "on her heart" (Hos 2:14). In Hosea's prophesy of redemption, the referent for the metaphorical wife of Yhwh vacillates between the land and the people. To the land, Yhwh will give "her vineyards, and make the Valley of Achor a door of hope," but Israel will respond as in her youth "when she came out of the land of Egypt" (Hos 2:15). The vacillation between land and people reinforces the idea that Yhwh's redemption of creation will encompass both the people and the land:

> I will make for you a covenant on that day with the wild animals, the birds of the air, and the creeping things of the ground; and I will abolish the bow, the sword, and war from the land; and I will make you lie down in safety. And I will take you for my wife forever ...
>
> On that day I will answer, says Yhwh,
> I will answer the heavens
> and they shall answer the land;
> and the land shall answer the grain, the wine, and the oil,
> and they shall answer Jezreel;
> and I will sow him for myself in the land. (Hos 2:18–23)

Yhwh's redemption of creation involves two reconciliations. First, Yhwh will establish a covenant to reconcile humans with the animal kingdom. Many commentators have interpreted the covenant with the animals to refer to the reversal of Yhwh's curse on the animals in Genesis 3: the enmity between humans and animals is reconciled; the creation becomes what it should have been. Although such an interpretation is possible and attractive in light of other similarities with the Yahwist creation myth, it is not persuasive in Hosea's context. Hosea's vision of collapse and new creation is not eschatological—that is, Hosea does not envision a transformation of time and space, a final end. The collapse and new creation take place in history, even though it is presented through myth. An apt parallel to Hosea's covenant with the wild animals from the prophecy of Ezekiel may be instructive. In that context, the prophet also envisions the redemption of creation, but for him redemption includes the removal of wild animals:

> I will make with them [the people] a covenant of peace and remove the wild animals from the land, so that they may live in the desert and sleep in the woods securely. (Ezek 34:25)

In the formulation of the covenant, wild animals are often included in God's judgments, if the people fail to keep the laws. Wild animals may be part of God's creation, but they are also a threat to human creation and are thus used to signal the collapse of creation. Just as the wild animals suffer the environmental consequences caused by Israel's sins (Hos 4:3), they devour the land's vines and fig trees as YHWH lays waste to the land in response to her promiscuity (Hos 2:12). The covenant with the animal kingdom in Hosea is simply the reconciliation of the hostilities that were provoked by Israel's sins. The relationship between the human and animal worlds is not otherwise transformed (see Tucker 2000; compare the eschatological vision in Isa 11:6–9).

Second, YHWH's redemption of creation will reconcile the fractured relationship between himself and his wife—the land and the people of Israel. Although redemption follows collapse, it is not inevitable or automatic. YHWH must initiate the new creation, and so YHWH rejuvenates the ecological web that unites the land and its people. With images reflective of the Yahwist creation myth, YHWH will cause rain to once again fall on the land, which will produce its crops to sustain the human community. Jezreel, YHWH's firstborn son, whose name resembles "Israel" and who represents the violent beginning of the House of Jehu, had been a sign of YHWH's judgment on Israel. In the new creation, YHWH will restore Jezreel to his household as the land will again flourish with agricultural bounty from YHWH's fertilizing rain; the human community will sprout up from the land in which YHWH has sown it—the name Jezreel means "God sows." But unlike in the Yahwist myth, no role for humans is mentioned in the new creation; the redemption of creation is YHWH's work alone.

LAMENTATION AND REPENTANCE

Climate change is the result of human sin. Just as Hosea proclaimed that Israel's promiscuity had disrupted the household of YHWH—the relationship between YHWH, the land, and the people—so also our sin has disrupted our relationship with the natural world and its creator. Although promiscuity is perhaps not the most appropriate metaphor for our context, the image of a household remains relevant. Both "ecology" and "economics" are based on the Greek *oikos*, "household." Both disciplines seek, from different perspectives, to understand the household in which we live, and each emphasizes a different facet of our sin. Ecology underscores pollution: we have polluted our household from the excessive burning of fossil fuels. Economics points out exploitation: capitalist property and social relations have exploited natural resources and human labor for the benefit of a few. In Hosea's prophecy, Yhwh's wife delighted and longed for the gifts she thought her lovers provided, not realizing that it was her husband, Yhwh, who had provided them for her all along (Hos 2:6, 8). Similarly, in our own household, we have delighted in all the benefits that economic growth—made possible by capitalist relations and fossil fuels—has provided, without realizing the environmental harm it has produced or for whom it has offered little benefit. Moreover, we have become addicted to economic growth, a dependency rooted in our capitalist relations and the social complexity they have produced, so that it is difficult to imagine living without it. We are like the heroin addict who will alienate his friends and destroy his family relations in order to maintain his habit, only to eventually overdose and die, if not treated. Our household is sick because of our sins, and we must change our ways in order to preserve it.

Hosea's prophecy aides us in diagnosing our sin, but is not so helpful in suggesting a treatment. For Hosea, the collapse of creation was inevitable, and thus he placed hope in the redemption of creation. But whether his prophecy is eschatological or not, such future-oriented prophecies of redemption are problematic in environmental contexts. They might lead some to minimize or even reject present concerns, for they seem to suggest that God will simply solve our environmental problems (see Horrell 2010, 88–114). This is particularly true in some forms of Christian fundamentalism where living in the "end-times" is embraced as a present reality. For these Christians, the destruction of the environment has no future significance other than perhaps signaling the coming of Jesus and the great apocalypse (see Scherer 2004). Influenced by dispensationalism and a literalist reading of the Bible, these Christians believe that they will be raptured into heaven while those left behind suffer in the wars and natural catastrophes of the tribulation. At the end of the tribulation, Jesus will return to destroy the kingdom of the anti-Christ and establish his reign in a millennial kingdom on a transformed earth. In this scenario, the environment is but a stage for the heavenly drama, with no intrinsic relationship to the human beings who live within it. Such thinking is detrimental to action on behalf of the environment and climate change here and now. However, I suspect that fewer Christians would have such an "eschatological" motive for their climate denial or inaction than environmental advocates such as Scherer would have us believe.

James Watt, the much-maligned Secretary of the Interior during the Reagan administration, is often put forward as a champion of this view of Christian eschatology.

He is reputed to have written in *The Saturday Evening Post* that the earth is "merely a temporary way station on the road to eternal life . . . The earth was put here by the Lord for His people to subdue and use for profitable purposes on their way to the hereafter."[9] Similarly, at a congressional hearing, he is regularly quoted as saying: "God has given us [natural resources] to use. After the last tree is felled, Christ will come back."[10] The problem is that Watt neither wrote nor said these statements. In fact, what he did write and say in these contexts is the direct opposite of what is attributed to him; he emphasized stewardship of the environment, which is a dominant biblical theme (see Bratton 1983). I suspect that most Christians, like Watt, would also temper the implication of their eschatological beliefs with environmental stewardship. Nevertheless, a future-oriented, otherworldly eschatology in which God saves us *from this world* may deter concern or care for the environment, especially when it requires substantial economic costs in order to curb climate change.

This Christian eschatology is also a distortion of the biblical tradition. Putting aside the dispensationalist framework, which has little credibility, human salvation in the biblical tradition is never separate from God's redemption of creation, nor is the material world somehow irrelevant to God's plan of salvation. The incarnation, in which God takes on material existence, should dispel this error. Even so, biblical prophecies of the redemption of creation in response to creation's collapse assign no role for humans. Unlike in the Yahwist creation myth where humans collaborate with Yhwh in creation, Yhwh redeems creation alone. But it would be a mistake to assume that the prophets expected nothing from their human audience. First, it is important to note that God's role in recreation follows the failure of humans to prevent the collapse of creation—whether from their sins or other causes. In other words, unlike the first creation in which humans *can* create, God's redemption of creation takes place when humans are *unable* to create further. Second, the vision of God's recreation is not historically specific—that is, it is not laying out a plan according to which God will act. It is not telling us when and how God will restore the earth from the abuse caused by human sin. Rather, the prophets present a moral vision about God, God's character, and God's intention for creation:

> The value of these texts lies not in their capacity to predict cosmic or human history in advance—that they cannot do—but in their capacity to *shape* our behavior now toward each other and the other denizens of the earthly ecosystem. (Towner 1996, 31)

---

9. A Google search found over forty citations attributable to Watt; numerous other citations are undoubtedly found in traditional print sources. No statement like this was ever written by Watt; compare what he actually wrote in Watt 1982.

10. Watt (2005) actually stated: "I do not know how many future generations we can count on before the Lord returns, whatever it is we have to manage with a skill to leave the resources needed for future generations." Unfortunately, when Watt is quoted correctly, usually only the first clause is cited, leaving an incorrect impression of his thought.

The prophetic vision can also inform us that our own redemption is integrally linked to the redemption of creation, providing *motivation* to work for the preservation of creation and *hope* for when the task is beyond our capabilities.

The threat of climate change to bring about the collapse of human civilization demands that we begin to act now on behalf of creation before the damage is irreparable and the collapse is close to being realized. We must stop burning fossil fuels, as much as possible, and reorganize our economy along lines other than capitalist relations. In the process, we need to reconcile the inequalities created from capitalism, both locally and globally, to ensure a just and equitable transition to a sustainable political economy. These are big tasks that can easily overwhelm individuals. They require the action of the political body to effect the necessary change in society, and so individuals need to contribute to the political processes. Much of the work that needs to be done will involve material changes—changes in how we live and work, changes in what we produce and consume, changes in how we use the land, water, and other natural resources—but we also need to respond theologically. And here, individuals can also make a significant contribution. We can reshape the ideology that governs our political economy. We can *take responsibility* for climate change: embrace our role in it, recognize it as the result of sin in which we participate, and then take responsibility for our behavior and values, both individually and collectively. This is the work of lamentation and repentance.

Although lamentation and repentance do not always belong together—one may mourn a loss for which one shares no responsibility, such as the death of a close friend or relative—in the case of climate change, which is anthropogenic, lamentation and repentance are needed in concert. The former mourns what has been lost, while the latter recognizes one's contribution to the loss, makes reparations, and alters one's behavior. Repentance is what effects a transformational change in a person—repentance demands the change that is necessary to curb climate change—but lamentation lays the groundwork for it. Lamentation provides time and space to acknowledge what has been lost with climate change and to grieve its disastrous effects, as well as to discern how we are complicit in climate change. Without lamentation, repentance may be hollow or performative, or it can be put off for another day. Without lamentation, repentance enables us to accept responsibility for climate change without adequately confronting the repercussions of our wrongdoing or recognizing the severity of the threat. This is a form of denial—we protect ourselves by claiming that climate change is *not that bad*—and it will impede how we can respond to climate change in the future. With lamentation, however, we recognize the full ramifications of our behavior, our complicity and our sin, and the existential threat it poses. When followed by repentance, lamentation prepares us to better navigate an uncertain future because it enables us to fully accept our participation in the sins that have produced climate change.

Hosea called Israel to lament and repent, even as the collapse of creation due to the people's sins was inevitable. The prophet Joel calls for the people to lament and repent in the *midst* of collapse. Little is known about the prophet Joel, who seems to have prophesied during the Persian period, and he may have also served as a priest or as a scribe associated with the temple in Jerusalem. In any case, the historical situation that seems to have inspired his prophecy was an unprecedented locust plague and the damage it inflicted on the environs of Jerusalem over multiple years (see Simkins 1991). The people's initial encounter with the plague consisted of a flying swarm of adult locusts, passing through the region during the spring around harvest time. The destruction of locusts seems unimaginable to those have not experienced it, but a flying swarm of perhaps a trillion locusts can consume all the vegetation in its path, and only after all edible food is consumed will they move onto the next region. In response to the utter devastation of the plague, Joel calls on the people to lament. Joel 1:5–14 consists of four calls to lamentation, each addressed to a different group of people who suffered from the plague. Then in Joel 1:15–20, the prophet issues his own lament:

> Alas for the day!
> > The day of Yhwh is near,
> > and like destruction from Shaddai it comes.
> Is not the food cut off before our eyes,
> > joy and gladness from the temple of our God?
> The seed shrivels under the clods.[11]
> Desolate are the storehouses,
> > ruined are the granaries,
> > for the grain is withered.
> How the animals groan!
> > the herds of cattle wander in confusion
> For they have no pasture,
> > even the flocks of sheep are appalled.
> To you, O Yhwh, I will cry,
> > for fire devoured the pastures of the steppe,
> > and flame scorched all the trees of the field.
> Even the wild animals long for you,
> > for the fountains of water are dried up,
> > and fire devoured the pastures of the steppe.

---

11. The preserved Hebrew text of verse 17a is corrupt and unintelligible. Each of the ancient versions offers a different translation. Scholars have suggested different emendations, mostly speculative, and none have been convincing. I have cited the text from the New Revised Standard Version, which is based on Rabbinic exegesis, but has little evidence to commend it (see further, Simkins 1991, 146–47).

Joel's lament is interesting for two reasons. First, Joel laments with the animals—wild and domestic—who have also suffered from the locust plague. It seems that Joel must convince the people to lament, while the animals instinctively know to lament. Both Joel and the animals grieve how all the vegetation has been consumed by the locusts. He compares the effects of the plague to the damage caused by fire and drought. Second, Joel associates the locust plague with the day of Yhwh. In the prophetic tradition, the day of Yhwh refers to Yhwh's war or judgment on his enemies, often with tropes from the conflict myth. Amos first used the expression in reference to Yhwh's judgment on his own people, Israel (5:18), but it is also used for Yhwh's judgment on the nations (Isa 34:8; Zech 14:1). Joel uses the expression five times in the book, interpreting the unprecedented locust plague as Yhwh's judgment and heralding a final, eschatological day of Yhwh in which the nations will be judged and Israel and the creation restored. In other words, Joel recognized in the locust plague the beginnings of the collapse of creation, and thus called the people to lament the devastation.

In Joel 2, the prophet again announces that the day of Yhwh is near, as a second wave of the locust plague, now in the form of immature hopper bands, assaults Jerusalem and its environs like an army (Joel 2:1–11). Their devastation is no less than the previous flying swarm, but now their assault is tied directly to the collapse of creation (2:10):

> The earth quakes before them,
>> The heavens shake;
> the sun and moon grow dark,
>> and the stars gather their light.

Then Joel issues his call to repentance (2:12–14):

> Yet even now, says Yhwh,
>> return to me will all your heart,
> with fasting, weeping, and lamentation.
>> Rend your hearts, not your garments.
> Return to Yhwh your God,
>> for he is gracious and compassionate,
> slow to anger, and abounding in kindness,
>> and relents from evil.
> Who knows whether he will turn and relent,
>> and leave behind him a blessing,
> a grain offering and a drink offering
>> for Yhwh your God.

Repentance is no guarantee of deliverance. Joel puts forward Yhwh's character as the basis for hope, but redemption remains uncertain—"who knows." Although Joel never articulates the people's sins—perhaps it was enough simply to emphasize the natural devastation—he calls the people to devote themselves to God. While lamentation brings clarity to the situation, repentance brings hope. For Hosea, the people's sins made the collapse of creation inevitable; hope only remained for Yhwh's new creation. For Joel, a reprieve from collapse is offered. Yhwh will drive away the locusts and restore the land and its vegetation (Joel 2:15–27). Nevertheless, the locust plague signals the certainty of Yhwh's eschatological day, which will entail the final collapse of creation, followed by Yhwh's recreation (Joel 2:28–3:21).

The collapse of human civilization that will result from climate change looms on the horizon. To many, the possibility of collapse is nothing more than a dystopian fiction—the world will continue as usual, and people will continue to prosper as the economy continues to grow. When I began writing this book in the fall of 2019, the U.S. economy was enjoying its longest, most prosperous period of economic growth in many years. Then the COVID-19 pandemic hit, and much of the economy ground to a halt. Three-quarters of a million global deaths later in the summer of 2020, as I finish writing this book, the future looks uncertain, with infections continuing to rise in the U.S. and elsewhere. The world can change quickly, and civilization is more fragile than we generally acknowledge. COVID-19 is not the direct consequence of climate change, though climate change does make it easier for such viruses to spread, nor is it an immediate threat to human civilization, though it may alter the way we interact with others for years to come. It is, however, a fitting reminder of our vulnerability.

Facing the devastation of an unprecedented locust plague, Joel called the people of Yhwh to lament the destruction and return to Yhwh because the plague signaled the coming day of Yhwh. It was the disposition needed for the people to endure the catastrophe. Climate change is not the day of Yhwh, but it does portend the looming collapse of human civilization. Thus, we should lament the ruin and loss that is resulting from climate change and repent of our sins. It will enable us to reconcile our affluence—our standard of living—with the damage we have caused the planet, and it will prepare us for the difficult tasks that curbing climate change entails.

> Let us recognize and mourn
>   what we are doing to the planet—
> degrading its lands,
>   polluting its waterways and oceans,
>   and emitting carbon dioxide into its atmosphere;
> let us grieve the loss of countless species
>   with whom we share this planet;
> let us acknowledge and lament the exploitation,
>   of nature and other human beings,
>   which makes possible our own affluence.

CONCLUSION

And let us repent and change our ways.

Who knows whether we might hold back the coming collapse.

Bibliography

Abou-Assaf, Ali, Pierre Bordreuil, and Alan R. Millard. 1982. *La statue de Tell Fekherye et son inscription bilingue assyro-araméenne*. Paris: Editions Recherche sur les civilisations.

Acker, Joan. 1988. "Class, Gender, and the Relations of Distribution." *Signs* 13:473–97.

———. 1992. "Gendered Institutions: From Sex Roles to Gendered Institutions." *Contemporary Sociology* 21:565–69.

Adams, Amanda S., and David W. Keith. 2013. "Are Global Wind Power Resource Estimates Overstated?" *Environmental Research Letters* 8. doi:10.1088/1748-9326/8/1/015021.

Aimé, Carla, and Frédéric Austerlitz. 2017. "Different Kinds of Genetic Markers Permit Inference of Paleolithic and Neolithic Expansions in Humans." *European Journal of Human Genetics* 25:360–65.

Albertz, Rainer. 2018. "The Recent Discussion on the Formation of the Pentateuch/Hexateuch." *Hebrew Studies* 59:65–92.

Alcott, Blake. 2005. "Jevon's Paradox." *Ecological Economic* 54:9–21.

———. 2010. "Impact Caps: Why Population, Affluence and Technology Strategies Should be Abandoned." *Journal of Cleaner Production* 18:552–60. doi:10.1016/j.jclepro.2009.08.001/.

Allen, James P. 1988. *Genesis in Egypt: The Philosophy of Ancient Egyptian Creation Accounts*. Yale Egyptological Studies 2. New Haven: Yale University Pres.

Anderson, Bernhard W. 1975. "Human Dominion over Nature." In *Biblical Studies in Contemporary Thought*, edited by M. Ward, 27–45. Somerville, MA: Greeno, Hadden.

———. 1978. "Unity and Diversity in God's Creation: A Study of the Babel Story." *Currents in Theology and Mission* 5:69–81.

Anderson, Blake, and Michael M'Gonigle. 2012. "Does Ecological Economics Have a Future? Contradiction and Reinvention in the Age of Climate Change." *Ecological Economics* 84:37–48. doi:10.1016/j.ecolecon.2012.06.009.

Anderson, Gary A. 1987. *Sacrifices and Offerings in Ancient Israel: Studies in Their Social and Political Importance*. Harvard Semitic Monographs 41. Atlanta: Scholars.

Anderson, Kevin, and Glen Peters. 2016. "The Trouble with Negative Emissions." *Science* 354 (6309):182–83.

Angus, Ian, 2016. *Facing the Anthropocene: Fossil Capitalism and the Crisis of the Earth System*. New York: Monthly Review.

Archer, David. 2005. "Fate of Fossil Fuel CO_2 in Geological Time." *Journal of Geophysical Research* 110, C9:1–6.

Arto, Iñaki, Iñigo Capellán-Pérez, Rosa Lago, Gorka Bueno, and Roberto Bermejo. 2016. "The Energy Requirements of a Developed World." *Energy for Sustainable Development* 33:1–16. doi:10.1016/j.esd.2016.04.001.

Asafu-Adjaye, John, Linus Blomqvist, Stewart Brand, Barry Brook, Ruth Defries, Erle Ellis, Christopher Foreman, et al. 2015. *An Ecomodernist Manifesto.* http://www.ecomodernism.org.

Asher-Greve, Julia M. 2002. "Decisive Sex, Essential Gender." In *Sex and Gender in the Ancient Near East: Proceeding of the 47th Rencontre Assyriologique Internationale, Helsinki, July 2–6, 2001*, edited by Simo Parpola and Robert M. Whiting, 11–26. Helsinki: Neo-Assyrian Text Corpus Project.

Asouti, Eleni, and Dorian Q. Fuller. 2013. "A Contextual Approach to the Emergence of Agriculture in Southwest Asia: Reconstructing Early Neolithic Plant-Food Production." *Current Anthropology* 54:299–345.

Athas, George. 2003. *The Tel Dan Inscription: A Reappraisal and a New Interpretation.* Journal for the Study of the Old Testament Supplements 360. London: T. & T. Clark.

Aurin, Hans-Christoph. 2008. "Your Urge Shall Be for Your Husband? A New Translation of Genesis 3:16b and a New Interpretation of Genesis 4:7." *Lectio Difficilior.* http://www.lectio.unibe.ch/08_1/pdf/aurin-lectio-EN.pdf.

Ayres, Robert U. 2007. "On the Practical Limits to Substitution." *Ecological Economics* 61:115–28.

———. 2017. "Gaps in Mainstream Economics: Energy, Growth, and Sustainability." In *Green Economy Reader: Lectures in Ecological Economics and Sustainability*, edited by Stanislav Shmelev, 39–54. Studies in Ecological Economics 6. Berlin: Springer.

Baden, Joel S. 2009. "The Tower of Babel: A Case Study in the Competing Methods of Historical and Modern Literary Criticism." *Journal of Biblical Literature* 128:209–24.

———. 2012. *The Composition of the Pentateuch: Renewing the Documentary Hypothesis.* New Haven: Yale University Press.

Baker, Heather D. 2001. "Degrees of Freedom: Slavery in Mid-First Millennium BC Baby-lonia." *World Archaeology* 33:18–26. https://www.academia.edu/245712/Baker_H_D_2001_Degrees_of_Freedom_Slavery_in_Mid_First_Millennium_BC_Babylonia.

Baker, Jill L. 2019. *Technology of the Ancient Near East: From the Neolithic to the Early Roman Period.* London: Routledge.

Ballentine, Debra Scoggins. 2015. *The Conflict Myth & the Biblical Tradition.* Oxford: Oxford University Press.

Baltzer, Klaus. 1971. *The Covenant Formulary: In Old Testament, Jewish, and Early Christian Writings.* Translated by David E. Green. Philadelphia: Fortress.

Baly, Denis. 1974. *The Geography of the Bible.* New and rev. ed. New York: Harper & Row.

Barker, David C., and David H. Bearce. 2012. "End-Times Theology, the Shadow of the Future, and Public Resistance to Addressing Global Climate Change." *Political Research Quarterly* 66:267–79.

Barnes, J. A. 1973. "Genetrix : Genitor :: Nature : Culture." In *The Character of Kinship*, edited by Jack Goody, 61–73. Cambridge: Cambridge University Press

Barr, James. 1972. "Man and Nature: The Ecological Controversy and the Old Testament." *Bulletin of the John Rylands Library* 55:9–32.

———. 1992. *The Garden of Eden and the Hope of Immortality.* Minneapolis: Fortress.

Barré, Lloyd M. 1988. "The Riddle of the Flood Chronology." *Journal for the Study of the Old Testament* 41:3–20.

Barrett, Matthew, and Ardel B. Caneday, eds. 2013. *Four Views on the Historical Adam*, with contributions from Denis O. Lamoureux, John H. Walton, C. John Collins, William D. Barrick, Gregory A. Boyd, and Philip G. Ryken. Grand Rapids: Zondervan.

Barrick, William D. 2013. "A Historical Adam: Young-Earth Creation View." In *Four Views on the Historical Adam*, edited by Matthew Barrett and Ardel B. Caneday, 197–227. Grand Rapids: Zondervan.

Bartholomew, Patriarch. 1997. "Remarks as Prepared for Delivery Address of His All Holiness Ecumenical Patriarch Bartholomew at the Environmental Symposium, Saint Barbara Greek Orthodox Church Santa Barbara, California." (Nov. 8). https://www.patriarchate.org/-/remarks-as-prepared-for-delivery-address-of-his-all-holiness-ecumenical-patriarch-b-a-r-t-h-o-l-o-m-e-w-at-the-environmental-symposium-saint-barbara-g.

Batto, Bernard F. 1992. *Slaying the Dragon: Mythmaking in the Biblical Tradition*. Louisville: Westminster John Knox.

———. 2013a. "The Combat Myth in Israelite Tradition Revisited." In *Creation and Chaos: A Reconsideration of Hermann Gunkel's* Chaoskampf *Hypothesis*, edited by JoAnn Scurlock and Richard H. Beal, 217–36. Winona Lake, IN: Eisenbrauns

———. 2013b. *In the Beginning: Essays on Creation Motifs in the Ancient Near East and the Bible*. Siphrut: Literature and Theology of the Hebrew Scriptures 9. Winona Lake, IN: Eisenbrauns.

Bauckham, Richard. 2010. *The Bible and Ecology: Rediscovering the Community of Creation*. Sarum Theological Lectures. Waco, TX: Baylor University Press.

Bauer, Andrew M., and Erle C. Ellis. 2018. "The Anthropocene Divide: Obscuring Understanding of Social-Environmental Change." *Current Anthropology* 59:209–27.

Beauvoir, Simone de. 1973. *The Second Sex*. Edited and translated by H. M. Parshley. 1952. Reprint, New York: Vintage.

Bechtel, Lyn M. 1991. "Shame as a Sanction of Social Control in Biblical Israel: Judicial Political, and Social Shaming." *Journal for the Study of the Old Testament* 49:47–76. doi.org/10.1177/030908929101604903.

———. 1995. Genesis 2:4b—3:24: A Myth About Human Maturation." *Journal for the Study of the Old Testament* 67:3–26.

Beckman, Gary M. 1983. *Hittite Birth Rituals*. Studien zu den Bogazköy-Texten 29. Wiesbaden: Harrassowitz.

Bedford, Peter R. 2007. "The Economic Role of the Jerusalem Temple in the Achaemenid Judah: Comparative Perspectives." In *Shai le-Sara Japhet: Studies in the Bible, Its Exegesis and Language Presented to Sara Japhet*, edited by Mosheh Bar-Asher and Sara Yefet, 3*–2*. Jerusalem: Bialik Institute.

———. 2015. "Temple Funding and Priestly Authority in Achaemenid Judah." In *Exile and Return: The Babylonian Conext*, edited by Jonathan Stökl and Caroline Waerzeggers, 336–51. Beihefte zur Zeitschrift für die alttestamentliche Wissenschaft 478. Berlin: de Gruyter.

Behrens, Arno, Stefan Giljum, Jan Kovanda, and Samuel Niza. 2007. "The Material Basis of the Global Economy: Worldwide Patterns of Natural Resource Extraction and Their Implications for Sustainable Resource Use Policies." *Ecological Economic* 64:444–53. doi: 10.1016/j.ecolecon.2007.02.034.

Bell, Michael Mayerfield. 2004. *Farming for Us All: Practical Agriculture and the Cultivation of Sustainability*. University Park: Pennsylvania State University Press.

Ben-Barak, Zafrira. 1981. "Meribaal and the System of Land Grants in Ancient Israel." *Biblica* 62:73–91. http://www.jstor.org/stable/42706921.

———. 2006. *Inheritance by Daughters in Israel and the Ancient Near East: A Social, Legal, and Ideological Revolution*. Jaffa: Archaeological Center Publications.

Bibliography

Bendell, Jem. 2018. "Deep Adaptation: A Map for Navigating Climate Tragedy." IFLAS Occasional Paper 2. http://lifeworth.com/deepadaptation.pdf.

Bendor, Shunya. 1996. *The Social Structure of Ancient Israel: The Institution of the Family (Beit Ab) from the Settlement to the End of the Monarchy*. Jerusalem Biblical Studies 7. Jerusalem: Simor.

Benedict XVI, Pope. 2008. "The Human Family, A Community of Peace." Message for the 41st World Day of Peace 2008. http://www.vatican.va/content/benedict-xvi/en/messages/peace/documents/hf_ben-xvi_mes_20071208_xli-world-day-peace.html.

———. 2009. *Charity in Truth: Caritas in Veritate*. San Francisco: Ignatius.

———. 2010. "If You Want to Cultivate Peace, Protect Creation." Message for the 43rd World Day of Peace 2010. http://www.vatican.va/content/benedict-xvi/en/messages/peace/documents/hf_ben-xvi_mes_20091208_xliii-world-day-peace.html.

Bennett, Carys E., Richard Thomas, Mark Williams, Jan Zalasiewicz, Matt Edgeworth, Holly Miller, Ben Coles, et al. 2018. "The Broiler Chicken as a Signal of a Human Reconfigured Biosphere." *Royal Society Open Science* 5:180325. doi:10.1098/rsos.180325.

Berlin, Adele. 2005. "The Wisdom of Creation in Psalm 104." In *Seeking Out the Wisdom of the Ancients: Essays Offered in Honor of Michael V. Fox on the Occasion of His Sixty-Fifth Birthday*, edited by R. L. Troxel, K. G. Friebel, and D. R. Magary, 71–83. Winona Lake, IN: Eisenbrauns.

Berna, Francesco, P. Goldberg, L. K. Horwitz, J. Brink, S. Holt, M. Bamford, and M. Chazan. 2012. "Microstratigraphic Evidence of In Situ Fire in the Acheulean Strata of Wonderwerk Cave, Northern Cape Provience, South Africa." *Proceedings of the National Academy of Sciences* 109, 20: E1215–20. doi:10.1073/pnas.1117620109.

Berry, Evan. 2013. "Religious Environmentalism and Environmental Religion in America." *Religion Compass* 7 (10):454–66.

Berry, Wendell. 1993. "Christianity and the Survival of Creation." *Cross Currents* 43 (2):149–63.

———. 2008 "Faustian Economics: Hell Hath No Limits." *Harper's Magazine* 316 (1896):35–42.

Biran, Avraham, and Joseph Naveh. 1993. "An Aramaic Stele Fragment from Tel Dan." *Israel Exploration Journal* 43 (2/3):81–98.

Bird, Phyllis A. 1981. "'Male and Female He Created Them': Genesis 1:27b in the Context of the Priestly Creation Account." *Harvard Theological Review* 74:129–59.

———. 1997. *Missing Persons and Mistaken Identities: Women and Gender in Ancient Israel*. Minneapolis: Fortress.

Bithas, Kostas, and Panos Kalimeris. 2017. "Unmasking Decoupling: Redefining the Resource Intensity of the Economy." *Science of the Total Environment* 619-20: 338–51. doi:10/1016/j.scitotenv.2017.11.061.

Black, Jacob. 1972. "Tyranny as a Strategy for Survival in an 'Egalitarian' Society: Luri Facts Versus an Anthropological Mystique." *Man* n.s. 7:614–34.

Blenkinsopp, Joseph. 1988. *Ezra–Nehemiah: A Commentary*. Old Testament Library. Louisville: Westminster John Knox.

———. 1996. "An Assessment of the Alleged Pre-Exilic Date for the Priestly Material in the Pentateuch." *Zeitschrift für die alttestamentliche Wissenschaft* 108:495–518.

———. 1997. "The Family in First Temple Israel." In *Families in Ancient Israel*, 48–103. Family, Religion, and Culture. Louisville: Westminster John Knox.

———. 2011. *Creation, Un-Creation, Re-Creation: A Discursive Commentary on Genesis 1–11*. London: T. & T. Clark.

Bloch-Smith, Elizabeth. 1992. *Judahite Burial Practices and Beliefs about the Dead.* Journal for the Study of the Old Testament Supplement 123. Sheffield: Sheffield Academic

Boer, Roland. 2007. "The Sacred Economy of Ancient 'Israel.'" *Scandinavian Journal of the Old Testament* 21 (1):29–48.

———. 2015. *The Sacred Economy of Ancient Israel*. Library of Ancient Israel. Louisville: Westminster John Knox.

Bollier, David. 2014. *Think Like a Commoner: A Short Introduction to the Life of the Commons*. Gabriola Island: New Society.

Boorse, Dorothy, et al. 2011. *Loving the Least of These: Addressing a Changing Environment*. Washington, DC: National Association of Evangelicals. http://nae.net/wp-content/uploads/2015/06/Loving-the-Least-of-These.pdf.

Borowski, Oded. 1987. *Agriculture in Iron Age Israel*. Winona Lake, IN: Eisenbrauns.

———. 1998. *Every Living Thing: Daily Use of Animals in Ancient Israel*. Walnut Creek, CA: AltaMira.

Bossio, D. A., S. C. Cook-Patton, P. W. Ellis, J. Fargione, J. Sanderman, P. Smith, S. Wood, et al. 2020. "The Role of Soil Carbon in Natural Climate Solutions." *Nature Sustainability* (Mar 16). doi:10.1038/s41893-020-0491-z.

Bottéro, Jean. 1992. *Mesopotamia: Writing, Reasoning, and the Gods*. Translated by Zainab Bahrani and Marc Van De Mieroop. Chicago: University of Chicago Press.

———. 2001. *Religion in Ancient Mesopotamia*. Translated by Teresa Lavender Fagen. Chicago: University of Chicago Press.

Boyd, Gregory A. 2013. "Whether or not There Was a Historical Adam, Our Faith is Secure." In *Four Views on the Historical Adam*, edited by Matthew Barrett and Ardel B. Caneday, 255–66. Grand Rapids: Zondervan.

Braaten, Laurie J. 2001. "Earth Community in Hosea 2." In *The Earth Story in the Psalms and the Prophets*, edited by Norman C. Habel, 185–203. Earth Bible 4. Sheffield: Sheffield Academic.

Bradford, Mark A., Chelsea J. Carey, Lesley Atwood, Deborah Bossio, Eli P. Fenichel, Sasha Gennet, Joseph Fargione, et al. 2019. "Soil Carbon Science for Policy and Practice." *Nature Sustainability* 2:1070–72. doi:10.1038/s41893-019-0431-y.

Bratton, Susan Power. 1983. "The Ecotheology of James Watt." *Environmental Ethics* 5:225–36.

Briant, Pierre. 2002. *From Cyrus to Alexander: A History of the Persian Empire*. Translated by Peter T. Daniels. Winona Lake, IN: Eisenbrauns.

Brichto, Herbert Chanan. 1973. "Kin, Cult, Land and Afterlife—A Biblical Complex." *Hebrew Union College Annual* 44:1–54.

Brody, Aaron J. 2011. "The Archaeology of the Extended Family: A Household Compound from Iron II Tell en-Nasbeh." In *Household Archaeology in Ancient Israel and Beyond*, edited by Assaf Yasur-Landau, Jennie R. Ebeling, and Laura B. Mazow, 237–54. Culture and History of the Ancient Near East 50. Leiden: Brill.

Brooke, John L. 2014. *Climate Change and the Course of Global History: A Rough Journey*. Studies in Environment and History. Cambridge: Cambridge University Press.

Brown, Gabe. 2018. *Dirt to Soil: One Family's Journey into Regenerative Agriculture*. White River Junction, VT: Chelsea Green.

Brown, James H., William R. Burnside, Ana D. Davidson, John P. DeLong, William C. Dunn, Marcus J. Hamilton, Norman Mercado-Silva, et al. 2011. "Energetic Limits to Economic Growth." *BioScience* 61:19–26.

Brown, William P. 2010. *The Seven Pillars of Creation: The Bible, Science, and the Ecology of Wonder*. New York: Oxford University Press.

Brueggemann, Walter. 2002. *The Land: Place as Gift, Promise, and Challenge in Biblical Faith*. 2nd ed. Overtures to Biblical Theology. Minneapolis: Fortress.

Buchholz, Todd G. 1988. "Biblical Laws and the Economic Growth of Ancient Israel." *Journal of Law and Religion* 6:389–427.

Bunker, Stephen G. 1996. "Raw Material and the Global Economy: Oversights and Distortions in Industrial Ecology." *Society and Natural Resources* 9:419–29.

Burton, Michael L., and Douglas R. White. 1984. "Sexual Division of Labor in Agriculture." *American Anthropologist* 86:568–83.

Burton, Michael L., Lilyan A. Brudner, Douglas R. White. 1977. "A Model of the Sexual Division of Labor." *American Ethnologist* 4:227–51.

Butler, Judith. 1986. "Sex and Gender in Simone de Beauvoir's *Second Sex*." *Yale French Studies* 72:35–49.

———. 2006. *Gender Trouble: Feminism and the Subversion of Identity*. New York: Routledge.

Cafaro, Philip, and Eileen Crist, eds. 2012. *Life on the Brink: Environmentalists Confront Overpopulation*. Athens: University of Georgia Press.

Callender, Dexter E., Jr. 1998. "Servants of God(s) and Servants of Kings in Israel and the Ancient Near East." *Semeia* 83/84:67–82.

———. 2000. *Adam in Myth and History: Ancient Israelite Perspectives on the Primal Human*. Harvard Semitic Studies 48. Winona Lake, IN: Eisenbrauns.

Campbell, J. K. 1964. *Honour, Family, and Patronage: A Study of Institutions and Moral Values in a Greek Mountain Community,*. Oxford: Oxford University Press.

Caradonna, Jeremy, Iris Borowy, Tom Green, Peter A. Victor, Maurie Cohen, Andrew Gow, Anna Ignatyeva, et al. 2015. "A Call to Look Past *An Ecomodernist Manifesto*: A Degrowth Critique." *Resilience* (May 6). https://www.resilience.org/stories/2015-05-06/a-degrowth-response-to-an-ecomodernist-manifesto.

Carr, David M. 1996. *Reading the Fractures of Genesis: Historical and Literary Approaches*. Louisville: Westminster John Knox.

———. 2000. "Gender and the Shaping of Desire in the Song of Songs and Its Interpretation." *Journal of Biblical Literature* 119:233–48.

Carrington, Damian. 2020. "World's Consumption of Materials Hits Record 100bn Tonnes a Year." *The Guardian* (January 22). https://www.theguardian.com/environment/2020/jan/22/worlds-consumption-of-materials-hits-record-100bn-tonnes-a-year.

Cataldo, Jeremiah. 2003. "Persian Policy and the Yehud Community during Nehemiah." *Journal for the Study of the Old Testament* 28:131–43.

Catton, William R., and Riley E. Dunlap. 1980. "A New Ecological Paradigm for Post-Exuberant Sociology." *American Behavioral Scientist* 24:15–47.

Chakrabarty, Dipesh. 2009. "The Climate of Histories: Four Theses." *Critical Inquiry* 35:197–222.

Chaney, Marvin L. 2017. *Peasants, Prophets, and Political Economy: The Hebrew Bible and Social Analysis*. Eugene, OR: Cascade Books.

Chapman, Cynthia R. 2004. *The Gendered Language of Warfare in the Israelite-Assyrian Encounter*. Harvard Semitic Monographs 62. Winona Lake, IN: Eisenbrauns.

———. 2016. *The House of the Mother: The Social Roles of Maternal Kin in Biblical Hebrew Narrative and Poetry*. Anchor Yale Bible Reference Library. New Haven: Yale University Press.

———. 2019. "The Breath of Life: Speech, Gender, and Authority in the Garden of Eden." *Journal of Biblical Literature* 138:241–62.

Chetty, Raj, David Grusky, Maximilian Hell, Nathaniel Hendren, Robert Manduca, and Jimmy Narang. 2017. "The Fading American Dream: Trends in Absolute Income Mobility since 1940." *Science* 356 (6336):398–406. doi:10.1126/science.aal4617.

Childs, James M., Jr. 2009. "The Ecology of Moral Authority: A Response to James A. Nash, 'The Bible vs. Biodiversity: The Case against Moral Argument from Scripture.'" *Journal for the Study of Religion, Nature and Culture* 3:254–59.

Chirichigno, Gregory C. 1993. *Debt-Slavery in Israel and the Ancient Near East*. Journal for the Study of the Old Testament Supplement 141. Sheffield: Sheffield Academic.

Cho, Adrian. 2016. "To Fight Global Warming, Senate Calls for Study of Making Earth Reflect More Light." *Science* (April 19). doi:10.1126/science.aaf9937.

Clack, Christopher T. M., Staffan A. Qvist, Jay Apt, Morgan Bazilian, Adam R. Brandt, Ken Caldeira, Steven J. Davis, et al. 2017. "Evaluation of a Proposal for Reliable Low-Cost Grid Power with 100% Wind, Water, and Solar." *Proceedings of the National Academy of Sciences of the USA* 114 (26):6722–27. doi:10.1073/pnas.1610381114.

Clark, Brett, and Richard York. 2008. "Rifts and Shift: Getting to the Root of Environmental Crises." *Monthly Review* 60 (6):13–24.

Clark, W. M. 1971. "The Flood and the Structure of the Pre-Patriarchal History." *Zeitschrift für die alttestamentliche Wissenschaft* 83:184–211.

Clifford, Richard J. 1972. *The Cosmic Mountain in Canaan and the Old Testament*. Harvard Semitic Monographs 4. Cambridge: Harvard University Press.

———. 1994. *Creation Accounts in the Ancient Near East and in the Bible*. Catholic Biblical Quarterly Monograph Series 26. Washington, DC: Catholic Biblical Association of America.

Clifford, Richard J., and John J. Collins, eds. 1992. *Creation in the Biblical Traditions*. Catholic Biblical Quarterly Monograph Series 24. Washington, DC: Catholic Biblical Association of America.

Cline, Eric H. 2014. *1177 B.C.: The Year Civilization Collapsed*. Princeton: Princeton University Press.

Clines, David J. A. 1990. *What Does Eve Do to Help? And Other Readerly Questions to the Old Testament*. Journal for the Study of the Old Testament Supplement 94. Sheffield: Sheffield Academic.

Clingerman, Forrest. 2012. "Between Babel and Pelagius: Religion, Theology, and Geoengineering." In *Engineering the Climate: The Ethics of Solar Radiation Management*, edited by Christopher J. Preston, 201–19. Lanham, MD: Lexington.

———. 2014. "Geoengineering, Theology, and the Meaning of Being Human." *Zygon* 49:6–21.

Clunies-Ross, Tracey, and Nicholas Hildyard. 1992. *The Politics of Industrial Agriculture*. London: Earthscan.

Cohen, Yehudi. 1969. "Ends and Means in Political Control: State Organization and Punishment of Adultery, Incest, and Violation of Celibacy." *American Anthropologist* 71:658–87.

Collins, C. John. 2010. "Adam and Eve as Historical People, and Why It Matters." *Perspectives on Science and Christian Faith* 62:147–65.

———. 2011. "Adam and Eve in the Old Testament." *Southern Baptist Journal of Theology* 15:4–25.

———. 2013. "A Historical Adam: An Old-Earth Creation View." In *Four Views on the Historical Adam*, edited by Matthew Barrett and Ardel B. Caneday, 143–75. Grand Rapids: Zondervan.

Commoner, Barry. 1972. "A Bulletin Dialogue on 'The Closing Circle': Response." *Bulletin of the Atomic Scientists* 28 (5): 17, 42–56.

Cook, J. M. 1983. *The Persian Empire*. New York: Schocken.

Coombe, Rosemary J. 1990. "Barren Ground: Re-Conceiving Honour and Shame in the Field of Mediterranean Ethnography." *Anthropologica* 32:221–38.

Coomber, Matthew J. M. 2010. *Re-Reading the Prophets through Corporate Globalization: A Cultural-Evolutionary Approach to Economic Injustice in the Hebrew Bible*. Biblical Intersections 4. Piscataway, NJ: Gorgias.

Cooper, Ryan. 2020. "The Real Potential of the Electric Vehicle Revolution." TheWeek.com (Feb. 17). https://theweek.com/articles/895479/real-potential-electric-vehicle-revolution.

Cooperman, Alan. 2006. "Evangelicals Will Not Take Stand on Global Warming." *Washington Post* (February 2): A08. http://www.washingtonpost.com/wp-dyn/content/article/2006/02/01/AR2006020102132.html.

Cornwall Alliance. 2009. "A Renewed Call to Truth, Prudence, and Protection of the Poor: An Evangelical Examination of the Theology, Science, and Economics of Global Warming." https://www.cornwallalliance.org/docs/a-renewed-call-to-truth-prudence-and-protection-of-the-poor.pdf.

Corry, Olaf. 2017. "The International Politics of Geoengineering: The Feasibility of Plan B for Tackling Climate Change." *Security Dialogue* 48:297–315.

Costanza, Robert. 1996. "Ecological Economics: Reintegrating the Study of Humans and Nature." *Ecological Applications* 6:978–90.

Costin, Cathy Lynne. 2013. "Gender and Textile Production in Prehistory." In *A Companion to Gender in Prehistory*, edited by Diane Bolger, 180–202. Hoboken, NJ: Wiley.

Craig, Kenneth M., Jr. 1999. "Questions Outside Eden (Genesis 4.1–16): Yahweh, Cain and Their Rhetorical Interchange." *Journal for the Study of the Old Testament* 86:107–28.

Craigie, Peter C. 1974. "The Comparison of Hebrew Poetry: Psalm 104 in the Light of Egyptian and Ugaritic Poetry." *Semitics* 4:10–21.

Credit Suisse. 2019. *Global Wealth Report 2019*. Credit Suisse Research Institute. https://www.credit-suisse.com/about-us/en/reports-research/global-wealth-report.html.

Crenshaw, James L. 1992. "When Form and Content Clash: The Theology of Job 38:1–40:5." In *Creation in the Biblical Traditions*, edited by Richard J. Clifford and John J. Collins, 70–84. Catholic Biblical Quarterly Monograph Series 24. Washington DC: Catholic Biblical Association of America.

Crist, Eileen. 2013. "On the Poverty of Our Nomenclature." *Environmental Humanities* 3:129–47.

———. 2019. *Abundant Earth: Toward an Ecological Civilization*. Chicago: University of Chicago Press.

Crook, Zeba A. 2006. "Reciprocity: Covenant Exchange as a Test Case." In *Ancient Israel: The Old Testament in Its Social Context*, edited by Philip F. Esler, 78–91. Minneapolis: Fortress.

———. 2009. "Honor, Shame, and Social Status Revisited." *Journal of Biblical Literature* 128:591–611.

Cross, Frank Moore. 1973. *Canaanite Myth and Hebrew Epic: Essays in the History of the Religion of Israel*. Cambridge: Harvard University Press.

Crüsemann, Frank. 1996. "Human Solidarity and Ethnic Identity: Israel's Self-Definition in the Genealogical System of Genesis." In *Ethnicity and the Bible*, edited by Mark G. Brett, 57–76. Biblical Interpretation Series 19. Leiden: Brill.

Crutzen, Paul J. 2002. "Geology of Mankind." *Nature* 415 (6867):23.

———. 2006. "Albedo Enhancement by Stratospheric Sulfur Injections: A Contribution to Resolve a Policy Dilemma?" *Climatic Change* 77:211–20.

Crutzen, Paul J., and Eugene F. Stoermer. 2000. "The 'Anthropocene.'" *Global Change Newsletter* 41 (May):17–18.

Culbertson, Laura, ed. 2011. *Slaves and Households in the Near East*. Oriental Institute Seminars 7. Chicago: The Oriental Institute of the University of Chicago.

Currid, John D. "Rectangular Storehouse Construction during the Israelite Iron Age." *Zeitschrift des deutschen Palästina-Vereins* 108:99–121.

Dalley, Stephanie. 1991. *Myths from Mesopotamia: Creation, The Flood, Gilgamesh and Others*. Oxford: Oxford University Press.

Daly, Herman. 2019. "Some Overlaps between the First and Second Thirty Years of Ecological Economics." *Ecological Economics* 164:106372. doi:10.1016/j.ecolecon.2019.106372.

Davis, Ellen F. 2009a. "The Agrarian Perspective of the Bible: A Response to James A. Nash, 'The Bible vs. Biodiversity: The Case against Moral Argument from Scripture.'" *Journal for the Study of Religion, Nature and Culture* 3:260–65.

———. 2009b. *Scripture, Culture, and Agriculture: An Agrarian Reading of the Bible*. Cambridge: Cambridge University Press.

Davis, John. 1977. *People of the Mediterranean: An Essay in Comparative Social Anthropology*. London: Routledge & Kegan Paul.

Deane-Drummond, Celia. 2009. "Response to James A. Nash, 'The Bible vs. Biodiversity: The Case against Moral Argument from Scripture.'" *Journal for the Study of Religion, Nature and Culture* 3:271–78.

———. 2016. "Pope Francis: Priest and Prophet in the Anthropocene." *Environmental Humanities* 8:256–62.

Dearman, John Andrew. 1988. *Property Rights in the Eighth-Century Prophets*. SBL Dissertation Series 106. Atlanta: Scholars.

DeFries, Ruth, Ottmar Edenhofer, Alex Halliday, Geoffrey Heal, Timothy Lenton, Michael Puma, James Rising, et al. 2019. *The Missing Economic Risks in Assessments of Climate Change Impacts*. doi: 10.7916/d8-6f8h-md45.

Delaney, Carol. 1986. "The Meaning of Paternity and the Virgin Birth Debate." *Man* 21:494–513.

———. 1987. "Seeds of Honor, Fields of Shame." In *Honor and Shame and the Unity of the Mediterranean*, edited by David D. Gilmore, 35–48. Special Publication of the American Anthropological Association 22. Washington, DC: American Anthropological Association.

———. 1991. *The Seed and the Soil: Gender and Cosmology in Turkish Village Society.* Berkeley: University of California Press.

Delucchi, Mark A., and Mark Z. Jacobson. 2011. "Providing All Global Energy with Wind, Water, and Solar Power, Part II: Reliability, System and Transmission Costs, and Policies." *Energy Policy* 39:1170–90. doi:10.1016/j.enpol.2010.11.045.

DeRoche, Michael. 1981. "The Reversal of Creation in Hosea." *Vetus Testamentum* 31:400–409.

Derr, Thomas Sieger. 1975. "Religion's Responsibility for the Ecological Crisis: An Argument Run Amok." *Worldview* 18:39–45.

Deurloo, Karel Adriaan. 1987. "*Teshuqah* 'Dependency,' Gen 4, 7." *Zeitschrift für die alttestamentliche Wissenschaft* 99:405–6.

Dever, William G. 1995. "Social Structure in Palestine in the Iron II Period on the Eve of Destruction." In *The Archaeology of Society in the Holy Land*, edited by Thomas E. Levy, 416–30. New York: Facts on File.

———. 2005. *Did God Have a Wife? Archaeology and Folk Religion in Ancient Israel.* Grand Rapids: Eerdmans.

Dick, Michael B. 2006. "The Neo-Assyrian Royal Lion Hunt and Yahweh's Answer to Job." *Journal of Biblical Literature* 125:243–70.

Djupe, Paul A., and Patrick Kieran Hunt. 2009. "Beyond the Lynn White Thesis: Congregational Effects on Environmental Concern." *Journal for the Scientific Study of Religion* 48:670–86.

Djupe, Paul A., and Gregory W. Gwiasda. 2010. "Evangelizing the Environment: Decision Process Effects in Political Persuasion." *Journal for the Scientific Study of Religion* 49:73–86.

Dominish, Elsa, Nick Florin, and Sven Teske. 2019. *Responsible Minerals Sourcing for Renewable Energy.* Report prepared for Earthworks by the Institute for Sustainable Futures, University of Technology Sydney.

Donham, Donald L. 1981. "Beyond the Domestic Mode of Production." *Man* n.s. 16:515–41.

———. 1999. *History, Power, Ideology: Central Issues in Marxism and Anthropology.* Berkeley: University of California Press.

Donner, Simon D. 2007. "Domain of the Gods: An Editorial Essay." *Climatic Change* 85:231–36.

Douglas, Mary. 1966. *Purity and Danger: An Analysis of the Concepts of Pollution and Taboo.* London: Ark.

———. 1970. *Natural Symbols: Explorations in Cosmology.* New York: Pantheon.

Dozeman, Thomas B. 2009. *Commentary on Exodus.* Eerdmans Critical Commentary. Grand Rapids: Eerdmans.

Dozeman, Thomas B., and Konrad Schmid, eds. 2006. *A Farewell to the Yahwist? The Composition of the Pentateuch in Recent European Interpretation.* Symposium Series 34. Atlanta: Society of Biblical Literature.

duBois, Page. 1988. *Sowing the Body: Psychoanalysis and Ancient Representations of Women.* Chicago: University of Chicago Press.

Dubos, René. 1972. *A God Within.* New York: Scribner.

Dutcher-Walls, Patricia. 2002. "The Circumscription of the King: Deuteronomy 17:16–17 in its Ancient Social Context." *Journal of Biblical Literature* 121:601–16.

Ebeling, Jennie R. 2010. *Women's Lives in Biblical Times.* London: T. & T. Clark.

Ehrlich, Paul R. 1970. *The Population Bomb: Population Control or Race to Oblivion*. New York: Ballantine.

Ehrlich, Paul R., and Anne H. Ehrlich. 2013. "Can a Collapse of Global Civilization Be Avoided?" *Proceedings of the Royal Society B* 280:20122845. doi:10.1098/rspb.2012.2845.

Ehrlich, Paul R., and John P. Holdren. 1971. "Impact of Population Growth." *Science* 171 (3977):1212–17.

———. 1972. "A Bulletin Dialogue on 'The Closing Circle': Critique." *Bulletin of the Atomic Scientists* 28 (5):16, 18–27.

Eilberg-Schwartz, Howard. 1990. *The Savage in Judaism: An Anthropology of Israelite Religion and Ancient Judaism*. Bloomington: Indiana University Press.

———. 1994. *God's Phallus and Other Problems for Men and Monotheism*. Boston: Beacon.

Eisenstadt, S. N. 1993. *The Political Systems of Empire*. New Brunswick: Transaction.

Eisenstadt, S. N., and L. Roniger. 1984. *Patrons, Clients and Friends: Interpersonal Relations and the Structure of Trust in Society*. Themes in the Social Sciences. Cambridge: Cambridge University Press.

Elat, Moshe. 1979. "The Monarchy and the Development of Trade in Ancient Israel." In *State and Temple Economy in the Ancient Near East*, edited by Edward Lipiński, 2:527–46. 2 vols. Orientalia Lovaniensia Analecta 6. Leuven: Departement Oriëntalistiek.

Eldardiry, Hisham, and Emad Habib. 2018. "Carbon Capture and Sequestration in Power Generation: Review of Impacts and Opportunities for Water Sustainability." *Energy, Sustainability and Society* 8 (6). doi:10.1186/s13705-018-0146-3.

Ellis, Erle. 2011. "Anthropogenic Transformation of the Terrestrial Biosphere." *Philosophical Transactions of the Royal Society A* 369:1010–35.

———. 2012. "The Planet of No Return: Human Resilience on an Artificial Earth." *Breakthrough Journal* 2 (January 6). https://thebreakthrough.org/journal/issue-2/the-planet-of-no-return.

———. 2015. "Ecology in an Anthropogenic Biosphere." *Ecological Monographs* 85:287–331.

Ellis, Erle, Dorian Q. Fuller, Jed O. Kaplan, and Wayne G. Lutters. 2013. "Dating the Anthropocene: Towards an Empirical Global History of Human Transformation of the Terrestrial Biosphere." *Elementa: Science of the Anthropocene* (December 4). doi:10.12952/journal.elementa.000018.

Ellis, Erle, Mark Maslin, Nicole Boivin, and Andrew Bauer. 2016. "Involve Social Scientists in Defining the Anthropocene." *Nature* 540 (7632):192–93.

Ember, Carol R. 1983. "The Relative Decline in Women's Contribution to Agriculture with Intensification." *American Anthropologist* 85:285–304.

Enns, Peter. 2012. *The Evolution of Adam: What the Bible Does and Doesn't Say About Human Origins*. Grand Rapids: Brazos.

Eph'al, I. 1988. "Syria–Palestine under Achaemenid Rule." In *The Cambridge Ancient History*. Volume IV: *Persia, Greece and the Western Mediterranean: c. 525 to 479 B.C.*, edited by John Boardman, N. G. L. Hammond, D. M. Lewis, and M. Ostwald, 139–64. 2nd ed. Cambridge: Cambridge University Press.

Erbele-Küster, Dorothea. 2011. "Gender and the Cult: 'Pure' and 'Impure' as Gender-Relevant Categories." In *Torah*, edited by Irmtraud Fischer and Mercedes Navarro Puerto, with Andrea Taschl-Erber, 375–405. The Bible and Women; Hebrew Bible/Old Testament 1.1. Atlanta: Society of Biblical Literature.

———. 2017. *Body, Gender and Purity in Leviticus 12 and 15*. Library of Hebrew Bible/Old Testament Studies 539. London: Bloomsbury T. & T. Clark.

Evangelical Climate Initiative. 2006. "Climate Change: An Evangelical Call to Action." https://www.npr.org/documents/2006/feb/evangelical/calltoaction.pdf.

FAO and ITPS. 2015. *Status of the World's Soil Resources: Technical Summary*. Rome: Food and Agriculture Organization of the United Nations and Intergovernmental Technical Panel on Soils.

Fager, Jeffrey A. 1993. *Land Tenure and the Biblical Jubilee: Uncovering Hebrew Ethics through the Sociology of Knowledge*. Journal for the Study of the Old Testament Supplement 155. Sheffield: Sheffield Academic.

Fairlie, Simon. 2018. "Is Grass-Fed Guilt-Free?" *The Land* 22:52–55.

Faramelli, Norm. 2009. "Whither the Bible in Environmental Ethics and Moral Argument." *Journal for the Study of Religion, Nature and Culture* 3:266–70.

Faulkner, Raymond O. 1969. *The Ancient Egyptian Pyramid Texts*. Oxford: Clarendon.

Faust, Avraham. 1999. "Differences in Family Structure between Cities and Villages in Iron Age II." *Tel Aviv* 26:233–52.

———. 2000. "The Rural Community in Ancient Israel during Iron Age II." *Bulletin of the American Schools of Oriental Research* 317:17–39.

———. 2011. "Household Economies in the Kingdoms of Israel and Judah." In *Household Archaeology in Ancient Israel and Beyond*, edited by Assaf Yasur-Landau, Jennie R. Ebeling, and Laura B. Mazow, 255–73. Culture and History of the Ancient Near East 50. Leiden: Brill.

———. 2012. *The Archaeology of Israelite Society in Iron Age II*. Translated by Ruth Ludlum. Winona Lake, IN: Eisenbrauns.

Fausto-Sterling, Anne. 1993. "The Five Sexes: Why Male and Female Are not Enough." *The Sciences* (March/April): 20–24.

Feig, Nurit. 2003. "Excavations at Beit Tsafafa: Iron Age II and Byzantine Agricultural Installations South of Jerusalem." *'Atiqot* 44:191–238.

Feldt, Laura. 2012. "Wilderness and Hebrew Bible Religion—Fertility, Apostasy and Religious Transformation in the Pentateuch." In *Wilderness in Mythology and Religion: Approaching Religious Spatialities, Cosmologies, and Ideas of Wild Nature*, edited by Laura Feldt, 55–94. Religion and Society 55. Berlin: de Gruyter.

Finkelstein, Israel. 1994. "The Archaeology of the Days of Manasseh." In *Scripture and Other Artifacts: Essays on the Bible and Archaeology in Honor of Philip J. King*, edited by Michael D. Coogan, J. Cheryl Exum, and Lawrence E. Stager, 164–87. Louisville: Westminster John Knox.

———. 1999. "State Formation in Israel and Judah: A Contrast in Context, A Contrast in Trajectory." *Near Eastern Archaeology* 62:35–52.

Finkelstein, Israel, Nadav Na'aman, and Thomas Römer. 2019. "Restoring Line 31 in the Mesha Stele: The 'House of David' or Biblical Balak?" *Tel Aviv* 46:3–11.

Fitz, Don. 2019. "What Is Energy Denial?" Resiliance.org (Sept. 12). https://www.resilience.org/stories/2019-09-12/what-is-energy-denial.

Fizaine, Florian, and Victor Court. 2016. "Energy Expenditure, Economic Growth, and the Minimum EROI of Society." *Energy Policy* 95:172–86. doi:10.1016/j.enpol.2016.04.039.

Fleishman, Joseph. 2011. *Father-Daughter Relations in Biblical Law*. Bethesda, MD: CDL.

Fletcher, Robert, and Crelis Rammelt. 2017. "Decoupling: A Key Fantasy of the Post-2015 Sustainable Development Agenda." *Globalization* 14:450–67.

Floyd, Joshua, Samuel Alexander, Manfred Lenzen, Patrick Moriarty, Graham Palmer, Sangeetha Chandra-Shekeran, Barney Foran, and Lorenz Keyßer. 2020. "Energy Descent as a Post-Carbon Transition Scenario: How 'Knowledge Humility' Reshapes Energy Futures for Post-Normal Times." *Futures* 122:102565. doi:10.1016/j.futures.2020.102565.

Foh, Susan T. 1979. "What Is the Woman's Desire?" *Westminster Theological Journal* 37:376–83.

Foster, George M. 1965. "Peasant Society and the Image of Limited Good." *American Anthropologist* 67:293–315.

Foster, John Bellamy, and Paul Burkett. 2000. "The Dialectic of Organic/Inorganic Relations." *Organization and Environment* 13:403–25.

Foster, John Bellamy, and Brett Clark. 2020. *The Robbery of Nature: Capitalism and the Ecological Rift*. New York: Monthly Review.

Foster, John Bellamy, Brett Clark, and Richard York. 2010. *The Ecological Rift: Capitalism's War on the Earth*. New York: Monthly Review.

Francis I, Pope. 2015. *Laudato Si': On Care for Our Common Home*. Vatican City: Vatican Press.

Franklin, Norma. 2017. "Entering the Arena: The Megiddo Stables Reconsidered." In *Rethinking Israel: Studies in the History and Archaeology of Ancient Israel in Honor of Israel Finkelstein*, edited by Oded Lipschits, Yuval Gadot, and Matthew J. Adams, 87–101. Winona Lake, IN: Eisenbrauns.

Frei, Peter. 2001. "Persian Imperial Authorization: A Summary." In *Persia and Torah: The Theory of Imperial Authorization of the Pentateuch*, edited by James W. Watts, 5–40. Symposium Series 17. Atlanta: Society of Biblical Literature.

Fremaux, Anne, and John Berry. 2019. "The 'Good Anthropocene' and Green Political Theory: Rethinking Environmentalism, Resisting Ecomodernism." In *Anthropocene Encounters: New Directions in Green Political Thinking*, edited by Frank Biermann and Eva Lövbrand, 171–90. Earth System Governance. Cambridge: Cambridge University Press.

Fretheim, Terence E. 2005. *God and World in the Old Testament: A Relational Theology of Creation*. Nashville: Abingdon.

Fried, Lisbeth S. 2004. *The Priest and the Great King: Temple-Palace Relations in the Persian Empire*. Biblical and Judaic Studies 10. Winona Lake, IN: Eisenbrauns.

———. 2015. "Exploitation of Depopulated Land in Achaemenid Judah." In *The Economy of Ancient Judah in Its Historical Context*, edited by Marvin Lloyd Miller, Ehud Ben Zvi, and Gary N. Knoppers, 151–64. Winona Lake, IN: Eisenbrauns.

———. 2018. "150 Men at Nehemiah's Table? The Role of the Governor's Meals in the Achaemenid Provincial Economy." *Journal of Biblical Literature* 137:821–31.

Frisch, Rob. 2020. Opinion, "On the Political Economy of Climate Change." Letter to the Editor, *Wall Street Journal* (Febrary 2). https://www.wsj.com/articles/on-the-political-economy-of-climate-change-11580670296.

Fritz, Volkmar, and Philip R. Davies, eds. 1996. *The Origins of the Ancient Israelite States*. Journal for the Study of the Old Testament Supplement 228. Sheffield: Sheffield Academic.

Frumhoff, Peter. 2014. "Global Warning Fact: More than Half of All Industrial CO_2 Pollution Has Been Emitted since 1988." *Union of Concerned Scientists Blog*, December 15. https://blog.ucsusa.org/peter-frumhoff/global-warming-fact-co2-emissions-since-1988-764.

Frumhoff, Peter, and Naomi Oreskes. 2015. "Fossil Fuel Firms are Still Bankrolling Climate Denial Lobby Groups." *The Guardian* (March 25). https://www.theguardian.com/

environment/2015/mar/25/fossil-fuel-firms-are-still-bankrolling-climate-denial-lobby-groups.

Frymer-Kensky, Tikva. 1987. "The Planting of Man: A Study in Biblical Imagery." In *Love & Death in the Ancient Near East: Essays in Honor of Marvin H. Pope*, edited by John H. Marks and Robert M. Good, 129–36. Guildford, CT: Four Quarters.

———. 1992. *In the Wake of the Goddess: Women, Culture, and the Biblical Transformation of Pagan Myth*. New York: Free Press.

———. 1998. "Virginity in the Bible." In *Gender and Law in the Hebrew Bible and the Ancient Near East*, edited by Victor H. Matthews, Bernard M. Levinson, and Tikva Frymer-Kensky, 79–96. Journal for the Study of the Old Testament Supplement 262. Sheffield: Sheffield Academic.

———. 2002. *Reading the Women of the Bible: A New Interpretation of Their Stories*. New York: Schocken.

Fuller, Dorian Q., George Willcox, and Robin G. Allaby. 2011. "Cultivation and Domestication Had Multiple Origins: Arguments against the Core Area Hypothesis for the Origins of Agriculture in the Near East." *World Archaeology* 43:628–52.

Gaiser, Frederick J. 2003. "Why Does It Rain? A Biblical Case Study in Divine Causality." *Horizons in Biblical Theology* 25:1–18.

García Bachmann, Mercedes L. 2013. *Woman at Work in the Deuteronomistic History*. International Voices in Biblical Studies 4. Atlanta: Society of Biblical Literature.

Garfinkel, Yosef, and Saar Ganor. 2008. "Khirbet Qeiyafa: Sha'arayim." *Journal of Hebrew Scriptures* 8, art. 22 (10pp). doi:10.5508/jhs.2008.v8.a22.

Garr, W. Randall. 2000, "'Image' and 'Likeness' in the Inscription from Tel Fakhariyeh." *Israel Exploration Journal* 50:227–34.

Geertz, Clifford. 1973. *The Interpretation of Cultures*. New York: Basic Books.

Gellner, Ernest, and John Waterbury. 1977. *Patrons and Clients in Mediterranean Societies*. London: Duckworth.

George, Mark K. 2009. *Israel's Tabernacle as Social Space*. Ancient Israel and Its Literature 2. Atlanta: Society of Biblical Literature.

Gertz, Jan C., Bernhard M. Levinson, Dalit Rom-Shiloni, and Konrad Schmid, eds. 2016. *The Formation of the Pentateuch: Bridging the Academic Cultures of Europe, Israel, and North America*. Forschungen zum Alten Testament 111. Tübingen: Mohr/Siebeck.

Gilmore, David D. 1982. "Anthropology of the Mediterranean Area." *Annual Review of Anthropology* 11:175–20.

———, ed. 1987. *Honor and Shame and the Unity of the Mediterranean*. American Anthropology Association Special Publication 22. Washington, DC: American Anthropology Association.

———. 1996. "Above and Below: Toward a Social Geometry of Gender." *American Anthropologist* n.s. 98:54–66.

Glacken, Clarence J. 1976. *Traces on the Rhodian Shore: Nature and Culture in Western Thought from Ancient Times to the End of the Eighteenth Century*. Berkeley: University of California Press.

Glass, Zipporah G. 2000. "Land, Slave Labor and Law: Engaging Ancient Israel's Economy." *Journal for the Study of the Old Testament* 91:27–39.

Glaub, Matthew, and Charles A. S. Hall. 2017. "Evolutionary Implications of Persistence Hunting: An Examination of Energy Return on Investment for !Kung Hunting." *Human Ecology* 45:393–401.

Global Carbon Project. 2019. "Global Carbon Budget" (December 4). https://www.globalcarbonproject.org/carbonbudget.

Godelier, Maurice. 1981. "The Origins of Male Domination." *New Left Review* 127:3–17.

Gordon, Cyrus. 1977. "Paternity at Two Levels." *Journal of Biblical Literature* 96:101.

———. 1982. "Khnum and El." *Scripta Hiersolymitana* 28:203–14.

Gorman, Frank H. Jr. 1990. *The Ideology of Ritual: Space, Time and Status in the Priestly Theology*. Journal for the Study of the Old Testament Supplement 91. Sheffield: Sheffield Academic.

Gottlieb, Roger S. 2007. "Religious Environmentalism: What It Is, Where It's Heading and Why We Should be Going in the Same Direction." *Journal for the Study of Religion, Nature and Culture* 1:81–91.

———, ed. 2010. *Religion and the Environment*. 4 vols. London: Routledge.

Gottwald, Norman K. 1979. *The Tribes of Yahweh: A Sociology of the Religion of Liberated Israel 1250–1050 B.C.E.* Maryknoll, NY: Orbis.

———. 1986. "The Participation of Free Agrarians in the Introduction of the Monarchy to Ancient Israel: An Application of H. A. Landsberger's Analysis of Peasant Movements." *Semeia* 37:77–106.

———. 1993. *The Hebrew Bible in Its Social World and in Ours*. Semeia Studies. Atlanta: Scholars.

———. 2016. "Early Israel as an Anti-Imperial Community." In *Social Justice and the Hebrew Bible*, 2:3–19. Eugene, OR: Cascade Books.

Gould, Stephen Jay. 1989. *Wonderful Life: The Burgess Shale and the Nature of History*. New York: Norton.

———. 1997. "Nonoverlapping Magisteria." *Natural History* 106 (March):16–22.

Gowdy, John M. 2000. "Terms and Concepts of Ecological Economics." *Wildlife Society Bulletin* 28 (1):26–33.

Graedel, T. E., E. M. Harper, N. T. Nassar, and Barbara K. Reck. 2015. "On the Material Basis of Society." *Proceedings of the National Academy of Sciences* 112:6295–6300.

GreenFaith. 2018. "Christian Teachings." https://greenfaith.org/christian_teachings.

Griethuysen, Pascal van. 2010. "Why Are We Growth-Addicted? The Hard Way towards Degrowth in the Involuntary Western Development Path." *Journal of Cleaner Production* 18:590–95. doi:10.1016/j.jclepro.2009.07.006.

Grey, William. 1998. "Environmental Value and Anthropocentrism." *Ethics and the Environment* 3:97–103.

Gudorf, Christine E. 1994. *Body, Sex, and Pleasure: Reconstructing Christian Sexual Ethics*. Cleveland: Pilgrim.

Guilford, Megan C., Charles A. S. Hall, Pete O'Connor, and Cutler J. Cleveland. 2011. "A New Long Term Assessment of Energy Return on Investment (EROI) for U.S. Oil and Gas Discovery and Production." *Sustainability* 3:1866–87. doi:10.3390/su3101866.

Guillaume, Philippe. 2010a. "Nehemiah 5: No Economic Crisis." *Journal of Hebrew Scriptures* 10, art. 8. doi:10.5508/jhs.2010.v10.a8.

———. 2010b. "The Hidden Benefits of Patronage: Debt." In *Anthropology and the Bible: Critical Perspectives*, edited by Emanuel Pfoh, 107–26. Biblical Intersections 3. Piscataway, NJ: Gorgias.

———. 2012. *Land, Credit and Crisis: Agrarian Finance in the Hebrew Bible*. Bible World Sheffield: Equinox.

———. 2015. "*Peru urbu* and the Seventh Year: Complementary Strategies for the Economic Recovery of Depopulated Yehud." In *The Economy of Ancient Judah in Its Historical Context*, edited by Marvin Lloyd Miller, Ehud Ben Zvi, and Gary N. Knoppers, 123–49. Winona Lake, IN: Eisenbrauns.

Gunkel, Hermann. 2006. *Creation and Chaos in the Primeval Era and the Eschaton: A Religio-Historical Study of Genesis 1 and Revelation 12* [1895]. Translated by K. William Whitney, Jr. Grand Rapids: Eerdmans.

Guth, James L., John C. Green, Lyman A. Kellstedt, and Corwin E. Smidt. 1995. "Faith and the Environment: Religious Beliefs and Attitudes on Environmental Policy." *American Journal of Political Science* 39:364–82.

Habel, Norman C. 1995. *The Land Is Mine: Six Biblical Land Ideologies*. Overtures to Biblical Theology. Minneapolis: Fortress.

———. 2000. "Introducing the Earth Bible." In *Readings from the Perspective of Earth*, edited by Norman C. Habel, 25–37. Earth Bible 1. Sheffield: Sheffield Academic.

Haddad, Brent M. 2003. "Property Rights, Ecosystem Management, and John Locke's Labor Theory of Ownership." *Ecological Economic* 46:19–31. doi:10.1016/S0921-8009(03)00079-X.

Hall, Charles A. S., Stephen Balogh, and David J. R. Murphy. 2009. "What is the Minimum EROI that a Sustainable Society Must Have?" *Energies* 2:25–47.

Hall, Charles A. S., and Kent A. Klitgaard. 2012. *Energy and the Wealth of Nations: Understanding the Biophysical Economy*. New York: Springer.

Hall, Charles A. S., Jessica G. Lambert, Stephen B. Balogh. 2014. "EROI of Different Fuels and the Implications for Society." *Energy Policy* 64:141–52. doi:10.1016/j.enpol.2013.05.049.

Halperin, Rhoda H. 1980. "Ecology and Mode of Production: Seasonal Variation and the Division of Labor by Sex Among Hunter-Gatherers." *Journal of Anthropological Research* 36 (3):379–99.

Halpern, Baruch. 1973. *The Emergence of Israel in Canaan*. SBL Monograph Series 29. Chico, CA: Scholars.

———. 1988. *The First Historians: The Hebrew Bible and History*. San Francisco: Harper & Row.

———. 1991. "Jerusalem and the Lineages in the Seventh Century BCE: Kinship and the Rise of Individual Moral Liability." In *Law and Ideology in Monarchic Israel*, edited by Baruch Halpern and Deborah W. Hobson, 11–107. Journal for the Study of the Old Testament Supplement 124.Sheffield: Sheffield Academic.

Hamilton, Clive. 2017. *Defiant Earth: The Fate of Humans in the Anthropocene*. Cambridge: Polity.

Hamilton, Victor P. 1990. *The Book of Genesis Chapters 1–17*. Grand Rapids: Eerdmans.

Hannis, Mike. 2017. "After Development? In Defense of Sustainability." *Global Discourse* 7 (1):28–38.

Hansen, James, Larissa Nazarenko, Reto Ruedy, Makiko Sato, Josh Willis, Anthony Del Genio, Dorothy Koch, et al. 2005. "Earth's Energy Imbalance: Confirmation and Implications." *Science* 308 (5727):1431–35.

Hansen, Kenneth, Christian Breyer, and Henrik Lund. 2019. "Status and Perspectives on 100% Renewable Energy Systems." *Energy* 175:471–80. doi:10.1016/j.energy.2019.03.092.

Hardin, James Walker. 2010. *Lahav II. Households and the Use of Domestic Space at Iron II Tell Halif: An Archaeology of Destruction*. Reports of the Lahav Research Project 2. Winona Lake, IN: Eisenbrauns.

———. 2011. "Understanding Houses, Households, and the Levantine Archaeological Record." In *Household Archaeology in Ancient Israel and Beyond*, edited by Assaf Yasur-Landau, Jennie R. Ebeling, and Laura B. Mazow, 9–25. Culture and History of the Ancient Near East 50. Leiden: Brill.

Hardin, Garrett. 1968. "The Tragedy of the Commons." *Science* 162 (3859):1243–48.

Hargrove, Eugene C. 1992. "Weak Anthropocentric Intrinsic Value." *The Monist* 75:183–207.

Harland, P. J. 1998. "Vertical or Horizontal: The Sin of Babel." *Vetus Testamentum* 48:515–33.

Harlow, Daniel C. 2010. "After Adam: Reading Genesis in an Age of Evolutionary Science." *Perspectives on Science and Christian Faith* 62:179–95.

Harrelson, Walter. 1975. "Of God's Care for the Earth: Psalm 104." *Currents in Theology and Mission* 2:19–22.

Harris, Jonathan M. 1995. "Ecological Economics: A New Perspective." *The Good Society* 5 (3):18–21.

Harrison, Peter. 1999. "Subduing the Earth: Genesis 1, Early Modern Science, and the Exploitation of Nature." *Journal of Religion* 79:86–109.

Haug, Frigga. 2002. "Towards a Theory of Gender Relations." *Socialism and Democracy* 16:33–46.

———. 2005. "Gender Relations." *Historical Materialism* 13:279–302.

Hauser, Alan J. 1980. "Linguistic and Thematic Links between Genesis 4:1–16 and Genesis 2–3." *Journal of the Evangelical Theological Society* 23:297–305.

Hawken, Paul, ed. 2017. *Drawdown: The Most Comprehensive Plan Ever Proposed to Reverse Global Warming*. New York: Penguin.

Hawkins, Troy R., Bhawna Singh, Guillaume Majeau-Bettez, and Anders Hammer Strømman. 2012. "Comparative Environmental Life Cycle Assessment of Conventional and Electric Vehicles." *Journal of Industrial Ecology* 17:53–64. doi:10.1111/j.1530-9290.2012.00532.x.

Hayhoe, Katharine. 2019. "I'm a Climate Scientist Who Believes in God. Hear Me Out." *New York Times* (October 31). https://nyti.ms/2oGcALj.

Heard, B. P., B. W. Brook, T. M. L. Wigley, and C. J. A. Bradshaw. 2017. "Burden of Proof: A Comprehensive Review of the Feasibility of 100% Renewable-Electricity Systems." *Renewable and Sustainable Energy Reviews* 76:1122–33. doi:10.1016/j.rser.2017.03.114.

Heinberg, Richard, and David Fridley. 2016. *Our Renewable Future: Laying the Path for 100% Clean Energy*. Washington, DC: Island.

Hendel, Ronald S. 1998. *The Text of Genesis 1–11: Textual Studies and Critical Edition*. New York: Oxford University Press

Herman, Menahem. 1991. *Tithe as Gift: The Institution in the Pentateuch and in Light of Mauss's Prestation Theory*. Distinguished Dissertation Series. San Francisco: Mellen Research University Press.

Herr, Larry G. 1988. "Tripartite Pillared Buildings and the Market Place in Iron Age Palestine." *Bulletin of the American Schools of Oriental Research* 272:47–67.

Herzfeld, Michael. 1980. "Honour and Shame: Problems in the Comparative Analysis of Moral Systems." *Man* n.s. 15:339–51.

———. 1984. "The Horns of the Mediterranean Dilemma." *American Ethnologist* 11:439–54.

———. 1987. *Anthropology through the Looking-Glass: Critical Ethnography on the Margins of Europe*. Cambridge: Cambridge University Press.

Hickel, Jason. 2019a. "Is It Possible to Achieve a Good Life for All within Planetary Boundaries?" *Third World Quarterly* 40:18–35. doi:10.1080/01436597.2018.1535895.

———. 2019b. "The Limits of Clean Energy." *Foreign Policy* (Sept. 6). https://foreignpolicy.com/2019/09/06/the-path-to-clean-energy-will-be-very-dirty-climate-change-renewables.

Hickel, Jason, and Giorgos Kallis. 2019. "Is Green Growth Possible?" *New Political Economy* (April 17). doi:10.1080/13563467.2019.1598964.

Hiebert, Theodore. 1996. *The Yahwist's Landscape: Nature and Religion in Early Israel*. New York: Oxford University Press.

———. 2007. "The Tower of Babel and the Origin of the World's Cultures." *Journal of Biblical Literature* 126:29–58.

Hiers, Richard H. 1984. "Ecology, Biblical Theology, and Methodology: Biblical Perspectives on the Environment." *Zygon* 19:43–59.

Higgs, Kerryn. 2014. *Collision Course: Endless Growth on a Finite Planet*. Cambridge: MIT Press.

Hobbs, T. R. 1997. "Reflections on Honor, Shame, and Covenant Relations." *Journal of Biblical Literature* 116:501–3

Hoffman, Andrew J., and Lloyd E. Sandelands. 2005. "Getting Right with Nature: Anthropocentrism, Ecocentrism, and Theocentrism." *Organization and Environment* 18:141–62.

Hoffmeier, James K. 1983. "Some Thoughts on Genesis 1 and 2 and Egyptian Cosmology." *Journal of the Ancient Near Eastern Society* 15:39–49.

Hoffner, Harry A. 1966. "Symbols for Masculinity and Femininity: Their Use in Ancient Near Eastern Sympathetic Magic Rituals." *Journal of Biblical Literature* 85:326–34.

Holladay, John S., Jr. 1986. "The Stables on Ancient Israel." In *The Archaeology of Jordan and Other Studies: Presented to Siegfried H. Horn*, edited by Lawrence T. Geraty and Larry G. Herr, 103–65. Berrien Springs: Andrews University Press.

———. 1995. "The Kingdoms of Israel and Judah: Political and Economic Centralization in Iron IIA–B (ca. 1000–750 BCE)." In *The Archaeology of Society in the Holy Land*, edited by Thomas E. Levy, 368–98. New York: Facts on File.

———. 2006. "Hezekiah's Tribute, Long-Distance Trade, and the Wealth of Nations ca. 1000–600 BC: A New Perspective." In *Confronting the Past: Archaeological and Historical Essays on Ancient Israel in Honor of William G. Dever*, edited by Seymour Gitin, J. Edward Wright, and J. P. Dessel, 309–31. Winona Lake, IN: Eisenbrauns.

Holleman, Hannah. 2018. *Dust Bowls of Empire: Imperialism, Environmental Politics, and the Injustice of "Green" Capitalism*. Yale Agrarian Studies Series. New Haven: Yale University Press.

Hood-Williams, John. 1996. "Goodbye to Sex and Gender." *Sociological Review* 44:1–16.

Hopkins, David C. 1985. *The Highlands of Canaan: Agricultural Life in the Early Iron Age*. Social World of Biblical Antiquity 3. Sheffield: Almond.

———. 1987. "Life on the Land: The Subsistence Struggles of Early Israel." *Biblical Archaeologist* 50:78–91.

———. 1996. "Putting Flesh on the Economics of Ancient Israel." In *The Origins of the Ancient Israelite States*, edited by Volkmar Fritz and Philip R. Davies, 121–39. Journal for the Study of the Old Testament Supplement 228. Sheffield: Sheffield Academic.

Horden, Peregrine, and Nicholas Purcell. 2000. *The Corrupting Sea: A Study of Mediterranean History*. Malden: Blackwell.

Hornung, Erik. 1982. *Conceptions of God in Ancient Egypt: The One and the Many*. Translated by J. Baines. Ithaca: Cornell University Press.

Horrell, David G. 2010. *The Bible and the Environment: Towards a Critical Ecological Biblical Theology*. Biblical Challenges in the Contemporary World. London: Equinox.

Horrigan, Leo, Robert S. Lawrence, and Polly Walker. 2002. "How Sustainable Agriculture Can Address the Environmental and Human Health Harms of Industrial Agriculture." *Environmental Health Perspectives* 110:445–56.

House, Kurt Zenz. 2009. "The Limits of Energy Storage Technology." *Bulletin of the Atomic Scientists* (Jan. 20). https://thebulletin.org/2009/01/the-limits-of-energy-storage-technology.

Houston, Walter J. 1993. *Purity and Monotheism: Clean and Unclean Animals in Biblical Law*. Journal for the Study of the Old Testament Supplements 140. Sheffield: Sheffield Academic.

———. 2006. *Contending for Justice: Ideologies and Theologies of Social Justice in the Old Testament*. Library of Hebrew Bible/Old Testament Studies 428. London: T. & T. Clark.

Hueting, Roefie. 2010. "Why Environmental Sustainability Can Most Probably not Be Attained with Growing Production." *Journal of Cleaner Production* 18:525–30. doi:10.1016/j.jclepro.2009.04.003.

Huffstutter, P. J. 2020. "U.S. Farm Bankruptcies Hit an Eight Year High: Court Data." *Reuters* (January 30). https://www.reuters.com/article/us-usa-farms-bankruptcy/us-farm-bankruptcies-hit-an-eight-year-high-court-data-idUSKBN1ZT2YE.

Hughes, J. Donald. 1975. *Ecology in Ancient Civilizations*. Albuquerque: University of New Mexico Press.

———. 2009. *An Environmental History of the World: Humankind's Changing Role in the Community of Life*. 2nd ed. London: Routledge.

Hunt, Robert C. 1991. "The Role of Bureaucracy in the Provisioning of Cities: A Framework for Analysis of the Ancient Near East." In *The Organization of Power: Aspects of Bureaucracy in the Ancient Near East*, edited by McGuire Gibson and Robert D. Biggs, 141–68. Studies in Ancient Oriental Civilization 46. Chicago: Oriental Institute.

IAASTD (International Assessment of Agricultural Knowledge, Science and Technology for Development). 2016. *Agriculture at the Crossroads: IAASTD Findings and Recommendations for Future Farming*, edited by Angelika Beck, Benedict Haerlin, and Lea Richter. Berlin: Foundation for Future Farming.

Ibn Ezra, Abraham ben Meir. 1988. *Ibn Ezra's Commentary on the Pentateuch*. Vol. 1, *Genesis (Bereshit)*. Translated and annotated by H. N. Strickman and A. M. Silver. New York: Menorah.

IMF (International Monetary Fund). 2019. *Fiscal Monitor* (October): *How to Mitigate Climate Change*. Washington, DC: International Monetary Fund.

IPBES (Intergovernmental Science-Policy Platform on Biodiversity and Ecosystem Services). 2018. "Media Release: Worsening Worldwide Land Degradation Now 'Critical,' Undermining Well-Being of 3.2 Billion People" (Mar. 23). https://ipbes.net/news/media-release-worsening-worldwide-land-degradation-now-'critical'-undermining-well-being-32.

IPCC (Intergovernmental Panel on Climate Change). 2014. *Climate Change 2014: Synthesis Report. Contribution of Working Groups I, II and III to the Fifth Assessment Report of the Intergovernmental Panel on Climate Change*, edited by Core Writing Team, R. K. Pachauri, and L. A. Meyer. Geneva: IPCC. http://ar5-syr.ipcc.ch.

———. 2018. *Global Warming of 1.5°C: An IPCC Special Report on the Impacts of Global Warming of 1.5°C above Pre-industrial Levels and Related Global Greenhouse Gas emission Pathways, in the Context of Strengthening the Global Response to the Threat of Climate Change, Sustainable Development, and Efforts to Eradicate Poverty*. Edited by V. Masson-Delmotte, P. Zhai, H.-O. Pörtner, D. Roberts, J. Skea, P. R. Shukla, A. Pirani, et al. Geneva: World Meteorological Organization. https://www.ipcc.ch/sr15.

———. 2020. *Climate Change and Land: An IPCC Special Report on Climate Change, Desertification, Land Degradation, Sustainable Land Management, Food Security, and Greenhouse Gas Fluxes in Terrestrial Ecosystems: Summary for Policy Makers*. Edited by V. Masson-Delmotte, P. Zhai, H.-O. Pörtner, D. Roberts, J. Skea, P. R. Shukla, E. C. Buendia, et al. Geneva: IPCC. https://www.ipcc.ch/srccl.

Irving, Peter J., Ben Kravitz, Mark G. Lawrence, and Helene Muri. 2016. "An Overview of the Earth System Science of Solar Geoengineering." *WIREs Climate Change* 7:815–33. doi:10.1002/wcc.423.

Jackson, Tim. 2009. *Prosperity without Growth: Economics for a Finite Planet*. London: Earthscan.

Jackson, Wes. 1980. *New Roots for Agriculture*. Reprint, Lincoln: University of Nebraska Press, 1985.

Jacobsen, Thorkild. 1970. *Toward the Image of Tammuz and Other Essays on Mesopotamian History and Culture*. Edited by William L. Moran. Cambridge: Harvard University Press.

———. 1976. *The Treasures of Darkness: A History of Mesopotamian Religion*. New Haven: Yale University Press.

———. 1984. *The Harab Myth*. Sources from the Ancient Near East 2/3. Malibu, CA: Undena.

———. 1987. *The Harps that Once . . . : Sumerian Poetry in Translation*. New Haven: Yale University Press.

Jacobson, Mark Z., and Mark A. Delucchi. 2011. "Providing All Global Energy with Wind, Water, and Solar Power, Part I: Technologies, Energy Resources, Quantities and Areas of Infrastructure, and Materials." *Energy Policy* 39:1154–69. doi:10.1016/j.enpol.2010.11.040.

Jacobson, Mark A., Mark A. Delucchi, Guillaume Bazouin, Zack A. F. Bauer, Christa C. Heavey, Emma Fisher, Sean B. Morris, et al. 2015. "100% Clean and Renewable Wind, Water, and Sunlight (WWS) All-Sector Energy Roadmaps for the 50 United States." *Energy and Environmental Science* 8:2093–2117. doi:10.1039/c5ee01283j.

Jacobson, Mark A., Mark A. Delucchi, Mary A. Cameron, and Bethany A. Frew. 2015. "Low-cost Solution to the Grid Reliability Problem with 100% Penetration of Intermittent Wind, Water, and Solar for All Purposes." *Proceedings of the National Academy of Sciences* 112 (49):15060–65. doi:10.1073/pnas.1510028112.

Jameson, Fredric. 2003. "Future City." *New Left Review* 21 (May–June):65–79.

Jamieson, Dale. 2006. "An American Paradox." *Climate Change* 77:97–102.

Jamieson-Drake, David W. 1991. *Scribes and Schools in Monarchic Judah: A Socio-Archaeological Approach*. Journal for the Study of the Old Testament Supplements 109. Sheffield: Almond.

Jenson, Philip Peter. 1992. *Graded Holiness: A Key to the Priestly Conception of the World*. Journal for the Study of the Old Testament Supplements 106. Sheffield: Sheffield Academic.

Jenkins, Willis. 2009. "After Lynn White: Religious Ethics and Environmental Problems." *Journal of Religious Ethics* 37:283–309.

———. 2013. *The Future of Ethics: Sustainability, Social Justice, and Religious Creativity*. Washington, DC: Georgetown University Press.

Jenkins, Willis, and Christopher Key Chapple. 2011. "Religion and Environment." *Annual Review of Environment and Resources* 36:441–63.

John Paul II, Pope. 1997. "Message to the Pontifical Academy of Sciences: On Evolution." *The Quarterly Review of Biology* 72:381–83.

Johnson, Mark. 1987. *The Body in the Mind: The Bodily Basis of Meaning, Imagination, and Reason*. Chicago: University of Chicago Press.

Johnson, Nancy Collins, Catherine Gehring, and Jan Jansa, eds. 2017. *Mycorrhizal Mediation of Soil: Fertility, Structure, and Carbon Storage*. Amsterdam: Elsevier.

Joyce, Paul. 1989. *Divine Initiative and Human Response in Ezekiel*. Journal for the Study of the Old Testament Supplements 51. Sheffield: Sheffield Academic.

Kallis, Giorgos. 2018. *Degrowth*. Newcastle, UK: Agenda.

Kalmanofsky, Amy. 2017. *Gender-Play in the Hebrew Bible: The Ways the Bible Challenges Its Gender Norms*. Routledge Interdisciplinary Perspectives on Biblical Criticism 2. London: Routledge.

Kaminsky, Joel S. 1995. *Corporate Responsibility in the Hebrew Bible*. Journal for the Study of the Old Testament Supplements 96. Sheffield: Sheffield Academic.

Kamionkowski, S. Tamar. 2003. *Gender Reversal and Cosmic Chaos: A Study on the Book of Ezekiel*. Journal for the Study of the Old Testament Supplement 368. Sheffield: Sheffield Academic.

Kaufman, Gordon D. 1971. "What Shall We Do with the Bible?" *Interpretation* 25:95–112.

Kay, Jeanne. 1988. "Concepts of Nature in the Hebrew Bible." *Environmental Ethics* 10:309–27.

———. 1989. "Human Dominion over Nature in the Hebrew Bible." *Annals of the Association of American Geographers* 79:214–32.

Kearney, Michael. 1984. *World View*. Novato: Chandler & Sharp.

Keefe, Alice A. 1995. "The Female Body, the Body Politic and the Land: A Sociopolitical Reading of Hosea 1–2." In *A Feminist Companion to the Latter Prophets*, edited by Athalya Brenner, 70–100. Feminist Companion to the Bible 8. Sheffield: Sheffield Academic.

Keith, David W. 2000. "Geoengineering the Climate: History and Prospect." *Annual Review of Energy and Environment* 25:245–84.

———. 2013. *The Case for Climate Engineering*. Cambridge: Massachusetts Institute of Technology Press.

Keith, David W., Geoffrey Holmes, David St. Angelo, and Kenton Heidel. 2018. "A Process for Capturing CO_2 from the Atmosphere." *Joule* 2:1573–94. doi:10.1016/j.joule.2018.05.006.

Keith, David W., and Douglas G. MacMartin. 2015. "A Temporary, Moderate and Responsive Scenario for Solar Geoengineering." *Nature Climate Change* 5 (February 16):201–6. doi:10.1038/nclimate2493.

Keller, David, ed. 2010. *Environmental Ethics: The Big Questions*. Chichester, UK: Wiley-Blackwell.

Kelly, Ronna, Susan Burns, and Mathis Wackernagel. 2015. "State of the States: A New Perspective on the Wealth of Our Nation." Global Footprint Network (July 15). https://www.footprintnetwork.org.

Kennedy, Christopher A., Iain Stewart, Angelo Facchini, Igor Cersosimo, Renata Mele, Bin Chen, Mariko Uda, et al. 2015. "Energy and Material Flows of Megacities." *Proceedings of the National Academy of Sciences* 112 (19):5985–90.

Kennedy, James M. 1990. "Peasants in Revolt: Political Allegory in Genesis 2–3." *Journal for the Study of the Old Testament* 47:3–14.

King, Philip J., and Lawrence E. Stager. 2001. *Life in Biblical Israel*. Library of Ancient Israel. Louisville: Westminster John Knox.

Klein, Naomi. 2014. *This Changes Everything: Capitalism vs. The Climate*. New York: Simon & Schuster.

Kluckhohn, Florence R., and Fred L. Strodtbeck. 1973. *Variations in Value Orientations*. reprint of 1961 edition. Evanston, IL: Row, Peterson.

Knight, Douglas A. 1985. "Cosmogony and Order in the Hebrew Tradition." In *Cosmogony and Ethical Order: New Studies in Comparative Ethics*, edited by Robin W. Lovin and Frank E. Reynolds, 133–57. Chicago: University of Chicago Press.

Knobnya, Svetlana. 2011. "God the Father in the Old Testament." *European Journal of Theology* 20:139–48.

Knohl, Israel. 1995. *The Sanctuary of Silence: The Priestly Torah and the Holiness School*. Minneapolis: Fortress.

Knoppers, Gary N. 1996. "The Deuteronomist and the Deuteronomic Law of the King: A Reexamination of a Relationship." *Zeitschrift für die alttestamentliche Wissenschaft* 108:329–46.

———. 2001a. "An Achaemenid Imperial Authorization of Torah in Yehud?" In *Persia and Torah: The Theory of Imperial Authorization of the Pentateuch*, edited by James W. Watts, 115–34. SBL Symposium Series 17. Atlanta: Society of Biblical Literature.

———. 2001b. "Rethinking the Relationship between Deuteronomy and the Deuteronomistic History: The Case of Kings." *Catholic Biblical Quarterly* 63:393–415.

———. 2015. "More Than Friends? The Economic Relationship between Huram and Solomon Reconsidered." In *The Economy of Ancient Judah in Its Historical Context*, edited by Marvin Lloyd Miller, Ehud Ben Zvi, and Gary N. Knoppers, 51–76. Winona Lake, IN: Eisenbrauns.

Koch, Klaus. 1983. "Is There a Doctrine of Retribution in the Old Testament?" In *Theodicy in the Old Testament*, edited by James L. Crenshaw, 57–87. Issues in Religion and Theology 4. Philadelphia: Fortress.

Kolbert, Elizabeth. 2014. *The Sixth Extinction: An Unnatural History*. New York: Holt.

Kopnina, Helen. 2012. "The Lorax Complex: Deep Ecology, Ecocentrism and Exclusion." *Journal of Integrative Environmental Sciences* 9:235–54.

Kopnina, Helen, Haydn Washington, Bron Taylor, and John J. Piccolo. 2018. "Anthropocentrism: More than Just a Misunderstood Problem." *Journal of Agricultural and Environmental Ethics* 31:109–27. doi:10.1007/s10806-018-9711-1.

Kramer, Samuel Noah. 1968. "The 'Babel of Tongues': A Sumerian Version." *Journal of the American Oriental Society* 88:108–11.

Kravitz, Ben, Ken Caldeira, Olivier Boucher, Alan Robock, Philip J. Rasch, Kari Alterskjaer, Diana Bou Karam, et al. 2013. "Climate Model Response from the Geoengineering Model Intercomparison Project (GeoMIP)." *Journal of Geophysical Research: Atmospheres* 118:8320–32.

Kubiszewski, Ida, Cutler J. Cleveland, and Peter K. Endres. 2010. "Meta-Analysis of Net Energy Return for Wind Power Systems." *Renewable Energy* 35:218–25. doi:10.1016/j.renene.2009.01.012.

Kugel, James L. 2007. *How to Read the Bible: A Guide to Scripture, Then and Now*. New York: Free Press.

Kuhrt, Amélie. 1998. "The Old Assyrian Merchants." In *Trade, Traders and the Ancient City*, edited by Helen Parkins and Christopher Smith, 16–30. London: Routledge.

Kurka, Robert C. 2013. "If Adam Be *Razed* Is Our Faith in Vain?" *Criswell Theological Review* 10:83–112.

Lacocque, André. 2009. "Whatever Happened in the Valley of Shinar? A Response to Theodore Hiebert." *Journal of Biblical Literature* 128:29–41.

Lakoff, George. 1987. *Women, Fire, and Dangerous Things: What Categories Reveal about the Mind*. Chicago: University of Chicago Press.

Lakoff, George, and Mark Johnson. 1980. *Metaphors We Live By*. Chicago: University of Chicago Press.

Lambert, W. G. 2013. *Babylonian Creation Myths*. Mesopotamian Civilizations 16. Winona Lake, IN: Eisenbrauns.

Lambert, W. G., and A. R. Millard. 1999. *Atra-hasis: The Babylonian Story of the Flood*. Winona Lake, IN: Eisenbrauns.

Lamoureux, Denis O. 2013. In *Four Views on the Historical Adam*, edited by Matthew Barrett and Ardel B. Caneday, 37–65. Grand Rapids: Zondervan.

Langgut, D., and Oded Lipschits. 2017. "Dry Climate during the Early Persian Period and Its Impact on the Establishment of Idumea." *Transeuphratène* 49:135–62. doi:10.2143/TE.49.0.3248524.

Lanser, Susan S. 1988. "(Feminist) Criticism in the Garden: Inferring Genesis 2–3." *Semeia* 41:67–84.

Latour, Bruno. 2004. "Why Has Critique Run out of Steam? From Matters of Fact to Matters of Concern." *Critical Inquiry* 30:225–48.

———. 2017. *Facing Gaia: Eight Lectures on the New Climate Regime*. Malden, MA: Polity.

LeCain, Timothy James. 2015. "Against the Anthropocene: A Neo-Materialist Perspective." *International Journal for History, Culture and Modernity* 3:1–28.

———. 2016. "Heralding a New Humanism: The Radical Implications of Chakrabarty's 'Four Theses.'" In "Whose Anthropocene? Revisiting Dipesh Chakrabarty's 'Four Theses,'" edited by Robert Emmett and Thomas Lekan. *RCC Perspectives: Transformations in Environment and Society* 2016/2:15–20. d El Chichón and Pinatobo doi:10.5282/rcc/7421.

Lee, Richard B. 1968. "What Hunters Do for a Living, or, How to Make Out on Scarce Resources." In *Man the Hunter*, edited by Richard B. Lee and Irven DeVore, 30–48. Chicago: Aldine.

Legaspi, Michael C. 2010. *The Death of Scripture and the Rise of Biblical Studies*. New York: Oxford University Press.

Leick, Gwendolyn. 1994. *Sex and Eroticism in Mesopotamian Literature*. London: Routledge.

Lemaire, André. 1994. "'House of David': Restored in Moabite Inscription." *Biblical Archaeology Review* 20 (3):30–37.

Lemche, Niels Peter. 1985. *Early Israel: Anthropological and Historical Studies on the Israelite Society before the Monarchy*. Vetus Testamentum Supplements 37. Leiden: Brill.

———. 1995a. "Justice in Western Asia in Antiquity, or: Why no Laws Were Needed!" *Chicago-Kent Law Review* 70:1695–716.

———. 1995b. "Kings and Clients: On Loyalty between the Ruler and the Ruled in Ancient 'Israel.'" *Semeia* 66:119–32.

———. 1996. "From Patronage Society to Patronage Society." In *The Origins of the Ancient Israelite States*, edited by Volkmar Fritz and Philip R. Davies, 106–20. Journal for the Study of the Old Testament Supplements 228. Sheffield: Sheffield Academic.

Lemos, T. M. 2010. *Marriage Gifts and Social Change in Ancient Palestine: 1200 BCE to 200 BCE*. Cambridge: Cambridge University Press.

———. 2011. "'Like the Eunuch Who Does Not Beget': Gender, Mutilation, and Negotiated Status in the Ancient Near East." In *Disability Studies and Biblical Literature*, edited by Candida R. Moss and Jeremy Schipper, 47–66. New York: Palgrave Macmillan.

———. 2017. *Violence and Personhood in Ancient Israel and Comparative Contexts*. Oxford: Oxford University Press.

Lenton, Timothy M., Herman Held, Elmar Kriegler, Jim W. Hall, Wolfgang Lucht, Stefan Rahmstorf, and Hans Joachim Schellnhuber. 2008. "Tipping Elements in the Earth's Climate System." *Proceedings of the National Academy of Sciences* 105:1786–93.

Lenton, Timothy M., Johan Rockström, Owen Gaffney, Stefan Rahmstorf, Katherine Richardson, Will Steffen, and Hans Joachim Schellnhuber. 2019. "Climate Tipping Points: Too Risky to Bet Against." *Nature* (Nov. 27). doi:10.1038/d41586-019-03595-0.

Léons, Madeline Barbara, and Frances Rothstein, eds. 1979. *New Directions in Political Economy: An Approach from Anthropology*. Contributions in Economics and Economic History 22. Westport: Greenwood.

Lesko, Leonard H. 1991. "Ancient Egyptian Cosmogonies and Cosmology." In *Religion in Ancient Egypt: Gods, Myths, and Personal Practice*, edited by Byron E. Shafer, 88–122. Ithaca, NY: Cornell University Press.

Levenson, Jon D. 1985. *Sinai & Zion: An Entry into the Jewish Bible*. San Francisco: Harper & Row.

———. 1988. *Creation and the Persistence of Evil: The Jewish Drama of Divine Omnipotence*. San Francisco: Harper & Row.

Levine, Baruch A. 1996. "Farewell to the Ancient Near East: Evaluating Biblical References to Ownership of Land in Comparative Perspective." In *Privatization in the Ancient Near East and Classical World*, edited by Michael Hudson and Baruch Levine, 223–52. Peabody Museum Bulletin 5. Cambridge: Peabody Museum of Archaeology and Ethnology, Harvard University.

———. 2002. "'Seed' versus 'Womb': Expressions of Male Dominance in Biblical Israel." In *Sex and Gender in the Ancient Near East: Proceeding of the 47th Rencontre Assyriologique Internationale, Helsinki, July 2–6, 2001*, edited by S. Parpola and R. M. Whiting, 337–43. Helsinki: Neo-Assyrian Text Corpus Project.

Levinson, Bernard M. 1997. *Deuteronomy and the Hermeneutics of Legal Innovation*. New York: Oxford University Press.

———. 2001. "The Reconceptualization of Kingship in Deuteronomy and the Deuteronomic History's Transformation of Torah." *Vetus Testamentum* 51:511–34.

Lewis, Theodore J. 1989. *Cults of the Dead in Ancient Israel and Ugarit*. Harvard Semitic Monographs 39. Atlanta: Scholars.

Lichtheim, Miriam. 1973. *Ancient Egyptian Literature*. Vol. 1, *The Old and Middle Kingdoms*. Berkeley: University of California Press.

———. 1976. *Ancient Egyptian Literature*. Vol. 2, *The New Kingdom*. Berkeley: University of California Press.

———. 1980. *Ancient Egyptian Literature*. Vol. 3, *The Late Period*. Berkeley: University of California Press.

Limburg, James. 1994. "Down-To-Earth Theology: Psalm 104 and the Environment." *Currents in Theology and Mission* 21:340–46.

Lipschits, Oded. 2012. "Archaeological Facts, Historical Speculations and the Date of the LMLK Storage Jars: A Rejoinder to David Ussishkin." *Journal of Hebrew Scriptures* 12, art. 4. doi:10.5508/jhs.2012.v12.a4.

Lipschits, Oded, and Joseph Blenkinsopp, eds. 2003. *Judah and the Judeans in the Neo-Babylonian Period*. Winona Lake, IN: Eisenbrauns.

Little, Amanda. 2019. *The Fate of Food: What We'll Eat in a Bigger, Hotter, Smarter World*. New York: Harmony.

Liverani, Mario. 1979. "Pharaoh's Letters to Rib-Adda." In *Three Amarna Essays*, 3–13. Monographs on the Ancient Near East 1, 5. Malibu: Undena.

———. 1983. "Political Lexicon and Political Ideologies in the Amarna Letters." *Berytus* 31:41–56.

———. 1984. "Land Tenure and Inheritance in the Ancient Near East: The Interaction between 'Palace' and 'Family' Sectors." In *Land Tenure and Social Transformation in the Middle East*, edited by T. Khalidi, 33–44. Beirut: American University of Beirut.

———. 1990. *Prestige and Interest: International Relations in the Near East ca. 1600–1100 B.C.* History of the Ancient Near East / Studies 1. Padova: Sargon.

———. 1998. *Uruk: The First City*. Bible World. London: Equinox.

Locke, John. 2017 [1689]. *Second Treatise of Government*, prepared and edited by Jonathan Bennett. https://www.earlymoderntexts.com/assets/pdfs/locke1689a.pdf.

Loftus, Peter J., Armond M. Cohen, Jane C. S. Long, and Jesse D. Jenkins. 2015. "A Critical Review of Global Decarbonization Scenarios: What Do They Tell Us about Feasibility?" *WIREs Climate Change* 6:93–112. doi:10.1002/wcc.324.

Lohfink, Norbert, SJ. 1991. "Poverty in the Laws of the Ancient Near East and of the Bible." *Theological Studies* 52:34–50.

Lohr, Joel N. 2011. "Sexual Desire? Eve, Genesis 3:16, and *teshuqah*." *Journal of Biblical Literature* 130:227–46.

Longo, Stefano B., Rebecca Clausen, and Brett Clark. 2015. *The Tragedy of the Commodity: Oceans, Fisheries, and Aquaculture*. Nature, Society, and Culture. New Brunswick, NJ: Rutgers University Press.

Lovejoy, C. Owen. 2009. "Reexamining Human Origins in Light of *Ardipithecus ramidus*." *Science* 326 (5949):74–74e8. doi:10.1126/science.1175834.

Lukacs, Martin. 2012. "World's Biggest Geoengineering Experiment 'Violates" UN Rules." *The Guardian* (October 15). https://www.theguardian.com/environment/2012/oct/15/pacific-iron-fertilisation-geoengineering.

Machmuller, Megan B., Marc G. Kramer, Taylor K. Cyle, Nick Hill, Dennis Hancock, and Aaron Thompson. 2015. "Emerging Land Use Practices Rapidly Increase Soil Organic Matter." *Nature Communications* 6 (6995). doi:10.1038/ncomms7995.

Macintosh, A. A. 2016. "The Meaning of Hebrew *teshuqah*." *Journal of Semitic Studies* 61:365–87.

MacMartin, Douglas G., Ben Kravitz, Jane C. S. Long, and Philip J. Rasch. 2016. "Geoengineering with Stratospheric Eerosols: What Do We not Know after a Decade of Research?" *Earth's Future* 4:543–48. doi:10.1002/2016EF000418.

Maeir, Aren M., and Itzhaq Shai. 2016. "Reassessing the Character of the Judahite Kingdom: Archaeological Evidence for Non-Centralized, Kinship-Based Components." In *From Sha'ar Hagolan to Shaaraim: Essays in Honor of Prof. Yosef Garfinkel*, edited by

Saar Ganor, Igor Kreimerman, Katharina Streit, and Madeleine Mumcuoglu, 323–40. Jerusalem: Israel Exploration Society.

Magdoff, Fred. 2013. "Global Resource Depletion: Is Population the Problem?" *Monthly Review* 64 (8):13–28.

Malina, Bruce J. 2001. *The New Testament World: Insights from Cultural Anthropology*. 3rd ed. Louisville: Westminster John Knox.

Malm, Andreas. 2016. *Fossil Capital: The Rise of Steam Power and the Roots of Global Warming*. London: Verso.

———. 2018. *The Progress of the Storm: Nature and Society in a Warming World*. London: Verso.

———. 2019. "Against Hybridism: Why We Need to Distinguish between Nature and Society, Now More than Ever." *Historical Materialism* 27:156–87.

Malm, Andreas, and Alf Hornborg. 2014. "The Geology of Mankind? A Critique of the Anthropocene Narrative." *The Anthropocene Review* 1:62–69.

Manning, J. G. 2018. *The Open Sea: The Economic Life of the Ancient Mediterranean World from the Iron Age to the Rise of Rome*. Princeton: Princeton University Press.

Marks, Robbin. 2001. *Cesspools of Shame: How Factory Farm Lagoons and Sprayfields Threaten Environmental and Public Health*. New York: Natural Resources Defense Council and the Clean Water Network.

Marshall, Jay W. 1993. *Israel and the Book of the Covenant: An Anthropological Approach to Biblical Law*. Society of Biblical Literature Dissertation Series 140. Atlanta: Scholars.

Martinez-Alier, Joan. 2011. "The EROI of Agriculture and Its Use by the Via Campesina." *Journal of Peasant Studies* 38:145–60.

Martinich, Jeremy, and Allison Crimmins. 2019. "Climate Damages and Adaptation Potential across Diverse Sectors of the United States." *Nature Climate Change* 9:397–404. doi: 10.1038/s41558-019-0444-6.

Marx, Karl. 1973 [1939]. *Grundrisse: Foundations of the Critique of Political Economy*. Translated by Martin Nicolaus. The Marx Library. New York: Vintage.

———. 1975. *Economic and Philosophical Manuscripts of 1844*. Translated by Martin Milligan and Dirk J. Struik, 229–346. Vol. 3 of *Karl Marx, Fredrick Engles, Collected Works*. New York: International.

———. 1992 [1894]. *Capital: A Critique of Political Economy*. Vol. 3. Translated by David Fernbach. London: Penguin.

———. 2004 [1867]. *Capital: A Critique of Political Economy*. Vol. 1. Translated by Ben Fowkes. London: Penguin.

Master, Daniel M. 2001. "State Formation Theory and the Kingdom of Ancient Israel." *Journal of Near Eastern Studies* 60:117–31.

———. 2003. "Trade and Politics: Ashkelon's Balancing Act in the Seventh Century B.C.E." *Bulletin of the American Schools of Oriental Research* 330:47–64.

———. 2014. "Economy and Exchange in the Iron Age Kingdoms of the Southern Levant." *Bulletin of the American Schools of Oriental Research* 372:81–97.

Matthews, Victor H. 1998. "Honor and Shame in Gender-Related Situations in the Hebrew Bible." In *Gender and Law in the Hebrew Bible and the Ancient Near East*, edited by Victor H. Matthews, Bernard M. Levinson, and Tikva Frymer-Kensky, 97–112. Journal for the Study of the Old Testament Supplements 262. Sheffield: Sheffield Academic.

Matthews, Victor H., and Don C. Benjamin, eds. 1996. *Honor and Shame in the World of the Bible*. Semeia 68. Atlanta: Scholars.

Mays, James Luther. 2006. "The Self in the Psalms and the Image of God." In *God and Human Dignity*, edited by R. Kendall Soulen and Linda Woodhead, 27–43. Grand Rapids: Eerdmans.

Mazar, Amihai. 1990. *Archaeology of the Land of the Bible: 10,000–586 B.C.E.* New York: Doubleday.

McCaffrey, Kathleen. 2002. "Reconsidering Gender Ambiguity in Mesopotamia: Is a Beard Just a Beard?" In *Sex and Gender in the Ancient Near East: Proceeding of the 47th Rencontre Assyriologique Internationale, Helsinki, July 2–6, 2001*, edited by S. Parpola and R. M. Whiting, 379–91. Helsinki: Neo-Assyrian Text Corpus Project.

McCalla, Arthur. 2006. *The Creationist Debate: The Encounter between the Bible and the Historical Mind*. London: T. & T. Clark.

McCarthy, Dennis J., SJ. 1965. "Notes on the Love of God in Deuteronomy and the Father-Son Relationship between Yahweh and Israel." *Catholic Biblical Quarterly* 27:144–47.

———. 1967. "'Creation' Motifs in Ancient Hebrew Poetry." *Catholic Biblical Quarterly* 29:87–100.

———. 1978. *Treaty and Covenant: A Study in Form in the Ancient Oriental Documents and in the Old Testament*. 2nd ed. Analecta Biblica 21. Rome: Pontifical Biblical Institute.

McDaniel, Jay. 2009. "The Manyness of God: A Tribute to James Nash." *Journal for the Study of Religion, Nature and Culture* 3:290–94.

McKay, David J. C. 2013. "Solar Energy in the Context of Energy Use, Energy Transportation and Energy Storage." *Philosophical Transactions of the Royal Society A* 371:20110431. doi:10.1098/rsta.2011.0431.

McKibben, Bill. 1989. *The End of Nature*. New York: Random House.

Medved, Goran. 2016. "The Fatherhood of God in the Old Testament." *KAIROS—Evangelical Journal of Theology* 10 (2):203–14.

Melgar-Melgar, Rigo E., and Charles A. S. Hall. 2019. "Why Ecological Economics Needs to Return to Its Roots: The Biophysical Foundation of Socio-economic Systems." *Ecological Economics* 169:106567. doi:10.1016/j.ecolecon.2019.106567.

Merchant, Carolyn. 1980. *The Death of Nature: Women, Ecology and the Scientific Revolution*. New York: Harper & Row.

———. 2006. "The Scientific Revolution and *The Death of Nature*." *Isis* 97:513–33.

Meyer, Esias E. 2010. "Dating the Priestly Text in the Pre-Exilic Period: Some Remarks about Anachronistic Slips and Other Obstacles." *Verbum et Ecclesia* 31, 1, art. #423. doi:10.4102/ve.v31i1.423.

Meyers, Carol. 1988. *Discovering Eve: Ancient Israelite Women in Context*. New York: Oxford University Press.

———. 2006. "Hierarchy or Heterarchy? Archaeology and the Theorizing of Israelite Society." In *Confronting the Past: Archaeological and Historical Essays on Ancient Israel in Honor of William G. Dever*, edited by S. Gitin, J. E. Wright, and J. P. Dessel, 245–54. Winona Lake, IN: Eisenbrauns.

———. 2007. "From Field Crop to Food: Attributing Gender and Meaning to Bread Production in Iron Age Israel." In *The Archaeology of Difference: Gender, Ethnicity, Class and the "Other" in Antiquity; Studies in Honor of Eric M. Meyers*, edited by Douglas R. Edwards and C. Thomas McCollough, 67–84. Boston: American Schools of Oriental Research.

———. 2012. "Food and the First Family: A Socioeconomic Perspective." In *The Book of Genesis: Composition, Reception, and Interpretation*, edited by Craig A. Evans, Joel N. Lohr, and David L Petersen, 137–57. Vetus Testamentum Supplements 152. Leiden: Brill.

Midgley, Mary. 1994. "The End of Anthropocentrism?" In *Philosophy and the Natural Environment*, edited by Robin Attfield and Andrew Belsey, 103–12. Royal Institute of Philosophy Supplement 36. Cambridge: Cambridge University Press.

Mies, Maria, and Veronika Bennholdt-Thomsen. 1999. *The Subsistence Perspective: Beyond the Globalized Economy*. London: Zed.

Mikayilov, Jeyhun, Fakhri J. Hasanov, and Marzio Galeotti. 2018. "Decoupling of CO_2 Emissions and GDP: A Time-Varying Cointegration Approach." *Ecological Indicators* 95:615–28. doi:10.1016/j.ecolind.2018.07.051.

Milgrom, Jacob. 2000. *Leviticus 17–22*. Anchor Bible 3A. New York: Doubleday.

Miller, L. M., F. Gans, and A. Kleidon. 2011. "Estimating Maximum Global Land Surface Wind Power Extractability and Associated Climatic Consequences." *Earth System Dynamics* 2:1–12. doi:10.5194/esd-2-1-2011.

Miller, Marvin Lloyd. 2010. "Nehemiah 5: A Response to Philippe Guillaume." *Journal of Hebrew Scriptures* 10, art. 13. doi:10.5508/jhs.2010.v10.a13.

Miller, Patrick D. 2000. *The Religion of Ancient Israel*. Library of Ancient Israel. Louisville: Westminster John Knox.

Miller, Robert D. 2015. "God and the Asiatic Mode of Production." In *The Highest Form of Wisdom: A Memorial Book in Honor of Professor Saul S. Friedman (1937–2013)*, edited by Jonathan C. Friedman and Robert D. Miller II, 1–16. New York: Ktav.

Minteer, Ben A., and Robert E. Manning. 2005. "An Appraisal of the Critique of Anthropocentrism and Three Lesser Known Themes in Lynn White's 'The Historical Roots of Our Ecologic Crisis.'" *Organization and Environment* 15:163–76.

Mitloehner, Frank M. 2018. "Yes, Eating Meat Affects the Environment, but Cows Are not Killing the Climate." *The Conversation* (Oct. 25). https://theconversation.com/yes-eating-meat-affects-the-environment-but-cows-are-not-killing-the-climate-94968.

Mizzoni, John. 2008. "Franciscan Biocentrism and the Franciscan Tradition." *Ethics and the Environment* 13:121–34.

Monberg, Torben. 1975. "Fathers Were not Genitors." *Man* 10:34–40.

Montgomery, David R. 2017. *Growing a Revolution: Bringing Our Soil Back to Life*. New York: Norton.

Moore, Henrietta L. 1988. *Feminism and Anthropology*. Minneapolis: University of Minnesota Press.

Mora, Camilo, Daniele Spirandelli, Erik C. Franklin, John Lynham, Michael B. Kantar, Wendy Miles, Charlotte Z. Smith, et al. 2018. "Broad Threat to Humanity from Cumulative Climate Hazards Intensified by Greenhouse Gas Emissions." *Nature Climate Change* 8:1062–71. doi:10.1038/s41558-018-0315-6.

Morenz, Siegfried. 1973. *Egyptian Religion*. Translated by A. E. Keep. Ithaca: Cornell University Press.

Moriarty, Patrick, and Damon Honnery. 2011. "Is There an Optimal Level for Renewable Energy?" *Energy Policy* 39:2748–53. doi:10.1016/j.enpol.2011.02.044.

———. 2012. "What Is the Global Potential for Renewable Energy?" *Renewable and Sustainable Energy Reviews* 16:244–52. doi:10.1016/j.rser.2011.07.151.

———. 2016. "Can Renewable Energy Power the Future?" *Energy Policy* 93:3–7. doi:10.1016/j.enpol.2016.02.051.

Morris, Rosalind C. 1995. "All Made Up: Performance Theory and the New Anthropology of Sex and Gender." *Annual Review of Anthropology* 24:567–92.

Morton, Oliver. 2015. *The Planet Remade: How Geoengineering Could Change the World.* Princeton: Princeton University Press.

Mummert, Amanda, Emily Esche, Joshua Robinson, and George J. Armelagos. 2011. "Stature and Robusticity during the Agricultural Transition: Evidence from the Bioarchaeological Record." *Economics and Human Biology* 9:284–301.

Murdock, George P., and Caterina Provost. 1973. "Factors in the Division of Labor by Sex: A Cross-Cultural Analysis." *Ethnology* 12:203–25.

Murphy, Nancey, and Warren S. Brown. 2007. *Did My Neurons Make Me Do It? Philosophical and Neurobiological Perspectives on Moral Responsibility and Free Will.* Oxford: Oxford University Press.

Na'aman, Nadav. 2005. *Ancient Israel and Its Neighbors: Interaction and Counteraction.* Vol. 1 of *Collected Essays.* Winona Lake, IN: Eisenbrauns.

———. 2014. "Dismissing the Myth of a Flood of Israelite Refugees in the Late Eighth Century BCE." *Zeitschrift für die alttestamentliche Wissenschaft* 126:1–14.

———. 2017. "Was Khirbet Qeiyafa a Judahite City? The Case against It." *Journal of Hebrew Scriptures* 17, 7. doi:10.5508/jhs.2017.v17.a7.

Nadan, Amos. 2006. *The Palestinian Peasant Economy under the Mandate: A Story of Colonial Bungling.* Harvard Middle Eastern Monographs 37. Cambridge: Harvard Center for Middle Eastern Studies.

Naidoff, Bruce D. 1978. "A Man to Work the Soil: A New Interpretation of Genesis 2–3." *Journal for the Study of the Old Testament* 5:2–14.

Nam, Roger S. 2012. "Power Relations in the Samaria Ostraca." *Palestine Exploration Quarterly* 144:155–63.

Nash, James A. 2009. "The Bible vs. Biodiversity: The Case against Moral Argument from Scripture." *Journal for the Study of Religion, Nature and Culture* 3:213–37.

National Academy of Sciences. 2015a. *Climate Intervention: Carbon Dioxide Removal and Reliable Sequestration.* Washington, DC: National Academies Press.

———. 2015b. *Climate Intervention: Reflecting Sunlight to Cool Earth.* Washington, DC: National Academies Press.

———. 2019. *Negative Emissions Technologies and Reliable Sequestration: A Research Agenda.* Washington, DC: National Academies Press.

Naville, Edouard. 1896. *The Temple of Deir El Bahari.* London: Egypt Exploration Fund.

Neumayer, Eric. 2000. "Scarce or Abundant? The Economics of Natural Resource Availability." *Journal of Economic Surveys* 14:307–35

Nichols, William Bradford. 2019. "What's Really behind Evangelicals' Climate Denial?" *The Humanist* (April 23). https://thehumanist.com/magazine/may-june-2019/features/whats-really-behind-evangelicals-climate-denial.

Nicholson, Simon. 2013. "The Promises and Perils of Geoengineering." In *State of the World 2013: Is Sustainability Still Possible?*, edited by Thomas Prugh and Linda Starke, 317–31. Washington, DC: Island Press and the Worldwatch Institute.

Niditch, Susan. 1985. *Chaos to Cosmos: Studies in Biblical Patterns of Creation.* Studies in the Humanities 6. Chico, CA: Scholars.

Niemann, Hermann Michael. 2008. "A New Look at the Samaria Ostraca: The King–Clan Relationship." *Tel Aviv* 35:249–66.

Nikiforuk, Andrew. 2012. *The Energy of Slaves: Oil and the New Servitude.* Vancouver: Greystone.

Noll, K. L. 2012. *Canaan and Israel in Antiquity: A Textbook on History and Religion.* 2nd ed. New York: T. & T. Clark.

Nordhaus, Ted, Michael Shellenberger, and Linus Blomqvist. 2012. *The Planetary Boundaries Hypothesis: A Review of the Evidence.* Breakthrough Institute. https://thebreakthrough.org/articles/planetary-boundaries.

Northcott, Michael. 2009. "Loving Scripture and Nature." *Journal for the Study of Religion, Nature and Culture* 3:247–53.

Norton, Bryan G. 1984. "Environmental Ethics and Weak Anthropocentrism." *Environmental Ethics* 6:131–48.

Noth, Martin. 1981. *A History of Pentateuchal Traditions.* Translated with an introduction by Bernhard W. Anderson. 1972. Reprint, Chico, CA: Scholars.

Oakman, Douglas E. 2018. "The Biblical World of Limited Good in Cultural, Social, and Technological Perspective." *Biblical Theology Bulletin* 48:97–105.

Oden, Robert A. 1981. "Divine Aspirations in Atrahasis and in Genesis 1–11." *Zeitschrift für die alttestamentliche Wissenschaft* 93:197–216.

Ohlson, Kristin. 2014. *The Soil Will Save Us: How Scientists, Farmers, and Foodies are Healing the Soil to Save the Planet.* New York: Rodale.

O'Keefe, John J. 2016. "Environmental Crisis and Christian Identity." In *Religion and Identity,* edited by Ronald A. Simkins and Thomas M. Kelly, 202–15. Journal of Religion & Society Supplement 13. http://moses.creighton.edu/jrs/toc/SS13.html.

Olivier, Hannes. 1996. "God as Friendly Patron: Reflections on Isaiah 5:1–7." *In die Skriflig* 30:293–303.

Olyan, Saul M. 1988. *Asherah and the Cult of Yahweh in Israel.* SBL Monograph Series 34. Atlanta: Scholars.

———. 1996. "Honor, Shame, and Covenant Relations in Ancient Israel and Its Environment." *Journal of Biblical Literature* 115:201–18.

O'Neill, Daniel W., Andrew L. Fanning, William F. Lamb, and Julia K. Steinberger. 2018. "A Good Life for All within Planetary Boundaries." *Nature Sustainability* 1:88–95. doi:10.1038/s41893-018-0021-4.

Orr, Isaac. 2019. "It Costs $532,000 to Decommission a Single Wind Turbine." Center of the American Experiment (Oct. 3). https://www.americanexperiment.org/2019/10/it-costs-532000-to-decommission-a-single-wind-turbine.

Oreskes, Naomi. 2004. "The Scientific Consensus on Climate Change." *Science* 306 (5702): 1686.

Oreskes, Naomi, and Erik M. Conway. 2010. *Merchants of Doubt: How a Handful of Scientists Obscured the Truth on Issues from Tobacco Smoke to Global Warming.* New York: Bloomsbury.

Ortner, Sherry B. 1974. "Is Female to Male as Nature Is to Culture?" In *Woman, Culture, and Society,* edited by Michelle Zimbalist Rosaldo and Louise Lamphere, 67–87. Stanford: Stanford University Press.

———. 1989–90. "Gender Hegemonies." *Cultural Critique* 14:35–80.

Ortner, Sherry B., and Harriet Whitehead, eds. 1981. *Sexual Meanings: The Cultural Construction of Gender and Sexuality.* Cambridge: Cambridge University Press.

Ossendrijver, Mathieu. 2016. "Conceptions of the Body in Mesopotamian Cosmology and Astral Science." In *SOMA: Körperkonzepte und körperliche Existenz in der antiken*

Philosophie und Literatur, edited by Thomas Buchheim, David Meissner, and Nora Wachsmann, 143–58. Archiv für Begriffsgeschichte 13. Hamburg: Meiner.

Ostling, Richard N. 2011. "The Search for the Historical Adam." *Christianity Today* (June):22–27.

Quinn, Naomi. 1991. "The Cultural Basis of Metaphor." In *Beyond Metaphor: The Theory of Tropes in Anthropology*, edited by J. W. Fernandez, 56–93. Stanford: Stanford University Press.

Quirke, Stephen. 1992. *Ancient Egyptian Religion*. New York: Dover.

Parker, Julie Faith. 2013. "Blaming Eve Alone: Translation, Omission, and Implications of *'mh* in Genesis 3:6b." *Journal of Biblical Literature* 132:729–47.

Perfecto, Ivette, John Vandermeer, and Angus Wright. 2019. *Nature's Matrix: Linking Agriculture, Biodiversity, Conservation and Food Sovereignty*. 2nd ed. London: Routledge.

Peristiany, John G. 1966. *Honor and Shame: The Values of Mediterranean Society*. Chicago: University of Chicago Press.

Peristiany, John G., and Julian A. Pitt-Rivers, eds. 1992. *Honor and Grace in Anthropology*. Cambridge Studies in Social and Cultural Anthropology 76. Cambridge: Cambridge University Press.

Perrings, Charles. 1995. "Ecology, Economics and Ecological Economics." *Ambio* 24: 60–64.

Perry, T. A. 2005. "Cain's Sin in Gen. 4:1–7: Oracular Ambiguity and How to Avoid It." *Prooftexts* 25:258–75

Pfoh, Emanuel. 2009a. *The Emergence of Israel in Ancient Palestine: Historical and Anthropological Perspectives*. Copenhagen International Seminar. London: Equinox.

———. 2009b. "Some Remarks on Patronage in Syria-Palestine during the Late Bronze Age." *Journal of the Economic and Social History of the Orient* 52:363–81.

———. 2013. "Loyal Servants of the King: A Political Anthropology of Subordination in Syria-Palestine (ca. 1600–600 BCE)." *Palamedes* 8:25–41.

Piketty, Thomas. 2014. *Capital in the Twenty-First Century*. Translated by Arthur Goldhammer. Cambridge, MA: Belnap.

Pimentel, David. 2006. "Soil Erosion: A Food and Environmental Threat." *Environment, Development and Sustainability* 8:119–37. doi:10.1007/s10668-005-1262-8.

Pimentel, David, and Michael Burgess. 2013. "Soil Erosion Threatens Food Production." *Agriculture* 3:443–63. doi:10.3390/agriculture3030443.

Pirgmaier, Elke. 2017 "The Neoclassical Trojan Horse of Steady-State Economics." *Ecological Economics* 133:52–61. doi:10.1016/j.ecolecon.2016.11.010.

Pitesky, Maurice E., Kimberly R. Stackhouse, and Frank M. Mitloehner. 2009. "Clearing the Air: Livestock's Contribution to Climate Change." *Advances in Agronomy* 103:1–40. doi:10.1016/S0065-2113(09)03001-6.

Pitt-Rivers, Julian A. 1977. *The Fate of Shechem; or the Politics of Sex: Essays in the Anthropology of the Mediterranean*. Cambridge Studies in Social Anthropology 19. Cambridge: Cambridge University Press.

Pius XII, Pope. 1950. *Humani Generis*. http://www.vatican.va/holy_father/pius_xii/encyclicals/documents/hf_p-xii_enc_12081950_humani-generis_en.html.

Pollan, Michael. 1991. *Second Nature: A Gardener's Education*. New York: Grove.

Pontifical Biblical Commission. 1993. *The Interpretation of the Bible in the Church*. Washington, DC: United States Catholic Conference.

Pope, Marvin H. 1965. *Job: A New Translation with Introduction and Commentary*. 3rd ed. Anchor Bible 15. Garden City: Doubleday.

Postgate, J. N. 1994. *Early Mesopotamia: Society and Economy at the Dawn of History.* London: Routledge.

Poulton, Paul, Johnny Johnston, Andy MacDonald, Roger White, and David Powlson. 2018. "Major Limitations to Achieving '4 per 1000' Increases in Soil Organic Carbon Stock in Temperate Regions: Evidence from Long-Term Experiments at Rothamsted Research, United Kingdom." *Global Change Biology* 24:2563–84. doi:10.1111/gcb.14066.

Premnath, D. N. 2003. *Eighth Century Prophets: A Social Analysis.* St. Louis: Chalice.

Pressler, Carolyn. 1993. *The View of Women Found in the Deuteronomic Family Laws.* Beihefte zur Zeitschrift für die alttestamentliche Wissenschaft 216. Berlin: de Gruyter.

———. 1994. "Sexual Violence and Deuteronomic Law." In *A Feminist Companion to Exodus to Deuteronomy*, edited by Athalia Brenner, 102–12. Feminist Companion to the Bible 6. Sheffield: Sheffield Academic.

Proctor, Jonathan, Solomon Hsiang, Jennifer Burney, Marshall Burke, and Wolfram Schlenker. 2018. "Estimating Global Agricultural Effects of Geoengineering Using Volcanic Eruptions." *Nature* 560 (7719):480–83. doi:10.1038/s41586-018-0417-3.

Pritchard, James B., ed. 1969. *Ancient Near Eastern Texts Related to the Old Testament.* 3rd ed. with supplement. Princeton: Princeton University Press.

Rad, Gerhard von. 1972. *Genesis.* Rev.d ed. Translated by J. H. Marks. Old Testament Library. Philadelphia: Westminster.

———. 1984. *The Problem of the Hexateuch and Other Essays.* Translated by E. W. Trueman Dicken. 1966. Reprint, London: SCM.

Rainey, Anson F. 1982. "Wine from Royal Vineyards." *Bulletin of the American Schools of Oriental Research* 245:57–62.

Ramsey, George W. 1988. "Is Name-Giving an Act of Domination in Genesis 2:23 and Elsewhere?" *Catholic Biblical Quarterly* 50:24–35.

Raudsepp-Hearne, Ciara, Garry D. Peterson, Maria Tengö, Elena M. Bennett, Tim Holland, Karina Benessaiah, Graham K. MacDonald, and Laura Pfeifer. 2010. "Untangling the Environmentalist's Paradox: Why Is Human Well-being Increasing as Ecosystem Services Degrade?" *Bioscience* 60 (8):576–89.

Raworth, Kate. 2017. *Doughnut Economics: Seven Ways to Think Like a 21st Century Economist.* White River Junction, VT: Chelsea Green.

Read, Rupert, and Samuel Alexander. 2019. *This Civilization is Finished: Conversations on the End of Empire—and What Lies Beyond.* Melbourne: Simplicity Institute.

Redman, Charles L. 1999. *Human Impact on Ancient Environments.* Tucson: University of Arizona Press.

REN21. 2019. *Renewables 2019 Global Status Report.* Paris: REN21 Secretariat.

Reviv, Hanoch. 1989. *The Elders in Ancient Israel: A Study of a Biblical Institution.* Translated by Lucy Plitmann. Jersualem: Magnes.

Rich, Nathaniel. 2019. *Losing Earth: A Recent History.* New York: MCD/Farrar, Straus & Giroux.

Ritchie, Hannah, and Max Roser. 2018. "Energy." *Our World in Data* (July). https://ourworldindata.org/energy.

———. 2019. "Land Use." *Our World in Data* (September). https://ourworldindata.org/land-use.

———. 2020. "Fossil Fuels." *Our World in Data.* https://ourworldindata.org/fossil-fuels.

Robb, Carol S. 2009. "Biblical Authority to Advocate for Biodiversity: A Response to James A. Nash." *Journal for the Study of Religion, Nature and Culture* 3:238–46.

Robinson, M. M., H. J. Dowsett, and M. A. Chandler. 2008. "Pliocene Role in Assessing Future Climate Impacts." *EOS* 89 (49):501–2.

Rockström, Johan. 2015. "Bounding the Planetary Future: Why We Need a Great Transition." *Great Transition Initiative* (April). https://greattransition.org/publication/bounding-the-planetary-future-why-we-need-a-great-transition.

Rockström, Johan, Will Steffan, Kevin Noone, Åsa Persson, F. Stuart III Chapin, Eric Lambin, Timothy M. Lenton, et al. 2009. "A Safe Operating Space for Humanity." *Nature* 461 (7263):472–75.

Rolston, Holmes, III. 1994. "Does Nature Need to Be Redeemed?" *Zygon* 29:205–29.

———. 1996. "The Bible and Ecology." *Interpretation* 50:16–26.

Roseberry, William. 1986. "The Ideology of Domestic Production." *LABOUR, Capital and Society* 19:70–93.

———. 1988a. "Issues and Agendas: Domestic Modes, Domesticated Models." *Journal of Historical Sociology* 1:423–30.

———. 1988b. "Political Economy." *Annual Review of Anthropology* 17:161–85.

Roser, Max. 2020. "Economic Growth." Our World in Data. https://ourworldindata.org/economic-growth.

Ruane, Nicole J. 2013. *Sacrifice and Gender in Biblical Law*. Cambridge: Cambridge University Press.

Ruddiman, William F. 2003. "The Anthropogenic Greenhouse Era Began Thousands of Years Ago." *Climate Change* 61:261–93.

Ruether, Rosemary Radford. 1978. "The Biblical Vision of the Ecological Crisis." *Christian Century* 95 (38):1129–32.

———. 2011. "Ecology and Theology: Ecojustice at the Center of the Church's Mission." *Interpretation* 65:354–63.

Russell, Stephen C. 2014. "The Hierarchy of Estates in Land and Naboth's Vineyard." *Journal for the Study of the Old Testament* 38:453–69.

Ryken, Philip G. 2013. "We Cannot Understand the World of Our Faith Without a Real, Historical Adam." In *Four Views on the Historical Adam*, edited by Matthew Barrett and Ardel B. Caneday, 267–79. Grand Rapids: Zondervan.

Sahlins, Marshall. 1972. *Stone Age Economics*. New York: Aldine de Gruyter.

Santmire, H. Paul. 1985. *The Travail of Nature: The Ambiguous Ecological Promise of Christian Theology*. Philadelphia: Fortress.

Sasson, Jack M. 1985. "*welo yitboshashu* (Gen 2.25) and Its Implications." *Biblica* 66:418–21.

Saunders, Harry D. 1992. "The Khazzoom-Brookes Postulate and Neoclassical Growth." *The Energy Journal* 13 (4):131–48.

Sauneron, Serge, and Jean Yoyotte. 1959. "La naissance du monde selon l'Égypte ancienne." In *La Naissance du Monde*, 17–91. Sources Orientales 1. Paris: Seuil.

Schandl, Heinz, Marina Fischer-Kowalski, James West, Stefan Giljum, Monika Dittrich, Nina Eisenmenger, Arne Geschke, et al. 2017. Global Material Flows and Resource Productivity: Forty Years of Evidence." *Journal of Industrial Ecology* 22:827–38. doi: 10.1111/jiec.12626.

Schaper, Joachim. 1995. "The Jerusalem Temple as an Instrument of the Achaemenid Fiscal Administration." *Vetus Testamentum* 45:528–39.

———. 1997. "The Temple Treasury Committee in the Times of Nehemiah and Ezra." *Vetus Testamentum* 47:200–206.

Scherer, Glenn. 2004. "The Godly Must Be Crazy: Christian-Right Views are Swaying Politicians and Threatening the Environment." *Grist* (Oct. 28). https://grist.org/politics/scherer-christian.

Schifferdecker, Kathryn. 2008. *Out of the Whirlwind: Creation Theology in the Book of Job*. Cambridge: Harvard Theological Studies.

Schloen, J. David. 2001. *The House of the Father as Fact and Symbol: Patrimonialism in Ugarit and the Ancient Near East*. Studies in the Archaeology and History of the Levant 2. Winona Lake, IN: Eisenbrauns.

Schmitt, John J. 1991. "Israel and Zion—Two Gendered Images: Biblical Speech Traditions and Their Contemporary Neglect." *Horizons* 18:18–32.

Schneider, John. 2012. "The Fall of 'Augustinian Adam': Original Fragility and Supralapsarian Purpose." *Zygon* 47:949–69.

Schultz, P. Wesley. 2000. "Empathizing with Nature: The Effects of Perspective Taking on Concern for Environmental Issues." *Journal of Social Issues* 56:391–406.

Schwartz, Judith C. 2013. *Cows Save the Planet: And Other Improbable Ways of Restoring Soil to Heal the Earth*. White River Junction, VT: Chelsea Green.

Scott, James C. 2017. *Against the Grain: A Deep History of the Earliest States*. New Haven: Yale University Press.

Scott, Joan Wallach. 1986. "Gender: A Useful Category of Historical Analysis." *American Historical Review* 91 (5):1053–75.

———. 2010. "Gender: Still a Useful Category of Analysis?" *Diogenes* 57:7–14.

SDG (Sustainable Development Goals). No date. United Nations website. https://www.un.org/sustainabledevelopment.

Sen, Amartya Kumar. 1962. "An Aspect of Indian Agriculture." *The Economic Weekly* 14 (February):243–46.

Sessions, George S. 1974. "Anthropocentrism and the Environmental Crisis." *Humboldt Journal of Social Relations* 2:71–81.

Shellenberger, Michael, and Ted Nordhaus. 2004. "The Death of Environmentalism: Global Warming in a Post-Environmental World." https://thebreakthrough.org/articles/the-death-of-environmentalism.

———. 2011. "Evolve." *Orion Magazine* (August 25). https://orionmagazine.org/article/evolve.

Sheng, Yu, Jiping Ding, and Jikun Huang. 2019. "The Relationship between Farm Size and Productivity in Agriculture: Evidence from Maize Production in Northern China." *American Journal of Agricultural Economics* 101:790–806.

Sherkat, Darren E., and Christopher G. Ellison. 2007. "Structuring the Religion-Environment Connection: Identifying Religious Influences on Environmental Concern and Activism." *Journal for the Scientific Study of Religion* 46:71–85.

Sideris, Lisa. 2016. "Anthropocene Convergences: A Report from the Field." In "Whose Anthropocene? Revisiting Dipesh Chakrabarty's 'Four Theses,'" edited by Robert Emmett and Thomas Lekan. *RCC Perspectives: Transformations in Environment and Society* 2016/2:89–96. doi:10.5282/rcc/7421.

———. 2017. *Consecrating Science: Wonder, Knowledge, and the Natural World*. Berkeley: University of California Press.

———. 2018. "Techno-Science, Integral Thought, and the Reality of Limits in *Laudato Si'*." *The Trumpeter* 34 (1):14–35.

Silverman, Jason M. 2019. *Persian Royal–Judaean Elite Engagements in the Early Teispid and Achaemenid Empire: The King's Acolytes*. Library of Hebrew Bible/Old Testament Studies 690. London: T. & T. Clark.

Simkins, Ronald A. 1991. *Yahweh's Activity in History and Nature in the Book of Joel*. Ancient Near Eastern Texts and Studies 10. Lewiston, NY: Mellen.

———. 1994. *Creator & Creation: Nature in the Worldview of Ancient Israel*. Peabody, MA: Hendrickson.

———. 2014. "The Bible and Anthropocentrism: Putting Humans in Their Place." *Dialectical Anthropology* 38:397–413. doi:10.1007/s10624-014-9348-z.

Simmons, Alan H. 2007. *The Neolithic Revolution in the Near East: Transforming the Human Landscape*. Tucson: University of Arizona Press.

Singer-Avitz, Lily. 1999. "Beersheva—A Gateway Community in Southern Arabian Long-Distance Trade in the Eighth Century B.C.E." *Tel Aviv* 26:3–74.

Siskind, Janet. 1978. "Kinship and Mode of Production." *American Anthropologist* 80:860–72.

Sivaram, Varun. 2018. *Taming the Sun: Innovations to Harness Solar Energy and Power the Planet*. Cambridge: MIT Press.

Skinner, John. 1930. *A Critical and Exegetical Commentary on Genesis*. 2nd ed. Edinburgh: T. & T. Clark.

Smil, Vaclav. 2011. "Global Energy: The Latest Infatuations." *American Scientist* 99 (May–June):212–19.

———. 2016a. *Power Density: A Key to Understanding Energy Sources and Uses*. Cambridge: MIT Press.

———. 2016b. "What I See When I See a Wind Turbine [Numbers Don't Lie]." *IEEE Spectrum* 53 (3):27. doi:10.1109/mspec.2016.7420393.

———. 2017. *Energy and Civilization: A History*. Cambridge: MIT Press.

———. 2018. "It'll Be Harder Than We Thought to Get the Carbon Out [Blueprints for a Miracle]." *IEEE Spectrum* 55:72–75. doi:10.1109/mspec.2018.8362233.

———. 2019. *Growth: From Microorganisms to Megacities*. Cambridge: MIT Press.

Smith, Claire Elizabeth, and Joseph Wayne Smith. 1996. "Economics, Ecology and Entropy: The Second Law of Thermodynamics and the Limits of Growth." *Population and Environment* 17:309–21.

Smith, Mark S. 2010. *The Priestly Vision of Genesis 1*. Minneapolis: Fortress.

Smith, Pete. 2016. "Soil Carbon Sequestration and Biochar as Negative Emission Technologies." *Global Change Biology* 22:1315–24. doi:10.1111/gcb.13178.

Smith, Pete, Steven J. Davis, Felix Creutzig, Sabine Fuss, Jan Minx, Benoit Gabrielle, Etsushi Kato, et al. 2016. "Biophysical and Economic Limits to Negative CO_2 Emissions." *Nature Climate Change* 6:42–50. doi:10.1038/nclimate2870.

Snaith, N. H. 1966. "The Daughters of Zelophehad." *Vetus Testamentum* 16:124–27.

Soga, Masashi, Kevin J. Gaston, and Yuichi Yamaura. 2017. "Gardening Is Beneficial for Heath: A Meta-Analysis." *Preventative Medical Reports* 5:92–99. doi:10.1016/j.pmedr.2016.11.007.

Solotaroff, Paul. 2013. "In the Belly of the Beast." *RollingStone* (Dec. 10). https://www.rollingstone.com/interactive/feature-belly-beast-meat-factory-farms-animal-activists.

Sommer, Benjamin D. 2011. "Dating Pentateuchal Text and the Perils of Pseudo-Historicism." In *The Pentateuch: International Perspectives on Current Research*, edited by Thomas B. Dozeman, Konrad Schmid, and Baruch J. Schwartz, 85–108. Forschungen zum Alten Testament 78. Tübingen: Mohr/Siebeck.

Sonik, Karen. 2009. "Gender Matters in *Enuma Elish*." In *In the Wake of Tikva Frymer-Kensky*, edited by Richard H. Beal, Steven W. Holloway, and JoAnn Scurlock, 85–101. Gorgias Précis Portfolios 4. Piscataway, NJ: Gorgias.

Sorrell, Steven. 2010. "Energy, Economic Growth and Environmental Sustainability: Five Propositions." *Sustainability* 2:1784–809. doi:10.3390/su2061784.

Spash, Clive L. 2019. "A Tale of Three Paradigms: Realising the Revolutionary Potential of Ecological Economics." *Ecological Economics* 169:106518. doi:10.1016/j.ecolecon.2019.106518.

Speiser, Ephraim A. 1982. *Genesis*. 3rd ed. Anchor Bible 1. Garden City, NY: Doubleday.

Spina, Frank Anthony. 1992. "The 'Ground' for Cain's Rejection (Gen 4): *adamah* in the Context of Gen 1–11." *Zeitschrift für die alttestamentliche Wissenschaft* 104:319–32.

Spitler, Gene. 1982. "Justifying a Respect for Nature." *Environmental Ethics* 4:255–60.

Spratt, David, and Ian Dunlop. 2018. *What Lies Beneath: The Understatement of Existential Climate Risk*. Rev. and updated. Melbourne: Breakthrough—National Centre for Climate Restoration.

SQS (Subcommission on Quaternary Stratigraphy). 2019. "Working Group on the 'Anthropocene.'" http://quaternary.stratigraphy.org/working-groups/anthropocene

Stacker, Jeffrey. 2015. "Holiness Code and Writings." In *The Oxford Encyclopedia of The Bible and Law*. Volume 1: ADM-LIT, edited by Brent A. Strawn, 389–96. Oxford: Oxford University Press.

Stager, Lawrence E. 1985. "The Archaeology of the Family in Ancient Israel." *Bulletin of the American Schools of Oriental Research* 260:1–35.

———. 1999. "Jerusalem and the Garden of Eden." *Eretz Israel* 26:183*–194*.

———. 2000. "Jerusalem as Eden." *Biblical Archaeology Review* 26.3:36–47, 66.

———. 2003. "The Patrimonial Kingdom of Solomon." In *Symbiosis, Symbolism, and the Power of the Past: Canaan, Ancient Israel, and Their Neighbors from the Late Bronze Age through Roman Palestina*, edited by William G. Dever and Seymour Gitin, 63–74. Winona Lake, IN: Eisenbrauns.

Steffen, Will, Wendy Broadgate, Lisa Deutsch, Owen Gaffney, and Cornelia Ludwig. 2015. "The Trajectory of the Anthropocene: The Great Acceleration." *Anthropocene Review* 2:81–98.

Steffen, Will, Paul J. Crutzen, and John R. McNeill. 2007. "The Anthropocene: Are Humans Now Overwhelming the Great Forces of Nature?" *Ambio* 36:614–21.

Steffen, Will, Jacques Grinevald, Paul Crutzen, and John McNeill. 2011. "The Anthropocene: Conceptual and Historical Perspectives." *Philosophical Transactions of the Royal Society A* 369:842–67.

Steffen, Will, Åsa Persson, Lisa Deutsch, Jan Zalasiewicz, Mark Williams, Katherine Richardson, Carole Crumley, et al. 2011. "The Anthropocene: From Global Change to Planetary Stewardship." *Ambio* 40:739–61.

Steffen, Will, Katherine Richardson, Johan Rockström, Sarah E. Cornell, Ingo Fetzer, Elena M. Bennet, Reinette Biggs, et al. 2015. "Planetary Boundaries: Guiding Human Development on a Changing Planet." *Science* 347 (6223):1259855. doi:10.1126/science.1259855.

Steffen, Will, Johan Rockström, Katherine Richardson, Timothy M. Lenton, Carl Folke, Diana Liverman, Collin P. Summerhayes, et al. 2018. "Trajectories of the Earth System in the Anthropocene." *Proceedings of the National Academy of Sciences* 115, 33: 8252–59.

Steffen, Will, Angelina Sanderson, Peter Tyson, Jill Jäger, Pamela Matson, Berrien Moore III, Frank Oldfield, et al. 2004. *Global Change and the Earth System: A Planet under Pressure.* Berlin: Springer.

Steinberg, Naomi. 1991. "The Deuteronomic Law Code and the Politics of State Centralization." In *The Bible and the Politics of Exegesis: Essays in Honor of Norman K. Gottwald on His Sixty-Fifth Birthday,* edited by Jobling, Peggy L. Day, and Gerald T. Sheppard, 161–70. Cleveland: Pilgrim.

———. 1993. *Kinship and Marriage in Genesis: A Household Economics Perspective.* Minneapolis: Fortress.

———. 2004. "Romancing the Widow: The Economic Distinctions between the *almanah,* the *ishah-almanah* and the *eshet-hammet.*" In *God's Word for Our World,* 327–43. Vol. 1 of *Biblical Studies in Honor of Simon John De Vries,* edited by J. Harold Ellens, Deborah L. Ellens, Rolf P. Knierim, and Isaac Kalimi. Journal for the Study of the Old Testament Supplements 388. London: T. & T. Clark.

Stephens, Jennie C., and Kevin Surprise. 2020. "The Hidden Injustices of Advancing Solar Geoengineering Research." *Global Sustainability* 3 (e2):1–6. doi:10.1017/sus.2019.28.

Stern, David I. 2011. "The Role of Energy in Economic Growth." *Annals of the New York Academy of Sciences* 1219:26–51. doi:10.1111/j.1749-6632.2010.05921.x.

Stordalen, Terje. 1992. "Man, Soil, Garden: Basic Plot in Genesis 2–3 Reconsidered." *Journal for the Study of the Old Testament* 53:3–36.

Streete, Gail Corrington. 1997. *The Strange Woman: Power and Sex in the Bible.* Louisville: Westminster John Knox.

Stulman, Louis. 1990. "Encroachment in Deuteronomy: An Analysis of the Social World of the D Code." *Journal of Biblical Literature* 109:613–32.

———. 1992. "Sex and Familial Crimes in the D Code: A Witness to Mores in Transition." *Journal for the Study of the Old Testament* 53:47–63.

Swimme, Brian Thomas, and Thomas Berry. 1992. *The Universe Story: From the Primordial Flaring Forth to the Ecozoic Era—A Celebration of the Unfolding of the Cosmos.* San Francisco: HarperSanFrancisco.

Synnott, Anthony. 1993. *The Body Social: Symbolism, Self and Society.* London: Routledge.

Tainter, Joseph A. 1988. *The Collapse of Complex Societies.* New Studies in Archaeology. Cambridge: Cambridge University Press.

Tappy, Ron E., and P. Kyle McCarter Jr., eds. 2008. *Literate Culture and Tenth-Century Canaan: The Tel Zayit Abecedary in Context.* Winona Lake, IN: Eisenbrauns.

Taylor, Bron. 2004. "A Green Future for Religion?" *Futures* 36:991–1008.

———. 2010. *Dark Green Religion: Nature Spirituality and the Planetary Future.* Berkeley: University of California Press

———. 2016. "The Greening of Religion Hypothesis (Part One): From Lynn White, Jr and Claims That Religions Can Promote Environmentally Destructive Attitudes and Behaviors to Assertions They Are Becoming Environmentally Friendly." *Journal for the Study of Religion, Nature and Culture* 10:268–305.

Taylor, Bron, Gretel Van Wieren, and Bernard Zaleha. 2016. "The Greening of Religion Hypothesis (Part Two): Assessing the Data from Lynn White, Jr, to Pope Francis." *Journal for the Study of Religion, Nature and Culture* 10:306–78.

Thompson, Lonnie G. 2010. "Climate Change: The Evidence and Our Options." *Behavior Analyst* 33:153–40.

Tigay, Jeffrey H. 1984. "The Image of God and the Flood: Some New Developments." In *Studies in Jewish Education and Judaica in Honor of Louis Newman*, edited by Alexander M. Shapiro and Burton I. Cohen, 169–82. New York: Ktav.

———. 1986. *You Shall Have No Other Gods: Israelite Religion in Light of Hebrew Inscriptions*. Harvard Semitic Studies 31. Atlanta: Scholars.

Tillich, Paul. 1957. *Dynamics of Faith*. New York: Harper and Row.

Tollefson, Jeff. 2008. "UN Decision Puts Brakes on Ocean Fertilization." *Nature* 453 (7196):704. doi:10.1038/453704b.

Toorn, K. van der, and P. W. van der Horst. 1990. "Nimrod Before and After the Bible." *Harvard Theological Review* 83:1–29.

Towner, W. Sibley. 1996. "The Future of Nature." *Interpretation* 50:27–35.

Townsend, Alan R., and Robert W. Howarth. 2010. "Fixing the Global Nitrogen Problem." *Scientific American* 302.2:64–71.

Trenberth, Kevin E., and Aiguo Dai. 2007. "Effects of Mount Pinatubo Volcanic Eruption on the Hydrological Cycle as an Analog of Geoengineering." *Geophysical Research Letters* 34 (15). doi:org.10.1029/2007GL030524.

Trible, Phyllis. 1971. "Ancient Priests and Modern Polluters." *Andover Newton Quarterly* 12:74–79.

———. 1978. *God and the Rhetoric of Sexuality*. Overtures to Biblical Theology. Philadelphia: Fortress.

Truelove, Heather Barnes, and Jeff Joireman. 2009. "Understanding the Relationship Between Christian Orthodoxy and Environmentalism: The Mediating Role of Perceived Environmental Consequences." *Environment and Behavior* 41:806–20.

Tuan, Yi-Fu. 1970. "Our Treatment of the Environment in Ideal and Actuality." *American Scientist* 58:244–49.

Tucker, Gene M. 1997. "Rain on a Land Where No One Lives: The Hebrew Bible on the Environment." *Journal of Biblical Literature* 116:3–17.

———. 2000. "The Peaceable Kingdom and a Covenant with the Wild Animals." In *God Who Creates: Essays in Honor of W. Sibley Towner*, edited by William P. Brown and S. Dean McBride, Jr., 215–25. Grand Rapids: Eerdmans.

Tucker, Mary Evelyn, and John Grim, eds. 1997–2004. *Religions of the World and Ecology* series. Cambridge: Harvard University Press.

———. 2017. "The Movement of Religion and Ecology." In *Routledge Handbook of Religion and Ecology*, edited by Willis Jenkins, Mary Evelyn Tucker, and John Grim, 3–12. Routledge International Handbooks. London: Routledge.

Tucker, W. Dennis, Jr. 2007. "Is Shame a Matter of Patronage in the Communal Laments?" *Journal for the Study of the Old Testament* 31:465–80.

Tuden, Arthur. 1979. "An Exploration of a Precapitalist Mode of Production." In *New Directions in Political Economy: An Approach from Anthropology*, edited by Madeline Barbara Léons and Frances Rothstein, 19–32. Contributions in Economics and Economic History 22. Westport, CT: Greenwood.

Tull, Patricia K. 2013. *Inhabiting Eden: Christians, the Bible, and the Ecological Crisis*. Louisville: Westminster John Knox.

Uehlinger, Christoph. 1990. *Weltreich und "eine Rede": Eine neue Deutung der sogenannten Turmbauerzählung (Gen 11,1–9)*. Orbis Biblicus et Orientalis 101. Freiburg, Schwitzerland: Universitätsverlag.

UNDP (United Nations Development Programme). 2014. "Sustaining Human Progress: Reducing Vulnerabilities and Building Resilience." Human Development Report 2014. http://hdr.undp.org/sites/default/files/hdr14-report-en-1.pdf.

UNEP (United Nations Environment Programme). 2011. *Decoupling Natural Resource Use and Environmental Impacts from Economic Growth: A Report of the Working Group on Decoupling to the International Resource Panel.* Marina Fischer-Kowalski, Mark Swilling, Ernst Ulrich von Weizsäcker, Yong Ren, Yuichi Moriguchi, Wendy Crane, Fridolin Krausmann, et al. Paris: United Nations Environment Programme.

———. 2014. *Decoupling 2: Technologies, Opportunities and Policy Options: A Report of the Working Group on Decoupling to the International Resource Panel.* Ernst Ulrich von Weizsäcker, Jacqueline Aloisi de Larderel, Karlson Hargrove, Christian Hudson, Michael Harrison Smith, and Maria Amelia Enriquez Rodrigues. Paris: United Nations Environment Programme.

———. 2016. *Global Materials Flow and Resource Productivity: An Assessment Study of the UNEP International Resource Panel.* Heinz Schandl, Marina Fischer-Kowalski, James West, Stefan Giljum, Monika Dittrich, Nina Eisenmenger, Arne Geschke, et al. Paris: United Nations Environment Programme.

Unruh, Gregory C. 2000. "Understanding Carbon Lock-In." *Energy Policy* 28:817–30.

USDA (United States Department of Agriculture). 2005. "The 20th Century Transformation of U.S. Agriculture and Farm Policy." *Economic Information Bulletin* 3 (June).

———. 2019a. "2017 Census of Agriculture." USDA Economic Research Service. https://www.nass.usda.gov/AgCensus.

———. 2019b. "Farmland Ownership and Tenure." USDA Economic Research Service. https://www.ers.usda.gov/topics/farm-economy/land-use-land-value-tenure/farmland-ownership-and-tenure.

———. 2020a. "Ag and Food Sectors and the Economy." USDA Economic Research. Service. https://www.ers.usda.gov/data-products/ag-and-food-statistics-charting-the-essentials/ag-and-food-sectors-and-the-economy.

———. 2020b. "Farming and Farm Income." USDA Economic Research Service. https://www.ers.usda.gov/data-products/ag-and-food-statistics-charting-the-essentials/farming-and-farm-income.

Vanderhooft, David S. 2009. "The Israelite *mishpahah*, the Priestly Writings, and Changing Valences in Israel's Kinship Terminology." In *Exploring the Longue Durée: Essays in Honor of Lawrence E. Stager*, edited by J. David Schloen, 485–96. Winona Lake, IN: Eisenbrauns.

Vatican II. 1965. *Dei Verbum*. http://www.vatican.va/archive/hist_councils/ii_vatican_council/documents/vat-ii_const_19651118_dei-verbum_en.html.

Venema, Dennis R. 2010. "Genesis and the Genome: Genomics Evidence for Human-Ape Common Ancestry and Ancestral Hominid Population Sizes." *Perspectives on Science and Christian Faith* 62:166–78.

Vikström, Hanna, Simon Davidsson, and Mikael Höök. 2013. "Lithium Availability and Future Production Outlooks." *Applied Energy* 110:252–66. doi:10.1016/apenergy.2013.04.005.

Visconti, Guido. 2014. "Anthropocene: Another Academic Invention?" *Rendiconti Lincei* 25:381–92.

Vogel, Steven. 1996. *Against Nature: The Concept of Nature in Critical Theory*. SUNY Series in Social and Political Thought. Albany: State University of New York Press.

Waggoner, P. E., and J. H. Ausubel. 2002. "A Framework to Sustainability Science: A Renovated IPAT Identity." *Proceedings of the National Academy of Sciences* 99.12:7860–65.

Wainwright, Joel, and Geoff Mann. 2020. *Climate Leviathan: A Political Theory of Our Planetary Future.* London: Verso.

Walker, Mike, Martin H. Head, Max Berklehammer, Svante Björck, Hai Cheng, Les Cwynar, David Fisher, et al. 2018. "Formal Ratification of the Subdivision of the Holocene Series/Epoch (Quaternary System/Period): Two New Global Boundary Stratotype Sections and Points (GSSPs) and Three New Stages/Subseries." *Episodes* 41.4:1–11.

Walker, Mike, Sigfus Johnsen, Sune Olander Rasmussen, Trevor Popp, Jørgen-Peder Steffensen, Phil Gibbard, Wim Hoek, et al. 2009. "Formal Definition and Dating of the GSSP (Global Stratotype Section and Point) for the Base of the Holocene Using the Greenland NGRIP Ice Core, and Selected Auxiliary Records." *Journal of Quaternary Science* 24:3–17.

Wallace, Howard N. 1985. *The Eden Narrative.* Harvard Semitic Monographs 32. Atlanta: Scholars.

Wallace-Hadrill, Andrew, ed. 1989. *Patronage in Ancient Society.* Leicester-Nottingham Studies in Ancient Society 1. London: Routledge.

Wallace-Wells, David. 2019. *The Uninhabitable Earth: Life after Warming.* New York: Duggan.

Walls, Neal. 2001. *Desire, Discord and Death: Approaches to Ancient Near Eastern Myth.* American Schools of Oriental Research Books 8. Boston: American Schools of Oriental Research.

Walsh, Jessica Fargen. 2020. "Nebraska Towns Pay More for Water." *Omaha World-Herald* (May 3):B1–B2.

Walton, John H. 2012. "Human Origins and the Bible." *Zygon* 47:875–89.

———. 2013. "A Historical Adam: Archetypal Creation View." In *Four Views on the Historical Adam*, edited by Matthew Barrett and Ardel B. Caneday, 89–118. Grand Rapids: Zondervan.

Ward, James D., Paul C. Sutton, Adrian D. Werner, Robert Costanza, Steve H. Mohr, and Craig T. Simmons. 2016. "Is Decoupling GDP Growth from Environmental Impact Possible?" *PLOS One* (October 14). doi:10.1371/journal.pone.0164733.

Washington, Harold C. 1998. "'Lest He Die in the Battle and Another Man Take Her': Violence and the Construction of Gender in the Laws of Deuteronomy 20–22." In *Gender and Law in the Hebrew Bible and the Ancient Near East*, edited by Victor H. Matthews, Bernard M. Levinson, and Tikva Frymer-Kensky, 185–213. Journal for the Study of the Old Testament Supplements 262. Sheffield: Sheffield Academic.

Watanabe, Chikako E. 2002. *Animal Symbolism in Mesopotamia: A Contextual Approach.* Wiener Offene Orientalistik 1. Vienna: Institut für Orientalistik der Universität.

Waters, Colin N., Jan Zalasiewicz, Colin Summerhayes, Anthony D. Barnosky, Clément Poirier, Agnieszka Galuszka, Alejandro Cearreta, et al. 2016. "The Anthropocene Is Functionally and Stratigraphically Distinct from the Holocene." *Science* 351 (6269):aad2622. doi:10.1126/science.aad2622.

Watt, James. 1982. "Ours Is the Earth." *The Saturday Evening Post* 254 (Jan./Feb.):74–75, 104.

———. 2005. "The Religious Left's Lies." *Washington Post* (May 21):A19. https://www.washingtonpost.com/wp-dyn/content/article/2005/05/20/AR2005052001333.html.

Weems, Renita J. 1995. *Battered Love: Marriage, Sex, and Violence in the Hebrew Prophets.* Overtures to Biblical Theology. Minneapolis: Fortress.

Wegner, Judith Romney. 1988. *Chattel or Person? The Status of Women in the Mishnah*. New York: Oxford University Press.

Weinberg, Joel. 1992. *The Citizen-Temple Community*. Translated by Daniel L. Smith-Christopher. Journal for the Study of the Old Testament Supplement 151. Sheffield: Sheffield Academic.

Weinfeld, Moshe. 1995. *Social Justice in Ancient Israel and in the Ancient Near East*. Jerusalem: Magnes.

Welti, Ellen A. R., Karl A. Roeder, Kirsten M. De Beurs, Anthony Joern, and Michael Kaspari. 2020. "Nutrient Dilution and Climate Cycles Underlie Declines in a Dominant Insect Herbivore." *Proceedings of the National Academy of Sciences* (March 9). doi:10.1073/pnas.1920012117.

Wenham, Gordon. 1987. *Genesis 1–15*. Word Biblical Commentary 1. Waco, TX: Word.

West, Candace, and Don H. Zimmerman. 1987. "Doing Gender." *Gender and Society* 1.2: 125–51.

Westbrook, Raymond. 1991. *Property and the Family in Biblical Law*. Journal for the Study of the Old Testament Supplement 113. Sheffield: Sheffield Academic.

———. 2009. "Patronage in the Ancient Near East." In *Law from the Tigris to the Tiber: The Writings of Raymond Westbrook. Volume 1: The Shared Tradition*, edited by Bruce Wells and F. Rachel Magdalene, 217–44. Winona Lake, IN: Eisenbrauns.

Westermann, Claus. 1978. *Blessing in the Bible and the Life of the Church*. Translated by K. Crim. Overtures to Biblical Theology. Philadelphia: Fortress.

———. 1984. *Genesis 1–11: A Commentary*. Translated by John J. Scullion, SJ. Continental Commentaries. Minneapolis: Augsburg.

Wheaton College. 2020. "Statement of Faith and Educational Purpose." https://www.wheaton.edu/about-wheaton/statement-of-faith-and-educational-purpose.

White, Lynn, Jr. 1967. "The Historical Roots of Our Ecologic Crisis." *Science* 155 (3767):1203–7.

Whitekettle, Richard. 2011. "A Communion of Subjects: Zoological Classification and Human/Animal Relations in Psalm 104." *Bulletin for Biblical Research* 21:173–88.

Whitney, Elspeth. 1993. "Lynn White, Ecotheology, and History." *Environmental Ethics* 15:151–69.

Wiedmann, Thomas O., Heinz Schandl, Manfred Lenzen, Daniel Moran, Sangwon Suh, James West, and Keiichiro Kanemoto. 2015. "The Material Footprint of Nations." *Proceedings of the National Academy of Sciences* 112 (20):6271–76.

Wikan, Unni. 1984. "Shame and Honour: A Contestable Pair." *Man* (n.s.) 19:635–52.

Wilberforce, Tabbi, Ahmad Baroutaji, Bassel Soudan, Abdul Hai Al-Alami, and Abdul Ghani Olabi. 2019. "Outlook of Carbon Capture Technology and Challenges." *Science of the Total Environment* 657:56–72.

Wilk, Richard R., and William L. Rathje. 1982. "Household Archaeology." *American Behavioral Scientist* 25:617–39.

Wilkinson, Richard, and Kate Pickett. 2009. *The Spirit Level: Why Greater Equality Makes Societies Stronger*. New York: Bloomsbury.

Williams, Raymond. 1977. *Marxism and Literature*. Oxford: Oxford University Press.

Willis, Timothy M. 2001. *The Elders of the City: A Study of the Elders-Laws in Deuteronomy*. Society of Biblical Literature Monograph Series 55. Atlanta: Society of Biblical Literature.

Wilson, Robert R. 1977. *Genealogy and History in the Biblical World*. Yale Near Eastern Researches 7. New Haven: Yale University Press.

Wise, Timothy A. 2019. *Eating Tomorrow: Agribusiness, Family Farmers, and the Battle for the Future of Food*. New York: New Press.

Wöhrle, Jacob. 2015. "Abraham amidst the Nations: The Priestly Concept of Covenant and the Persian Imperial Ideology." In *Covenant in the Persian Period: From Genesis to Chronicles*, edited by Richard J. Bautch and Gary N. Knoppers, 23–39. Winona Lake, IN: Eisenbrauns.

Wolde, Ellen van. 1991. "The Story of Cain and Abel: A Narrative Study." *Journal for the Study of the Old Testament* 51:25–41.

Wolf, Eric R. 1966. "Kinship, Friendship, and Patron–Client Relations in Complex Societies." In *The Social Anthropology of Complex Societies*, edited by M. Banton, 1–22. A.S.A. Monographs 4. London: Tavistock.

Wood, Ellen Meiksins. 2017. *The Origin of Capitalism: A Longer View*. London: Verso.

Wood, Neal. 1984. *John Locke and Agrarian Capitalism*. Berkeley: University of California Press.

Wright, David P. 1987. *The Disposal of Impurity: Elimination Rites in the Bible and in Hittite and Mesopotamian Literature*. Society of Biblical Literature Dissertation Series 101. Atlanta: Scholars.

Wyatt, Nicolas. 2014. "A Royal Garden: The Ideology of Eden." *Scandinavian Journal of the Old Testament* 28.1:1–35.

Xu, Yan, Jinhui Li, Quanyin Tan, Anesia Lauren Peters, and Congren Yang. 2018. "Global Status of Recycling Waste Solar Panels: A Review." *Waste Management* 75:450–58. doi:10.1016/.wasman.2018.01.036.

Yee, Gale A. 2003. *Poor Banished Children of Eve: Women as Evil in the Hebrew Bible*. Minneapolis: Fortress.

———. 2017. "'He Will Take the Best of Your Fields': Royal Feasts and Rural Extraction." *Journal of Biblical Literature* 136:821–38.

York, Richard. 2012. "Do Alternative Energy Sources Displace Fossil Fuels?" *Nature Climate Change* 2:441–43. doi:10.1038/nclimate1451.

York, Richard, Eugene A. Rosa, and Thomas Dietz. 2003. "STIRPAT, IPAT, and ImPACT: Analytical Tools for Unpacking the Driving Forces of Environmental Impacts." *Ecological Economics* 46:351–65. doi:10.1016/S0921-8009(03)00188-5.

———. 2005. "The Ecological Footprint Intensity of National Economies." *Journal of Industrial Ecology* 8.4:139–54.

Young, Davis A. 1995. "The Antiquity and the Unity of the Human Race Revisited." *Christian Scholar's Review* 25:380–96.

Zalasiewicz, Jan, Colin N. Waters, Martin J. Head, Will Steffen, J. P. Syvitski, Davor Vidas Colin Summerhayes, and Mark Williams. 2018. "The Geological and Earth System Reality of the Anthropocene." *Current Anthropology* 58:220–23.

Zalasiewicz, Jan, Colin N. Waters, Mark Williams, Colin Summerhayes, eds. 2019. *The Anthropocene as a Geological Time Unit: A Guide to the Scientific Evidence and Current Debate*. Cambridge: Cambridge University Press.

Zalasiewicz, Jan, Colin N. Waters, Alexander P. Wolfe, Anthony D. Barnosky, Alejandro Cearreta, Matt Edgeworth, Erle C. Ellis, et al. 2017. "Making the Case for a Formal Anthropocene Epoch: An Analysis of Ongoing Critiques." *Newletters on Stratigraphy* 50.2:205–26. doi:10.1127/nos/2017/0385.

Zalasiewicz, Jan, and Mark Williams, 2012. *The Goldilocks Planet: The Four Billion Year Story of Earth's Climate*. Oxford: Oxford University Press.

Zalasiewicz, Jan, Mark Williams, Richard Fortey, Alan Smith, Tiffany L. Barry, Angela L. Coe, Paul R. Bown, et al. 2011. "Stratigraphy of the Anthropocene." *Philosophical Transactions of the Royal Society A* 369:1036–55.

Zaleha, Bernard Daley. 2009. "James Nash as Christian Deep Ecologist: Forging a New Ecotheology for the Third Millennium." *Journal for the Study of Religion, Nature and Culture* 3:279–89.

Zaleha, Bernard Daley, and Andrew Szasz. 2015. "Why Conservative Christians Don't Believe in Climate Change." *Bulletin of the Atomic Scientists* 71.5: 19–30.

Zalk, John van, and Paul Behrens. 2018. "The Spatial Extent of Renewable and Non-Renewable Power Generation: A Review and Meta-Analysis of Power Densities and their Application in the U.S." *Energy Policy* 123:83–91. doi:10.1016/j.enpol.2018.08.023.

Zeder, Melinda A. 2011. "The Origins of Agriculture in the Near East." *Current Anthropology* 52 (S4):S221–35.

Zehner, Ozzie. 2012. *Green Illusions: The Dirty Secrets of Clean Energy and the Future of Environmentalism.* Lincoln: University of Nebraska Press.

———. 2013. "Unclean at Any Speed: Electric Cars Don't Solve the Automobile's Environmental Problem." *IEEE Spectrum* 50.7:40–45. doi:10.1109/MSPEC.2013.6545121.

Zevit, Ziony. 2013. *What Really Happened in the Garden of Eden?* New Haven: Yale University Press.

Zürn, Michael, and Stefan Schäfer. 2013. "The Paradox of Climate Engineering." *Global Policy* 4:266–77. doi:10.1111/1758-5899.12004.

Ancient Documents Index

ANCIENT NEAR EASTERN DOCUMENTS

Adapa
15, 44n21

Atrahasis
15, 33n8, 34–35, 36, 74–75, 77, 123, 169

Creation of the Pickax
123–24

Edict of Ammisaduqa
225

Enki and Ninmah
122–23

Enuma Elish
15, 124–25, 260, 274

Epic of Gilgamesh
42n18, 44n21, 172

Great Hymn to Aten
128–29

Great Hymn to Khnum
35–36

Heliopolitan Cosmogony
126, 170

Hittite Soldiers' Oath
140

Hymn to Ptah
126–27

Hymns to Khnum from the Temple at Esna
129

Law Code of Hammurabi
109

Memphite Theology
127

Morning Hymn to Khnum
129

Theogony of Dunnu
125–26

Short Hymn to Aten
128

Sumerian Hymn to E-engur
123

Ancient Documents Index

HEBREW BIBLE / OLD TESTAMENT

Genesis

	10–11, 77
1:1—2:3	76, 77, 95–96, 107, 109, 114–15, 133, 135, 150, 154, 157, 160, 164–65, 171, 172, 267, 268, 271, 274–75, 277, 278, 280, 294
1:3	33
1:26–28	95
1:26–27	109
1:27–28	107
1:28	157, 159, 258
1:28	76
2	41, 154
2:4b—3:24	15–17, 32–45, 59, 62, 75–76, 77, 86, 94–96, 101, 105, 114, 119, 123, 131, 132–33, 160, 161–64, 171, 269–73, 277, 278, 280, 295
2:4b	33
2:5–6	298
2:5	34, 38n14, 161
2:6–7	34
2:7	270
2:8–9	38, 270
2:15	38, 155
2:16–17	38
2:18–20	270
2:18	39
2:19–20	39
2:20–24	38n12
2:21–23	39, 270
2:24	39, 94–95
2:25	39, 41, 270
3	39, 165, 299
3:1–7	270
3:1	43
3:2–3	43
3:4–5	43
3:5	42, 161
3:6	39, 41, 43
3:14–19	271
3:15	161
3:16–19	162
3:16	43, 45, 46, 48, 49n27
3:17–19	44, 256
3:17	39, 44, 45
3:19	37, 49n27, 273
3:20	39, 40, 45
3:21–24	271
3:21	39
3:22–23	38n12
3:22	39, 44n21, 262
3:23–24	41
3:23	39n14, 44, 270
3:24	39
4–11	273
4:1–16	46–50
4:4–5	47
4:6–7	46n23, 47
4:7	46, 48
4:11–12	256
4:17	256
4:23–24	256
5:29	44, 271
6:1–4	256
6:5—8:22	256
6:5–6	257
6:5	273
6:11–12	257
8:20–22	44, 46, 162
8:21	162, 258, 271, 273
9:1	158
9:2–6	255
9:2–5	158
9:2	165
9:3–4	157
10	111
10:8–10	260
11:1–9	258–63
11:3–4	261
11:6–7	261
11:6	261
16	50n28
16:2	45
16:13	40
17:8	185
20:1–18	139
21	50n28
24:38	80, 81
25:21	45
29:14	94
29:31—30:24	98
29:31	45
30:2	45
30:17	45
30:22	45
31	50n28
49	98n8

Exodus

14	275, 276
15:1–12	275
19	77n18
20:8–11	76
20:12	28

20:22–23:19	95n5, 221, 227
21:2	223
21:7–11	137, 223n38
21:15	28, 137
21:17	28, 137
21:20–21	137
21:26–27	137
21:26–27	87
22:16–18	99
22:16–17	137
22:21–24	222
22:25–27	222
22:25	228
24	77n18
29:43	110
30:13	111
31:13–17	76–77
32–34	77n18

Leviticus

1–7	256
7:28–36	111
11–15	135
11	110, 154
12:1–5	136
14:34	185
15	31n6
15:2–15	136
15:2	135
15:16–18	136
15:19–24	136
15:25–30	136
17–26	96n7, 101n11
17:3–7	111
18	31n6, 136
18:6–18	112
18:6	136
18:11	112
18:16	112
18:19	136
18:20	136
18:22–23	136
19:2	255
19:9–10	113, 226
19:26	101
19:31	101
20:6	101
20:10–21	112
20:27	101
21:14	113, 114n23
22:13	113
23:22	113, 226
25:8–55	226
25:8–25	185
25:8–17	220
25:23	38, 184, 220
25:25–55	228
25:29–34	185
25:36–37	228
26	62, 78
26:3–45	174, 186
26:3–13	256
26:6	163
26:14–39	256
27:30–33	111, 226

Numbers

1	108, 111
1:2	59n7
18:21–32	111
18:21–24	226
26	80, 108, 111
26:2	108
26:19–22	80
26:30–33	104
26:42	79
26:52–56	184, 220
27:1–11	80n22, 103–4
32:22	109
32:29	109
36:1–12	81n22, 103–5
36:5–9	81

Deuteronomy

	94, 96, 97, 99, 100n10, 101, 112, 113, 114, 225
1:31	37
5:12–15	76
6:5–9	86
8:5	37
8:17–18	160
11:13–17	38, 62, 174, 186
12:5–7	99
12:20–24	111
14:22–29	110
14:24–26	88n26
14:28–29	225
14:29	112
15:1–18	225
15:1–17	228
15:1	225
15:2	225
15:12–18	225
15:12–17	137
16:1–17	99
16:9–15	225
16:11	112

Deuteronomy (continued)

16:14	112
16:18	99
17:14–15	97
18:10–11	101
19:14	184
20:5–7	141
20:7	102
21:10–14	102
21:15–17	100
21:18–21	100
21:19	80
22:13–21	100, 141–42
22:22–27	102
22:28–29	99, 102, 142n9
23:19–20	228
24:5	102, 141
24:10–15	225
24:10–11	141
24:16	101
24:19–21	112, 225
25:5–10	103, 112n21, 114n23
26:14	100n10
26:16–19	101n12
28:1–68	62, 174, 186
28:11	160
28:15–68	160
28:26	163
33	98n8

Joshua

7:14–18	79
13–21	80
13–19	184
17:3–6	104
18:1	109
21	184

Judges

4	52–53
5	53, 98n8
5:24	53
5:25–27	53
5:30	53
9:2	94

Ruth

4:5	112n21

1 Samuel

2:5–8	52
8:11–17	87, 92
8:20	87
11	96
13–14	96
20:6	80n21
22:2	84
22:7–8	84, 185
24:11	84
25:2–13	84, 138n7
25:18–31	138n7
26:17–25	84

2 Samuel

1:19–27	140
1:22	140
3:29	140
5:1	94
7	87, 93
8:15	222
9:7	185
11–12	92n1
15–19	92n1
19:12–13	94
20	92n1
20:6	80
24	92n1

1 Kings

1–2	92
3:16–28	52
4–5	92
4:24	109
10:1–13	89
11:4	50
11:26	112n21
12	92
12:1–19	87
21	184, 185

2 Kings

2:3	84
2:12	84
4:1–7	137
5:13	84
16:5–9	84
18:4	98
21:3	105
22:8—23:25	97
23:4–20	99

Ezra

	108, 111, 114
9–10	107

Nehemiah

	108, 111, 114
1:3	142–43
2:17	143
5:1–13	107, 108, 229
5:1–5	137
5:7	108
5:14–19	106
7:5b—10:39	114

Job

	62n9, 175, 264–65, 268
10:8–11	131
38–42	160, 164, 167–68
38:4—39:30	167, 175
38:13–15	167
38:25–27	167
39:29–30	168
40:15—41:34	167, 168, 176
40:15	168
40:19	168, 176
40:25	168
41:18–21	279–80
41:33–34	168, 176

Isaiah

5:1–6	130
11:6–9	163, 300
18:6	163
27:1	275, 279
34–35	295
34:8	305
34:11	163
34:13–15	163
37:22	142
29:15–16	131
40–55	114n24
40:6–8	130
47:1–3	144
51:9–11	276–77
51:9	279
62:5	142
66:8–13	142

Jeremiah

2–3	51
3	78
3:19	37
4:23–26	294
14:1–9	294
15:3	163
17:8	130
18:3–6	131
31:9	37
31:27–28	130
31:29–30	x, 101n12
32:41	130
34:8–22	228
50:11–16	144
50:37	144
51:30	140, 144
51:34–37	276

Lamentations

1:1	142

Ezekiel

5:17	163
16	51
16:15–22	142
18	101n12
23	51
28	38n12
29:3–5	276
32:2–5	276
34:25	163, 300

Hosea

1–3	295–300
1:2	296
2	51, 296
2:2–5	297
2:6–7	297n7
2:6	301
2:8	296n5, 298, 301
2:9–13	298
2:11	298
2:12	163, 300
2:14–20	296n5
2:14	299
2:15	299
2:18–23	299
3	296
4:1–3	174–75, 293–94
4:3	300
4:12–19	298
8:4–5	298
8:9–10	299

Hosea (continued)

10:5	298
11:1–2	298
12:1	299
13:2	298

Joel

1:5–14	304
1:11–12	143
1:15–20	304
2:1–11	305
2:9	143
2:10	305
2:12–14	305
2:15–27	306
2:26–27	143
2:28—3:21	306

Amos

4:1–5	227
5:18	305
6:4–7	227
8:4–8	227
9:15	130

Micah

2:1–5	227

Nahum

3:4	144
3:5	144
3:13	140, 144

Habakkuk

3	276

Zephaniah

1:2–3	294

Haggai

	114n24

Zechariah

1–8	114n24
14:1	305

Psalm

1:3	130
2	87
2:7	97, 173
7–10	158
7:9–16	158–59
8	154, 157–59, 160
8:3–8	158
9:19–20	159
10:2–4	159
24:1	59n7, 160, 166, 171, 184, 219
29	62
65	62
72	87, 132
72:1–4	222
72:6	173
72:16	173
74	276
74:12–17	131–32, 173, 274
74:13–14	164
74:18	279
74:22–23	132
74:22	279
77:16–20	275–76
89	87, 276
89:9–14	173
89:25	173
89:46	279
90:5–6	130
93:3–4	131
103:15–16	130
104	160, 164–66, 167, 268–69, 271, 277, 280
104:1–9	131
104:1–4	268
104:2	268
104:5–9	268
104:10	268
104:14–15	268
104:14	268
104:19	268
104:23	268
104:26	164, 269
104:27–30	166
104:35	166, 269
115:16	187
127:3–5	140
139:13	131
139:15	36, 131

Proverbs

24:30–34	174
31:10–31	139

Song of Songs
7:10 — 48

APOCRYPHA

Judith — 52

Sirach
26:1–27 — 139

NEW TESTAMENT

Matthew
19:4 — 15

Romans
5:12–20 — 15

www.ingramcontent.com/pod-product-compliance
Lightning Source LLC
Chambersburg PA
CBHW080803020526
44114CB00046B/2738